handbook
Key Notes • Terms • Definitions • Flow Charts

Biology

Highly Important for **Class XI & XII** Students,
Medical Entrances Aspirants

handbook
Key Notes • Terms • Definitions • Flow Charts

Biology

*Highly Important for **Class XI & XII** Students,
Medical Entrances Aspirants*

Multi-Purpose Quick **Revision** Resource

Sanjay Sharma

Supported By
Kavita Thareja • Shailesh Shukla

ARIHANT PRAKASHAN, MEERUT

Arihant Prakashan, Meerut

All rights reserved

※ © Publishers

No part of this publication may be re-produced, stored in a retrieval system or distributed in any form or by any means, electronic, mechanical, photocopying, recording, scanning, web or otherwise without the written permission of the publisher. Arihant has obtained all the information in this book from the sources believed to be reliable and true. However, Arihant or its editors or authors or illustrators don't take any responsibility for the absolute accuracy of any information published, and the damages or loss suffered thereupon.

※ Administrative & Production Offices

Corporate Office: 4577/15, Agarwal Road, Darya Ganj, New Delhi -110002
Tele: 011- 47630600, 23280316; Fax: 011- 23280316

Head Office: Kalindi, TP Nagar, Meerut (UP) - 250002
Tele: 0121-2401479, 2512970, 4004199; Fax: 0121-2401648

All disputes subject to Meerut (UP) jurisdiction only.

※ Sales & Support Offices

Agra, Ahmedabad, Bengaluru, Bhubaneswar, Chennai, Delhi (I, II & III), Guwahati, Haldwani, Hyderabad Jaipur, Jalandhar, Kolkata, Kota, Lucknow (I & II), Nagpur, Meerut & Pune

※ **ISBN** 978-93-5176-452-6

Typeset by Arihant DTP Unit at Meerut

PRINTED & BOUND IN INDIA
Printed at Repro Knowledgecast Limited, Thane

For further information about the products from Arihant
log on to **www.arihantbooks.com** or email to **info@arihantbooks.com**

PREFACE

Handbook means reference book listing brief facts on a subject. So, to facilitate the students in this we have released this **Handbook of Biology**. This book has been prepared to serve the special purpose of the students, to rectify any query or any concern point of a particular subject.

This book will be of highly use whether students are looking for a quick revision before the board exams or just before other Medical Entrances like **AIPMT, AIIMS, CPMT** etc.

This handbook can even be used for revision of a subject in the time between two shift of the exams, even this handbook can be used while travelling to Examination Centre or whenever you have time, less sufficient or more.

The format of this handbook has been developed particularly so that it can be carried around by the students conveniently.

The objectives of publishing these handbooks are:
- To support students in their revision of a subject just before an examination.
- To provide a focus to students to clear up their doubts about particular concepts which were not clear to them earlier.
- To give confidence to the students just before they attempt important examinations.

However, we have put our best efforts in preparing this book, but if any error or what so ever has been skipped out, we will by heart welcome your suggestions. A part from all those who helped in the compilation of this book a special note of thanks to Miss Abhilasha Chauhan.

Authors

CONTENTS

1. **Cell: The Unit of Life**   1-15
   - Cell
   - Cell Theory
   - Types of Cells
   - Components of a Cell

2. **Biomolecules**   16-37
   - How to Analyse Chemical Composition?
   - Biomolecules
   - Carbohydrates
   - Monosaccharides
   - Oligosaccharides
   - Polysaccharides
   - Proteins
   - Lipids
   - Nucleic Acids
   - DNA
   - RNA
   - Enzymes
   - Metabolites

3. **Cell Cycle and Cell Division**   38-43
   - Cell Cycle
   - Interphase
   - Mitosis or *M*-phase
   - Amitosis
   - Meiosis

4. **The Living World**   44-49
   - Characteristic of Living Forms
   - Biodiversity
   - Systematics
   - Identification
   - Classification
   - Nomenclature
   - Taxonomy

5. **Biological Classification**   50-66
   - Biology : Nature and Scope
   - Classification of Living Organisms
   - Monera
   - Protista
   - Fungi
   - Plantae
   - Animalia
   - Viruses and Viroids
   - Viroids

6. Plant Kingdom   67-85
- Plants: Producers of the Ecosystem
- Algae
- Nutrition
- Algin, Carrageenan and Agar
- Bryophyta
- Pteridophytes
- Heterospory in Pteridophytes
- Gymnosperms
- Angiosperms

7. Animal Kingdom   86-114
- Phylum-Chordata
- Phylum-Porifera
- Phylum-Coelenterata/Cnidaria
- Phylum-Platyhelminthes
- Phylum-Aschelminthes
- Phylum-Annelida
- Phylum-Arthropoda
- Phylum-Mollusca
- Phylum-Echinodermata
- Phylum-Hemichordata
- Phylum-Chordata

8. Structural Organisation in Animals   115-145
- Tissues
- Epithelial Tissue(By Ruysch)
- Connective Tissue
- Muscular Tissue
- Neural Tissue
- Earthworm
- Cockroach
- Frog

9. Digestion and Absorption   146-162
- Human Digestive System
- Alimentary Canal
- Zygomatic Gland
- Ebner's Glands
- Tonsils
- Waldeyer's Ring
- Circopharyngeal Sphincter
- Cardiac Sphincter
- Valves of Kerkring
- Dentition
- Molars
- Cusps
- Digestive Glands
- Absorption of Nutrients

10. Breathing and Exchange of Gases   163-173
- Respiration
- Human Respiratory System
- Breathing
- Lungs
- Dead Space
- Exchange of Gases
- Transport of Gases
- Regulation of Respiration
- Disorders of Respiration System

11. Body Fluids and Circulation — 174-194
- Body Fluids
- Blood
- Lymph
- Circulatory System
- Human Circulatory System
- Human Heart
- Electrocardiogram
- Blood Vascular System
- Portal System

12. Locomotion and Movement — 195-218
- Locomotion
- Movement
- Muscles
- All-or-None Law
- Oxygen Debt
- Cori's Cycle
- Skeletal System

13. Excretory Products and Their Elimination — 219-228
- Excretion
- Excretory Products
- Human Excretory System
- Urine Formation
- Glomerular Filtration Rate
- Effective Filtration Pressure
- Mechanism of Filtrate Concentration
- Regulation of Kidney Function
- Micturition

14. Neural Control and Coordination — 229-259
- Human Neural System
- Central Nervous System
- Neuron of Cerebral Cortex
- Brain Ventricles
- Cerebrospinal Fluid
- Peripheral Nervous System
- Spinal Nerves
- Autonomic Nervous System
- Reflex Action
- Reflex Arc
- Sense Organs
- The Visual Sense-The Eye
- Human Ear-Organ of Hearing and Balance
- Nerve Impulse
- Synapse

15. Chemical Coordination and Integration — 260-270
- Glands
- Human Endocrine System
- Endocrine Disorders
- Hormones
- Mechanism of Hormone Action
- Control of Hormone Action

16. Human Reproduction 271-294
- Male Reproduction System
- Female Reproduction System
- Gametogenesis
- Spermatogenesis
- Sperm
- Hormonal Control of Male Reproductive System
- Oogenesis
- Hormonal Control of Female Reproductive System
- The Menstrual Cycle
- Menopause
- Fertilisation
- Implantation
- Embryonic Development
- Foetal Development
- Placenta
- Lactation
- The Lactating Breast

17. Reproductive Health 295-305
- Problems Related to Reproductive Health
- Population Explosion
- Strategies to Improve Reproductive Health
- Medical Termination of Pregnancy
- Sexually Transmitted Diseases
- Acquired Immuno Deficiency Syndrome
- Infertility
- Assisted Reproductive Technology
- Detection of Foetal Disorders during Early Pregnancy

18. Human Health and Disease 306-327
- Common Diseases in Humans
- Immunity and Immune System
- Criterias for Antigenicity
- Structure of Antibodies
- Classes of Immunoglobulins
- Complement System
- Vaccination and Immunisation
- Allergies
- Autoimmunity
- Acquired Immuno Deficiency Syndrome
- Cancer
- Drugs
- Addiction
- De-addiction
- Adolescence

19. Morphology of Flowering Plants 328-357
- Types of the Root
- Modifications of Roots
- The stem
- The leaf
- The inflorescence
- The flower
- The fruit
- The seed

20. Anatomy of Flowering Plants 358-375
- The tissues
- Chief theories related to SAM and RAM
- Permanent tissues
- Components of Xylem
- The Tissue System
- Anatomy of Dicot and Monocot Plants

21. Mineral Nutrition in Plants 376-382
- Classification of Mineral Nutrients
- Deficiency Symptoms of Essential Mineral Nutrients
- Toxicity of Micronutrients
- Hydroponics
- Metabolism of Nitrogen
- Soil as Reservoir of Essential Elements

22. Photosynthesis in Higher Plants 383-394
- Chemistry and Thermodynamics of Photosynthesis
- Historical Timeline of Photosynthesis
- Chloroplast: Photosynthetic Organ of Cell
- Photosynthetic Pigments
- Factors Affecting Photosynthesis
- Law of Limiting Factors
- Photorespiration

23. Transport in Plants 395-406
- Plant Water Relation
- Osmotic Pressure
- Chemical Potential
- Water Potential
- Osmotic Potential
- Diffusion Pressure Deficit
- Mechanism of Water Absorption
- Factors Affecting the Rate of Water Absorption
- Transpiration
- Translocation and Storage of Food in Plants
- Mass or Pressure Flow Theory
- Diffusion Theory

24. Respiration in Plants 407-417
- Cellular Respiration
- Schematic Representation of EMP Pathway
- Kerbs' Cycle or Tricarboxylic Acid Cycle
- Electron Transport Chain
- Oxidative Phosphorylation
- Pentose phosphate Pathway
- Amphibolic Pathway
- Factor Affecting Respiration

25. Plant Growth and Development 418-426
- Growth
- Growth Rate
- Differentiation, Dedifferentiation and Redifferentiation
- Plant Hormones/ Phytohormones Plant Growth Regulators
- Plant Hormones, their Function and Location
- Applications of Phytohormones
- Photoperiodism
- Abscission of Plant Parts

26. Reproduction in Organisms 427-431
- Reproduction in Animals
- Reproduction in Plants
- Events in Sexual Reproduction of Both Plants and Animals

27. Sexual Reproduction in Flowering Plants　432-445
- Pollen Grain Formation
- Embryo Sac Formation
- Development of Embryo Sac
- Pollination
- Fertilisation
- Endosperm
- Development of Embryo/Embryogenesis

28. Principles of Inheritance and Variation　446-468
- Heredity
- Variations
- Gregor Johann Mendel
- Mendel's Laws of Inheritance in which Monohybrid Cross is Applied
- Chromosomal Theory of Inheritance
- Sex Determination
- Linkage
- Mutation
- Pedigree Analysis

29. Molecular Basis of Inheritance　469-487
- DNA as Genetic Material
- DNA
- RNA
- Gene Expression
- Genetic Code
- Wobble Hypothesis
- Regulation of Gene Expression
- Human Genome Project

30. Biotechnology: Principles and Processes　488-500
- Principle of Biotechnology
- Genetic Engineering/Recombinant DNA Technology/Gene Cloning
- Tools of *r*DNA Technology
- Gel Electrophoresis
- Bioreactors
- Down Stream Processing

31. Biotechnology and Its Application　501-513
- Red Biotechnology
- White Biotechnology
- Green Biotechnology
- *Bt* Cotton
- Application of Biotechnology in Medicine
- Cystic Fibrosis
- Application of Biotechnology in Industry

32. Strategies for Enhancement in Food Production　514-528
- Animal Husbandry
- Improvement of Animals through Breeding
- Pisciculture/ Fish Farming/ Culture Fishery
- Apiculture/Bee-Farming
- Sericulture
- Lac Culture
- Plant Breeding
- Single Cell Protein

33. Microbes in Human Welfare 529-538
- Microbes in Household Products
- Microbes in Industrial Product
- Biopesticides
- Bioherbicides
- Bioinsecticides
- Microbes in Biofules

34. Evolution 539-569
- Origin of Universe
- Origin of Life
- Adaptive Radiation
- Theories of Evolution
- Darwinism
- Mutation Theory
- Evolution of Human
- Human and Other Primates

35. Ecosystem 570-588
- Classification of Ecosystem
- Components of Ecosystem
- Ecosystem: Structure and Characteristics
- Features of Ecosystem
- Food Chain
- Food Web
- Ecosystem Services

36. Organisms and Population 589-599
- Organism and its Environment
- Responses to Abiotic Factors
- Adaptation
- Mimicry
- Population and Community
- Characteristics of Population

37. Biodiversity and Conservation 600-613
- Levels of Biodiversity
- Patterns of Biodiversity
- Importance of Biodiversity
- Loss of Biodiversity
- IUCN and Red List Categories
- Biodiversity Conservation

38. Environmental Issues 614-634
- Pollution
- Greenhouse Effect
- Global Warming
- Acid Rain
- Ozone Layer Depletion
- Deforestation

- **Appendix** 635-640

1
Cell : *The Unit of Life*

Cell
The cell is the basic structural, functional and biological unit of all known living organisms.

Robert Hooke (1665) observed honey-comb like dead cells in a thin slice of cork and named them 'cell'. **Anton van Leeuwenhoek** (1667) was the first to describe a living cell.

The properties of a living organism depend on those of its individual cells. Cells contain DNA which is found specifically in the chromosome and RNA found in the cell nucleus and cytoplasm.

All cells are basically the same in chemical composition in organisms of similar species. Energy flow (metabolism and biochemistry) occurs within cells.

Cell Theory (Magna Carta of Cell Study)
MJ Schleiden; 1838 and **Theodor Schwann; 1839**.

The postulates are
- All living beings are made up of cells (cell is the basic unit of life).
- All cells arise from pre-existing cells *(Omnis cellula e cellula–* Rudolf Virchow).
- Cell is the smallest independent unit of life.

Types of Cells

Cells are classified into two types, i.e., prokaryotic and eukaryotic cells.

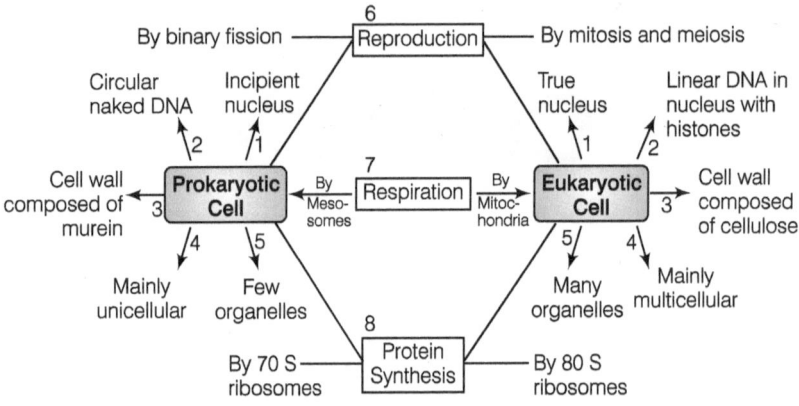

Process of prokaryotic and eukaryotic cell

Size of biological cell is generally too small to be seen without a microscope. There are exceptions as well as considerable range in the sizes of various cell types.

Relative size of different cells is given below

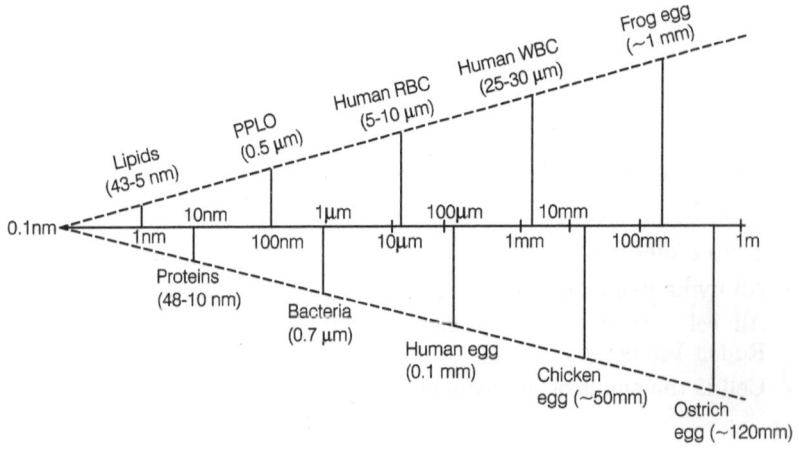

Relative size of different cells

Components of a Cell

1. Cell Wall

A typical cell wall consists of four layer namely

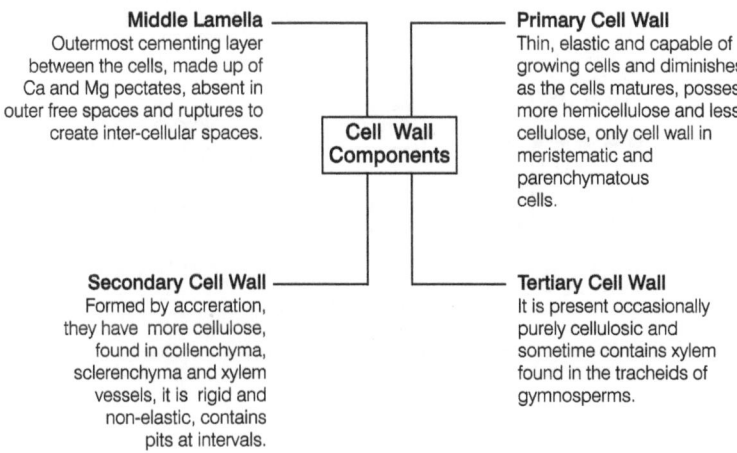

Components of cell wall

Growth of Cell Wall

The growth and formation of cell wall occurs by two ways

(i) **By intussusception** It is the deposition of wall material in the form of fine grains.

(ii) **By apposition** In this method, the new cell wall material secreted by protoplasm is deposited by definite thin plates one after other.

Functions of the Cell Wall

- It maintains the shape of plant cell and protects it from mechanical injury.
- It wards off the effect of pathogens.

2. Plasma Membrane

Plasmalemma contains about 58-59% proteins, 40% lipids and 1-2% carbohydrates.

To explain the structure of plasma membrane various models were proposed by different scientist which are discussed below.

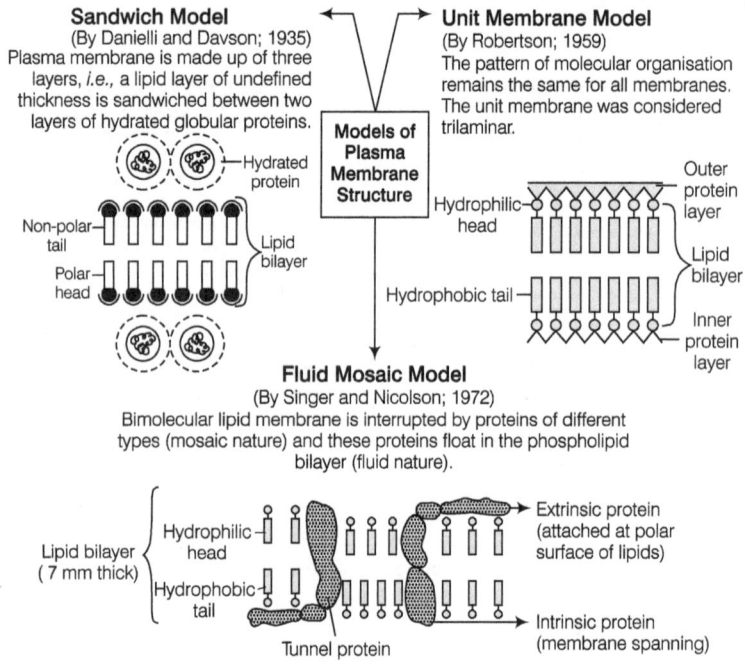

Model of plasma membrane structure

Functions of Plasma Membrane

- The cell membranes cause **compartmentalisation**. As plasma membranes separate the cells from their external environment. As organelle coverings, they allow the cells organelles to maintain their identity, internal environment and functional individuality.
- Plasma membrane protects the cell from injury.
- The membranes allow the flow of materials and information between different organelles of the same cell as well as between one cell and another.
- As plasmodesmata and gap junctions the biomembranes provide organic connections between adjacent cells.

Handbook of BIOLOGY

3. Nucleus

Nucleus or **karyon** was first discovered by **Robert Brown** (1831) in the cells of orchids roots. It is darkly stained, spherical and the largest cell organelle whose composition is as follows : 9-12% DNA, 15% histones (basic proteins), 15% enzymes, 5% RNA, 3% lipids, 65% acid and neutral proteins.

Nucleus has an outer double layered nuclear membrane with nuclear pores, a transparent granular matrix (nucleoplasm/karyolymph), chromatin network composed of DNA and histones and a directly stainable spherical body called nucleolus.

4. Chromosomes

They are rod-shaped and thread-like condensed chromatin fibres which appear during karyokinesis. Each chromosome have halves or **chromatids,** which are attached to each other by **centromere** or **primary constriction.**

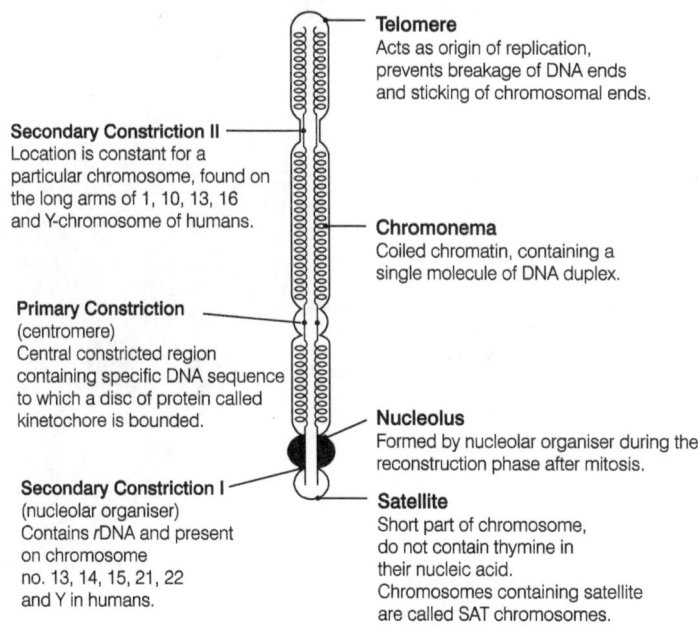

Structure outline of a typical chromosome

Structure and Components of Cell
(Plant and Animal)

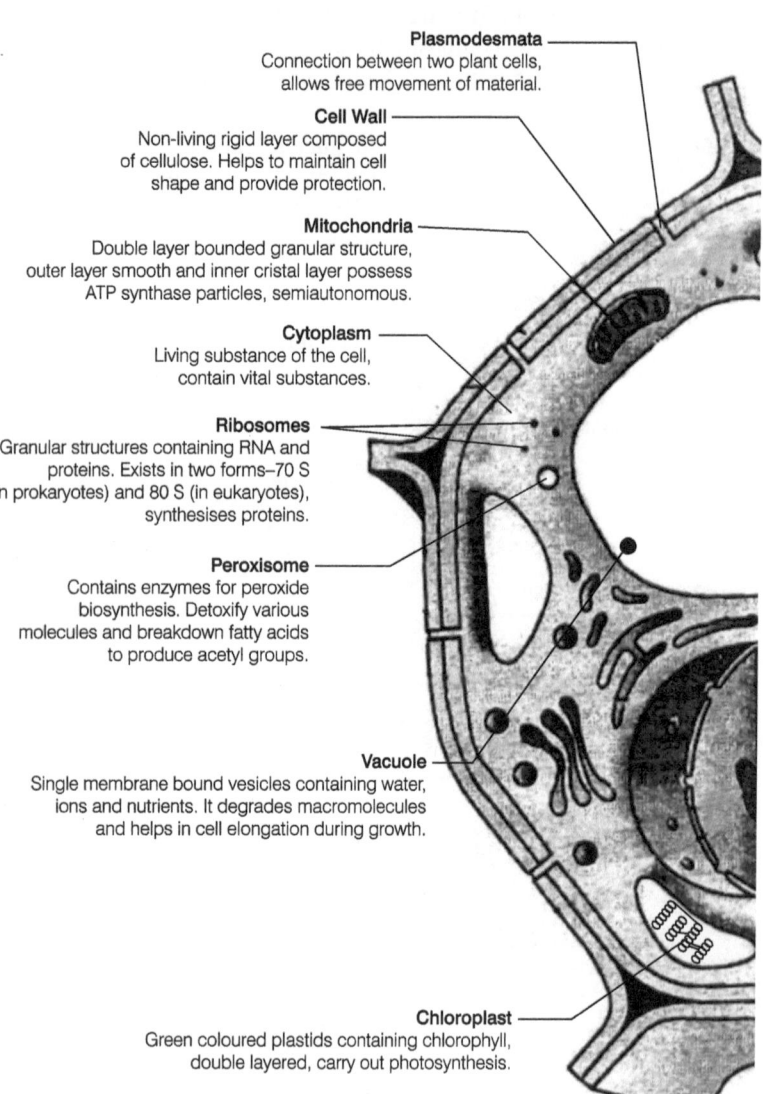

Plasmodesmata
Connection between two plant cells, allows free movement of material.

Cell Wall
Non-living rigid layer composed of cellulose. Helps to maintain cell shape and provide protection.

Mitochondria
Double layer bounded granular structure, outer layer smooth and inner cristal layer possess ATP synthase particles, semiautonomous.

Cytoplasm
Living substance of the cell, contain vital substances.

Ribosomes
Granular structures containing RNA and proteins. Exists in two forms–70 S (in prokaryotes) and 80 S (in eukaryotes), synthesises proteins.

Peroxisome
Contains enzymes for peroxide biosynthesis. Detoxify various molecules and breakdown fatty acids to produce acetyl groups.

Vacuole
Single membrane bound vesicles containing water, ions and nutrients. It degrades macromolecules and helps in cell elongation during growth.

Chloroplast
Green coloured plastids containing chlorophyll, double layered, carry out photosynthesis.

Structure of plant cell

Handbook of BIOLOGY

Microvilli
Outgrowth of plasma membrane, increases absorptive surface area.

Plasma Membrane
Quasifluid, elastic cell membranes, control movement of molecules in and out of the cell, aids in cell-cell signalling and cell-adhesion.

Golgi Apparatus
Densely stained reticular structures consists of sacs and cisternae. Process and sort lysosomal, secreted and membrane proteins to release their content.

Centriole
Contained in centrosome as a paired structure, lying perpendicular to each other. Form basal bodies of cilia and flagella.

Nuclear Envelope
Double membrane with perinuclear space. Outer membrane is continuous with RER, possess nuclear pores.

Lysosomes
Membrane bound vesicular structure, contain hydrolytic enzymes, degrade worn-out material, active at acidic pH.

Nucleus
Filled with chromatin, composed of DNA and proteins synthesises $mRNA$ and $tRNA$ in dividing cells.

Smooth ER
Do not possess ribosomes, major site of lipid synthesis.

Nucleolus
Nuclear compartments where most of $rRNA$ is synthesised.

Rough ER
Possess ribosomes on their surface, synthesise, process and sort secreted and lysosomal proteins.

Structure of animal cell

Types of Chromosomes

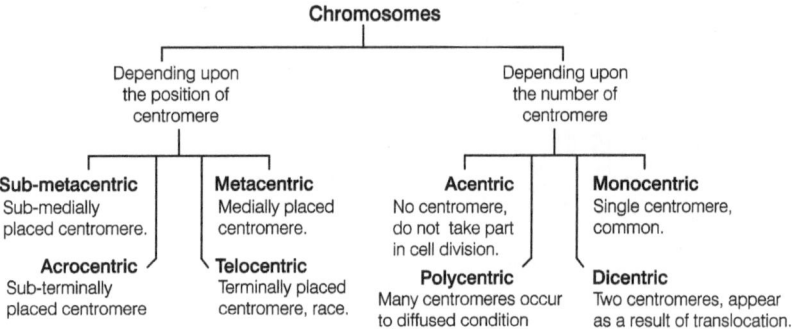

Besides, chromosomes can also be categorised on the basis of their specific properties. *These are*

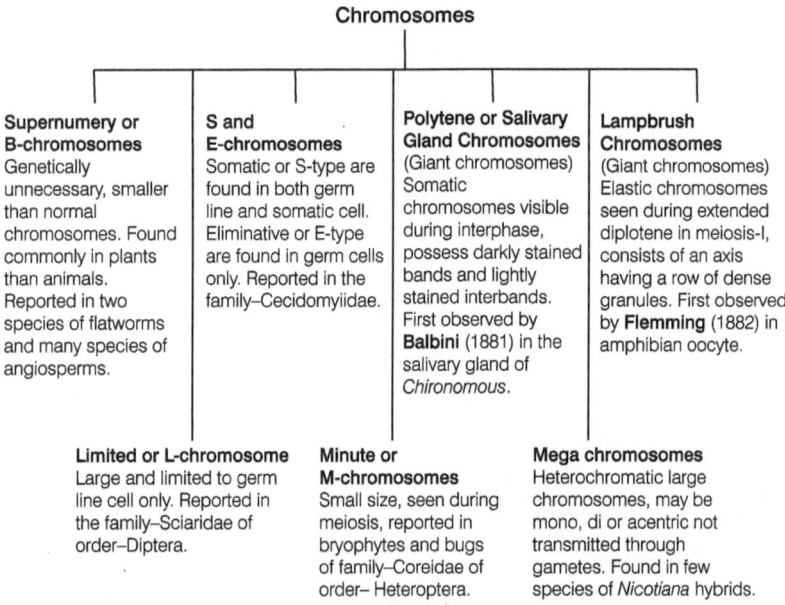

On the basis of genes they possess, the chromosomes can be of following types

Autosomes These are the somatic chromosomes which do not take part in fertilisation process. These are also called **allosomes** and they are 44 in number in human body.

Handbook of BIOLOGY

Sex chromosomes These are involved in fertilisation process and helps to pass information from one generation to another. These are also called **heterosomes** and are two in number in human body.

Functions of Chromosomes
- They carry hereditary information in the genes from parents to offspring.
- The SAT (stands for Satellite or Sine Acid Thymonucleonics means where thymine containing acid is absent) chromosomes form nucleoli in daughter cells at nucleolar organiser regions.
- Sex chromosomes (X and Y) play role in sex determination.
- They undergo crossing over and mutations and thus contribute to the evolutions.

5. Mitochondria

It is a spherical or rod-shaped, two-layered granular structure which was first seen by **Kolliker** (1850) in the striated muscles and called them **sarcosomes**. Because of the formation of ATP, they are also called as power houses of the cell.

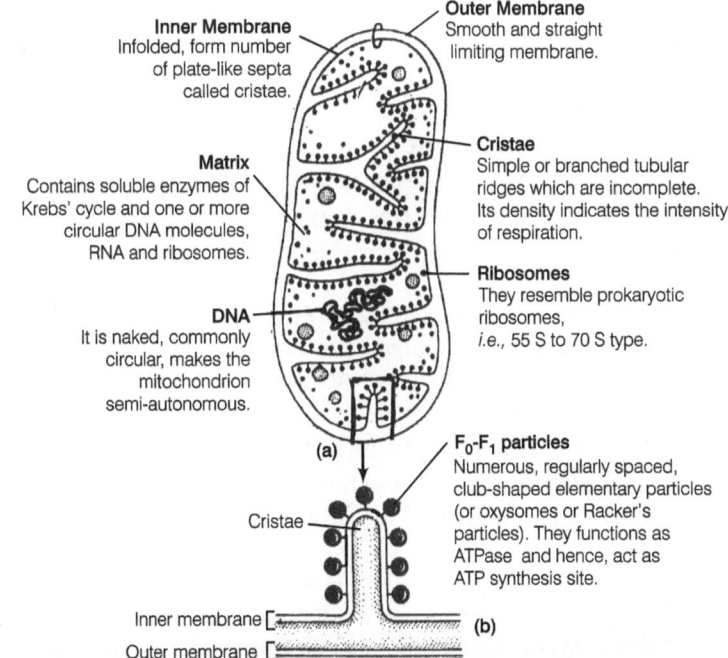

Mitochondria (a) Internal structure of mitochondria
(b) One cristae magnified

Each F_0-F_1 particle posseses head, a stalk and a base *which is shown in the figure below*

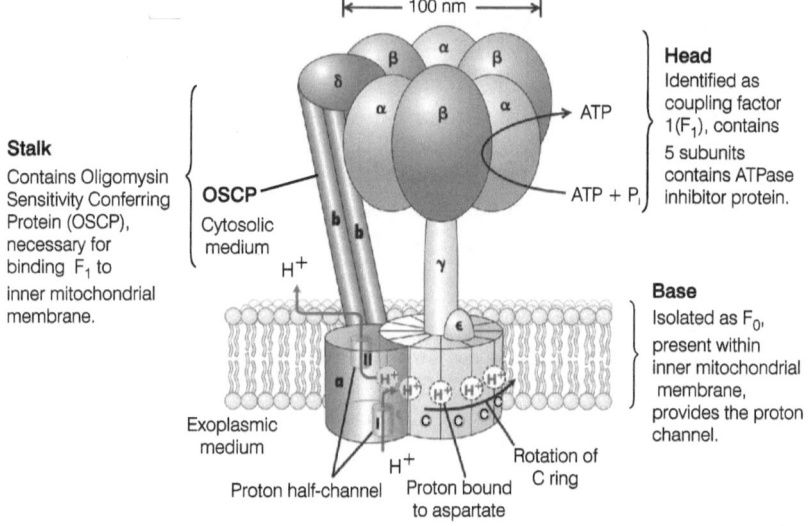

Structure of ATP synthetase

Functions of Mitochondria
- Synthesise and store ATP during aerobic respiration.
- Contains many lipid synthesising enzymes.

6. Plastids
These are the small bodies found free in most plant cells. They are not found in fungi, some bacteria, algae and multicellular animals. These double membrane bound structures are semi-autonomous organelles having their own DNA.

Based on the type of pigment they are of three types

(i) **Chromoplasts** They are yellow or red in colour due to the presence of carotenoids. They are found in fruits, flower and leaves.

(ii) **Leucoplasts** They are colourless plastids which generally occurs near the nucleus in non-green cells. They are further of three types depending upon the type of food stored, *e.g.*, amyloplasts (starch), aleuronoplasts (proteins) and elaioplasts (lipids).

(iii) **Chloroplasts** These are green coloured plastids containing chlorophylls and carotenoids. These double membraned structures contain thylakoids in their stroma. The stroma also contains enzymes required for the synthesis of carbohydrates and proteins.

Functions of Plastids
- Chromoplast trap electromagnetic radiations.
- Leucoplast store food material.
- Chloroplast are the centres of photosynthesis.

7. Endoplasmic Reticulum (ER)

These are membrane bound channels, which are seen in the form of a network of delicate strands and vesicles in the cytoplasm. These were first observed by **Porter, Claude** and **Fullam** (1945).

They are not found in mature erythrocytes and prokaryotes. Two basic morphological types of ER are Rough Endoplasmic Reticulum (RER) and Smooth Endoplasmic Reticulum (SER).

RER is granular where as SER is agranular depending on the basis of presence or absence of ribosomes on their surface. The ER membranes may assume the shape of cisternae, tubules or vesicles.

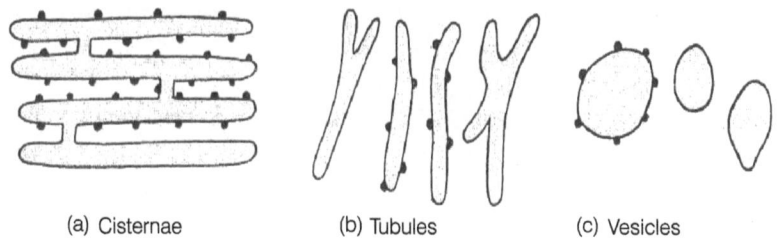

(a) Cisternae　　　(b) Tubules　　　(c) Vesicles

Morphology of the endoplasmic reticulum

Functions of ER
- RER is involved in protein synthesis and secretion.
- SER is the major site for the synthesis of lipids.
- The SER membrane shown to possess enzyme system with detoxification activities.

8. Golgi Apparatus

These are the flattened stacks of membranes found within the endomembrane system. This complex cytoplasmic structure is made up of cisternae, vesicles and vacuoles.

They are absent in prokaryotic cells, sieve tubes of plants, sperms of bryophytes pteridophytes and RBCs of mammals. Golgi bodies were first described by **Camillo Golgi** in 1989. **Perroncito** (1910) used the term 'Dictyosomes' for smaller dividing units of Golgi apparatus.

Mollenhauer and **Whaley** (1963) suggested the polarised nature of Golgi complex. According to them, the margins of cisternae are slightly curved. So each cisternae has a convex *cis* (forming face) facing towards nucleus and a concave *trans* (maturing face) facing towards the plasma membrane.

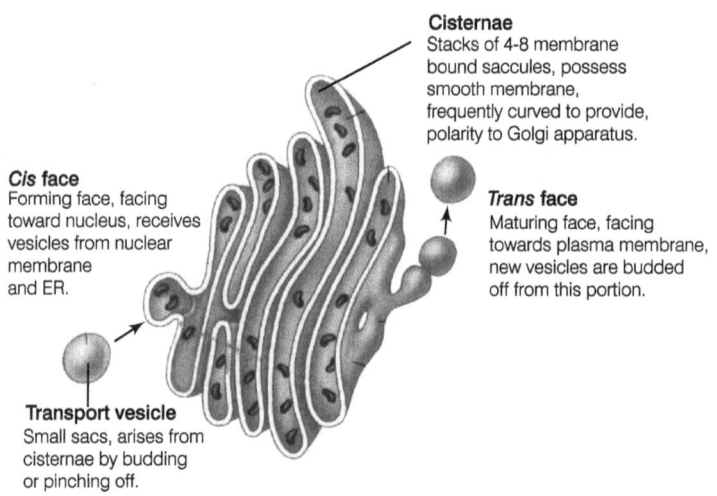

Cisternae
Stacks of 4-8 membrane bound saccules, possess smooth membrane, frequently curved to provide, polarity to Golgi apparatus.

***Cis* face**
Forming face, facing toward nucleus, receives vesicles from nuclear membrane and ER.

***Trans* face**
Maturing face, facing towards plasma membrane, new vesicles are budded off from this portion.

Transport vesicle
Small sacs, arises from cisternae by budding or pinching off.

Structure of Golgi apparatus

Functions of Golgi Apparatus

- Helps in the formation of acrosome of sperms.
- Important sites for the formation of glycoproteins and glycolipids.
- Studies by autoradiographic ^{3}H glucose and ^{3}H galactose labelling have provided direct evidence of polysaccharide synthesis in Golgi apparatus.

9. Ribosomes

They are large non-membranous RNA-protein complexes which are necessary for protein synthesis. These dense granules are found either in free state or attached to the outside of cytoplasmic membrane through ribophorins.

These are also called **Palade** particles as they were first observed by **Palade** in 1955. In plants, they were reported by **Robinson** and **Brown** in the bean roots.

Types of Ribosomes

Ribosomes are of two basic types, *i.e.*, **70 S** and **80 S**, where 'S' refers to **Svedberg** unit of sedimentation coefficient.

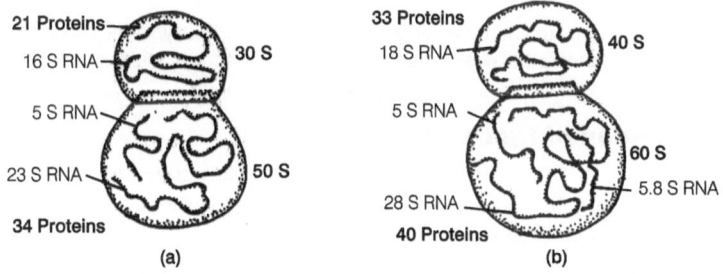

Ribosomes : (a) 70 S (in prokaryotes)   (b) 80 S (in eukaryotes)

Functions of Riosomes

- They are the sites for polypeptide or protein synthesis (protein factories).
- They provide enzymes (peptidyl transferase) and factors for condensation of amino acids to form polypeptides.

10. Lysosomes

They are single membrane bound structures, supposed to contain hydrolytic enzymes in them. Therefore, they are known as suicidal bags of the cell. They were first observed by **C de Duve** (1949) in the liver cells. They were reported in plant cells by **P Matile**.

There are two basic types of lysosomes namely **primary lysosomes** and **secondary lysosomes**. Primary lysosomes are further categorised to phagosomes, autophagic vacuoles and residual bodies.

Autolysis is the phenomenon of self destruction of a cell with the help of lysosomes. Because of close relationship between Golgi complex, ER and lysosomes, **Novikoff** *et al.* (1961-64) denoted endomembrane system as **GERL system**, *i.e.*, Golgi complex, ER and lysosome system.

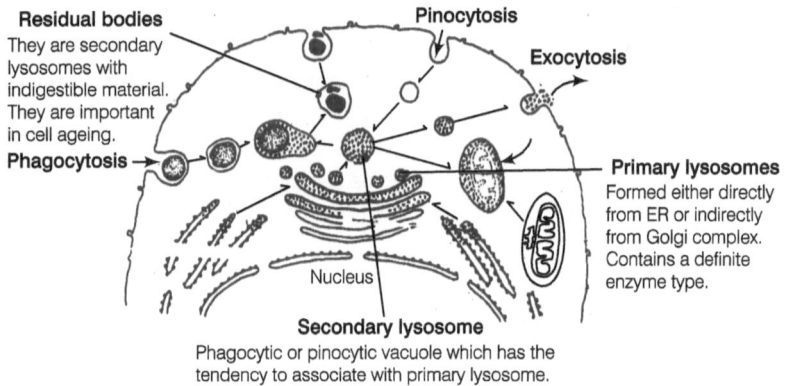

Representing the dynamic aspects of the GERL system. Observe the relationship between the processes of phagocytosis, pinocytosis, exocytosis and autophagy

Functions of Lysosomes
- They help in intracellular and extracellular digestion.
- They help in the secretion of thyroid hormones and regulation of hormone secretion in mammotrophs.
- Acrosome of sperm is considerd as giant lysosome. It contains hyaluronidase and proteases which are helpful in dissolving the covering of ovum. It is formed by the modification of Golgi body.

11. Microbodies
They are small, single membrane bounded cell organelles which absorb molecular oxygen and take part in oxidation. They were first seen by **Rhodin** (1954) in mouse kidney tubule cells.

They are of two types

(i) **Peroxisomes** They contain enzymes for peroxide biosynthesis. They are found in both plant and animal cells in the closed association of ER, mitochondria and chloroplasts. Despite absence of DNA, they are believed to be able to replicate like plastids and mitochondria.

(ii) **Glyoxysomes** They contain enzymes for β-oxidation of fatty acids and glyoxylate pathway. They usually occurs in fat rich plants. They are more prominent in plant seedlings and generally found in yeast and *Neurospora* cells. They are considered to be special peroxisomes. They were first reported by **Beevers** in 1969 in the endosperm of germinating seeds.

Functions of Microbodies
- Peroxisomes can metabolise unusual substances or xenobiotics.
- Glyoxysomes metabolise acetyl Co-A in glyoxylate cycle to produce carbohydrates.
- Peroxiomes are associated with lipid metabolism in animal cells in particular the oxidation of amino acid and uric acid.

12. Cytoskeletal Elements
These consist of following types

(i) **Microtubules** They are unbranched, hollow tubules made up of tubulin, protein. They contains 13 protofilaments and are 25nm in diameter (Roberts and Franchi). They occur in centrioles, basal bodies, cilia/filagella, astral rays, spindle fibres, etc. They are non-contractile in nature.

(ii) **Microfilaments** They are long, narrow, cylindrical rods made up of actin protein. They are contractile, solid structures having diameter of about 7nm. They occur below cell membrane and at the interphase of plasma gel-plasmasol.

Functions of Cytoskeletal Elements
- Microtubules helps in the movement of nuclei during division.
- Microfilament are responsible for cellular movements like contraction, crawling, pinching during division and formation of cellular extensions.

2
Biomolecules

Simply, chemistry is the foundation of biology, as a number of chemicals (over 5000) are found in cells with a great quantitative and qualitative variations. These chemicals and the interaction between them are responsible for the formation of all the biological molecules or compounds which primarily has carbon as its constituents. These biological molecules can be collectivily termed as **biomolecules**.

A quantitative (in percentage) account of four main organic compounds present in protoplasm of animal and plant cell is shown in below figure (pie diagram).

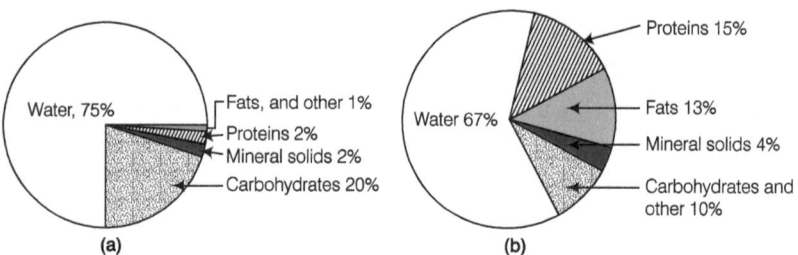

Chemical constituents of the protoplasm : (a) Plants (b) Animals

Before discussing the biomolecules in detail, we need to take a look on the methods of chemical analysis to determine the composition of any cell or tissue in living state.

How to Analyse Chemical Composition?

We generally perform the chemical analysis to get an idea about the molecular formula and probable structure of a compound.

There are two general methods of analysis

(i) Grind the living matter in trichloroacetic acid (Cl$_3$CCOOH) and filter it through a cheese cloth. Two fractions are obtained. One is called **filtrate** or **acid soluble fraction** containing **micromolecules** and second one is called **pellet** or **acid insoluble fraction** containing **macromolecules**.

(ii) The composition of living tissues can also be confirmed after burning. All the oxidisable compounds, oxidised in form of gases and the inorganic compounds remains in form of **ash**.

A comparative account of elements present in living and non-living matters is given in following table

Composition of Earth's Crust and Human Body

Elements	% Weight of	
	Earth's Crust	Human Body
Hydrogen (H)	0.14	0.5
Carbon (C)	0.03	18.5
Oxygen (O)	46.6	65.0
Nitrogen (N)	Very little	3.3
Sulphur (S)	0.03	0.3
Sodium (Na)	2.8	0.2
Calcium (Ca)	3.6	1.5
Magnesium (Mg)	2.1	0.1
Silicon (Si)	27.7	Negligible

Biomolecules

The collection or sum total of different types of biomolecule, compounds and ions present in a cell is called the **cellular pool.** A comprehensive account of various components of cellular pool are given below

The following flow chart provides a glance view of biomolecules

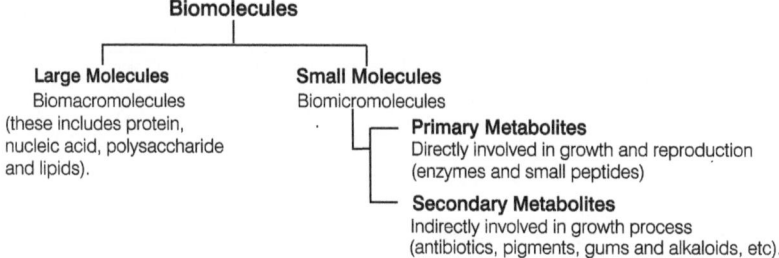

Bonds Involved in Biomolecules

Despite having several basic bondings between their structure, some modified bonds and linkages also involved in the organisation of biomolecules.

Some of them are discussed here briefly

Name	Occurrence/Formed between	Diagram/Detail
Peptide bond	Protein/Two amino acids	O=C⋯N—H, Peptide bond
Glycosidic bond	Carbohydrate/Two monosaccharides	Sugar—O—Sugar
Phosphodiester bond	Nucleic acid/Phosphate and hydroxyl group of sugar	OCH_2—Thymine ring, O=P—OH Phosphodiester bond, CH_2—Guanine ring
Hydrogen bond	Nucleic acid/Two nitrogenous bases	Guanine ⋯ Cytosine, Hydrogen bonds
Hydrophobic interaction	Protein/Two non-polar side chains of neutral amino acids	The interaction formed between two molecules as a strategy to avoid the contact with water.
Disulphide bonds	Protein/Two sulphur containing molecules	—S—S— Disulphide bond

Carbohydrates (Saccharides)

These are among the most widely distributed compounds both in plants as well as in animal kingdom. These are defined as polyhydroxy aldolases, ketoses and their condensation products.

The organic substance having carbon, hydrogen and oxygen, where oxygen and hydrogen occur in ratio of 1 : 2. The carbohydrate shows the general formula $C_n(H_2O)_n$ or $(CH_2O)_n$.

On the basis of the products of hydrolysis, the carbohydrates are divided into three major groups

Carbohydrates
- **Monosaccharides** — Such carbohydrates, which on further hydrolysis give compounds other than carbohydrates.
- **Oligosaccharides** (Gr. *oligo* – few; *saccharon* – sugar). — Such carbohydrates, which on further hydrolysis yield 3 to 9 monosaccharide units.
- **Polysaccharides** (Gr. *poly* – many; *saccharon* – sugar). — Such carbohydrates, which give many monosaccharide units on hydrolysis

Monosaccharides

These are simplest sugar which cannot hydrolysed further. These can be **trioses** (3C), **tetroses** (4C), pentoses (5C), **hexoses** (6C) and **heptoses** (7C). On the basis of presence of **aldehydes group** (*i.e.,* $-\overset{\parallel}{\underset{O}{C}}-H$) and **ketone group** (*i.e.,* $-\overset{\parallel}{\underset{O}{C}}-$), these may be **aldoses** and **ketoses** respectively.

On reacting with alcoholic and nitrogen group of other organic compounds, the aldoses and ketoses form a bond called **glycosidic bond** (C—O—C or C—N—C). Pentoses and hexoses exist in both open chain as well as ring forms.

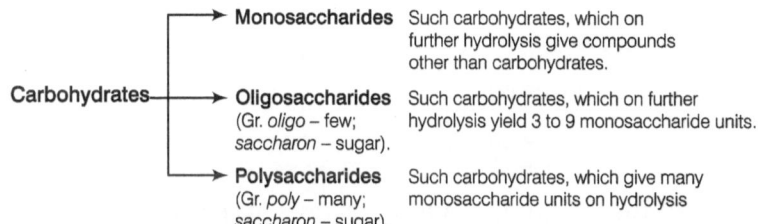

Structure of monosaccharides : (a) Open chain glucose (6C) (b) Pyranose ring form (6C) (c) Furanose ring form (5C)

Monosaccharides are sweet tasting, colourless solids having solubility in water, but sparingly soluble in alcohol and insoluble in ether. These have at least one **asymmetric carbon atom** (except dihydroxyacetone), hence they exist in different isomeric forms *i.e.*, dextro or laevorotatory.

Examples of Monosaccharides

(a) **Trioses** ($C_3H_6O_3$) These are glyceraldehyde and dihydroxy acetone.

(b) **Tetroses** ($C_4H_8O_4$) *These are erythrose and threose as*

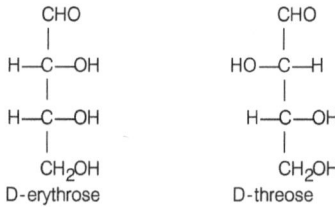

(c) **Pentoses** ($C_5H_{10}O_5$), *Among pentoses the important ones are*

Ribose This is found in Ribonucleic acid (RNA), coenzymes, ATP, FAD, NAD and NADP.

Deoxyribose This is found in Deoxyribonucleic Acid (DNA).

D-arabinose This occurs as glycoside of tuberculosis bacilli.

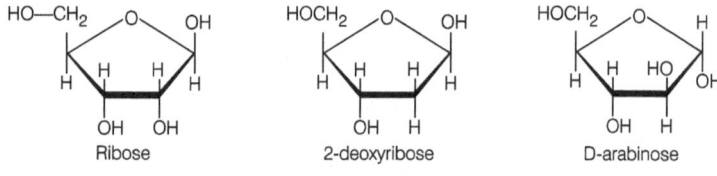

Some pentose sugars

Ribulose An important pentose of photosynthetic pathway.

(d) **Hexoses** ($C_6H_{12}O_6$)

D-glucose This is the most widely distributed sugar. It is also known by the name of **blood sugar**. It is a component of sucrose.

D-galactose This is found in glycolipids of nervous tissue. It is a **component of milk sugar** and lactose.

D-mannose This is widely distributed as mannans in plants. In small amounts, it is also present in some glycoproteins. It is converted to glucose in animals.

D-fructose This is sweetest of all the sugars. It is found in fruit juices, honey and seminal fluid.

(e) **Heptoses** ($C_7H_{14}O_7$) Sedoheptuloses act as intermediate in Calvin cycle.

On the basis of reaction with different substances, monosaccharides can be divided into various categories

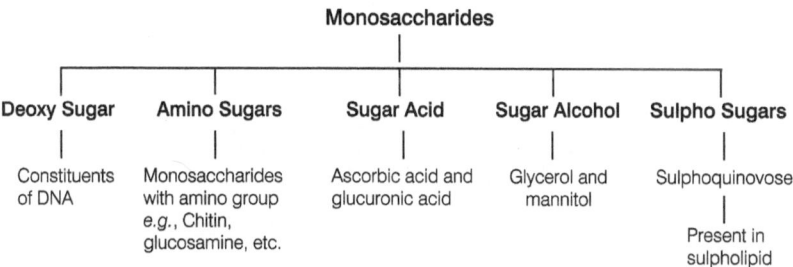

Oligosaccharides

These are the group of compounds which are formed by condensation of **2-9 monosaccharide**. These units are joined with the help of specialised **glycosidic linkges.**

Examples of Oligosaccharides

(a) **Lactose or Milk sugar** It is present in milk of mammals and made up of **one glucose** and **one galactose** units. It is reducing sugar. Souring of milk is due to the conversion of lactose to lactic acid.

(b) **Maltose or Malt sugar** It is named because of its occurrence in malted grain of Barley. Mostly found in germinating seeds and tissue where starch is broken down. It is a reducing sugar and formed by condensation of 2 glucose units.

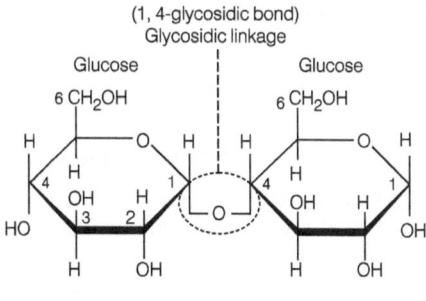

Maltose

(c) **Sucrose or Table sugar** It is also known as **cane sugar** or **invert sugar**. In this fructose occurs in **pentagon** form, while glucose is in **hexagon** form. It is a non-reducing sugar.

Sucrose

(d) **Raffinose** ($C_{18}H_{32}O_{16}$) It is a **trisaccharide**, contains glucose, galactose and fructose.

Polysaccharides

The term is usually employed to polymers containing minimum ten monosaccharide units. *Polysaccharides are of following two types*

(i) **Homopolysaccharides** or **Homoglycans** They have only one type of monosaccharide units in them.

Some of the better known homoglycans are

 (a) **Glucans**, *i.e.,* which contain only glucose units, *e.g.,* starch, glycogen, cellulose, chitin, etc.

 (b) **Galactans**, *i.e,* which contain galactose units only, *e.g.,* agar, pectin, galactan from snails.

 (c) **Mannans**, *i.e,* which contain only mannose units, *e.g.,* yeast mannan.

 (d) **Xylans**, *i.e,* which contain xylose units, *e.g.,* hemicellulose xylan.

 (e) **Fructans**, *i.e,* those with fructose monomers, *e.g.,* inulin.

(ii) **Heteropolysaccharides** or **Heteroglycans** They have atleast two types of monosaccharide units in them.

Chief polysaccharides are explained in details as

Starch

Starch $(C_6H_{10}O_5)_n$ is a polymer of D-glucopyranose units linked by α-1, 4-glycosidic linkages. It consists of a mixture of **amylose** (linear, 200-500 glucose units) and **amylopectin** (branched, more than 1000 glucose units) in 1 : 4 ratio respectively. It is reserve food material in plants.

The structure of amylose and amylopectin are as follows

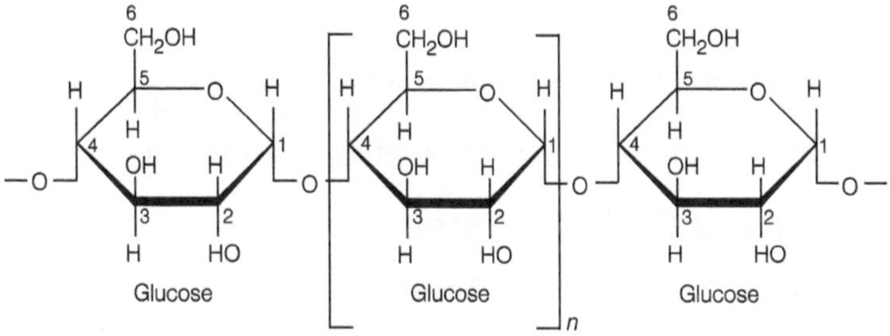

Structure of amylose

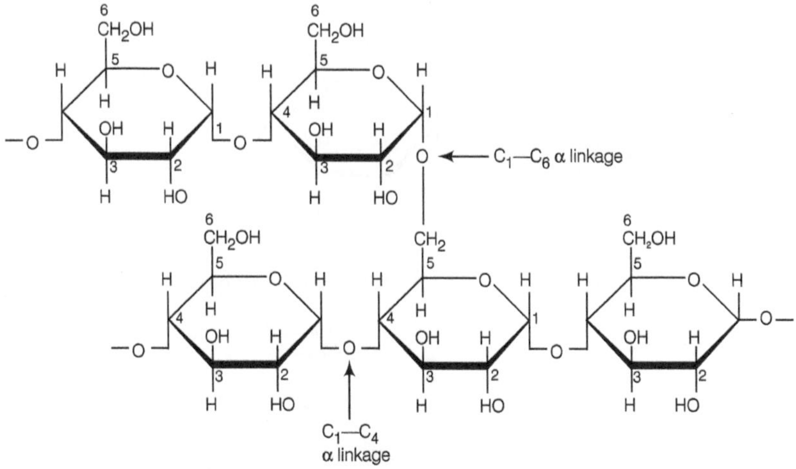

Structures of amylopectin

Glycogen

About 5000-15000 glucose units make up glycogen $(C_6H_{10}O_5)_n$. It is extensively branched and formed the reserve food material in animals hence, also called as **animal starch**.

Cellulose

It is a linear polymer of β-D-glucose units connected through β-1, 4-glycosidic linkage. It is important structural component of the cell wall of plants.

Chitin

It is the second most abundant organic substance. It is complex polymer of heteropolysaccharide type, which is the structural component of fungal walls and exoskeletons of arthropods.

Properties of Carbohydrates

Reducing and Non-Reducing Sugar

The sugars which have unlinked potential aldehyde group at their first C-atom, called **reducing sugar** and those which have aldehyde group in linked condition, called as **non-reducing sugars.**

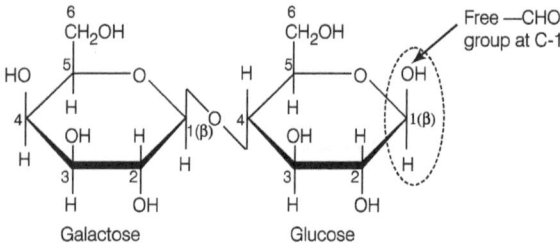

Reducing sugar : Lactose (β-1, 4-linkage)

Non-reducing sugar : Sucrose (α-1, 2-linkage)

Enantiomers

Optical isomers which are mirror image of each other. The d (+) and l (+) forms of carbohydrates are classified on this basis. The sugar solution which rotates the axis of plane polarised light clockwise called d (+) isomers, while those rotates it to anticlockwise termed as l (−) isomers.

Diastereomers

The isomers which are not the mirror image of each other.

Epimers

The diastereomers which have configurational change at a single interstitial C-atom.

Anomers

These are specialised diastereomers which shows configurational change at terminal carbon called **anomeric carbon** (the carbon which involved in ring formation and contains functional group). Two anomers of glucose are defined, *i.e.*, α-form and β-forms.

D and L Isomers

These are classified on the basis of direction of —OH group on **farthest chiral carbon** from functional group.

Proteins

The word protein (Gk. *proteios* – first or foremost) was first coined by **Berzelius** (1837) and **Mulder** (1838). It constitutes about 15% of our body and by mass involved in various functions like structural, storage, transport, signalling, movement, etc.

These are natural heteropolymer of substances like amino acids. To understand the detail structure of protein, we first take a close view of amino acids.

Amino Acids

The compound which contain both amino (—NH$_2$) and acid (–COOH) groups in them. *The generalised structure is as follows*

Amino group → H_2N—C—COOH Carboxylic group
with R (Alkyl/Aryl group) above C and H below.

To form peptide (or proteins), amino acids linked serially by **peptide bonds** (— CO—NH—) formed between amino group of one amino acid and the carboxylic group of the adjascent one.

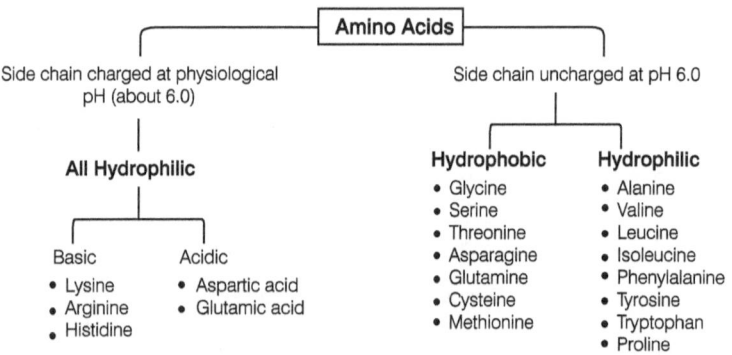

Following flow chart, indicate the physiological nature of amino acids

```
                            Amino Acids
            ┌───────────────────┴───────────────────┐
Side chain charged at physiological         Side chain uncharged at pH 6.0
        pH (about 6.0)
              │                              ┌──────┴──────┐
        All Hydrophilic                 Hydrophobic    Hydrophilic
         ┌────┴────┐                    • Glycine      • Alanine
       Basic     Acidic                 • Serine       • Valine
     • Lysine   • Aspartic acid         • Threonine    • Leucine
     • Arginine • Glutamic acid         • Asparagine   • Isoleucine
     • Histidine                        • Glutamine    • Phenylalanine
                                        • Cysteine     • Tyrosine
                                        • Methionine   • Tryptophan
                                                       • Proline
```

Amino acids and their physiological nature

There are 20 amino acids, which form proteins. These are called **proteinous amino acids**. Amino acids have both three letter and one letter code for convenient study. Following table gives information about the chemical nature and codes for amino acids.

Proteinous Amino Acids (with three letter code) **and** (one letter code in brackets)

Neutral	Glycine (Gly), (G)
	Alanine (Ala), (A)
	Valine (Val), (V)
	Leucine (Leu), (U)
	Isoleucine (Ile), (I)
Acidic	Aspartic acid (Asp), (D)
	Asparagine (Asn), (N)
	Glutamic acid (Glu), (Q)
	Glutamine (Gln), (E)
Basic	Arginine (Arg), (R)
	Lysine (Lys), (K)
S-Containing	Cysteine (Cys), (C)
	Methionine (Met), (M)
Alcoholic	Serine (Ser), (S)
	Threonine (Thr), (T)
Aromatic	Phenylalanine (Phe), (F)
	Tyrosine (Tyr), (Y)
	Tryptophan (Try), (W)
Heterocyclic	Histidine (His), (H)
	Proline (Pro), (P)

Non-Proteinous Amino Acids

They have physiological importance but not form proteins.

Some of them are

(i) **β-alanine** Component of Co-A and pentothenic acid (vitamin-B_5).

(ii) **γ-amino-butyric Acid** (GABA) Inhibitony neurotransmitter of CNS.

(iii) **Creatine** Important constituents of muscles.

(iv) **Ornithine and Citrulline** Intermediate in urea biosynthesis.

(v) **Histamine** Vasodilator, involved in allergic reaction.

(vi) **Serotonin** Vasoconstrictor, stimulate the contraction of smooth muscles.

(vii) **Epinephrine or Adrenaline** Derivative of tyrosine.

Structural Level of Proteins

There are four structural levels in proteins

(i) **Primary structure** This includes number of polypeptide, number and sequence of amino acids in each polypeptide.

(ii) **Secondary structure** There are three types of secondary structures α-helix, **β-pleated sheet** and **collagen helix.** The turns of helices and sheets are attached by hydrogen bond.

(iii) **Tertiary structure** Tertiary structure is stabilised by several types of bonds, hydrogen bonds, ionic bonds, Van der Waal's interaction, like covalent bonds and hydrophobic bonds. It gives 3-D conformation to protein.

(iv) **Quaternary structure** Found only in multimeric proteins, where two tertiary structure joins as a subunit.

Lipids

Lipids are chemically diverse group of compounds which are characterised by their relative insolubility in water and solubility in organic solvents. *These can be defined as* 'The easters of fatty acids and alcohol'.

The lipids have wide distribution in both animal and plant kingdom.

Classification of Lipids

On the basis of their chemical structure, the lipids are classified into following classes

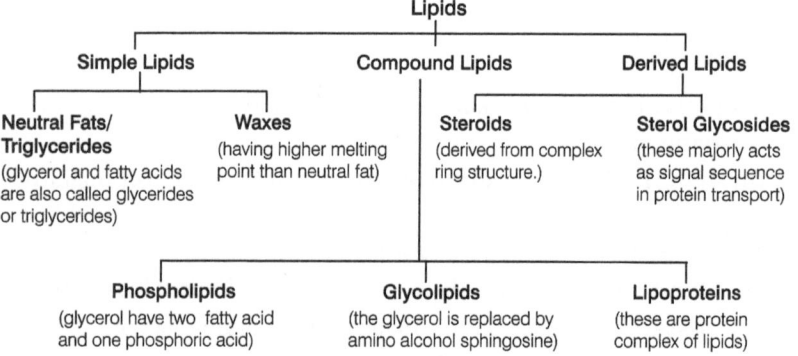

Handbook of BIOLOGY

The detailed explanation of these classes of lipids is given below

Triglycerides (Neutral Fats)

Neutral fats such as butter and vegetables oils are mostly triglycerides. Each has three fatty acid linked to a glycerol (glycerine or trihydroxy propane). In fats, when all three fatty acids are similar they are called as **pure fats** and when these fatty acids are dissimilar they termed as **mixed fat**.

Waxes

These are long chain fatty acid linked to long chain of alcohol or carbon ring. All waxes have firm consistency and repel water. In plants, it cover the surface of leaf and other aerial surfaces to avoid excess transpiration. In animals, **cutaneous glands** secrete wax, **lanolin** for forming a protective water insoluble coating on animal fur.

Glycolipids

These contains sphingosine with a fatty acid and monosaccharide sugar, *e.g.*, cerebrosides, terpenes and gangliosides.

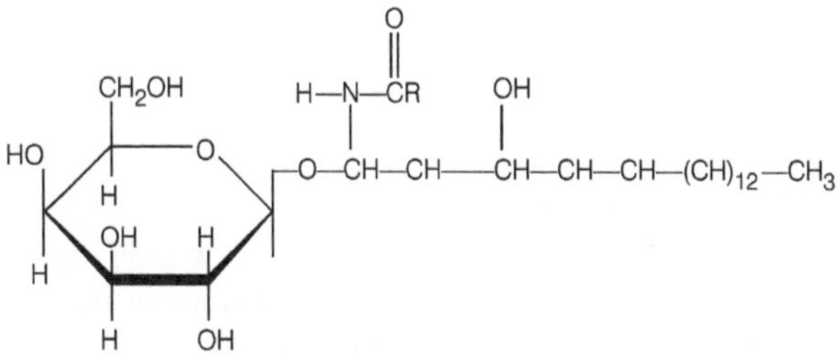

Glycolipids

Phospholipids (Common Membrane Lipid)

These are triglyceride lipids with one fatty acid is replaced by phosphoric acid which is often linked to additional nitrogenous group like choline, ethanolamine, etc.

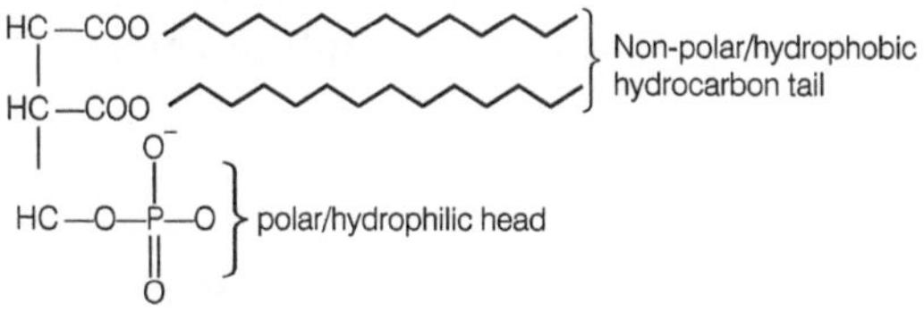

Phospholipids

Lipoproteins

These are the complex of lipids and proteins and are present in blood, milk and egg yolk. *On the basis of compactness, these can be devided into*

(a) **LDL** Deposition of bad cholesterol

(b) **HDL** Removal of bad cholesterol

Steroids

The group of complex lipids that possess a rigid backbone of four fused-together carbon rings. Sterols are the components of every eukaryotic cell membrane.

The most common type in animal tissue is cholesterol. Chemically these contain cyclopentanoperhydrophenanthrene nucleus.

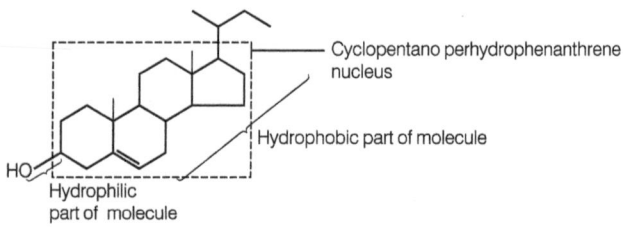

Terms Related to Lipids

(i) **Emulsion** Due to its insolubility in water, lipids form a colloidal complex and get dispersed uniformly in water in the form of minute droplets, called emulsions.

(ii) **Oils** Oils are those fats, which are liquid at room temperature of 20°C, *e.g.,* groundnut, cotton seed oil, etc.

(iii) **Hydrogenation** The process of conversion of unsaturated fatty acids to saturated form is called **hydrogenation**.

(iv) **Wax-D** Tuberculosis and leprosy bacteria produces a wax called wax-D. It is a major factor for their pathogenicity.

(v) **Amphipathic** The lipid which contain both the hydrophilic and hydrophobic groups called **amphipathic**.

Handbook of BIOLOGY

Functions of Lipids

Lipids generally perform following functions

```
                            Functions
    ┌──────────────────────────┼──────────────────────────┐
Energy Storage            Thermal Insulation          Buoyancy
    ┌──────┴──────┐        ┌──────┴──────┐
Animals      Plants     Animals      Plants
```

Energy Storage
- Animals
  - Fats (triglycerides)
  - In adipocytes
- Plants
  - Oil
  - In seeds and other tissues.

Thermal Insulation
- Animals
  - Fat in form other than triglycerides.
- Plants
  - Protective covering over leaf and stem provides heat protection.

Buoyancy
- In plants the leaf and stem have lipid covering to avoid wetting of plant and maintain buoyancy.

Nucleic Acids

Nucleic acid are long chain macromolecule which are formed by end to end polymerisation of large number of units called **nucleotides**. The two most important nucleic acids, present in living cells are Deoxyribonucleic Acids (DNA) and Ribonucleic Acid (RNA).

Components of Nucleic Acids

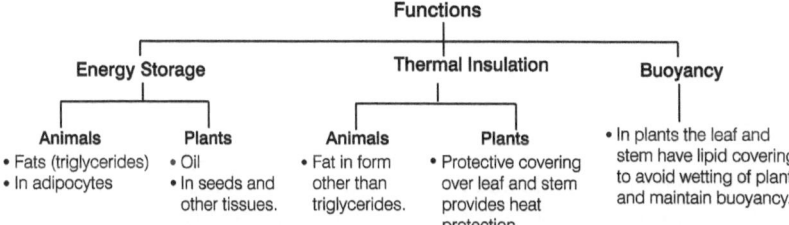

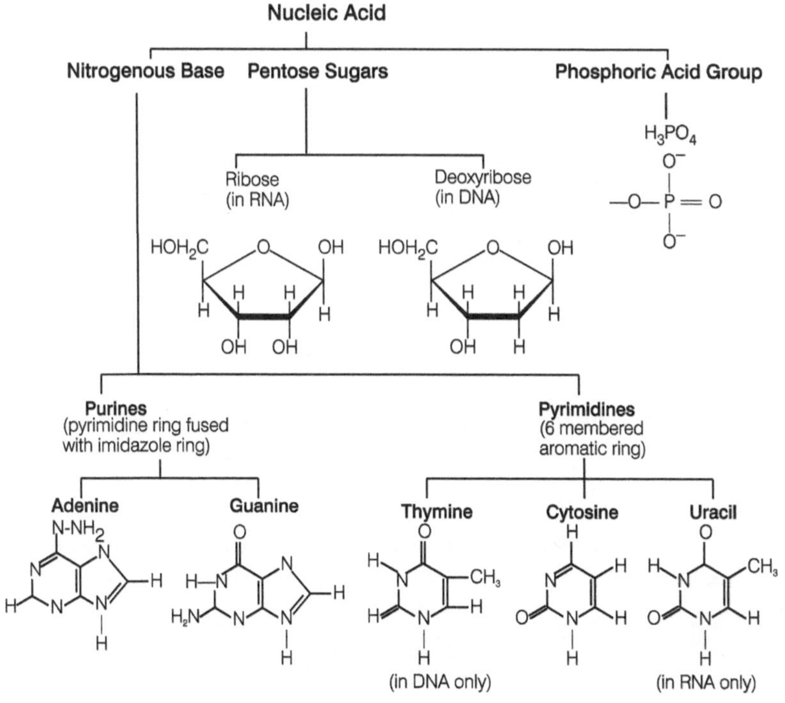

Components of nucleic acid

DNA

The DNA molecule is a polymer of several thousands pair of nucleotide monomers. A nucleotide is formed by the union of a phosphate group with a nucleosides.

Nucleoside = Nitrogenous base + Sugar

Nucleotide = Nucleoside + Phosphate group

DNA form a double helical structure in which two strends are bonded through hydrogen bonds and are antiparallel to each other. The coiling pattern and antiparallel structure of DNA, *can be seen as*

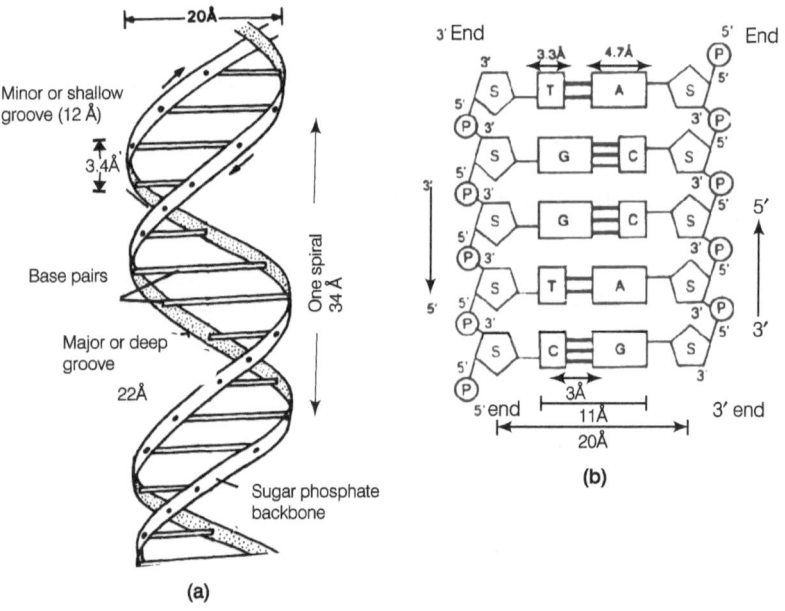

DNA structure : (a) Coiling of two strands
(b) Antiparallel strands and bond details

RNA

RNA is single stranded genetic material present in **lower organism**. In higher organism it present with DNA and perform various functions.

The main types of RNAs are
  (i) *m*RNA (messanger RNA)
  (ii) *t*RNA (transfer RNA)
  (iii) *r*RNA (ribosomal RNA)
  (iv) *hn*RNA (heteronuclear RNA)
  (v) *mt*RNA (mitochondrial RNA)
  (vi) *cp*RNA (chloroplastidal RNA)

Enzymes

An enzyme is a specific protein produced within the organism, that is capable of catalysing specific chemical reactions. As they are of biological origin and catalyse various reactions, are called **biocatalyst.**

The term 'Enzyme' was coined by **Kuhne** (1878) for catalytically active substances previously called **ferments.** Protein nature of the enzyme was first found out by **Sumner** (1926). Like catalysts, the enzyme do not start a chemical reaction or change its equilibrium, but enhance the rate of reaction.

Chemical Nature of Enzymes

All enzymes are globular proteins with the exception of recently discovered RNA enzymes. Some enzyme may additionally contain a non-protein group.

There are two types of enzymes on the basis of composition
  (i) **Simple enzymes** The enzyme which completely made up of protein, *e.g.,* pepsin, trypsin, urease, etc.
  (ii) **Conjugate enzyme** *It is the enzyme formed by two parts*

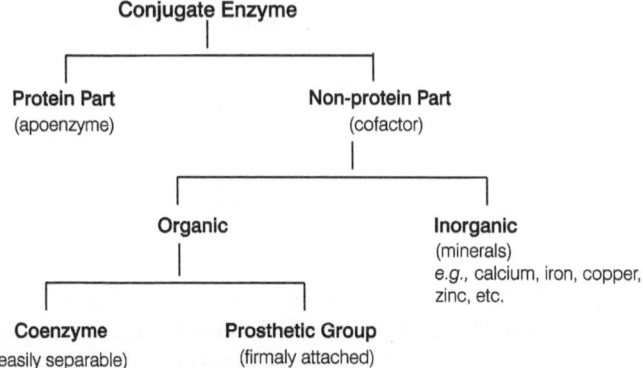

Enzyme and their constituents

Classification of Enzymes

On the basis of reaction they performed, enzymes are classified into six categories

(i) **Oxidoreductases** Oxidase, reductase and dehydrogenases are included in this class of enzymes.

(ii) **Transferases** These enzymes perform group transfer reaction.

(iii) **Hydrolases** These enzyme induce hydrolysis, *e.g.*, amylase, lactase, etc.

(iv) **Lyases** They induced the cleavage without hydrolysis and addition of double bond takes place, *e.g.*, aldolase.

(v) **Isomerases** Rearrangement of molecular structure, *e.g.*, isomerase, epimerase, mutase, etc.

(vi) **Ligases/Synthetases** These enzymes induced the bonding of two molecule after taking energy from ATP.

Nomenclature of Enzymes

Enzymes are named by adding the suffix-ase after the substrate (*e.g.*, lipase, amylase, maltase, etc.) or chemical reaction (*e.g.*, succinate dehydrogenase). Some old names also persist as pepsin, trypsin, etc.

Mechanism of Enzyme Action

The general mechanism of enzyme action has two steps

(i) Formation of Enzyme-Substrate Complex

When an enzyme acts upon a substrate, it forms an enzyme-substrate complex. Subsquently this complex decomposes the substrate, undergoes chemical change and the enzyme is regenerated afterwards.

$$E + S \rightarrow ES$$
$$ES \rightarrow E + P$$

Following two models has been put forth to explain the formation of ES complex

(a) **Lock and key model** Proposed by **Emil Fisher** in 1890s. He states that the both the components (*i.e.*, enzyme and substrate) have strictly complementary structure.

(b) **Induced fit model** Proposed by **D Koshland** in 1966. According to this when enzyme bind to substrate, the change in shape of active sites of enzyme takes place.

(ii) Lowering of Activation Energy

All chemical reactions have a potential energy barrier that must be overcome before the reactants can be converted into products. The energy required to break this barrier is equivalent to activation energy.

The enzyme lowers the energy of activation during its complexing with substrate. After the combination of enzyme and substrate, the energy level of substrate gets raised, and it reacts faster.

The diagrammatic representation of the process is as follows

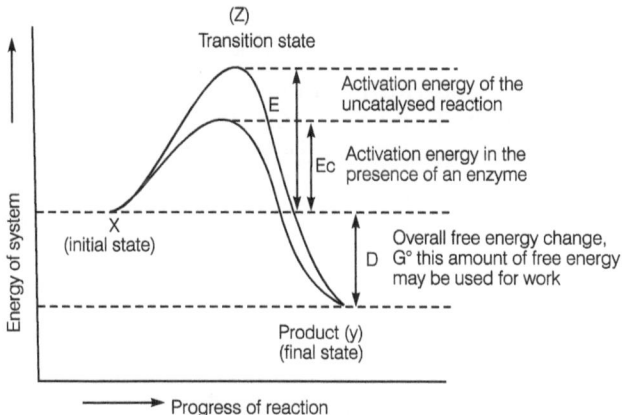

Graphical representation of enzyme catalysis

Turnover Number

Being large sized protein molecule, enzyme exists as colloid. Substrate molecule changed per minute into product is called **turn over number**, *e.g.,* 36 millions for carbonic anhydrase, 5 millions for catalase, etc.

Factors Affecting Enzyme Activity

The activity of an enzyme can be affected by a change in the conditions which can alter the tertiary structure of the protein.

(i) **Substrate concentration** Enzyme activity increase with increase in concentration of the substrate to a maximum and then it levels off.

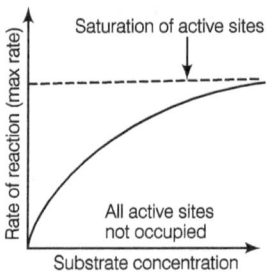

(ii) **Enzyme concentration** In general the rate of reaction will increase with increasing enzyme concentration, due to availability of more active sites for reaction.

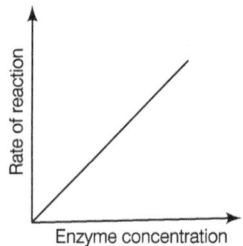

(iii) **Temperature and pH** In most of the enzymatic reactions, rise of 10°C in the temperature doubles the rate of reaction between 5-40°C. Enzymes are **denatured** (secondary and above level of structures degraded) at higher temperature due to proteinaceous nature and rate of reaction drops.

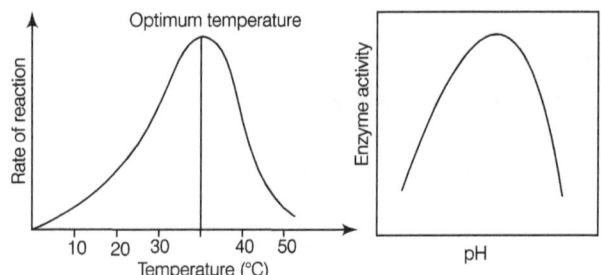

(iv) **Redox potential** Enzymes are sensitive to redox-potential of the cell also. Many enzymes are affected by redox potential due to presence of oxidisable SH-group.

Enzyme Inhibition

Reduction or stoppage of enzyme activity due to certain adverse conditions or chemicals is called **enzyme inhibition**.

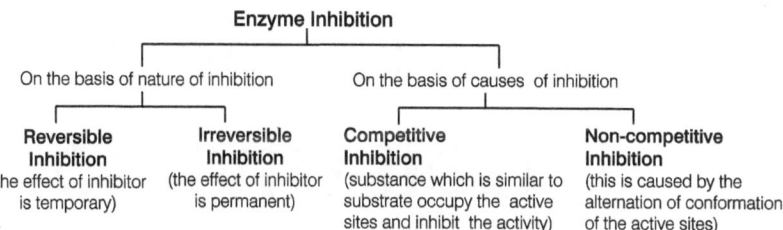

Metabolites

Plants and animals produce thousands types of chemicals. Some of the organic compounds like carbohydrate, fat, protein, nucleic acid, chlorophyll and heme, etc., are required for basic metabolic processes and found the whole plant and animal kingdom. These are called **primary metabolites.**

Many plants, fungi and microbes synthesise a number of organic substances, which are not involved in primary metabolisms (as respiration, reproduction, photosynthesis, protein and lipid metabolism) and seen to have no direct function in growth and development of these organisms, called **secondary metabolites.** *These are as follows*

Class of Secondary Metabolites	Examples	Chief Functions
Pigments	Carotenoids, anthocyanins, etc.	Attract pollinators and help in seed dispersal.
Alkaloids	Morphine, codeine, etc.	Defense against herbivore and pathogens.
Terpenoides	Monoterpenes, diterpenes, etc.	Provide characteristic smell to plants.
Essential oils	Lemon grass oil, etc.	Protection against pathogens.
Toxins	Abrin, ricin	To kill pathogens.
Drugs	Vinblastin, curcumin, etc.	Stop the growth of bacteria and other pathogen.
Polymeric substances	Rubber, gums and cellulose	To inhibit the entry of pathogens.

3
Cell Cycle and Cell Division

Cell Cycle (Howard and Pelc; 1953)

It is a genetically controlled series of events occurring in a co-ordinated manner in newly formed cell by which it undergoes growth and divides to form two daughter cells. The cell cycle is divided into two parts, *i.e.,* **interphase** and **cell division** (M-phase).

Interphase

It is the phase of the cell cycle in which the cell prepares itself for the initiation of cell division. It comprises G_1, S and G_2-phase. It represents the stage between two successive M-phase. The cells are actively involved in metabolic activities during this phase.

G_0-Phase It is the quiscent phase during which the cell cycle is arrested for an indefinite period. Bone, muscle and nerve cells remain in this phase permanently. The cells remain metabolically active but do not proliferate.

These two groups are further divided into sub-groups

Mitosis or M-phase (Flemming; 1882)

It is the frequent process of nuclear division in somatic cells by which two daughter nuclei are produced, each identical to the parent nuclei.

Mitosis is achieved in two phases

(a) **Karyokinesis** It is a type of indirect nuclear division, which involves the division of nucleus. It is divided into four phases, *i.e.*, prophase, metaphase, anaphase and telophase.

(b) **Cytokinesis** It invsolves the division of cytoplasm. Cytokinesis normally starts towards the middle anaphase and is completed simultaneously with the telophase. It is different in animal and plant cell. In animals, it occurs by **cleavage furrow method** whereas in plants, it is carried out by **cell plate method**.

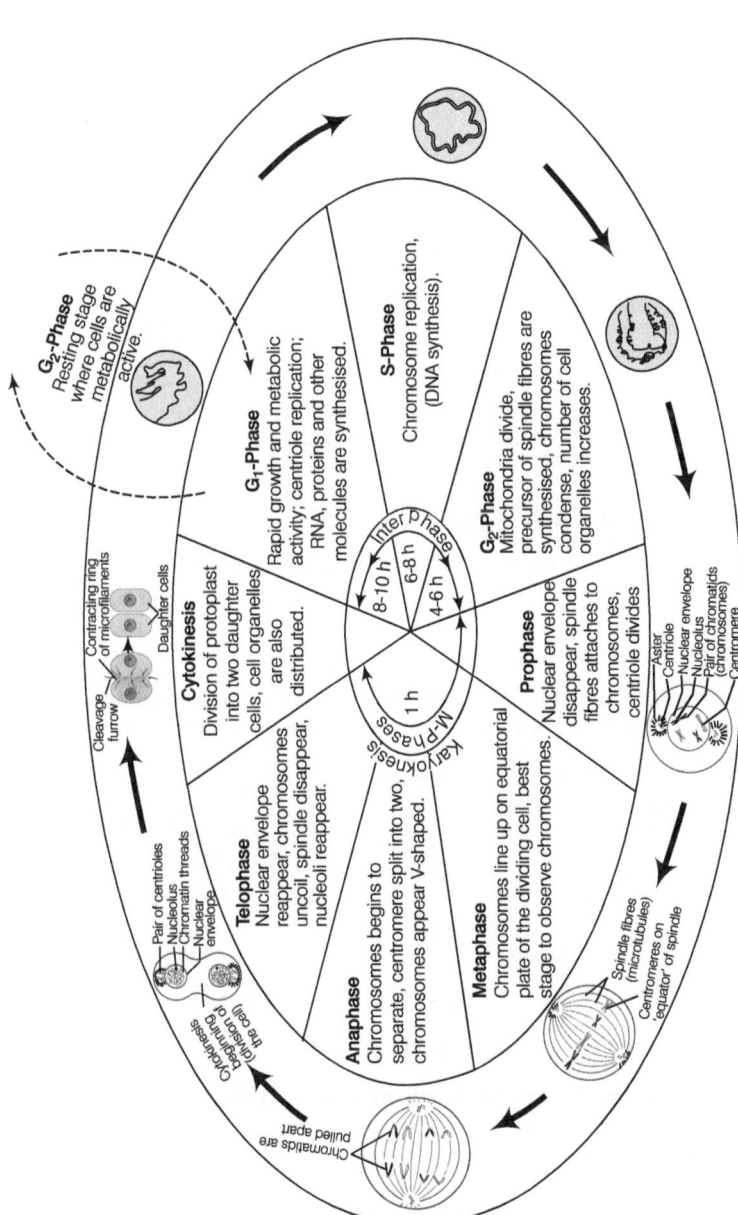

Cell cycle (pictorial view with events)

Significance of Mitosis

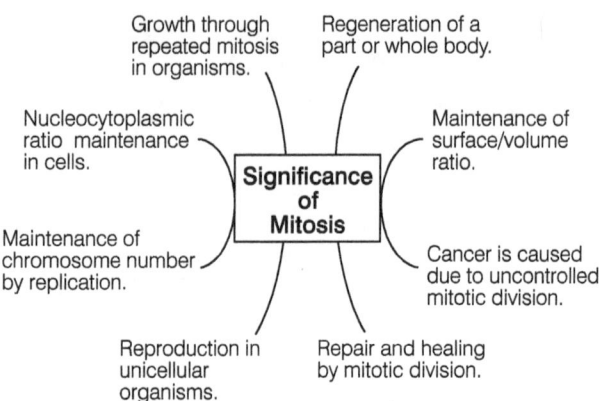

Significance of Cell Cycle

(i) It helps to maintain, controlled proliferation of cells.

(ii) Deregulation of cell cycle may lead to tumour formation.

Amitosis (Remak; 1855)

It is a direct cell division by simple cleavage of nucleus and cytoplasm without the formation of chromosomes. It is seen in few monerans.

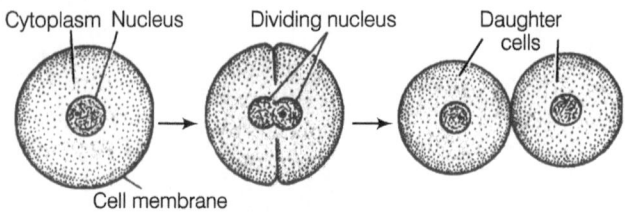

Amitosis

Meiosis (Farmer and Moore; 1905)

It is a type of indirect division, which occurs in diploid sex cells and gives rise to four haploid cells, each having half number of chromosomes as compared to parent cell.

Handbook of BIOLOGY

It consists of two division
- Meiosis I
- Meiosis II

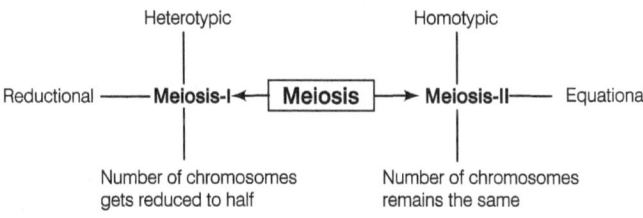

Important processes seen during meiosis are

Synapsis (Montgomery; 1901) It is the side-by-side pairing of homologous chromosomes **during the zygotene** phase of meiosis prophase-I.

Depending upon the place of origin of pairing, it is **procentric** (starting from centromere), **proterminal** (starting from the ends) and **intermediate** (starting at various places).

Crossing-over It is an enzyme mediated process of exchange of genetic material or chromatid segments between two homologous chromosomes occurring **during the pachytene phase** of meiosis-I.

The temporary jointsor point of attachment between chromosomes during crossing-over are called **chiasmata**. Formation of these structures is an indication of completion of crossing-over and bigennning of separation of chomosomes, *i.e.*, process of **terminalisation**. In the process of terminalisation chiasmata start moving towards their terminals. The complete process in pictorial view in given on next page.

Handbook of BIOLOGY

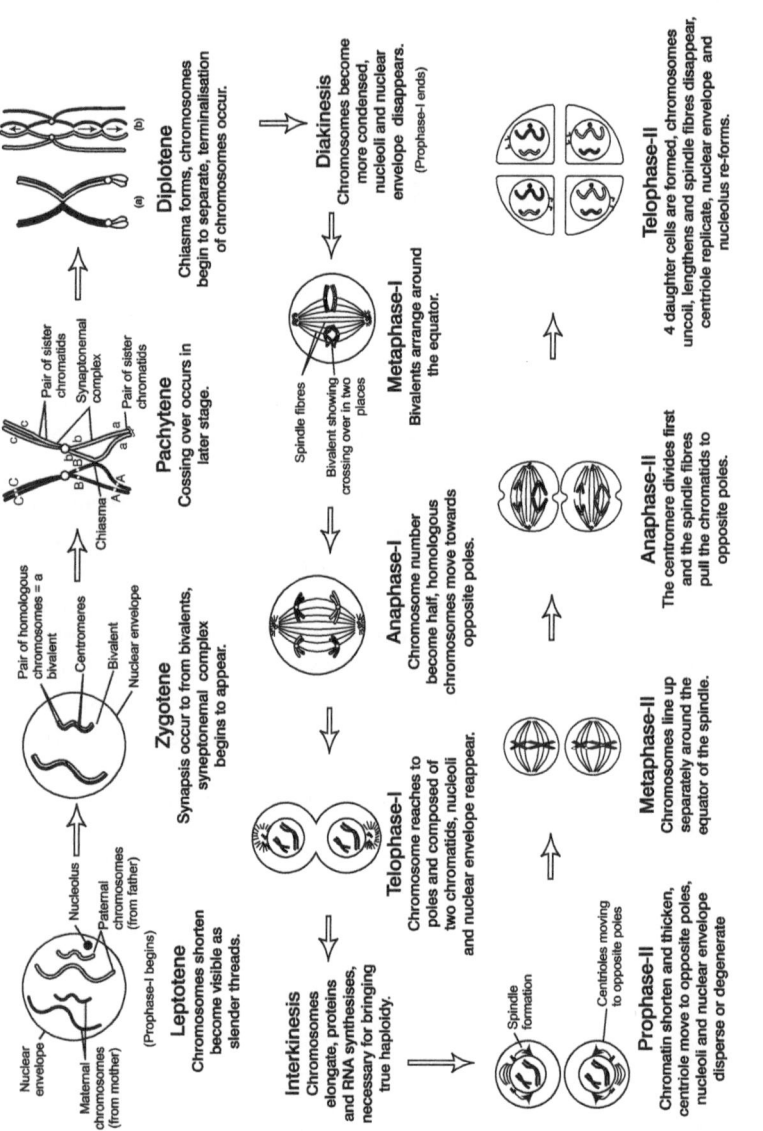

Stages of meiosis

Handbook of BIOLOGY

Significance of Meiosis

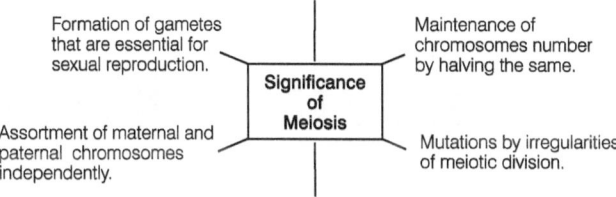

Differences between Mitosis and Meiosis

Mitosis	Meiosis
G_2-period of interphase is normal.	G_2-period is short or non-existent.
Division phase of one or two hours.	Division phase lasts several days to several years.
Occurs in most body (somatic) cells.	Occurs only in germ cells in the gonads.
Accounts for growth of body, repair and regeneration of injured parts and embryonic development.	Accounts for formation of gametes in sexual reproduction.
One chromosomal duplication is followed by one cell division, producing two diploid daughter cells.	One chromosomal duplication is followed by two consecutive divisions, producing four haploid daughter cells.
Resultant daughter cells are genetically similar to each other and to the parent cell.	Resultant daughter cells are genetically dissimilar to each other and to the parent cell.
Prophase relatively short and less complicated.	Prophase of first meiosis very long and complicated.
No synapsis, chiasmata-formation and crossing-over between homologous chromosomes.	Synapsis, chiasmata-formation and crossing-over between homologous chromosomes in prophase of first meiosis.
It is always the chromatids that segregate into resultant daughter cells.	It is the homologous chromosomes that segregate into resultant daughter cells in first meiosis and chromatids in the second.
Cytokinesis includes a single equatorial furrow around the parental cell.	Cytokinesis includes two furrows at right angles around the parent cell.
Occurs in body throughout life.	Occurs in gonads only when these are mature for sexual reproduction.

4
The Living World

Life is a characteristic quality that differentiate an inanimate (non-living) object from the animate (living) forms.

Characteristic of Living Forms

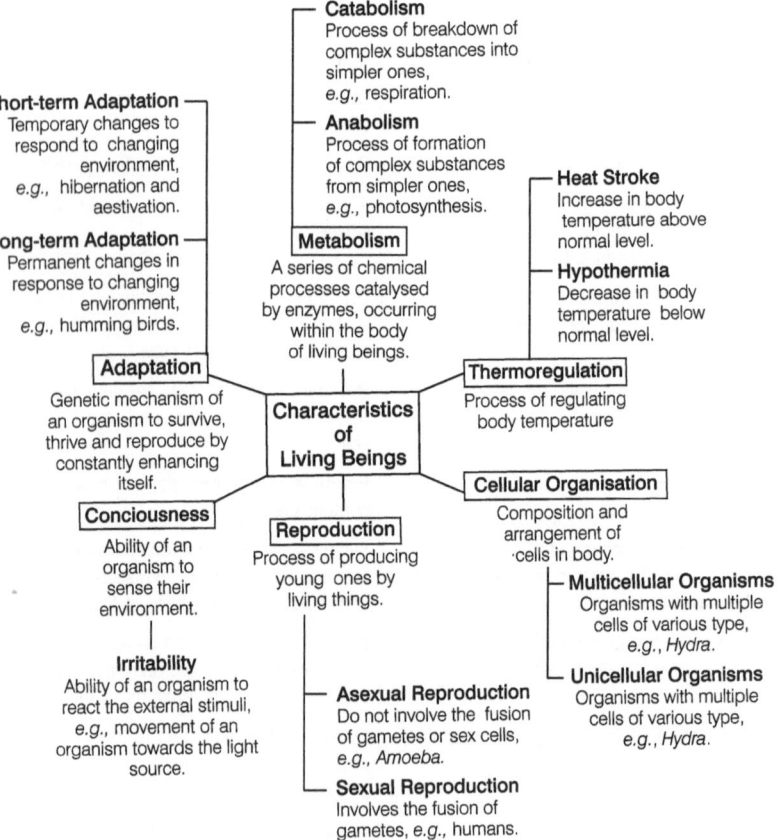

Biodiversity

Biodiversity is the degree of variability among living organisms. It includes all the varieties of plants and animals. It encompasses all the ecological complexes (in which the diversity occurs), ecosystem, community diversity, species diversity and genetic diversity. It comprises all the millions of species and the genetic differences between them.

Systematics

Systematics is the study of the units of the biodiversity. It attempts to classify the diversity of organisms on the basis of following four fields *viz*, identification, classification, nomenclature and taxonomy.

Identification

It aims to identify the correct name and position of an organism in the already established classification system. It is done with the help of keys. **Key** is a list of alternate characters. An organism can be identified easily by selecting and eliminating the characters present in the key.

Classification

It involves the scientific grouping of identified organisms into convenient categories or taxa based on some easily observable and fundamental characters. The various categories are kingdom, phylum, class, order, family, genus and species.

Nomenclature

After classification, organisms are subjected to a format of two-word naming system called **binomial nomenclature**. It consists of two components, *i.e.*, generic name and specific epithet. For example, in *Mangifera indica*, '*Mangifera*' is the generic name and '*indica*' is the specific name of mango. This system was proposed by **C Linnaeus** (a Swedish Botanist) in (1753) in his book *Species Plantarum*.

Polynomial System of Nomenclature is a type of naming system containing more than two words. Trinomial system is a component of polynomial system and contains three words. Third word represents the sub-species and first two-words remains the same as in binomial system.

Codes of Biological Nomenclature

There are five codes of nomenclature which helps to avoid errors, duplication and ambiguity in scientific names.

Handbook of BIOLOGY

These codes are as follows

- **ICBN**   International Code of Botanical Nomenclature
- **ICZN**   International Code of Zoological Nomenclature
- **ICVN**   International Code of Viral Nomenclature
- **ICBN**   International Code of Bacteriological Nomenclature
- **ICNCP** International Code of Nomenclature for Cultivated Plants

Types of Specification in Nomenclature

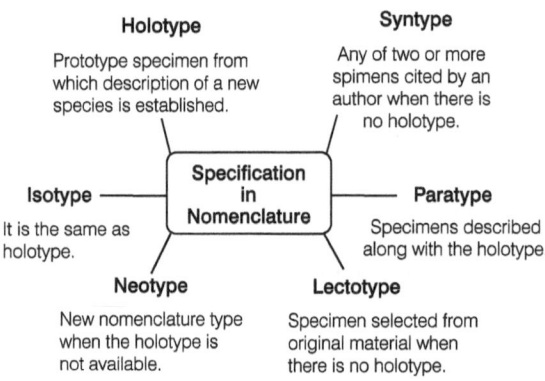

Taxonomy

It deals with the principles and procedures of identification, nomenclature and classification of organisms. It reflets the natural and phylogenetic relationships among organisms. It also provides the details of external and internal structure, cellular structure and ecological information of organisms.

Various Branches of Taxonomy

Taxonomic Field	Basis
Classical (alpha) Taxonomy	Morphological traits
Artificial Taxonomy	Habit and habitat of organisms
Natural Taxonomy	Natural similarity among organisms
Chemotaxonomy	Presence or absence of chemicals in cells or tissues
Cytotaxonomy	Cytological studies
Numerical or Phenetic Taxonomy	Number of shared characters of various organisms
Phylogenetic or Omega Taxonomy	Phylogenetic relationships

Handbook of BIOLOGY

Classical Taxonomy

It is also known as old taxonomy. In classical taxonomy, species is the basic unit and it can be described on the basis of one or few preserved specimens. Organisms are classified on the basis of some limited features.

Modern Taxonomy/New Systematics

The concept of modern taxonomy was given by **Julian Huxley** (1940). According to it, species are dynamic and ever-changing entity. Studies of organisms are done on a huge number of variations. It includes cytotaxonomy, numerical taxonomy, chemotaxonomy, etc.

Taxonomic Categories

Classification is not a single step process. It involves hierarchy of steps in which each step represents a rank or category. Since, the category is a part of overall taxonomic arrangement, it is called the **taxonomic category** and all categories together constitutes the **taxonomic hierarchy**.

The taxonomic categories, which are always used in hierarchical classification of organisms are called **obligate categories**.

The sub-categories like sub-species, sub-class, sub-family, etc., which facilitate more sound and scientific placement of various taxa are called **intermediate categories**.

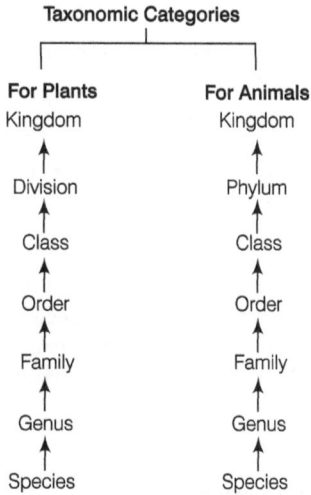

Taxonomic categories showing hierarchical

Taxon represents the rank, of each category and referred to as a unit of classification. The term 'Taxon' was first introduced by ICBN during 1956. According to Mayr (1964), taxon is a group of any rank that is sufficiently distinct to be worthy of being assigned a definite category. In simple words, taxon refers to a group of similar, genetically related individuals having certain characters distinct from those of other groups.

Taxonomic Hierarchy

Arrangement of taxonomic categories in a descending order during the classification of an animal is called **taxonomic hierarchy**. It was first introduced by **Linnaeus** (1751) and hence, it is also known as **Linnaean Hierarchy**.

Kingdom

It is the highest category in taxonomy. A kingdom includes all the organisms, which share a set of distinguished characters.

Phylum or Division

Phylum or Division (Cuvier, Eichler) is a taxonomic category higher than class and lower in rank to kingdom. The term 'Phylum' is used for animals, while 'Division' is commonly employed for plants. It consists of more than one class having some similar correlated characters.

Class

Class (Linnaeus) is a major category, which includes related orders.

Order

An order (Linnaeus) is a group of one or more related families that possess some similar correlated characters, which are lesser in number as compared to a family or genera.

Family

Family (John Ray) is a group of related genera with less number of similarities as compared to genus and species. All the genera of a family have some common or correlated features. They are separable from genera of a related family by important differences in both vegetative and reproductive features.

Genus

Genus (Term by John Ray) comprises a group of related species, which has more characters common in comparison to species of other genera. In other words genera are the aggregates of closely related species.

Species

Taxonomic studies consider a group of individual organisms with fundamental similarities as a species (John Ray). Species is the lowest or basic taxonomic category, which consists of one or more individuals of a populations.

Taxonomical Aids

They include techniques, procedures and stored information that are useful in identification and classification of organisms.

Some of the taxonomical aids are as follows

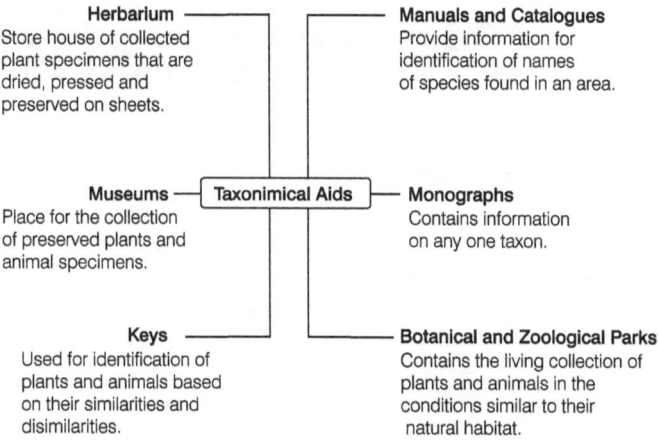

Importance of Taxonomical Aids

These aids helps to store and preserve the information as well the specimens. The collection of actual specimens of plants and animals species is essential and is the prime source of taxonomic studies.

These are also essential for training in systematics which is used for classification of an organism. Hence, taxonomic aids facilitate identification, naming and classification of organisms using actual specimens collected from the fields and preserved as referrals in the from of herbaria, museums, etc.

5
Biological Classification

Biology : Nature and Scope
Biology (L. *bios* – life; *logos* – knowledge) is the branch of science, which deals with the study of living organisms and their life processes. **Aristotle** is called the Father of Biology, but the term 'Biology' was first coined by **Lamarck** and **Treviranus** in 1802. It has two main branches, *i.e.*, Botany (study of plants) and Zoology (study of animals).
- *Father of Zoology* **Aristotle**
- *Father of Botany* **Theophrastus**

Classification of Living Organisms
Classification is an arrangement of living organisms according to their common characteristics and placing the group within taxonomic hierarchy.

The branch of science which deals with description, nomenclature, identification and classification of organisms is called taxonomy. *Some major branches of taxonomy are*

Numerical Taxonomy It is based on all observable characteristics. Number and codes are assigned to characters and data is processed through computers.

Cytotaxonomy In this taxonomy the detailed cytological information, is used to categorise organisms.

Chemotaxonomy The chemical constituents are taken as the basis for classification of organisms.

On the basis of reference criteria, the classification of living organisms can be of three types

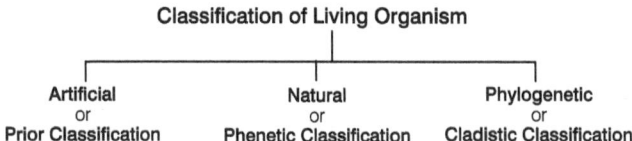

Artificial or Prior Classification

In this system of classification one or very few characters are considered as the key feature of classification. This classification system, never throws light on affinities or relationship between the plants.

Natural or Phenetic Classification

The classification system in which the organism is classified on the basis of their permanent vegetative character. In this classification system, the grouping of heterogenous group (unrelated) of organism avoided.

Cladistic Classification or Phylogenetic Classification

This classification may be monophyletic (*i.e.*, one ancestry), polyphyletic (*i.e.*, the organism derived from two ancestors) and paraphyletic (*i.e.*, the organism does not include all the descendents of common ancestor).

Cladistics is a method of classification of organism based upon their genetic and ancestral relationship, which are more scientific and natural.

The most accepted, five kingdom system of classification of living organism is proposed by **RH Whittakar**. *These five kingdoms are* **Monera, Protista, Fungi, Animalia** and **Plantae**.

Other Classification Systems

- Two Kingdom System–**Carolus Linnaeus** (Animals and Plants).
- Three Kingdom System–**Ernst Haeckel** (Protista, Animals and Plants).
- Four Kingdom System–**Copeland** (Monera, Protista, Animals and Plants).
- Six Kingdom System (Most Recent)–**Carl Woese** (Archaebacteria, Eubacteria, Protista, Fungi, Animalia and Plantae).

Monera (Prokaryotic, Unicellular Organisms)

Kingdom–Monera contains bacteria, archaebacteria, mycoplasma, actinomycetes, cyanobacteria and rickettsia.

Bacteria

Unicellular, prokaryotic organisms contain cell wall (features of plant cells only). Approximately 4000 species of bacteria, with cosmopolitan occurrence. Bacteria can be regarded both friends and foes, on the basis of interaction with human being.

An average weight human (~ 70 kg) has about 2.5 kg of bacteria in form of gut microflora to supplement the proper digestion and other metabolic functions.

Facts related to bacteria can be visualised in a nutshell as

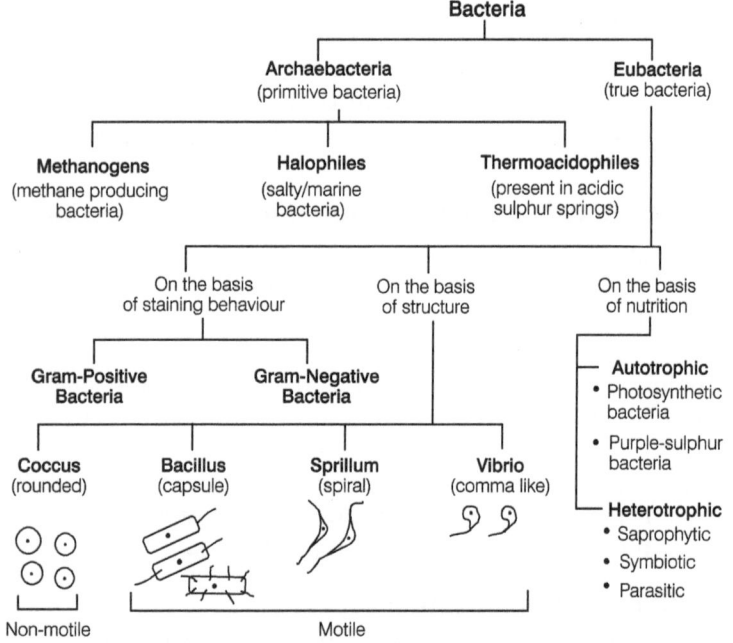

Archaebacteria

This is a group of most primitive prokaryotes. They have the cell wall, made up of protein and non-cellulosic polysaccharides. The presence of 16 *sr*RNA, makes them unique and helps in placing in a separate domain called **archaea** between bacteria and eukarya.

Handbook of BIOLOGY

Archaebacteria can live under extreme hostile conditions like salt pans, salt marshes and hot sulphur springs. They are also known as **living fossil**, because they represent the earliest form of life on earth.

Archaebacteria can be used as
  (i) Experimentation for absorption of solar radiation.
  (ii) Production of gobar gas from dung and sewage.
  (iii) Cause fermentation of cellulose in **ruminants**.

Eubacteria

Eubacteria are 'true bacteria' which lack nucleus and membrane bound organalles like mitochondria, chloroplasts, etc. Eubacteria are usually divided into five phylums– Spirochetes, Chlamydias, Gram-positive bacteria, Cyanobacteria and Proteobacteria.

The structural detail of a typical eubacterial cell is given as follows

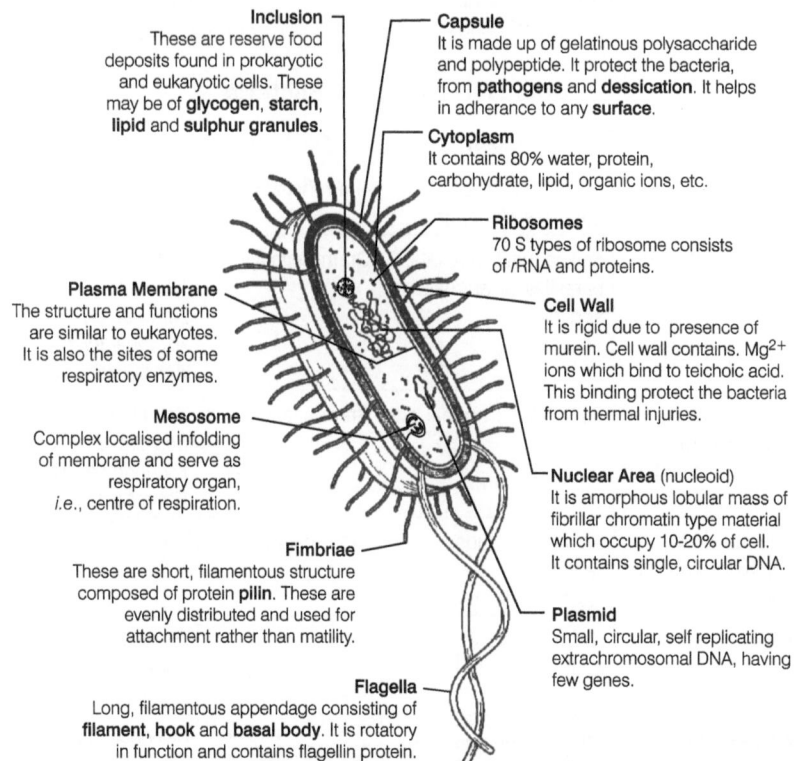

Detailed structure of bacteria

Nutrition in Bacteria

The process of acquiring energy and material is called nutrition. On the basis of mode of nutrition, bacteria is of two types—**autotrophic** and **heterotrophic**. About 1% bacteria show autotrophic mode of nutrition and the rest are of heterotrophic habit.

Autotrophic (*i.e.,* photosynthetic) bacteria and **heterotrophic bacteria** with their related details are mentioned in following tables.

Some Photosynthetic Bacteria

Group	Main Habitats	Cell Wall	Representatives
Prochlorobacteria	Live in tissues of marine invertebrates.	Gram-negative	*Prochloron*
Purple or green bacteria	Generally anaerobic and resides on sediments of lakes and ponds.	Gram-negative	*Rhodospirillum* and *Chlorobium*

Some Heterotrophic Bacteria

Group	Main Habitats	Cell Wall	Representatives
Spirochaetes	Aquatic habitats; parasites of animals	Gram-negative	*Spirochaeta* and *Treponema*.
Aerobic rods and cocci	Soil, aquatic habitats; parasites of animals and plants	Gram-negative	*Pseudomonas, Neisseria, Nitrobacter, Azotobacter* and *Agrobacterium*
Facultative anaerobic rods (enterobacteria)	Soil, plants, animal gut	Gram-negative	*Salmonella, Shigella, Proteus, Escherichia* and *Photobacterium*
Sulphur and sulphate reducing bacteria	Anaerobic muds, sediments (as in bogs, marshes)	Gram-negative	*Desulfovibrio*
Myxobacteria	Decaying plant, animal matter, bark of living trees	Gram-negative	*Myxococcus* and *Chondromyces*
Mycoplasmas	Parasites of plants, animals	Cell wall absent	*Mycoplasma*

Group	Main Habitats	Cell Wall	Representatives
Gram-positive cocci	Soil, skin and mucous membranes of animals	Gram-positive	*Staphylococcus* and *Streptococcus*
Endospore-forming rods and cocci	Soil; animal gut	Gram-positive	*Bacillus* and *Clostridium*
Non-sporulating rods	Fermenting plant, animal material, human oral cavity, gut vaginal tract	Gram-positive	*Lactobacillus* and *Listeria*
Chemoautotrophes	Soil, aquatic habitat	Gram-negative	*Halothiobacillus* and *Acidothiobacillus*

Reproduction in Bacteria

Bacteria reproduce both **asexually** and **sexually**.

Asexual Methods

Asexually, bacteria reproduces by following methods

- **Fission** Bacteria divide both laterally and longitudinally.
- **Budding** Vegetative outgrowths results into new organism after maturity.
- **Spore formation** Non-motile spore like **conidia, oidia** and **endospores** are formed.

Sexual Methods

Although sexes are not differentiated in bacteria, but still following methods of genetic recombination are categorised under sexual reproduction in bacteria

- **Transformation** F Griffith (1928), Genetic material of one bacteria transferred to other through **conjugation tube**.
- **Conjugation** Lederberg and Tatum (1946), Transfer of genetic material through **sex pili.**
- **Transduction** Zinder and Lederberg (1952), Transfer of genetic material by **bacteriophage.**

Economic Importance

Economically, some bacteria are useful in producing various useful substances like curd, cheese antibiotics and vinegar, etc. While other bacteria causes several chronic diseases in human, plants and other animals, etc.

Other Monerans

1. Mycoplasma

It was discovered by **Nocard** and **Roux** in 1898. These are cell wall less, aerobic and non-motile organisms. Due to absence of cell wall and pleomorphic nature, they are commonly called as **jokers of living world**.

The mycoplasmas are also known as **Pleuro Pneumonia Like Organisms** (PPLO). These are the smallest living cell yet discovered, can survive without oxygen and are typically about 0.1 µm in diameter.

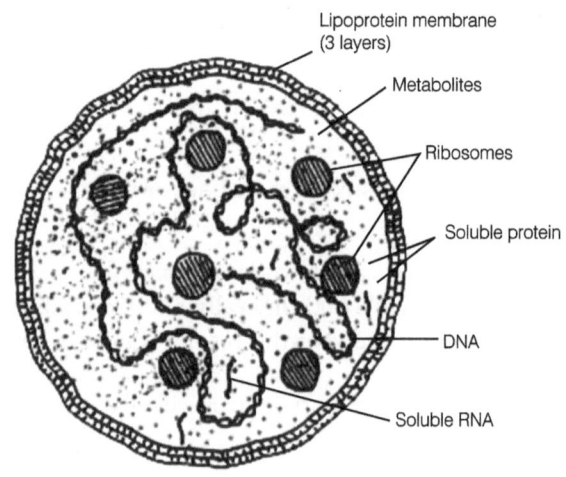

Structure of *Mycoplasma*

2. Actinomycetes

Actinomycetes, member of a heterogeneous group of Gram-positive, generally anaerobic bacteria noted for a filamentous and branching growth pattern that results, in most forms, in an extensive colony, or **mycelium**.

Morphologically they resemble fungi because of their elongated cells that branch into filaments or hyphae. During the process of composting, mainly thermophilic and thermotolerent actinomyces are responsible for decomposition of the organic matter at elevated temperature.

Generally, Actinomycetes grow on fresh substrates more slowly than other bacteria and fungi. During the composting process the Actinomycetes degrade natural substances such as chitin or cellulose.

Natural habitats of thermophilic Actinomycetes are silos, corn mills, air conditioning systems and closed stables. Some Actinomycetes are found responsible for allergic symptoms in the respiratory tract, *e.g.*, Extrinsic Allergic Alveolitis (EAA).

3. Cyanobacteria/Blue-Green Algae (BGA)

They are Gram-negative photosynthetic prokaryote which perform oxygenic photosynthesis. These can live in both freshwater and marine habitat and responsible for 'blooms' in polluted water (eutrophication).

They have photosynthetic pigments **chlorophyll-*a* carotenoids** and **phycobilins** and food is stored in form of cyanophycean starch, lipid globule and protein granules.

Cyanobacteria has cell wall formed of peptidoglycan, naked DNA, 70 S ribosomes and absence of membrane bound organalles like ectoplasmic reticulum, mitochondria, Golgi bodies, etc.

The red sea is named after the colouration provided by red coloured cyanobacteria *i.e.*, *Trichodesmium erythraeum*.

Cyanobacteria can fix atmospheric nitrogen through a specific structure called **heterocyst** these are modified cells in which photosystem-II is absent hence, non-cyclic photophosphorylation doesn't takes place. Nitrogen fixation is performed through enzyme nitrogenase, present in it.

4. *Rickettsia*

These are small, aerobic and Gram-negative bacteria. They belongs to phylum–Alpha-protobacteria which are capable of growing in low level of nutrients and have long generation time relative to other Gram-negative bacteria.

Rocky Mountain Spotted Fever (RMSF) is a tick borne human disease caused by *Rickettsia rickettsii*, an obligate, intracellular bacteria.

Protista (Eukaryotic, Unicellular Organisms)

Kingdom–Protista include three broad groups, explained in following flow chart

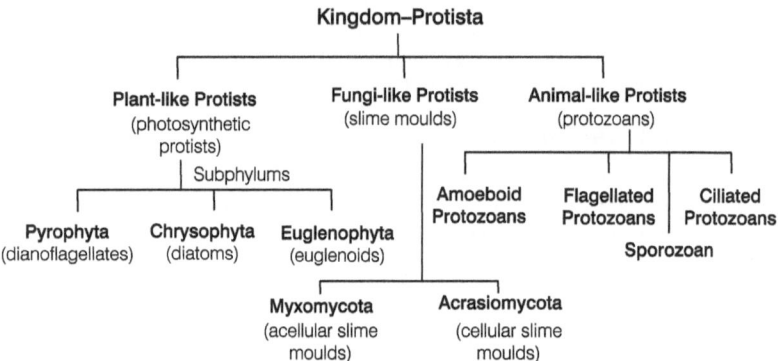

In view of evolution, the **kingdom–Protista** acts as a connecting link between the prokaryotic kingdom–Monera and multicellular kingdoms like Fungi, Plantae and Animalia. The term 'Protista' was given by German biologist **Ernst Haeckel** in 1866.

The group Protista shows following characteristics in common

(i) These are mostly aquatic.
(ii) Eukaryotic cell of protista possess well defined nucleus.
(iii) Mambrane bound organelles present.
(iv) Protists reproduce both asexually and sexually by a process involving cell fusion and zygote formation.
(v) They may be autotrophic and heterotrophic (*i.e.,* parasitic).

The detailed description of protistian groups is as follows

A. Photosynthetic (Plant-like) Protists

These can be

1. Dianoflagellates

The group of 1000 species of photosynthetic protists belongs to division–**Pyrophyta** and class–**Dinophyceae**. They are unicellular, motile and biflagellate golden-brown coloured protists. They forms the important components of phytoplanktons.

Their macronucleus possess condensed chromosome even in interphase, called as **mesokaryon** (Dodge; 1966). Sometimes they exhibit the phenomenon of bioluminescence. Some dianoflagellates are known as **oceli**.

2. Chrysophytes

These include **diatoms** and **desmids.** Diatoms are mostly aquatic and sometimes present in moist terrestrial habitat. They are very **good pollution indicator.**

The diatoms not decayed easily as their body covered by **siliceous shell.** They pile up at the bottom of water body and form **diatomite** or **diatomaceous earth** (can be used as fuel after mining).

3. Euglenoids

These are *Euglena* like unicellular flagellate found mostly in stagnant freshwater. Instead of a cell wall, they have a protein rich layer called **pellicle**, which makes their body flexible. *They have two types of flagella*

(a) **Long** Whiplash

(b) **Short** Tinsel

The food is stored in proteinaceous granules called **pyrenoid.** Photosynthetic euglenoids, behaves like heterotrophs in dark, this mode of nutrition is called **mixotrophic.**

The chief member of this group, *i.e., Euglena* is regarded as connecting link between animals and plants.

B. Fungi-Like Protists (Slime Moulds)

They possess the characters of both animal and fungi therefore, combinely called as **fungus-animals.** They shows saprophytic food habit and consume organic matter. Under suitable condition, they form *Plasmodium*. *On the basis of occurrence of Plasmodium, these are of two types*

(i) **Acellular/Plasmodial slime moulds**, *e.g., Physarum, Fuligo septica*, etc.

(ii) **Cellular slime moulds,** *e.g., Dictyostelium, Polysphondylium,* etc.

C. Animal-Like Protists (Protozoans)

The most primitive relative of animals, protozoans are heterotrophic (predator or parasitic) organisms, *divided into four major groups*

(i) **Amoeboid protozoans** They live in freshwater, moist soil and salt water as parasite. They move with the help of **pseudopodia** as in *Amoeba*.

Other members of this group are

Entamoeba histolytica, E. gingivalis causes various digestive and oral diseases when engulfed through polluted water.

(ii) **Flagellated protozoans** They are either free-living or parasitic in nature. *Chief members are*
  (a) *Trypanosoma* sp.–carried by **tse-ts efly** cause **African sleeping sickness.**
  (b) *Leismania* sp. carried by **sand fly** cause **kala azar** or **dum dum-fever**.
  (c) *Giardia* sp. cause **giardiasis**.
  (d) *Tricomonas vaginalis* — Cause **leucorrhoea**.
(iii) **Ciliated protozoans** They are aquatic and move actively due to presence of cilia. They shows nuclear dimorphism (macro and micronucleus), *e.g., Paramecium*, etc.

  Macronucleus/Vegetative Nucleus Control metabolic activity and growth.

  Micronucleus/Reproductive Nucleus Control reproduction.
(iv) **Sporozoans** They have an infectious, spore like stage in their life cycle. All are endoparasite. Locomotory organs are cilia, flagella and pseudopodia, *e.g., Plasmodium, Monocystis*, etc.

Fungi (Eukaryotic, Heterotrophic Organisms)

Fungi is a group of eukaryotic, achlorophyllous, non-photosynthetic and heterotrophic organism.

The basic features of fungi includes

1. Fungi lacks chlorophyll, hence they are heterotrophic.
2. They cannot ingest solid food, but absorb it after digestion. The digestive enzyme are secreted on food, then it absorb.
3. On the basis of food source, they may be saprophyte or parasites. Cell wall in fungi is made up of nitrogen containing polysaccharides, chitin. Reserved food material is glycogen or oil. As their nutritional habit, along with certain bacteria, saprotrophic fungi function as the main decomposers of organic remains.

Handbook of BIOLOGY

Classification of Fungi (Martin; 1961)

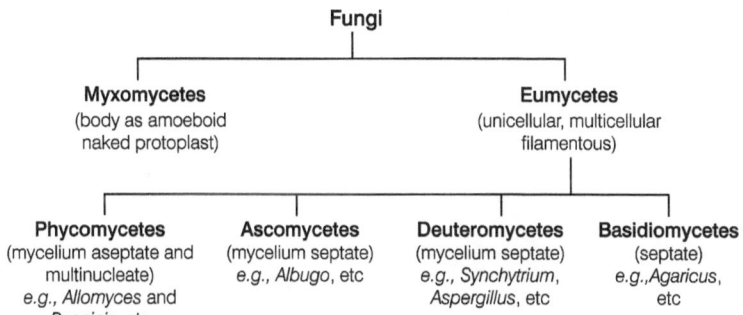

Reproduction in Fungi

Three types of reproduction occur in fungi

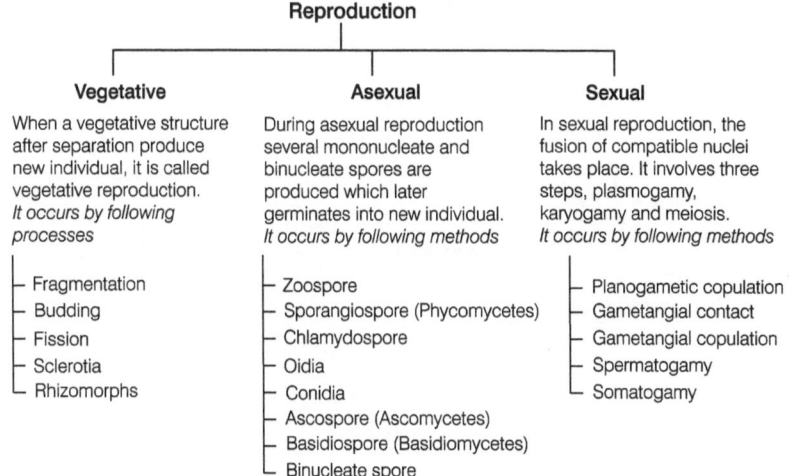

Life Cycles of Some Fungi

(i) Life Cycle of *Rhizopus*

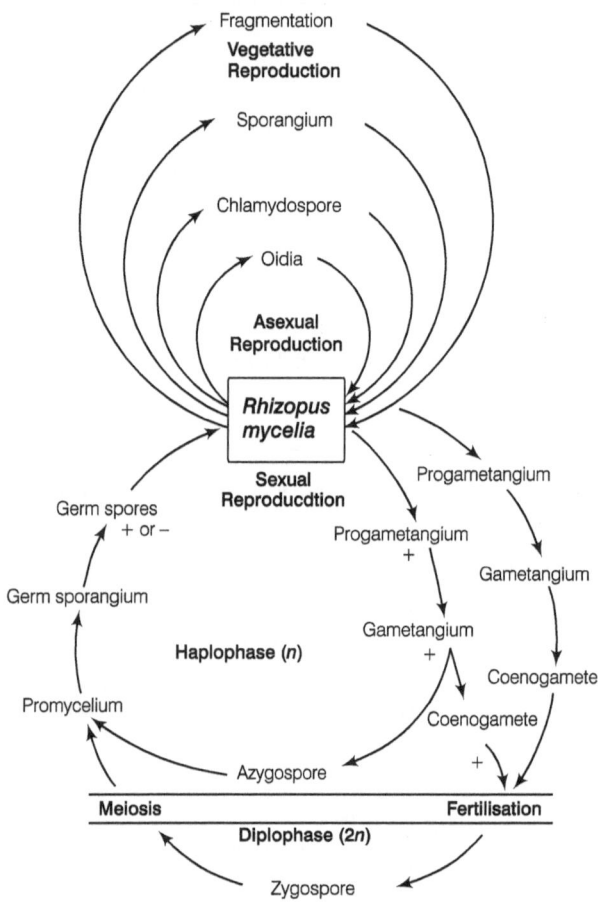

Life cycle of *Rhizopus*

Handbook of BIOLOGY

(ii) Life Cycle of Yeast

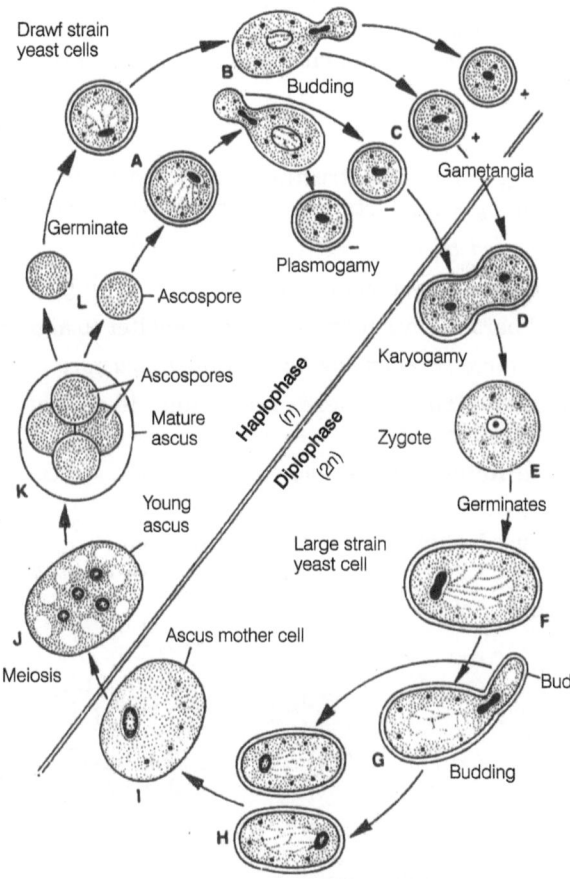

Sexual cycle in *Saccharomyces cerevisiae*

Heterothallism

The phenomenon of having two genetically different and compatible sexual strain in two different thalli is called heterothallism. It was discovered by **Blakeslee** in *Mucor*.

Mushroom and Fairy Rings

Agaricus compestris is an edible mushroom. It is also called **white button mushroom.** The fruiting body of *Agaricus*, arise in concentric rings (called fairy rings or fungal flowers) from the mycelium present in the soil.

Lichens

Lichens, having composite structure and consist of two dissimilar organisms forming a symbiotic relationship between them.

Lichens are formed by

(i) Algal Part — Phycobiont — Provide food to fungi
(ii) Fungal part — Mycobiont — Provide shelter to algae
⎬ Lichen

Lichens are of three types on the basis of their structure

(i) **Crustose lichen** These are paint like, flat lichens, *e.g., Caloplaca flave.*

(ii) **Foliose lichen** These lichens have leafy structure, *e.g., Hypogymnia physodes.*

(iii) **Fruticose lichen** These are branched lichen, from filamentous branching, *e.g., Cladonia evansii, Usnea australis,* etc.

Various forms of lichens are given as follows

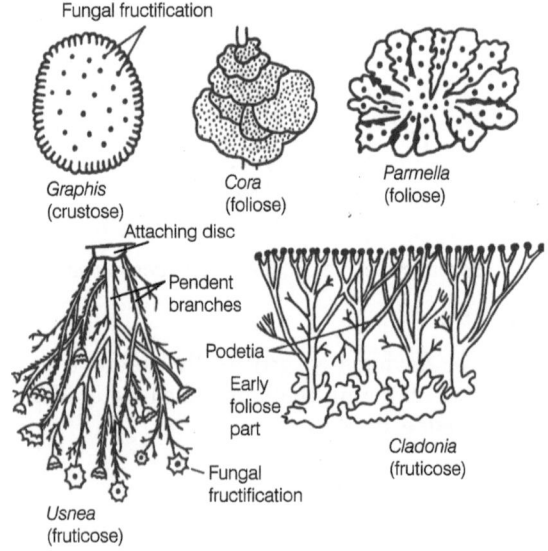

Forms of lichens

Plantae (Eukaryotic, Chlorophilous Organisms)
These are chlorophillous and embryo forming organism. Mostly non-motile and functions as the producers in **ecosystem** as they can fix solar energy into chemical energy through the process of photosynthesis. The cell wall in plants is cellulosic and stored food material is in form of starch.
A detailed account of plant kingdom is given in chapter 6.

Animalia (Unicellular, Eukaryotic Organisms)
The heterotrophic, eukaryotic organism which are multicellular and lacks cell wall, present in this kingdom. Animals have advanced level of tissue organisation, in which the division of labour is highly specific. The two main groups among animals are Non-chordata and Chordata divided on the basis of presence of notochord present in them.
A detailed account of animal kingdom is given is chapter 7.

Viruses and Viroids

Viruses

The term 'Virus' means **poisonous fluid**. The word was coined by **Louis Pasteur**. Viruses are very small (0.05-0.2 µm), infective, nucleoprotein particle, which can be called as **living** because of presence of nucleic acid as genetic material and ability to produce their own copy-viruses shows only some properties of living, otherwise it behaves like non-living. Hence, these are referred as the **connecting link between living and non-living**.

On the basis if nature of genetic material, the viruses are of two types

  (i) **Adenovirus**   DNA containing, *e.g.,* HIV, etc.

  (ii) **Retrovirus**   RNA containing, *e.g.,* Rous sarcoma virus, etc.

On the basis of their host, the viruses can be categorised as

  (i) **Animal virus** (Zoophagineae), *e.g.,* HIV, sarcoma, etc.

  (ii) **Plant virus** (Phytophagineae), *e.g.,* TMV, etc.

  (iii) **Bacterial viruses** (Phagineae), *e.g.,* T_4 phage, etc.

Characteristics of Viruses

Living
- They can replicate.
- In host body, they can synthesise protein.
- They cause disease like other living organism.
- Similar gene mutation as living organism.

Non-living

- Do not have protoplasm, not performing metabolism.
- These can be crystallised.
- They do not respire.
- *In vitro* culture is not possible.

Structure of Viruses

(a) Viruses are non-cellular and ultramicroscopic.
(b) *Virus has two components*
   (i) A core of nucleic acid called **nucleoid**.
   (ii) A protein coat called **capsid**.

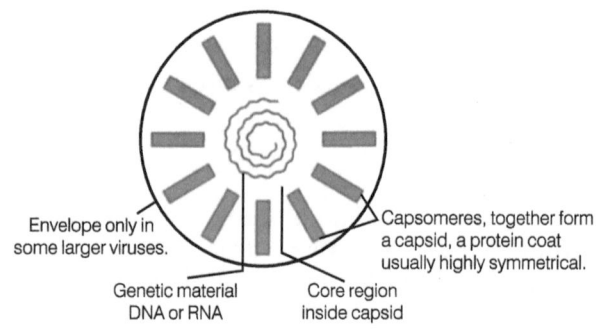

Structure of a virus (generalised)

Viroids (RNA without a Capsid)

TO Diener (1917) introduced the term as 'Subviral pathogens'. Viroids are 100 times smaller that smallest virus. They are known to be infectious for plants only (no any animal), *e.g.,* potato spindle tube caused by viroids.

Virion

An intact, inert, complete virus particle capable of infecting the host lying outside the host cell in cell free environment is called **virion.**

Virusoids

Virusoids are like viroids, but located inside the protein coat of a true virus. Virusoid RNA can be circular or linear. These are non-infectious as they are replicated only in their host.

Prions/Slow Virus

The prions are smallest. Proteinaceous infectious particles, *i.e.,* disease causing agent that can be transmitted from one animal to other.

6

Plant Kingdom

Plants : Producers of the Ecosystem

Plants are multicellular, photoautotrophic and embryo forming (excluding algae) organisms placed in kingdom–Plantae. They have cell wall, which is made up of cellulose and reserve food material in form of starch (sometimes fat as in seeds).

Plants, referred as producers, because they have unique ability to fix solar energy in form of chemical energy, through the process of **photosynthesis** and supplies the energy in ecosystem to other living organisms, hence they are referred as producers.

The plant kingdom is classified as

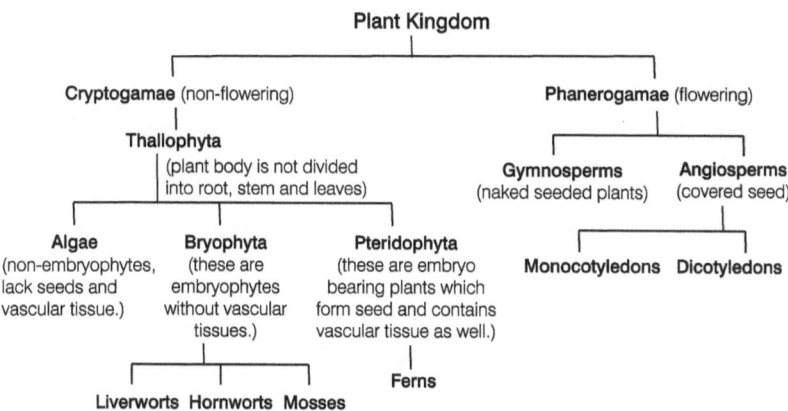

Algae (L. alga–sea weeds)

Algae are eukaryotic, autotrophic (holophytic), chlorophyll containing, non-vascular thallophytes. These are characterised by absence of embryonic stage and presence of non-jacketed gametengia. Mostly they are of aquatic habitat (both freshwater and marine).

The branch of Botany which deals with the study of algae is termed as 'Algology or Phycology'. **FE Fritsch** is known as Father of Algology. (Prof. MOP Iyengar is regarded as Father of Indian Algology).

Structure of Algae

Algae may be unicellular and multicellular, *i.e.*,

1. Unicellular

It is of two types
- (a) **Motile**, *e.g., Chlamydomonas*, etc.
- (b) **Non-motile**, *e.g., Chlorella*, etc.

2. Multicellular

It is of following types
- (a) **Colonial** *e.g., Volvox, Hydrodictyon*, etc.
- (b) **Aggregation** *e.g., Tetraspora, Prasinocladus*, etc.
- (c) **Filamentous** *e.g., Ulothrix, Cladophora*, etc.
- (d) **Pseudoparenchymatous** *e.g., Nemalion*, etc.
- (e) **Siphonous** *e.g., Vaucheria*, etc.
- (f) **Parenchymatous** *e.g., Ulva, Fritschella*, etc.
- (g) **Well developed thallus** *e.g., Chara, Sargassum*, etc.

Nutrition

Mostly algae are autotrophic, due to presence of chlorophyll. Some are parasitic, *e.g., Cephaleuros*, causes rust of tea.

Classification of Algae (FE Fritsch; 1935)

Algal Class	Colour	Reserve Food	Examples
Chlorophyceae	Grass green	Starch	*Chlamydomonas* and *Spirogyra*.
Xanthophyceae	Yellow-green	Fat	*Microspora* and *Botrydium*.
Chrysophyceae	Yellow-green and golden-brown	Carbohydrate and leucosin	*Amphipleura* and *Chrysosphaera*.
Bacillariophyceae	Brown and green	Fat and volutin	*Pinnularia* and *Melosira*.
Cryptophyceae	Red and green-blue	Carbohydrate and starch	*Cryptomonas*.
Dinophyceae	Dark yellow, brown-red	Starch and oil	*Peridinium* and *Glenodinium*.
Chloromonadineae	Bright green	Fatty compounds	*Vaucheria* and *Trentonia*.
Euglenophyceae	Grass green	Paramylum	*Euglena* and *Phacus*.
Phaeophyceae	Brown coloured	Laminarin and mannitol	*Laminaria* and *Fucus*.
Rhodophyceae	Red coloured	Floridean starch	*Polysiphonia* and *Batrachospermum*.
Myxophyceae	Blue-green algae	Protein granules	*Nostoc* and *Anabaena*.

Reproduction

Algae reproduced by
1. Vegetative methods
2. Asexual methods
3. Sexual methods

Vegetative Reproduction

Algae reproduce vegetatively by two methods
1. **Fragmentation**, *e.g., Fucus, Chara,* etc.
2. **By hormogones**, *e.g., Oscillatoria, Nostoc,* etc.

Asexual Reproduction

In this process some cells form motile or non-motile spore. After release, this spore gives rise to new plant. *Following spores are involved*
1. **By zoospore**, *e.g., Ulothrix, Oedogonium,* etc.
2. **By aplanospore**, *e.g., Chlorella,* etc.
3. **By hypnospore**, *e.g., Vaucheria,* etc.
4. **By palmella stage**, *e.g., Chlamydomonas, Ulothrix,* etc.
5. **By endospore**, *e.g., Anabaena, Nostoc,* etc.
6. **By akinete**, *e.g., Chara, Oedogonium,* etc.

Sexual Reproduction

On the basis of shape, size, morphology and behaviour of gametes.
The sexual reproduction is of following types

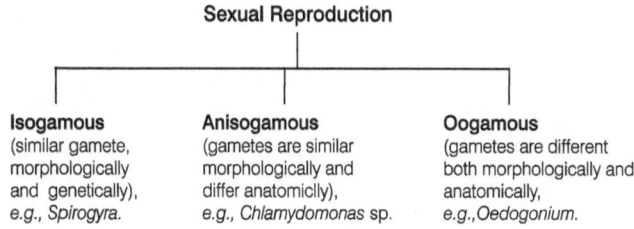

Isogamous
(similar gamete, morphologically and genetically), *e.g., Spirogyra.*

Anisogamous
(gametes are similar morphologically and differ anatomiclly), *e.g., Chlamydomonas* sp.

Oogamous
(gametes are different both morphologically and anatomically, *e.g., Oedogonium.*

Life Cycle of Algae

Various algae shows different type of life cycle. Life cycles of *Spirogyra* and *Ulothrix* are discussed here.

Life cycle of *Spirogyra* It is a green algae of filamentous shape. *The detailed life cycle is given as follows*

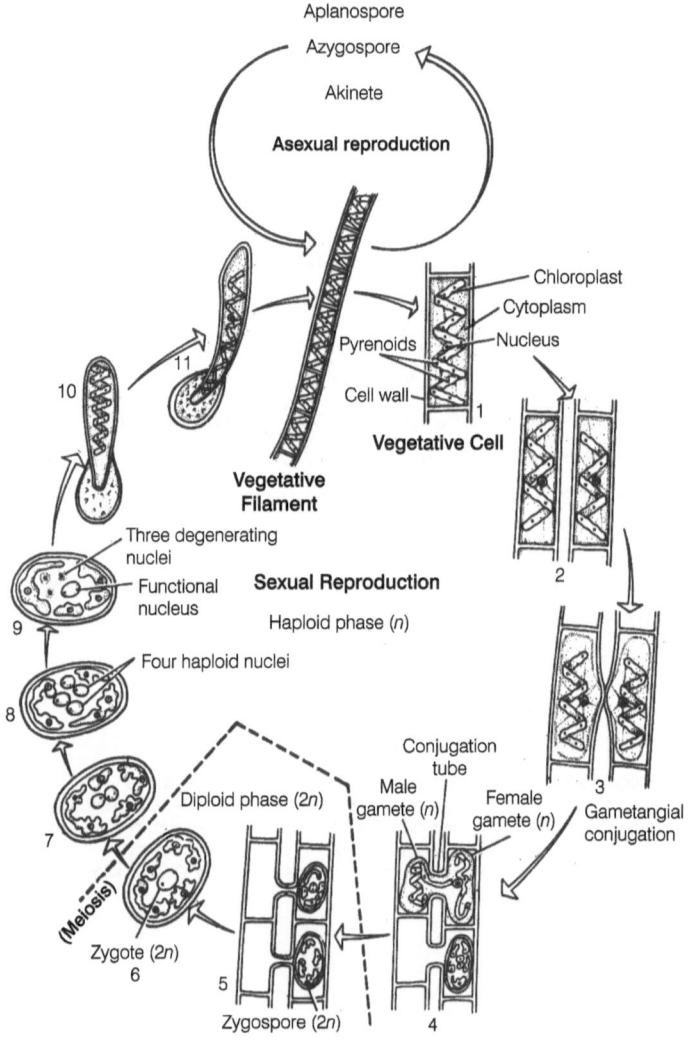

Life cycle of *Spirogyra*

Handbook of BIOLOGY

Life cycle of *Ulothrix* The diagrammatic representation of life cycle of *Ulothrix* is given here.

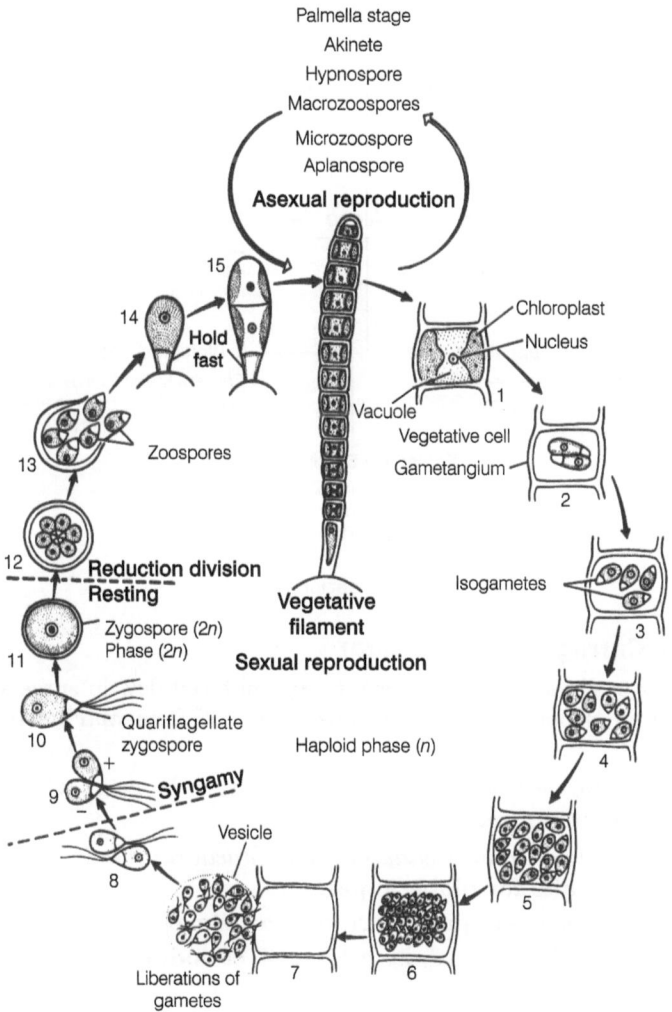

Life cycle of *Ulothrix*

Economic Importance

Algae can be both useful and harmful, the detailed economic importance is as follows. Several useful algal species with their uses are mentioned here

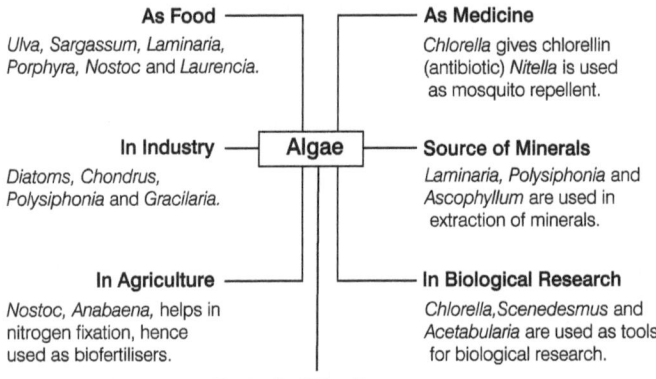

Useful applications of algae

Algin, Carrageenan and Agar

Algin is used as **artificial fibre,** to control blood flow in surgery and production of non-inflammable films, extracted from **marine brown algae.**

Carrageenan, extracted from seaweeds used in **cosmetics, boot polish, ice cream, paints,** etc.

Agar, extracted from *Gelidium* and *Gracilaria* used in culture medium, **biscuits for diabetic patients**, etc.

- *Sargassum* is used in manufacture of **artificial wool.**
- *Laminaria, Fucus* used in extraction of **iodine, bromine** and **acetone.**

Harmful Algae

Group of algae like (*Microcystis, Oscillatoria* and *Anabaena*) cause water blooms (eutrophication) and death and reduction of aquatic organisms.

Bryophyta (L. bryon–leaf-like; phyton–plant body)

Bryophyta is the simplest and primitive group of land plants, they are also known as **amphibians of plant kingdom** because of their habitat adaptability in both aquatic and terrestrial environment. They are situated as the **connecting link between algae and pteridophytes**. Bryophytes are autotrophic, non-seeded, **cryptogamic** plant. The plant body is gametophytic and may be differentiated into stem, leaves and rhizoids.

- Bryophytes do not have true vascular tissue (xylem and phloem), but some of them have **hydroids** (similar to xylem) and **leptoids** (similar to phloem) into them which helps in conduction of water and food respectivily.
- The sex organs in bryophytes are multicellular, male sex organ is called **antheridium** and female sex organ is called **archegonium**. Sexual reproduction in bryophytes is highly **oogamous type**.

Classification of Bryophytes

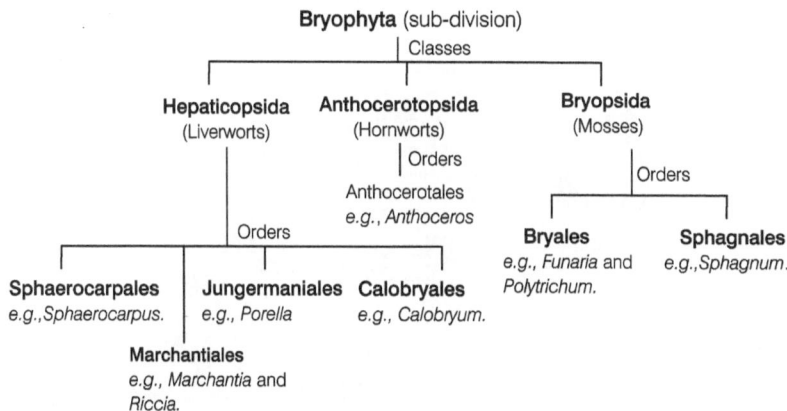

Reproduction in Bryophytes

Bryophytes reproduced by both vegetative and sexual methods of reproduction.

Vegetative Reproduction

Following methods of vegetative reproduction are reported in bryophytes

(a) **By fragmentation** The two fragments resulted by progressive death and decay of thallus, results into new thallus. *e.g., Riccia.*

(b) **By adventitious branches** Special adventitious branches arised from the mid-ventral surface of the thallus, *e.g., Riccia fluitans.*

(c) **By tubers** Some species form perennating tubers at the apices of thallus, *e.g., Riccia, Marchantia,* etc.

(d) **By persistent apices** The underground part in soil of thallus remains living and grows into plant, *e.g., Riccia, Pellia,* etc.

Sexual Reproduction

The sex organs are highly differentiated and well developed in bryophytes. The **antherozoid** or **sperm** (minute, slender, curved body, having two whiplash flagella) released from antheridium and reach to archegonium, through neck canal cells. The antherozoid fuses with **egg cell** to produce sporophytic generation.

Life Cycle in Bryophyta

A typical bryophyte shows following type of life cycle

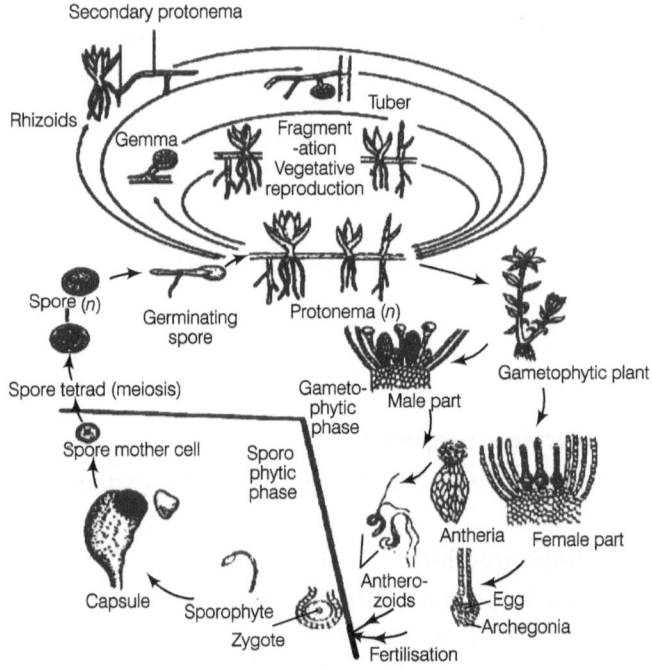

A typical bryophytic life cycle

Economic Importance

Bryophytes have limited economic importance, *they can be used in following ways*
- (i) They help in **soil formation** (pedogenesis) and act as agent for biological succession.
- (ii) Peat from *Sphagnum* can be used as fuel in preparation of ethyl alcohol.
- (iii) They help in protecting soil from erosion.
- (iv) Some bryophytes are used as **fodder** for cattle.
- (v) Due to high water retention capacity, *Sphagnum* can be used in preserving living materials and used in **grafting of plants**.

Pteridophytes (*pteron*–feather; *phyton*–plant)

Pteridophytes are seedless, vascular cryptogams. They reproduce by means of spore and reach to the tree-like hights (30-40 feets).

General Characteristics

- (i) The plant body is differentiated into **root, stem** and **leaves.**
- (ii) The stem may be aerial or underground and is generally herbaceous, rarely solid and stout.
- (iii) Vascular tissues consist of **xylem** (without vessels) and **phloem** (without companion cells)
- (iv) **Alternation of generation** find here, gametophyte is autotrophic and independent.
- (v) Sporangia containing leaves are called **sporophylls**.
- (vi) Antherozoids (flagellated male gametes) formed in **antheridia**.
- (vii) Reproduction is both vegetative and sexual types.
- (viii) On the basis of development of sporangia, *they are of two types*
    - (a) **Eusporangiate** From a group of superficial initial cells.
    - (b) **Leptosporangiate** From a single superficial initial cell.

Classification
(Smith; 1955, Bold; 1955-57, Benson; 1957)

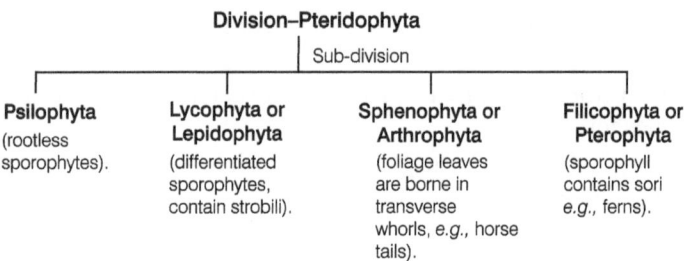

Reproduction
Pteridophytes reproduced by vegetative, asexual and sexual methods.

Vegetative Reproduction
It takes place by two methods
  (a) Death and decay of older tissue lead to separation of new branches, which can grow into new plants.
  (b) Adventitive buds develop from petiole and later on rooting and gets separated.

Asexual Reproduction
It is done by meiospore
When pteridophytic plants get mature, the special spore bearing structure develops under the surface of pinnules.

These structures are
  (a) **Sporangium** These are differentiated into capsule and the stalk. Capsule has a single layer of thick wall, which consists of specialised cell along with the normal wall cells.
  (b) **Spores** These are minute, bilateral body of brown colour. The spore coat is two layered, *i.e.*, thick, exine and thin, intine.

Sexual Reproduction
It is of advanced type in which the multicellular sex organs (*i.e.*, antheridia and archegonia) are borne on the underside of prothallus. The mucilagenous substance oozes out form archegonia, which contain **malic acid** after diffusing into water it attracts antherozoids through **chemotaxis.** The male nucleus fuses with the egg nucleus and forms zygote.

Life Cycle of Pteridophytes

Most pteridophytic plast shows similar type of life cycle. *Which is diagrammatically represented as follows*

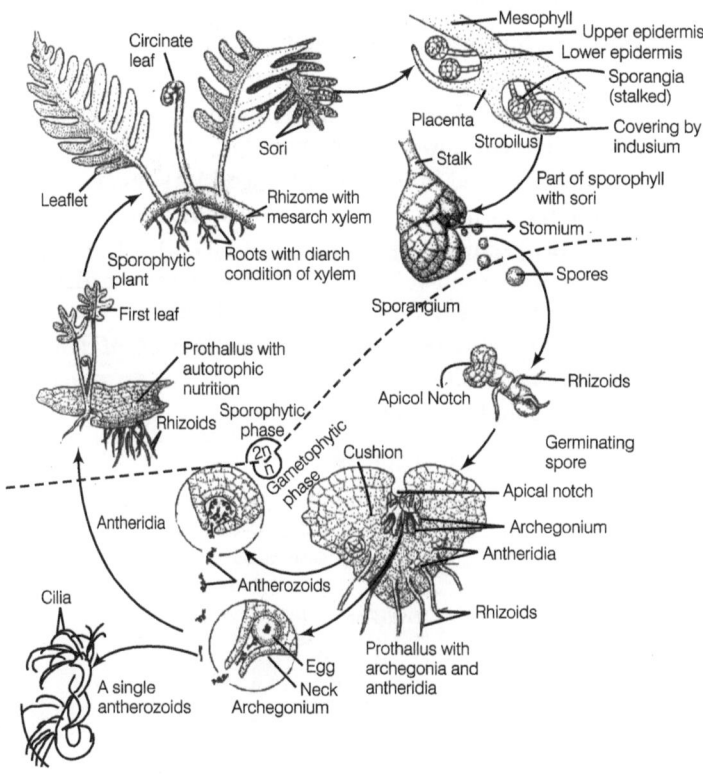

Life cycle of *Dryopteris*

Heterospory in Pteridophytes

In heterosporous plants, a sporophyte produces two types of *Sporangia*–**micro** and **megasporangia**. Microsporangia contain microspore mother cell (mmc) each which undergoes meiosis and produce **microspores**. Megasporangia contain **megaspore mother cell**, which after going to meiosis produce **megaspores**.

$$\text{Microspore} \xrightarrow{\text{Germinate}} \text{Microgametophyte}$$
(possess antheridia)

$$\text{Microspore} \xrightarrow{\text{Germinate}} \text{Megagametophyte}$$
(possess archegonia)

The differentiation between male and female gametophyte ensures cross fertilisation. This set of conditions occurs in **marsiliaceae** and **Salviniaceae**.

Economic Importance

Pteridophytes are economically important group of plants.

Some of them are

(i) Pteridophytes **used in horticulture**, since they resist wilting, can be used in cut flower arrangements.

(ii) Some ferns are used in **handicrafts and basketery**.

(iii) *Pteridium* leaves are used in making **green dyes**.

(iv) Club mosses are used for making **industrial lubricant** since its spore contains non-volatile oils. These spores are also used as finger print powder in forensic investigation.

(v) Some pteridophytes are used as **biofertiliser** (*Azolla*) due to its nitrogen fixing ability.

(vi) Some pteridophytes are **eaten as foods**.

Stelar System in Pteridophytes

Stele is central vascular tissue surrounded by cortex. *It is of two types*

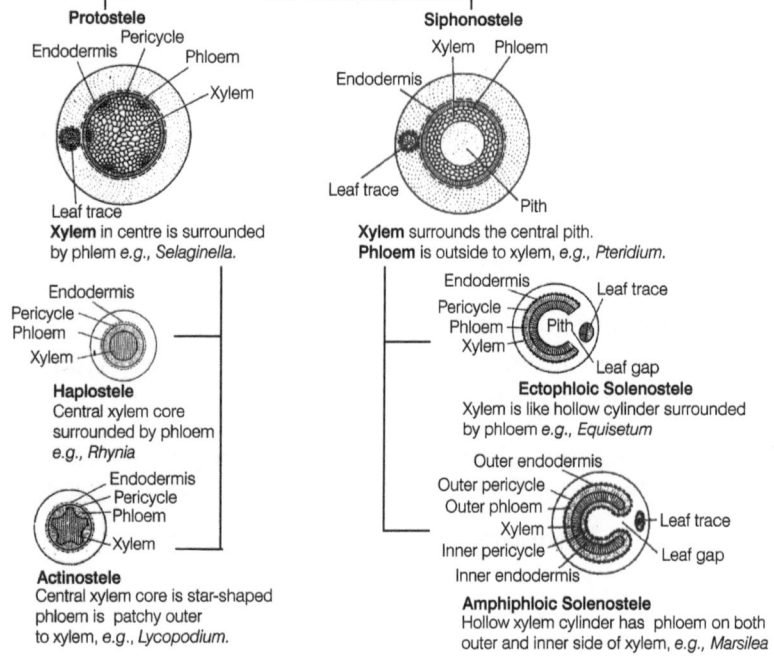

Gymnosperms (*gymnos* – naked; *sperma* – seed)

Gymnosperms are naked seeded plants, which evolved earlier than the flowering plants. They have their seeds exposed on the megasporophylls, *i.e.*, carpels. Probably, they are the first surviving seed plants (evolved during Jurassic period).

General Characteristics

(i) Plants are sporophyte, differentiated into root, stem and leaves.

(ii) Always **heterosporous**, *i.e.*, contains two types of spores (one spore (microspore) produces male gametophyte and other (megaspore) produces female gametophyte after germination).

(iii) Root system is well developed, *i.e.*, **tap root system**, some have **coralloid** root (*e.g., Cycas*).

(iv) Formed various structures through symbiotic relationships, *i.e.*, coralloid root (with algae) and **mycorrhizae** (with fungi).

(v) *Leaves are dimorphic, are of two types*

   (a) **Foliage leaves** Green, simple, needle-shaped and pinnately compound.

   (b) **Scaly leaves** Minute and deciduous.

(vi) Flowers are unisexual, simple, reduced and naked, *i.e.*, without perianth (except *Gnetum*).

Classification of Gymnosperms

Classification of gymnosperms was described by **A Arnold** (1948) and modified by **Pilger** and **Melchior** (1954).

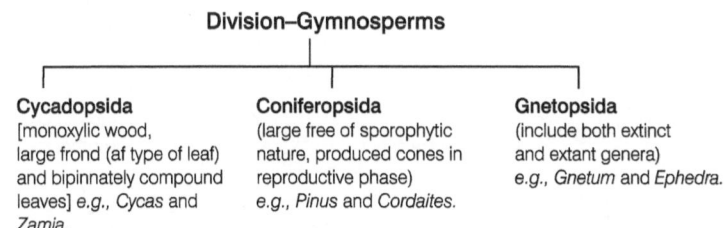

Reproduction in Gymnosperms

Gymnosperms reproduced by both vegetative and sexual methods.

Vegetative Reproduction

This is done by **bulbils**, which commonly arise on trunk. These bulbils get separated from plants and germinates into new plants.

Sexual Reproduction

The life cycle of gymnosperms is also characterised by alternation of generations. The green leafy parts of the plant is the sporophyte, the cones contain the male and female gametophytes.

Upon landing on the female cone, the tube cell of the pollen forms the pollen tube, through which the generative cells migrate towards the female gametophyte.

The generative cells splits into two sperm nuclei, one of which fuses with the egg, while the other degenerates. After fertilisation of the egg, the diploid zygote is formed, which divides by mitosis to form embryo.

The seed is covered by a seed coat, which is derived from the female sporophyte. No fruit formation takes place as gymnosperms do not have true seed covering.

Life Cycle of Gymnosperms

The gymnosperms are higher plants with advanced life cycle. *The descriptive account of life cycle of both Cycas and Pinus are given as follows*

Life Cycle of *Cycas*

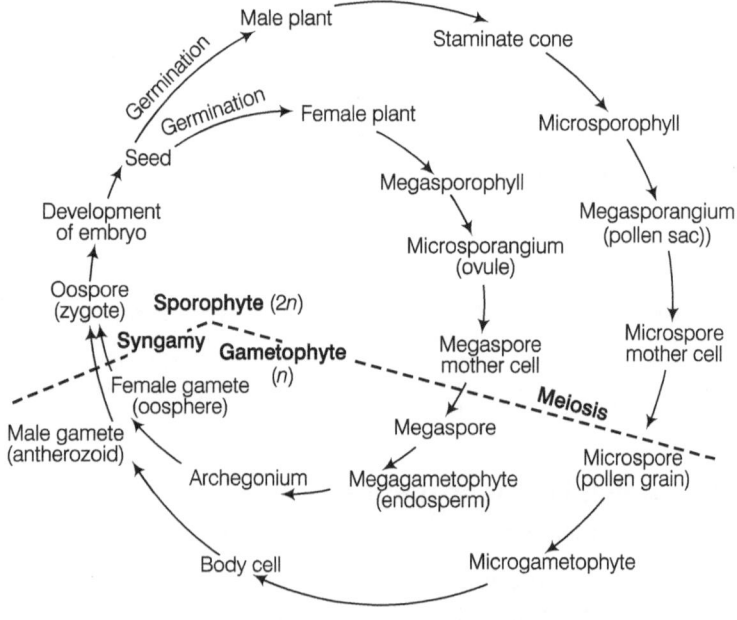

Cycas : topographical representation of life cycle

Life Cycle of *Pinus*

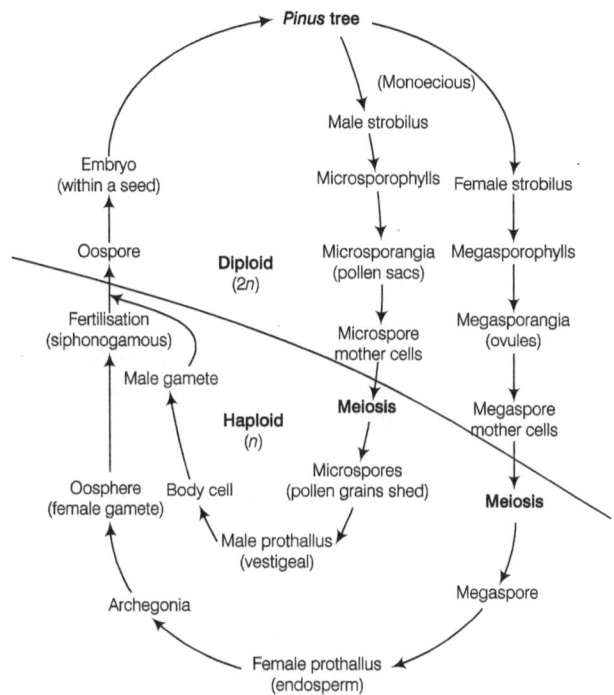

Pinus : Topographical representation of the life cycle

Economic Importance of Gymnosperms

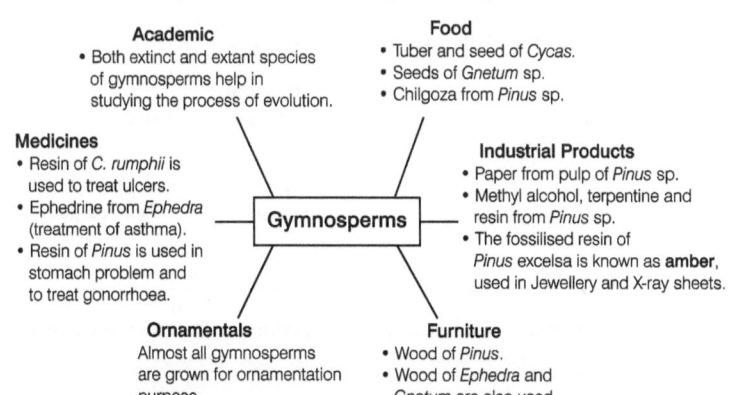

Academic
- Both extinct and extant species of gymnosperms help in studying the process of evolution.

Food
- Tuber and seed of *Cycas*.
- Seeds of *Gnetum* sp.
- Chilgoza from *Pinus* sp.

Medicines
- Resin of *C. rumphii* is used to treat ulcers.
- Ephedrine from *Ephedra* (treatment of asthma).
- Resin of *Pinus* is used in stomach problem and to treat gonorrhoea.

Industrial Products
- Paper from pulp of *Pinus* sp.
- Methyl alcohol, terpentine and resin from *Pinus* sp.
- The fossilised resin of *Pinus* excelsa is known as **amber**, used in Jewellery and X-ray sheets.

Ornamentals
Almost all gymnosperms are grown for ornamentation purpose.

Furniture
- Wood of *Pinus*.
- Wood of *Ephedra* and *Gnetum* are also used.

Angiosperms
(Gk. *ang*–vessel; *sperma*–seed)

Angiosperms constitute a distinct group of flowering plant, which form covered seed. With about 250000 species, it can be regarded as the most successful group of plants. They arose in middle of cretaceous period.

General Characteristics
(i) Angiosperms range from microscopic *Wolffia* to largest tree such as *Eucalyptus*.
(ii) The pollen grains and ovules develop in their flower and the seeds are formed within the fruits.
(iii) Nutritionally they may be **autotrophic** (wheat, corn, etc.), **parasitic** (*Cuscuta, Santalum*, etc.), **saprophytic** (*Monotrapa*, etc.) and **insectivorous** (*Drosera, Utricularia*, etc.).
(iv) They may be herb, shrub and trees.
(v) Their life times may be **ephemeral, annual, biennial** and perennial.
(vi) Angiosperms are adapted to various habitats as they may be hydrophytes, xerophytes and mesophytes.
(vii) A flower is modified shoot comprised of four whorls, *i.e.*, **sepal, petal, androecium** and **gynoecium.**

Classification of Angiosperms
A natural system of classification was given by **George Bentham** and **JD Hooker** in 1862-63 in his book *Genera Plantarum* (3 volumes) in Latin.

The outlines of the above mentioned classification is as follows

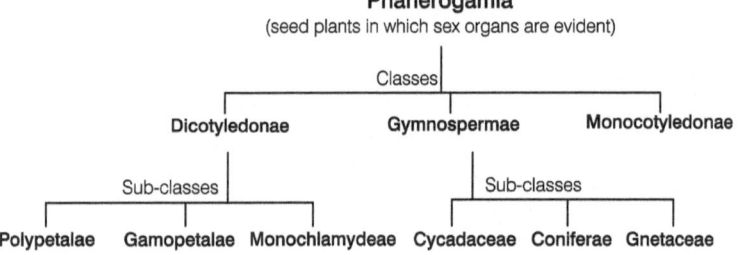

Some important plant families with their representative genera are as follows

Ranunculaceae, **Brassicaceae** (*e.g.*, mustard), **Malvaceae** (*e.g.*, gurhal), **Asteraceae** (*e.g.*, sunflower), **Laminaceae** (*e.g.*, tulsi), **Solanaceae** (*e.g.*, potato), **Leguminoceae** (*e.g.*, pea), **Cucurbitaceae**, **Euphorbiaceae**, **Orchidaceae**, **Palmae** (*e.g.*, cashewnut), **Poaceae** (*e.g.*, Paddy) and **Liliaceae** (*e.g.*, onion), etc.

Reproduction in Angiosperms

Angiosperms are type of plants that bear fruits and flowers, these are plant's reproductive structures. Reproduction in angiosperm (mostly sexual type) occurs when the pollen from an anther is transferred to stigma.

When the ovule gets fertilised, they will develop into seeds. Non-reproductive structures like petals, sepals etc. of the flowers fall of leaving only the ovary behind, which will develop into a fruit.

Economic Importance

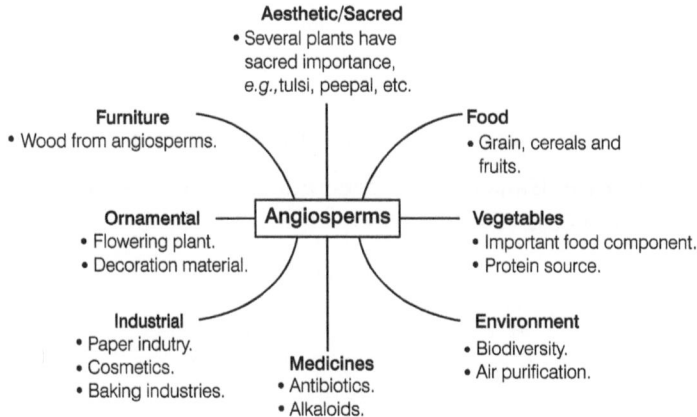

Useful applicatien of angiosperms

Alternation of Generation

It can also be termed as 'Patterns of life cycle'. Plants divide mostly through mitotic divisions and form different plant bodies (these may be haploid or diploid).

The inter conversion of the haploid and diploid plant body in alternate manner is called **alternation of generation.** *Generally, it is of three types*

(i) **Haplontic** Sporophytic generation is not prominent, *e.g.,* algae, etc.

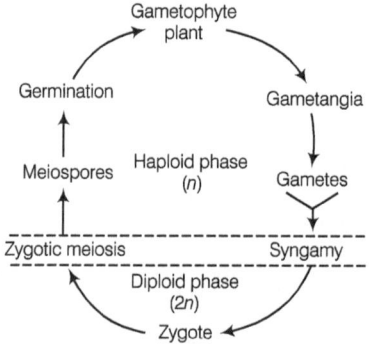

Diagrammatic outline of a haplontic life cycle

(ii) **Diplontic** Gametophytic generation is of very short duration, *e.g.,* gymnosperms and angiosperms, etc.

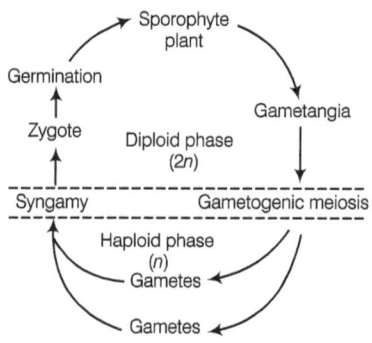

Diagrammatic outline of a diplontic life cycle

Handbook of BIOLOGY

(iii) **Haplo-Diplontic** Both gametophytic (n) and sporophytic ($2n$) are free living, independent and multicellular phases, *e.g.,* bryophytes, pteridophytes, etc.

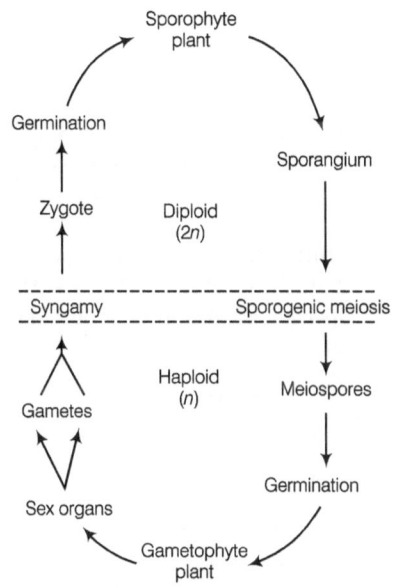

Diagrammatic outline a haplodiplontic life cycle

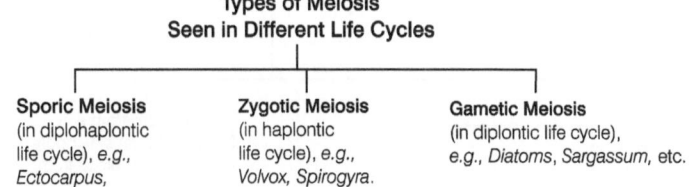

Types of Meiosis Seen in Different Life Cycles

Sporic Meiosis
(in diplohaplontic life cycle), *e.g., Ectocarpus, Laminaria,* etc.

Zygotic Meiosis
(in haplontic life cycle), *e.g., Volvox, Spirogyra.*

Gametic Meiosis
(in diplontic life cycle), *e.g., Diatoms, Sargassum,* etc.

7

Animal Kingdom

Animal kingdom (Animalia) is characterised by multicellular, eukaryotic animal forms. It is also known as **Metazoa**. It includes around 1.2 million species of animals from sponges to mammals (other than protozoans).

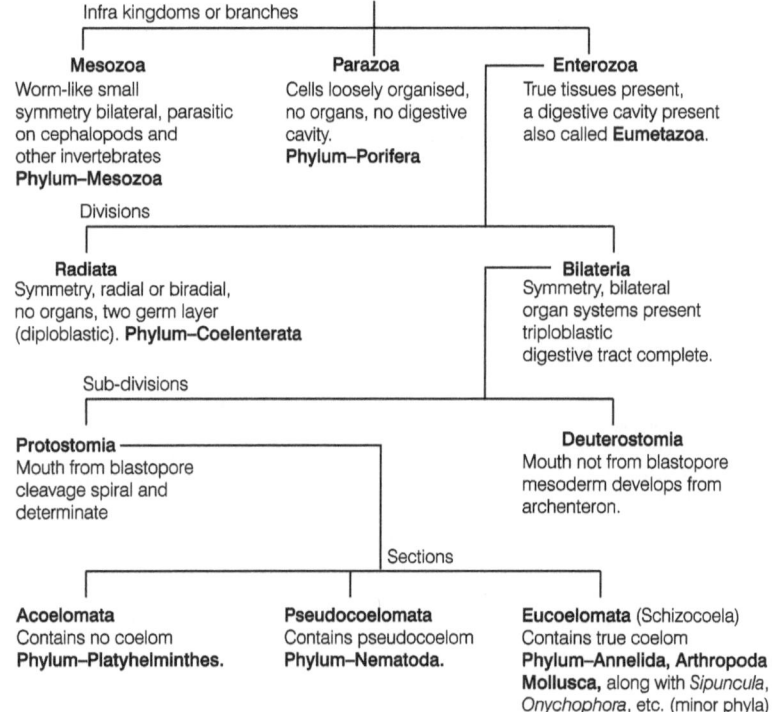

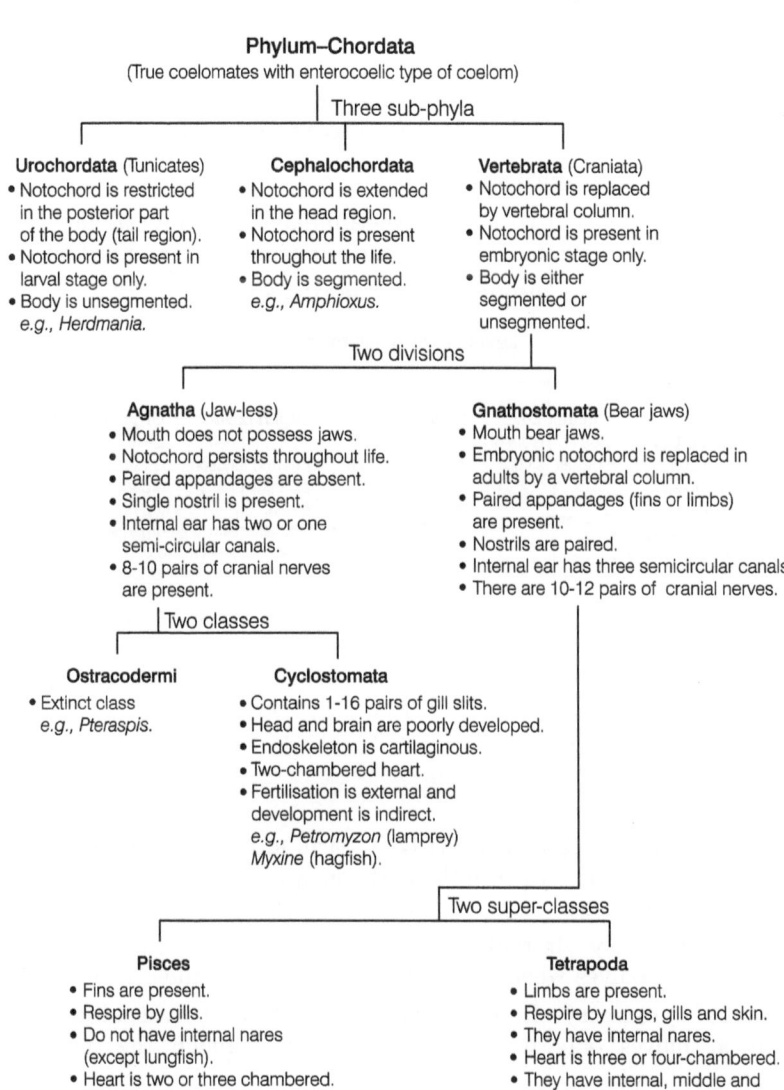

Basis of Classification

There are few fundamental common features to various animal groups, which form the basis of classification. *These features are as follows*

1. Level of Organisation

Though, all the members of kingdom–Animalia are multicellular, yet all of them do not exhibit the same pattern of cellular organisation. *Different levels of organisation are discussed below*

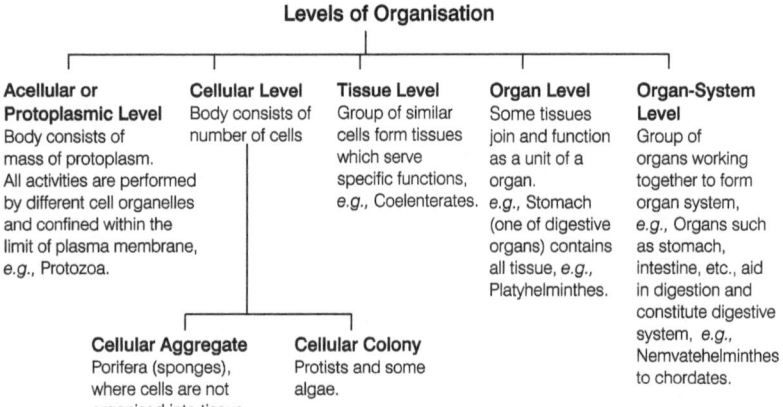

2. Symmetry

It refers to the correspondence of body parts in all major respect like size, shape, position, etc., with the parts on opposite side when divided from the central axis.

Radial symmetry In radial symmetry, the animal gets divided into two identical halves when any plane passes through the central axis.

Bilateral symmetry In bilateral symmetry, body is divided into two identical halves only when a plane passes through the median longitudinal axis.

3. Coelom

It is a large fluid-filled space or cavity lying between the outer body wall and inner digestive tube.

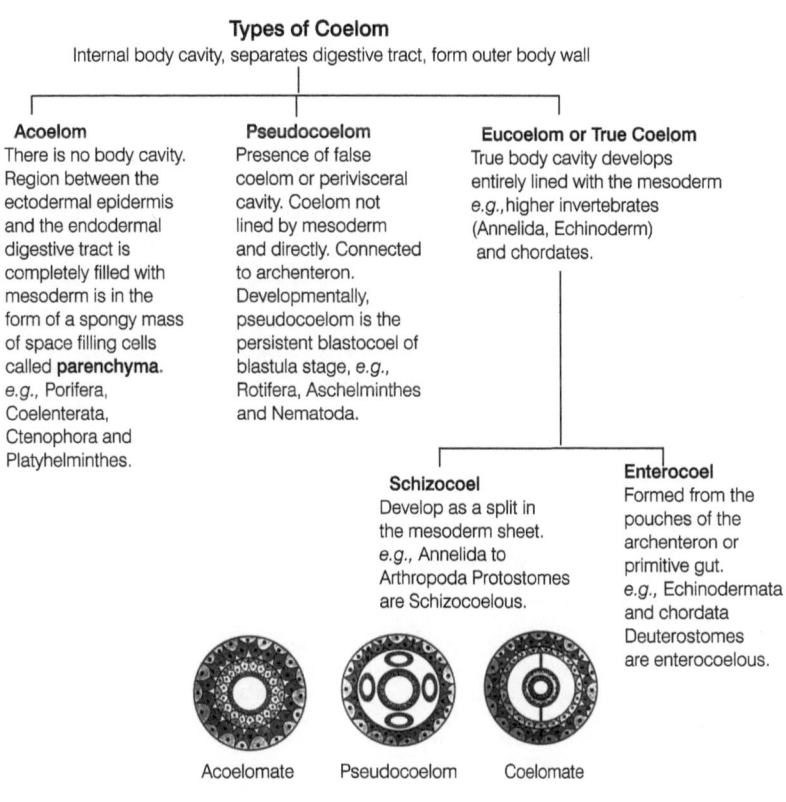

Digrammatic sectional view of coelom

4. Notochord

It is a rod-like structure present on the dorsal side of the animal body. It is derived from the embryonic mesoderm. Based on its presence and absence, animals are non-chordates (phylum–Porifera to Echinodermata) and chordates (phylum–Chordata).

Major differences between Chordata and Non-chordata are as follows

Chordata	Non-chordata
Bilaterally symmetrical.	Asymmetrical, radially symmetrical or bilaterally symmetrical.
True metamerism.	Non-segmented, false segmented or true metamerically segmented.
True coelomates.	Acoelomate, pseudocoelomate or true coelomates.
Post-anal tail usually present.	It is usually absent.
Triploblastic animals.	Cellular, diploblastic or triploblastic animals.
Alimentary canal is always ventrally placed to nerve cord. Heart is ventrally placed.	It is always dorsally placed to the nerve cord. Heart is dorsal or absent.
Central nervous system is hollow, dorsal and single.	Central nervous system is ventral, solid and double.
Pharynx is perforated by gill slits.	Gill slits are absent.

5. Segmentation

It is the serial repetition of similar parts along the length of an animal.

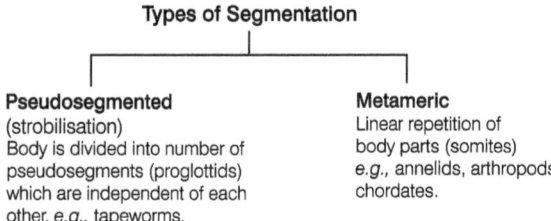

Pseudosegmented (strobilisation)
Body is divided into number of pseudosegments (proglottids) which are independent of each other, *e.g.,* tapeworms.

Metameric
Linear repetition of body parts (somites) *e.g.,* annelids, arthropods chordates.

6. Germ Layers

These are the groups of cells behaving as a unit during early stages of embryonic development. On the basis of number of germ layers, animals are placed in two groups, *i.e.,* diploblastic and triploblastic. These groups are divided at the gastrulation stage.

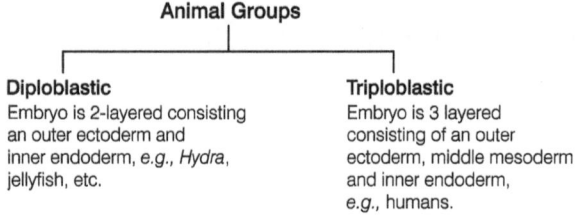

Diploblastic
Embryo is 2-layered consisting an outer ectoderm and inner endoderm, *e.g., Hydra,* jellyfish, etc.

Triploblastic
Embryo is 3 layered consisting of an outer ectoderm, middle mesoderm and inner endoderm, *e.g.,* humans.

Phylum—Porifera

General Characteristics

Poriferans bears numerous minute pores called **ostia** on the body wall which leads into a central cavity called **spongocoel** or **paragastric cavity**. The spongocoel opens to outside by **osculum**.

Majority of poriferans (sponges) are marine and sedantry. They are diploblastic animals and contain an outer dermal layer of pinacocytes and inner gastral layer of choanocytes.

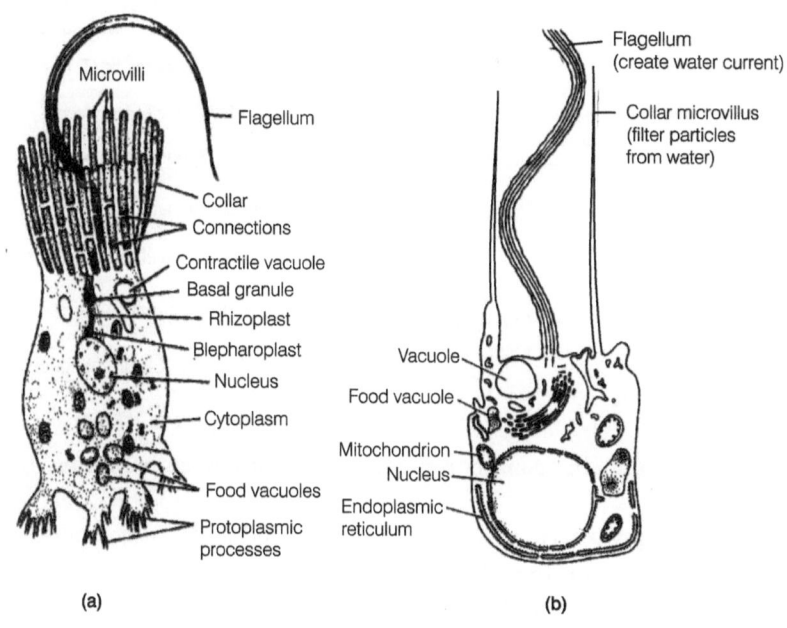

Choanocyte : (a) Light microscopic view
(b) Electron microscopic view

Canal System Canal system (aquiferous system) is a system of interconnected canals through which water circulates and helps in a number of metabolic activities of a sedentary sponge. In sponges, canal system is of three types, *i.e.*, asconoid, syconoid and leuconoid.

Different Types of Canal System

Asconoid Canal System	Syconoid Canal System	Leuconoid Canal System
Simplest type with thin walls.	Complex type with thick walls.	Much complex type with highly folded thick walls.
Spongocoel is large and spacious.	Spongocoel is narrow.	Spongocoel is either reduced or absent.
Choanocytes forms the gastral layer and lines the whole spongocoel.	Choanocytes are restricted in radial canals only.	Choanocytes are confined in the flagellated chambers which are formed by the evagination of radial canals.
Route of water is Outside water $\xrightarrow{\text{Dermal Ostia}}$ Outside $\xleftarrow{\text{Osculum}}$ Spongocoel e.g., *Leucosolenia*.	**Route of water is** Outside water $\xrightarrow{\text{Dermal Ostia}}$ $\xrightarrow{\text{Prosopyle}}$ Incurrent canal Radial canal $\xrightarrow{\text{Apopyle}}$ $\xrightarrow{\text{Gastral Ostia}}$ Excurrent canal Spongocoel $\xrightarrow{\text{Osculum}}$ Outside e.g., *Grantia*.	**Route of water is (T.T)** Outside water $\xrightarrow{\text{Dermal Ostia}}$ Hypodermal spaces Incurrent canals $\xrightarrow{\text{Prosophyle}}$ $\xrightarrow{\text{Apopyle}}$ Flagellated chambers Excurrent canal Osculum Excurrent spaces Outside, e.g., *Plakina*.

Reproduction In sponges, reproduction occurs by both asexual and sexual means.

Asexual Reproduction Mainly occurs by budding and gemmules.

Sexual Reproduction Occurs with the help of amoebocyte or archeocytes or sometimes through choanocytes.

Classification

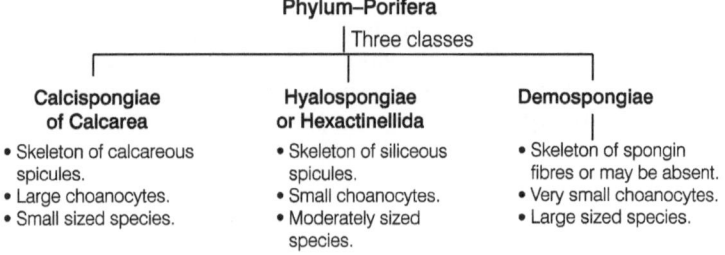

Handbook of BIOLOGY

Common and Scientific Name of Some Members of Porifera

Common Species of Porifera	Scientific Name	Common Species of Porifera	Scientific Name
Glass rope sponge	Hyalonema	Venus flower basket	Euplectella
Bath sponge	Euspongia	Bowl sponge	Pheronema
Freshwater sponge	Spongilla	Dead man's finger sponge	Chalina
Urn sponge	Scypha	Boring sponge	Cliona

Economic Importance

- They are used commercially for bathing/cleaning sponges.
- They help to clean-up the ocean floor by boring into dead shells and corals releasing chemicals to break them down.

Phylum–Coelenterata/Cnidaria

Coelenterates are the group of animals bearing a special body cavity called **coelenteron** (gastrovascular cavity). They exhibit dimorphism and display two major forms namely polyp (sedentary) and medusa (swimming). They also exhibit trimorphism (*e.g., Siphonophora*) and polymorphism (*e.g., Porpita*).

Body wall They are diploblastic animals and their body wall contains several types of cells, *e.g.,* **stinging cells** (cnidoblast/nematocyst), **interstitial cells** (totipotent cells), **sensory cells, nerve cells**, etc.

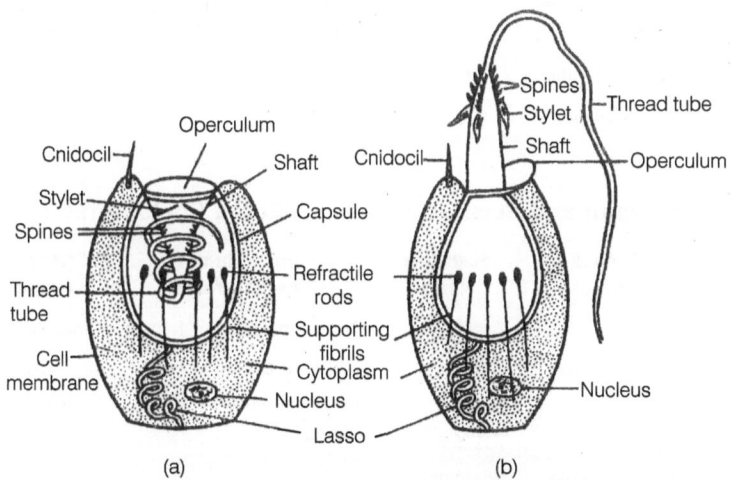

Cnidoblasts : (a) Undischarged (b) Discharged

Skeleton In coelenterates, skeleton may be endoskeleton, exoskeleton or absent.

Endoskeleton *e.g.*, *Alcyonium* (fleshy mesogloea), *Pennatula* (axial rod of calcified horn).

Exoskeleton *e.g.*, *Millipore* (Coenosteum), *Gorgonia* (gorgorin), *Madrepora* (corallum).

Absent *e.g.*, sea anemones.

Metagenesis It is like the alternation of generation between the sexual (medusa) and asexual (polyp) form. In contrast to alternation of generation, in metagenesis it is difficult to distinguish between asexual and sexual forms as both the individuals are diploid.

Reproduction It occurs both by sexual and asexual means.

Asexual Reproduction By external budding.

Sexual Reproduction By sexual medusae. The development is usually indirect which occur through *Ephyra*, *Plamula* and *Hydrula* larvae.

Classification

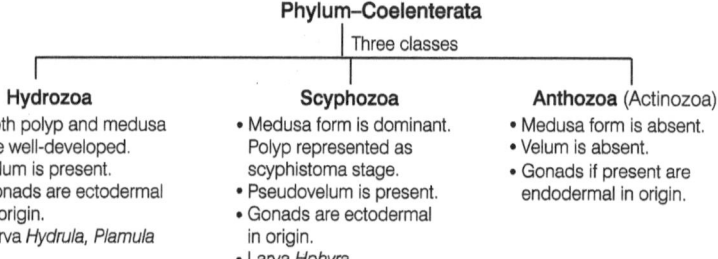

Common and Scientific Name of Some Coelenterates

Common Names of Coelenterates	Scientific Name	Common Names of Coelenterates	Scientific Name
Sail-by-wind	*Valella*	Organ pipe coral	*Tubipora*
Portuguese man of war	*Physalia*	Stag horn coral	*Madrepora*
Stinging coral	*Millipora*	Mushroom coral	*Fungia*
Sea anemone	*Metridium*	Star coral	*Astraea*
Dead's man finger coral	*Alcyonium*		

Economic Importance

- They take part in the formation of coral reefs, *e.g.*, *Millipora* (stinging coral).
- Their skeleton has medicinal value, *e.g.*, *Tubipora* (organ-pipe coral).
- They have ornamental value, *e.g.*, *Astraea* (star coral).

Phylum–Platyhelminthes

General Characteristics

Platyhelminthes are the dorsoventrally flat animals having either unsegmented and leaf-like (*e.g.*, flukes) or segmented and ribbon-like (*Taenia*) body. They are the first animals to have bilateral symmetry and to undergo **cephalisation**.

Habitat Platyhelminthes are mostly found as free living forms, but few of them are parasitic in their habitat.

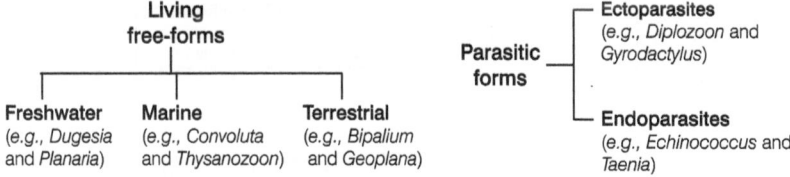

Peculiar Features of Platyhelminthes

These are the first animals with **triploblastic layers** in body wall and **organ-system organisation**. They are **acoelomates** due to the presence of a mesodermal connective tissue, **parenchyma**, in between the visceral organs. These animals have ladder-type nervous system and peculiar cells called **flame cells or protonephridia for excretion**. These cells are modified mesenchymal cells.

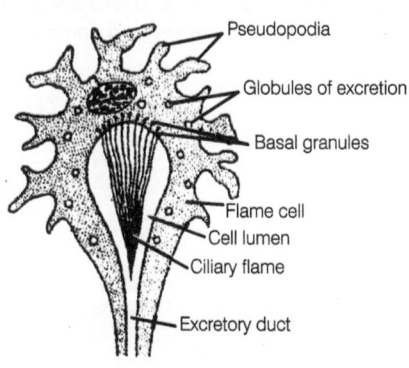

Flame cell (Solenocyte)

Reproduction These animals are generally bisexual. **Cross-fertilisation** occurs in trematodes, while **self-fertilisation** occurs in cestodes. Fertilisation is always internal. Turbellarians reproduce by **transverse fission**.

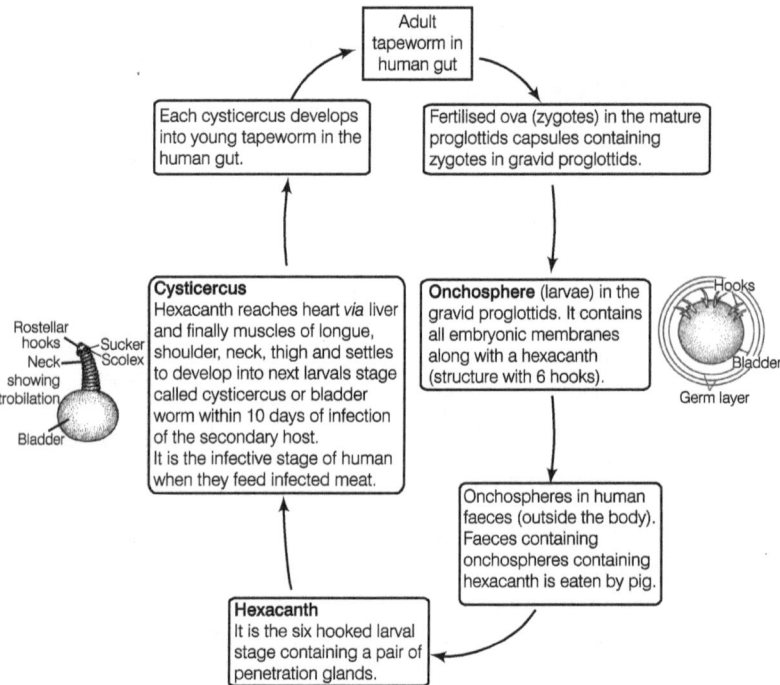

The graphical representation of life cycle of *Taenia solium* depicting different larval stages and adult form the primary and secondary host

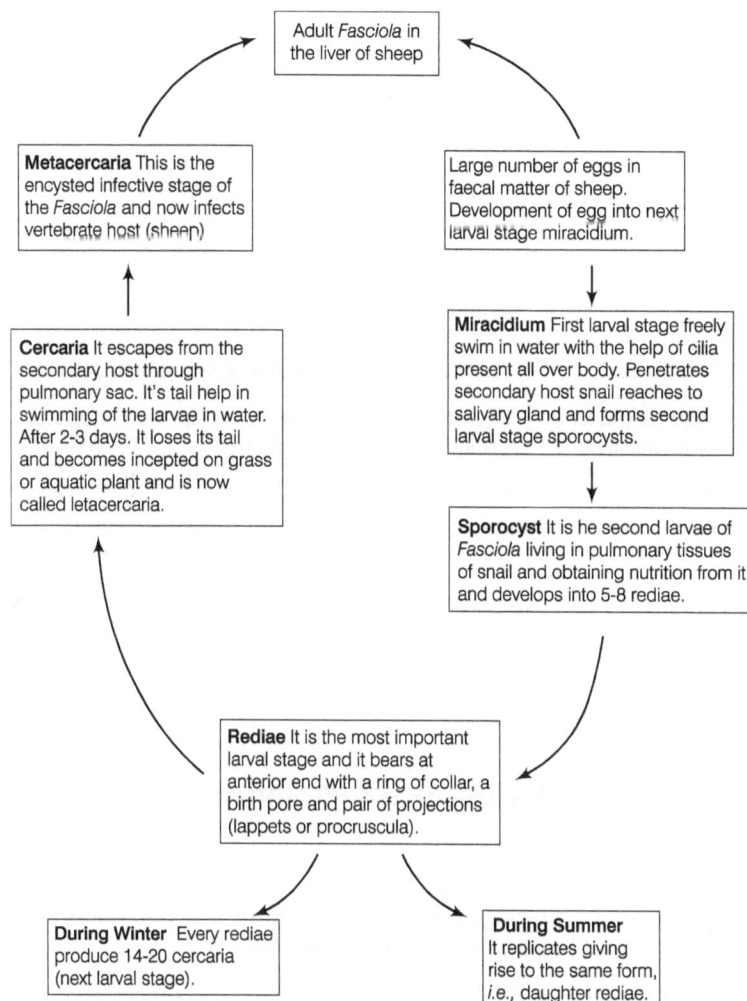

Graphical representation of life cycle of *Fasciola hepatica* depicting polyembryony along with different larval stages

Classification

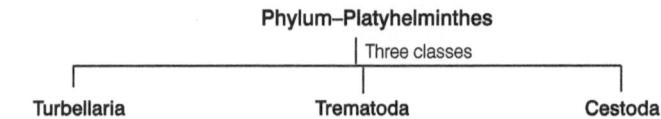

Turbellaria
- Mostly non-parasitic and free living.
- Unsegmented and flat leaf-like.
- Body wall contains syncytial epidermis with rod-shaped rhabditis.
e.g., *Planaria*.

Trematoda
- Ecto or endoparasites.
- Unsegmented and flat leaf-like.
- Body wall contains cuticular spines.
e.g., *Fasciola*.

Cestoda
- Exclusively endoparasites
- Segmented and ribbon-like.
- Body wall is lined by microvilli.
e.g., *Taenia*.

Common and Scientific Name of Some Platyhelminthes

Common Names of Platyhelminthes	Scientific Name	Common Names of Platyhelminthes	Scientific Name
Liver fluke	*Fasciola hepatica*	Pork tapeworm	*Taenia solium*
Planarian	*Dugesia*	Hydatid worm or dog tapeworm	*Echinococcus granulosus*

Economic Importance

- *Fasciola* causes **fascioliosis** or **liver rot** which is characterised by hepatitis.
- *Echinococcus* causes hydatid disease which is characterised by enlargement of liver.

Phylum–Aschelminthes

General Characteristics

Aschelminthes are long, cylindrical, unsegmented and thread-like animals with no lateral appandages, so these are commonly called **roundworms** or **bagworms** or **threadworms**.

Peculiar Features of Aschelminthes

Body wall of these pseudocoelomate animals is composed of complex cuticle, syncytial epidermis and only longitudinal muscles. They have **tube-within-tube plan of digestive system.**

They have fixed number of cells in every organ of the body (eutylic condition). Excretory system is H-shaped and contains **rennet cells.**

Handbook of BIOLOGY

Reproduction

Sexual dimorphism is present and males are smaller than females. Fertilisation is internal and it may be direct or indirect.

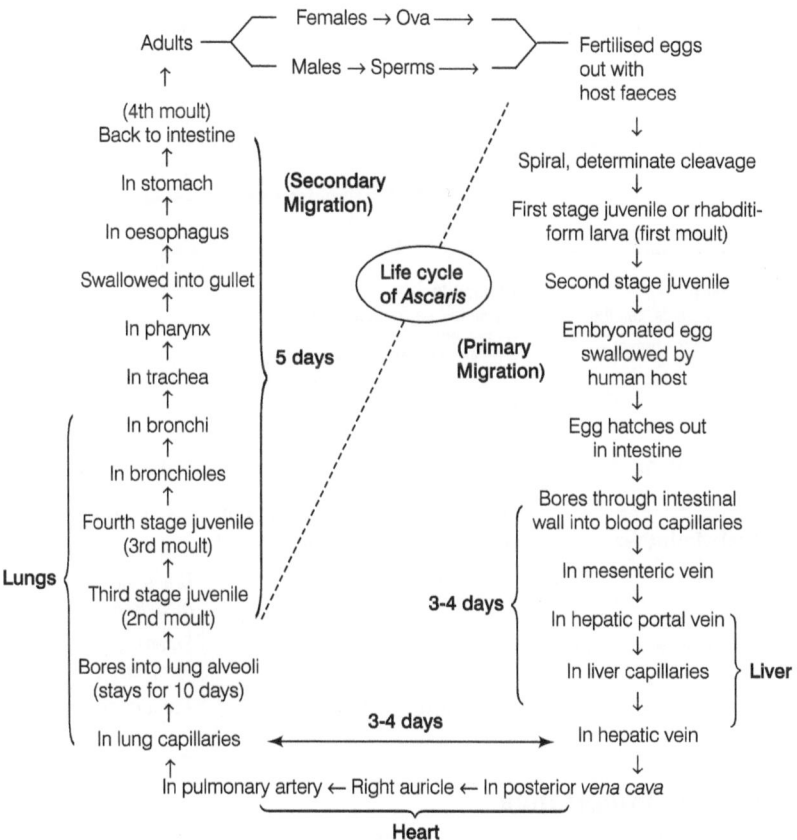

A graphical representation of *Ascaris* life cycle

Classification

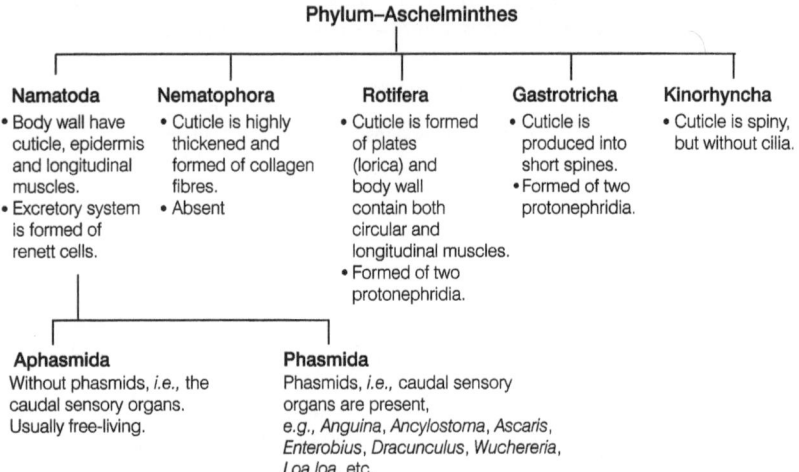

Common and Scientific Name of Some Aschelminthes

Common Names of Aschelminthes	Scientific Name	Common Names of Aschelminthes	Scientific Name
Roundworm	Ascaris lumbricoides	Guinea worm	Dracunculus medinesis
Root-knot eel worm	Meloidogyne marioni	Pinworm	Enterobius vermicularis
Filarial worm	Wuchereria bancrofti	Whipworm	Trichuris trichiura
Eye worm	Loa loa		

Economic Importance

- *Ascaris* cause ascariasis in humans.
- *Meloidogyne* is a harmful phytoparasitic nematode.

Phylum–Annelida

General Characteristics

Annelids are the segmented worms with an elongated body possessing triploblastic layers. Their musculature is formed of only smooth muscle fibres of two types, *i.e.*, longitudinal (inner) and circular (outer) muscles.

Peculiar Features of Annelids

- These animals show **metameric segmentation**, *i.e.*, the external division of the body by annuli corresponds to internal division of coelom by septa.
- These are the first animals to have circulatory system.
- Locomotory organs are minute rod-like chitinous **setae** or **suckers** which are embedded over **parapodia**.
- A characteristic **circumoesophageal ring** is present in the anterioe part of CNS.
- Special structures called nephridia are present for excretion.

Reproduction

Asexual Reproduction by fragmentation is seen in some polychaetes.

Sexual Reproduction Sexes are either united (*e.g.*, oligochaetes) or separate (*e.g.*, polychaetes). Fertilisation is internal (*e.g.*, *Hirudinaria*) or external (*e.g.*, earthworm). Development is direct in monoecious forms and indirect in dioecious forms involving a free-swimming trochophore larva.

Classification

Phylum–Annelida
Three classes

Polychaeta
- Marine, fossorial or tubicolous.
- Distinct head bearing tentacles, palps and eyes.
- Bristle-like setae and parapodia for locomotion
- Clitellum is absent.
- Unisexual
e.g., *Aphrodite* and *Chaetopterus*.

Oligochaeta
- Terrestrial, freshwater
- Distinct head with eyes (palps and tentacles are absent).
- Locomotion by peristalies, parapodia is absent.
- Permanent clitellum is present.
- Bisexual
e.g., *Pheretima* and *Tubifex*.

Hirudinea
- Mostly freshwater, few marine.
- No cephalisation
- Locomotion by anterior and posterior suckers. Clitellum appears during
- breeding season. Bisexual
- e.g., *Hirudinaria* and *Acanthobdella*.

Common and Scientific Name of Some Annelids

Common Names of Annelids	Scientific Names	Common Names of Annelids	Scientific Names
Earthworm	*Pheretima posthuma*	Paddle worm	*Chaetopterus*
Clam worm	*Nereis*	Blood worm	*Tubifex*
Polalo worm	*Eunice*	Skate sucker	*Pontobdella*
Sea mouse	*Aphrodite*	Lung worm	*Arenicola*

Economic Importance
- Earthworms are used as fish-bait and for improving the soil fertility.
- *Polynoe* shows bio-luminescence and this phenomenon is used in self defence.
- *Tubifex* has putrefaction ability and is grown in filter beds of sewage disposal plants.
- *Pontobdella* causes huge food loss to man when present in large number.

Phylum–Arthropoda

General Characteristics
It is the largest phylum of Animalia which includes insects with jointed legs and sclerotized exoskeleton. Their body is divided into three parts or tegmata *i.e.*, head, thorax and abdomen. They are haemocoelomates, *i.e.*, true coelom is replaced by haemocoel (pseudocoel with blood). The body appandages are variously modified in different arthropods to perform various functions.

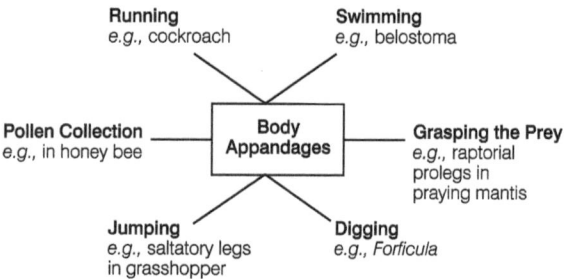

Peculiar Features of Arthropoda
- They are the first animals to have an **endoskeleton** and **voluntary muscles** in their body wall.
- They have well developed sensory organs which include antennae, sensory hair, simple or compound eyes, auditory organs and statocyst.
- They have well developed **endocrine system** containing glands like corpora cardiaca, corpora allata, etc.
- Mouth is always surrounded by mouth parts of different types in different animals.

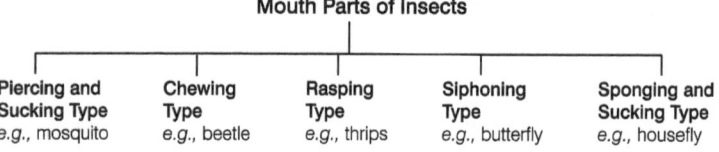

Handbook of BIOLOGY

Arthropods have special respiratory and excretory structures as follows

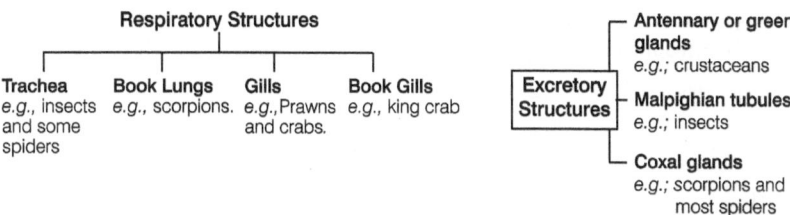

- Their nervous system possess all the three types, *i.e.*, **central**, **peripheral** and **autonomic**.

Reproduction Sexes are separate and fertilisation is internal. These animals are generally oviparous or ovoviviparous.

Development may be direct (*e.g.*, cockroach) or indirect. Some arthropods undergo parthenogenesis *e.g.*, drones of honeybee.

Classification

Phylum–Arthropoda
Three sub-phyla

Chelicerata
- Body is divided into cephalothorax (prosoma) and abdomen (opisthosoma), cephalothorax is covered by a carapace. Antennae are absent.
- Mandible absent.

Trilobitomorpha
- Extinct group

Mandibulata
- Body is divided into cephalothorax and abdomen.
- One or two pair of antennae present.
- One pair of mandible present.

Three classes

Mesostomata
- Aquatic (marine)
- Abdomen ends into a spike-like telson, *e.g., Limulus* and *Eurypterus.*

Arachnida
- Mostly terrestrial, some parasitic.
- Abdomen lacks locomotory appandages. *e.g., Aranaea, Palamnaeus*

Pycnogonida
- Marine
- Abdomen is reduced.

Four classes

Crustacea
- Mostly aquatic, few are terrestrial or parasitic.
- Body is divisible into two parts–cephalothorax and abdomen.
- Exoskeleton is calcified.
- Excretion by green glands *e.g., Cyclops* and *Sacculina.*

Chilopoda
- Terrestrial
- Body is divisible into two part, *i.e.*, head and trunk.
- Exoskeleton is uncalcified.
- One pair of Malpighian tubule is present. *e.g., Scolopendra* and *Lithobius.*

Diplopoda
- Terrestrial
- Body is divisible into three parts–head, thorax and abdomen.
- Calcified
- Two pair of Malpighian tubules present. *e.g., Julus* and *Glomeris.*

Insecta
- Found in all habitats.
- Body is divisible into three parts *i.e.*, head, thorax and abdomen.
- Uncalcified
- Two to many pairs of Malpighian tubules are present. *e.g., Mantis* and *Lepisma.*

Common and Scientific Name of Some Arthropods

Common Names of Arthropods	Scientific Name	Common Names of Arthropods	Scientific Name
Walking worm	*Peripatus*	Grasshopper	*Poecilocercus*
Prawn	*Palaemon*	House cricket	*Gryllus*
Spiny lobster	*Palinurus*	Praying mantis	*Mantis religiosa*
Crab	*Cancer*	Earwig	*Forficula*
Root-headed barnacle	*Sacculina*	Dragon fly	*Sympetrum*
Hermit crab	*Eupagurus*	Silkmoth	*Bombyx mori*
Goose-barnacle	*Lepas*	Yellow wasp	*Polistes*
Rock barnacle	*Balanus*	Honeybee	*Apis indica*
Silverfish	*Lepisma*	Millipede	*Thyroglutus*
Cockroach	*Periplaneta*	Centipede	*Scolopendra*
Desert locust	*Schistocerca*	Horseshoe crab	*Limulus*

Economic Importance

- *Limulus* is a living fossil.
- Honeybee produces wax and honey.
- *Peripatus* acts as a connecting link between Arthropoda and Annelida.
- Prawn and lobster are used as food in many countries.
- *Microtreme* (white ant-termite) causes loss to furniture and other wooden articles.

Phylum–Mollusca

General Characteristics

Phylum–Mollusca is the second most abundant phylum which contains soft bodied animals usually protected by a calcareous shell and a ventral muscular foot. The study of molluscs is called **Malacology**, while study of molluscan shell is called **Choncology**.

Peculiar Features of Mollusca

- They generally have an exoskeleton of calcareous shell which may be internal or absent.
- Body is divisible into three parts *i.e.*, head, foot and mantle cavity.
- A glandular fold called **mantle** or **pallium** is present in the body wall.
- A rasping organ called **radula** is present in buccal cavity of most of molluscs.
- A peculiar sense organ called **osphradium** check the quality of water.

Handbook of BIOLOGY

Respiration occurs by the following structures

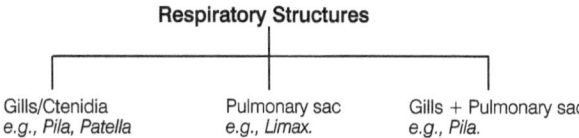

Excretion occurs by 1 or 2 pairs of metanephridial tubules called **kidneys** or **organs of Bojanus**. Pelecypods also have a large, reddish-brown **Keber's organ** in front of pericardium for excretion. Nervous system is formed of 3 paired ganglia, *i.e.,* cerebral, pedal and visceral ganglia.

Reproduction

Sexes are usually dioecious, but some are hermaphrodite, *e.g., Doris, Limax,* etc. Most forms are oviparous, but only a few are viviparous (*e.g., Pecten*) fertilisation is external (*e.g., Patella*) or internal (*e.g., Pila*).

Development is either direct (*e.g.,* all pulmonates and cephalopods) or indirect including **trochophore,** (*e.g., Chiton*) or **glochidium** (*e.g., Unio*) or **velliger** (*e.g., Dentalium*) larvae.

Classification

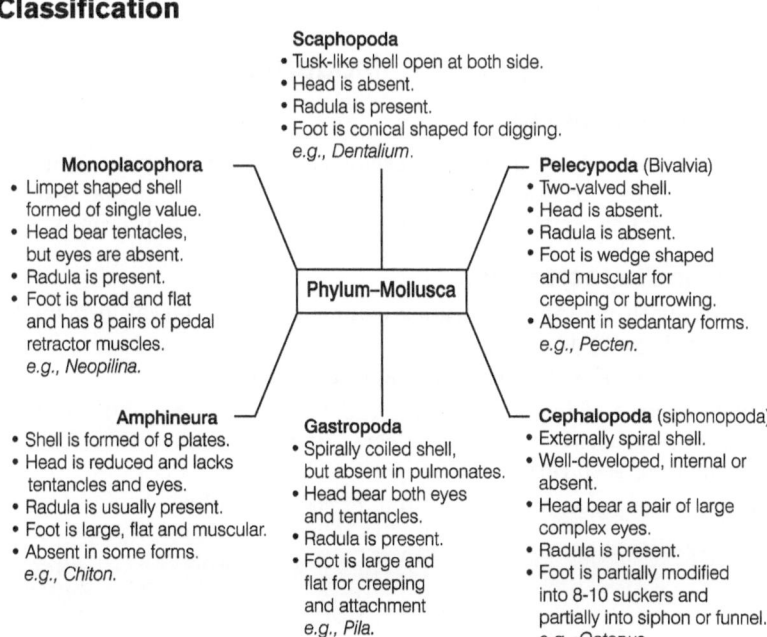

Common and Scientific Name of Some Molluscs

Common Names of Molluscans	Scientific Name	Common Names of Molluscans	Scientific Name
Sea mussel	Mytilus	Sea lemon	Doris
Edible oyster	Ostrea	Grey slug	Limax
Cockle	Cardium	Squid	Loligo
Rock-borer	Pholas	Cuttlefish	Sepia
Razor clam	Solen	Devil fish	Octopus
Scallop	Pecten	Pearly nautilus	Nautilus
Ear shell	Haliotis	Tusk shell	Dentalium
True limpet	Patella	Coat of mail shell	Chiton
Sea hare	Aplysia		

Economic Importance
- Molluscans like oyster, squid and cuttlefish are used as food in many countries.
- Shell of many molluscans is of ornamental value.
- *Dentalium* is used as decorative piece.
- *Sepia* ink has medicinal value.

Phylum–Echinodermata

General Characteristics
Echinodermata is a group of exclusively marine, spiny skinned animals. These triploblastic animals form the only phyla (except Chordata) which contains true endoskeleton (mesodermal origin).

Peculiar Characteristics
- Adults with pentamerous radial symmetry, while larval forms with bilateral symmetry.
- Good power of **autotomy** and **regeneration**.
- Body surface of five symmetrical radiating areas or ambulacra and alternating between interambulacra. Ambulacra have tube feet for locomotion, respiration, etc.
- Presence of water-vascular system of coelomic origin.

Handbook of BIOLOGY

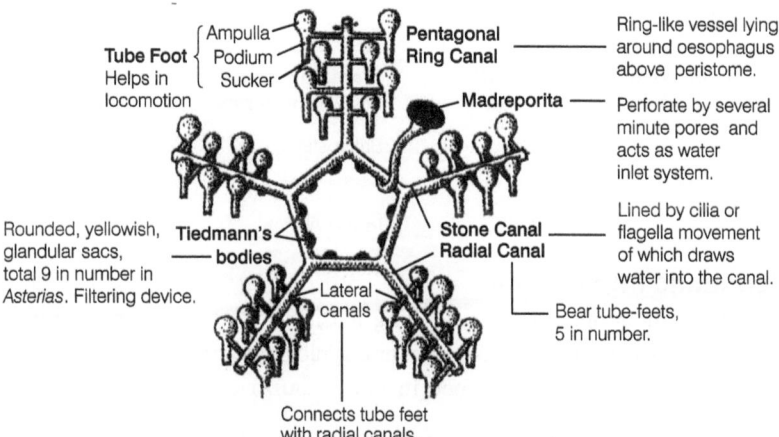

Water vascular system in *Asterias*

Degenerate Characters

- Head, respiratory pigment and excretory organs are absent.
- Sense organs are poorly developed.
- Nervous system is formed of nerve plexi.
- Circulatory system is of open type

Classification of Echinodermata

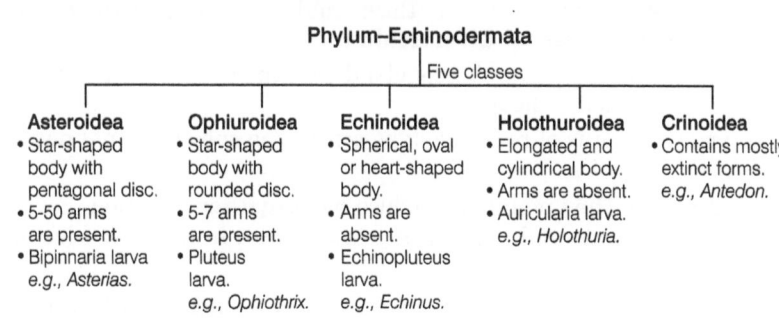

Common echinoderms with their common names and scientific name given here

Common Names of Echinoderms	Scientific Name	Common Names of Echinoderms	Scientific Name
Starfish	Asterias	Brittle star	Ophiothrix
Sea cucumber	Echinus	Feather star	Antedon
Brittle star	Ophiothrix	Basket star	Astrophyton

Economic Importance
- *Antedon* is supposed to be a living fossil.
- Eggs of sea urchin are used for embryological studies.
- Sea cucumber is used as food in many countries.

Phylum–Hemichordata

General Characteristics
Hemichordates include the acorn worms or tongue worms. These are commonly called half chordates or pre-chordates. They are exclusively marine, mostly tubicolous, primitive chordates. They are bilaterally symmetrical, triploblastic and enterocoelic true coelomates.

Peculiar Characteristics
- Body is divided into three regions, *i.e.*, proboscis, collar and trunk.
- Their foregut gives out a thick and stiff outgrowth called **stomochord** or **buccal diverticulum**.
- Excretion occurs by a proboscis gland or glomerulus present in the proboscis in front of heart.
- Nervous system is of primitive type containing sub-epidermal nerve plexus.

Reproduction They mainly reproduce by sexual reproduction. Sexes are usually separate and number of gonads varies from one to several pairs.

Fertilisation is external. Development is direct or indirect with a free swimming tornaria larva.

Economic Importance
They show affinities with annelids, echinoderms and chordates.

Phylum–Chordata

General Characteristics

Animals belonging to phylum–Chordata are characterised by the presence of notochord, dorsal tubular nerve cord and gill-clefts. These three structures are found in the embryological stages of all chordates.

Notochord It serves as a primitive internal skeleton. It may persist throughout life, as in cephalochordata, cyclostomata and some fishes or it may be replaced partially or completely by a backbone or vertebral column.

Dorsal Tubular Nerve Cord lies above the notochord and persists throughout life in most chordates, but in a few it degenerates before maturity.

Gill Clefts Gill clefts appear during the development of every chordate, but in many aquatic forms they are lined with vascular lamellae which form gill for respiration.

In terrestrial chordates which never breathe by gills, traces of gill-clefts are present during early development, but disappear before adult life.

The various sub-phyla and divisions are already explained in the chapter starting. *Major classes of Chordata are discussed below*

Pisces
Classes

Chondrichthyes	Osteichthyes	Placodermi
• Cartilaginous endoskeleton.	• Bony endoskeleton.	• Includes earlier fossils
• Exoskeleton is of placoid scales (dermal origin).	• Exoskeleton comprieses cycloid, ctenoid or ganoid scales (mesodermal origin).	• Body is with an external protective armour of bony scales or plates
• Mouth is placed ventrally.	• Mouth is terminal.	• Jaws are kimitive with teeth e.g., *Climatius*, *Palaeospondyeus*.
• External nares are ventral to head.	• External nares are dorsal to head.	
• Caudal fin is heterocercal.	• Caudal fin is homocercal.	
• 5-7 pairs of gills are present.	• Four pairs of gills are present.	
• Swim bladder is absent.	• Swim bladder is present.	
• Gills are not covered by operculum.	• Gills are covered by operculum.	
• Electric organs (e.g., *Torpedo*) and poison sting (e.g., *Trygon*) are present.	• Electric organs all absent	
• Mostly viviparous. e.g., *Scoliodon* (dog fish), *Pristis* (saw fish), *Trygon* (sting ray), *Carcharodon* (great white shark), *Chimaera* (rabbit fish) and *Rhinobatos*.	• Mostly ovisparous e.g., *Labeo* (rohu), *Clarias* (magur), *Pterophyllum* (angel fish), *Betta* (fighting fish), *Catla* and *Exocoetus* (flying fish).	

```
                              Tetrapoda
                              |  Classes
    ┌─────────────────┬───────────────────┬──────────────────┬─────────────────┐
   Amphibia          Reptilia            Aves               Mammals
```

Amphibia	Reptilia	Aves	Mammals
• Cold-blooded	• Cold-blooded	• Warm blooded	• Warm-blooded
• Skin is smooth and glandular.	• Skin is cornified and covered with scales	• Skin is covered by feathers	• Skin is covered by epidermal hairs.
• Heart is with two auricles and one ventricle.	• Heart consists of two auricles and partly divided ventricle.	• Heart contains two auricles and two ventricles.	• Heart contains two part auricle and two ventricles.
• Respiration occurs by lungs, buccopharyngeal cavity, skin and gills.	• Respiration occurs by lungs.	• Rispiration occur by lungs provided by air sacs.	• Respiration occurs by lungs.
• RBCs are nucleated.	• RBCs are nucleated.	• RBCs are nucleated	• RBCs are enucleated.
• They have largest RBCs of animal kingdom.	• Two pairs of pentadactyl limbs, each with 5 digits bearing clames corneoscutes. In snakes limbs are absent.	• Forelimbs are modified to wings and hindlimbs are modified for walking, swimming and pearching.	• Quadraped limbs whose digit ends with claws or nails or hooves.
• Two pairs of limbs, each with five-toes.		• Hindlimbs bear claws and scales (fects).	• In whales and dolphins, limbs are absent.
• Skull is dicondylic	• Skull is monocondylic.	• Skull is monocondylic.	• Skull is dicondylic.
• Mesonephric kidney 10 pairs of cranial nerves	• Metanephric kidney 12 pairs of cranial nerves.	• Metanephric kidney.	• Metanephric kidney.
• Fertilisation is external, oviparous.	• Thecodont teeth	• 12 pairs of cranial nerves.	• 12 pairs of cranial nerves.
	• Fertilisation is internal, oviparous.	• Teeth are absent and upper and lower jaws are modified into beak.	• Thecodont, heterodont and diphyodont teeth.
		• Fertilisation is internal, oviparous.	• Fertilisation is internal, both oviparous and viviparous.

Amphibia

Class-Amphibia consists of two sub-classes, *i.e.*, **Stegocephalia** (extinct) and Lissamphibia (modern living amphibians). In contrast to Stegocephalia whose skin bear scales and bony plates, Lissamphibians do not possess bony dermal skeleton.

Lissamphibia is further divided into three orders as follows

Lissamphibia | Orders

Apoda/Gymnophiona/Caecillians
- Also called **limbless amphibians**.
- Long worm-like, burrowing, dermal scales present in skin.
- Tail short or absent, cloaca terminal.
- Skull compact, roofed with bone.
- Males have protrisible copulatory organ.
- Larva has 3 pairs of external gills, gills also present in adult stage.
- e.g., *Ichthyophis* (blindworm), *Ureotyphus*.

Anura/Salientia
- Also called tail-less amphibians.
- Commonly includes frogs and toads.
- Forelimbs shorter then hindlimbs.
- Adults without gills.
- Skin loosely fitting, scaleless, teeth pre only on upper jaw or absent.
- Vertebral column very small of 5-9 proc
- Vertebrae and a slender urostyle.
- Fertilisation always external.
- Full metamorphosis without neotenic to e.g., *Rana, Bufo, Hyla* and *Rhacophorus*.

Urodela/Caudata
- Also called tailed amphibians lizard-like, limbs two pairs of weak and equal size.
- Commonly called newts and salamanders.
- Skin devoids of scales and tympanum.
- Possess largest RBC.
- Gills permanant or lost in adults. (*Necturus, Proteus, Siren* and Axolotl larva have external gills).
- Fertilisation is internal.
- Larva aquatic, adult-like with teeth. e.g., *Nectunes, Salotrandra* and *Ambystoma*.

Reptilia

On the basis of presence of temporal fossae, class—Reptilia is sub-divided into three sub-classes, *i.e.*, Anapsida, Parapsida and Diapsida.

These sub-classes are further divided into orders and sub-orders as follows

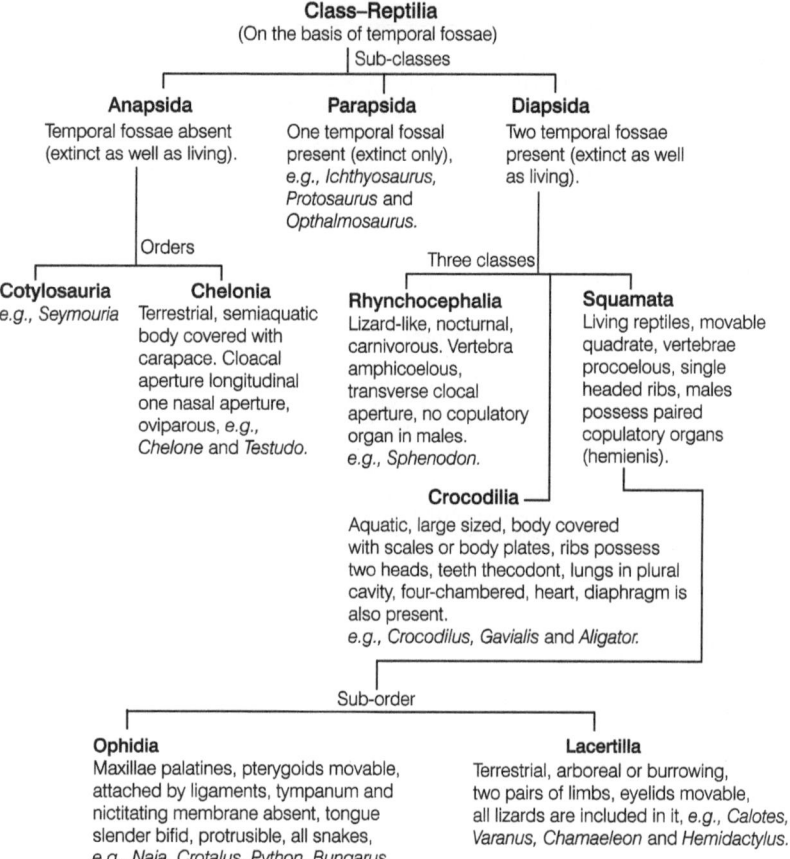

Aves

Class–Aves possesses various peculiar characteristics which are not found in other animal groups. They possess long bones with air cavities, *i.e.,* **pneumatic** bones which reduces their body weight and hence, helpful in flight. Their bones also lack bone marrow.

Their sternum is large and bears a keel for the attachment of flight muscles. They do not possess skin glands except the cutaneous oil glands or **green glands** (or uropygial glands) that are located at the root of the tail. These glands are absent in parrot and ostrich.

Class–Aves is further divided into sub-classes and orders as follows

Class–Aves
Sub-classes

Archaeornithes
(Gk. *archios*–ancient; *ornithes*–bird)
(Includes extinct (in Mesozoic era) birds homodont (same type of teeth) teeth in both the jaw, long tapering tail, weak, vertebrae are amphicoelous, keeled sternum, non-pneumatic bones, hand with clawed fingerswings are primitive with little power of flight. e.g., *Archaeopteryx lithographica* (ancient or lizard bird) and *Archaeornithes*.

Neonithes
(Includes extinct as well as living birds) Teeth absent except in some fossil birds, wings are well development and adapted for flight, tail short and reduced, fingers of the wings are without claw.

Super-orders

Odontognathae
(Extinct cretaceous birds) jaw bear teeth for catching fish.
e.g., *Hesperornis*, *Ichthyornis*.

Palaeognathae
(Flight less running birds)
- Wings vestigial or rudimentary, feathers without any interlocking mechanism.
- Oil gland is absent except in *Tinamus* and kiwi.
- Sternal keel is vestigial, flat or raft-like.
- Pygostyle is penis or reduced.
- Syrinx is absent.
- Male has a penis.
e.g., *Struthio camelus* (African ostrich), *Rhea americana* (American ostrich), *Dromaeus* (emu), *Casurarius* (cassowary) *Apteryx* (kiwi), *Tinamus* (tinamou).

Impennae
- The superorder includes modern aquatic flightless birds with paddle like wings or flippers.
- Feet are webbed.
- The skeleton is solid, air sacs are absent.
- The integument is a fatty insulating layer
e.g., *Aptenodytes* (emperor penguin), *Eudyptes* (rock hopper penguin).

Neognathae (Carinatar)
- Modern flying birds, with well-developed wings and feathers with interlocking mechanism.
- Sternum with developed keel.
- Males have no copulatory organ.
- *Some important order of flying birds are*
Gaviiformes
e.g., divers.
Procellariiformes,
e.g., albatross.
Anseriformes.
e.g., swans, geese and ducks.
Falconiformes
e.g., vultures, eagles, hawks and falkons.
Gruiformes.
e.g., pheasants.
Columbiformes,
e.g., pigeons.
Psittaciformes,
e.g., parrots.
Cuculiformes,
e.g., cuckoo.
Coraciiformes,
e.g., kingfishers.
Passeriformes,
e.g., crow and thrashers.

Mammalia

Class–Mammalia is the considered superior of all animal groups. This class is further divided into two sub-classes.

The detailed classification of class–Mammalia is as follows

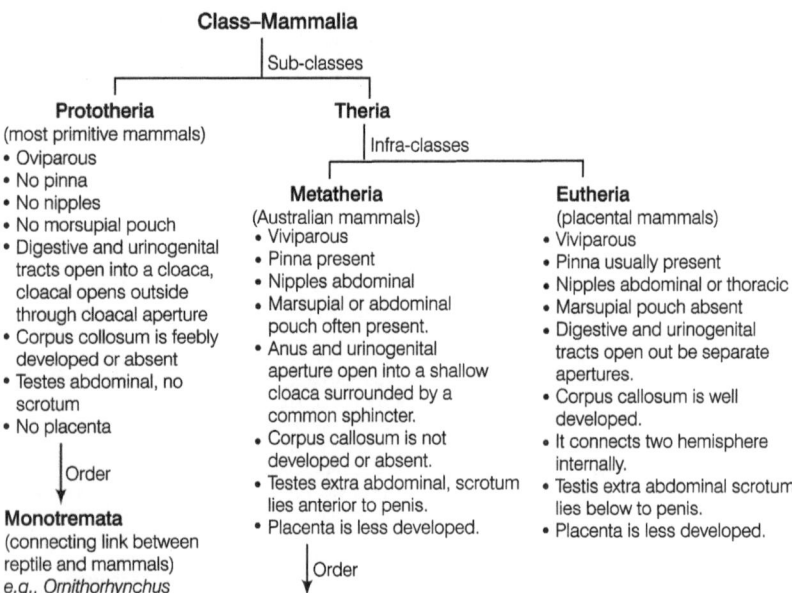

Class–Mammalia

Sub-classes

Prototheria
(most primitive mammals)
- Oviparous
- No pinna
- No nipples
- No morsupial pouch
- Digestive and urinogenital tracts open into a cloaca, cloacal opens outside through cloacal aperture
- Corpus collosum is feebly developed or absent
- Testes abdominal, no scrotum
- No placenta

Order

Monotremata
(connecting link between reptile and mammals)
e.g., Ornithorhynchus (duck-billed platypus), *Tachyglossus* or *Echidna* (spiny anteater).

Theria

Infra-classes

Metatheria
(Australian mammals)
- Viviparous
- Pinna present
- Nipples abdominal
- Marsupial or abdominal pouch often present.
- Anus and urinogenital aperture open into a shallow cloaca surrounded by a common sphincter.
- Corpus callosum is not developed or absent.
- Testes extra abdominal, scrotum lies anterior to penis.
- Placenta is less developed.

Order

Marsupialia
(pouched mammals)
e.g., Macropus (kangaroo), *Phascolarctos* (kolabear), *Didelphys* (opossum).

Eutheria
(placental mammals)
- Viviparous
- Pinna usually present
- Nipples abdominal or thoracic
- Marsupial pouch absent
- Digestive and urinogenital tracts open out be separate apertures.
- Corpus callosum is well developed.
- It connects two hemisphere internally.
- Testis extra abdominal scrotum lies below to penis.
- Placenta is less developed.

Structural Organisation in Animals

Tissues (By Bichat; Father of Histology)

It is a group of one or more cell types and their intercellular substances that perform a particular function.

Based on structure, function and location, *animal tissues are of four types*

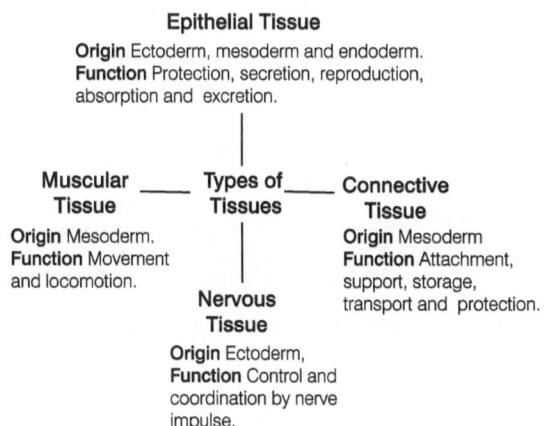

Epithelial Tissue (By Ruysch)

It consists of a sheet of tightly packed cells with the minimum of intercellular material and rest upon a non-cellular basement membrane or lamina propria. *Epithelial tissues are of two types*

(i) Simple Epithelium

It consists of a single cellular layer and all the cells rest on the basement membrane. It covers the surface with little wear and tear activity. It performs secretory, absorptive and protective functions.

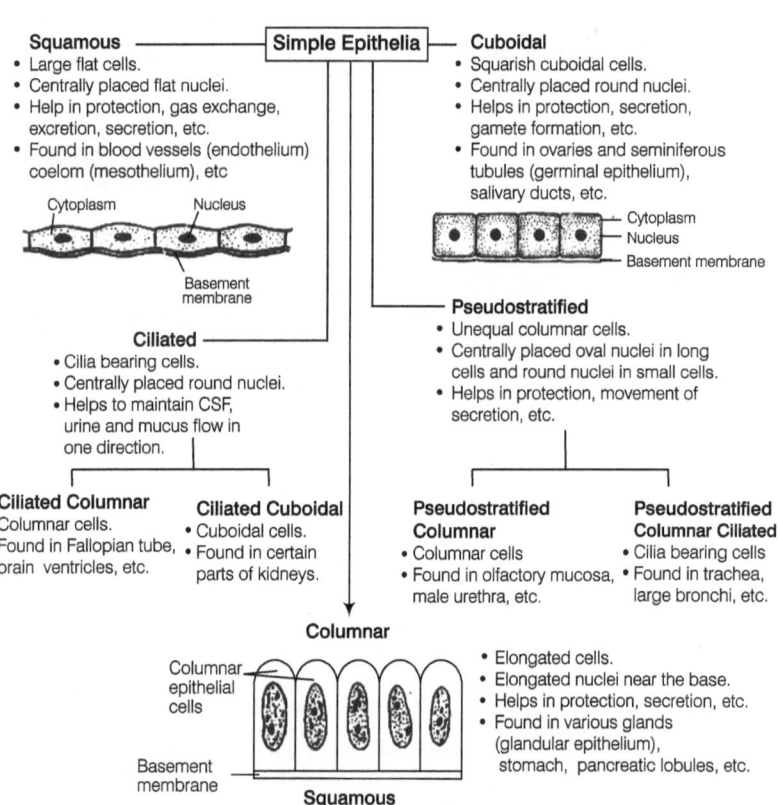

Types of simple epithelium

(ii) Compound Epithelium

It consists of multicellular layers and the cells of deepest layer rest on the basement membrane. It covers the surfaces with maximum wear and tear activity. It performs protective functions.

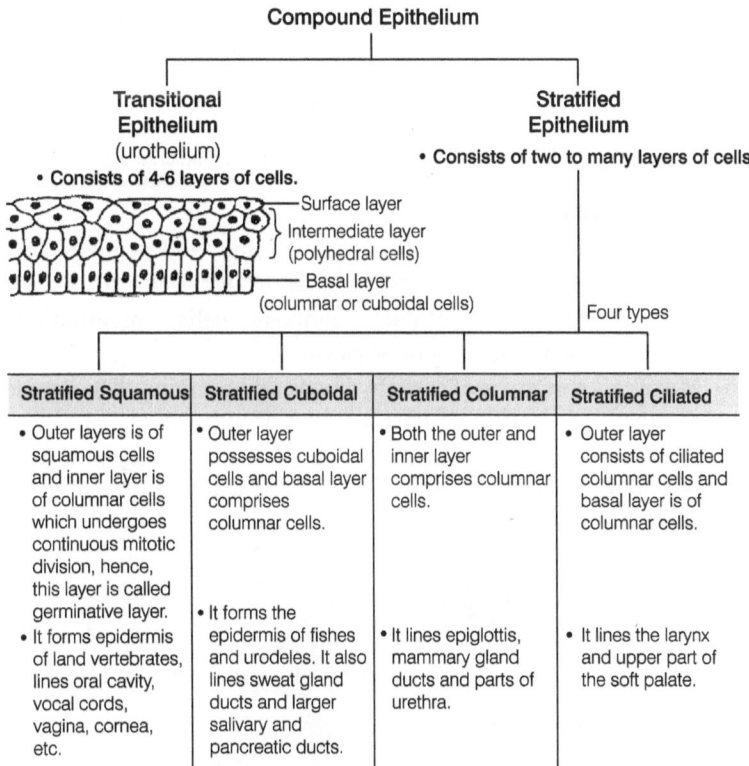

Stratified squamous epithelium is further of two types

(a) **Keratinised epithelium** Keratin is present in the dead superficial cells. It is impermeable to water and forms well protective covering against abrasions. It forms epidermis of skin of land vertebrates.

(b) **Non-keratinised epithelium** Its superficial cells are living and keratin is absent. It is permeable to water and forms moderately protective covering against abrasions. It lines the buccal cavity, pharynx, oesophagus, etc.

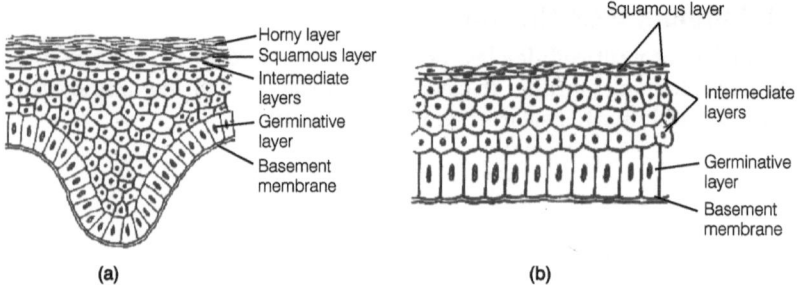

(a) Keratinised epithelium (b) Non-keratinised epithelium

Connective Tissue

Most abundant and widely spread tissue, link and support other tissues of the body. *Basic components of connective tissue are*

(i) **Cells** including fibroblast, adipose cells, macrophages, mesenchyme cells, plasma cells, etc.

(ii) **Matrix** is a mixture of carbohydrates and proteins. The common mucopolysaccharide in matrix is hyaluronic acid.

(iii) **Fibres** including collagen fibres of white collagen protein, reticular fibres of reticulin protein and elastic fibres of yellow elastin protein.

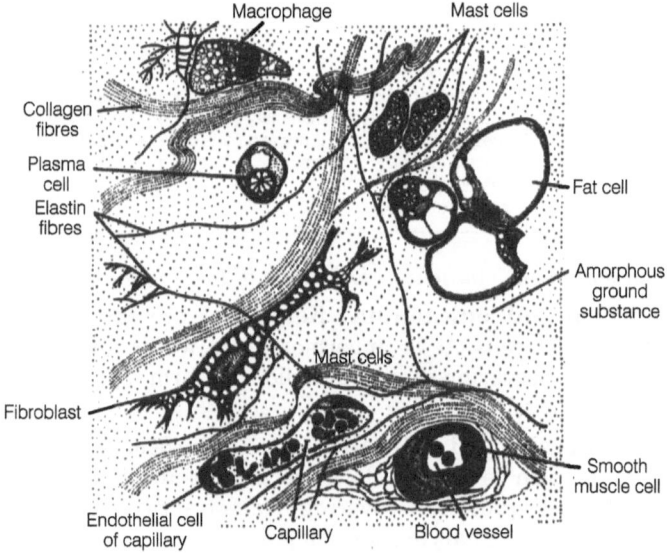

Connective tissue (generalised)

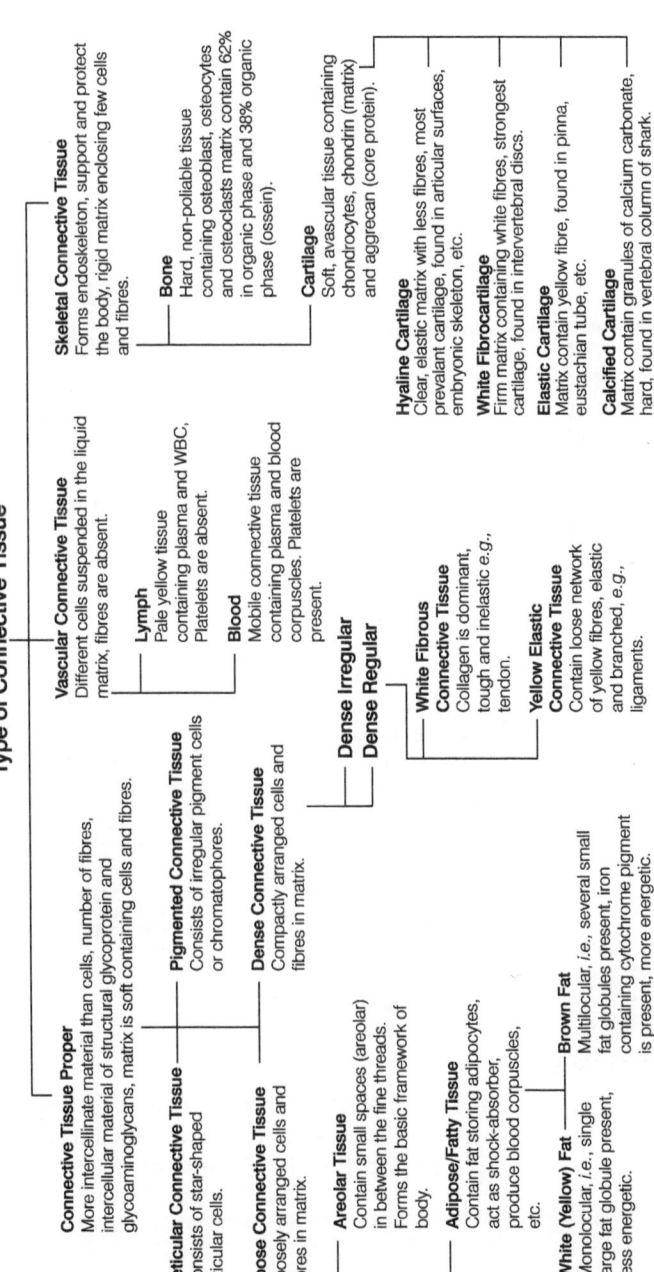

Muscular Tissue

Contractile tissue containing numerous fine fibrils called **myofibrils** in the cytoplasm (sarcoplasm). Muscle cells (myocytes) develop from myoblasts. Muscles have the capacity to respond to a stimulus (irrilability) by two basic phenomena, *i.e.*, response to a stimulus and conductivity.

Muscular tissues are of following three types

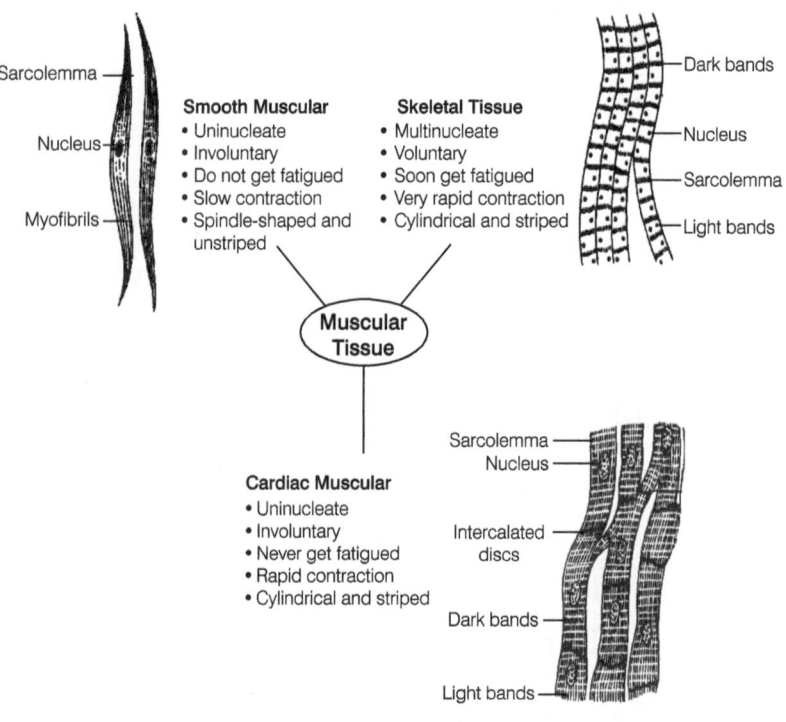

Types of muscles

Neural Tissue

This tissue is the second specialised tissue with the property of exicitability and conductivity. It consists of nerve cells and glial cells. Neurons are the structural and functional units of neural (nervous) tissue.

Handbook of BIOLOGY

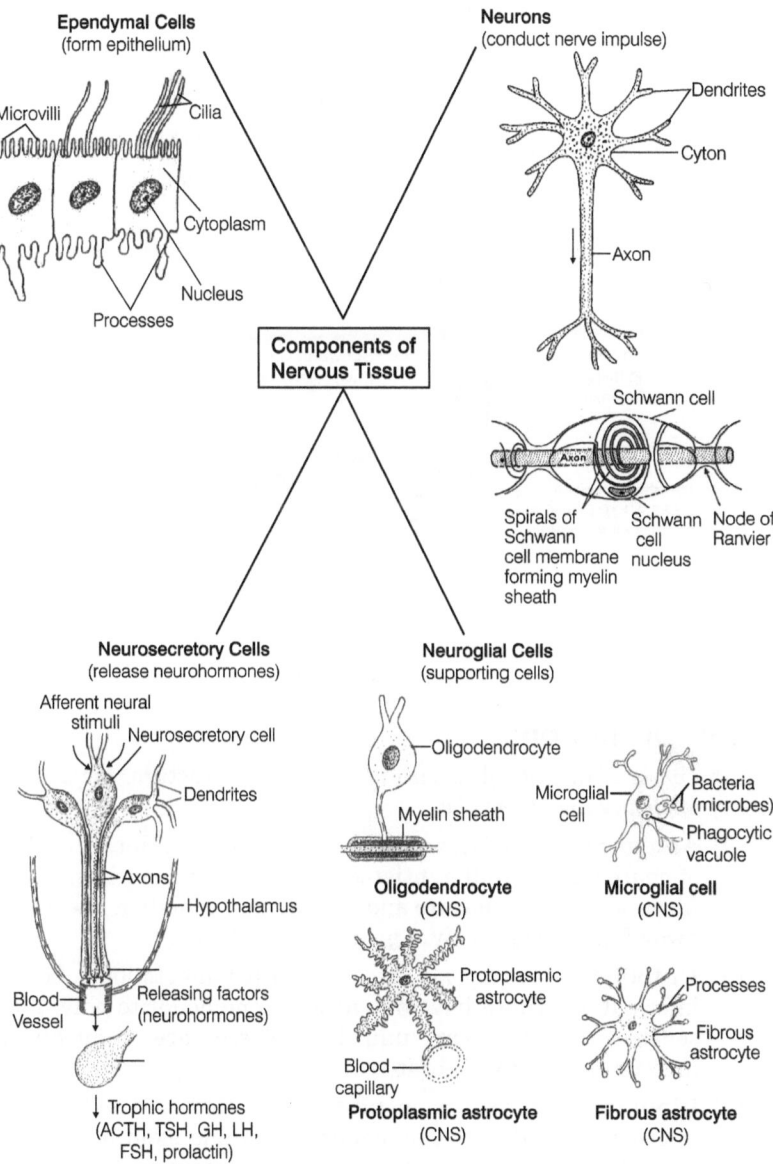

Components of Nervous Tissue

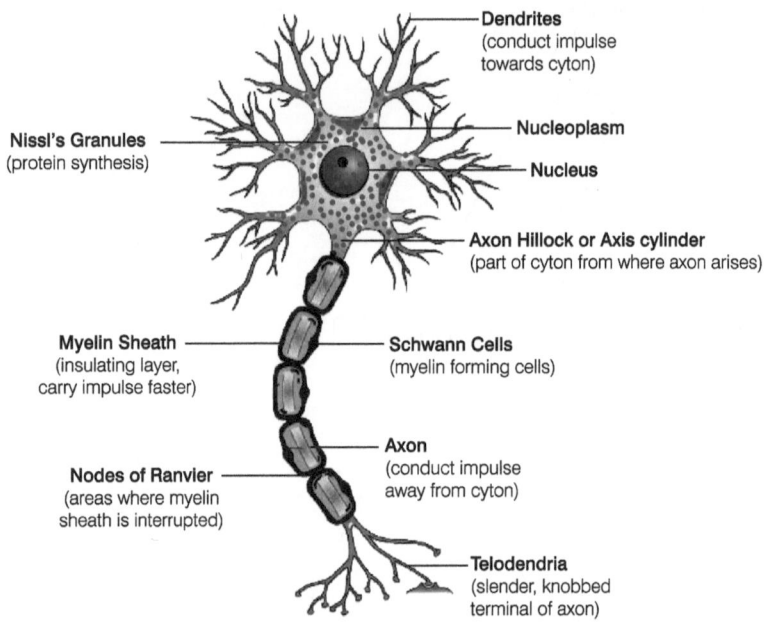

Structure of a neuron

Types of Neurons

On the basis of functional nature in relation to structure, *the neurons are of following four types*, i.e.,

  (i) **Apolar neurons**, *i.e.,* neurons without polarity. Here, the fibres of neuron are not differentiated into axon and dendrites. All the fibres are of same nature and can carry information towards or away from the cell body, *e.g.,* neurons of *Hydra*.

 (ii) **Unipolar neurons**, *i.e.,* neurons with unidirectional flow of information. These have one axon or one dendrite only. Most sensory neurons are unipolar. These are common in invertebrate and vertebrate embryos.

(iii) **Bipolar neurons**, *i.e.,* neurons with unidirectional flow of information, but with one dendron and one axon at opposite poles. These occur in the retina of eyes, olfactory epithelium, etc.

(iv) **Multipolar neurons**, *i.e.,* neurons with unidirectional flow of information, but with one axon and many dendrites. They occur in the nervous system of adult vertebrates.

Neurons can also be classified according to their functions as
  (i) **Sensory or Afferent neurons**, *i.e.,* these connect sensory or receptor cells or organs to the CNS and conduct sensory impulses. Branched or unbranched and naked or encapsulated free endings of numerous sensory neurons found scattered in skin epidermis. These serve as cutaneous sense organs or **exteroceptors**. Similar endings scattered in skeletal muscles, bone joints, ligaments and tendons serve as **interceptors**.
  (ii) **Motor or Efferent neurons**, *i.e.,* these connect the CNS to effectors (muscles and glands) and conduct motor impulses.
  (iii) **Internuncial or Interneurons** These occur only in the CNS and serve to connect two or more neurons for distant transmission of impulses.

Similary nerve fibres can be categorised as

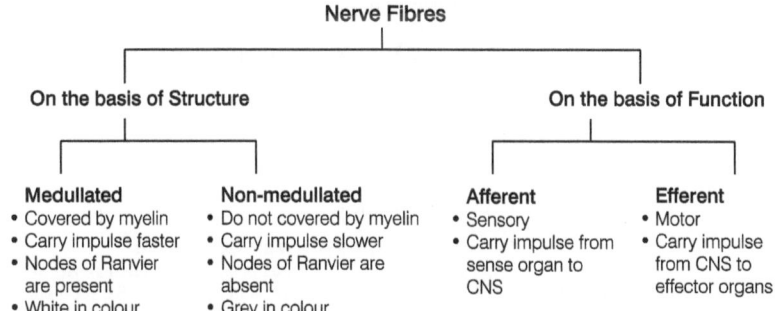

Earthworm

It is a raddish-brown terrestrial invertebrate that inhabits the upper layer of the moist soil. The common Indian earthworms are *Pheretima* and *Lumbricus*.

Morphology

Bilaterally symmetrical with elongated, narrow and cylindrical body. It appears brown due to the presence of porphyrin pigment in the body wall. Dorsal body surface is demarkated by the ventral surface due to the presence of dark mid-dorsal line. Their body is metamerically segmented.

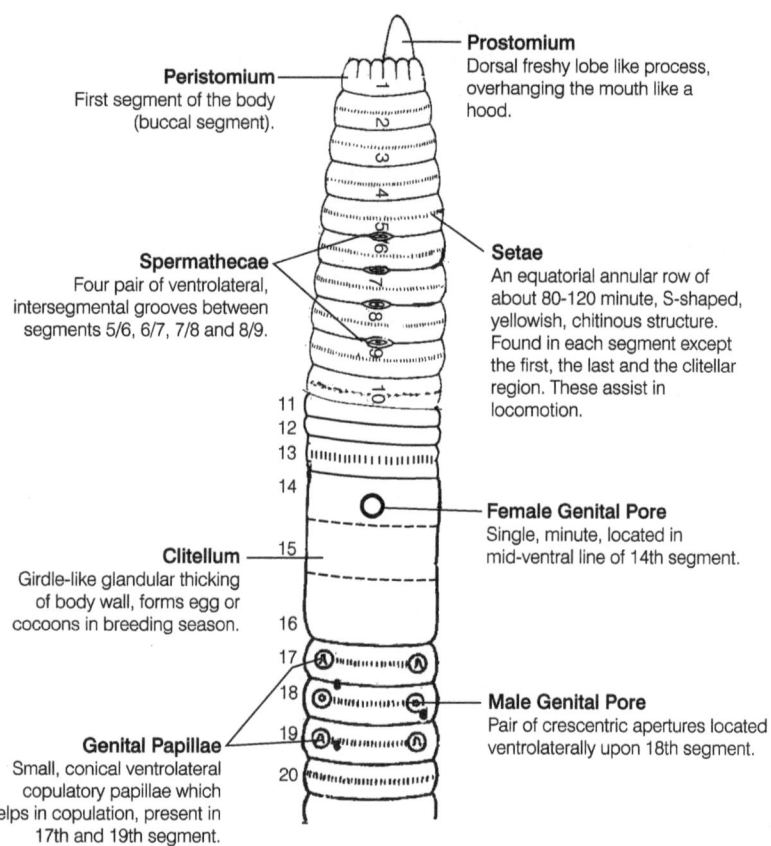

External structure of earthworm

Metamerism

It is the repetition of organs and tissues at intervals along the body of an animal, thus dividing the body into a linear series of similar parts or segments (metamers). It is an internal mesodermal phenomenon and helps in more efficient locomotion.

Nephridiopores

They are 200-250 minute pores per segment from 7th segment onwards. Their number increases to 2000 to 2500 in the clitellar region.

Anatomy and Physiology

- **Locomotion** It is brought about by a coordinated contraction and relaxation of circular and longitudinal muscles of body wall, assisted by setae, mouth and the hydrostatic pressure of coelomic fluid.
- **Digestive System** Earthworm possesses a straight alimentary canal from mouth to anus. The canal is differentiated into six regions-buccal chamber, pharynx, oesophagus, gizzard, stomach and intestine.

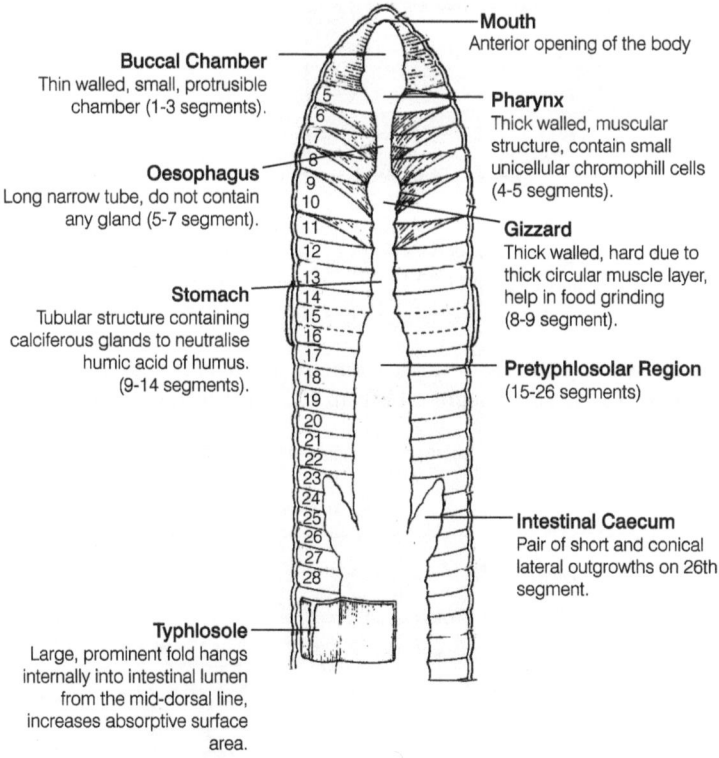

Mouth
Anterior opening of the body

Buccal Chamber
Thin walled, small, protrusible chamber (1-3 segments).

Pharynx
Thick walled, muscular structure, contain small unicellular chromophill cells (4-5 segments).

Oesophagus
Long narrow tube, do not contain any gland (5-7 segment).

Gizzard
Thick walled, hard due to thick circular muscle layer, help in food grinding (8-9 segment).

Stomach
Tubular structure containing calciferous glands to neutralise humic acid of humus. (9-14 segments).

Pretyphlosolar Region
(15-26 segments)

Intestinal Caecum
Pair of short and conical lateral outgrowths on 26th segment.

Typhlosole
Large, prominent fold hangs internally into intestinal lumen from the mid-dorsal line, increases absorptive surface area.

Internal structure of earthworm

Circulatory System

Closed circulatory system, **haemoglobin** (erythrocruorin) dissolved in blood plasma. Three main blood vessels in body are dorsal, ventral and sub-neural. **Dorsal blood vessel** is the largest blood vessel of the body. **Blood glands** are present on the 4th, 5th and 6th segments and they produce blood cells and haemoglobin. Blood cells are phagocytic in nature. Their heart do not have any kind of pulsative activity.

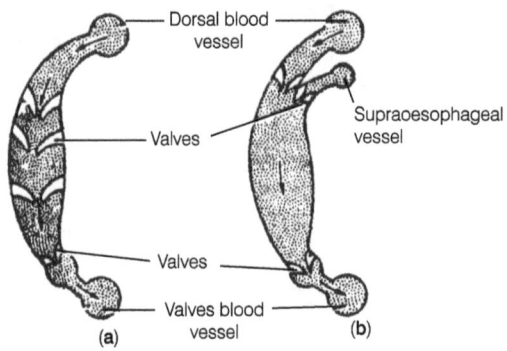

Heart of *Pheretima* : (a) Lateral heart (7th and 9th segment) (b) Lateral oesophageal heart (12th and 13th segment)

The number, nature and arrangement of blood vessels are very different in the first 13 segments from that in the rest of the body.

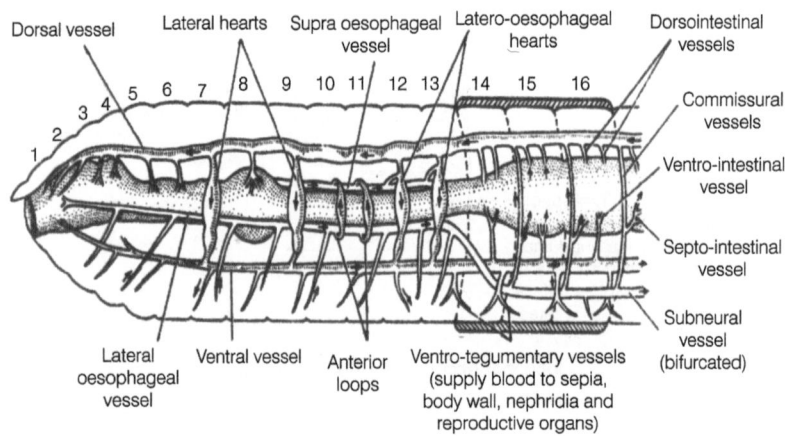

Pattern of blood vascular system in first 13 segments

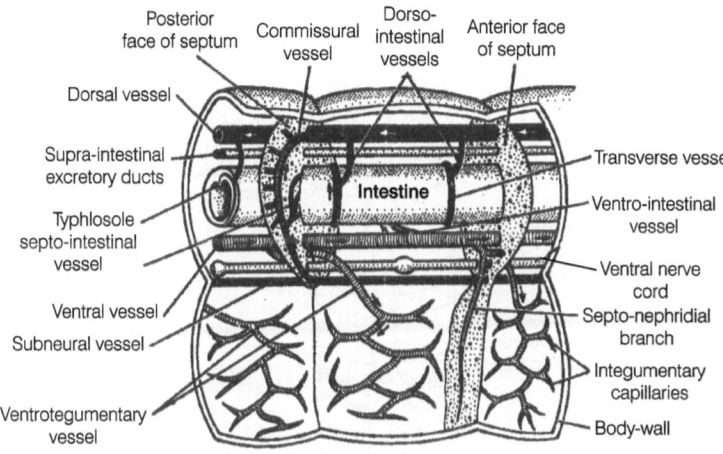

Pattern of blood vascular system behind 13th segment

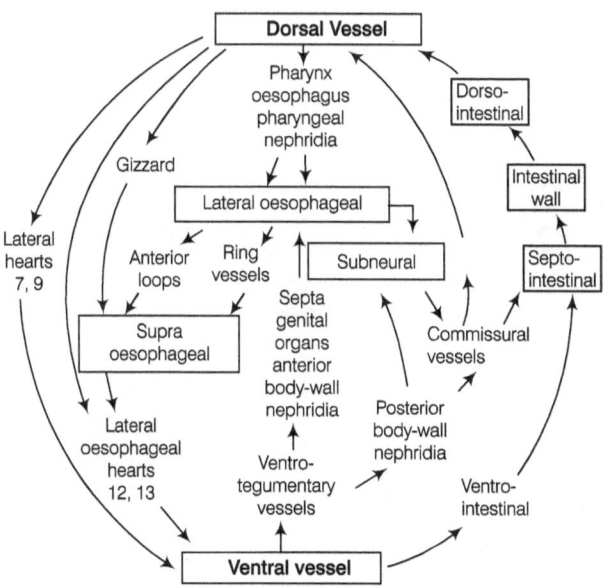

Complete circulation plan of earthworm

- **Respiratory System** The animal is aerobic and gaseous exchange takes place through general body surface.
- **Excretory System** It is made up of segmentally arranged **nephridia** of **three types**.

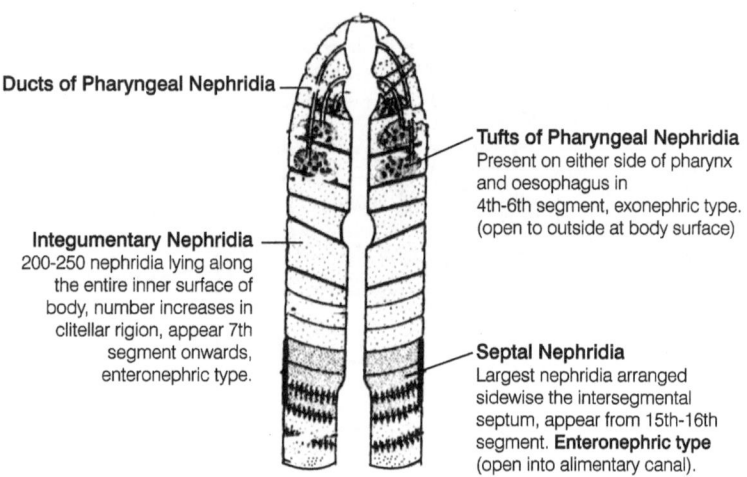

Types of nephridia

Nervous System

Metamerically segmented, divisible into three sections, *viz.*, central, peripheral and autonomic. All nerves are mixed, having both sensory and motor fibres.

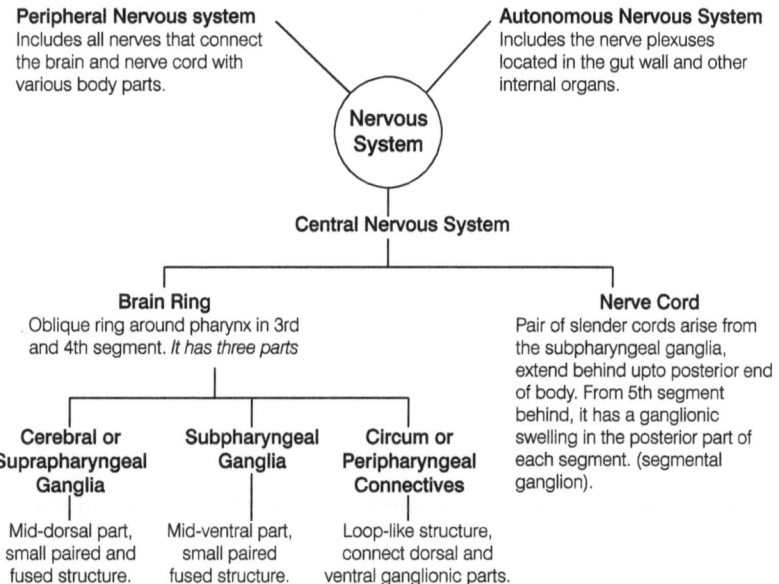

Reproductive System

Animal is hermaphrodite and reproduce only sexually.

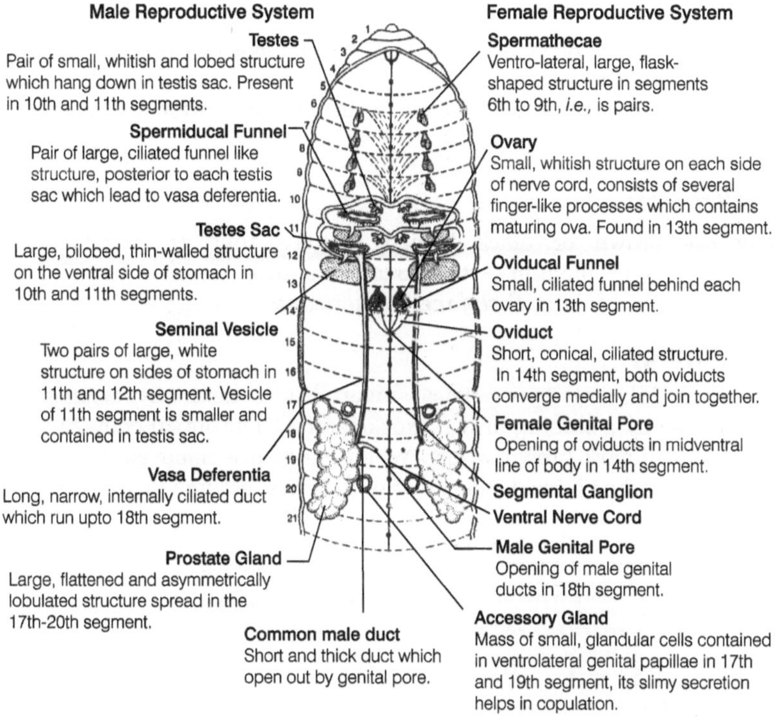

Male Reproductive System
Testes
Pair of small, whitish and lobed structure which hang down in testis sac. Present in 10th and 11th segments.
Spermiducal Funnel
Pair of large, ciliated funnel like structure, posterior to each testis sac which lead to vasa deferentia.
Testes Sac
Large, bilobed, thin-walled structure on the ventral side of stomach in 10th and 11th segments.
Seminal Vesicle
Two pairs of large, white structure on sides of stomach in 11th and 12th segment. Vesicle of 11th segment is smaller and contained in testis sac.
Vasa Deferentia
Long, narrow, internally ciliated duct which run upto 18th segment.
Prostate Gland
Large, flattened and asymmetrically lobulated structure spread in the 17th-20th segment.
Common male duct
Short and thick duct which open out by genital pore.
Female Reproductive System
Spermathecae
Ventro-lateral, large, flask-shaped structure in segments 6th to 9th, *i.e.*, is pairs.
Ovary
Small, whitish structure on each side of nerve cord, consists of several finger-like processes which contains maturing ova. Found in 13th segment.
Oviducal Funnel
Small, ciliated funnel behind each ovary in 13th segment.
Oviduct
Short, conical, ciliated structure. In 14th segment, both oviducts converge medially and join together.
Female Genital Pore
Opening of oviducts in midventral line of body in 14th segment.
Segmental Ganglion
Ventral Nerve Cord
Male Genital Pore
Opening of male genital ducts in 18th segment.
Accessory Gland
Mass of small, glandular cells contained in ventrolateral genital papillae in 17th and 19th segment, its slimy secretion helps in copulation.

Reproductive system of earthworm

Reproduction

Copulation → Sperms reaches in spermatheca → Secretion of clitellum forms cocoon → Mature ova discharge into cocoon → Worm wriggles backward and cocoon slips towards the spermathecal segments → Cocoon receives numerous eggs in spermathecal segments. → With advancement, it receives albuminous secretion of epidermal gland cells. → Worm wriggles out completely through cocoon and left free in the moist soil. → In 2-3 weeks, developing embryo become young adult worm. → Copulation

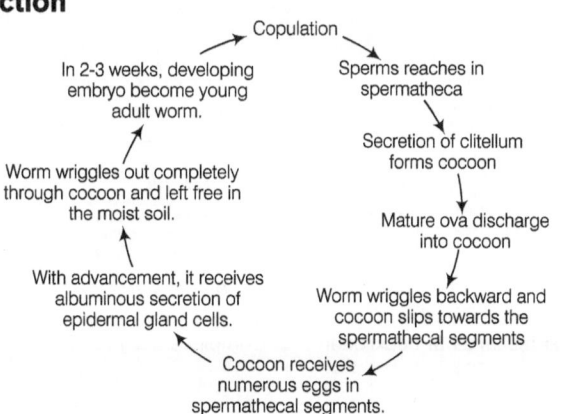

Events of reproduction in earthworm

Economic Importance of Earthworm
- They are used as bait for fishing.
- Their burrowing habit increases the fertility of soil.
- Their burrows causes the loss of water by seepage from ditches in irrigated lands.
- They are easily obtained and are of convenient size for dissections in laboratories.

Cockroach

They are brown or black bodied animals that are included in class–Insecta of phylum–Arthropoda. The most common species of cockroaches in India is *Periplaneta americana*.

Morphology

Nocturnal, bilateral symmetrical invertebrate, distinctly segmented and covered by a shining brown exoskeleton. Their dorsal body surface is covered by dark brown wings. When wings are removed, the three regions of the body–head, thorax and abdomen become visible.

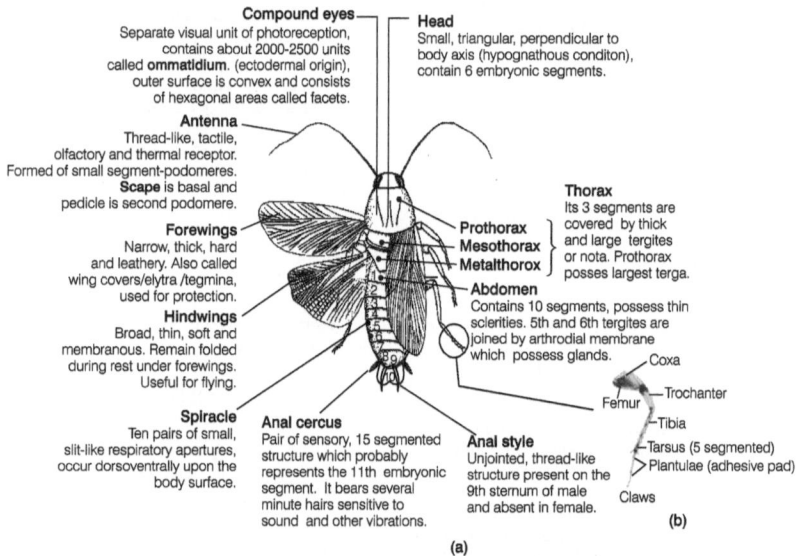

External features of cockroach : (a) Complete body (b) One walking leg

Sclerites

Small plate-like structures which forms the exoskeleton. These structures are joined together by soft, intersegmental, flexible membrane called **arthrodial membrane.**

The dorsal sclerites are called **tergites, ventral** one are **sternites,** which the lateral ones are called **pleurites.**

Anatomy and Physiology

Locomotion

Cockroaches are good runners, but poor fliers as the muscles associated with the jointed legs are much more developed than those associated with the wings.

Digestive System

The mouth in animal is surrounded by well defined appendages which can be seen as

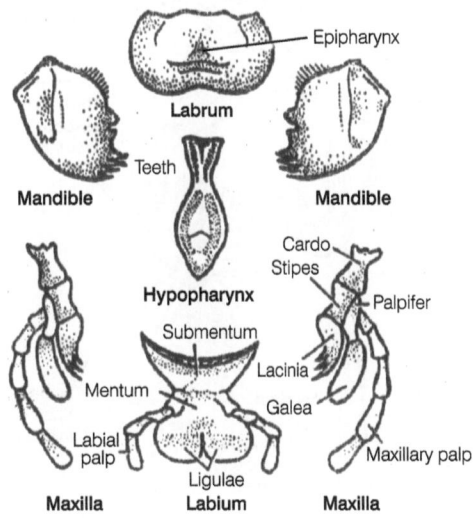

Mouth parts of cockroach

Alimentary canal is complete and well differentiated in accordance with omnivorous mode of feeding. *It is divisible into following parts*

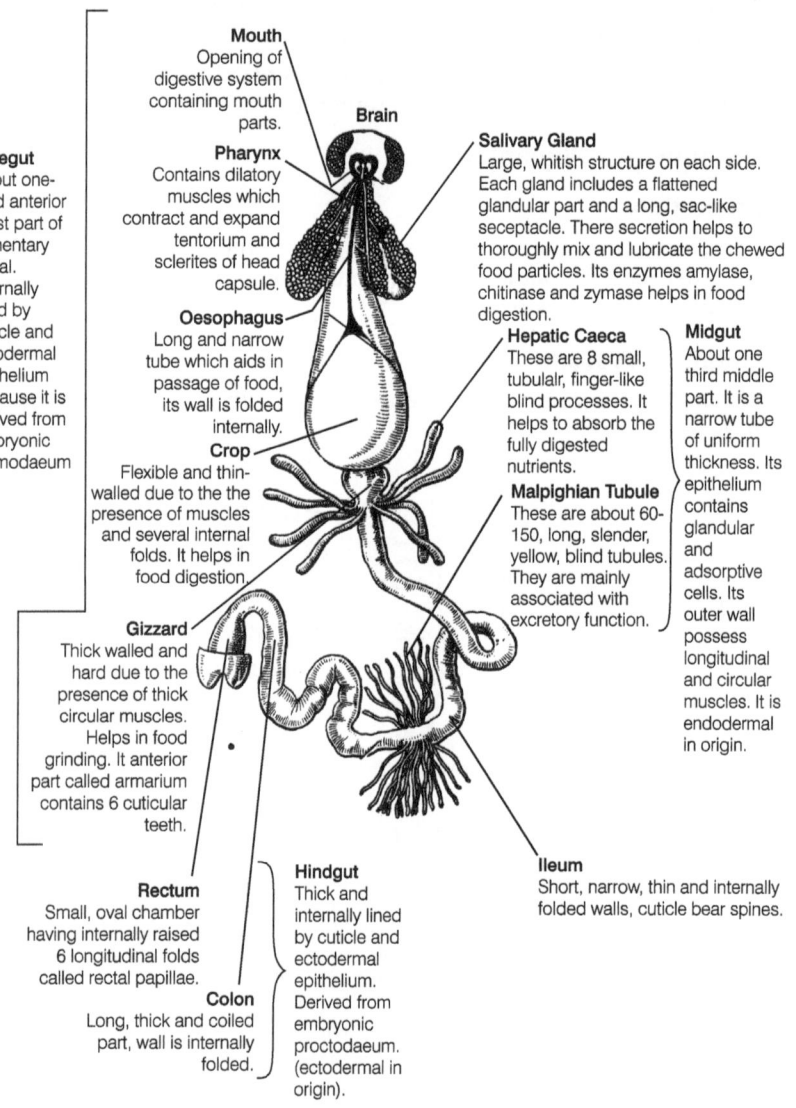

Foregut
About one-third anterior most part of alimentary canal. Internally lined by cuticle and ectodermal epithelium because it is derived from embryonic stomodaeum.

Mouth
Opening of digestive system containing mouth parts.

Pharynx
Contains dilatory muscles which contract and expand tentorium and sclerites of head capsule.

Oesophagus
Long and narrow tube which aids in passage of food, its wall is folded internally.

Crop
Flexible and thin-walled due to the the presence of muscles and several internal folds. It helps in food digestion.

Gizzard
Thick walled and hard due to the presence of thick circular muscles. Helps in food grinding. It anterior part called armarium contains 6 cuticular teeth.

Brain

Salivary Gland
Large, whitish structure on each side. Each gland includes a flattened glandular part and a long, sac-like seceptacle. There secretion helps to thoroughly mix and lubricate the chewed food particles. Its enzymes amylase, chitinase and zymase helps in food digestion.

Hepatic Caeca
These are 8 small, tubulalr, finger-like blind processes. It helps to absorb the fully digested nutrients.

Malpighian Tubule
These are about 60-150, long, slender, yellow, blind tubules. They are mainly associated with excretory function.

Midgut
About one third middle part. It is a narrow tube of uniform thickness. Its epithelium contains glandular and adsorptive cells. Its outer wall possess longitudinal and circular muscles. It is endodermal in origin.

Rectum
Small, oval chamber having internally raised 6 longitudinal folds called rectal papillae.

Colon
Long, thick and coiled part, wall is internally folded.

Hindgut
Thick and internally lined by cuticle and ectodermal epithelium. Derived from embryonic proctodaeum. (ectodermal in origin).

Ileum
Short, narrow, thin and internally folded walls, cuticle bear spines.

Digestive system of cockroach

Respiratory System

Every tissue of body is in direct communication with atmospheric air due to the absence of respiratory pigment in the blood.

It consists of following components

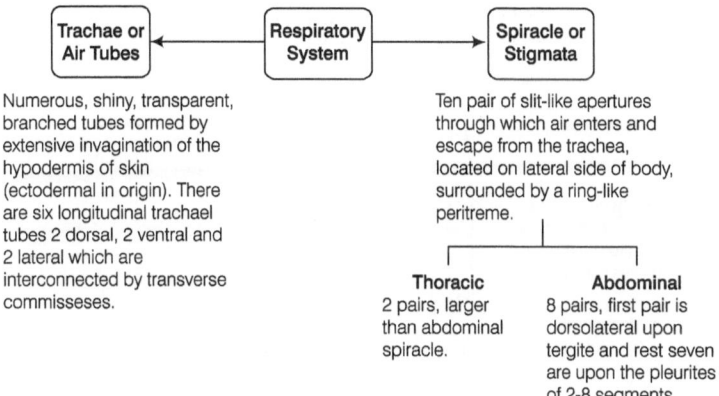

Circulatory System

Cockroach possesses open type of circulatory system with blood flowing in the blood spaces or lacunae. The blood is without respiratory pigment and called haemolymph (possess plasma and haemocytes). Body consists of three sinuses mainly with one head sinus.

The flow of blood within the body lookes like

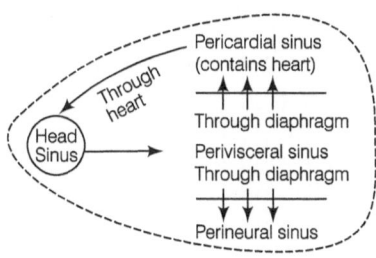

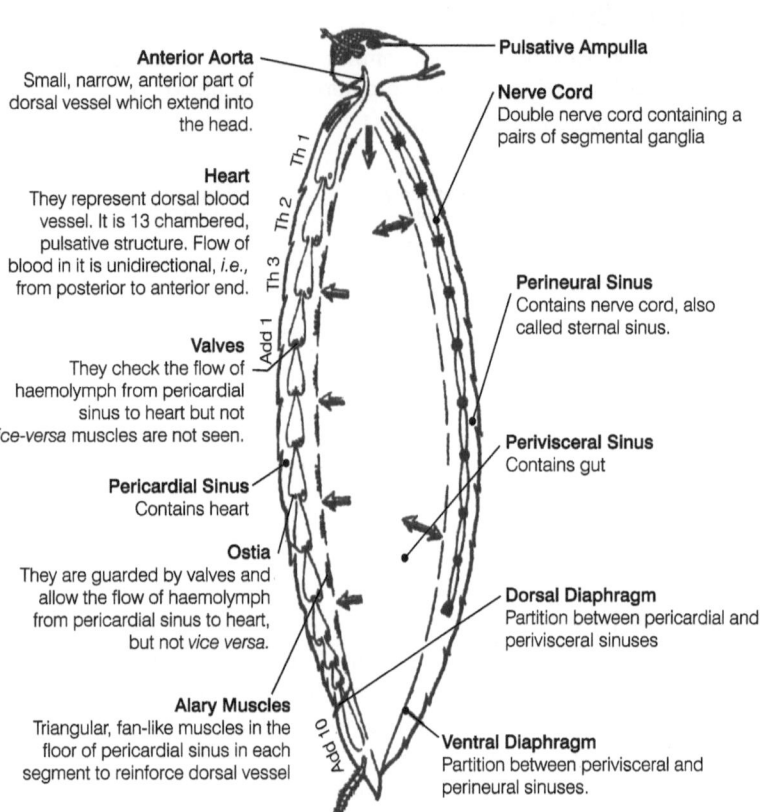

Circulatory system of cockroach

Handbook of BIOLOGY

Excretory System

The animal is uricotelic and excretion occurs through the following structures

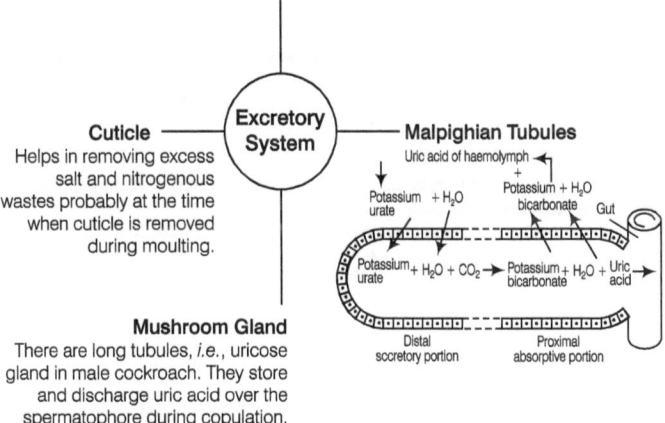

Excretory system in cockroach

Fat Body
It has urate cells which obtain nitrogenous waste from haemolymph and store it in the form of uric acid. Mycetocyte cells of fat body contain symbiotic bacteria which decompose uric acid into protein during protein deficiency.

Cuticle
Helps in removing excess salt and nitrogenous wastes probably at the time when cuticle is removed during moulting.

Malpighian Tubules

Mushroom Gland
There are long tubules, *i.e.*, uricose gland in male cockroach. They store and discharge uric acid over the spermatophore during copulation.

Nervous System

It is well-developed and divided into following three types

(i) **Central nervous system** It includes a nerve ring and a double ventral nerve cord.

(ii) **Peripheral nervous system** It includes the nerves that connect the various ganglia of CNS to different body parts.

(iii) **Autonomic nervous system** It is of sympathetic type and also called **visceral nervous system**. It performs both nervous and endocrine functions.

It is divided into three parts

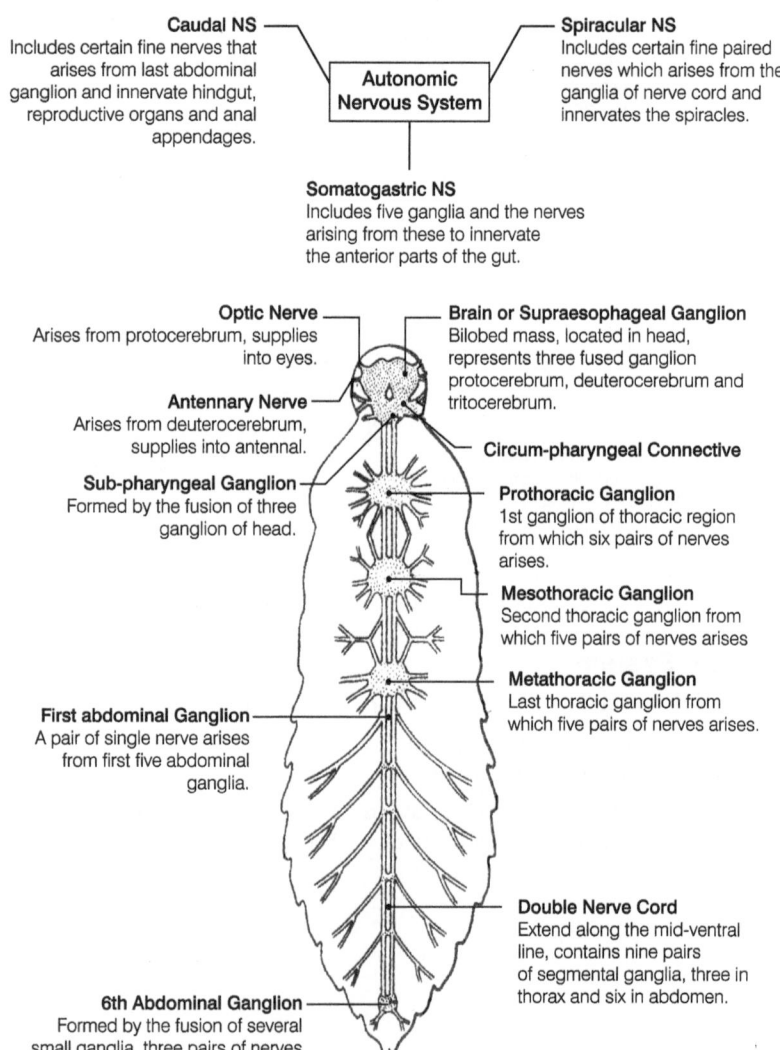

Central and peripheral nervous system of cockroach

Handbook of BIOLOGY

Reproductive System

Sexes are separate and sexual dimorphism is also seen

Female Cockroach	Male Cockroach
Body relatively larger and thicker.	Body relatively smaller and more flattened.
Abdomen has seven distinct segments.	Abdomen has nine distinct segments.
Hind end of abdomen is blunt and boat-shaped.	Hind end of abdomen is somewhat pointed.
Seventh sternite is divided.	Seventh sternite is undivided.
Anal styles all absent.	A pair of anal styles are articulated with 9th abdominal sternite.
Wings are smaller, extend only upto the hind end part of body.	Wings are relatively large, extend somewhat beyond the hindend of body.

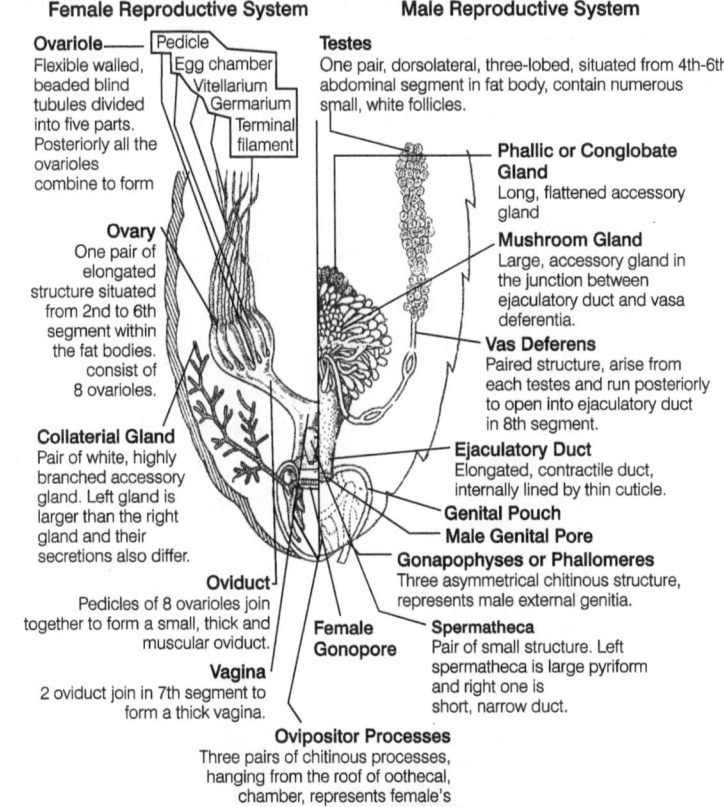

Female Reproductive System

Ovariole — Pedicle — Egg chamber — Vitellarium — Germarium — Terminal filament
Flexible walled, beaded blind tubules divided into five parts. Posteriorly all the ovarioles combine to form

Ovary
One pair of elongated structure situated from 2nd to 6th segment within the fat bodies. consist of 8 ovarioles.

Collaterial Gland
Pair of white, highly branched accessory gland. Left gland is larger than the right gland and their secretions also differ.

Oviduct
Pedicles of 8 ovarioles join together to form a small, thick and muscular oviduct.

Vagina
2 oviduct join in 7th segment to form a thick vagina.

Female Gonopore

Ovipositor Processes
Three pairs of chitinous processes, hanging from the roof of oothecal, chamber, represents female's external genitalia.

Male Reproductive System

Testes
One pair, dorsolateral, three-lobed, situated from 4th-6th abdominal segment in fat body, contain numerous small, white follicles.

Phallic or Conglobate Gland
Long, flattened accessory gland

Mushroom Gland
Large, accessory gland in the junction between ejaculatory duct and vasa deferentia.

Vas Deferens
Paired structure, arise from each testes and run posteriorly to open into ejaculatory duct in 8th segment.

Ejaculatory Duct
Elongated, contractile duct, internally lined by thin cuticle.

Genital Pouch

Male Genital Pore

Gonapophyses or Phallomeres
Three asymmetrical chitinous structure, represents male external genitia.

Spermatheca
Pair of small structure. Left spermatheca is large pyriform and right one is short, narrow duct.

Reproductive system in cockroach

Suspensory Filament

Thin, thread-like terminal filament formed of a syncytial chord of cytoplasm. It is terminally inserted upon dorsal body wall and serves to suspend the ovarioles into the perivisceral sinus.

Germarium

A small, multicellular structure in which oogonia form and mature into oocytes.

Vitellarium

A long and narrow structure which receives the actively growing oocytes from germarium. It appears beaded due to gradually growing sizes of contained oocytes.

Egg Chamber

A small, thick and elliptical structure which contains, at a time, a single, large, mature ovum.

Pedicel

A small, hollow structure which unite to form oviduct.

Spermatophore

It is a three-layered, pear-shaped, tough structure which centrally contains spermatozoa in the nourishing fluid secreted by small tubules or utriculi breviores of male's mushroom gland.

Physiology of Reproduction

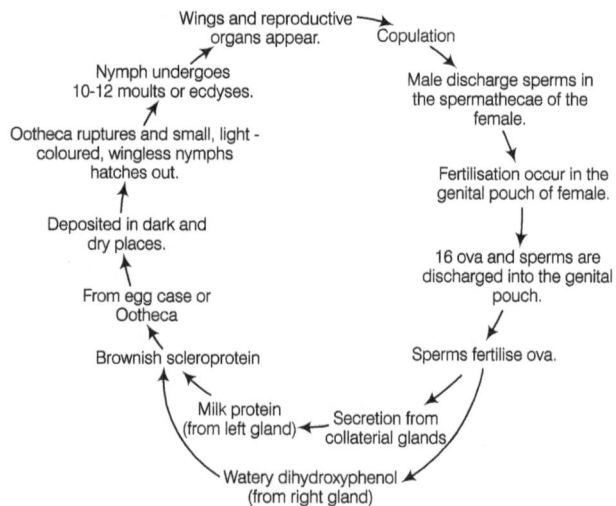

Process of reproduction in cockroach

Economic Importance of Cockroach
- They can be used as tools for the research of insect physiology and toxicology.
- They do not sting or bite, they transport human pathogens.

Frog
They are called amphibians because they can live both on land and in freshwater. The most common species of frog is *Rana tigrina*.

Morphology
Frog is a dorsoventrally flattened and streamlined animal, adapted for an amphibious mode of life. Its body is divisible into head and trunk.

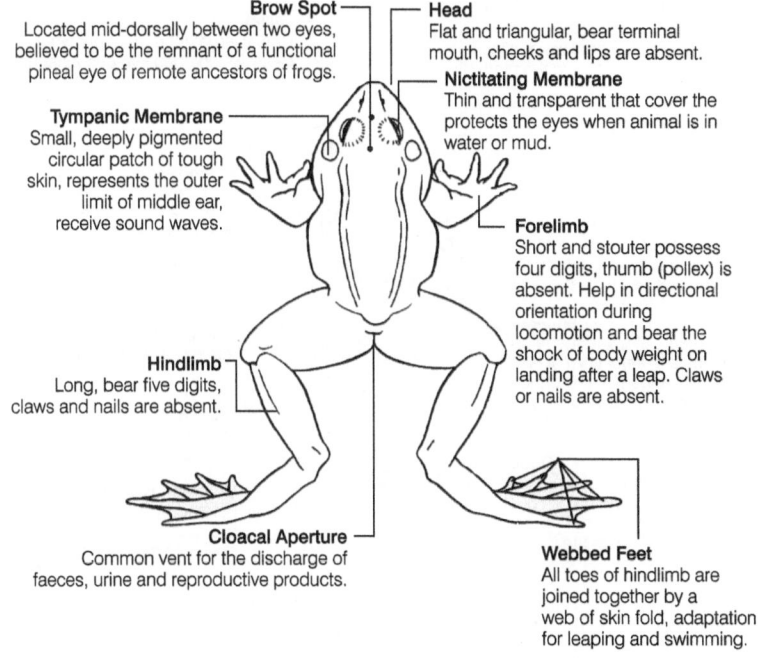

External structure of frog

Croaking
During the rainy season or breeding season, the frogs make peculiar sound with the help of their vocal cords to attract the females for mating. The male frogs croak louder than the females.

Metachrosis

It is the capability of frog to change its body colour with the change in its surroundings and climatic conditions.

Nuptial Pad

It is a dark swelling on the inner finger of the male frog which helps the male frog in mating.

Anatomy

Digestive System

Frogs are holozoic and carnivorous. Their alimentary canal is long, *coiled tube consisting of following structures*

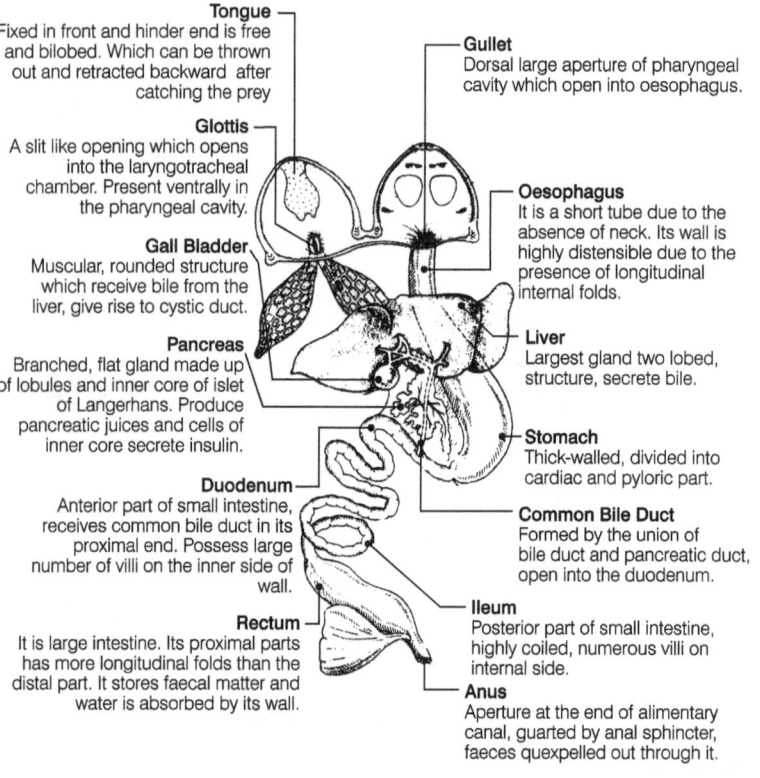

Tongue — Fixed in front and hinder end is free and bilobed. Which can be thrown out and retracted backward after catching the prey

Glottis — A slit like opening which opens into the laryngotracheal chamber. Present ventrally in the pharyngeal cavity.

Gall Bladder — Muscular, rounded structure which receive bile from the liver, give rise to cystic duct.

Pancreas — Branched, flat gland made up of lobules and inner core of islet of Langerhans. Produce pancreatic juices and cells of inner core secrete insulin.

Duodenum — Anterior part of small intestine, receives common bile duct in its proximal end. Possess large number of villi on the inner side of wall.

Rectum — It is large intestine. Its proximal parts has more longitudinal folds than the distal part. It stores faecal matter and water is absorbed by its wall.

Gullet — Dorsal large aperture of pharyngeal cavity which open into oesophagus.

Oesophagus — It is a short tube due to the absence of neck. Its wall is highly distensible due to the presence of longitudinal internal folds.

Liver — Largest gland two lobed, structure, secrete bile.

Stomach — Thick-walled, divided into cardiac and pyloric part.

Common Bile Duct — Formed by the union of bile duct and pancreatic duct, open into the duodenum.

Ileum — Posterior part of small intestine, highly coiled, numerous villi on internal side.

Anus — Aperture at the end of alimentary canal, guarted by anal sphincter, faeces quexpelled out through it.

Digestive system of frog

Respiratory System

Respiration in frog occurs through three modes

(a) **Cutaneous respiration** Frog's skin is ideally adapted for the process of gaseous exchange as it is without exoskeleton, highly vascularised skin, always remain moist due to the secretions of mucous glands. **It is most common mode, especially during hibernation** and **aestivation**.

(b) **Buccopharyngeal respiration** Mucosa of buccopharyngeal cavity is highly vascularised which aids in gaseous exchange. By showing oscillatory movements of the floor of buccal cavity and keeping the mouth, gullet and glottis closed breathing process is carried out. **Sternohyal** and **pterohyal** muscles help in the oscillatory movements. It is carried out in water and on land.

(c) **Pulmonary respiration** It involves the lungs, which are positive pressure type with hollow, highly distensible walls. They are endodermal in origin. Inspiration and expiration involves **gulping movements** in between oscillatory motion of buccopharyngeal respiration.

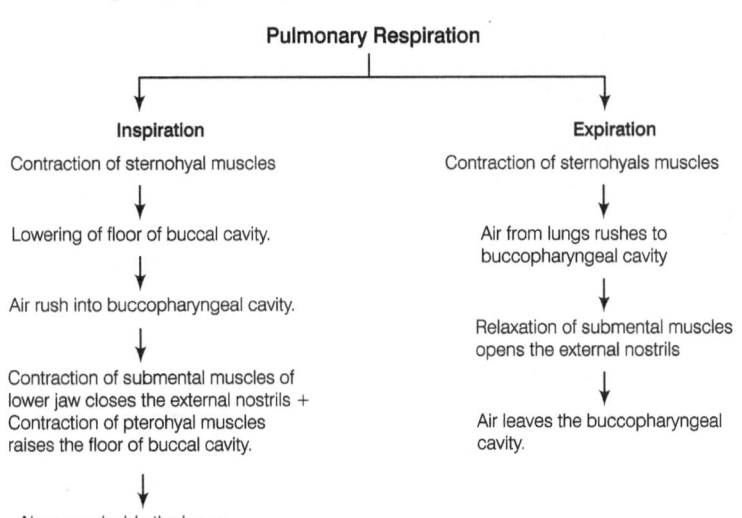

Circulatory System

It consists of blood vascular system of closed type which represents the incomplete double circulation. *i.e.,* both oxygenated and deoxygenated blood enters the heart and get mixed in the ventricle. Blood vascular system comprises blood, heart and blood vessels. Their heart is myogenic.

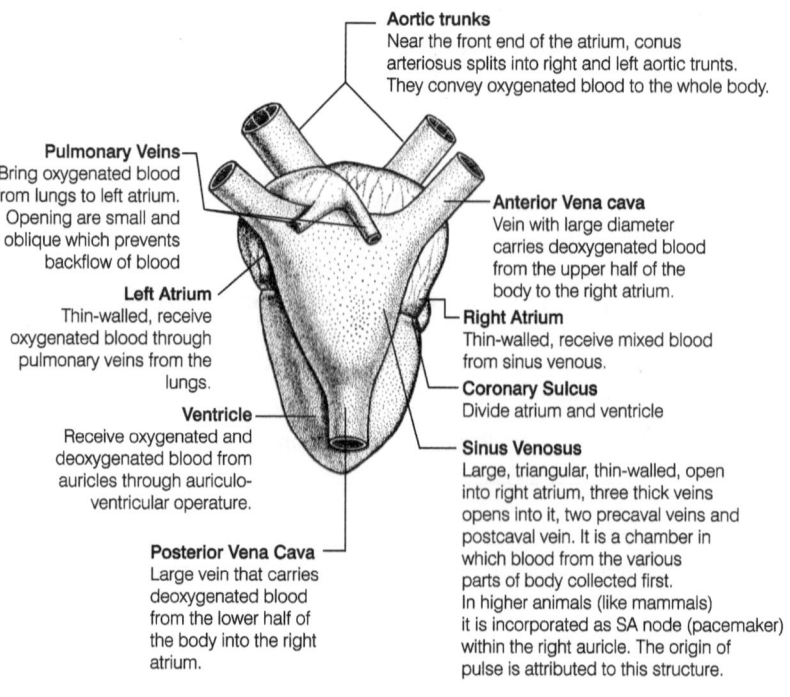

Aortic trunks
Near the front end of the atrium, conus arteriosus splits into right and left aortic trunts. They convey oxygenated blood to the whole body.

Pulmonary Veins
Bring oxygenated blood from lungs to left atrium. Opening are small and oblique which prevents backflow of blood

Anterior Vena cava
Vein with large diameter carries deoxygenated blood from the upper half of the body to the right atrium.

Left Atrium
Thin-walled, receive oxygenated blood through pulmonary veins from the lungs.

Right Atrium
Thin-walled, receive mixed blood from sinus venous.

Coronary Sulcus
Divide atrium and ventricle

Ventricle
Receive oxygenated and deoxygenated blood from auricles through auriculo-ventricular operature.

Sinus Venosus
Large, triangular, thin-walled, open into right atrium, three thick veins opens into it, two precaval veins and postcaval vein. It is a chamber in which blood from the various parts of body collected first. In higher animals (like mammals) it is incorporated as SA node (pacemaker) within the right auricle. The origin of pulse is attributed to this structure.

Posterior Vena Cava
Large vein that carries deoxygenated blood from the lower half of the body into the right atrium.

Circulatory system of frog

Conus or Truncus Arteriosus

This accessory chamber is present towards the ventral side. It contains a spiral valve inside because of which its cavity is divided into cavum pulmocutaneum and cavum aorticum.

Pylangium

The proximal, more muscular and longer portion of conus arteriosus. It is also called as **bulbus arteriosus**. It contains pulsative cardiac muscles.

Handbook of BIOLOGY

Synangium
The distal, less muscular portion of conus arteriosus. It is also called as **ventral aorta**.

Columnae Carneae
These are the major muscle columns of ventricle. These columns are connected with the flaps of valves through elastic chords of fibres called **chordae tendineae**.

Mixed blood is pumped by frog's heart due to incomplete double circuit (*i.e.*, due to the presence of only one ventricle).

Lymphatic system of frog consists of lymphatic capillaries, sinuses, lymph hearts and lymph.

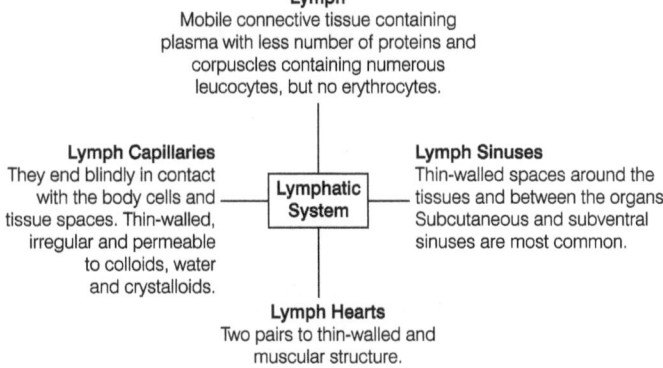

Excretory System
It consists of two kidneys, ureter, urinogenital ducts and bladder. The kidneys are of **mesonephric type**, *i.e.*, it develops from the middle part of intermediate mesoderm.

The nephron is not much differentiated. In embryonic conditions, **nephrostomes** are functional and in adults, they get replaced by **glomerulus**. Frog is **ureotelic**.

Nervous System
It comprises CNS, PNS and ANS

(a) **Central nervous system** It comprises brain and spinal cord. Brain is enveloped by two membranous meninges. **Pia arachnoid** (inner, soft, highly vascularised) and **Dura mater** (outer, tough, collagen fibre covering).

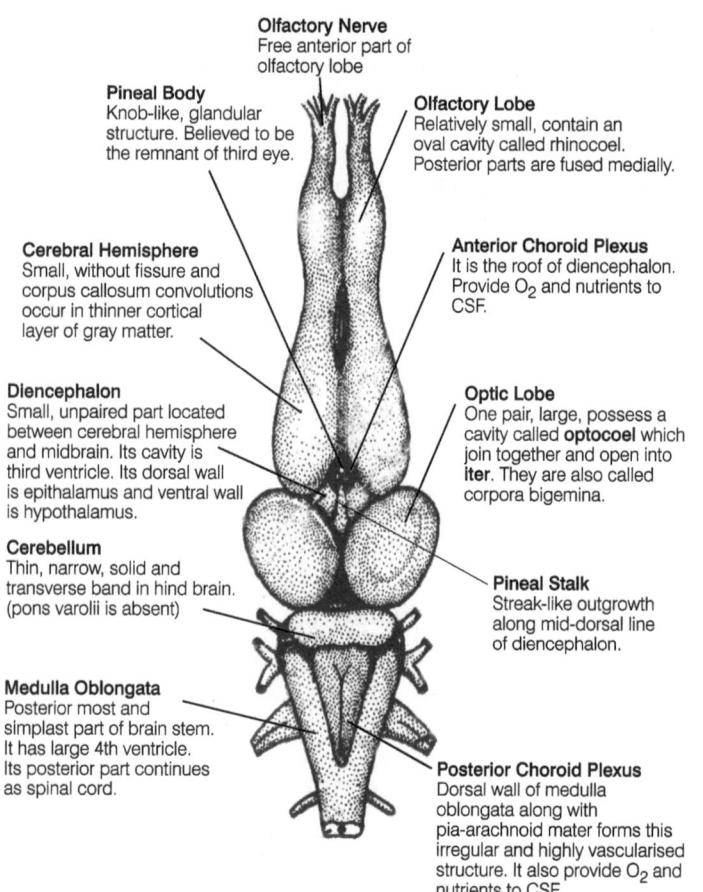

Nervous system of frog

Exceptions to Frog's Brain as Compared to Humans

- Rhienecphalon is anterior in position, but not in humans.
- Optic lobes are one pair, whereas they are two pairs in humans.
- Corpus striatum are present upon the floor of cavities of cerebral hemisphere in frog.
- Hippocampi, corpus callosum and pons varolii are absent in frogs.
- Frog's vision is monolucular and its binocular in humans.

Peripheral Nervous System It is represented by cranial and spinal nerves.

There are 10 pairs of cranial nerves in frog.

Handbook of BIOLOGY

Spinal accessory nerves and hypoglossal nerves are absent in it.

The number of spinal nerves in frog is 10 pairs, *i.e.*, 20.

Autonomic Nervous System It controls the involuntary activities such as homeostasis. *It comprises two antagonistic parts*

(i) **Sympathetic NS** It generally acts to stimulate the body to cope with stress. Its nerve endings are cholinergic and adrenergic.

(ii) **Parasympathetic NS** It functions to calm the body. Its nerve endings are cholinergic.

Reproductive System

The sexes are separate and sexual dimorphism can be seen. The vocal sacs and nuptial pad can be observed in male frogs in breeding season.

Male Reproductive System

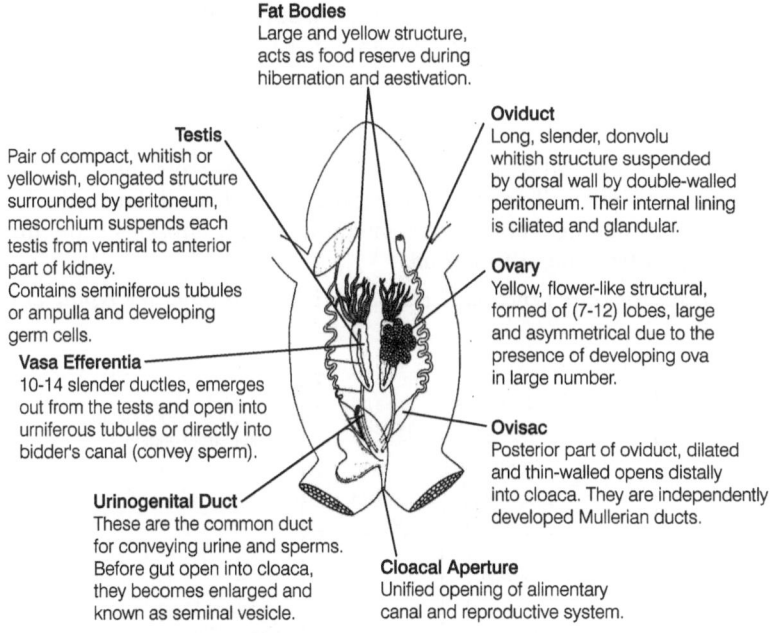

Fat Bodies
Large and yellow structure, acts as food reserve during hibernation and aestivation.

Testis
Pair of compact, whitish or yellowish, elongated structure surrounded by peritoneum, mesorchium suspends each testis from ventral to anterior part of kidney.
Contains seminiferous tubules or ampulla and developing germ cells.

Vasa Efferentia
10-14 slender ductles, emerges out from the tests and open into urniferous tubules or directly into bidder's canal (convey sperm).

Urinogenital Duct
These are the common duct for conveying urine and sperms. Before gut open into cloaca, they becomes enlarged and known as seminal vesicle.

Oviduct
Long, slender, donvolu whitish structure suspended by dorsal wall by double-walled peritoneum. Their internal lining is ciliated and glandular.

Ovary
Yellow, flower-like structural, formed of (7-12) lobes, large and asymmetrical due to the presence of developing ova in large number.

Ovisac
Posterior part of oviduct, dilated and thin-walled opens distally into cloaca. They are independently developed Mullerian ducts.

Cloacal Aperture
Unified opening of alimentary canal and reproductive system.

Male reproductive system in frog

Economic Importance of Frog

- They control bugs and help keep the ecosystem in balance.
- They maintain the balance in food chain and food web by acting as consumers.

Digestion and Absorption

Human Digestive System

The organ system of human body responsible for breaking our complex food into simple food particles, so that, it can be utilised by our cells, is called **Digestive System**. In humans, it consists of two main parts, *i.e.,* alimentary canal and digestive glands.

Alimentary Canal

It is the first visceral organ to evolve. It is the tube responsible for the conversion of intracellular mode of digestion to extracellular mode. It is the tubular passage of mucous membrane and muscles extending about 8.3 m from mouth to anus.

The structural and functional classification of alimentary canal is as follows

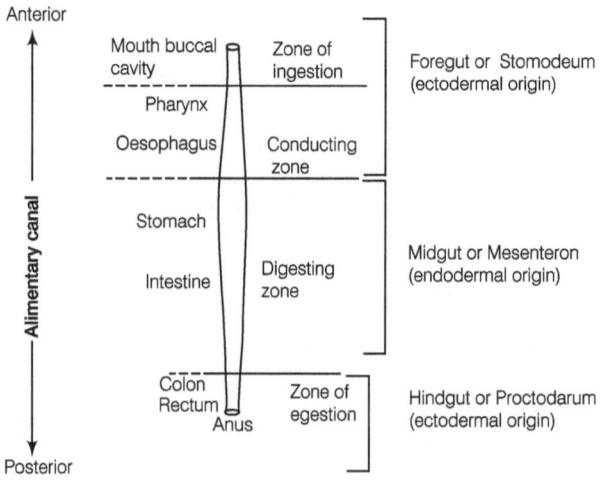

Rest of the components of digestive system are discussed below

Zygomatic Gland

It is the fourth type of major salivary gland (rest 3 are parotid, submadibular and sublingual). It is also the compound racemose gland and pour their secretion into the mouth. It is not seen in humans and rabbit. They are present below the eyes in dogs and cats and hence called infraorbital glands.

Ebner's Glands

These are zymogenic or enzyme secreting accessory glands. They secrete minute quantities of salivary lipase. They are found in the mucous membrane of lips (labial), cheeks (buccal), tongue (lingual) and palates (palatine).

Mucous secreting minor or accessory glands are
Unicellular goblet cells, Nuhn's gland and Weber's gland.

Tonsils

The lymphoid tissue of pharynx and oral cavity is seen as lymph nodes called tonsils. *Types of tonsil include*

(a) **Tubal tonsils** These are present near the opening of eustachian tube as a collection of lymphoid tissue.

(b) **Nasopharyngeal tonsils** These are present in the porterior wall of nasopharynx. These tonsils may get enlarged in children and cause an obstruction in normal breathing. This condition is called **adenoids**.

Waldeyer's Ring

Within the pharynx, tonsils are arranged in the form of a ring from top to bottom. *This ring consists of following tonsils*

(a) **Lingual tonsils** Irregular masses of lymphoid tissue near the basal part of the tongue.

(b) **Palatine or faucial tonsils** These are present as two masses in the lateral walls of oropharynx.

Circopharyngeal Sphincter

It is the upper sphincter of oesophagus, which prevents the air passing into the oesophagus during inspiration and expiration of oesophageal content.

Cardiac Sphincter

It is the lower sphincter of oesophagus, which prevents the reflux of acidic contents of gastric juice into the oesophagus.

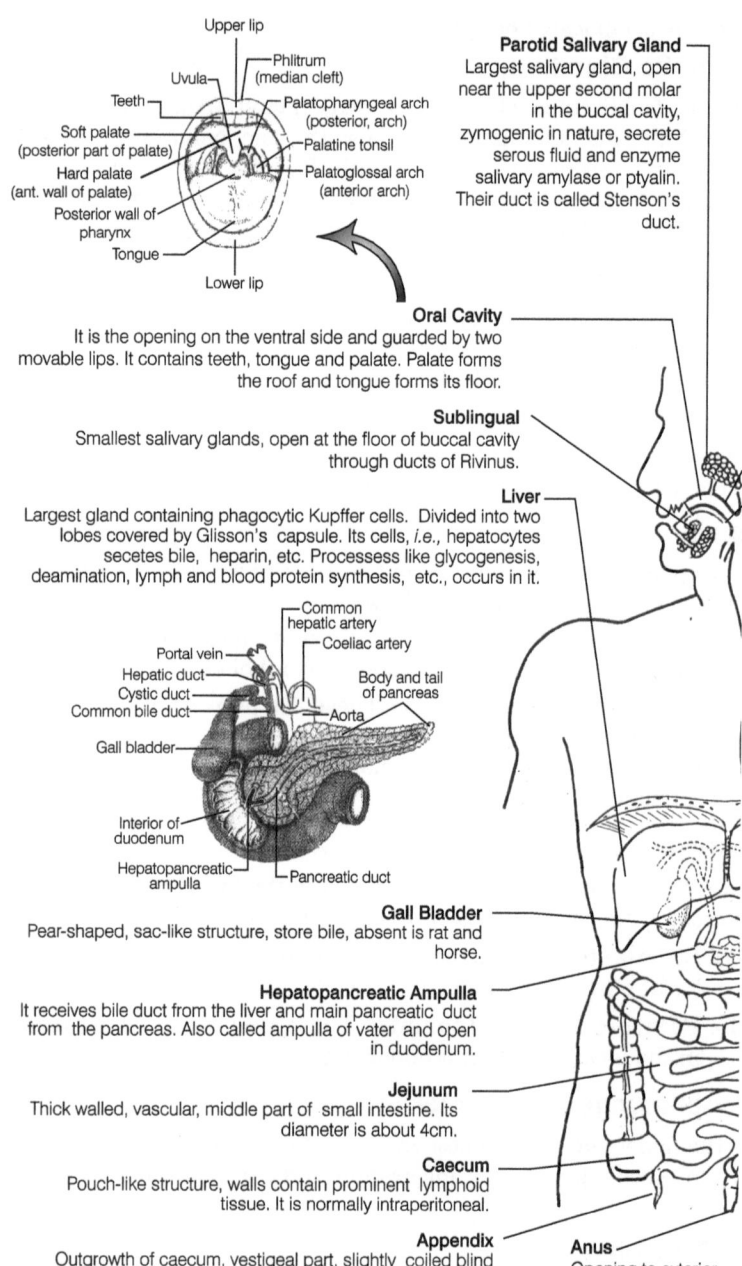

Parotid Salivary Gland
Largest salivary gland, open near the upper second molar in the buccal cavity, zymogenic in nature, secrete serous fluid and enzyme salivary amylase or ptyalin. Their duct is called Stenson's duct.

Oral Cavity
It is the opening on the ventral side and guarded by two movable lips. It contains teeth, tongue and palate. Palate forms the roof and tongue forms its floor.

Sublingual
Smallest salivary glands, open at the floor of buccal cavity through ducts of Rivinus.

Liver
Largest gland containing phagocytic Kupffer cells. Divided into two lobes covered by Glisson's capsule. Its cells, *i.e.,* hepatocytes secetes bile, heparin, etc. Processess like glycogenesis, deamination, lymph and blood protein synthesis, etc., occurs in it.

Gall Bladder
Pear-shaped, sac-like structure, store bile, absent is rat and horse.

Hepatopancreatic Ampulla
It receives bile duct from the liver and main pancreatic duct from the pancreas. Also called ampulla of vater and open in duodenum.

Jejunum
Thick walled, vascular, middle part of small intestine. Its diameter is about 4cm.

Caecum
Pouch-like structure, walls contain prominent lymphoid tissue. It is normally intraperitoneal.

Appendix
Outgrowth of caecum, vestigeal part, slightly coiled blind tube.

Anus
Opening to exterior.

Posterior alimentary canal

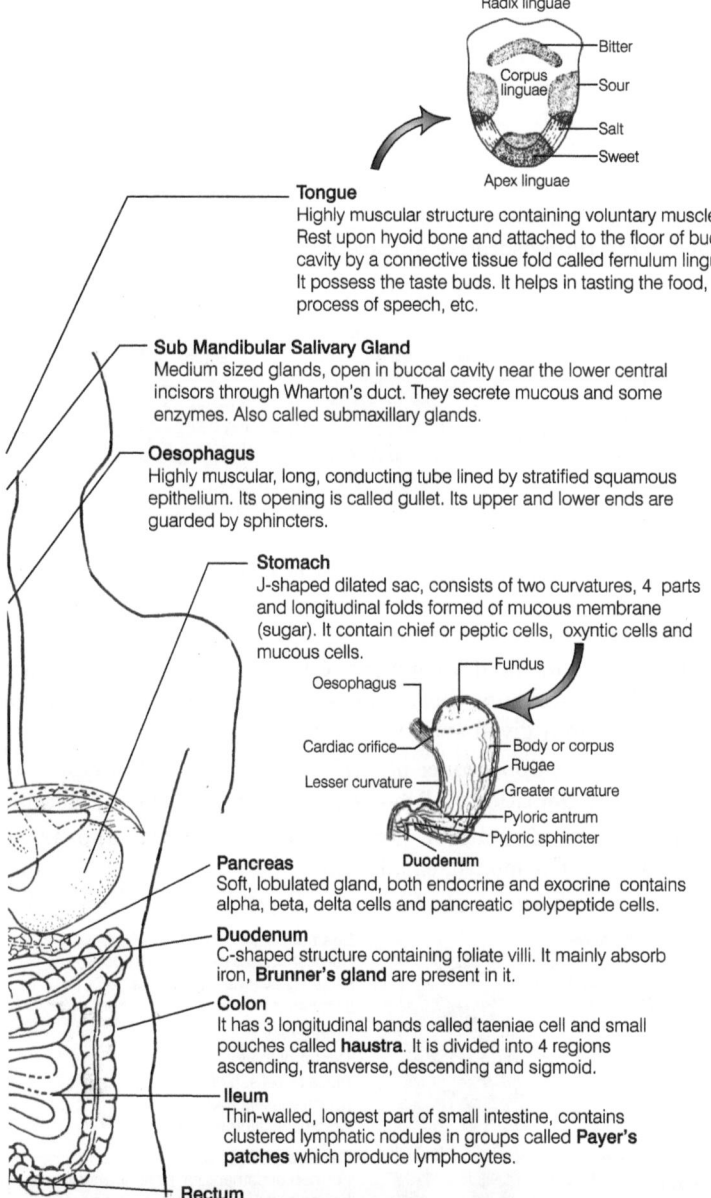

Tongue
Highly muscular structure containing voluntary muscles. Rest upon hyoid bone and attached to the floor of buccal cavity by a connective tissue fold called fernulum linguae. It possess the taste buds. It helps in tasting the food, process of speech, etc.

Sub Mandibular Salivary Gland
Medium sized glands, open in buccal cavity near the lower central incisors through Wharton's duct. They secrete mucous and some enzymes. Also called submaxillary glands.

Oesophagus
Highly muscular, long, conducting tube lined by stratified squamous epithelium. Its opening is called gullet. Its upper and lower ends are guarded by sphincters.

Stomach
J-shaped dilated sac, consists of two curvatures, 4 parts and longitudinal folds formed of mucous membrane (sugar). It contain chief or peptic cells, oxyntic cells and mucous cells.

Pancreas
Soft, lobulated gland, both endocrine and exocrine contains alpha, beta, delta cells and pancreatic polypeptide cells.

Duodenum
C-shaped structure containing foliate villi. It mainly absorb iron, **Brunner's gland** are present in it.

Colon
It has 3 longitudinal bands called taeniae cell and small pouches called **haustra**. It is divided into 4 regions ascending, transverse, descending and sigmoid.

Ileum
Thin-walled, longest part of small intestine, contains clustered lymphatic nodules in groups called **Payer's patches** which produce lymphocytes.

Rectum
Terminal part of large intestine and digestive tract. Composed of two parts pelvic part containing ampulla of rectum and perineal part containing anal canal.

Anterior alimentary canal

Valves of Kerkring

These are the circular folds of the mucous membrane present along the entire small intestine. They are more prominent in the jejunum and increases the absorptive surface area considerably. They are also called **plicae circulares**.

These contain villi over their exposed surface. A single villi on the other hand contains brush bordered or microvilli bearing cells over it, thus increasing the absorptive surface area many fold.

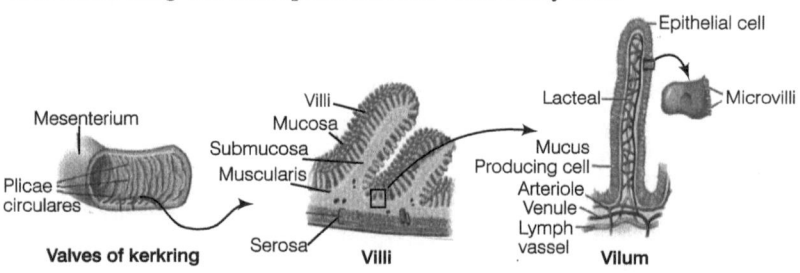

Valves of kerking showing arrangement of villi and microvili

Dentition

Dentition pertains to the development of teeth and their arrangement in the mouth. It accounts the characteristic arrangement, kind and number of teeth in a given species at a given age.

Depending upon the appearance of teeth, dentition is of two types

(a) **Homodont dentition** All the teeth in the jaw are alike, *e.g.*, alligator.

(b) **Heterodont dentition** Teeth differ in general appearance throughout the mouth, *e.g.*, human.

A tooth with its structure looks like

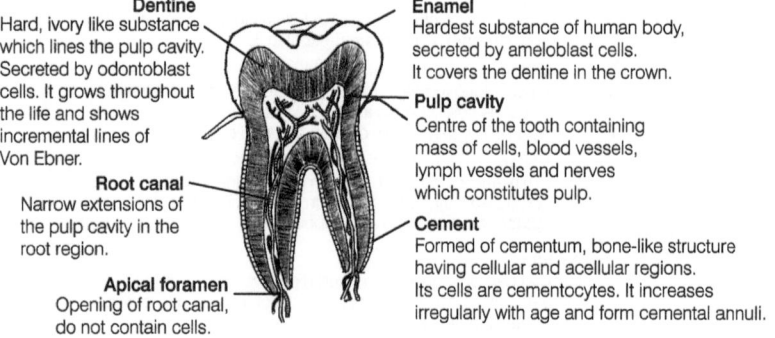

Internal structure of tooth

Handbook of BIOLOGY 151

Few important terms related to teeth structure are given below

Peridontal Ligament
It is a layer of thick collagen fibres, which helps in the fixation of teeth within the sockets. These collagen fibres are called **sharpey's fibres**.

Closed Pulp Cavities
This condition is seen in humans where apical foramen closes after the teeth is fully grown and no cell type is present in this region.

Open or Rootless Pulp
This condition can be seen in rabbit, rat, etc., where apical foramen of some teeth like incisors, contains a group of ameloblast cells. Such teeth grow throughout life, but there size remains the constant.

Different Classes of Teeth
On the basis of their persistance, teeth are of two types

(i) **Deciduous teeth** These are temporary or milk teeth which erupt in early stages of life. They have thinner layers of enamel and dentin. They do not possess premolars and number of molars present is two. They are 20 in number in humans and soon replaced by permanent teeth.

(ii) **Permanent teeth** They are stronger than the milk teeth and persist for a longer period. They possess premolars and three molars.

However, on the basis of attachment and appearance the teeth may be

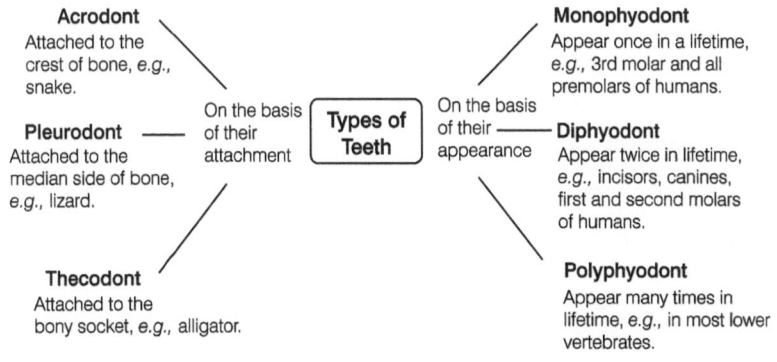

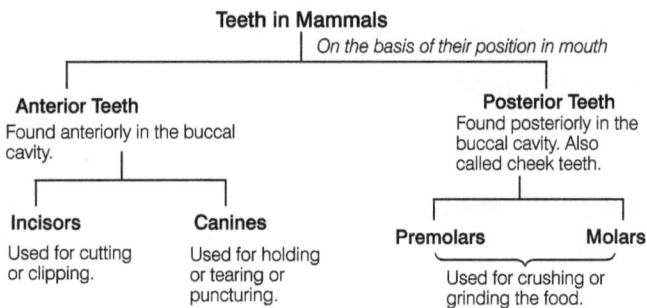

Molars

On the basis of length of crown and root, the molars can be of two types

(i) **Hypsodont** Teeth are long, crown with short roots, e.g., horses.

(ii) **Brachydont** Teeth are short, crown with deep roots, e.g., humans.

Cusps

Cheek or molariform teeth have specialised medial depressions over their crowns known as cusps.

According to the food and feeding habits, the cheek teeth are of various types depending upon the shape of cusps.

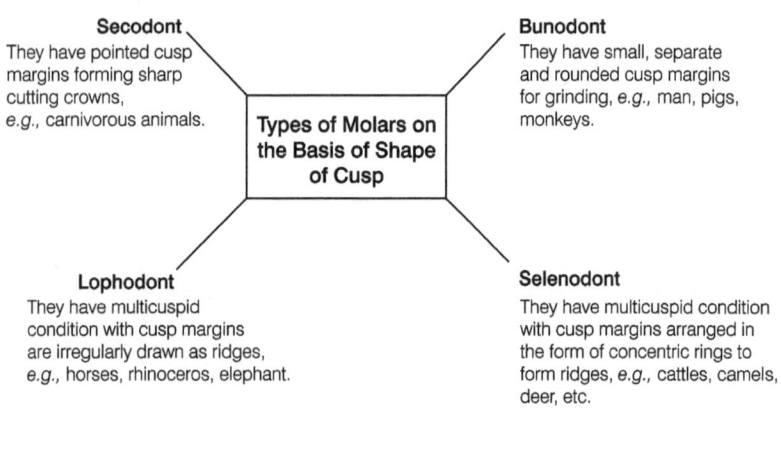

Dental Formula

The number and kinds of teeth in mammals are represented by an equation called dental formula. Since, two halves of each jaw are identical hence, the teeth of only one side are recorded.

Dental formula is represented as
$$\frac{ICP_m\ M}{ICP_m\ M}$$

where,   I = Incisors, C = Canines, P_m = Premolar, M = Molar

Total number of teeth = No. of teeth in dental formula × 2

Dental Formula of Some Animals

Animals	Dental Formula	Animals	Dental Formula
Pig and Mole	$\frac{3143}{3143} \times 2 = 44$	Cow, Sheep and Goat	$\frac{0033}{3133} \times 2 = 32$
Opossum	$\frac{5134}{4134} \times 2 = 50$	Cat	$\frac{3131}{3121} \times 2 = 30$
Dog	$\frac{3142}{3143} \times 2 = 42$	Rabbit	$\frac{2033}{1023} \times 2 = 28$
Lemur	$\frac{2133}{2133} \times 2 = 36$	Squirrel	$\frac{1023}{1013} \times 2 = 22$
Kangaroo	$\frac{3124}{1024} \times 2 = 34$	Rat	$\frac{1003}{1003} \times 2 = 16$
Man	$\frac{2123}{2123} \times 2 = 32$	Elephant	$\frac{1003}{0003} \times 2 = 14$

Digestive Glands

They include salivary glands, gastric glands (containing chief cells, oxyntic cells and mucous cells), liver, pancreas (containing alpha cells, beta cells, delta cells and pancreatic polypeptides) and intestinal glands (crypts of Lieberkuhn and Brunner's gland). Salivary glands and liver have already been discussed earlier in this chapter.

The other glands are

1. Pancreatic Glands

It consists of two parts, i.e., exocrine part and endocrine part.

(i) **Exocrine part** This part consists of rounded lobules (acini) that secrete an alkaline pancreatic juice with pH 8.4. It contains sodium bicarbonate and 3 proenzymes namely trypsinogen, chymotrypsinogen and procarboxy peptidase. It also contains some enzymes such as lipase, elastase, α-amylase, DNase, RNase, etc. The pancreatic juices help in the digestion of starch, proteins, fats and nucleic acids.

(ii) **Endocrine part** This part consists of groups of islets of langerhans. They are most numerous in the tail of the pancreas.

They consists of following types of cells

(a) **Alpha (α) cells** More numerous towards the periphery of the islet and constitute about 15% of the islet of langerhans. They produce glucagon hormone.

(b) **Beta (β) cells** More numerous towards the middle of the islet and constitute 65% of it. They produce insulin hormone.

(c) **Delta (δ) cells** They are found towards the periphery of islet and constitute 5% of it. They secrete somatostation hormone.

(d) **Pancreatic Polypeptide (PP) cells** They constitute about 15% of the islet of langerhans and secrete pancreatic polypeptides, which inhibits the release of pancreatic juice. These are also called **F-cells**.

2. Gastric Glands

They are microscopic, tubular glands formed by the epithelium of the stomach. They contains chief cells, oxyntic cells, mucous cells and endocrine cells (G cells and Argentaffin cells).

3. Intestinal Glands

They are formed by the surface epithelium of small intestine. These are of two types, *i.e.*, crypts of Lieberkuhn and Brunner's gland. Crypts of Lieberkuhn consists of **Paneth cells** and **Argentaffin cells** at its base.

Oxyntic Cell (Parietal cell)
Large and most numerous on the side walls of the gastric glands, against the basement membrane. They secrete HCl and castle intrinsic factor. They stain strongly with eosin.

Chief Cells
Also called peptic cells or zymogenic cells as they secrete digestive enzymes as proenzymes or zymogens, pepsinogen and prorennin.
They also produce gastric amylase and lipase. They are basal in location.

Mucous Cells
They are present throughout the epithelium and secrete mucous. Their secretions make the gastric juices acidic (pH 1.5-2.5).

Argentaffin Cell
These endocrine cells produce serotonin, somatostatin and histamine.

Gastrin (G) Cells
These endocrine cells are present in the pyloric region and secrete and store gastrin hormone.

(a)

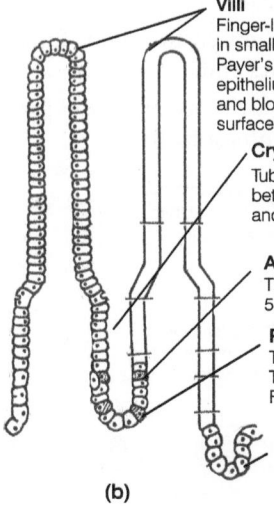

Villi
Finger-like projections of the mucosa in small intestine. They are absent over Payer's patches. They are covered with epithelium and contains a lymph capillary and blood capillaries. They increases the surface area of small intestine.

Crypts of Lieberkuhn
Tubular structures, occur throughout small intestine between villi. They possess goblet cells (mucous) and enterocytes (secrete water and electrolytes).

Argentaffin Cells
They synthesise secretin hormone and 5-hydroxytryptamine.

Paneth Cells
They are rich in zinc and contain acidophilic granules. They are capable of phagocytosis and secrete lysozyme. Found in duodenum.

Brunner's Gland
They secrete little enzyme and mucus. The mucus protects the duodenal wall from getting digested.

(b)

(a) Gastric glands; (b) Intestinal glands

Physiology of Digestion

Digestion

The process in which large macromolecules of food are broken up into smaller usable molecules with the help of enzymes is called **digestion**.

The process or physiology of digestion begins with the following processes

(i) **Mastication** It is the process of biting and grinding the food in mouth with the help of teeth so as to make it soft enough to swallow. Saliva plays a major role in it.

(ii) **Deglutition** It is the process of swallowing, *i.e.,* the collection of food or bolus is pushed inward through the pharynx into the oesophagus. Swallowing is controlled by swallowing centre located in the medulla oblongata and lower pons Varolii of the brain.

(iii) **Peristalsis** It is the wave of contraction and relaxation produced by the involuntary contraction of circular muscles in the oesophagus and simultaneous contraction of longitudinal muscles. It helps to push the food toward the stomach.

Digestive Enzymes

These are present in digestive juices and secreted by various components of alimentary canal. Depending upon their functional site, they are categorised as exo and endoenzymes.

(i) **Exoenzymes** They require a terminus for their functional ability, *i.e.,* cut the substrate from its end.

(ii) **Endoenzymes** They do not require any stimulus for their functioning, *i.e.,* cut the substrate interstitially.

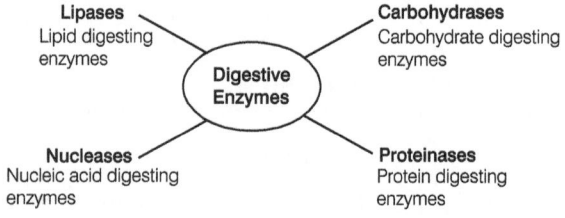

Process of Digestion in Alimentary Canal

Digestive Juice	pH	Source	Stimulation by	Proenzyme (inactive)	Activator	Enzyme	Substrates	End Products
Saliva	6.8	Salivary glands	Neuronal reflex	...	...	Ptyalin	Some polysaccharides	Disaccharide maltose
Gastric juice	1.0 - 3.5	Gastric glands	Neuronal reflexes and gastrin hormone	Pepsinogen	HCl	Pepsin*	Proteins	Proteoses, peptones and large polypeptides
				Prorenin	HCl	Renin**	Milk proteins	Calcium paracaseinate
				...	...	Gastric lipase, gastric amylase	Fats, starches	Negligible Negligible
Bile***	7.7	Liver	Secretin and CCK hormones	...	...	...	Fats	Emulsified fats
Pancreatic juice	7.5 - 8.3	Pancreas	Neuronal reflexes, secretin an CCK hormones	...	...	Amylopsin or pancreatic amylase	Polysaccharides	Maltose
						Steapsin or pancreatic lipase	Emulsified fats	Monoglycerides, fatty acids, cholesterol
				Trypsinogen	Enterokinase	Trypsin	Proteins, proteoses, peptones, large peptides	Small peptides
				Chymotrypsinogen	Trypsin	Chymotrypsin	Proteins, proteoses, peptones, large peptides	Small peptides

			Procarboxy-polypeptidase		Carboxypoly-peptidase	Small peptides	Amino acids
					Deoxyribonuclease	DNA	Nucleotides → Nucleosides
					Ribonuclease	RNA	Nucleotides → Nucleosides
Intestinal juice or succus entricus	7.5 - 8.0	Intestinal glands	Neuronal reflex enterokinin hormone	.....	Erepsin group (exopeptidase)	Small peptides and dipeptides	Amino acids
					Maltase	Maltose	Glucose (2 molecules)
					Sucrase	Sucrose	Glucose and fructose
					Lactase	Lactose	Glucose and galactose
					α-dextrimax	α-dextrin	Glucose
					Enterokinase	Trypsinogen	Active trypsin
					Intestinal Lipase	Emulsified fats	Fatty acids and glycerol
					Nucleases and Nucleosidases	Nucleotides and nucleosides	Nitrogeneous bases and pentose sugars
Symbiotic bacteria and Protozoa of caecum	.....	.....	.....	.....	.....	Cellulose	Sugars

(Carbohydrases bracket covers Maltase/Sucrase/Lactase row)

* **Pepsin** Secreted as pepsinogen (inactive form) and activated by HCl, exopeptidase in nature. Convert protein molecules into proteoses, peptones and ultimately into large polypeptides.

****Renin** Secreted as prorenin (inactive form) and activated by HCl. Convert milk protein - casein to paracasein. Paracasein combine with calcium to form calcium paracaseinate (curd). This action is required so that, the liquid milk does not leave stomach without being acted upon by the pepsin (act on calcium paracaseinate to form peptones).

*** **Bile** Greenish-blue, alkaline (pH 7.7) fluid containing 92%. water, 6%. bile salts, 0.3% bile pigments (bilirubin and biliverdin), 0.3-1.2% fatty acids and 0.3 to 0.9% cholesterol along with 0.3% lecithin. It do not contain any digestive enzyme.

Digestive Hormones

These hormones are involved in the regulation of digestive secretions.

Gastrointestinal Hormones

Hormone	Source	Target Organ	Action
Gastrin	Pyloric region of stomach	Stomach	Stimulates gastric glands to secrete and release the gastric juice. It also stimulates gastric mobility and HCl secretion.
Enterogastrone (Gastric Inhibitory Peptide–GIP)	Duodenum epithelium	Stomach	Inhibits gastric secretion and motility (slows gastric contraction).
Secretin first hormone discovered by scientists	Duodenum epithelium	Pancreas liver stomach	Released bicarbonates in the pancreatic juice. Increases secretion of bile. Decreases gastric secretion and motality.
Cholecystokinin-Pancreozymin (CCK-Pz)	Small intestine entire epithelium	Gall bladder and pancreas	Contracts the gall bladder to release bile. Stimulates pancreas to secrete and release digestive enzymes in the pancreatic juice.
Duocrinin	Duodenum epithelium	Duodenum	Stimulates the Brunner's glands to release mucus and enzymes into the intestinal juice.
Enterocrinin	Small intestine entire epithelium	Small intestine	Stimulates the crypts of Lieberkuhn to release enzymes into the intestinal juice.
Vasoactive Intestinal Peptide (VIP)	Small intestine entire epithelium	Small intestine and stomach	Dilates peripheral blood vessels of gut. Inhibits gastric acid secretion.
Villikinin	Small intestine entire epithelium	Small intestine	Accelerates movements of villi.
Somatostatin (SS)	Delta cells of islets of langerhans of pancreas.	Pancreas and gastrointestinal tract	Inhibits the secretion of glucagon by alpha cells and insulin by beta cells. It also inhibits a absorption of nutrients from the gastrointestinal tract.
	Argentaffin cells of gastric and intestinal glands	Gastrointestinal tract	Supresses the release of hormones from the digestive tract.
Pancreatic Polypeptide (PP)	Pancreatic polypeptide cells of islet of langerhans.	Pancreas	Inhibits the release of pancreatic juice from the pancreas.

Handbook of BIOLOGY

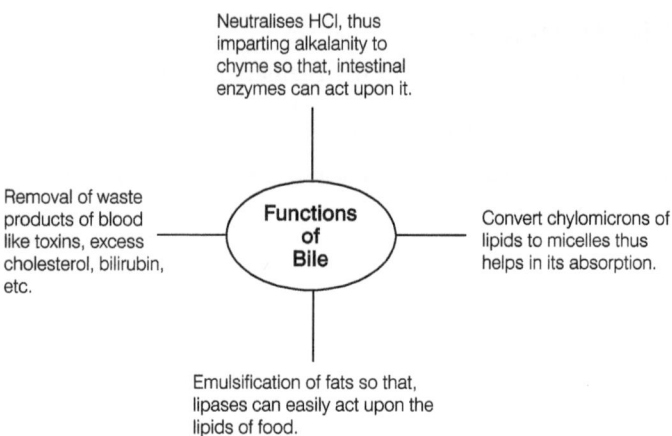

- Bile is alkaline in man, but in cats and dogs, it is acidic in nature.

Absorption of Nutrients

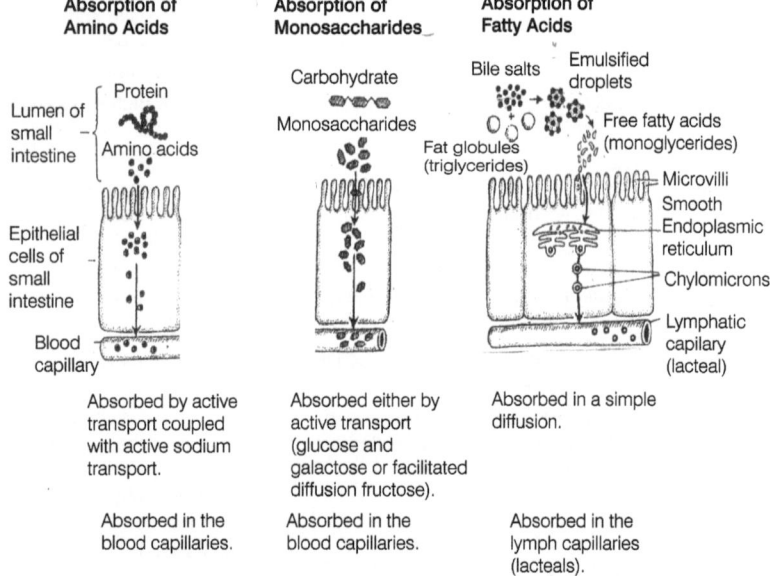

Micelles These are the small, spherical, water soluble molecules. The products of fat digestion are incorporated into them with the help of bile salts and phospholipids. Hence, the fat molecules are absorbed into the intestinal cells in the form of micelles and reach directly to lymph in lymph vessels (lacteals).

Chylomicrons These are the products of fat digestion, which are used for synthesising new fats. These are released by the intestinal cells into the lymph, in the form of droplets. Hence, the synthesised fats are liberated from the intestinal cells in the form of chylomicrons.

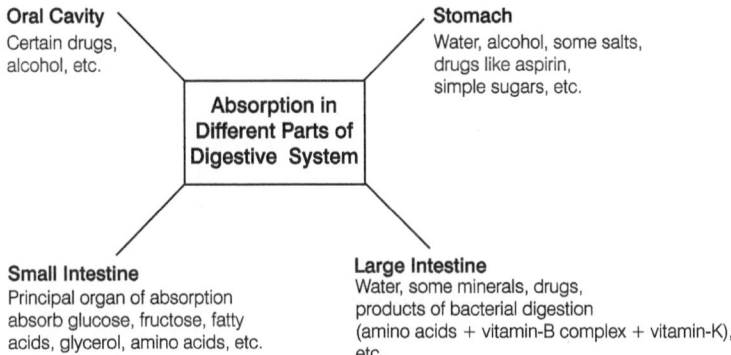

Chyle The lacteals after absorption of lipids contain white coloured liquid inside them known as chyle.

Disorders of Digestive System

Deficiency Diseases They include Protein Energy Malnutrition (PEM) and disorders due to the deficiency of vitamins, iodine, etc.

PEM is of two types *i.e.*, kwashiorkor and marasmus.

Deficient Nutrient	Name of Deficiency	Deficiency Symptoms
Protein (PEM)	Kwashiorkor (usually observed in children in the age group of 1-5 years)	Wastes muscles, thin limbs, retarded growth of body and brain, swelling of legs due to retention of water (oedema), reddish hair, pot belly and diarrhoea.
Protein and calorie (PEM)	Marasmus (it usually affects infants below age of one year)	Impaired growth and replacement of tissue proteins, thin limbs and prominent ribs (very less fat in the body), dry, wrinkled and thin skin, diarrhoea.
Vitamin-A	Nyctalopia (night blindness)	Difficulty to see in night due to the deficiency of retinol.
Vitamin-D	Rickets	Pigeon breast, bow legs, knock knee due to low calcification of developing bones.
Vitamin-E	Macrocytic anaemia	Increased fragility and haemolysis of RBCs.

Deficient Nutrient	Name of Deficiency	Deficiency Symptoms
Vitamin-K	Hypoprothrombinemia	Deficiency of prothrombin in blood.
Vitamin-B_1 (thiamine)	Beri-beri	Retarded growth, degeneration of bones and muscles.
Vitamin-B_2 (riboflavin or vitamin-G)	Dermatitis	Rough, dry and scaly skin.
Vitamin-B_3 (niacin)	Pellagra	3D disease as its symptoms include dermatitis, diarrhoea and dementia.
Vitamin-B_5	Achromotrichia	Premature graying of hairs.
Vitamin-B_7 (vitamin-H)	Acne vulgaris	Appearance of pimples and boils in young people.
Vitamin-B_{10} (vitamin-M or folic acid)	Sprue	Ulceration of mouth, diarrhoea, etc.
Vitamin-B_{12}	Pernicious anaemia	Large, oval and fragile RBC formation in bone marrow.
Vitamin-C (ascorbic acid)	Scurvy	Swelling and bleeding of gums.

Vomiting

Ejection of stomach content through the mouth. This reflex action is controlled by the vomiting centre located in the medulla oblongata.

Ulcerative Colitis

This inflammatory disease affects the large intestine, diarrhoea occurs when waste products move through the large intestine quickly and constipation occurs when this movement is too slow.

Constipation

It is infrequent or difficult defecation caused by decreased motility of the intestines. Due to the prolonged collection of faeces in the colon, excessive water absorption occurs and faeces become dry and hard. Due to this, their egestion becomes difficult.

Cirrhosis

It is the scarring of the liver due to the loss of liver cells. Alcohol and viral hepatitis-B and C are the common causes of cirrhosis. It may cause weakness, loss of appetite, jaundice, etc. Jaundice is characterised by yellowish colouration of the sclerae, skin and mucous membrane due to the accumulation of yellow compound called **bilirubin**.

10

Breathing and Exchange of Gases

Respiration
It is the oxidation reaction process in cellular metabolism that involves the sequential degradation of food substances and generation of energy.

It is of two types
   1. **Aerobic Respiration**   Oxidation in the presence of oxygen.
   2. **Anaerobic Respiration**   Oxidation in the absence of oxygen.

In complicated organisms, aerobic respiration is a compulsion. As involvement of oxygen is essential, hence, breathing becomes the most important step of respiration.

Human Respiratory System
The special feature of mammalian respiratory system are presence of a nose, elongation of nasal passage and its complete separation from buccal passage through palate, long wind pipe due to the presence of well defined neck, spongy and solid lungs.

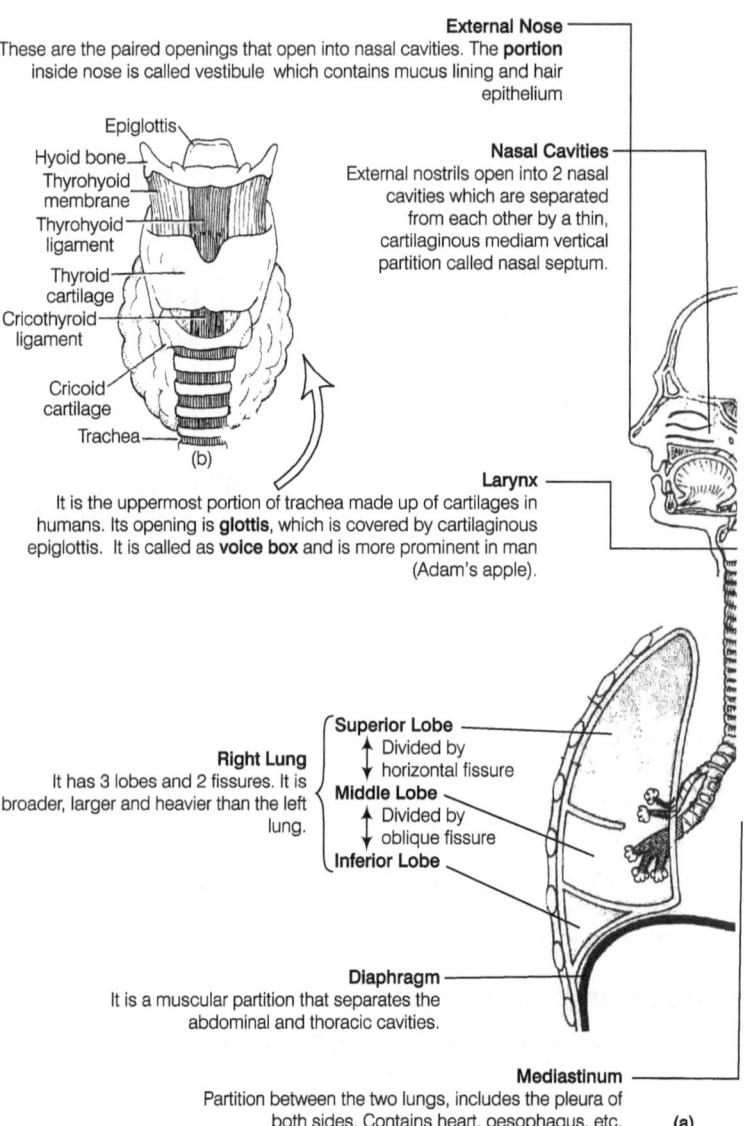

External Nose
These are the paired openings that open into nasal cavities. The **portion** inside nose is called vestibule which contains mucus lining and hair epithelium

Nasal Cavities
External nostrils open into 2 nasal cavities which are separated from each other by a thin, cartilaginous medium vertical partition called nasal septum.

Larynx
It is the uppermost portion of trachea made up of cartilages in humans. Its opening is **glottis**, which is covered by cartilaginous epiglottis. It is called as **voice box** and is more prominent in man (Adam's apple).

Right Lung
It has 3 lobes and 2 fissures. It is broader, larger and heavier than the left lung.

- **Superior Lobe** — Divided by horizontal fissure
- **Middle Lobe** — Divided by oblique fissure
- **Inferior Lobe**

Diaphragm
It is a muscular partition that separates the abdominal and thoracic cavities.

Mediastinum
Partition between the two lungs, includes the pleura of both sides. Contains heart, oesophagus, etc.

(a) Respiratory system in humans (b) A magnified larynx

Handbook of BIOLOGY

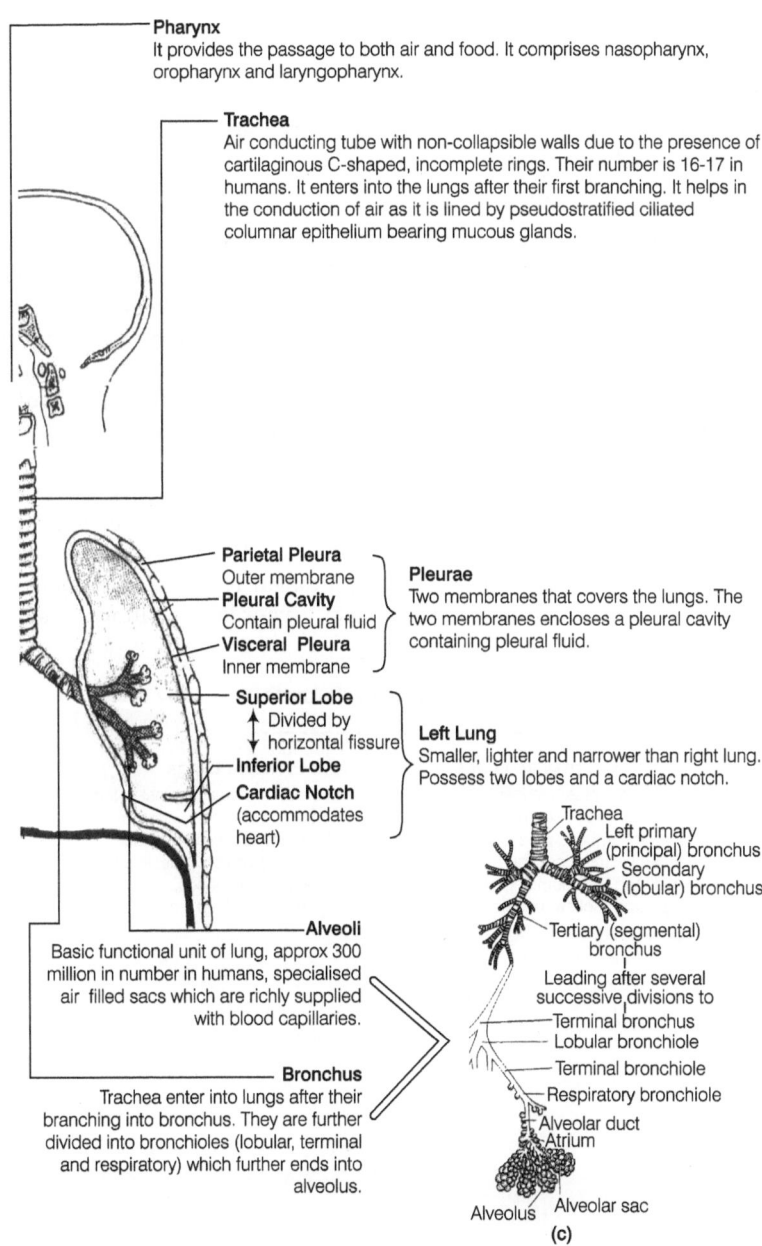

Pharynx
It provides the passage to both air and food. It comprises nasopharynx, oropharynx and laryngopharynx.

Trachea
Air conducting tube with non-collapsible walls due to the presence of cartilaginous C-shaped, incomplete rings. Their number is 16-17 in humans. It enters into the lungs after their first branching. It helps in the conduction of air as it is lined by pseudostratified ciliated columnar epithelium bearing mucous glands.

Parietal Pleura
Outer membrane
Pleural Cavity
Contain pleural fluid
Visceral Pleura
Inner membrane

Pleurae
Two membranes that covers the lungs. The two membranes encloses a pleural cavity containing pleural fluid.

Superior Lobe
↕ Divided by horizontal fissure
Inferior Lobe
Cardiac Notch
(accommodates heart)

Left Lung
Smaller, lighter and narrower than right lung. Possess two lobes and a cardiac notch.

Trachea
Left primary (principal) bronchus
Secondary (lobular) bronchus
Tertiary (segmental) bronchus
Leading after several successive divisions to
Terminal bronchus
Lobular bronchiole
Terminal bronchiole
Respiratory bronchiole
Alveolar duct
Atrium
Alveolus Alveolar sac
(c)

Alveoli
Basic functional unit of lung, approx 300 million in number in humans, specialised air filled sacs which are richly supplied with blood capillaries.

Bronchus
Trachea enter into lungs after their branching into bronchus. They are further divided into bronchioles (lobular, terminal and respiratory) which further ends into alveolus.

(c) A magnified bronchus

Breathing

It is the process of exchange of oxygen (O_2) from the atmosphere with carbon dioxide (CO_2) produced by the cells.

The process of breathing is carried out in different forms with the help of gaseous exchange devices,

which are of two types

(a) **Diffusion devices** Exchange of gases with environment takes place through the process of diffusion, *e.g.*, diffusion lungs found in *Pila* (pulmonary sac), spiders (book lungs), etc.

(b) **Ventilating devices** Gaseous exchange structures are not in direct contact with the environmental air. The air is taken to the gaseous apparatus with the help of specialised tubular network, *e.g.*, trachea or wind pipe, ventilating lungs, etc.

Lungs

These are the organs associated with the gaseous exchange. They are also called pulmones. It is the characteristic feature of vertebrates. These can operate through diffusion (diffusion lungs of *Pila*, spiders, etc.) or operate through ventilation (ventilating lungs as of vertebrates).

Ventilating Lungs (Pulmones)

+ve Pressure Lungs	−ve Pressure Lungs
In this, the pressure inside the lungs is +ve in comparison to the atmospheric pressure at the time of inspiration, Thus, in take of air requires pumping action *e.g.*, frog (hollow lungs).	In these, the pressure inside the lungs is −ve as compared to atmospheric pressure at the time of inspiration. Thus, intake of air in spontaneous, *e.g.*, humans (solid lungs).

Physiology of Breathing

Breathing is associated with the inflow (inspiration) and outflow (expiration) of air between atmosphere and the alveoli of the lungs.

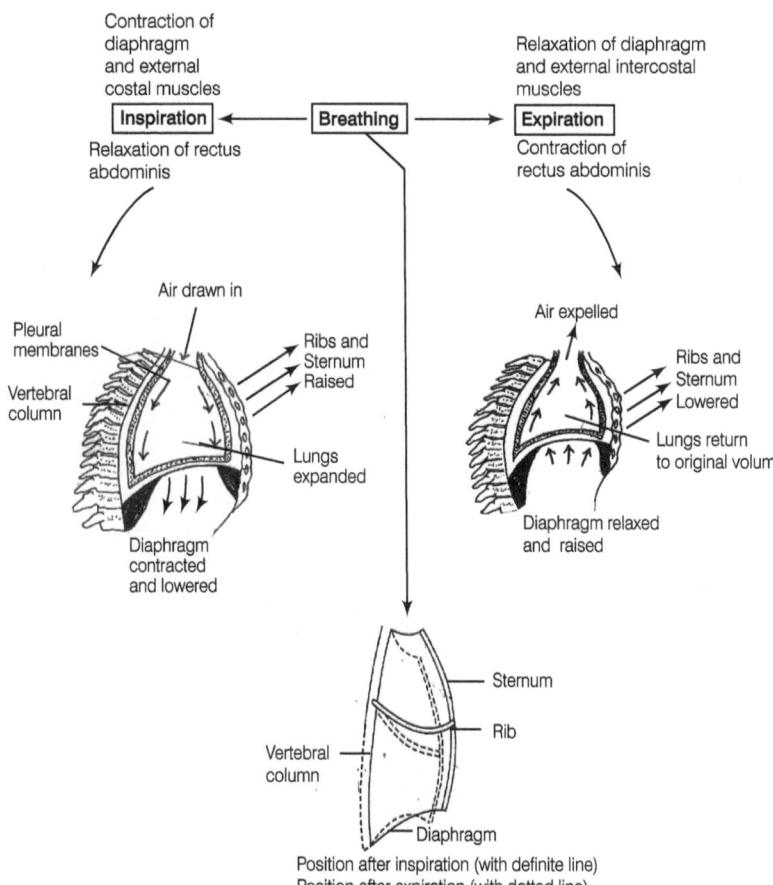

Process of breathing in human

- Movement of fresh air into the lungs

    External nares → Nasal cavities → Internal nares →
    Bronchi ← Trachea ← Larynx ← Glottis ← Pharynx ←┘
    → Bronchioles → Alveolar duct → Alveoli

Movement of foul air out of the lungs occurs in reverse pathway, *i.e.*, from alveoli to external nares.

Lung Volume and Capacities

Terms	Symbols	Descriptions
Vital Capacity	VC	Maximal volume of air exhaled after forced inspiration (includes TV, IRV and ERV).
Tidal Volume	TV	Volume of air inhaled or exhaled during quiet breathing.
Inspiratory Reserve Volume	IRV	Maximal air that can be inhaled after a quiet inspiration.
Expiratory Reserve Volume	ERV	Maximal air that can be expelled out after quiet expiration.
Residual Volume	RV	Volume of air remaining in lungs after full expiration.
Inspiratory Vital Capacity	IVC	Maximal volume of air inhaled after full expiration.
Forced Expiratory Volume, per time interval in seconds	FEV	Volume of air exhaled in a given period during a complete forced expiration (FVC).
Maximal Expiratory Flow Rate	MEFR	Volume of air exhaled per second measured between the 200 mL and 1200 mL volumes of the forced expiratory spirogram.
Maximal Mid-expiratory Flow	MMF	Volume of air per second exhaled during middle half of expired volume of forced expiratory spirogram.
Maximal Voluntary Ventilation	MVV	Maximum breathing capacity litre/minute. Subject can breathe with maximal voluntray effort (actual measurement twelve seconds).

Dead Space

In lungs the volume occupied by gas which does not participate in gaseous exchange is called dead space. A fixed quantity of each tidal volume goes to the dead space.

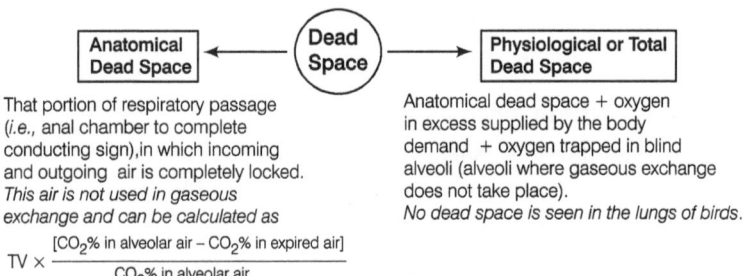

Anatomical Dead Space ← Dead Space → Physiological or Total Dead Space

That portion of respiratory passage (*i.e.*, anal chamber to complete conducting sign), in which incoming and outgoing air is completely locked. *This air is not used in gaseous exchange and can be calculated as*

$$TV \times \frac{[CO_2\% \text{ in alveolar air} - CO_2\% \text{ in expired air}]}{CO_2\% \text{ in alveolar air}}$$

Anatomical dead space + oxygen in excess supplied by the body demand + oxygen trapped in blind alveoli (alveoli where gaseous exchange does not take place).
No dead space is seen in the lungs of birds.

Exchange of Gases

In the process of respiration, gaseous exchange occurs at two level, i.e., (i) between alveoli and blood (external respiration) and (ii) between blood and tissue cells (internal respiration).

(i) Exchange of gases between alveoli and blood.

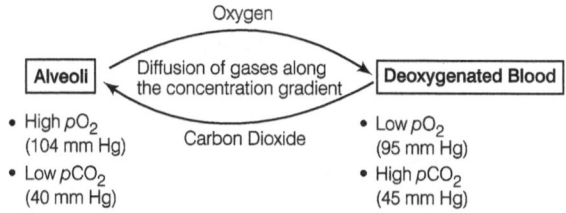

(ii) Exchange of gases between blood and tissue cells.

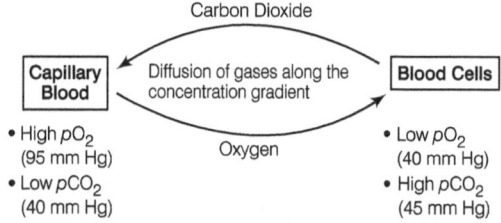

The whole process of gaseous exchange can be summarised as

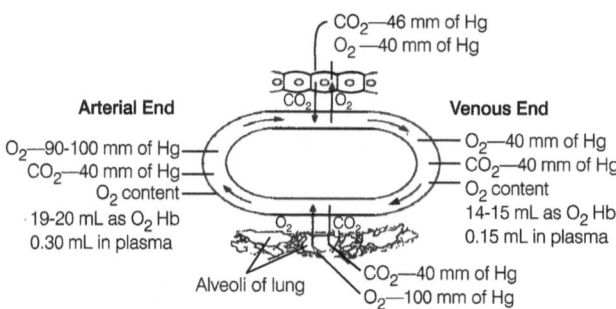

Transport of Gases

Blood is the medium of transport for O_2 and CO_2.

(a) Transport of Oxygen

Oxygen enters the venous blood in the lungs and leaves the blood stream in the tissue capillaries and goes to the tissue cells.

Oxygen is carried in the blood in the following forms
  (i) **As dissolved gas** Under normal conditions of temperature and pressure, about 0.30 mL of O_2 is carried in physical solution in 100 mL of atrerial blood.
  (ii) **As chemical compound** Oxygen is carried in combination with haemoglobin as oxyhaemoglobain

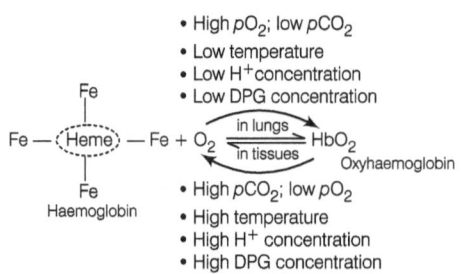

Where,   Fe = Iron (have strong affinity for oxygen).

DPG = Diphosphoglyceraldehyde

O_2 – Hb Dissociation Curve

This curve is the graphical representation of per cent saturation of haemoglobin at various partial pressure of oxygen.

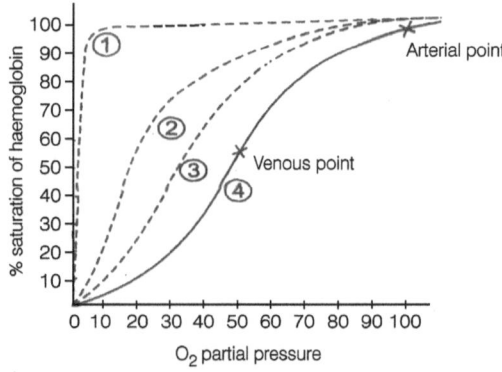

Where,   1 = At room temperature with CO_2.
             2 = At body temperature without CO_2.
             3 = At body temperature + 20 mm of Hg CO_2.
             4 = At body temperature + 40 mm of Hg CO_2.

Handbook of BIOLOGY

Following interpretations can be made from the given curve
  (i) The curve is sigmoid or S-shaped under normal condition.
  (ii) With increased CO_2 levels and increased temperatures, the curve is shifted towards right and *vice versa*.
  (iii) The curve is completely sigmoid for strong electrolytes, while it is hyperbolic for weak electrolytes.
  (iv) The curve for foetal haemoglobin is towards the left hand side as compared to maternal haemoglobin. It shows that foetal haemoglobin have greater affinity for oxygen as compared to that of mother.
  (v) Oxyhaemoglobin dissociation curve for myoglobin is rectangular hyperbola with more towards left end side.
  (vi) The partial pressure of oxygen at which 50% saturation of haemoglobin takes place is called p_{50} value.

$$p_{50} \text{ value} \propto \frac{1}{\text{affinity of blood for } O_2}$$

- Under normal body conditions, what so ever increase occurs in partial pressure of O_2 (even upto 100 mm of Hg), the haemoglobin is never fully saturated because of the presence of CO_2 and temperature conditions in body.
- The entry of CO_2 in blood helps in the dissociation of oxyhaemoglobin and to increase acidity (decreased pH) of blood which promotes the lesser affinity of blood for oxygen (Bohr effect).
- The entry of O_2 in blood (*i.e.*, more and more formation of oxyhaemoglobin) is more responsible for more and more replacement of CO_2 from the venous blood.

(b) Transport of Carbon Dioxide

Transportation of CO_2 is much easier due to its high solubility in water. *CO_2 is transported in three ways*

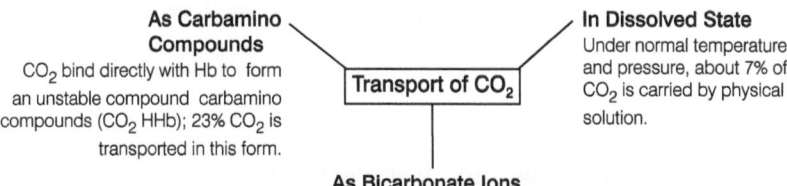

As Carbamino Compounds
CO_2 bind directly with Hb to form an unstable compound carbamino compounds (CO_2 HHb); 23% CO_2 is transported in this form.

Transport of CO_2

In Dissolved State
Under normal temperature and pressure, about 7% of CO_2 is carried by physical solution.

As Bicarbonate Ions
CO_2 reacts with water to form carbonic acid (H_2CO_3) in the presence of carbonic anhydrase in RBC. (H_2CO_3) dissociate into hydrogen and bicarbonate ions (HCO_3).

The whole reaction preceeds as follows

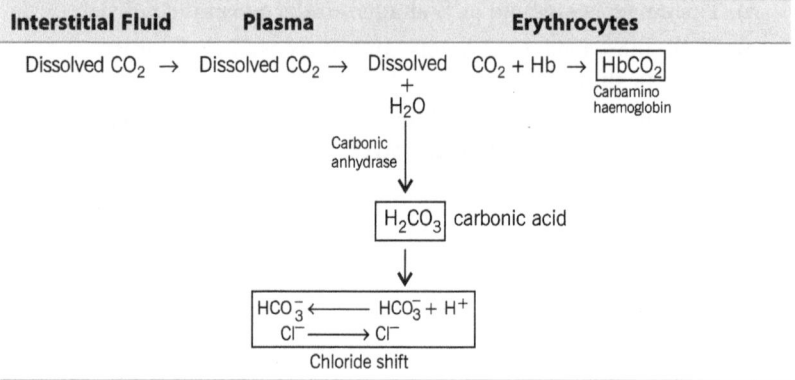

Chloride Shift Most of the bicarbonate ions move out of the erythrocytes into the plasma *via* a transporter that exchanges one bicarbonate for one chloride ion. This is called **chloride shift** or **Hamburger phenomenon**.

Regulation of Respiration

Process of respiration is under both nervous and chemical control

(a) **Neural regulation** The groups of neurons located in the medulla oblongata and pons varolii acts as the respiratory centre which is composed of groups of neurons. Hence, respiratory centre is divided into the medullary respiratory centre and pons respiratory centre.

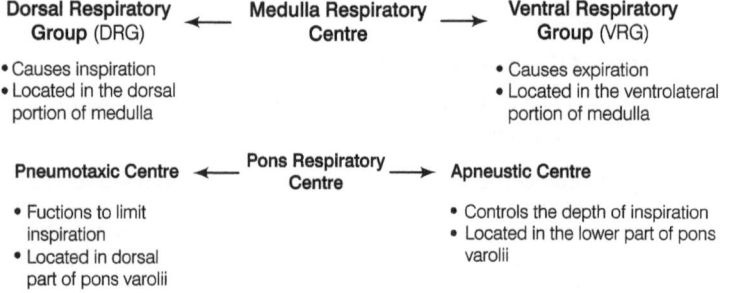

(b) **Chemical regulation** It includes the affect of CO_2, O_2 and H^+ concentration in blood. Its receptors are located in **carotid bodies** (largest number), **aortic bodies** and in brain.

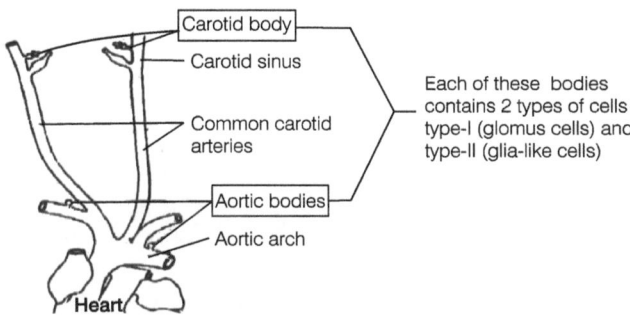

Carotid and Aortic bodies

Carotid bodies and aortic bodies are the peripheral cheoreceptors, where, as these located in brain are called central chemoreceptors.

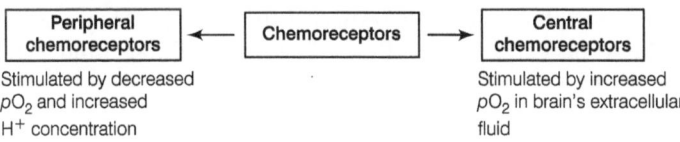

Stimulated by decreased pO_2 and increased H^+ concentration

Stimulated by increased pO_2 in brain's extracellular fluid

Disorders of Respiratory System

(a) **Bronchitis** Inflammation of the bronchi caused by irritants such as cigarette smoke, air pollution or infection. The inflammation results in the swelling of mucous membrane lining of bronchi, increased mucous production and decreased movement of mucous by cilia which impairs the ventilation process.

(b) **Emphysema** It results in the destruction of the alveolar walls due to the decreased respiratory surface, which decreases gaseous exchange. Its symptoms include shortness of breath and enlargement of thoracic cavity. The progress of emphysema can be slowed, but these is no cure.

(c) **Asthma** It is associated with the periodic episodes of contraction of bronchial smooth muscles, which restricts the air movement. It results from allergic responses to pollen, dust animal dander or other substance.

(d) **Pulmonary fibrosis** It is an occupational lung disease. it involves the replacement of lung tissue with fibrous connective tissue, making the lungs less elastic and breathing more difficult. Its common causes include the exposure to silica, asbestos or coal dust.

11
Body Fluids *and* Circulation

Body Fluids
Body fluids are the medium of transport in the body. They may either intracellular or extracellular fluid. The intracellular fluid contains large amount of potassium ions, phosphate ions and proteins. Extracellular fluids include blood, lymph, cerebrospinal fluid, etc.

Blood
It is the most common body fluid in higher organisms, consisting of plasma, blood corpuscles, etc. This extracellular fluid is slightly alkaline having pH 7.4.

Blood is composed of a watery fluid called **plasma** and floating bodies called **formed elements** (blood cells).

Blood Plasma
Crystallo-colloidal mixture, makes 55-60% of blood, contains 90-92% of water and 0.9% salts, slightly alkaline, constitutes about 5% of the body weight.

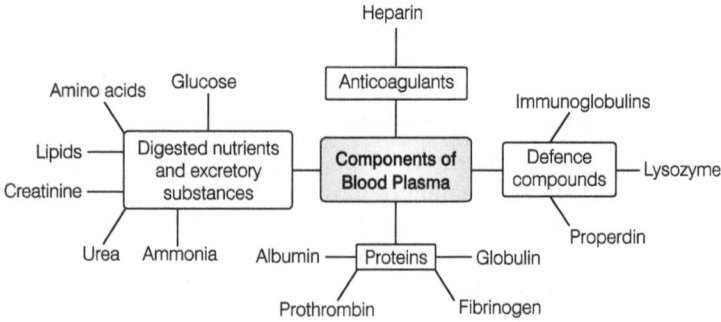

Blood Cells

They constitute about 40-45% of the blood. They have specific gravity of about 1.09, *i.e.,* these are slightly heavier than the plasma.

The three types of cellular elements in blood are

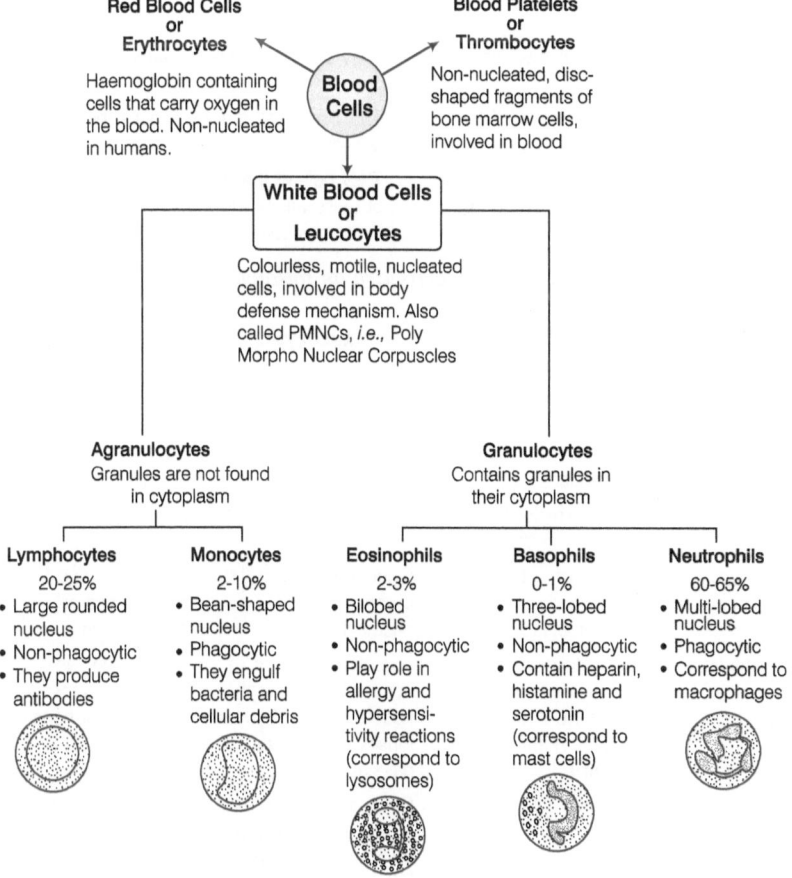

Lymphocytes exist in two major groups in circulation, *i.e.,* B-lymphocytes and T-lymphocytes.

B-lymphocytes (B-cells) and T-lymphocytes (T-cells)

B-Cells	T-Cells
They form a part of the humoral immune system.	They form a part of the cell-mediated immune system.
They are processed in the liver or bone marrow.	They are processed in the thymus gland.
They release the antibodies which finally enter the blood.	They do not release the antibodies.
They produce antibodies to kill the antigens.	The whole cell directly attacks the antigens.
They defend the body against invading bacteria/virus. They do not reach against transplants and cancerous tissues.	They defend the body against pathogens, but also attack the transplants and the cancerous cells.

Major characteristics of blood cells are as follows

Characteristic Features	Erythrocytes	Leucocytes	Thrombocytes
Number	4.5-5 million mm^3 of blood	6000-8000 mm^3 of blood	1,50,000-3,50,000 mm^3 of blood
Shape	Biconcave and circular	Rounded or irregular	Rounded or oval disc like bodies.
Size	7-8 μm in diameter 1-2 mm thick	12-20 μm in diameter	2-3 μm in diameter
Colour	Red (due to the presence of haemoglobin)	Colourless (due to the absence of haemoglobin)	Colourless (due to the absence of haemoglobin)
Formation	Erythropoiesis occur in liver and spleen (before birth) and in bone marrow (after birth).	Leucopoiesis occur in bone marrow, lymph nodes, spleen, thymus, tonsils and Peyer's patches.	Thrombopoiesis occur from very large cells of bone marrow, *i.e.,* megakaryotes.
Life span	About 120 days	Few hours to few days (granulocytes) or few months (agranulocytes).	About 8-10 days.

Blood Groups

There are more than 30 antigens on the surface of blood cells that gives rise to different blood groups. During agglutination, reaction occurs between antigens (agglutinogens) in red blood cells and antibodies (agglutins) in blood plasma.

Two types of blood grouping are widely used all over the world namely; ABO blood group and Rh (rhesus) blood group.

Handbook of BIOLOGY

ABO Blood Groups

Reported first time by **Karl Landsteiner** in human beings. AB blood group was reported by **de Castell** and **Steini**.

Phenotype	Genotype	Antigen on RBC Membrane	Antibody In Plasma	Can Receive Blood From	Can Donate Blood To
A (40%)	$I^A I^A$ or $I^A I^O$	A antigen	Anti-B antibodies	A, O	A, AB
B (10%)	$I^B I^B$ or $I^B I^O$	B antigen	Anti-A antibodies	B, O	B, AB
AB (4%)	$I_A I^B$	A antigen B antigen	No antibodies	A, B, AB, O (universal acceptor)	AB
O (46%)	$I^O I^O$	No antigen	Anti-A and Anti-B antibodies	O	A, B, AB, O (universal donor)

I represents isoagglutinin gene possessing 3 alleles-I^A, I^B, I^O.

Rhesus (Rh) Blood Group

It was discovered by **Landsteiner** and **Wiener** in the blood of **rhesus monkey**. Depending upon the presence or absence of rhesus antigen on the surface of red blood corpuscles, individuals are categorised as **Rh positive** (Rh^+) and **Rh negative** (Rh^-), respectively. Rh^+ is dominant to Rh^-.

Rh Incompatibility During Pregnancy

It is seen when father's blood is Rh^+ and mother's blood is Rh^-.

Rh^+ being a dominant character expresses in the foetus and causes a serious problem.

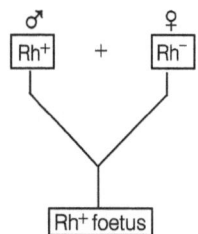

The first child of Rh^- mother will not suffer, but Rh^+ blood of foetus stimulates the formation of anti-Rh^- factors in the mother's blood.
In the subsequent pregnancies with foetus, the anti-Rh antibodies in the mother's blood destroy the foetal RBCs and results in **Haemolytic Diseases of the Newborn** (HDN) or **erythroblastosis foetalis**.

Rh Incompatibility During Blood Transfusion

The first transfusion between Rh^+ and Rh^- blood causes no harm, because Rh^- person develops anti Rh antibodies in his blood. But in the second transfusion of Rh^+ blood to Rh^- blood, the anti Rh antibodies in the latter's blood destroy the RBCs of the donor.

Coagulation of Blood

Coagulation or clotting is one of the characteristic feature of blood. It is defined as 'conversion of normal viscous blood fluid into jelly-like mass within 3-10 minutes after its exposure to air'.

The pathways of mechanism of blood clotting are as follows

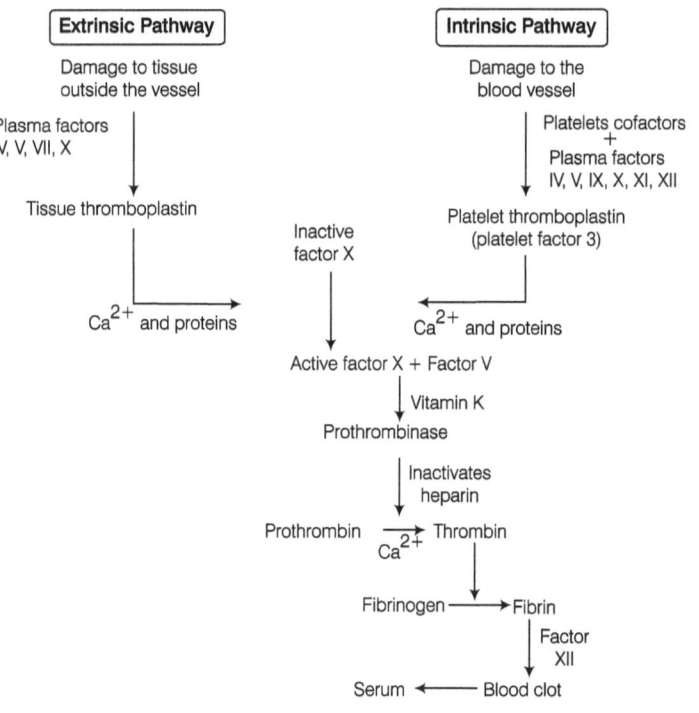

Description of various clotting factors

Clotting Factor	Synonym	Characteristic
Factor I	Fibrinogen	Glycoprotein, synthesise in liver, contain 3 pairs of non-identical polypeptide chains, soluble in plasma
Factor II	Prothrombin	Glycoprotein, synthesise in liver by vitamin-K
Factor III	Thromboplastin or tissue factor	Lipoprotein, secreted in inactive form, prothromboplastin which gets activated by proconvertin of plasma tissues
Factor IV	Calcium ions	Required for the formation of intrinsic and extrinsic thromboplastin and for the conversion of prothrombin to thrombin
Factor V	Proaccelerin or labile factor	Glycoprotein, heat labile, synthesised in liver, absent in serum
Factor VI	Accelerin	Hypothetical activation product of proaccelerin
Factor VII	Serum Prothrombin Accelerator (SPA) or stable factor or autoprothrombin	Synthesise in liver by vitamin-K, associated with prothrombin and accelerates tissue thromboplastin formation from damaged tissues
Factor VIII	Anti-haemophilic factor or platelet cofactor	Glycoprotein, synthesise in liver, required for prothrombin activator formation from blood constituents, its deficiency causes haemophilia-A
Factor IX	Anti-prothrombin II or platelet cofactor II or Plasma Thromboplastin Component (PTC)	Glycoprotein, synthesise in liver by vitamin-K, its deficiency causes haemophilia-B
Factor X	Stuart factor	Glycoprotein, synthesises in liver by vitamin-K, its deficiency causes nose bleeding (epistaxis)
Factor XI	Plasma Thromboplastin Antecadent (PTA)	Glycoprotein, required for stage 1 of intrinsic pathway, synthesis in liver, deficiency, cause haemophilia-C
Factor XII	Hageman factor or surface factor	Glycoprotein, present in both plasma and serum, required for the formation of prothrombin activator complex, deficiency results in delayed blood clotting
Factor XIII	Fibrin stabilising factor	Glycoprotein, causes polymerisation of soluble fibrinogen to-insoluble fibrin, deficiency causes haemorrhagic state

Lymph

It is an interstitial mobile connective tissue comprising lymph plasma and lymph corpuscles. It contains little O_2 but lot of CO_2 and metabolic waste.

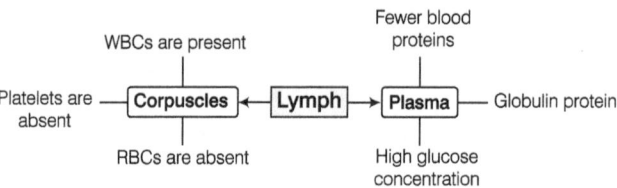

Infact, when blood flows from arterial end to venous end of a capillary most of its contents move into tissue third (at the arterial end) 90% of these constituents return back at the venous end which remaining 10% constitute the lymph.

Lymphoid Organs

These are the lymph secreting/accumulating organs. They include lymph nodes, tonsils, thymus, spleen and peyer's patches. The spleen is the largest lymphoid organ in the body.

Functions of Lymph

- Its white blood corpuscles helps in defense mechanism, tissue, repair and healing.
- It is an important carrier for nutrients, hormones, etc.
- It helps in the absorption of fats in the lacteals present in the intestinal villi.

Circulatory System

This system is primarily concerned with the circulation of substances through body fluids like blood and lymph.

The two types of circulatory system found in animals are

Open Circulatory System

Blood pumped by the heart passes through large vessels into open spaces or body cavities called **sinuses**. It is found in arthropods and molluces.

Closed Circulatory System

Blood pumped by the heart circulates through a closed network of blood vessels. It is found in annelids and chrodates.

Handbook of BIOLOGY

The general vertebrate closed circulatory systems can be
(a) Single circuit,
(b) Double circuit (complete or incomplete).

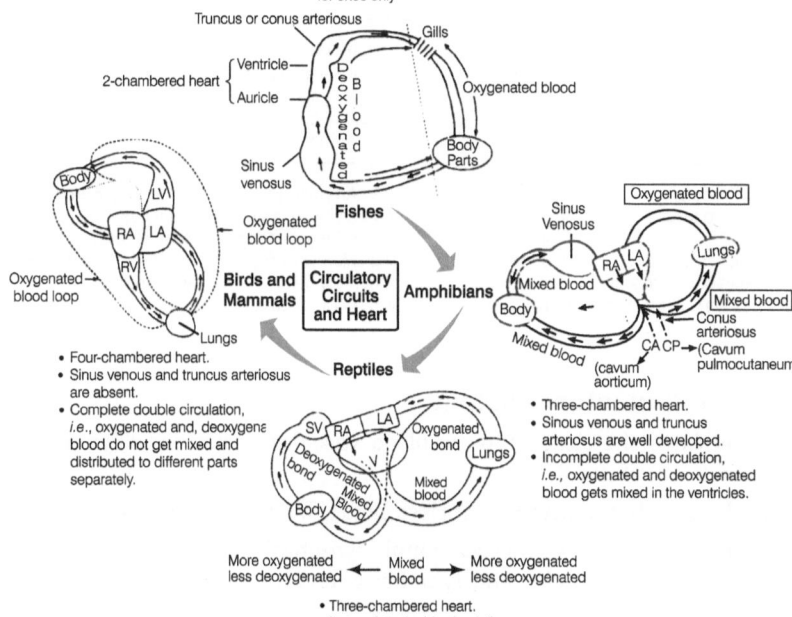

Circulatory circuits and heart

Types of Heart

Heart can be classified into different types on the basis of origin of impulse for contraction and their structure.

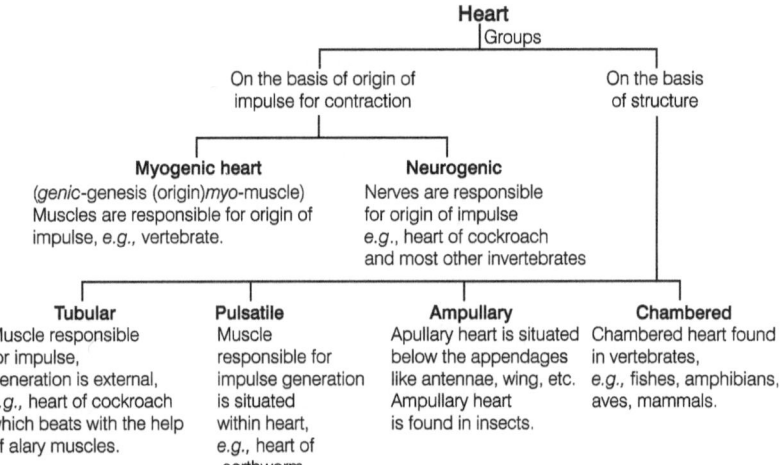

Human Circulatory System

It constitutes the closed type of blood vascular system and lymphatic system.

Blood vascular system comprises heart, blood and blood vessels.

Lymphatic system comprises lymph, lymphatic capillaries, lymphatic vessels, lymphatic nodes and lymphatic ducts.

Human Heart

The heart is a hollow, fibromuscular organ of somewhat conical or pyramidal form with upper broad part, the base and the lower narrow apex which is slightly directed to the left.

Histologically, the heart consists of three layers

(i) **Pericardium** Outermost smooth coelomic epithelium.

(ii) **Myocardium** Thick muscular middle layer, composed of cardiac muscle fibres.

(iii) **Endothelium** Innermost layer consisting of simple squamous epithelial cells.

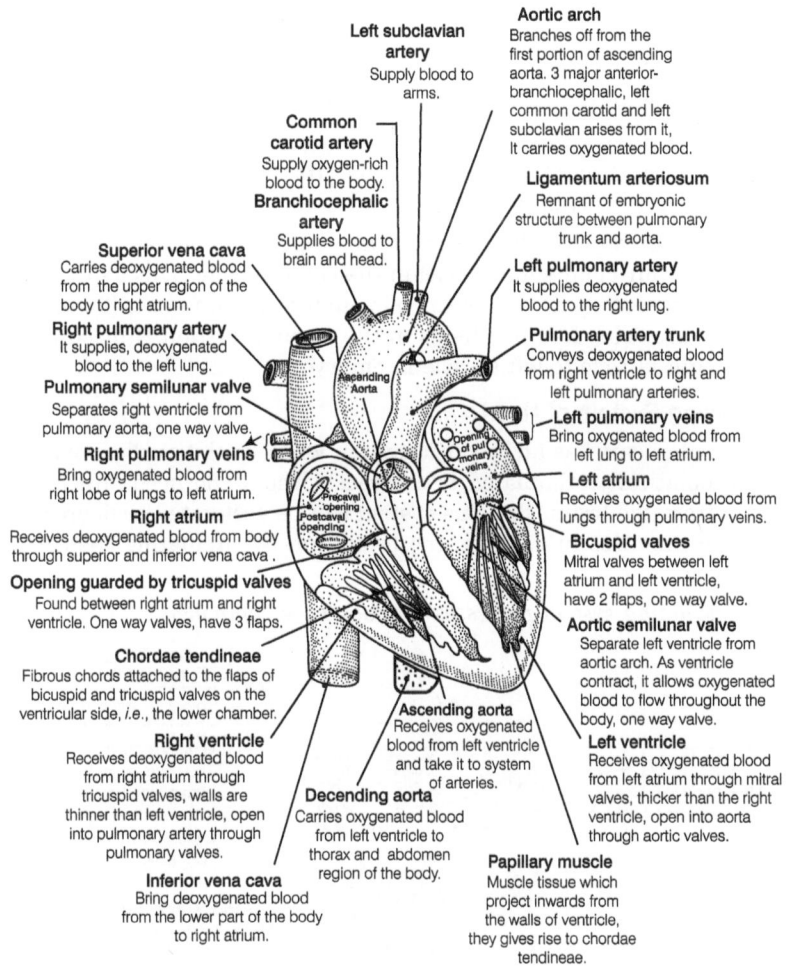

Human heart

Other components of heart which are not shown in the figure are described below

(i) **Grooves** (Sulci) These are the partitions that separate the various components of the heart. *These are*

  (a) **Interatrial groove or sulcus** The left and right atria are separated by this shallow, vertical groove.

  (b) **Atrioventricular sulcus** It divides the atria from the ventricle.

(c) **Interventricular sulcus** It divides the right and the left ventricle

(d) **Coronary sulcus** It separates atria and ventricles

(ii) **Coronary sinus** It delivers deoxygenated blood into the right atrium through coronary veins. Its opening is guarded by coronary valves or the besian valve.

(iii) **Fossa ovalis** It is an oval depression present in the interauricular septum within the right auricle. This depression is present as an oval foramen in embryo and known as **foramen ovale**. This foramen helps in the communication of blood from right auricle to left auricle in embryo.

Conducting System of Heart

The human heart has an intrinsic system whereby the cardiac muscles are automatically stimulated to contract without the need of a nerve supply from the brain. But this system can be accelerated or depressed by nerve impulses initiated in the brain and by circulating chemicals (hormones).

The conducting system possesses the following components

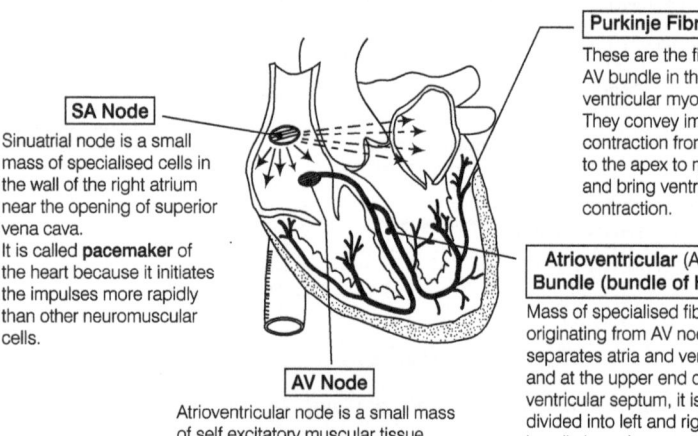

Purkinje Fibres
These are the fine fibres of AV bundle in the ventricular myocardium. They convey impulse of contraction from AV node to the apex to myocardium and bring ventricular contraction.

SA Node
Sinuatrial node is a small mass of specialised cells in the wall of the right atrium near the opening of superior vena cava.
It is called **pacemaker** of the heart because it initiates the impulses more rapidly than other neuromuscular cells.

Atrioventricular (AV) Bundle (bundle of His)
Mass of specialised fibres originating from AV node. It separates atria and ventricle and at the upper end of ventricular septum, it is divided into left and right bundle branches.

AV Node
Atrioventricular node is a small mass of self excitatory muscular tissue situated in the wall of atrial septum near the atrioventricular valves. It is stimulated by impulses that sweep over atrial myocardium. It is capable of initiating own impulses, but at slower rate. It is called **pacesetter** of heart.

Components of heart's conducting system

Cardiac Cycle

It is the event during which one heart beat or one cycle of contraction and relaxation of cardiac muscle occurs.

The time of cardiac cycle is in reverse ratio of the rate of heart beat. In man, the heart rate is about 72 times/min, therefore time of a cardiac cycle is 60/72 = 0.8 sec approx.

Time Taken	Atria		Ventricle	
	Systole	Diastole	Systole	Diastole
	0.1 sec	0.7 sec	0.3 sec	0.5 sec

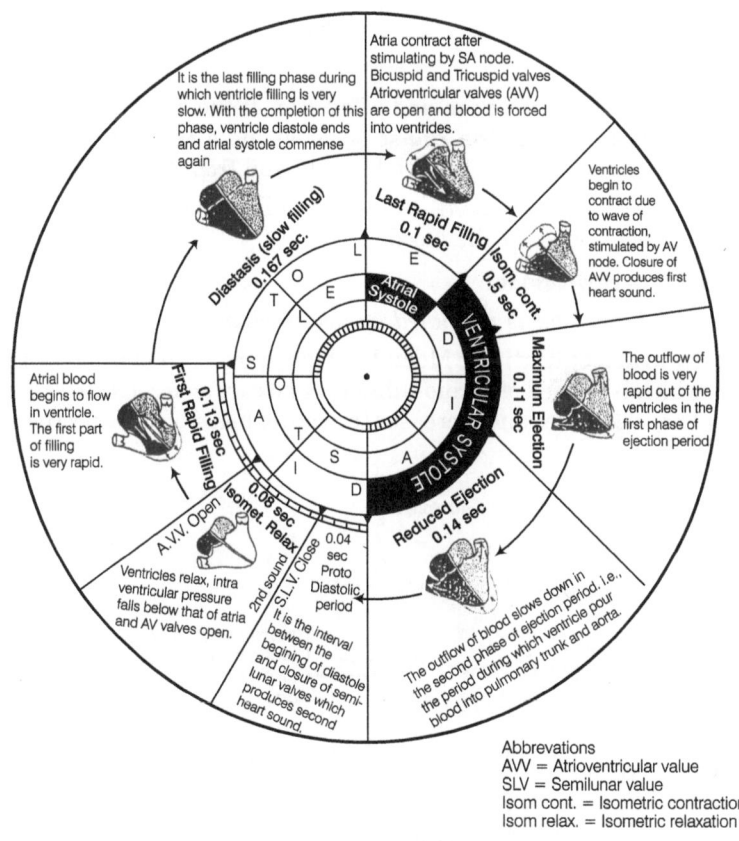

Abbreviations
AVV = Atrioventricular value
SLV = Semilunar value
Isom cont. = Isometric contraction
Isom relax. = Isometric relaxation

Cardiac cycle

Heart Sounds

The beating of heart produces characteristic sounds which can be heard by placing the ear or stethoscope against the chest. The two sounds are produced per heart beat, *i.e.,* 'lubb' and 'dubb'.

Differences between First and Second Heart Sounds

First Heart Sound	Second Heart Sound
It is produced by the closure of bicuspid and tricuspid valves.	It is produced by the closure of aortic and pulmonary semilunar valves.
It is low pitched, less loud and of long duration.	It is higher pitched, louder and of short duration.
It lasts for 0.15 sec.	It lasts for 0.1 sec.

Heart Beat

It is the rhythmic contraction and relaxation of the heart. Each heart beat includes a **contraction phase** (systole) and a **relaxation phase** (diastole) to distribute and receive blood to and from the body.

Adult healthy heart beats 72 times per minute (average) to pump approximately 5 litres of the blood.

Regulation of Heart Beat

The rate of heart beat is regulated by two mechanism

(a) **Neural regulation** Medulla oblongata is the cardiac centre which is formed of cardio-inhibitor and cardio-accelerator parts. They decreases and increases the rate of heart beat respectively.

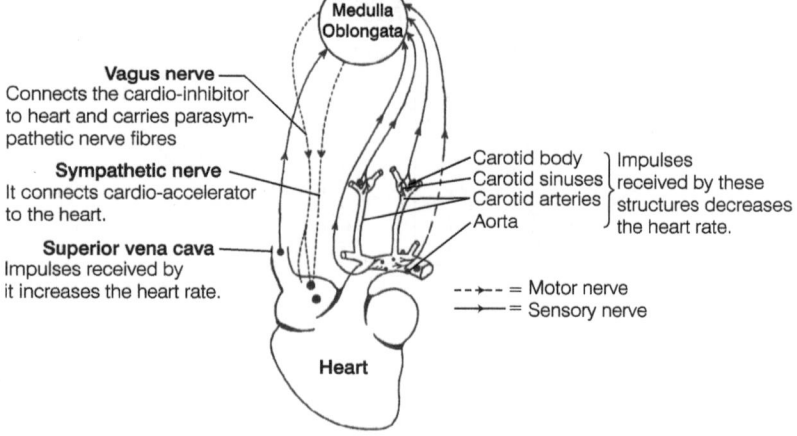

Neural regulation of heart beat

(b) **Hormonal regulation** Hormones secreted by the medulla region of adrenal gland helps is regulating the heart beat.

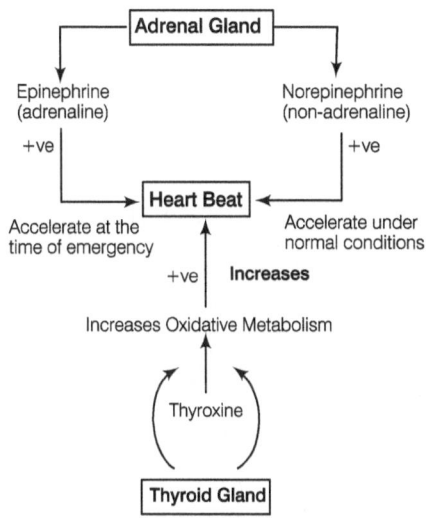

Hormonal regulation of heart beat

Cardiac Output

It is the amount of blood pumped by heart per minute

Cardiac output = Normal heart rate of an adult per minute × Amount of blood pumped by heart per minute

= 72 × 70

= 5040 mL per minute (5 L/min).

Electrocardiogram (ECG)

ECG is a graphic record of the electric current produced by the excitation of the cardiac muscles.

Electrocardiograph It is the machine by which the electrocardiogram is recorded.

Waller (1887) first recorded the ECG, but Einthoven (1903) studied ECG in detail and got Nobel Prize in 1924 for the discovery of electrocardiography. He also considered "Father of Electrocardiography".

A human electrocardiogram shows the following 5 consecutive waves, i.e., P Q R S T

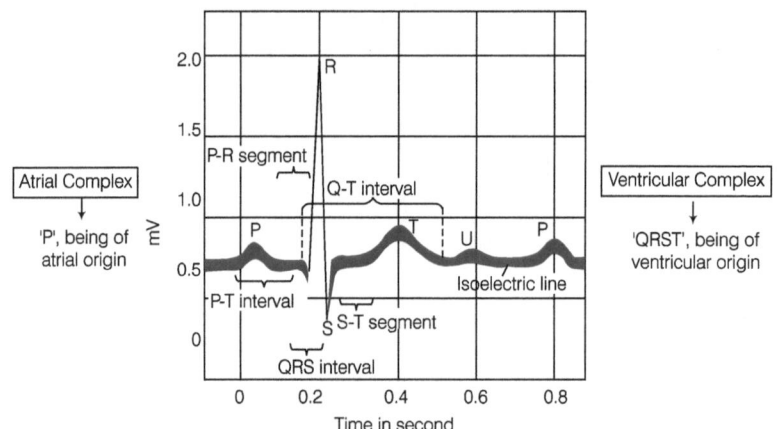

There are two isoelectric period in ECG
  (a) The shorter one, between P and Q.
  (b) The longer one, between S and T.

Waves involved in ECG are described below

P Wave
Represents **atrial depolarisation**, impulse is originating at SA node, these is no defect of conduction.

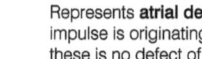

T Wave ——— ECG ——— **Q Wave**

T Wave: Broad, smoothly rounded deflection, caused by the contraction of the basal part of ventricles, represents **ventricular repolarisation**.

Q Wave: Caused by the activity of septum. It is small, negative, often inconspicuous deflection.

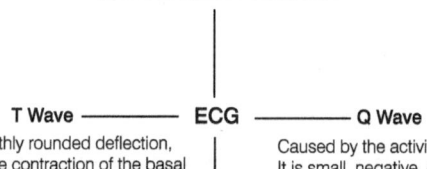

R and S Wave
R is the most constant and conspicuous wave having tallest amplitude, represents first positive deflection during **ventricular depolarisation** 'S' is downward deflection, constant and inconspicuous.

U Wave This wave is often seen just after the T wave. It is possibly due to slow repolarisation of the intraventricular conducting system.

Significance of different intervals involved in ECG

R-R interval Rhythmical depolarisation of ventricles.

P-P interval Rhythmical depolarisation of atrium.

P-R interval Measure conduction time of the impulse from SA node to the ventricles. It varies from 0.13-0.16 sec.

Q-R-S interval Measures total ventricular depolarisation time. It varies from 0.08-0.1 sec.

Q-T interval Measures the ventricular total systolic time. It is about 0.36 sec.

T-P interval Measures the diastolic period of the heart.

Abnormalities in ECG and their significance

(i) **Inverted P wave** Indicates that SA node fails to initiate the impulse and atrial muscles depolarised by the impulse originating in AV node.

(ii) **Enlarged P wave** Enlargement of the atria.

(iii) **Absent Q wave** Infants suffering from congenital patency of the septum.

(iv) **Abnormal T wave** Serious myocardial damage, cardiac hypoxia.

(v) **Enlarged P-R interval** Inflammation of atria and AV node.

(vi) **Repressed S-T segment** Heart muscles receives insufficient oxygen.

Blood Vascular System

Blood vascular system consists of a system of vessels that supply the blood throughout the body. Oxygenated and deoxygenated blood is transported to different body parts through different vessels namely **arteries** and **veins**, respectively.

The walls of artery and veins consists of 3 coats as follows

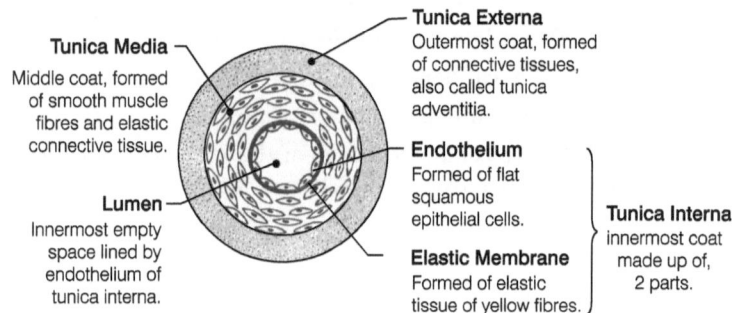

Tunica Media
Middle coat, formed of smooth muscle fibres and elastic connective tissue.

Lumen
Innermost empty space lined by endothelium of tunica interna.

Tunica Externa
Outermost coat, formed of connective tissues, also called tunica adventitia.

Endothelium
Formed of flat squamous epithelial cells.

Elastic Membrane
Formed of elastic tissue of yellow fibres.

Tunica Interna
innermost coat made up of, 2 parts.

TS of artery and veins

Arteries	Veins
Arteries distribute blood from the heart to the different parts of the body.	Veins collect blood from different parts of the body and pour it into the heart.
Tunica media is thick, having more muscle fibres.	Tunica media is thin, having fewer muscle fibres.
Tunica interna has strong elastic membrane and more elongated endothelial cells.	Tunica interna has simple, elastic membrane and elongated endothelial cells.
The walls of the arteries are thick and muscular.	The walls of the veins are thin and non-muscular.
Arteries are not collapsible as they have thick walls.	Veins are collapsible because they have thin walls.
Arteries have no valves.	Veins have valves which prevent backward flow of blood.
The flow of the blood is fast as the blood in them is under great pressure.	The flow of blood in veins is not so fast because the blood in veins is under low pressure.
Except the pulmonary arteries all the arteries carry oxygenated blood.	Except pulmonary veins all the veins carry deoxygenated blood.

Some Major Arteries and Veins of Human Body

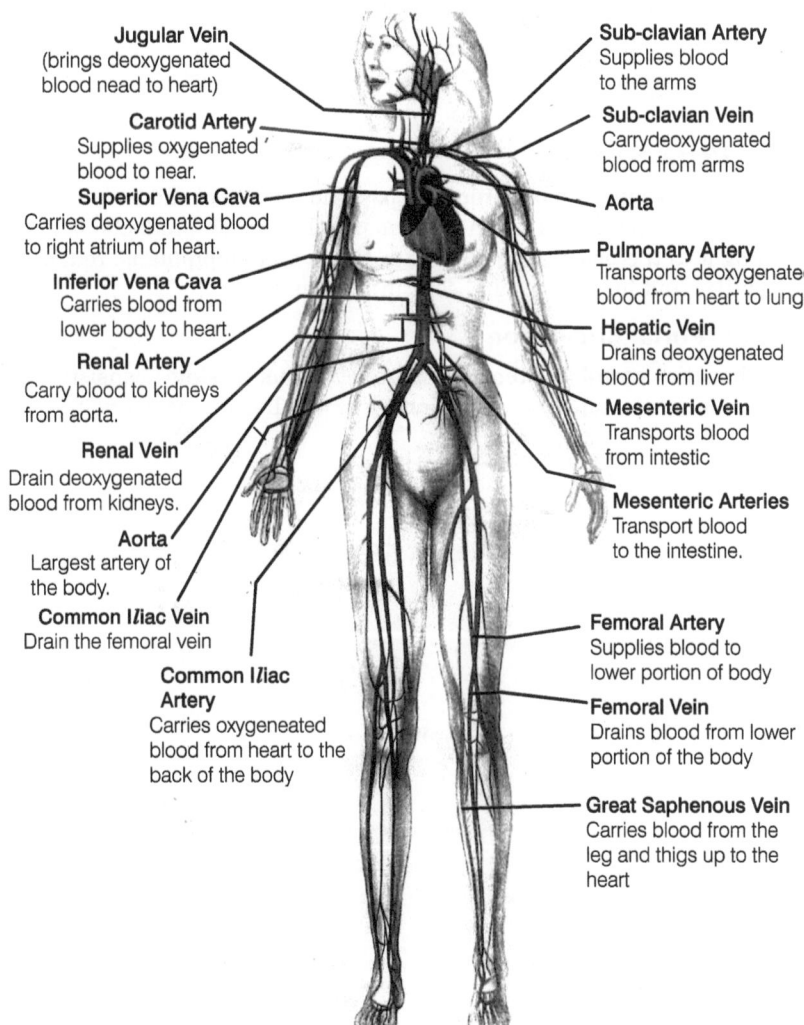

Jugular Vein (brings deoxygenated blood nead to heart)

Carotid Artery Supplies oxygenated blood to near.

Superior Vena Cava Carries deoxygenated blood to right atrium of heart.

Inferior Vena Cava Carries blood from lower body to heart.

Renal Artery Carry blood to kidneys from aorta.

Renal Vein Drain deoxygenated blood from kidneys.

Aorta Largest artery of the body.

Common Iliac Vein Drain the femoral vein

Common Iliac Artery Carries oxygeneated blood from heart to the back of the body

Sub-clavian Artery Supplies blood to the arms

Sub-clavian Vein Carrydeoxygenated blood from arms

Aorta

Pulmonary Artery Transports deoxygenated blood from heart to lungs

Hepatic Vein Drains deoxygenated blood from liver

Mesenteric Vein Transports blood from intestic

Mesenteric Arteries Transport blood to the intestine.

Femoral Artery Supplies blood to lower portion of body

Femoral Vein Drains blood from lower portion of the body

Great Saphenous Vein Carries blood from the leg and thigs up to the heart

Portal System

It is a part of venous circulation which is present between the two groups of capillaries, *i.e.*, it starts in capillaries and ends in capillaries.

Portal Vein It is the vein that drains blood into organs other than heart. This vein along with other small veins constitute a portal system.

Renal Portal System

This system supplies blood from the posterior region of the body to the kidneys by renal portal vein to remove the waste products before sending it to the heart. It is present in fishes and amphibians, reduced in reptiles and birds, and is absent in mammals.

Hepatic Portal Circulation

The hepatic portal system or portal venous system consists of numerous veins and tributaries, including the hepatic portal vein.

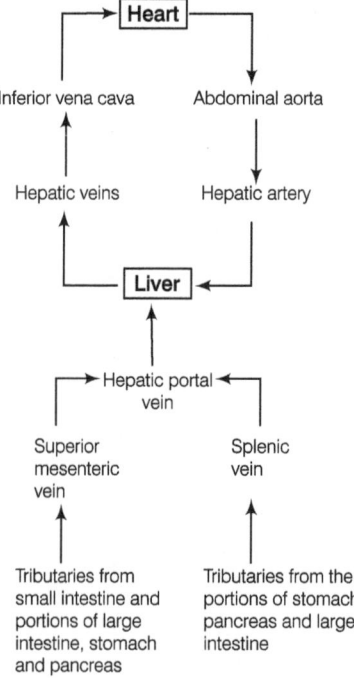

Importance of Hepatic Portal System

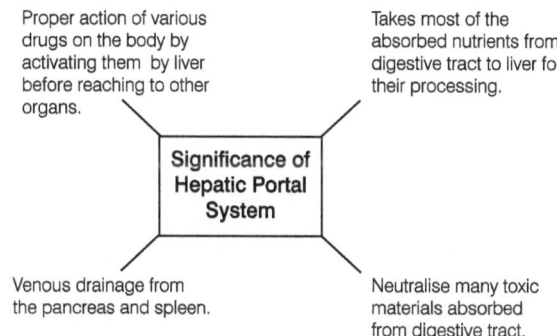

Hypophysial Portal Circulation

This system carry blood from the hypothalamus of the brain to the anterior lobe of pituitary gland. It allows the endocrine communication between the two structures.

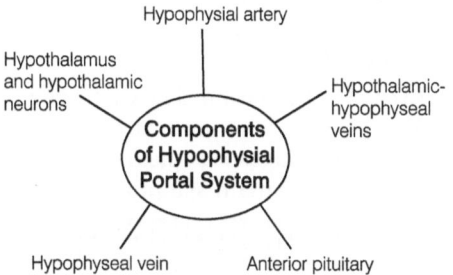

Significance of Hypophysial Portal System

- It allows a fast communication between pituitary gland and hypothalamus.
- The fenestral structure of the hypophyseal portal system needs only a small amount of hormones to tolerate a rapid exchange between two structures.

Disorders of Circulatory System

(a) **Angina** It is also called **angina pectoris** means chest pain. In this disease enough oxygen does not reach the heart muscles. The patient experiences pain in chest.

(b) **Arteriosclerosis** It refers to the hardening and loss of elasticity of the arteries. In arteriosclerosis, calcium salts precipitate with the cholesterol which forms plaques.

Calcification of the plaques makes the walls of the arteries stiff and rigid. The affected arteries lose their elasticity and their walls may get ruptured. The blood coming out of the ruptured walls may clot and block the blood flow which further may load to heart attack.

(c) **Coronary Artery Disease (CAD) or Atherosclerosis** It is the deposition of fatty substances specially cholesterol and triglycerides in the tunica interna and smooth muscles of arteries. Such a deposition is called **atheromatous plaque** which deforms the arterial wall. These plaque reduces the lumen of artery which interfere with the blood flow to the heart. This may result in heart stroke or heart attack.

(d) **Fibrillation** It is a condition in which the heart muscles contracts very rapidly but in uncoordinated fashion. There are atrial and ventricular fibrillation. Ventricular fibrillation is life threatening unless it can be stopped by defibrillation.

(e) **Heart attack** (Myocardial infarction) It is the death of a part of heart muscle following cessation of blood supply to it. It is an acute heart attack. The heart muscles suddenly get damaged by inadequate blood supply.

(f) **Heart failure** It is the condition when heart does not pump blood effectively enough to meet the need of the body. It is sometimes called congestive heart failure because, lung congestion is one of the main symptom of this disease.

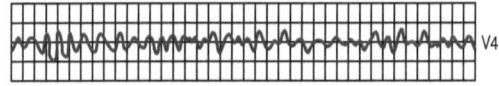

Ventricular fibrillation

(g) **Ventricular premature beat or extra-systole** The series of ventricular premature beat or extra-systole are shown in then fig. given below, Sometimes, a portion of the myocardium becomes irritable and **ectopic beat** occurs before the **expected next normal beat**. This ectopic beat causes **transient** interruptions of the **cardiac rhythm**. This type of ectopic beat is known as **ventricular extra-systole or premature beat**.

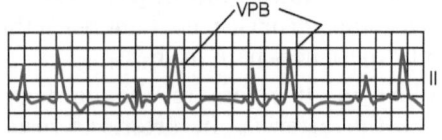

Ventricular premature beat

12

Locomotion and Movement

Locomotion
It is the self-propelled movement or the ability of an individual to move from one place to another. An animal cannot locomote without movement.

Movement
It refers to the change of position that does not entail the change of location. Movements are brought about by internal or external forces.

The movement of a non-living object is induced (due to external force) while the movements of living things are autonomic (self-sustained).

Following types of movements are shown by the different cells of the human body

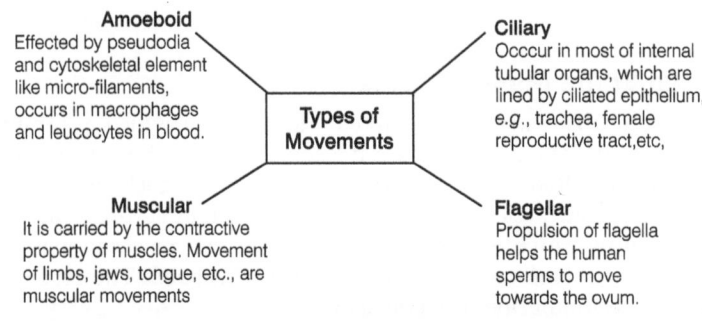

Amoeboid
Effected by pseudodia and cytoskeletal element like micro-filaments, occurs in macrophages and leucocytes in blood.

Ciliary
Occur in most of internal tubular organs, which are lined by ciliated epithelium, e.g., trachea, female reproductive tract, etc,

Muscular
It is carried by the contractive property of muscles. Movement of limbs, jaws, tongue, etc., are muscular movements

Flagellar
Propulsion of flagella helps the human sperms to move towards the ovum.

Muscles

Muscle is a specialised contractile tissue that bring about the movement of different body parts. It is mesodermal in origin and contributes to 40-50% of the body weight.

Based on their location, muscles are of 3 types, i.e., striated, non-striated and cardiac.

Striated	Non-striated	Cardiac
They are present in the limbs, body walls, tongue, pharynx and beginning of oesophagus.	They are present in the oesophagus (posterior part only), urino-genital tract, urinary bladder, vessels, iris of eye, dermis of skin and arrector pili muscles of hair.	They are present in the wall of the heart, pulmonary veins and superior vena cava.
Cylindrical.	Spindle shaped.	Cylindrical.
Fibres unbranched.	Fibres unbranched.	Fibres branched.
Multinucleate.	Uninucleate.	Uninucleate.
Bounded by sarcolemma.	Bounded by plasmalemma.	Bounded by sarcolemma.
Light and dark bands present.	Light and dark bands absent.	Faint light and dark bands present.
No oblique bridges and intercalated discs.	No oblique bridges and intercalated discs.	Oblique bridges and intercalated discs present.
Nerve supply from central nervous system.	Nerve supply from autonomic nervous system.	Nerve supply from the brain and autonomic nervous system.
Blood supply is abundant.	Blood supply is scanty.	Blood supply is abundant.
Very rapid contraction.	Slow contraction.	Rapid contraction.
They soon get fatigued.	They do not get fatigued.	They never get fatigued.
Voluntary.	Involuntary.	Involuntary.

Red and White Muscle Fibres

Red muscle fibres are those striated muscle fibres, which are thinner but dark-red in colour. The dark red colour is due to the accumulation of **myoglobin**. Red muscle fibres are rich in mitochondria. They perform slow contractions. Because of this, red muscle fibres are also known as **slow muscle fibres**. However, they can perform sustained contraction over long periods with out getting fatigued. The reason for this is non-accumulation of lactic acid.

Red muscle fibres are more abundant in athletes like long distance runners and cyclist. Extensor muscles present on the back of human body are rich in red muscle fibres because these are required to undergo prolonged contraction for the maintenance of erect posture against the force of gravity. Avial flight muscles used in prolonged slow flying (*e.g.*, kite) are also rich in red muscles fibres.

White muscles fibres are a type of striated muscle fibres which are thicker and of pale-yellow colour. These muscle fibres do not contain myoglobin and mitochondria are fewer in number. White muscle fibres contract very quickly but for short durations that's why these are also termed as **fast muscle fibres**.

Theser fibres mostly perform anaerobic glycolysis for liberation of energy. Therefore, white muscle fibres get fatigued quickly. White muscle fibres are more abundant in short distance runner and other athletes. Muscles which move our eyeballs are rich in white fibres. Similarly, **avial flight** muscles used in short distance but fast flying (*e.g.*, sparrow) have white fibres only.

Structure of Skeletal Muscle

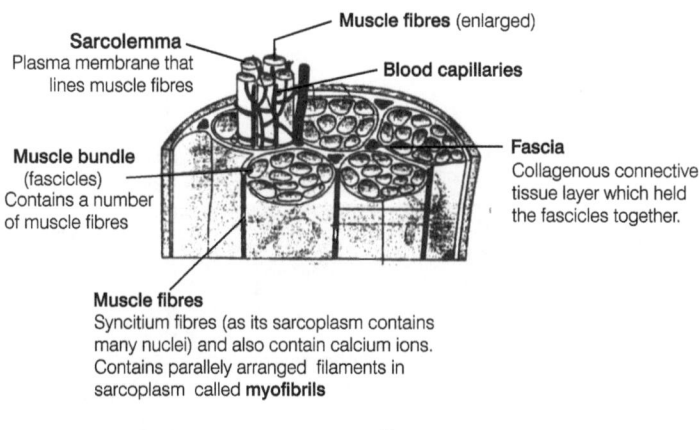

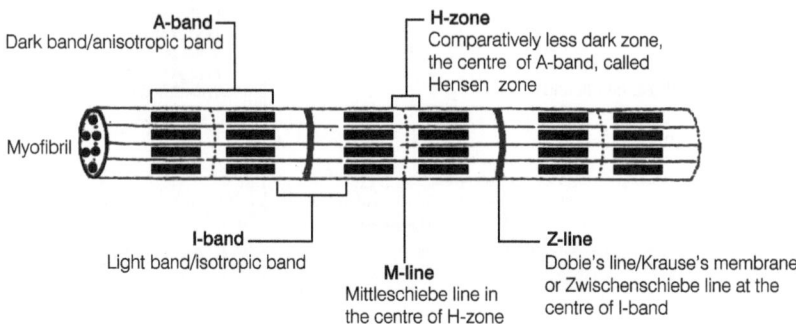

The part of myofibril between two successive Z-lines is **sarcomere** (functional unit of myofibril).

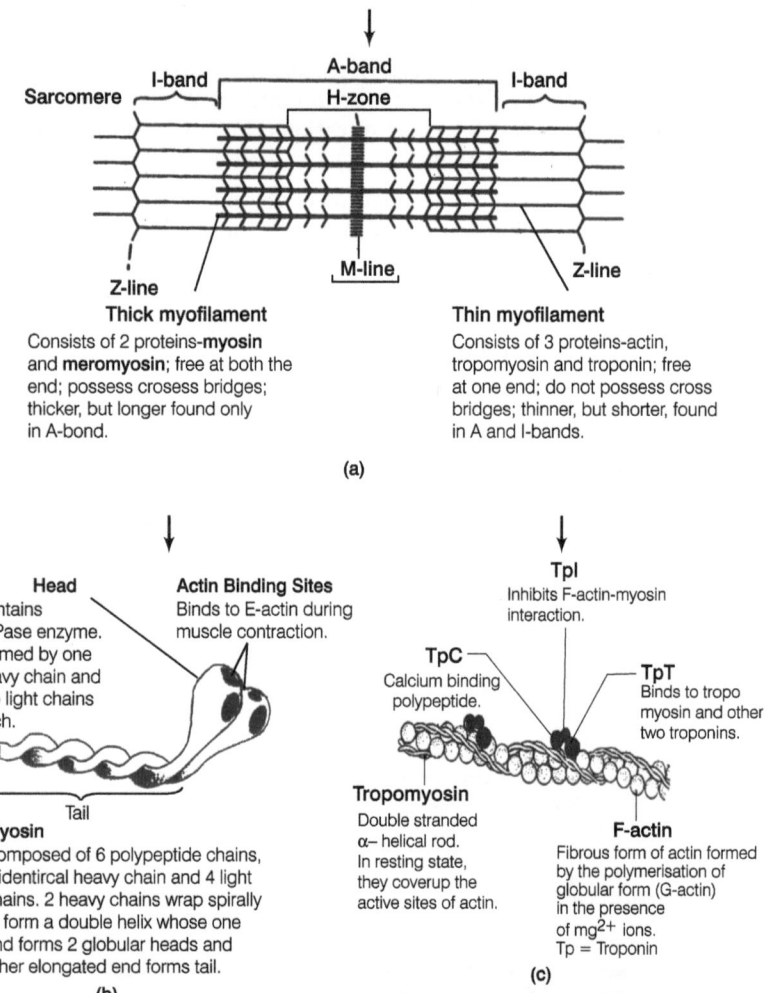

Muscle structure : (a) A sarcomer (enlarged) (b) Myosin filament (c) Actin filament

Handbook of BIOLOGY

Mechanism of Muscle Contraction

Sliding filament theory proposed by **Huxley** and **Hanson** (1954) best explains the mechanism of muscle contraction. *The essential features of this theory are*

- During the process of muscle contraction, the thin myofilaments show sliding inward towards the H-zone.
- The sarcomere shortens, without changing the length of thin and thick myofilaments.
- The crossbridges of the thick myofilaments connect with the portions of actin of the thin myofilaments. These cross bridges move on the surface of the thin myofilaments resulting in sliding of thin and thick myofilaments over each other.
- The lengths of the thick and thin myofilaments does not change during muscle contraction.

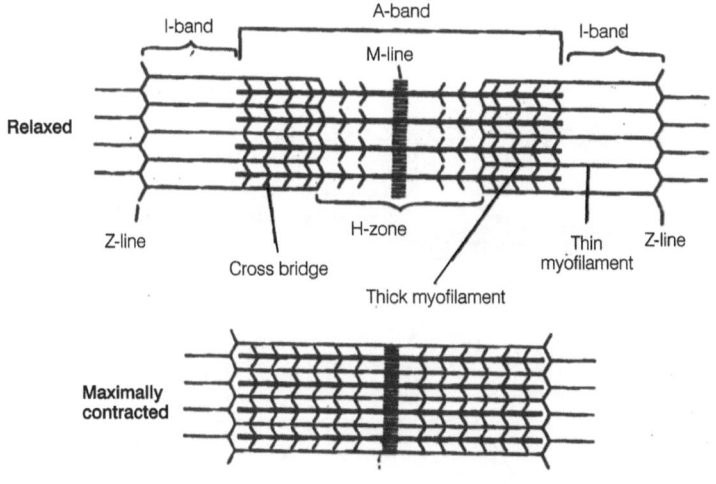

Contraction in a sarcomere of muscle

Electrical and Biochemical Events in Muscle Contraction

These events have been worked out by **Albert Szent Gyorgyi** and others and involve sliding filament procedures as well.

These are as follows

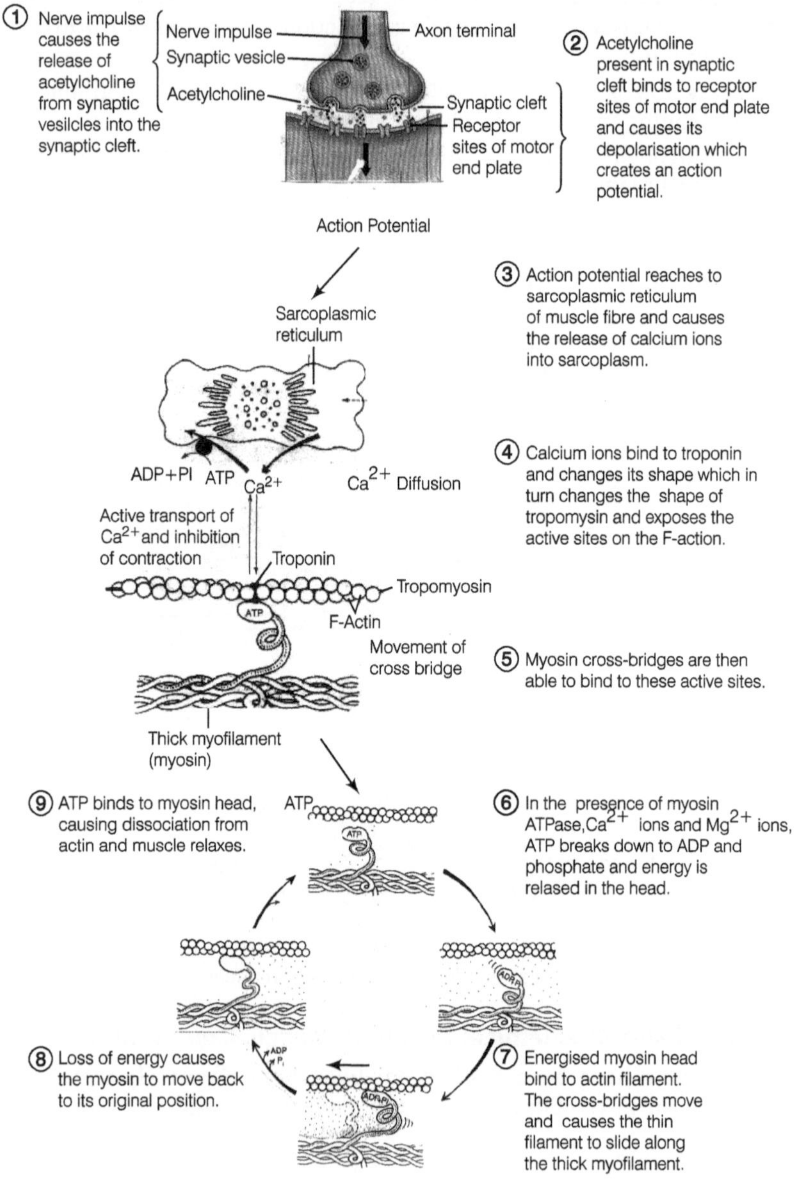

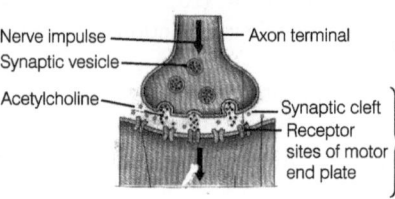

① Nerve impulse causes the release of acetylcholine from synaptic vesilcles into the synaptic cleft.

② Acetylcholine present in synaptic cleft binds to receptor sites of motor end plate and causes its depolarisation which creates an action potential.

③ Action potential reaches to sarcoplasmic reticulum of muscle fibre and causes the release of calcium ions into sarcoplasm.

④ Calcium ions bind to troponin and changes its shape which in turn changes the shape of tropomysin and exposes the active sites on the F-action.

⑤ Myosin cross-bridges are then able to bind to these active sites.

⑥ In the presence of myosin ATPase, Ca^{2+} ions and Mg^{2+} ions, ATP breaks down to ADP and phosphate and energy is relased in the head.

⑦ Energised myosin head bind to actin filament. The cross-bridges move and causes the thin filament to slide along the thick myofilament.

⑧ Loss of energy causes the myosin to move back to its original position.

⑨ ATP binds to myosin head, causing dissociation from actin and muscle relaxes.

Types of Muscle Contraction

A skeletal muscle contraction may be any of several types. *These are as follows*

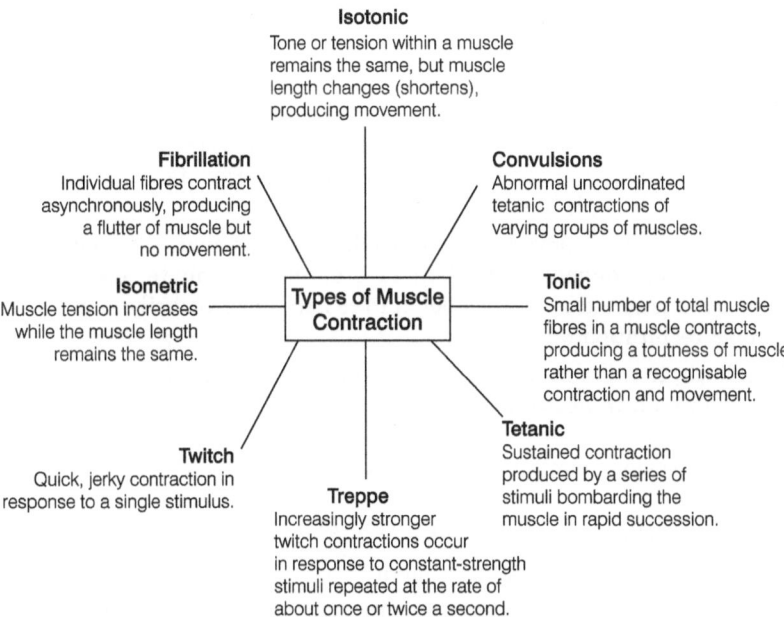

All-or-None Law

All-or-none law or **Bowditch's law** is a principle which states that response of a muscle/nerve to a stimulus is not proportionate to the intensity of stimulus but is either present in full strength or completely absent.

A single muscle fibre (striated, unstriated or cardiac) does not show any gradation in contraction in relation to the degree to stimulus, *i.e.*, like a nerve fibre, a muscle fibre does not respond to a stimulus till it is equal to or above a minimum (threshold) value.

The degree of contraction also shows independence with the intensity of stimulus. At or above all the threshold value, a muscle fibre will always contract with the maximum force irrespective of the strength of the stimulus.

However, the force of contraction may increase or decrease with the change in pH, temperature, stretching of muscle fibre, etc., though even under such condition increase of decrease in the value of stimulus would not alter the force of contraction. Further, the entire muscle does not follow the all-or-none rule.

Oxygen Debt

It is the extra oxygen required by the body muscles during relaxation or recovery period over the resting state. During strenuous exercise, the requirement of oxygen and hence, energy far exceeds its availability through breathing.

Therefore, other sources are tapped. These include oxygen from oxymyoglobin, dephosphorylation of creatine phosphate, etc. After their exhaustion, the muscles begin to respire anaerobically along with aerobic respiration.

Muscle contraction or activity under anaerobic conditions is termed as **anaerobic contraction**. The lactic acid produced here accumulates in the muscle. When exercise is stopped, the recovery process starts. During recovery, extra oxygen is required for which deep breathing continues.

The extra (extra to normal aerobic breathing) is used in

(a) Regeneration of oxymyoglobin
(b) Oxidation of accumulated lactic acid
(c) Restoration of depleted ATP
(d) Restoration of creatine phosphate.

Oxygen debt decreases with regular exercise because the regular exercise increases oxymyoglobin content of the muscles and allows sufficient deep breathing during exercise to perform aerobic contractions.

Cori's Cycle

A cyclic process involving the formation of lactic acid in the muscles and regeneration of glycogen from it (in the liver) in order to reduce accumulation of lactic acid in muscles and increased maintain continued supply of glucose to them.

This cycle was discovered by **Cori** and involves lactic acid formed in the muscle passes into the blood stream and reaches the liver where roughly 4/5 of it is changed to glycogen while rest 1/5 is oxidised to CO_2 and H_2O.

Handbook of BIOLOGY

Afterwards, this glycogen in hydrolysed to form glucose that passes into the blood stream and reaches the muscles for the liberation of energy and the production of fresh lactic acid.

Importance With the help of **Cori's cycle**, lactic acid is not allowed to accumulate beyond a certain concentration within the muscles.

This protects the neuro-muscular junction which is sensitive to lactic acid. The cycle also replenishes glucose/glycogen in the muscles.

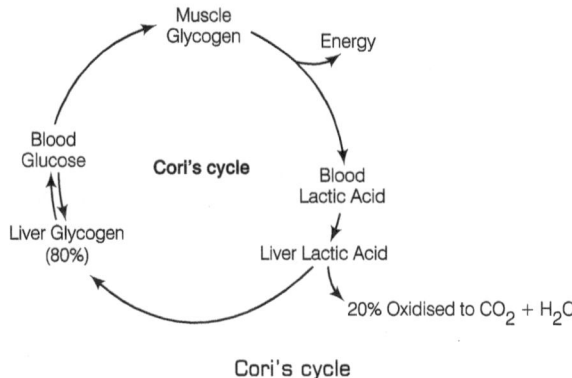

Cori's cycle

Muscle Fatigue

The decrease in the force of contraction of a muscle after prolonged stimulation is called **muscle fatigue**.

Cause A muscle is able to contract for a short time in the absence of oxygen. But it gets fatigued sooner because in the absence of oxygen, the metabolic products of glycolysis (mainly lactic acid) accumulates around it.

This accumulation leads to muscle fatigue. Normally, pain is experienced in the fatigued muscle. The site of fatigue is the neuromuscular junction.

Functional Classification of Skeletal Muscles

Type of Skeletal Muscle	Function	Example
Flexors	Muscles which bend one part of the body over the other.	**Biceps** bending forearm towards upper arm.
Extensors	Muscles which extend or straighten the limbs.	**Triceps** extending forearm and is antagonous to biceps.
Abductors	Muscles which pull a limb away from the median line.	**Deltoides** of shoulder.
Adductors	Muscles which bring a limb towards the median line of the body.	**Latissimus dorsi** which draw the whole forelimb towards the body and is antagonous to deltoides.
Depressors	Muscles which lower some parts.	**Depressor mandibularis** lowers the lower jaw (similarly pectoralis major is the depressor muscle for the wings of birds).
Elevators	Antagonistic to depressors as they raise a body part.	**Masseter** which lifts the lower jaw (similarly pectoralis minor is the elevator muscle for the wings of birds).
Pronators	The muscle that turns the palm downward or backward.	**Pronator teres** in mammalian limbs.
Supinators	Antagonistic to pronator, *i.e.,* turns the palm upward or forward.	**Supinator** in human forelimbs.
Sphinctors	Decreases the size of an opening and close it.	**Pyloric sphincter** of alimentary canal.
Dilators	The muscles around the openings, which increases their size and open them. Antagonistic to sphinctors.	**Iris**.
Ratators	Associated with rotatory movements of a body part.	**Pyriformis** which raises and rotates the thigh.

Skeletal System

It consists of a framework of bones and cartilages. They forms the internal framework (endoskeleton) of the body. Tendons and ligament are also associated connective tissues of the skeletal system.

Handbook of BIOLOGY

Components of Skeletal System

Bone

Hardest tissue, homeostatic reservoir of calcium, magnesium, phosphorus, etc. It is the major component of vertebrate endoskeleton.

Types of Bones

A. *On the basis of shape, there are following categories of bone*

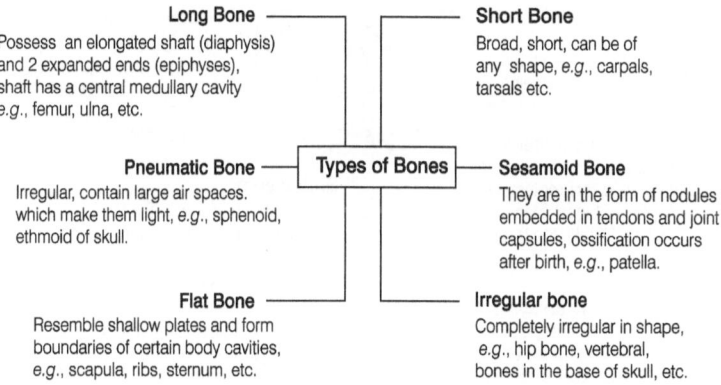

B. *On the basis of development, bones are of three types*

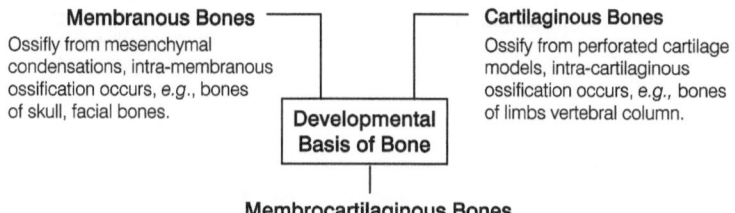

C. *Based on their histological structure, there are two major types of bone*
   (i) **Compact bone** It forms most of the diaphysis (shaft) of long bones and the thinner surfaces of all other bones. Their lamellae is surrounded into sets of concentric ring, with each set surrounding a **haversian** or **central canal**.
   (ii) **Spongy bone** It is mainly located in the epiphysis (ends) of long bones. It forms the interior of all other bones. It consists of delicate inconnecting rods or plates of bone called **trabeculae**, which add strength to bone without adding the weight.

Various components of the bone and their arrangements is shown in the figure below

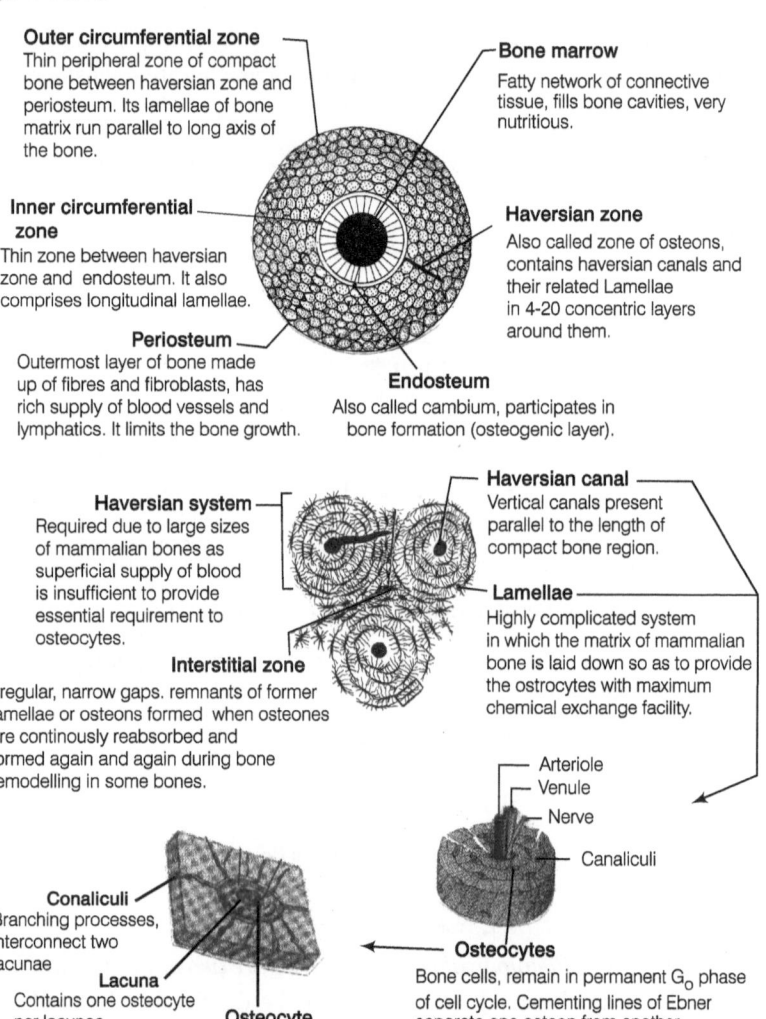

Outer circumferential zone
Thin peripheral zone of compact bone between haversian zone and periosteum. Its lamellae of bone matrix run parallel to long axis of the bone.

Bone marrow
Fatty network of connective tissue, fills bone cavities, very nutritious.

Inner circumferential zone
Thin zone between haversian zone and endosteum. It also comprises longitudinal lamellae.

Haversian zone
Also called zone of osteons, contains haversian canals and their related Lamellae in 4-20 concentric layers around them.

Periosteum
Outermost layer of bone made up of fibres and fibroblasts, has rich supply of blood vessels and lymphatics. It limits the bone growth.

Endosteum
Also called cambium, participates in bone formation (osteogenic layer).

Haversian system
Required due to large sizes of mammalian bones as superficial supply of blood is insufficient to provide essential requirement to osteocytes.

Haversian canal
Vertical canals present parallel to the length of compact bone region.

Lamellae
Highly complicated system in which the matrix of mammalian bone is laid down so as to provide the ostrocytes with maximum chemical exchange facility.

Interstitial zone
Irregular, narrow gaps. remnants of former lamellae or osteons formed when osteones are continuously reabsorbed and formed again and again during bone remodelling in some bones.

- Arteriole
- Venule
- Nerve
- Canaliculi

Conaliculi
Branching processes, interconnect two lacunae

Lacuna
Contains one osteocyte per lacunae.

Osteocyte

Osteocytes
Bone cells, remain in permanent G_O phase of cell cycle. Cementing lines of Ebner separate one osteon from another.

Generalised internal structure of bone

Cartilage

It is a semi-rigid dense connective tissue composed of cells called **chondrocytes** dispersed in a firm gel-like ground substance called **matrix**. It is non-vascular and do not contain blood vessels. Nutrients are diffused through the matrix enriched with glycosaminoglycans, proteoglycans and macromolecules that interact with collagen and elastic fibres.

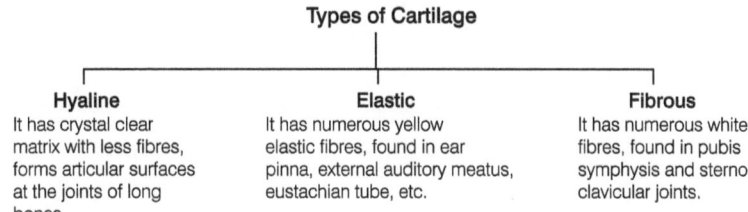

Hyaline
It has crystal clear matrix with less fibres, forms articular surfaces at the joints of long bones.

Elastic
It has numerous yellow elastic fibres, found in ear pinna, external auditory meatus, eustachian tube, etc.

Fibrous
It has numerous white fibres, found in pubis symphysis and sterno clavicular joints.

Perichondrium It is a fibrous membrane that surrounds the cartilage. It contains chondroblasts with the potential of cartilage formation. Articular cartilage that covers the bones of movable joints is devoid of perichondrium.

Joints

A joint or an articulation is a place where two bones of the skeletal system meet. **Arthrology** is the science of joint structure, function and dysfunction.

Based on the degree of motion, joints are of following types

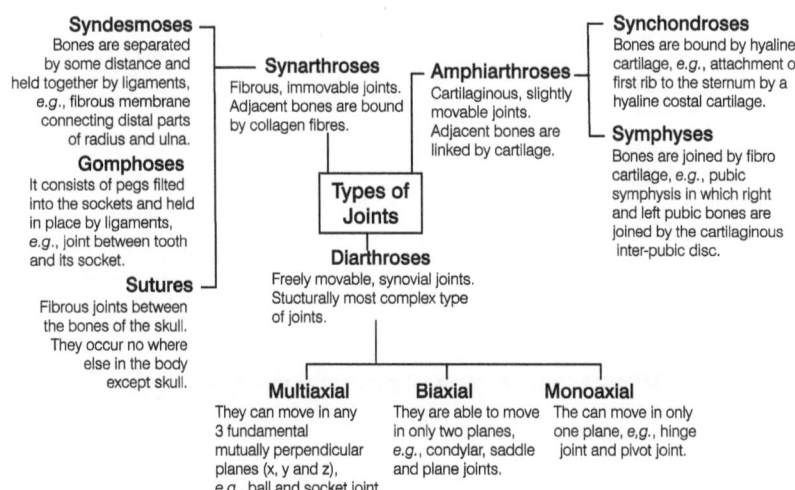

Structure of Synovial Joints (Diarthroses)

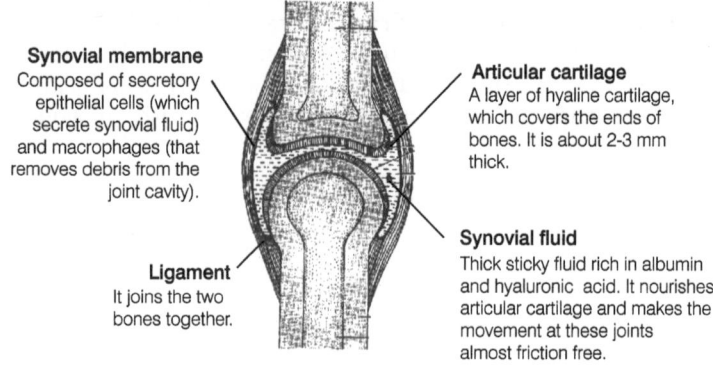

Synovial membrane
Composed of secretory epithelial cells (which secrete synovial fluid) and macrophages (that removes debris from the joint cavity).

Articular cartilage
A layer of hyaline cartilage, which covers the ends of bones. It is about 2-3 mm thick.

Ligament
It joins the two bones together.

Synovial fluid
Thick sticky fluid rich in albumin and hyaluronic acid. It nourishes articular cartilage and makes the movement at these joints almost friction free.

Types of Synovial Joint

Various type of synovail joints and their respective position in the body is given in the following figure

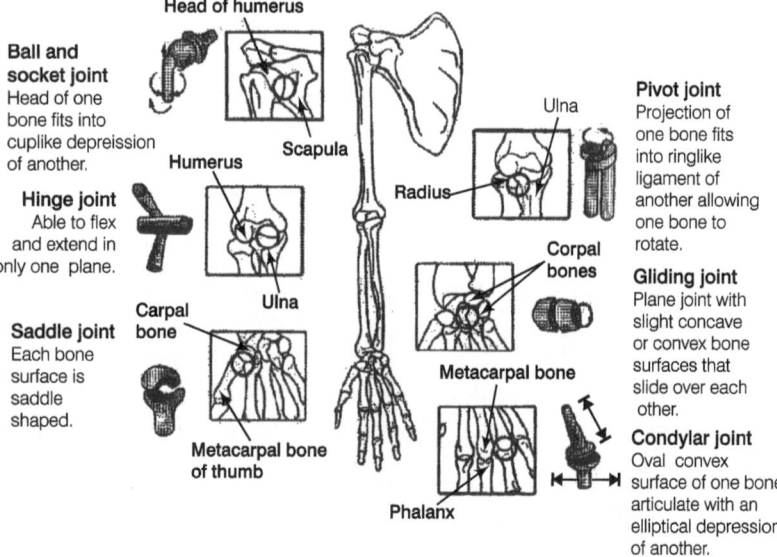

Ball and socket joint
Head of one bone fits into cuplike depreission of another.

Hinge joint
Able to flex and extend in only one plane.

Saddle joint
Each bone surface is saddle shaped.

Pivot joint
Projection of one bone fits into ringlike ligament of another allowing one bone to rotate.

Gliding joint
Plane joint with slight concave or convex bone surfaces that slide over each other.

Condylar joint
Oval convex surface of one bone articulate with an elliptical depression of another.

Different types of synovial joints in human forelimb

Types of Skeletal System

On the basis of the position of the skeletal structures in the body, *the endoskeleton is of two types*

```
                    Skeletal System
                   |              |
           Axial Skeleton    Appendicular Skeleton
```

Axial Skeleton
Present on the median longitudinal axis of the body. It consists of skull, vertebral column, sternum and ribs.

Appendicular Skeleton
Present at the lateral sides which extend outwards from the principal axis. It consists of pectoral and pelvic girdle and bones of arms and legs.

Axial Skeleton

The axial skeleton consists of 80 bones. *The various components of axial skeleton are as follows*

Bones		Numbers
Axial Skeleton		
Skull		
Braincase		
Paired	Parietal	2
	Temporal	2
Unpaired	Frontal	1
	Occipital	1
	Sphenoid	1
	Ethmoid	1
Face		
Paired	Maxilla	2
	Zygomatic	2
	Palatine	2
	Nasal	2
	Lacrimal	2
	Inferior nasal concha	2
Unpaired	Mandible	1
	Vomer	1
	Total Skull	22
Auditory Ossicles	Malleus (outer)	2
	Incus (middle)	2
	Stapes (inner)	2
	Total Auditory Ossides	6

Bones	Numbers
Hyoid	1
Vertebral Column	
Cervical vertebrae	7
Thoracic vertebrae	12
Lumbar vertebrae	5
Sacrum	1
Coccyx	1
Total Vertebral Column	26
Thoracic Cage	
Ribs	24
Sternum (3 parts, sometimes considered 3 bones)	1
Total thoracic cage	25
Total axial skeleton	80

(a) **Skull** The skull of human beings is **tropibasic**, *i.e.*, the eyes are not situated much apart and the brain and eyes are present at different planes in the skull in well defined sockets. Human skull is **dicondylic**, *i.e.*, with two occipital condyles, which connects the skull with the vertebral column.

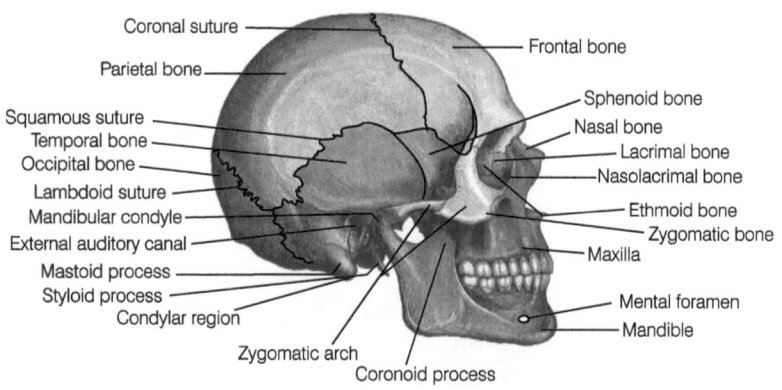

Human skull showing its various components

Handbook of BIOLOGY

Functions of Skull
This bony covering protects the brain from injuries.

The skull bears jaws (craniostylic suspension), which helps the animal for cutting and masticating the food.

(b) **Vertebral column** It is the main bone present at the axis of an individual body. Vertebrae centrum is the portion which contains the vestiges of notochord. Hence, the centrum is the main identifiable part of a vertebrae.

Various types of centrum in different animal groups are as follows

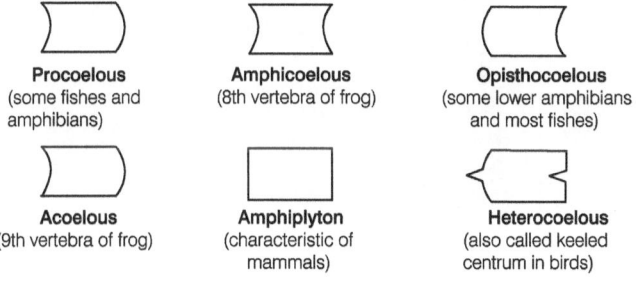

Types of cetrum

Structure of a Typical Vertebrae
Basic components of a typical vertebral include neural canal, neural arch, centrum, neural spine, and various process. *These structures in outline diagrammatic view are as follows*

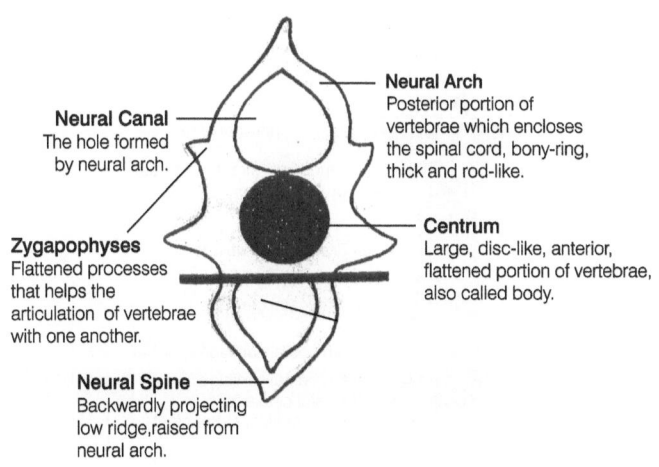

Typical vertebrae

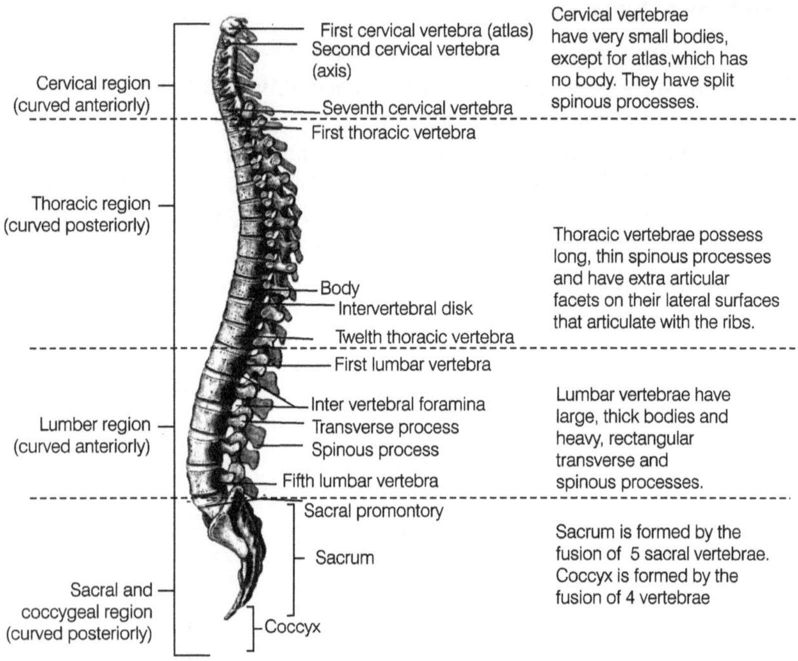

212 Handbook of BIOLOGY

Cervical region (curved anteriorly) — First cervical vertebra (atlas); Second cervical vertebra (axis); Seventh cervical vertebra; First thoracic vertebra

Cervical vertebrae have very small bodies, except for atlas, which has no body. They have split spinous processes.

Thoracic region (curved posteriorly) — Body; Intervertebral disk; Twelfth thoracic vertebra

Thoracic vertebrae possess long, thin spinous processes and have extra articular facets on their lateral surfaces that articulate with the ribs.

Lumber region (curved anteriorly) — First lumbar vertebra; Inter vertebral foramina; Transverse process; Spinous process; Fifth lumbar vertebra

Lumbar vertebrae have large, thick bodies and heavy, rectangular transverse and spinous processes.

Sacral and coccygeal region (curved posteriorly) — Sacral promontory; Sacrum; Coccyx

Sacrum is formed by the fusion of 5 sacral vertebrae. Coccyx is formed by the fusion of 4 vertebrae

Vertebral column (right leteral view)

(c) **Thoracic cage** It consists of **sternum** and **ribs**. The sternum or breast bone is a flat bone which is made up of 8 skeletal elements (sternebrae).

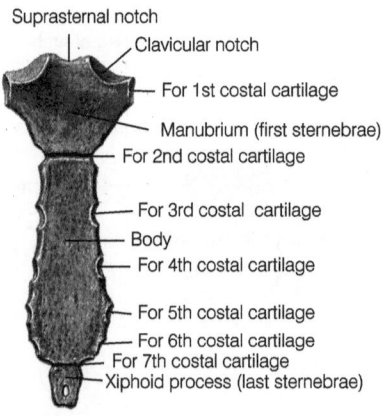

The sternum (posterior view)

In mammals, the number of thoracic ribs are equal to the number of thoracic vertebrae, *i.e.,* humans has 12 number of thoracic ribs.

A generalised rib consists of a vertebral (dorsal) part and a sternal (ventral) part.

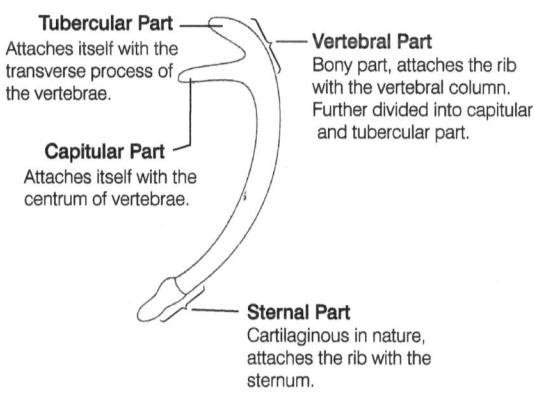

Generalised structure of a rib

Thoracic ribs of humans are double headed and classified as **true ribs**, **false ribs** and **floating ribs**. *The attachment and arrangement of ribs and sternum looks like*

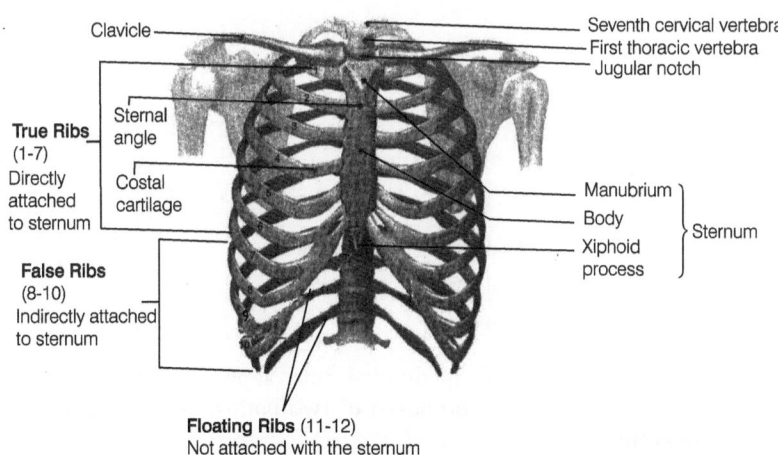

The sternum and rib cage

Appendicular Skeleton

The appendicular skeleton consists of total 126 bones. *The various components of it are as follows*

Bones	Number
Appendicular Skeleton	
Pectoral Girdle	
Scapula	2
Clavicle	2
Upper Limb	
Humerus	2
Ulna	2
Radius	2
Carpal bones	16
Metacarpal bones	10
Phalanges	28
Total girdle and upper limb	64
Pelvic Girdle	
Coxal bone	2
Lower Limb	
Femur	2
Tibia	2
Fibula	2
Patella	2
Tarsal bones	14
Metatarsal bones	10
Phalanges	28
Total girdle and lower limb	62
Total appendicular skeleton	126
Total bones	206

(a) **Pectoral girdle** It is divided into separate right and left halves. Each half is composed of two bones, *i.e.,* **scapula** and **clavicle**.

Handbook of BIOLOGY

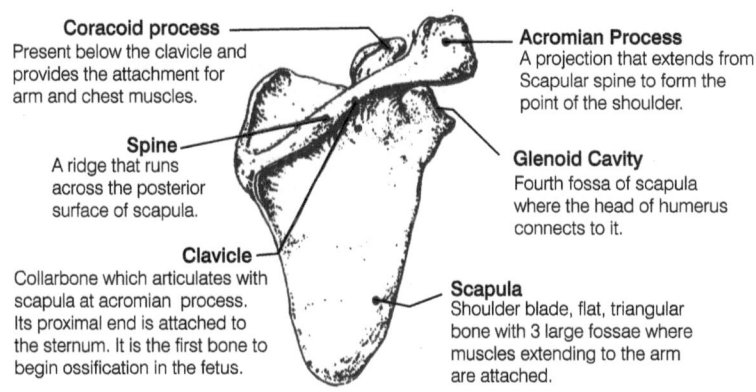

Coracoid process
Present below the clavicle and provides the attachment for arm and chest muscles.

Acromian Process
A projection that extends from Scapular spine to form the point of the shoulder.

Spine
A ridge that runs across the posterior surface of scapula.

Glenoid Cavity
Fourth fossa of scapula where the head of humerus connects to it.

Clavicle
Collarbone which articulates with scapula at acromian process. Its proximal end is attached to the sternum. It is the first bone to begin ossification in the fetus.

Scapula
Shoulder blade, flat, triangular bone with 3 large fossae where muscles extending to the arm are attached.

Components of pectoral girdle

(b) **Bones of arm or forelimb** It consists of total 60 bones including the humerus, ulna, radius, carpals, metacarpals and phallanges.

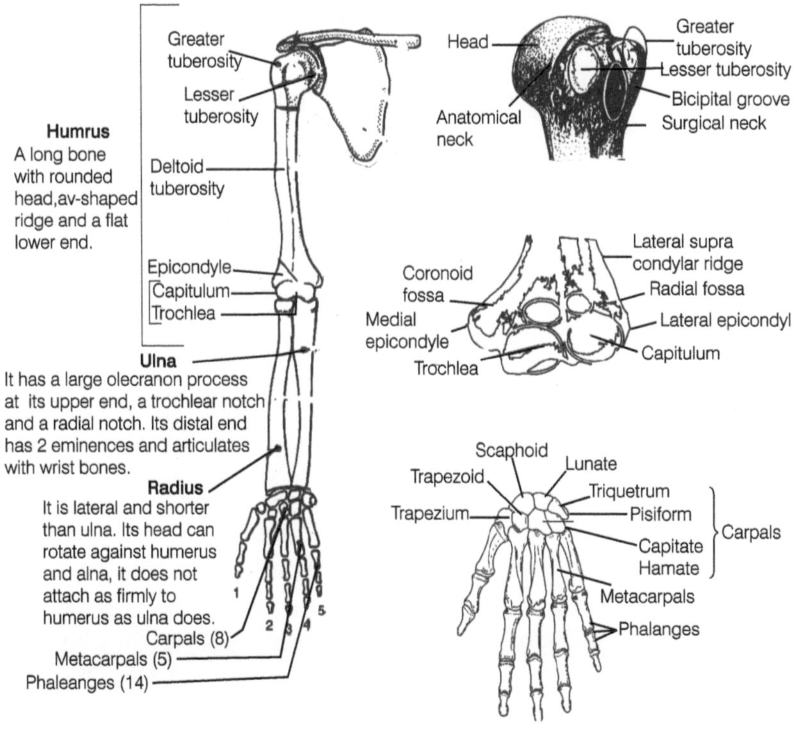

Humrus
A long bone with rounded head, av-shaped ridge and a flat lower end.

Greater tuberosity
Lesser tuberosity
Deltoid tuberosity
Epicondyle
Capitulum
Trochlea

Head
Anatomical neck
Coronoid fossa
Medial epicondyle
Trochlea

Greater tuberosity
Lesser tuberosity
Bicipital groove
Surgical neck
Lateral supra condylar ridge
Radial fossa
Lateral epicondyl
Capitulum

Ulna
It has a large olecranon process at its upper end, a trochlear notch and a radial notch. Its distal end has 2 eminences and articulates with wrist bones.

Radius
It is lateral and shorter than ulna. Its head can rotate against humerus and alna, it does not attach as firmly to humerus as ulna does.
Carpals (8)
Metacarpals (5)
Phaleanges (14)

Scaphoid
Lunate
Trapezoid
Triquetrum
Trapezium
Pisiform
Capitate
Hamate
} Carpals
Metacarpals
Phalanges

Bones of forelimb

(c) **Pelvic girdle** Each half of pelvic girdle is known as coxal or innominate bone. The right and left **coxal** or **hip bones** joins each other anteriorly and the sacrum posteriorly to form a ring of bone called the pelvic girdle.

Each coxal bone is formed by three bones fused to one another to form a single bone. The **ilium** is the most superior, the **ischium** is inferior and posterior and the **pubis** is inferior and anterior.

Acetabulum It is the socket of the hip joint. All the three bone, *i.e.*, ilium, ischium and pubis participate equally in the formation of acetabulum.

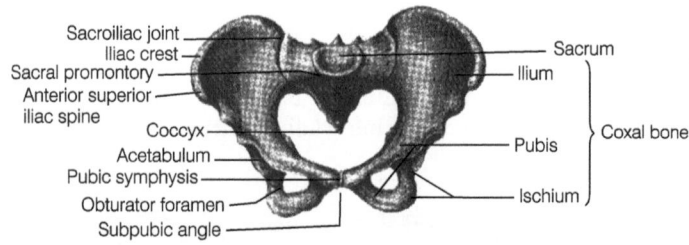

Anterosuperior view of pelvis

Handbook of **BIOLOGY**   **217**

(d) **Bones of leg or hindlimb** It consist of total 60 bones including femur, tibia, fibula, patella, tarsals, metatarsals and phallanges.

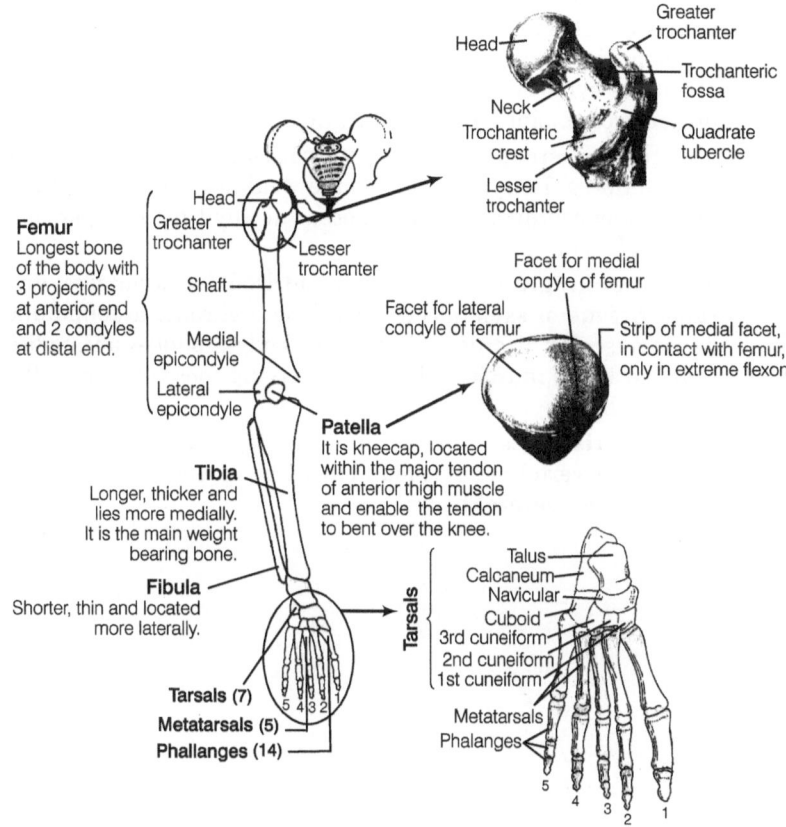

Bones of hindlimb

Disorders of Muscular and Skeletal System

(a) **Arthritis** It refers to the group of inflammatory and degenerative conditions that causes stiffness, swelling and pain in the joints.

There are several different types of arthritis each having different characteristics.

(i) **Osteoarthritis** It most often involves the knees, hips and hands and usually affects middle-aged and older people.

(ii) **Rheumatioid arthritis** It is a damaging condition that causes inflammation in joints and in other body tissues, such as heart coverings, lungs and eyes, It affects individual of all age groups.

(b) **Bursitis** It is the inflammation of the bursae present within the synovial joints as small membrane bound sockets which holds the synovial fluid. It mainly occurs due to an injury or pressure on a joint for a long duration.

(c) **Muscular dystrophy** It is a genetic disease that damages the muscle fibres. Its symptoms include weakness, loss of mobility and lack of coordination. It can occur at any time in a person's life and has no cure.

(d) **Myasthenia gravis** It is characterised by weakness and rapid fatigue of skeletal muscles. It is a chronic autoimmune neuromuscular disorder in which the body produces antibodies that block the muscle cells from receiving messages from the nerve cells.

(e) **Spondylitis** It is a chronic and developed form of arthritis that affects vertebrae. It is found in a person who keeps bending their neck for several hours.

13

Excretory Products and Their Elimination

Excretion

Excretion is the elimination of metabolic waste products from the animal body to regulate the cosmposition of the body fluids and tissues.

Various type of metabolic waste (excretory) products in animals are nitrogenous waste material, mineral salts, vitamins, hormones, etc.

Excretory Products

Depending upon the type of nitrogenous waste excreted, *animals are of three types*

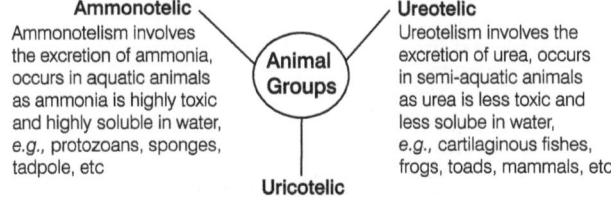

Ammonotelic
Ammonotelism involves the excretion of ammonia, occurs in aquatic animals as ammonia is highly toxic and highly soluble in water, *e.g.,* protozoans, sponges, tadpole, etc

Ureotelic
Ureotelism involves the excretion of urea, occurs in semi-aquatic animals as urea is less toxic and less solube in water, *e.g.,* cartilaginous fishes, frogs, toads, mammals, etc.

Uricotelic
Uricotelism is the excretion of uric acid, occurs in animals living in dry conditions to conserve water in their bodies, uric acid crystals are non-toxic and almost insoluble in water, *e.g.,* land crustaceans, land snails, birds, etc.

Other excretory products in different animals include
(a) **Allantoin** is the oxidation product of uric acid. The name given to this compound is because of the fact that it is excreted through the extra embryonic membrane allantois.
(b) **Hippuric acid** is seen among the excretory products only when benzoic acid is present in diet. This benzoic acid reacts with glycine to form the hippuric acid. It is present in traces in human urine.
(c) **Amino acids** are excreted in certain invertebrates like *Unio*, *Limnaea* (molluscans) and *Asterias* (echinoderm). These animals are called aminotelic and the phenomenon is called **Aminotelism**.
(d) **Guanine** is the excretory material of spiders. The mode of formation of guanine is not clear. It is excreted in almost solid form.
(e) **Creatine** is seen as excretory product in foetus, pregnant and the lactating women. It is most probably associated with the processes of histolysis and histogenesis going on in above written examples.
(f) **Creatinine** is the end product of creatine metabolism.

Human Excretory System

The human excretory system functions to remove waste products from the human body. This system consists of specialised structures and capillary networks that assist in the excretory processes. The human excretory system includes two kidneys (possessing its functional unit, the nephron), two ureters, urinary bladder and urethra.

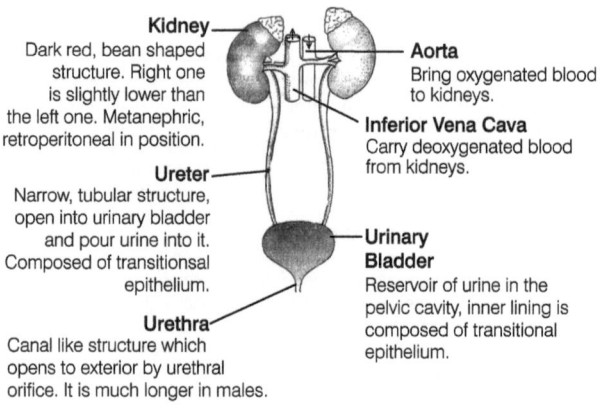

Human urinary system

Handbook of BIOLOGY

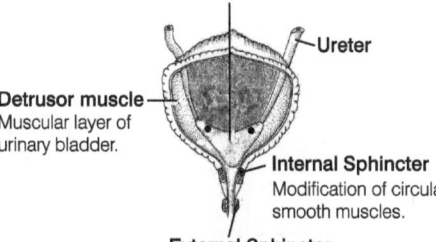

Trigone
Consists of 3 openings, 2 of ureters and one through which urethra leaves the bladder.

Ureter

Detrusor muscle
Muscular layer of urinary bladder.

Internal Sphincter
Modification of circular smooth muscles.

External Sphincter
Made up of skeleton muscles which is under voluntary control of nervous system.

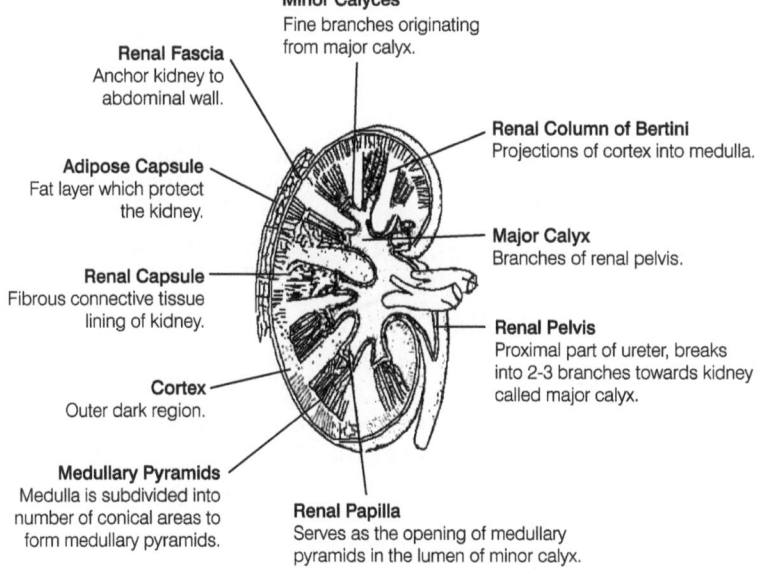

Minor Calyces
Fine branches originating from major calyx.

Renal Fascia
Anchor kidney to abdominal wall.

Renal Column of Bertini
Projections of cortex into medulla.

Adipose Capsule
Fat layer which protect the kidney.

Major Calyx
Branches of renal pelvis.

Renal Capsule
Fibrous connective tissue lining of kidney.

Renal Pelvis
Proximal part of ureter, breaks into 2-3 branches towards kidney called major calyx.

Cortex
Outer dark region.

Medullary Pyramids
Medulla is subdivided into number of conical areas to form medullary pyramids.

Renal Papilla
Serves as the opening of medullary pyramids in the lumen of minor calyx.

Longitudinal section of kidney

Handbook of BIOLOGY

Proximal Convoluted Tubule
Lined by single layer cuboidal cells bearing microvilli, in between microvilli apical canaliculi occurs which are involved in the cellular mechanism of protein from the filtrate.

Malpighian Corpuscle { **Glomerulus**, **Bowman's Capsule** }

Descending Limb
Lined by simple cuboidal epithelium with few cells and small microvilli

Ascending Limb
Length of cells increases in this region, cells are not brush bordered

Main Loop
Length of cells is minimised in this region

Collecting Duct
20 mm long tube, lined by cuboidal cells. Several collecting tubes join to form the duct of Bellini.

Distal Convoluted Tubule
Situated in the cortex region of kidney, lined by cuboidal epithelium without true brush border

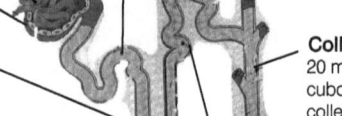

Nephron showing blood vessels, duct and tubule

Afferent Arteriole
Short and wide capillaries, which break up into 20-50 glomerular tufts.

Efferent Arteriole
Narrow and long capillaries which forms a fine peritubular capillary network around renal tubule a part of which form vasa rector (runparalled to henle loop)

Bowman's Capsule
Double walled epithetial sac consisting of outer parietal and inner visceral layer. Parietal layer consists of squamous epithelium and visceral layer bears podocyte.

Glomerulus
Capillary tuft present in the concavity of Bowman's capsule, capillaries have arterial parts at both the ends. Blood pressure in glomerulus is much higher than else where in the body

Malpighian body

Urine Formation

Urine formation in human beings occurs in following two steps

1. Urea Formation within the Liver

The centre process of urea formation takes place with the cycle called **ornithine cycle** or **Kreb Hanseleit cycle**.

Handbook of **BIOLOGY**

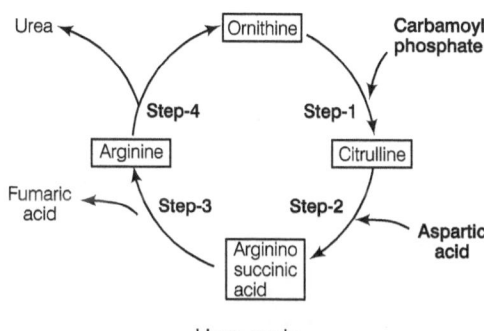

Urea cycle

2. Formation of Urine by the Kidney

It can be divided into following three sub-categories
  (i) Glomerular filtration or ultrafiltration
  (ii) Selective reabsorption
  (iii) Tubular secretion

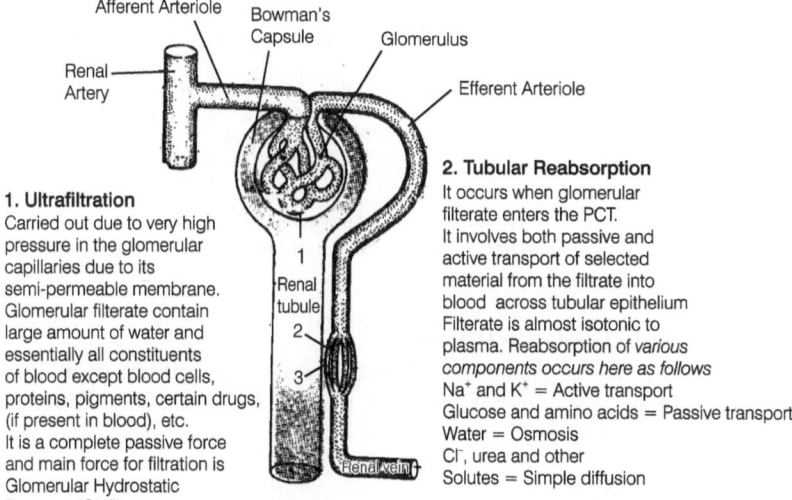

1. Ultrafiltration
Carried out due to very high pressure in the glomerular capillaries due to its semi-permeable membrane. Glomerular filtrate contain large amount of water and essentially all constituents of blood except blood cells, proteins, pigments, certain drugs, (if present in blood), etc.
It is a complete passive force and main force for filtration is Glomerular Hydrostatic Pressure (GHP).

2. Tubular Reabsorption
It occurs when glomerular filterate enters the PCT.
It involves both passive and active transport of selected material from the filtrate into blood across tubular epithelium Filterate is almost isotonic to plasma. Reabsorption of *various components occurs here as follows*
Na^+ and K^+ = Active transport
Glucose and amino acids = Passive transport
Water = Osmosis
Cl^-, urea and other
Solutes = Simple diffusion

3. Tubular Secretion
It is the removal of selected components from the blood of the peritubular blood capillaries into the nephric filtrate. It involves the active transport of ammonia, urea, uric acid, creatine, hippuric acid, drugs like penicillin, etc.

Processes involved in urine formation by kidney

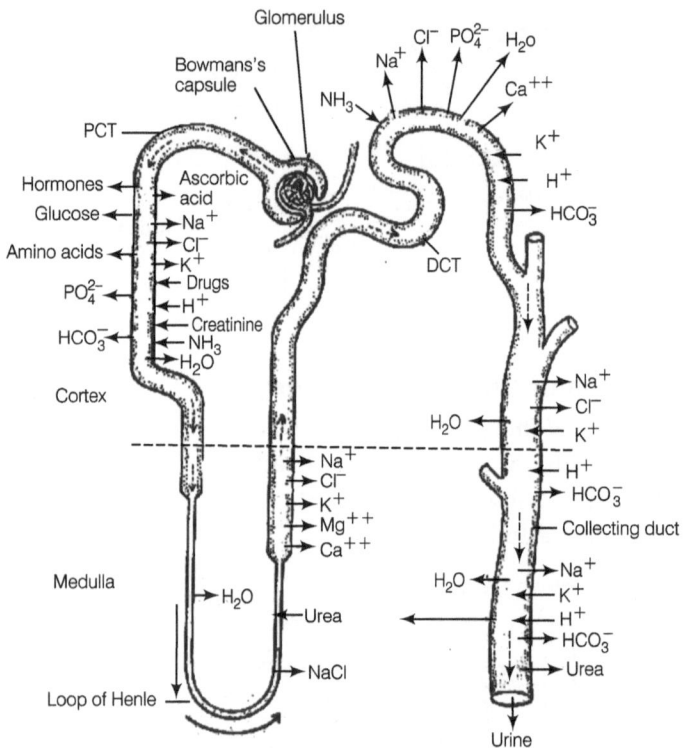

Tubular reabsorption and secretion of major substances in mammalian nephron.

Glomerular Filtration Rate (GFR)

It is the quantity of glomerular filtrate formed per minute in all the nephrons of both kidneys. In normal person, GFR is 125 ml/min or about 180 litres per day.

Filtration Fraction

It is the fraction of the renal plasma which becomes the filtrate. It is the ratio between the renal plasma flow and glomerular filtrate which is expressed in percentage. The normal filtration fraction varies from 15-20%.

Handbook of BIOLOGY

$$\text{Filtration Fraction} = \frac{\text{Glomerular filtration rate}}{\text{Renal plasma flow}} \times 100$$

$$= \frac{125}{650 - 700}$$

$$= 17.8 - 19.2\%$$

(The renal plasma flow is about 650-700 mL/m or about 940 litres/day.)

Pressures in the Renal Circulation

During renal circulation, pressure varies at different region of nephron as follows

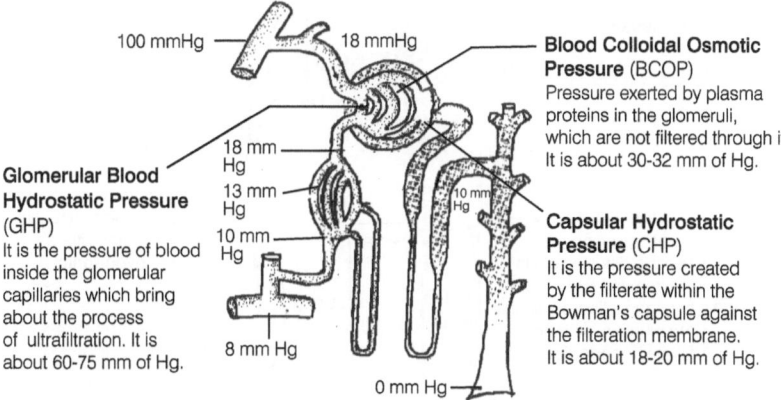

Pressures at different points in the vessels and tubules of nephron

Effective Filtration Pressure (EFP)

It is the total pressure that promotes filtration (as both BCOP and CHP opposes the process of filtration).

It can be calculated as

$$\text{EFP} = \text{GHP} - (\text{BCOP} + \text{CHP})$$
$$= 60 - 75 \text{ mmHg} (30 - 30 \text{ mmHg} + 18 - 20 \text{ mmHg})$$
$$= 10 - 25 \text{ mmHg}.$$

Thus, a pressure of about 10 – 25 mmHg causes a normal amount of blood plasma to filter from the glomerulus into the Bowman's capsule.

Mechanism of Filtrate Concentration

Mammals have the ability to produce a concentrated or hypertonic urine. The different phases through which the urine becomes hypertonic in relation to body fluids have been studied by **Wirz** and associates (1951) and later on by **Bray** (1960).

It is a complex process and related to the anatomical distribution of tubules along with Na$^+$ ion concentration at different depths from the cortex towards the medulla of kidney.

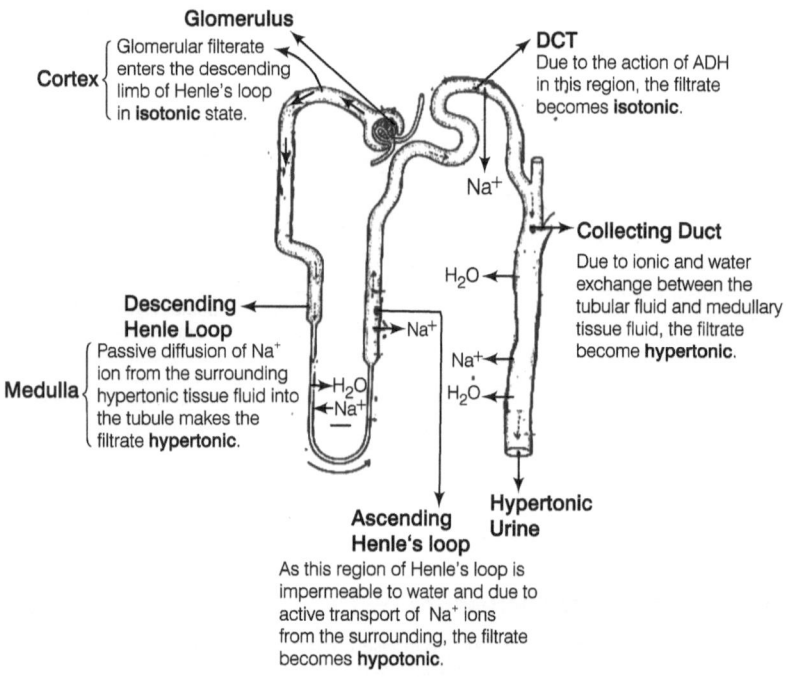

Mechanism of tubular reabsorption and secretion

Countercurrent Mechanism

The theory of countercurrent mechanism was given by **Berliner** *et. al.* (1958). According to this theory, the role vasa recta is very important in urine concentration.

The flow of the filtrate in the two limbs of vasa recta is in opposite direction similarly as in the two limbs of Henle's loop.

The arrangement of vasa recta and Henle's loop can be seen as side wise.

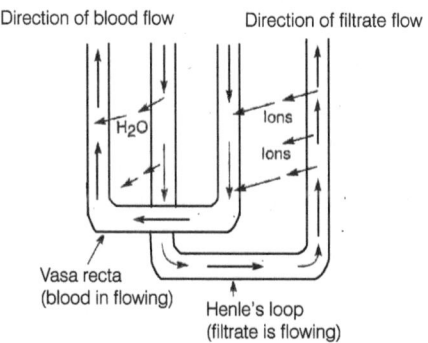

Arrangement of vasa recta and Henle's loop

As the descending limb of vasa recta gradually enters deep into the medulla some water diffuses out from it and more ions are taken in. In the ascending limb, on the other hand, the diffusion process is just in opposite direction thus isotonic blood leaves the medulla.

The counter exchange reduces the rate of dessipation thus reduces the rate at which the counter current multiplier must pump Na^+ to maintain any given gradient.

Regulation of Kidney Function

The functions of kidneys are regulated by following three mechanism

Control by JGA

Juxta Glomerular Apparatus works through RAAS, *i.e.*, renin-Angiotensin-Aldosteron-system when the blood pressure is decreased.
In response, **Renin** enzyme is released from JG cells. Rennin act upon plasma protein **angiotensinogen** and convert it to a protein **angiotension II**. Angiotensin II increases blood pressure by constricting the thearterioles, by increasing water and NaCl reabsorption in PCT and by stimulating adrenal gland to secrete **aldosterone** which work on DCT for the same cause.

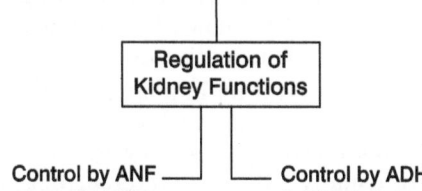

Control by ANF
Atrial natriuretic factor opposes the RAAS. ANF is released by atrial walls in response to increased blood pressure. It inhibits the release of renin from JGA, reduces aldosterone release from adrenal gland and inhibit NaCl reabsorption by collecting duct.

Control by ADH
Antidiuretic hormone is produced by hypothalamus and secreted by posterior lobe of pituitary gland. When osmolarity of blood increases above 300 mos mL^{-1}. In response, osmoreceptors of hypothalamus promote thirst.

Micturition

The expulsion of urine from the urinary bladder is called micturition. It is a reflex process, but in grown up children and adults, it can be controlled voluntarily.

The urinary bladder and the internal sphincter are supplied by both sympathetic and parasympathetic nerves whereas, the external sphincter is supplied by the somatic nerve.

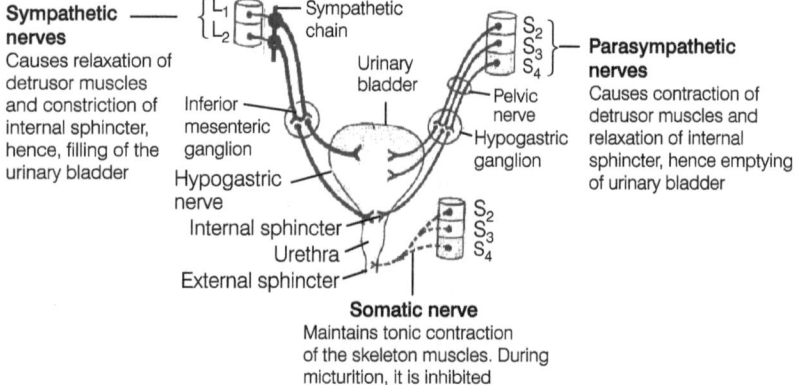

Nerve supply to urethra and urinary bladder

Disorders of Excretory System

(a) **Glomerulonephritis** It is also called Bright's disease which is caused by the injury to the kidney, by congenital kidney defects or by an allergic reaction to the toxins of bacteria such as Streptococci. The glomeruli become inflamed and engorged with blood. Proteins and red blood cells enter the filtrate.

(b) **Kidney stone** The stone in the kidney gives rise to severe colic pain starting in the back and radiating down to the front of the thigh. It may come down in the bladder and would cause frequent and painful urination and blood in urine.

(c) **Pyelonephritis** It is an inflammation of the renal pelvis and the medullary tissue of the kidney. It is usually caused by bacteria that reaches the kidney by the way of urethra and ureter. It usually affects countercurrent mechanism in the medulla. Affected person has inability to concentrate his urine.

(d) **Renal tubular acidosis** In this condition, the person is unable to secrete the adequate quantities of hydrogen ions and as a result, large amount of sodium bicarbonate are continuously lost into the urine.

14

Neural Control *and* Coordination

Nervous system is the master controlling and communicating system of the body by means of which the activities of the animal and its awareness and reaction to outside environment are co-ordinated.

Human Neural System

Humans have highly integrated nervous (or neural) system and for the convenience of study it can be divided into two principal parts.

Human Neural System

Central Nervous System
Dorsally placed structure lying along the mid-dorsal axis of the body. It is the integrating and command centre of the nervous system.

Peripheral Nervous System
This system consists of nerves that extend from the brain and spinal cord and known as cranial nerves and spinal nerves, respectively.

Brain
Anterior most part, lodged in the cranial cavity of skull.

Spinal Cord
Posterior part, run mid-dorsally within vertebral column.

Sensory or Afferent Division
Consists of nerve fibres that convey impulses to CNS from sensory receptors located in the body.

Motor or Efferent Division
Consists of nerve fibres that transmit impulses from the CNS to effector organs, *i.e.*, muscles and glands.

Somatic Nervous System (SNS)
Consists of somatic motor fibres (axons) that conduct impulse from CNS to skeletal muscles, allows conscious control over skeletal muscles (voluntary nervous system).

Autonomic Nervous System (ANS)
Consists of visceral motor fibres that regulate the activities of smooth muscles, cardiac muscles and glands. (involuntary nervous system).

Sympathetic NS
It mobilise body during emergency situations.

Parasympathetic NS
This system conserve energy and promotes non-emergency functions.

Central Nervous System

It consists of two major divisions, *i.e.*, brain and spinal cord.

Brain

It is the highly coordinated centre of the human body which weighs about 1220 to 1400 grams.

The human brain is covered by three membranes or **meninges** (sing. *meninx*) namely piameter, arachnoid membrane and duramater.

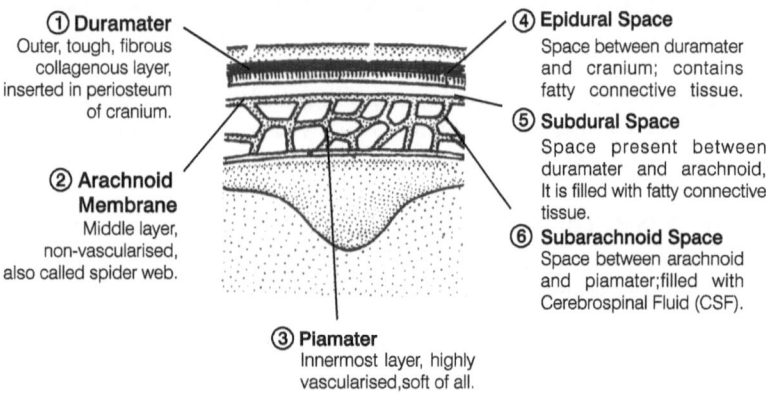

① **Duramater** Outer, tough, fibrous collagenous layer, inserted in periosteum of cranium.

② **Arachnoid Membrane** Middle layer, non-vascularised, also called spider web.

③ **Piamater** Innermost layer, highly vascularised, soft of all.

④ **Epidural Space** Space between duramater and cranium; contains fatty connective tissue.

⑤ **Subdural Space** Space present between duramater and arachnoid, It is filled with fatty connective tissue.

⑥ **Subarachnoid Space** Space between arachnoid and piamater; filled with Cerebrospinal Fluid (CSF).

Meninges of brain: (1), (2) and (3) = Meninges; (4), (5) and (6) = Space between them

The human brain is divisible into three parts as follows

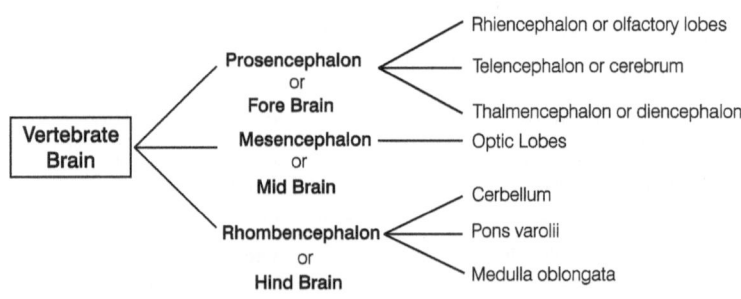

Forebrain

(a) **Rhiencephalon** Anterioventral part of forebrain, functionally related to smell, consists of olfactory lobes as paired, fused posterior portion.

Handbook of BIOLOGY

The variations in rhiencephalon in different animal groups is shown in the figures below

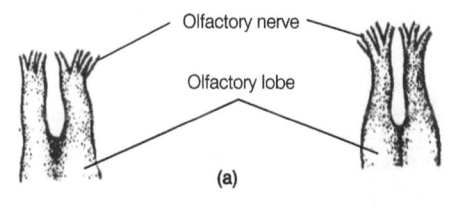

Olfactory region relatively smaller, major part is formed by olfactory lobes, anterior most portion runs as olfactory nerves into nasal chambers.

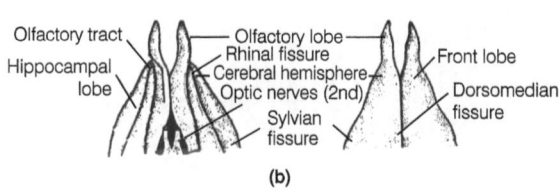

Olfactory region relatively larger, lobes are smaller, major part is formed by olfactory tract, a rhynial fissure separate both lobes from cerebral lobes.

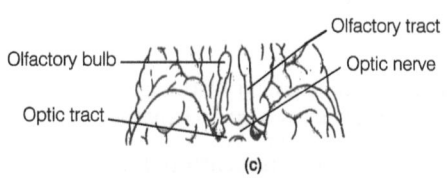

Anterior portion is lost Hence, the lobes look ventral in position as olfactory bulbs.

Olfactory lobes : (a) frog, (b) rabbit (c) human

(b) **Telencephalon** Most developed part in humans, perform specialised functions like intelligence, learning skills, memory, speech, etc. It has shown maximum development during evolution, in particular its **roof** (pallium) in vertebrates other than mammals.

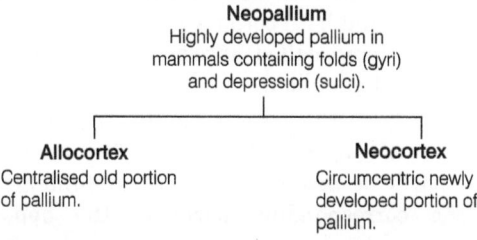

Lobes of Cerebrum Cerebrum consists of two lobes, *i.e.*, right and left, which are separated by a deep **longitudinal fissure**.

Each hemisphere has a thick central core of **white matter** containing bundles of myelinated axons.

Cerebral cortex Forms the thin outer layer of **grey matter**, containing the cell bodies of the neurons.

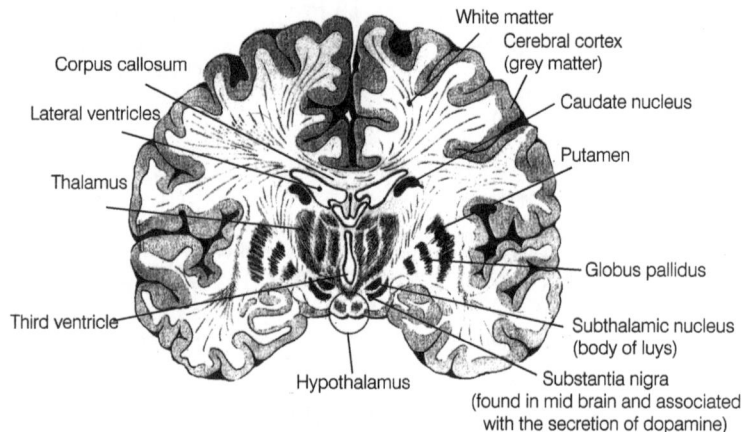

Transverse section of brain showing white matter, grey matter and components of basal ganglion

Basal Ganglion (or nuclei) These are the scattered masses or bulges of grey matter, which are submerged into the white matter (subcortex) of cerebrum.

They constitutes the five structures namely, **caudate nucleus, putamen, globus pallidus, subthalamic nuclei** and **substantia nigra.** The main function of basal nuclei is to control and regulate stereotypic (3D) movements.

Corpus Striatum It is the structure formed by the association of caudate nucleus, putamen and globus pallidus. In mammals, it is present in frontal lobe and both corpora striate are connected with the help of a nerve fibre band called anterior commissure. It forms the largest nucleus of basal ganglion.

Corpus Callosum It is the largest bundle of fibres which connect the two hemispheres of cerebrum. Most of the fibres of corpus callosum arises from the parts of neocortex of one cerebral hemisphere and terminate in the corresponding parts of the opposite cerebral hemisphere. It is a unique feature of mammals.

It is divided into 4 parts namely rostrum, genu, body (or trunk) and splenium. It is the characteristic feature of mammals only.

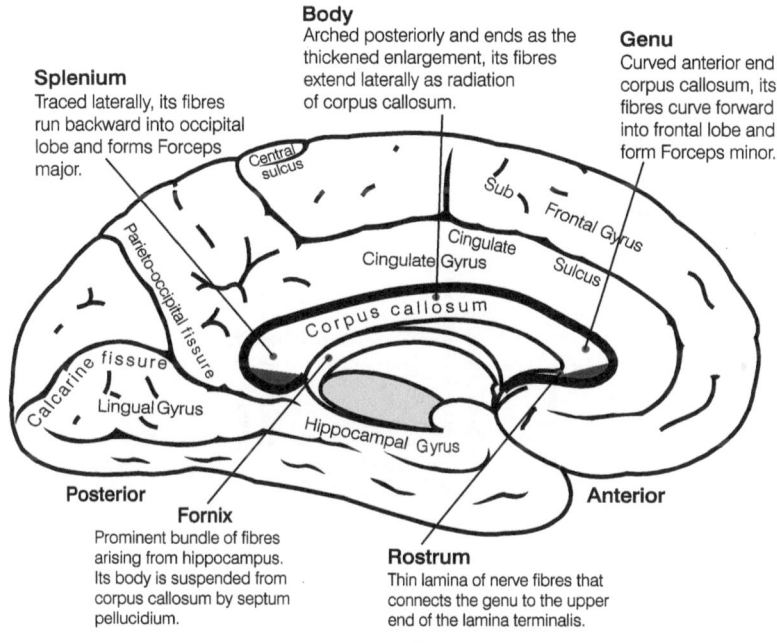

Corpus callosum

Each cerebral hemisphere is further divided into five lobes namely parietal, occipital, temporal, frontal and insular (not visible from outside).

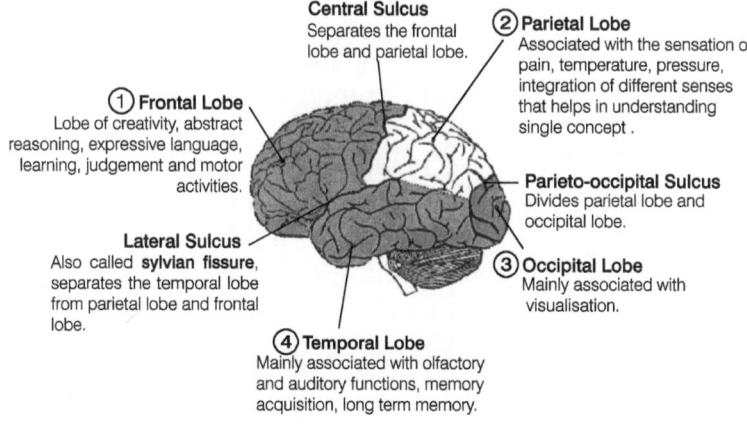

Major lobes and sulcus of brain

Specialised Regions Present in Cerebral Hemisphere

The cerebral cortex has three principal functions
  (i) Receiving sensory input
  (ii) Integrating sensory information
  (iii) Generating motor responses.

These functions are performed by special areas in cerebrum, which are described in the figure below

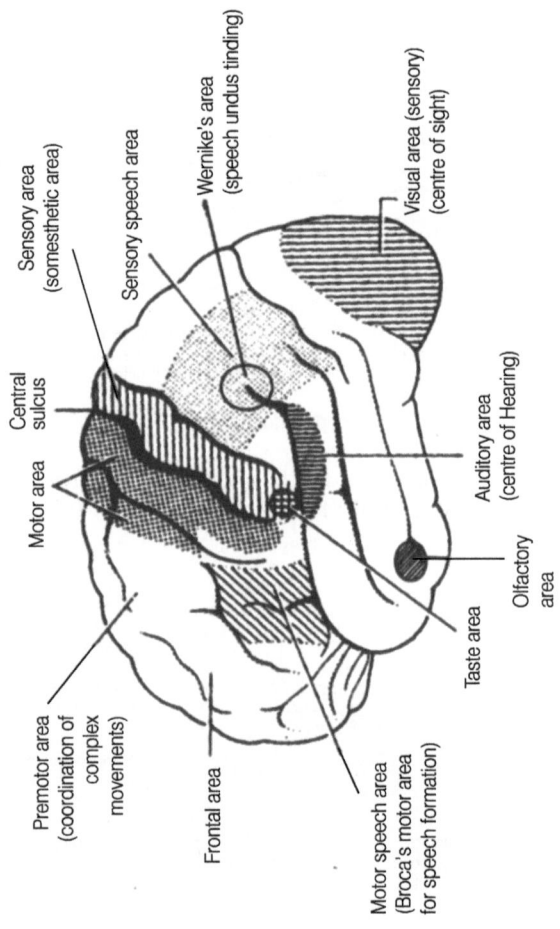

The three major specialised regions of the cerebrum are

(i) **The primary motor cortex** It occupies a single ridge on each hemisphere in front of central sulcus.

The pathway of voluntary movements carried out by primary motor cortex is as follows

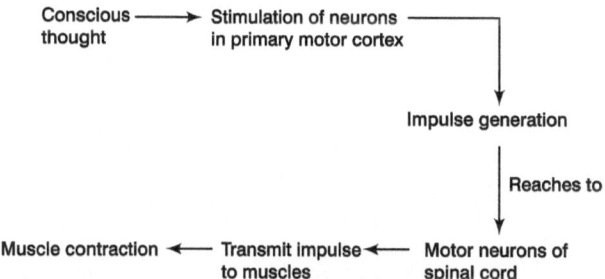

(ii) **The primary sensory cortex** It lies just behind the central sulcus as a ridge of tissue running parallel to the primary motor cortex. It is the final destination of many sensory impulses travelling to the brain. It receives the sensory information from the body.

(iii) **Association cortex** It consists of large regions of cerebral cortex where integration occurs. Here, information is interpreted, made sense of, and acted upon. It also carries out more complex functions.

Neuron of Cerebral Cortex

Cerebral cortex is composed of two major types of neurons, i.e.,

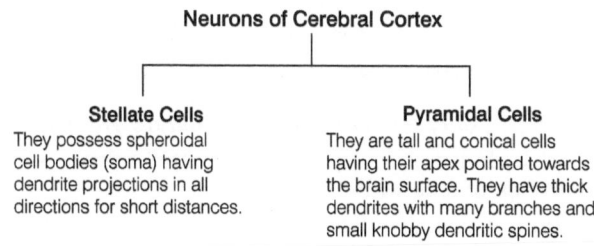

Limbic System The medial border of temporal lobe is called limbic system. It is a loop of cortical structures, surrounding the corpus callosum and thalamus. Its four major components are hippocampus, amygdala, septal nuclei and mammillary bodies.

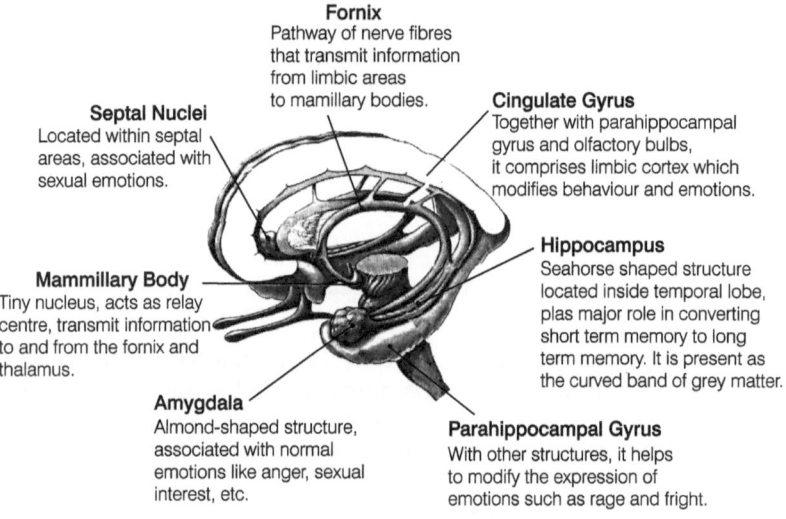

Limbic system and its associated structures

Diencephalon *It is the posterioventral part of the brain and formed by three structures as follows*

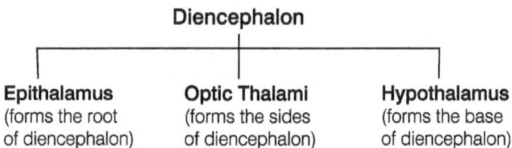

In case of humans, only two parts of diencephalon are defined
- **Thalamus** Includes roof (epithalamus) and upper portion with medial portions of side walls.
- **Hypothalamus** Includes floor along with lower side walls.

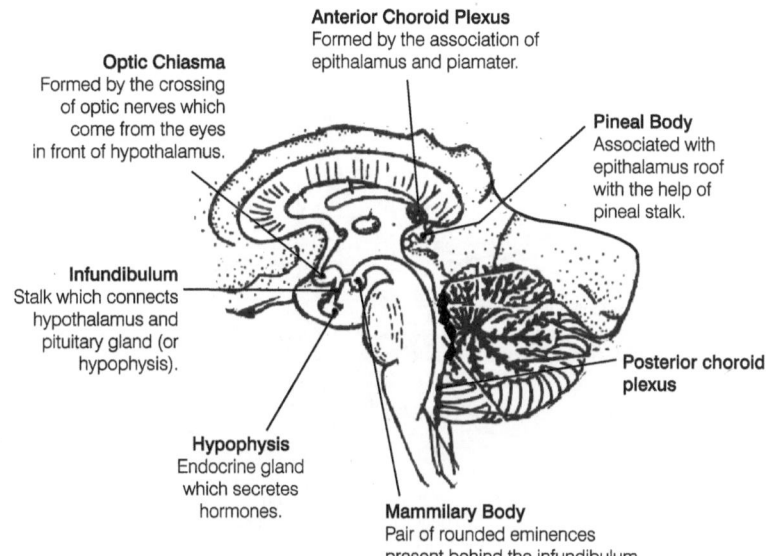

Components of diencephalon

Thalamus It is present just beneath the cerebrum. It is a relay centre. It receives all sensory inputs, except for smell, and then relays it to the sensory and association cortex.

Hypothalamus It is present beneath the thalamus. It consists of many groups of nerve cells called **nuclei** which control a variety of autonomic functions and helps to maintain homeostasis (such as appetite, body temperature, blood pressure, etc). It also regulates the functioning of pituitary gland.

Midbrain

The midbrain contains optic lobes. These lobes are two in case of frog and called as **corpora bigemina** (hollow structures).

In case of humans, they are four in number and called as **corpora quadrigemina** (solid structures).

In humans, the four lobes are defined in two pairs as superior and inferior colliculus.

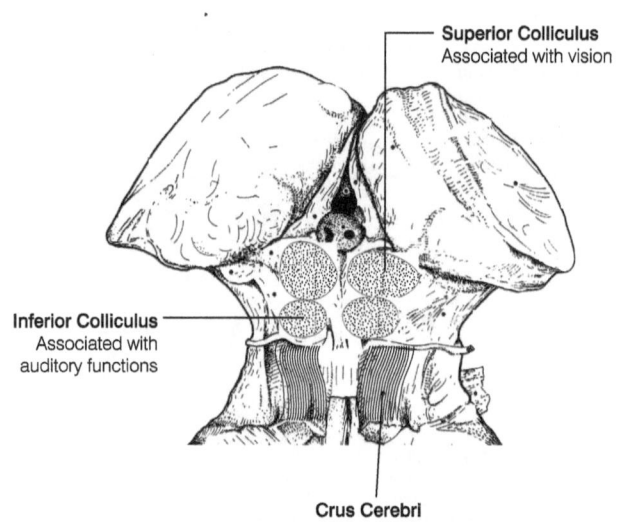

Posterior view of brain showing the components of midbrain

The functions performed by superior and inferior colliculi are originally taken up by cerebrum. Crus cerebri functions to relay impulses back and forth between the cerebrum, cerebellum, pons and medulla.

Hindbrain

It basically consists of cerebellum (metencephalon), medulla oblongata (myelencephalon) and pons varolii. Collectively, these three structures forms the **brain stem**.

(i) Cerebellum

It is the second largest part of brain and considered as small brain or little cerebrum. From birth with the age of 2 yrs, it grows faster than the rest of the brain.

It consist of 2 cerebellar hemispheres with a central worm-shaped vermis.

The various structural components of cerebellum are as follows

(a) **Arbor vitae** It is the tree of life present in the internal region of cerebellum. It is the profuse ramifications of white matter into the grey matter. Externally, its surface contains gyri and sulci.

(b) **Cerebellar peduncles** These are the bundles of fibres connecting the cerebellum with the underlying brainstem. *On the basis of their position, they are of three types*

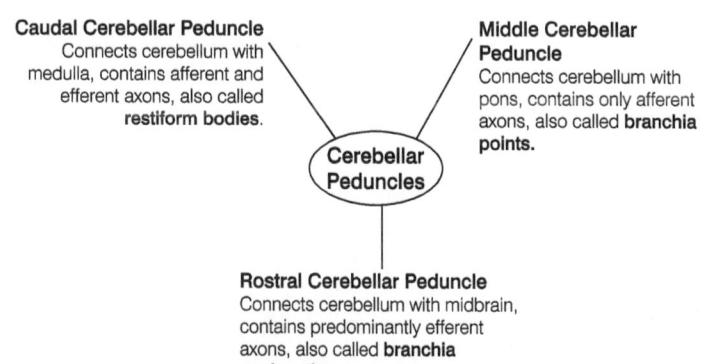

(c) **Cerebellar cortex** It is the surface grey matter of the cerebellum. *It consists of three layers as follows*

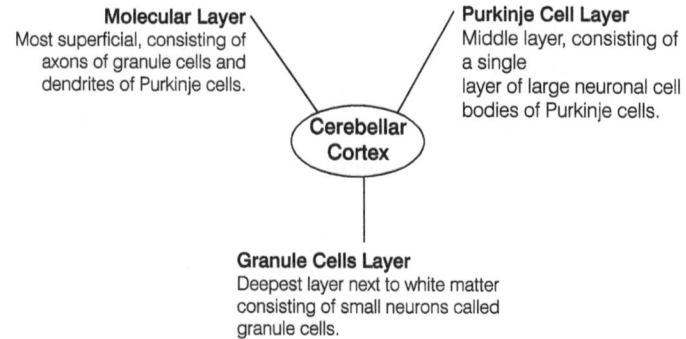

Cerebellar cortex also contains various cell types as follows

- **Purkinje cells** These are the only output neuron from the cerebellar cortex; it utilises the neurotrans mitter GABA (Gamma Amino Butyric Acid) to inhibit neurons in deep cerebellar nuclei. These flask-shaped Purkinje cells are considered as one of the largest and most complex neurons.
- **Granule cells** These are the intrinsic cells of cerebellar cortex; they use glutamate as an excitatory transmitter; they excites Purkinje cells *via* axonal branches called parallel fibres.
- **Basket cells** These are the inhibitory interneurons, they utilises GABA to inhibit Purkinje cells.

Functions of Cerebellum

- Maintenance of balance and posture.
- Coordination of voluntary movements by modulating timing and force of muscle groups.
- Motor learning through adaptation and fine-tuning in solving a motor problem.
- Cognitive functions associated with language.

(ii) Pons Varolii

It is present at the axis of brain in front of cerebellum below the midbrain and above medulla oblongata. It is considered as a link between upper portion of brain and spinal cord through medulla oblongata.

It contain nerve fibres which forms a bridge called **pons bridge** in between the two cerebellar hemispheres.

Function

It contains pneumotoxic centre and helps in regulating breathing movements.

(iii) Medulla Oblongata

It is the triangular part of the brain. Its roof is associated with overlying piamater to form the posterior choroid plexus.

Function

(i) It receive and integrate signals from spinal cord and send them to cerebellum and thalamus.

(ii) It regulates heart rate, blood pressure, swallowing salivation, vomiting and some other involuntary movements.

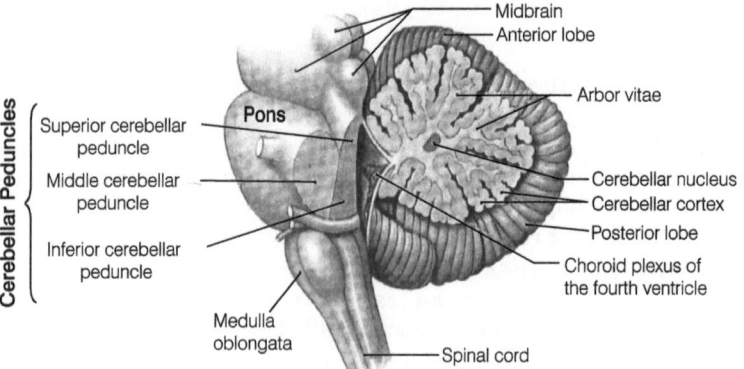

Lateral view of brain showing the components of hindbrain

Brain Ventricles

The ventricles consists of four hollow, fluid filled spaces inside the brain. *These are as follows*

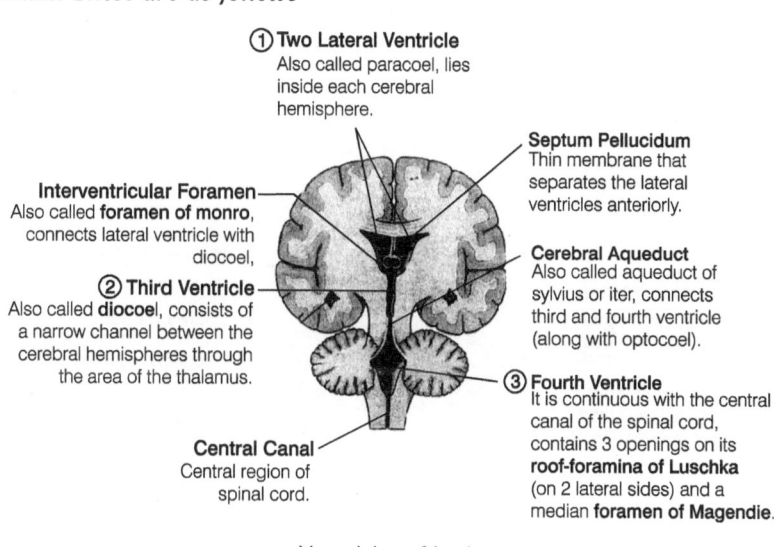

Ventricles of brain

Cerebrospinal Fluid (CSF)

It is the watery liquid that is found between the inner and outer layers of meninges. It also fills the internal cavities in the brain and spinal cord. CSF is secreted by anterior and posterior choroid plexus. It is similar in composition to blood plasma and interstitial fluid.

Function of CSF

(i) **Protection of brain and spinal cord** CSF protects the delicate brain and spinal cord by providing shock-absorbing medium. It acts as **cushion jolts** to the central nervous system.

(ii) **Buoyancy to the brain** Since, the brain is immersed in the CSF, the net weight of the brain is reduced from about 1.4 kg to about 0.18 kg. Thus, the pressure at the base is reduced.

(iii) **Excretion** CSF carries harmful metabolic wastes, drugs and other substances from the brain to the blood.

(iv) **Detection of infections** As CSF bathes the CNS, examining small amounts of CSF can provide physicians a means of detecting infections in the brain, spinal cord and meninges. Samples of CSF are obtained by inserting a needle between 3rd and 4th lumbar vertebrae (lumbar puncture).

Spinal Cord

Spinal cord is the part of dorsal nerve cord present in continuation with brain. It lies in the neural canal of the vertebral column. Like rain, it is also surrounded by 3 meninges namely piamater (inner), arachnoid membrane (middle) and duramater (outer).

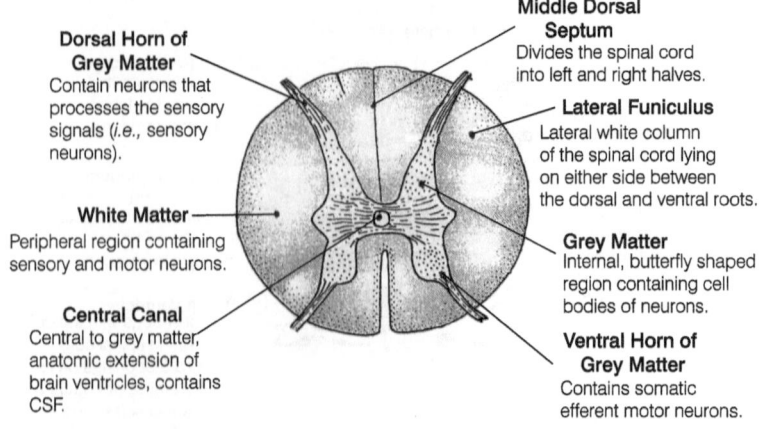

T.S. of spinalcord

Horns These are the projections of grey matter into the white matter and their presence gives a butterfly appearance to the spinal cord in TS.

Conus terminalis or medullaris It is the termination point of the spinal cord. In humans, this point is situated in L-2 region.

Filum terminal It is a long slender filament at the end of the spinal cord in the caudal region. It consists of vascular meninges, i.e., piamater or pia arachnoid matter. It anchors the spinal cord within the vertebral column.

In the TS of spinal cord, certain tracts are also seen. These tracts are meant for the vertical communication of spinal cord with brain. *These are*

(a) **Ascending tracts** They take information to the brain.

(b) **Descending tracts** They bring information from the brain.

Peripheral Nervous System (PNS)

The PNS transmits information to and from the CNS and plays a major role in regulating movements and internal environment. It consists of cranial and spinal nerves.

Cranial nerves They originate in the brain and terminate mostly in the organs of the head and upper body. Mammals have 12 pairs of cranial nerves.

Cranial Nerves in Humans

	Types of Cranial Nerves	From	To	Nature
I	**Olfactory**	Olfactory lobe	Olfactory epithelium	S
II	**Optic**	Optic chiasma	Eye retina	S
III	**Oculomotor**	Crus cerebrum	Four muscles of eye ball, iris, ciliary body	Mo
IV	**Trochlear** (smallest nerve)	Midbrain	Superior oblique muscles of eye	Mo
V	**Trigeminal** (largest nerve)	Pons varolii		Mix
	V_1- Ophthalmic		Eye, eyelids, snout	S
	V_2- Maxillary		Upper jaw, cheeks and lower eyelids	S
	V_3- Mandibular		Lower jaw, lip, tongue, external ear	Mix
VI	**Abducens**	Pons	Lateral rectus muscles of eye	Mo
VII	**Facial**	Pons		Mix
	VII_1- Palatinus		Palate	S
	VII_2- Tympani		Tongue, salivary gland, taste buds	S
	VII_3- Hyomandibular		Lower Jaw, pinna, neck, hyoid	Mix
VIII	**Auditory**	Medulla		S
	VIII_1- Vestibular		Internal ear	S
	VIII_2- Cochlear		Cochlea	S
IX	**Glossopharyngeal**	Medulla		Mix
	IX_1- Lingual		Tongue, pharynx	Mix
	IX_2- Pharyngeal		Pharynx, salivary gland	Mix
X	**Vagus**	Medulla		
	X_1- Superior laryngeal		Laryngeal muscles	Mix
	X_2- Recurrent laryngeal		All muscles of larynx	Mo
	X_3- Cardiac		Cardiac muscles	Mo
	X_4- Pneumogastric		Lungs, oesophagus, stomach, ileum	Mo
	X_5- Depressor		Diaphragm	Mix
XI	**Spinal accessory**	Medulla	Pharynx, larynx, neck, shoulder	Mo
XII	**Hypoglossal**	Medulla	Tongue, hyoid	Mo

S— Sensory, Mo— Motor, Mix— Mixed.

Spinal Nerves

They originate in the spinal cord and extend to the different body parts below the head. There are 31 pairs of spinal nerves in humans. All spinal nerves contain axons of both sensory and motor neurons.

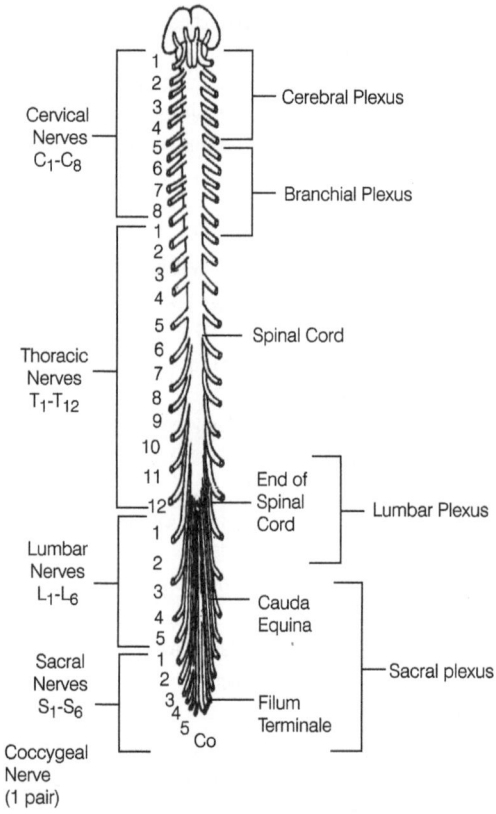

Spinal nerves in human

Autonomic Nervous System (ANS)

The ANS regulates the internal environment of the animal's body by controlling smooth and cardiac muscles and other involuntary actions.

Autonomic Nervous System

Sympathetic Nervous System	Parasympathetic Nervous System
Vasoconstriction in general and vasodilation (brain, heart, lungs and skeletal muscles)	Vasodilation of coronary vessel
Dilates pupil	Constricts pupil
Increases lacrimal glands secretion	Inhibits lacrimal glands secretion
Inhibits salivary and digestive glands	Stimulates them
Accelerates heart beat	Retards heart beat
Dilates trachea, bronchi, lungs	Constricts these organs
Inhibits gut peristalsis	Stimulates gut peristalsis
Contracts anal sphincter	Relaxes anal sphincter
Relaxes urinary bladder	Contracts urinary bladder

Reflex Action

Reflex action is a spontaneous automatic mechanical response to a stimulus involuntarily (without the will).

It is of following types

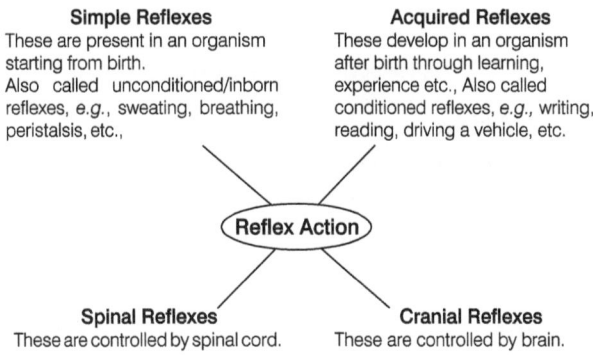

Simple Reflexes
These are present in an organism starting from birth.
Also called unconditioned/inborn reflexes, *e.g.*, sweating, breathing, peristalsis, etc.,

Acquired Reflexes
These develop in an organism after birth through learning, experience etc., Also called conditioned reflexes, *e.g.*, writing, reading, driving a vehicle, etc.

Spinal Reflexes
These are controlled by spinal cord.

Cranial Reflexes
These are controlled by brain.

Reflex Arc

Reflex arc is the pathway covered by nerve impulses (generated at the receptor due to the stimulus) to reach the effector organ during a reflex action. *It has following five components*

1. **Receptor** It is a cell/tissue/organ, which receives an external or internal stimulus, *e.g.*, skin, eye, ear.
2. **Sensory/Afferent nerve fibres** They carry the sensory nerve impulses generated by the receptor to the central nervous system.

3. **Part of Central Nervous System** It may be spinal cord or brain or ganglion.
4. **Motor/Efferent Nerve Fibres** These carry the motor nerve impulse generated in the CNS to the specific effector organs.
5. **Effector Organ** It may be organ/muscle/gland which on being activated by a motor nerve impulse, help to deal with the stimulus.

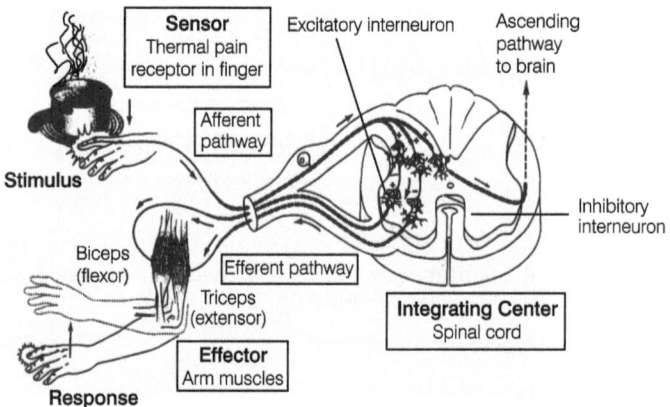

Reflex action and reflex arc

Importance of Reflex Arc
(a) Controls a number of body activities.
(b) Response to harmful stimulus is fast.
(c) Response to stimulus is accurate and useful.
(d) Coordinate body activities.

Sense Organs

The human body contain receptors that monitor numerous internal and external stimuli essential for homeostasis and our well-being. These receptors are located in the skin, internal organs, muscles, etc.

They detect stimuli that gives rise to **general senses** like pain, pressure, etc.

The human body is also endowed with five additional **special senses**, *i.e.*, taste, smell, sight, hearing and balance.

Handbook of BIOLOGY

General and Special Senses

Sense	Stimulus	Receptor
General senses	Pain	Naked nerve endings
	Light touch	Merkel's discs; naked nerve endings around hair follicles; Meissner's corpuscles; Ruffini's corpuscles, Krause's end-bulbs
	Pressure	Pacinian corpuscles
	Temperature	Naked nerve endings
	Proprioception	Golgi tendor organs; muscle spindles; receptors similar to Meissner's corpuscles in joints
Special senses	Taste	Taste buds
	Smell	Olfactory epithelium
	Sight	Retina
	Hearing	Organ of Corti
	Balance	Crista ampularis in the semicircular canals, maculae in utricle and saccule

Receptors in humans, involved in the general and special senses *fall into five categories as follows*

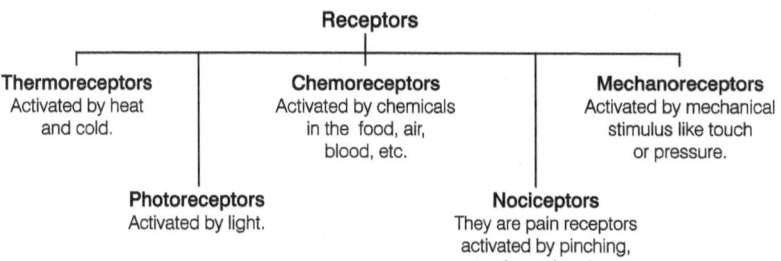

Based on kinds of stimulus, the sensory receptors fall into following two categories

1. **Exteroceptors** These receive external stimuli.
2. **Interceptors** These receive internal stimuli coming from the internal body organs, changes in muscles and joint movements.

The Visual Sense–The Eye

Human eye is one of the most extraordinary product of evolution. It contains a patch of photoreceptors that permit us to perceive the diverse and colourful environment.

Anatomy of Eye

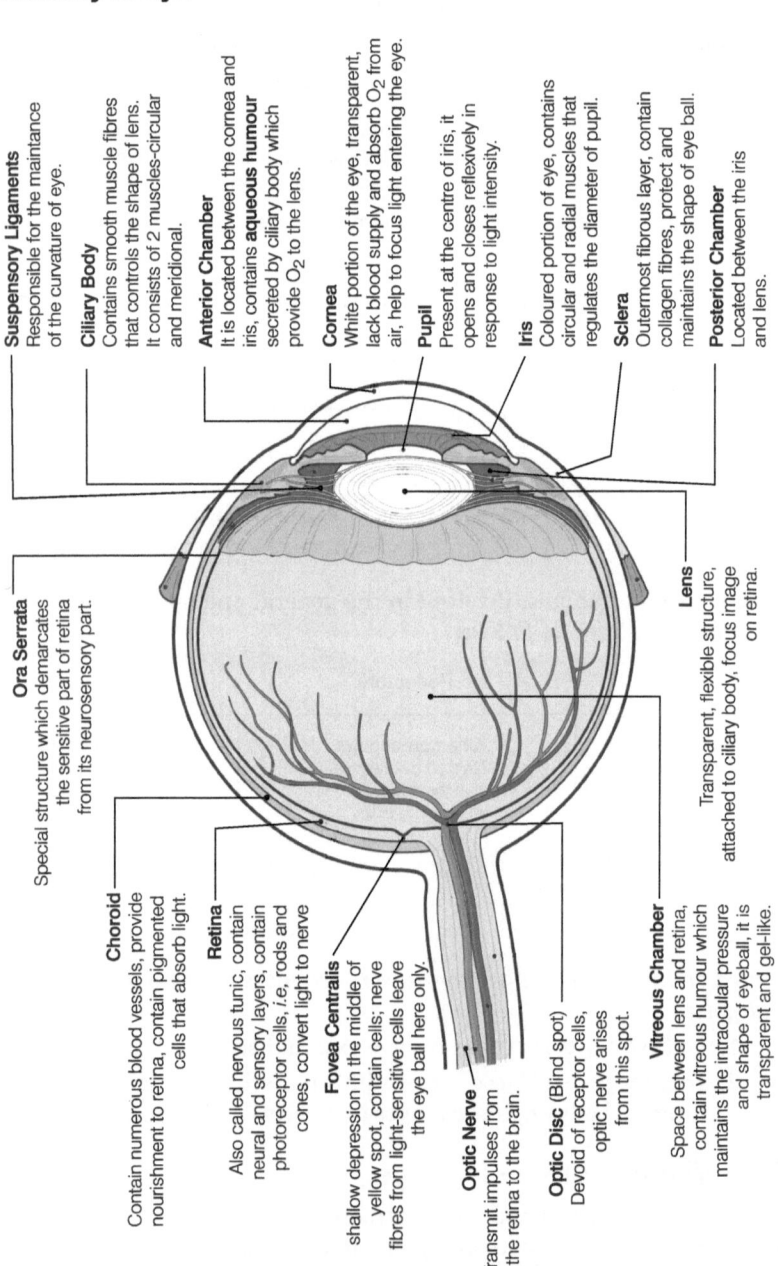

Various layers of retina are as follows

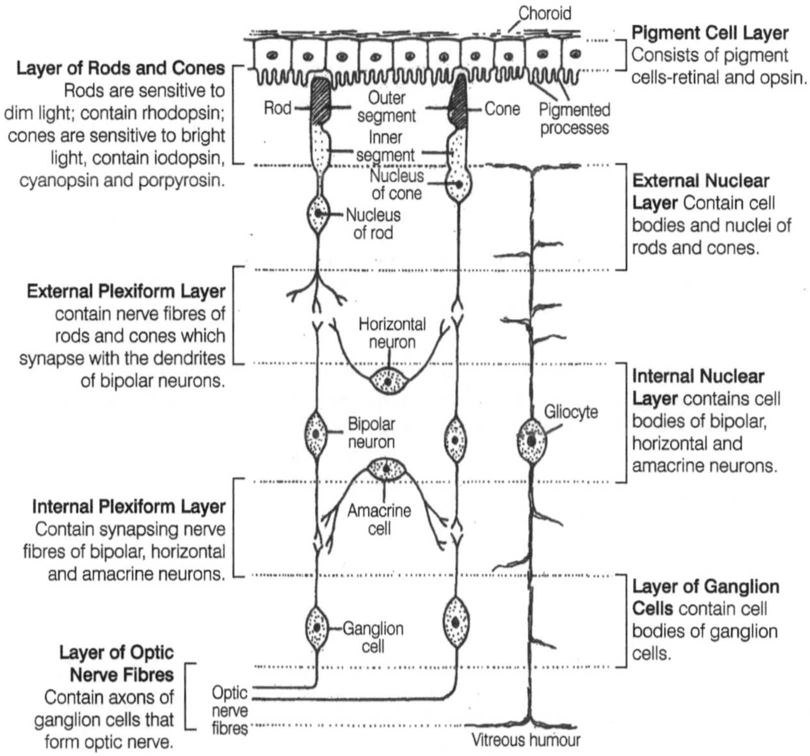

Choroid
Pigment Cell Layer Consists of pigment cells-retinal and opsin.
Layer of Rods and Cones Rods are sensitive to dim light; contain rhodopsin; cones are sensitive to bright light, contain iodopsin, cyanopsin and porpyrosin.
Rod
Outer segment
Cone
Pigmented processes
Inner segment
Nucleus of cone
Nucleus of rod
External Nuclear Layer Contain cell bodies and nuclei of rods and cones.
External Plexiform Layer contain nerve fibres of rods and cones which synapse with the dendrites of bipolar neurons.
Horizontal neuron
Internal Nuclear Layer contains cell bodies of bipolar, horizontal and amacrine neurons.
Gliocyte
Bipolar neuron
Internal Plexiform Layer Contain synapsing nerve fibres of bipolar, horizontal and amacrine neurons.
Amacrine cell
Layer of Ganglion Cells contain cell bodies of ganglion cells.
Ganglion cell
Layer of Optic Nerve Fibres Contain axons of ganglion cells that form optic nerve.
Optic nerve fibres
Vitreous humour

Layers of retina

- Rhodopsin pigment (visual purple) is formed by combining **retinene** with **scotopsin** in the presence of energy.
- Iodine is the main constituent of iodopsin pigment (visual violet)
- On the basis of sensitivity to a particular colour, the cones are of three types.

Erythrolable Cones Sensitive to red colour.
Chlorolable Cones Sensitive to green colour.
Cone Cells
Cyanolable Cones Sensitive to blue colour.

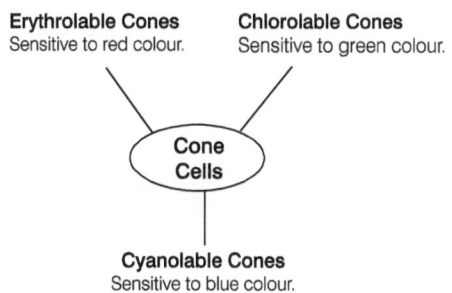

Rest of the colours are detected by the combination of these basic colours.

Few Important Terms Related to Eye

1. **Uvea** It is the name given to the vascular layer (tunic) of the eye which comprises posterior choriodeal, intermediate ciliary body and an anterior iris, perforated with pupil.
2. **Canal of Schlemm** Aqueous humour secreted by ciliary body is continuously drained to anterior part of eye through this canal. Its blockage may cause glucoma or kala motia.
3. **Tapetum Lucidum** It is the refractive layer of guanine particles in the iris of many mammals and elasmobranch fishes.
4. **Tapetum Fibrosum** It is the tapetum containing glistening white fibres of tendon type in marsupials, elephant, whale and hoofed mammals.
5. **Tapetum Cellulosum** It is the tapetum composed of cellulose like crystalline material instead of guanine in carnivore mammals, seals and lower primates.

Accessory Organs of the Eye

The eye is a delicate organ which is protected by several structures, i.e., eyebrows, eyelids, eyelashes, lacrimal apparatus, etc.

Lacrimal Gland
Situated on the lateral sides of eye in frontal bones behind suborbital margins, composed of secretory epithelial cells, secrete tears, water antibodies and lysozyme (a bactericidal enzyme).

Eyelid Margins
Contains modified sebaceous gland called **Meibomian glands** (tarsal glands), These glands secrete oily material which keeps the eyes wet and delays evaporation of tears.

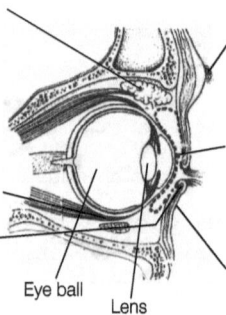

Eye ball   Lens

Eye Brows
2 arched ridges of suborbital margins of the frontal, possess numerous hairs which protects the eyes from sweat, dust, etc.

Conjunctiva
Transparent membrane, lines the eyelids, consists of highly vascular columnar epithelium, protects the cornea and front of the eye.

Eyelids
Also called palpebrae, movable folds of tissue, possess eyelashes (short curved hairs).

Accessory structures of human eye

Handbook of **BIOLOGY**

Mechanism of Vision

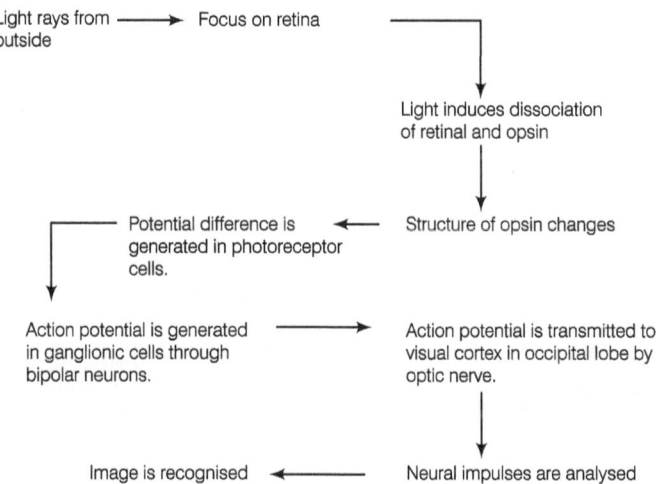

Accommodation It is the automatic adjustment in the curvature of lens as it focuses on different objects.

Accomodation for Distant Objects	Accomodation for Near Objects
Light rays are parallel from the distant objects when they strike the eye.	Light rays are divergent from the near objects when they strike the light.
Lens is pulled thin.	Lens is allowed to shrink.
Suspensory ligament is stretched tightly.	Suspensory ligament's tension is relaxed.
Ciliary muscles are stretched.	Ciliary muscles are contracted.

Binocular Vision When both the eyes can be focused simultaneously on a common object, it is called binocular vision, *e.g.*, humans.

Monocular Vision In this vision, eye focuses its own object and both the eyes cannot focus on one object, *e.g.*, rabbit.

Human Ear-Organ of Hearing and Balance

The human ear is an organ of special senses. It serves two functions; it detects sound and enable us to maintain balance.

Anatomy of Ear

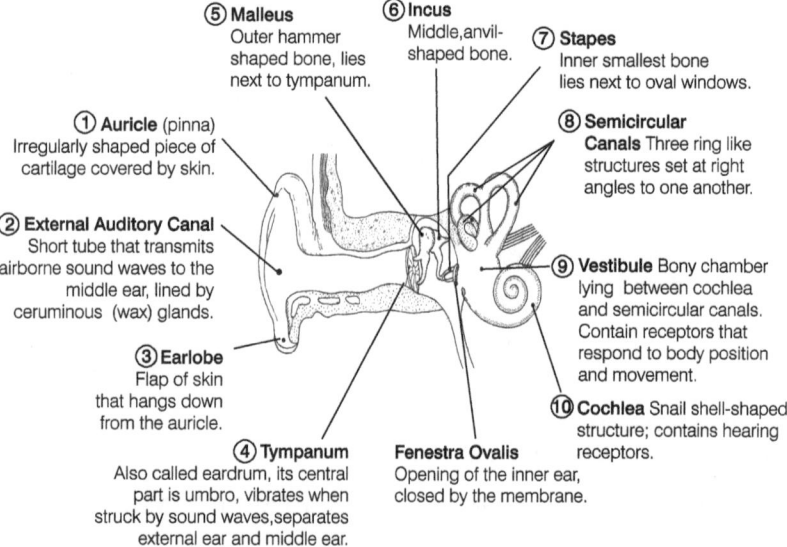

① **Auricle** (pinna) Irregularly shaped piece of cartilage covered by skin.

② **External Auditory Canal** Short tube that transmits airborne sound waves to the middle ear, lined by ceruminous (wax) glands.

③ **Earlobe** Flap of skin that hangs down from the auricle.

④ **Tympanum** Also called eardrum, its central part is umbro, vibrates when struck by sound waves, separates external ear and middle ear.

⑤ **Malleus** Outer hammer shaped bone, lies next to tympanum.

⑥ **Incus** Middle, anvil-shaped bone.

⑦ **Stapes** Inner smallest bone lies next to oval windows.

Fenestra Ovalis Opening of the inner ear, closed by the membrane.

⑧ **Semicircular Canals** Three ring like structures set at right angles to one another.

⑨ **Vestibule** Bony chamber lying between cochlea and semicircular canals. Contain receptors that respond to body position and movement.

⑩ **Cochlea** Snail shell-shaped structure; contains hearing receptors.

Human Ear (1), (2), (3), (4) = External ear; (5), (6), (7) = Middle ear; (8), (9), (10) = Internal ear

Structure and Function of Cochlea

The cochlea is a hollow structure containing 3 fluid-filled canals, sound receptors (organ of Corti) and a basilar membrane.

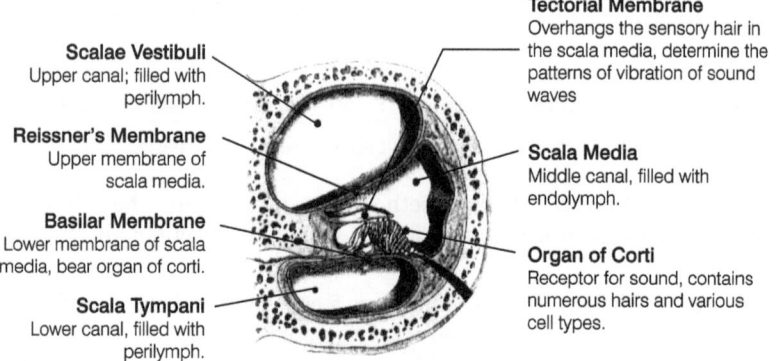

Scalae Vestibuli Upper canal; filled with perilymph.

Reissner's Membrane Upper membrane of scala media.

Basilar Membrane Lower membrane of scala media, bear organ of corti.

Scala Tympani Lower canal, filled with perilymph.

Tectorial Membrane Overhangs the sensory hair in the scala media, determine the patterns of vibration of sound waves

Scala Media Middle canal, filled with endolymph.

Organ of Corti Receptor for sound, contains numerous hairs and various cell types.

Cross section through the cochlea

Handbook of BIOLOGY

Function It is the main organ of hearing which converts the fluid waves to nerve impulses.

The Vestibular Apparatus

It consists of two parts the semicircular canals and the vestibule. Both are involved in proprioception.

The Semicircular Canals The three semicircular canals are filled with a fluid (endolymph). These are anterior, posterior and lateral semicircular canals or ducts.

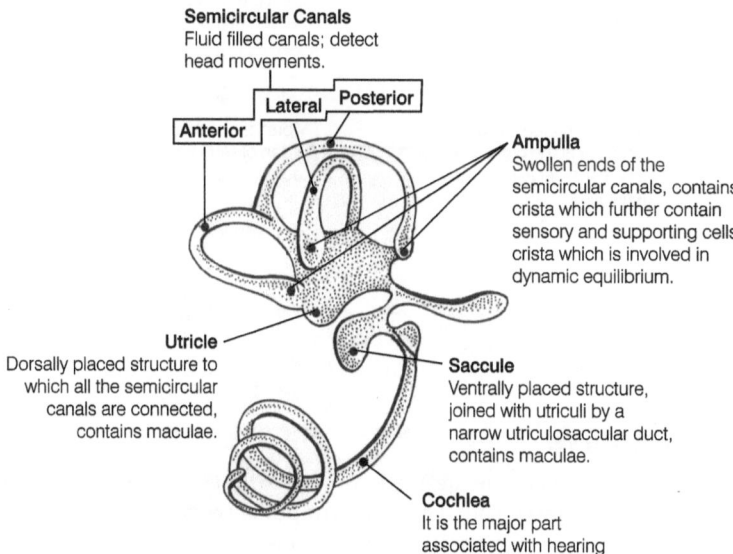

Membranous labyrinth of internal ear

Maculae It is concerned with the static equilibrium and respond to linear acceleration and tilling of the head.

Mechanism of Hearing

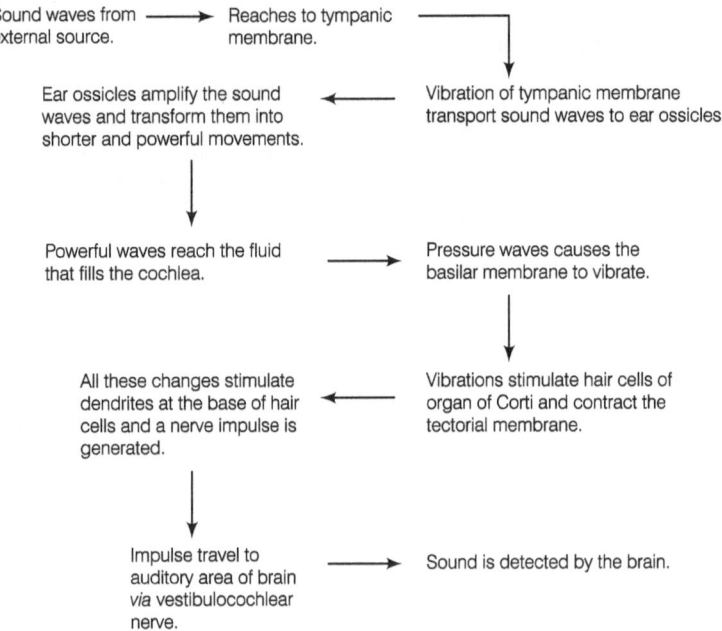

Nerve Impulse

A nerve impulse may be defined as wave of depolarisation of the membrane of the nerve cell. The nerve impulse travels along a neuron or across a synapse (junction), between one neuron and another, or between a neuron and an effector, such as a muscle or gland.

Membrane Theory of Nerve Impulse

This theory was proposed by English neurophysiologists **Hodgkin** and **Huxley** in the late 1930s. This theory states that electrical events in the nerve fibre are governed by the **differential permeability** of its membrane to sodium and potassium ions and that these permeabilities are regulated by the **electric field** across the membrane.

The interaction of differential permeability and electric field makes a critical threshold of charge essential to excite the nerve fibre.

According to this theory, the process of nerve impulse conduction is divisible into two main phases *i.e.,* **resting membrane potential of nerve** and **action membrane potential of nerve**.

Membrane Potentials

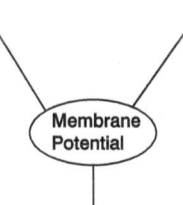

Positive Over Potential
It is the small action potential generated following the termination of spike. It consists of an initial negative deflection followed by a positive deflection both being of smaller amplitude than action potential Represented by '**d**' in the graph below.

Resting Membrane Potential
(Polarised state)
It is about 90 mV for a resting large resting nerve fibre, *i.e.*, potential inside the fibre is 90 mV more negative than the potential in the extracellular fluid on the outside of the fibre. Represented by '**a**' in the graph below.

Action Membrane Potential
It is responsible for transmitting the nerve signals. Action potential is generated due to rapid changes in membrane potential when a threshold stimulus is applied. The membrane potential changes from negative to positive.

Depolarisation Stage
Normal 90 mV polarised stage is lost, potential rises rapidly to positive direction due to tremendous inflow of Na^+ ions inside the axion. Represented by '**b**' in the graph below.

Repolarisation Stage
Caused due to excessive diffusion of K^+ ions to exterior which establish normal negative resting membrane potential. Represented by '**c**' in the graph below.

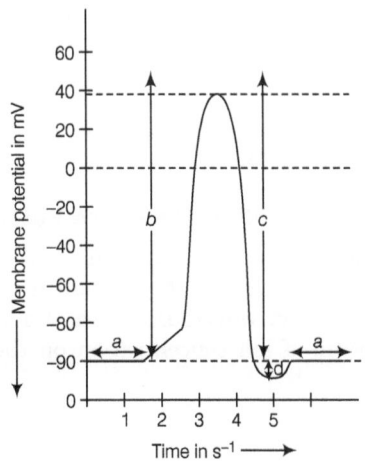

Causes of Membrane Potential

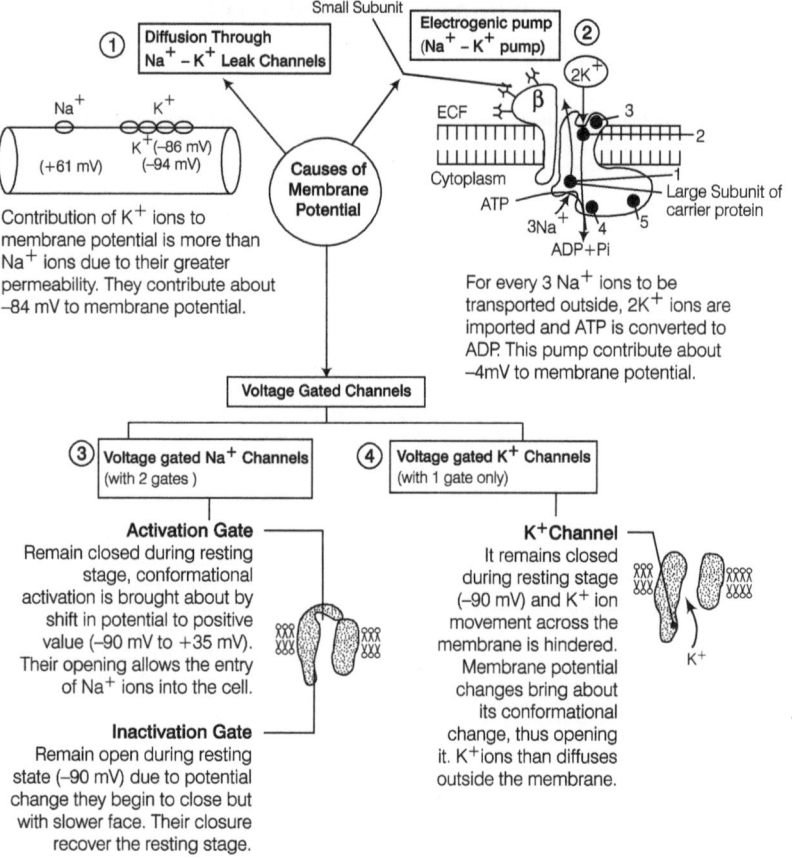

Causes of membrane potential (1) and (2) for resting potenial (3) and (4) for action potential

Calculation of Nernst Equation and Nerve Potential

The potential level across the membrane that will exactly prevent net diffusion of an ion in either direction through a membrane is called **Nernst potential of that particular ion**. Its magnitude can be determined by the ratio of ion concentration on the two sides of the membrane.

The following equation called **Nernst equation** is used to calculate the **Nernst potential** for any univalent ion at normal body temperature of 37°C.

$$\text{EMF (milli volts)} = \pm 61 \log \frac{\text{Concentration inside}}{\text{Concentration outside}}$$

When using this formula, it is assumed that the potential outside the membrane always remains exactly at zero and Nernst potential is calculated in the potential membrane.

Diffusion potential occurs when membrane is permeable to several different ions. *In this condition, the diffusion potential that develops, depend upon three factors*

(i) The polarity of electric charge of each ion.

(ii) The permeability of membrane (P) of each ion.

(iii) The concentration (c) of respective ions on the inside (i) and outside (o) to the membrane.

Thus, the following formula called the **Goldman equation** or **Goldman-Hodgkin-Katz equation** gives the calculated membrane potentials when the Na^+, K^+, Cl^- ions are involved. *The equation is*

EMF (milli volts)

$$= -61 \log \frac{CNa_i^+ \cdot PNa_i^+ + CK_i^+ \, PK_i^+ + CCl_O^- \cdot PCl_O^-}{CNa_O^+ \cdot PNa_O^+ + CK_O^+ \cdot PK_O^+ + CCl_i^- \cdot PCl_i^-}$$

Here, C is the concentration of respective ion, P is the partial pressure and permeability of concerning ion, i represent inside, 'o' represents outside.

Synapse

A **synapse** is formed by the membranes of a pre-synaptic neuron and a post-synaptic neuron which may or may not be separated by a gap called **synaptic cleft**. *There are two types of synapses*

(i) At **electrical synapse**, the membranes of pre-and post-synaptic neurons are in very close proximity. Electrical current can flow directly from one neuron to the other, across these synapses.

Impulse transmission across an electrical synapse is always faster than that across a chemical synapse. Electrical synapses are rare in our system.

(ii) At **chemical synapse**, the membranes of pre-and post-synaptic neurons are separated by a fluid-filled space called as **synaptic cleft**.

Conduction Through Synaptic Cleft

The pre-synaptic neuron synthesises the neurotransmitter and packages it in **synaptic vesicles** which are stored in the neuron's synaptic terminals. Hundreds of synaptic terminals may interact with the cell body and dendrites of a post-synaptic neuron.

When an action potential reaches a synaptic terminal, it depolarises the terminal membrane, opening the **voltage-gated calcium channels** in the membrane. Calcium ions (Ca^{2+}) then diffuse into the terminal and the rise in Ca^{2+} concentration in the terminal causes some of the synaptic vesicles to fuse with the terminal membrane, releasing the **neurotransmitter**.

The neurotransmitter diffuses across the **synaptic cleft**, a narrow gap that separates the pre-synaptic neuron from the post-synaptic neuron. The released neurotransmitter binds to the specific **receptors**, present on the post-synaptic neuron. This binding open the ion channels allowing the entry of ions which can generate a new potential in the post-synaptic neuron.

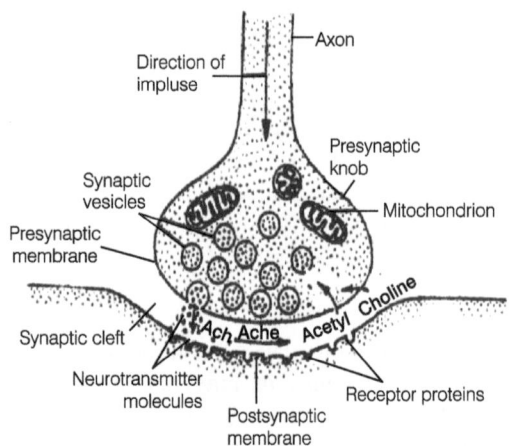

Transmission of nerve impulse at a chemical synapse

Neurotransmitters

Neurotransmitters are **chemical messengers** secreted by the axon terminals for transmitting impulses to the next neuron. At most synapses, information is passed from the transmitting neuron (pre-synaptic cell) to the receiving cell (post-synaptic cell) by neurotransmitters. Each neurotransmitter bind to its own group of receptors. Some neurotransmitters have many different receptors, which can produce different effects in the post-synaptic cell.

Various kinds of neurotransmitters are listed below
  (i) **Acetylcholine** is a common neurotransmitter present in the neuromuscular junctions, voluntary neural synapses, synapses of pre-ganglionic nerve fibres, synapses of post-ganglionic parasympathetic nerve fibres. **Cholinergic** nerve fibres release acetylcholine. It has excitatory effect on the skeletal muscles and excitatory or inhibitory effect at other sites.
 (ii) **Norepinephrine** (noradrenaline) is formed at synapses and neuromuscular junctions of the post-ganglionic sympathetic nerve fibres. The nerve fibres are called **adrenergic**. It has excitatory or inhibitory effects.

   Peripheral nervous system generally uses acetylcholine, noradrenaline and adrenaline.
(iii) **Glycine, Dopamine** and **Gamma Amino Butyric Acid** (GABA) are inhibitory transmitters.
(iv) **Glutamate** is excitatory in function.
 (v) **Serotonin** inhibits pain pathways of spinal cord. It generally controls mood and induces sleep.

15

Chemical Coordination *and* Integration

Glands

Glands are the group to cells that are specialised for the secretion of a particular substance. *Glands can be classified into different groups as follows*

Types of Glands

Exocrine Glands
The secretion of these glands are carried by the ducts to a particular organ, *e.g.,* salivary glands, liver, etc.

Endocrine Glands
These glands do not possess ducts and they pour their secretions directly into the blood, *e.g.,* hypothalamus, thyroid, etc.

Holocrine Glands
They secrete only hormones, *e.g.,* thyroid, adrenal, etc

Heterocrine Glands
They have dual functions, *i.e.,* secretion of hormones and other physiological functions, *e.g.,* testes, pancreas, etc.

Handbook of BIOLOGY

Gland	Hormone	Type	Action
Hypothalamus	Oxytocin	Peptide	Moves to posterior pituitary for storage.
	Antidiuretic Hormone (Vasopressin)	Peptide	Moves to posterior pituitary for storage.
	Regulatory Hormones (RH and IH) of anterior Pituitary gland		Act on anterior pituitary to stimulate or inhibit the hormone production.
Pituitary gland			
Anterior			
1. Pars distalis	Growth Hormone (GH)	Protein	Stimulates body growth.
	Prolactin	Protein	Promotes lactation.
	Follicle-Stimulating Hormone (FSH)	Glycoprotein	Stimulates follicle maturation and production of estrogen; stimulates sperm production.
	Luteinizing Hormone (LH)	Glycoprotein	Triggers ovulation and production of estrogen and progesterone by ovary, promotes sperm production.
	Thyroid-Stimulating Hormone (TSH)	Glycoprotein	Stimulates the releases of T_3 and T_4.
	Adrenocorticotropic Hormone (ACTH)	Peptide	Promotes the release of glucocorticoids and androgens from adrenal cortex.
2. Pars intermedia	Melanocyte-Stimulating Hormone (MSH)	Peptide	Maintenance of lipid content in body.
Posterior	Oxytocin Vasopression (ADH)	Peptide	Initiates labor, initiates milk ejection. controls osmotic concentration of body fluids in particular water reabsorption by kidneys.
Thyroid gland	T_3 (Triiodothyronine)	Amine	Increases metabolism and blood pressure, regulates tissue growth, five times more potent than T_4.
	T_4 (Thyroxine)	Amine	Increases metabolism and blood pressure, regulates tissue growth.
	Calcitonin	Peptide	Childhood regulation of blood calcium levels through uptake by bone.

Human Endocrine System

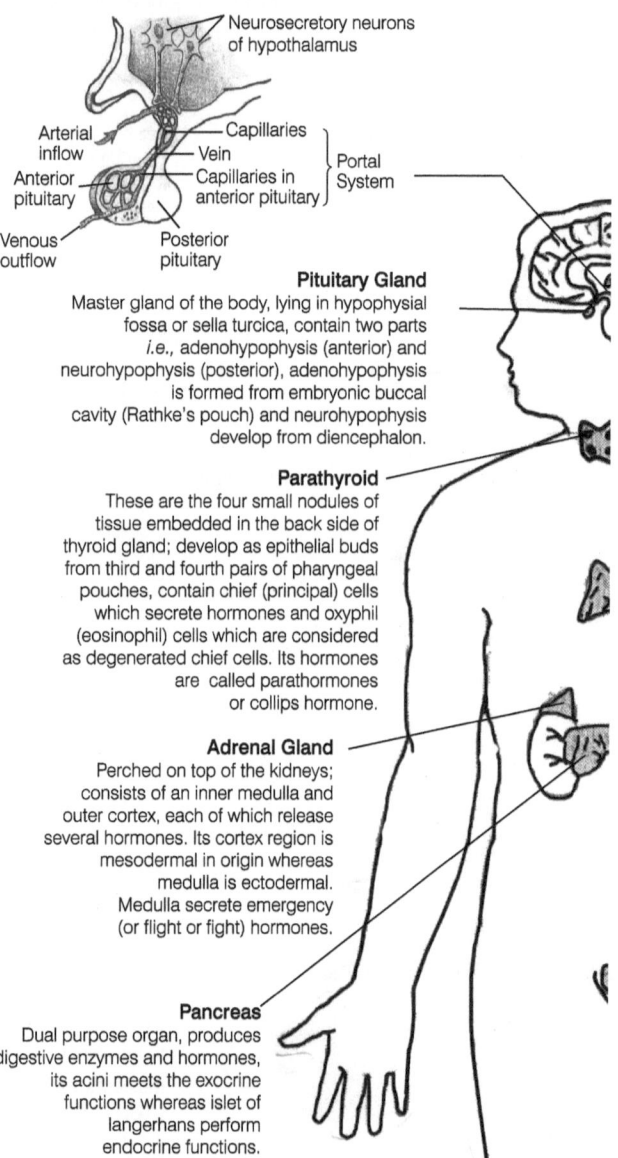

Pituitary Gland
Master gland of the body, lying in hypophysial fossa or sella turcica, contain two parts i.e., adenohypophysis (anterior) and neurohypophysis (posterior), adenohypophysis is formed from embryonic buccal cavity (Rathke's pouch) and neurohypophysis develop from diencephalon.

Parathyroid
These are the four small nodules of tissue embedded in the back side of thyroid gland; develop as epithelial buds from third and fourth pairs of pharyngeal pouches, contain chief (principal) cells which secrete hormones and oxyphil (eosinophil) cells which are considered as degenerated chief cells. Its hormones are called parathormones or collips hormone.

Adrenal Gland
Perched on top of the kidneys; consists of an inner medulla and outer cortex, each of which release several hormones. Its cortex region is mesodermal in origin whereas medulla is ectodermal. Medulla secrete emergency (or flight or fight) hormones.

Pancreas
Dual purpose organ, produces digestive enzymes and hormones, its acini meets the exocrine functions whereas islet of langerhans perform endocrine functions.

Anterior human endocrine system

Handbook of BIOLOGY

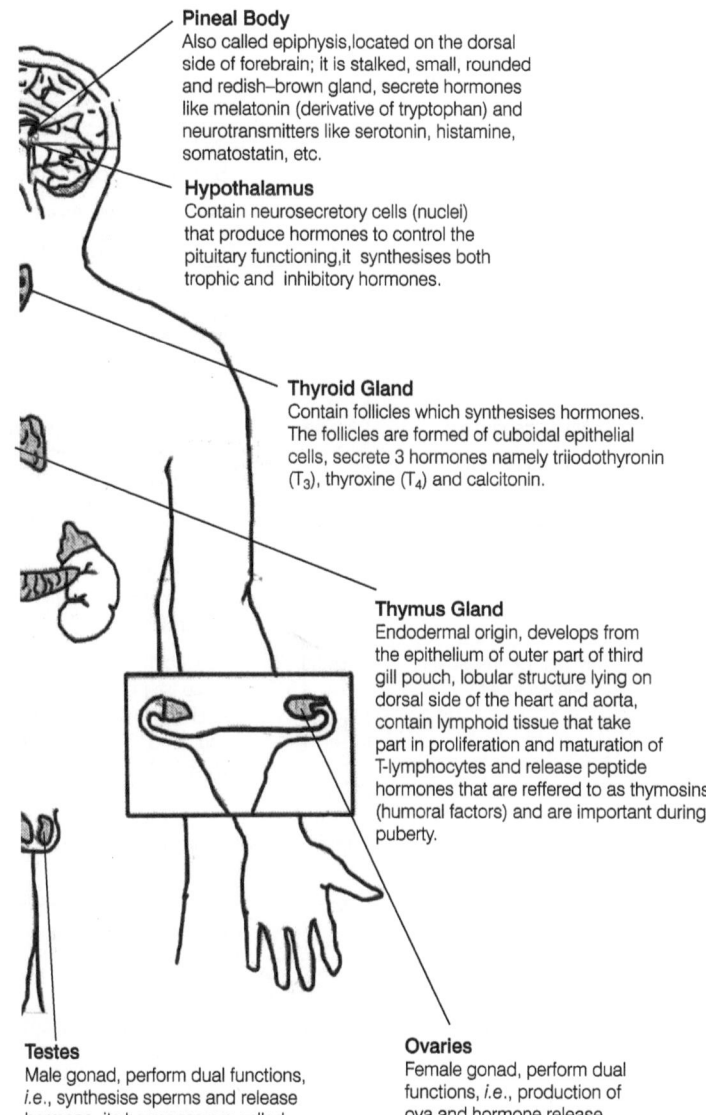

Pineal Body
Also called epiphysis, located on the dorsal side of forebrain; it is stalked, small, rounded and redish–brown gland, secrete hormones like melatonin (derivative of tryptophan) and neurotransmitters like serotonin, histamine, somatostatin, etc.

Hypothalamus
Contain neurosecretory cells (nuclei) that produce hormones to control the pituitary functioning, it synthesises both trophic and inhibitory hormones.

Thyroid Gland
Contain follicles which synthesises hormones. The follicles are formed of cuboidal epithelial cells, secrete 3 hormones namely triiodothyronin (T_3), thyroxine (T_4) and calcitonin.

Thymus Gland
Endodermal origin, develops from the epithelium of outer part of third gill pouch, lobular structure lying on dorsal side of the heart and aorta, contain lymphoid tissue that take part in proliferation and maturation of T-lymphocytes and release peptide hormones that are reffered to as thymosins (humoral factors) and are important during puberty.

Testes
Male gonad, perform dual functions, i.e., synthesise sperms and release hormone, its hormones are called androgens.

Ovaries
Female gonad, perform dual functions, i.e., production of ova and hormone release.

Posterior human endocrine system

Gland	Hormone	Type	Action
Parathyroid gland	Parathyroid hormone (parathormones or collip hormones).	Peptide	Increases blood calcium levels through action on bone, kidneys and intestine.
Pancreas	Insulin (α-cells)	Protein	Reduces blood sugar level by regulating cell uptake.
	Glucagon (β-cells)	Protein	Increases blood sugar levels.
Adrenal glands Adrenal medulla	Epinephrine (Adrenaline)	Amine	Affect PNS either by stimulating or inhibiting it, increases respiration rate, heart rate and muscle contraction.
	Norepinephrine (Nor.aadrenaline)	Amine	Stress hormone, increases blood pressure, heart rate and glucose level.
Adrenal cortex	Glucocorticoids (cortisol)	Steroid	Long-term stress response–increased blood glucose levels, blood volume maintenance, immune suppression.
	Mineralocorticoids (Aldosterone)	Steroid	Long-term stress response-blood volume and pressure maintenance, sodium and water retention by kidneys.
Gonads			
Testes	Androgens (Testosterone)	Steroid	Reproductive maturation, sperm production.
Ovaries	Estrogen	Steroid	Stimulates hypothalamus to release GnRH before ovulation, maintain follicular, growth.
	Progesterone	Steroid	Maintain pregnancy and uterus wall thickening, Inhibit the release of estrogen.
Pineal gland	Melatonin	Amine	Circadian timing (rhythm).
Thymus	Thymosin	Peptide	Development of T-lymphocytes.

Endocrine Disorders

(i) **Acromegaly** It is caused by the hypersecretion of GH after bone growth has stopped.

It symptoms include skin and tongue thicking, enlarged hands and feets, facial features become coarse.

(ii) **Addison's disease** It is caused due to the decrease production of hormones from adrenal gland usually due to autoimmune reactions.

Its symptoms include loss of weight and appetite, fatigue, weakness, complete renal failure.

(iii) **Cushing's syndrome** It is caused due to the hyposecretion of hormones from adrenal glands.

In this disease face and body become fatter, loss of muscle mass, weakness, fatigue, osteoporosis.

(iv) **Cretinism** (Hypothyroidism) The retarded mental and physical development is associated with the hyposecretion of thyroid hormones. The child receives hormones from the mother before birth, so appears normal at first, but within a few weeks or months it becomes evident the physical and mental development are retarded.

Symptoms are disproportionately short limbs, a large protruding tongue, coarse dry skin, poor abdominal muscle tone and an umbilical hernia.

(v) **Diabetes insipidus** It is caused due to the hyposecretion of ADH and characterised by excessive thirst, urination and constipation.

(vi) **Diabetes mellitus** It is caused due to the insufficient insulin production in body. It can be of two types, *i.e.,* Type 1 or Insulin Dependent Diabetes Mallitus (IDDM) and Type 2 or Non-Insulin Dependent Diabetes Mallitus (NIDDM).

It is characterised by poor wound healing, urinary tract infection, excess glucose in urine, fatigue and apathy.

(vii) **Eunuchoidism** It is a hormonal disorder due to the deficient secretion of testosterone in males. In this case, the secondary male sex organs, such as prostate gland, seminal vesicle and penis are underdeveloped and non-functional. The external male sex characters like beard, moustaches and masculine voice fails to develop, sperms are not formed.

(viii) **Grave's disease** (Hyperthyroidism) It is caused due to the hypersecretion of thyroxine.

Its symptoms include protrusion of eye balls (exopthalamus), excessive fat near the eyes, weight loss, nervousness, excess sweating.

Toxic nodular goitre (Plummer's Disease) It is caused due to the excess secretion of T_3 and T_4 and is characterised by the presence of glandular tissue in the form of limps.

Simple goitre It is caused due to the deficient secretion of T_3 and T_4 hormones which results in the enlargement of thyroid gland.

(ix) **Gigantism** It is caused by excess of growth hormone from early age. It is characterised by large and well proportioned body.

(x) **Gynaecomastia** It is the development of breast tissue in males, gynaecomastia occurs mainly due to the disturbance in oestrogen and testosterone ratio.

(xi) **Hyperparathyroidism** It is caused due to the excessive parathromones secretion usually due to tumour in parathyroid gland.

Its symptoms include kidney stones, indigestion, depression, loss of calcium from bones, muscle weakness.

(xii) **Hypoparathyroidism** (Tetany) It is caused due to the hyposecretion of parathyroid hormones.

Its symptoms include muscle spasm, dry skin, numbness in hands and feets.

(xiii) **Hypogonadism** It occurs due to the defect in hypothalamus, pituitary, testes or ovaries. In males, less production of testosterone occurs affecting the development of male secondary sexual features. In females, deficient production of oestrogen occurs resulting in very less development of secondary sex characters.

(xiv) **Simmond's disease** It is caused due to the atrophy or degeneration of anterior lobe of pituitary gland. In this disease, the skin of face becomes dry and wrinkled and shows premature ageing.

Handbook of BIOLOGY

Hormones (Bayliss and Starling; 1903)

Hormones are the chemical substances that are produced or released by cells or group of cells that form the endocrine (ductless) glands.

Target cells are the cells affected by a hormone. These target cells are selective or exclusive to a hormone due the presence of protein receptors on them.

Types of Hormones

(i) *Hormones fall into two broad categories*

(a) **Tropic hormones** These hormones stimulate other endocrine glands to produce and secrete hormones, *e.g.*, Thyroid Stimulating Hormone (TSH) produced by pituitary gland stimulates the release of thyroxine hormone from thyroid gland. Thyroxine in turn stimulates metabolism in many types of body cells. Thus, TSH is a tropic hormone (thyroxine is a non-tropic hormone).

(b) **Non-tropic hormones** These hormones stimulates vital cellular processes including metabolism, but do not stimulate the release of other hormones, *e.g.*, prolactin secreted by anterior pituitary stimulates the production of milk in a women's breast tissue.

(ii) According to their chemical composition, *hormones can be classified into following groups*

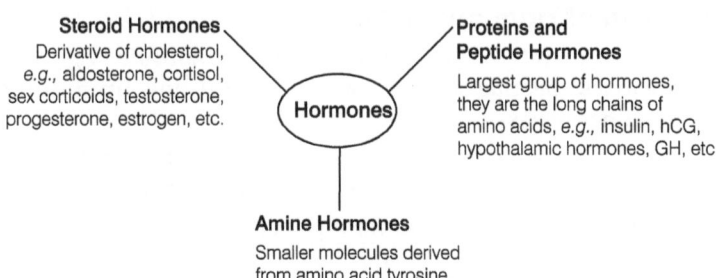

(iii) **Local hormones** These are secreted by the cells, but not by glands and widely dispersed in the body. These are considered as tissue hormones or non-endocrine hormone.

Different type of local hormones are as follows

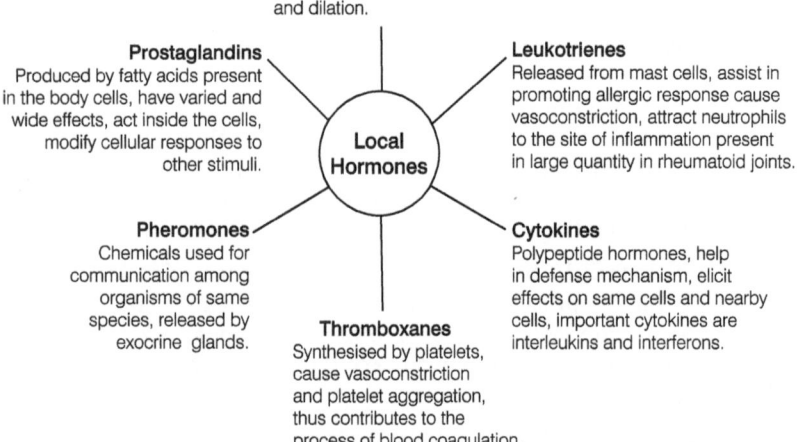

Mechanism of Hormone Action

Hormones are mainly of two types *i.e.,* **water soluble** (*e.g.,* amino acid derivatives, peptide and protein hormones) and **lipid soluble** (*e.g.,* steroid hormones).

Water-soluble hormones require extracellular receptors and generate **second messengers** (*e.g.,* cAMP) for carrying out their activity.

Lipid soluble hormones can pass through cell membranes and directly enter the cell.

(i) Peptide hormone action through extracellular receptors

These hormones act at the surface of target cell as **primary messengers** and bind to the cell-surface receptor forming the **hormone-receptor complex**.

This mechanism was discovered by **EW Sutherland** in 1950 for which he got the Nobel Prize.

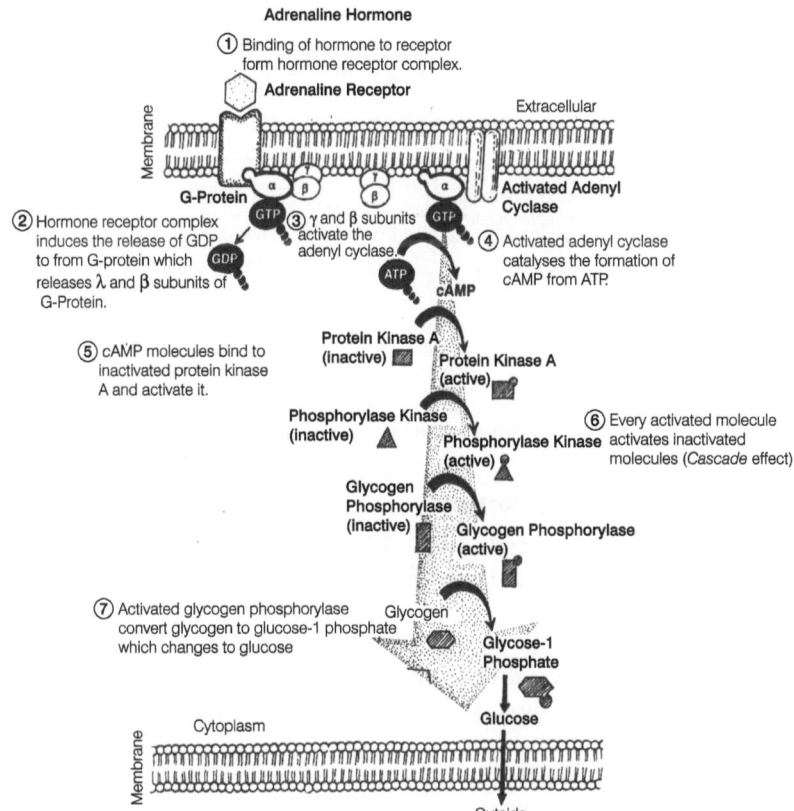

Mechanism of protein hormone action

Hence, single molecule of adrenaline may lead to the release of 100 million glucose molecules.

(ii) **Steroid hormone action through intracellular receptors**

These hormones easily pass through the cell membrane of a target cell and bind to specific intracellular receptors (protein) to form a hormone receptor complex.

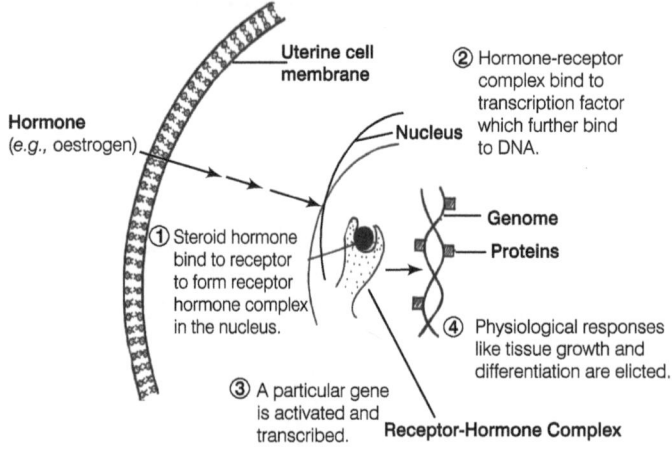

Mechanism of steroid hormone action

Control of Hormone Action

Hormones help to control many homeostatic mechanisms. Their production and release are generally controlled by positive or negative feedback loop.

In positive feedback loop hormones released by one gland stimulates the other gland which further lead to even more significant changes in the same direction. It acts as self-amplifying cycle that accelerate a process.

While in **negative feedback loop**, the end product of a biochemical process inhibits its own production.

16
Human Reproduction

Human beings show sexual reproduction and they have separate sexes (unisexual). As we can identify male and female from their physical appearence means sexual dimorphism is present. *The secondary sexual characters of Man and Woman are as follows*

Secondary Sexual Features in Man and Woman

Character	Man	Woman
General build up	More muscular	Less muscular
Aggressiveness	More marked	Less marked
Hair growth		
(i) Facial	Beard, moustache present	Absent
(ii) Axillary	Present	Present
(iii) Pubic	Hair distribution more lateral and upwards towards umbilicus	Upward growth not so, marked and is more horizontal
(iv) Chest	Present	Absent
Mammary glands	Undeveloped	Well developed
Pelvis	Not broad	More broad
Larynx	More apparent	Less apparent
Voice	Low pitched	High pitched
Breathing	Predominantly abdominal	Predominantly thoracic
BMR	High due to greater activity	Not so high as compared to man

Male Reproductive System

The male has two visible sex organs, the testes and penis, which can be seen from the outside. The testes are the **primary male sexual organ** in males whereas prostate, seminal vesicles, vas deferentia and penis are the **secondary sexual organs**.

Male reproductive system

Ureter
Convey the urine from kidneys to urinary bladder.

Seminal Vesicle
One pair of sac-like structure near the base of the bladder, produce alkaline secretion which forms 60% of semen volume, its fluid pH is 7.4, contain fructose, prostaglandins and cloting factors. The fructose provide energy to semen.

Bulbourethral Gland
Also called cowper's gland, secrete alkaline fluid, called seminal plasma which is rich is fructose, calcium and certain enzymes; it also secrete mucous that helps in the lubrication of penis.

Epididymis
Long, narrow, coiled tubule lying along the inner side of the testis, it stores sperms, secrete fluid, which nourishes the sperms.

Testes
Primary sex organ, produce sperms and male sex steroids, suspended in the scrotum by the spermatic cords called gubernaculum, lined by mesorchium, which protects the testis.

Urinary Bladder
Muscular structure that stores the urine.

Vas Deferens
Energes from cauda epididymis, leaves scortal sac and enters abdominal cavity, they are thick, 2 in numbers possess many stereocilia, carry sperms from epididymis to ejaculatory ducts.

Prostate Gland
Single large gland that surrounds the urethra, produce milky secretion with pH 6.5 which forms 25% of semen volume, its secretion contain citric acid, prostaglandins, and enzymes like amylose, pepsinogen, etc. Due to the presence of citric acid, semen is slightly acidic. Prostaglandins causes the uterus muscles to contract.

Ejaculatory Duct
2 short tubes, each formed by the union of duct from seminal vesicle and vas deferens, it passes through prots state gland and joins the urethra; composed of fibrous, muscular, columnar epithelium, function to convey sperms.

Scrotum
Pouch of deeply pigmented skin, contain testis, its temperature is 2-2.5°C lower than the normal body temperature which favours the production of sperms, remain connected to abdomen by inguinal canal.

Urethra
Provides common pathway for sperms and urine, its opening possess 2 sphincters, its external opening is called urethral meatus.

Penis
Male copulatory organ, conduct both urine and semen.

Glans penis
Corpus spongiosum enlargement at the end of penis

Spongy Erectile Tissue
3 cylindrical masses–2 dorsal corpora covernosa and 1 ventral corpus spongiosum

Prepuce
Foreskin which covers the glans penis

L.S. of Penis

T.S. of Penis
- Dorsal veins
- Artery
- Corpus spongiosum
- Urethra
- Corpora cavernosa

Testis:
- Nerve
- Blood vessels
- Vas deferens
- Epididymis
- Connective tissue
- Seminiferous tubules
- Testis

Handbook of BIOLOGY

The testis in transverse section shows different cell types at various stages.

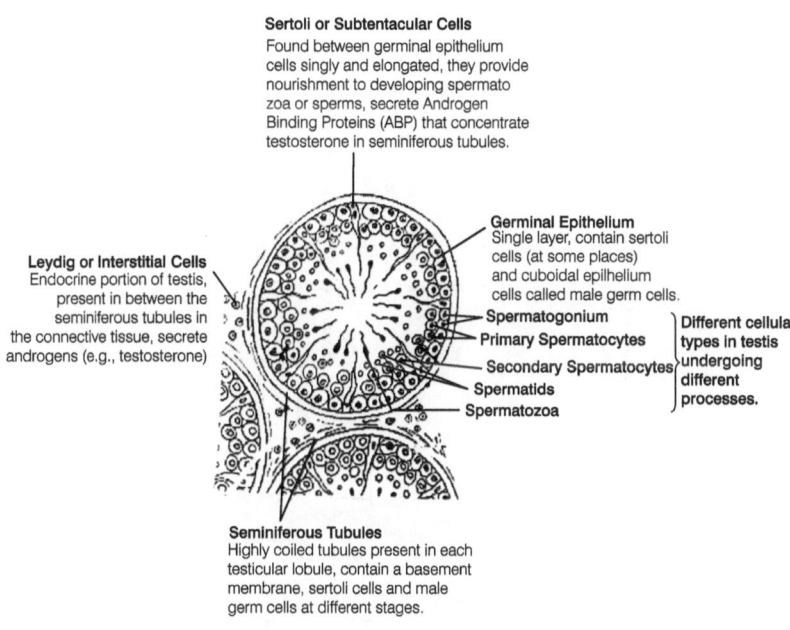

TS of testis

Female Reproductive System

It consists of ovaries which are the primary sex organs in human female. The secondary sex organs in human female are Fallopian tubes (oviducts), uterus, vagina and mammary glands.

Various components of female's internal reproductive system are shown in the given figure

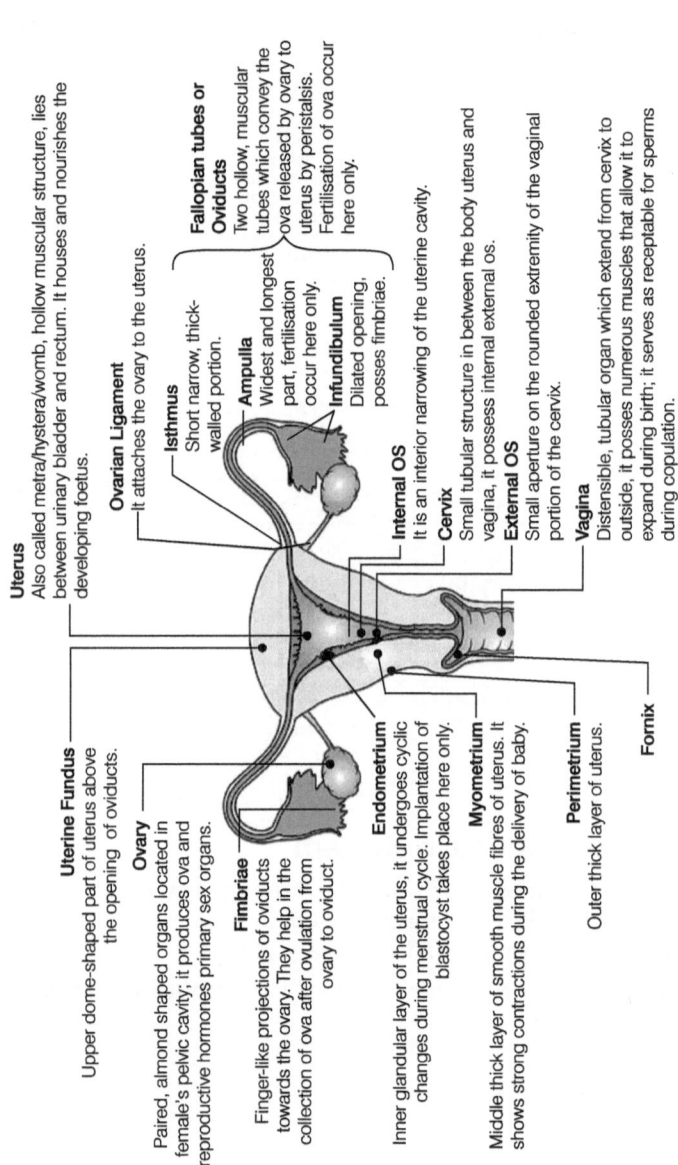

Female reproductive system

Handbook of BIOLOGY

The primary sex organ of human females, *i.e.*, ovaries consists of a dense outer layer called **cortex** and a less dense inner portion called **medulla**. A section of ovary shows the growing follicles at different stages.

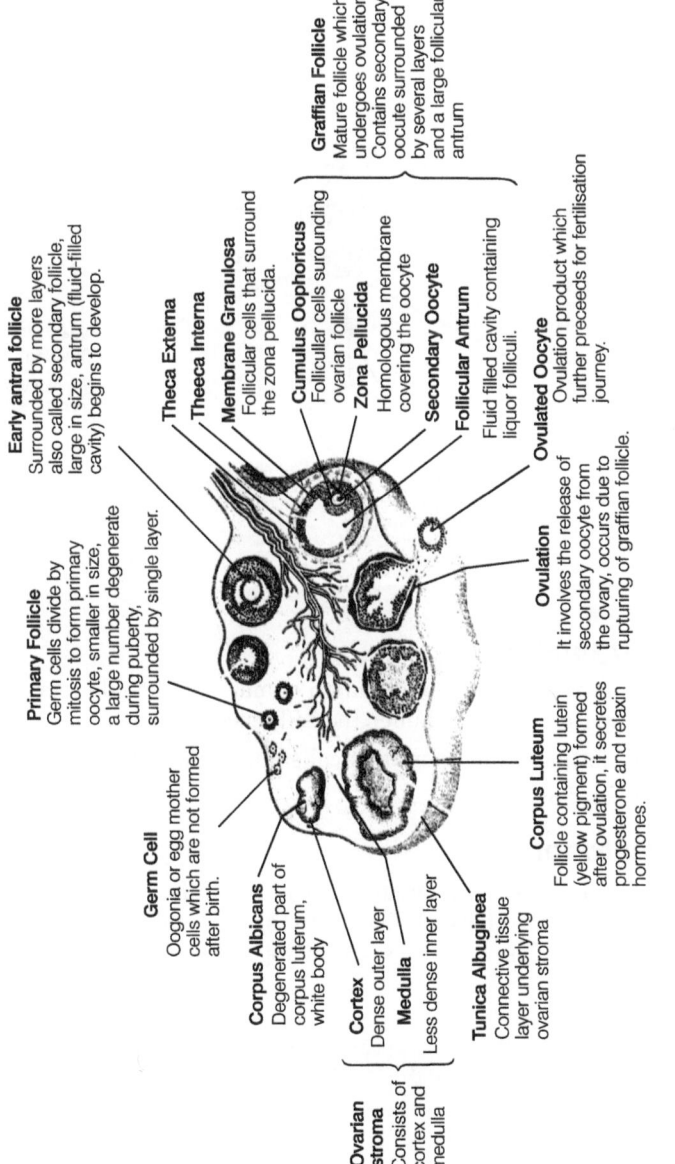

T.S of ovary

The external genitilia or vulva of female consists of following parts.

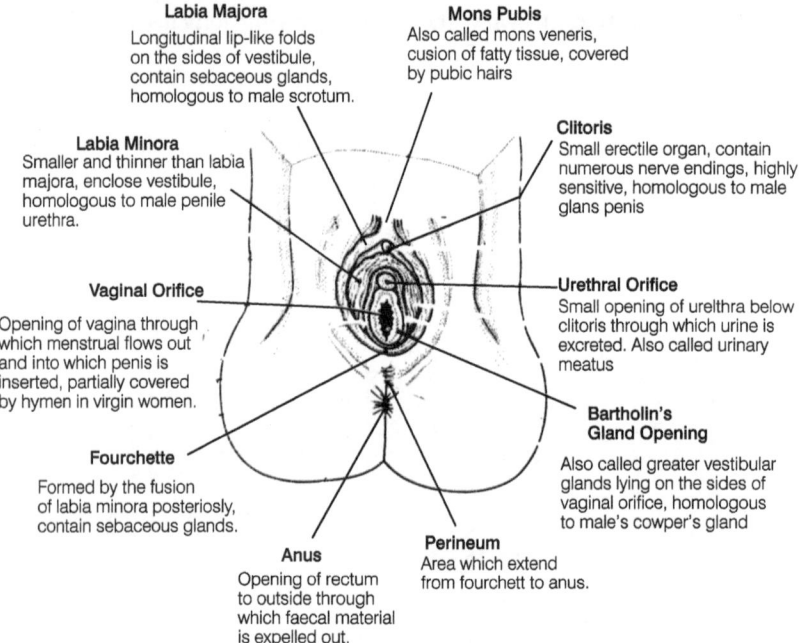

Labia Majora
Longitudinal lip-like folds on the sides of vestibule, contain sebaceous glands, homologous to male scrotum.

Mons Pubis
Also called mons veneris, cusion of fatty tissue, covered by pubic hairs

Labia Minora
Smaller and thinner than labia majora, enclose vestibule, homologous to male penile urethra.

Clitoris
Small erectile organ, contain numerous nerve endings, highly sensitive, homologous to male glans penis

Vaginal Orifice
Opening of vagina through which menstrual flows out and into which penis is inserted, partially covered by hymen in virgin women.

Urethral Orifice
Small opening of urelthra below clitoris through which urine is excreted. Also called urinary meatus

Fourchette
Formed by the fusion of labia minora posteriosly, contain sebaceous glands.

Bartholin's Gland Opening
Also called greater vestibular glands lying on the sides of vaginal orifice, homologous to male's cowper's gland

Anus
Opening of rectum to outside through which faecal material is expelled out.

Perineum
Area which extend from fourchett to anus.

Gametogenesis

Gametogenesis involves the formation of male and female reproductive cells, *i.e.,* sperms and ova under the influence of hormones.

Process of formation of sperms is called spermatogenesis and that of ova is called oogenesis.

Spermatogenesis

The formation of sperms occurs in the seminiferous tubules of the testis. Sperms are formed from the special cells present in the periphery of tubules, known as spermatogonia.

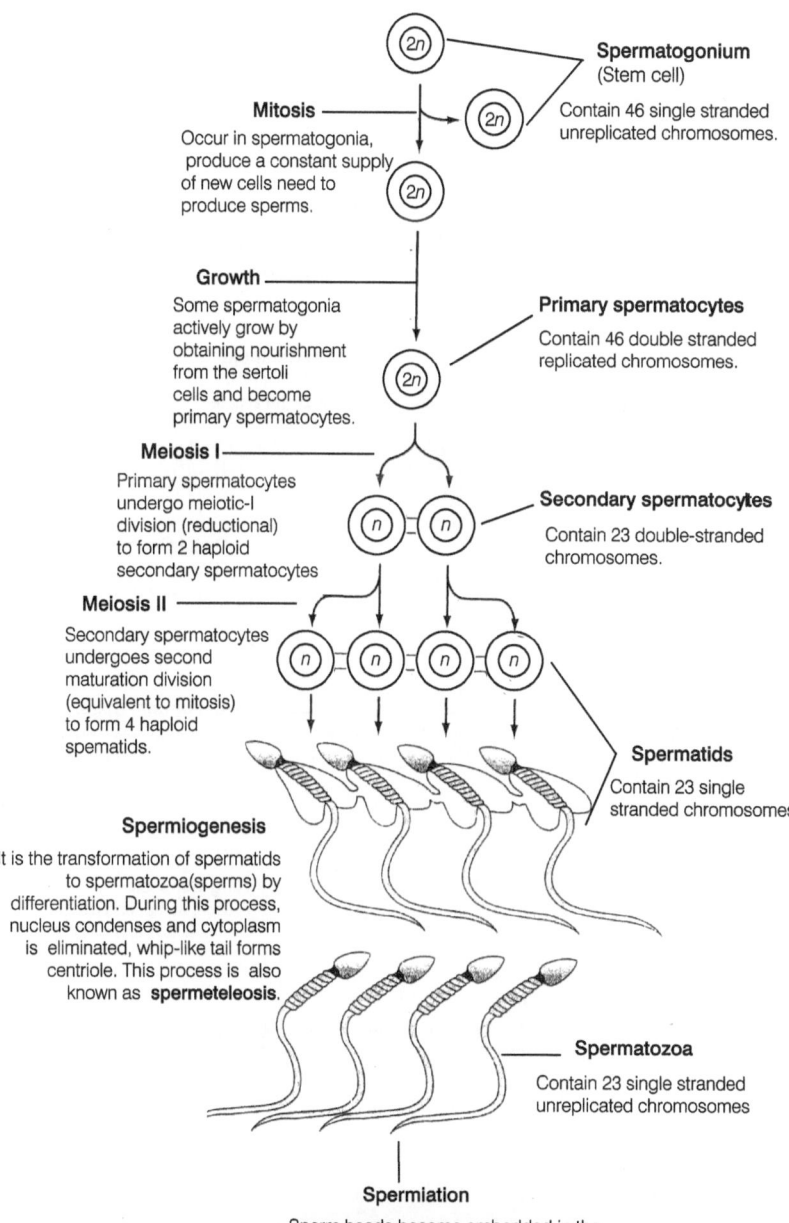

Stages in spermatogenesis

Sperm (Spermatozoan)

The sperms are microscopic and motile cells. Sperms remain alive and retain their ability to fertilise the ovum from 24 to 48 hours after being entered in the female reproductive tract.

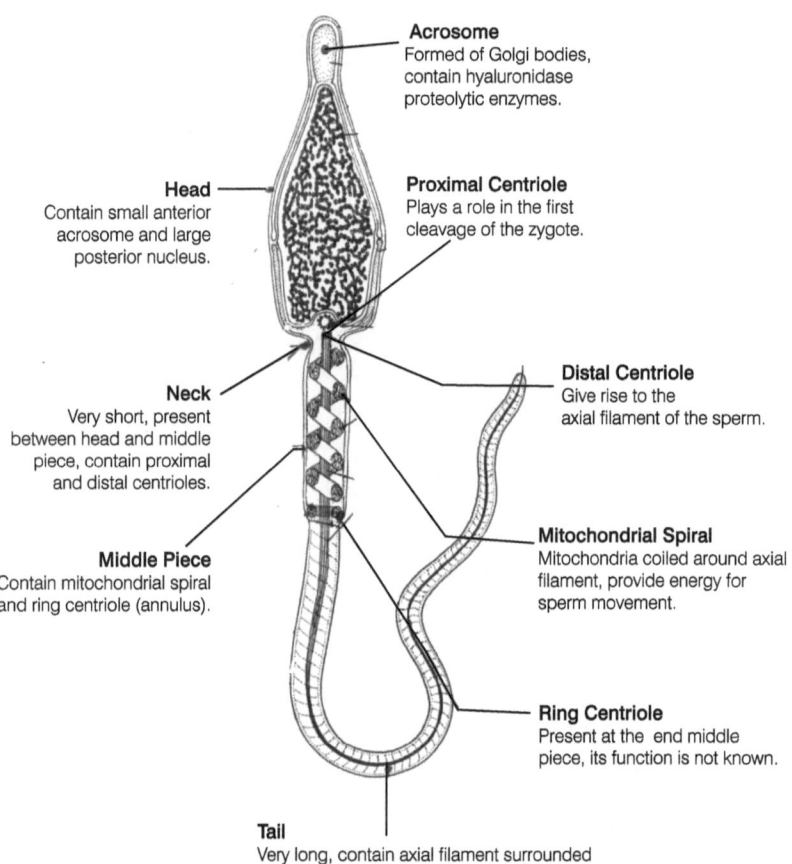

Human sperm

Hormonal Control of Male Reproductive System

The growth, maintenance and functions of male reproductive organs are under the control of steroid hormones–mainly testosterone. These hormones, in turn are controlled by negative feedback mechanisms.

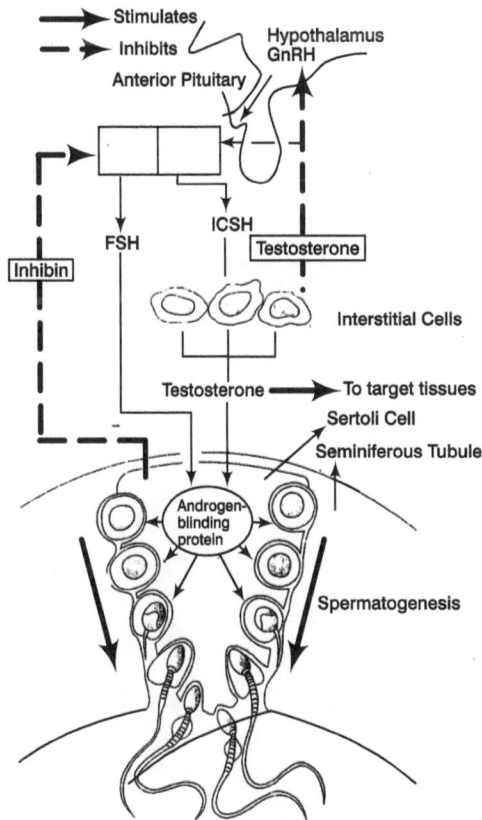

GnRH released from hypothalamus stimulates anterior pituitary to release FSH and LH (ICSH in males). ICSH act upon interstitial cells to secrete testosterone and FSH act upon the sertoli cells. Both FSH and testosterone promote spermatogenesis in seminiferous tubules.

Negative Feedback Control

The secretion of GnRH and ICSH is controlled by the testosterone in a negative feedback loop. Dip in the testosterone level in the blood increases the production of GnRH and ICSH whereas when the testosterone level becomes normal, GnRH release subsides, as does ICSH level. Similarly, FSH secretion is controlled by inhibin by negative feedback loop. When excess FSH level is detected in blood, sertoli cells secrete inhibin which in turn inhibits the release of FSH from anterior pituitary.

Hormonal control of male reproductive system

Oogenesis

It is the process of formation of a mature female gamete (ovum), occurring in the primary female gonads, *i.e.*, ovaries.

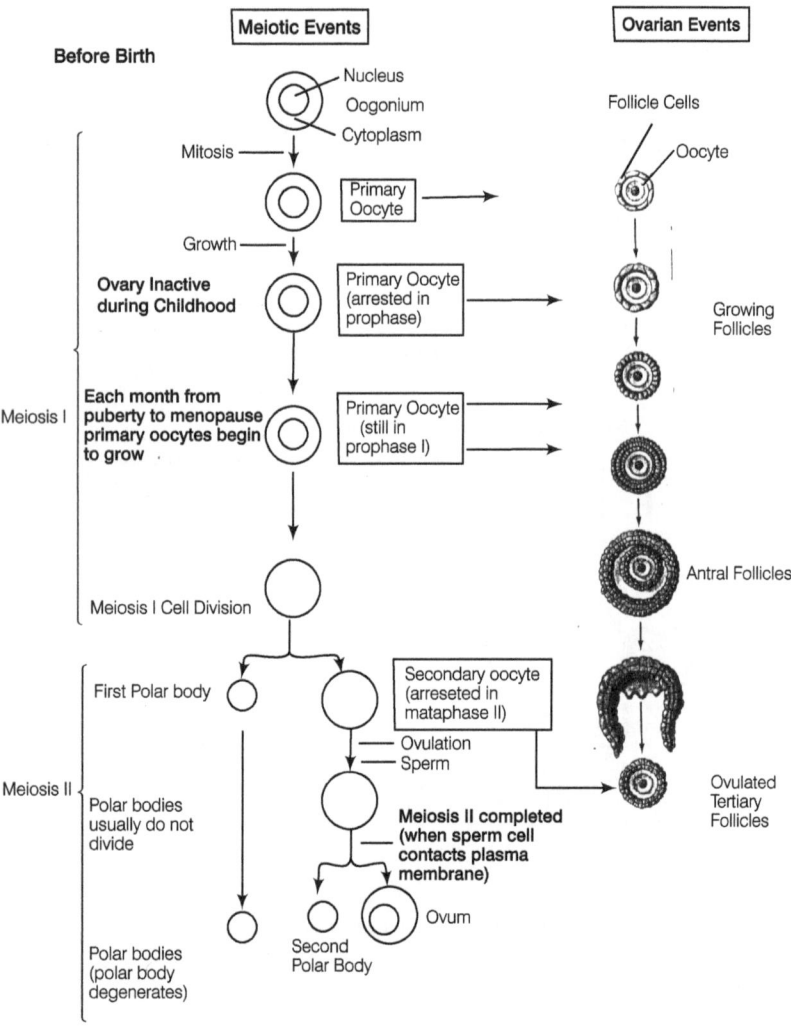

Process of oogensis

Hormonal Control of Female Reproductive System

The growth, maintenance and functions of the female reproductive organs are under the hormonal control as described below.

GnRH is secreted by the hypothalamus which stimulates the anterior lobe of pituitary gland to secrete LH and FSH. FSH stimulates the growth of the ovarian follicles and also increases the development of egg/oocyte within the follicle to complete the meiosis I to form secondary oocyte. FSH also stimulates the formation of estrogens. LH stimulates the corpus luteum to secrete progesterone. Rising level of progesterone inhibits the release of GnRH, which in turn, inhibits the production of FSH, LH and progesterone.

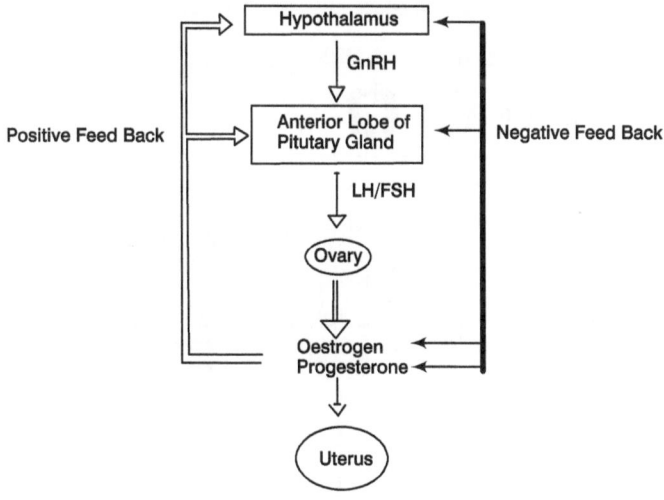

Hormonal control of female reproductive system

The Menstrual Cycle

Women of reproductive age undergoes a series of anatomical and physiological changes each month known as the menstrual cycle.

These changes occur in three areas—hormone levels, ovarian structure and uterine structure.

On average, the menstrual cycle repeats itself every 28 days. Ovulation usually occurs approximately at the midpoint of the 28-day cycle, *i.e.*, at day 14.

The average length of menstrual cycle is 28 days which may vary in different or even in the same women.

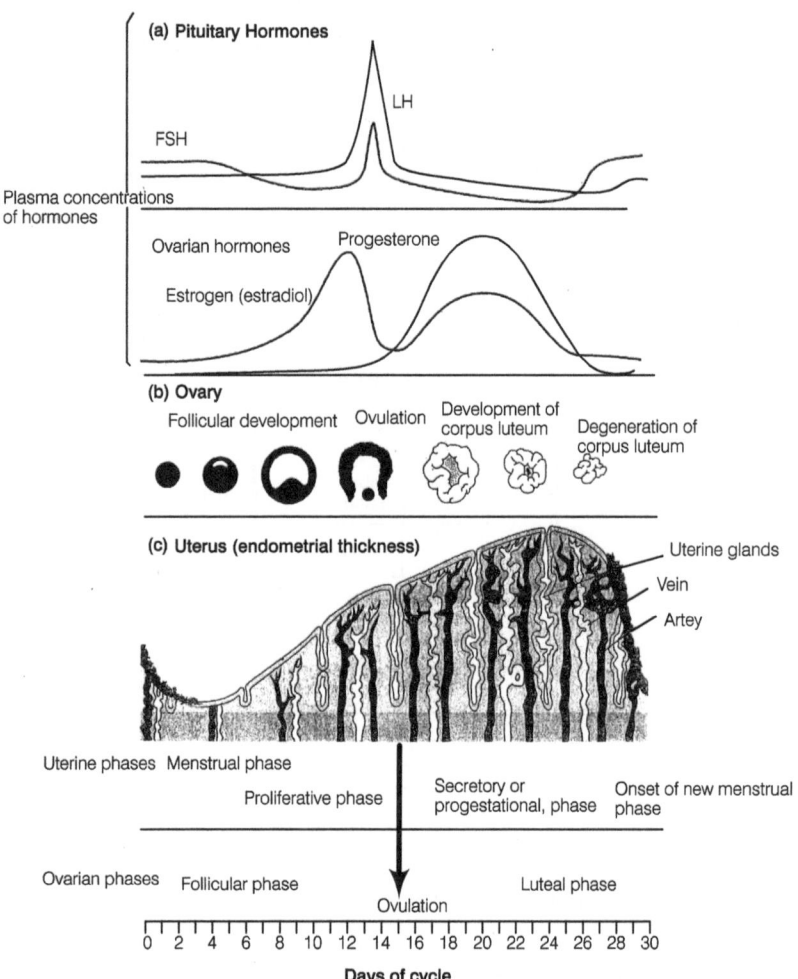

The menstrual cycle : (a) Hormonal cycle
(b) The ovarian cycle (c) The uterine cycle

Menopause

It is the complete cessation of the menstrual cycle, occur between the ages 40-50. All the follicles present in the ovary gets degenerated or ovulated, decline in estrogen production and vaginal secretions occurs. It results in temporary behavioral changes such as irritability and depression. In can also lead to osteoporosis.

Fertilisation

It is the first step in human development where union of sperm and ova occurs to form a diploid **zygote**.

It occurs in the ampullary-isthmic junction of the oviduct.

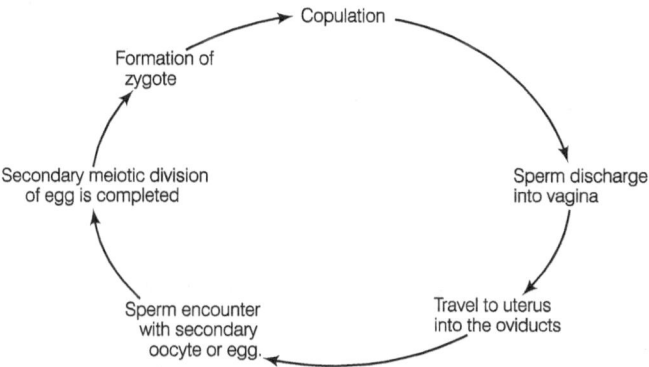

Although many millions of sperm are deposited in the vagina, only a tiny fraction make it into the oviducts. The rest are killed by the acidic secretions of the vagina or fail to find their way into the cervix.

Sperm Capacitation

It is the process in which the sperm acquire the capacity to fertilise the eggs by the secretions of the female genital tract.

It involves the removal of coating substances present on the surface of sperms so that the receptor sites on acrosome are exposed and sperm become active to penetrate the egg.

It takes about 5 to 6 hours.

Acrosome Reaction

It involves the release of various chemicals (**spermlysins**) contained in the acrosome of capacitated sperm.

Acrosome reaction occurs in three steps which are carried out by three different sperm lysins as follows

(i) **Hyaluronidase** act on the ground substances of the follicle cells.

(ii) **Corona penetrating enzyme** dissolves the **corona radiata** (radiating crown) cells that surrounds the female gamete.

(iii) **Zona lysins** (acrosin) digest the **zona pellucida** (the clear zone), a clear gel like layer immediately surrounding the oocyte.

The Block to Polyspermy

Polyspermy is the entry of more than one sperm into the oocyte.

To prevent polyspermy and to ensure monospermy (entry of one sperm into oocyte) *following events occur*

(i) **Fast Block to Polyspermy**

Rapid depolarisation of the egg's plasma membrane as soon as first sperm contracts the plasma membrane.

(ii) **Slow Block to Polyspermy** (Cortical Reaction)

Just after the penetration of sperm into egg, cortical granules (present beneath the plasma membrane of egg) fuses with the plasma membrane and release **cortical enzymes**.

These enzyme hardens the zona pellucida and convert it into the **fertilisation envelope** hence, blocking other sperm from reaching the oocyte.

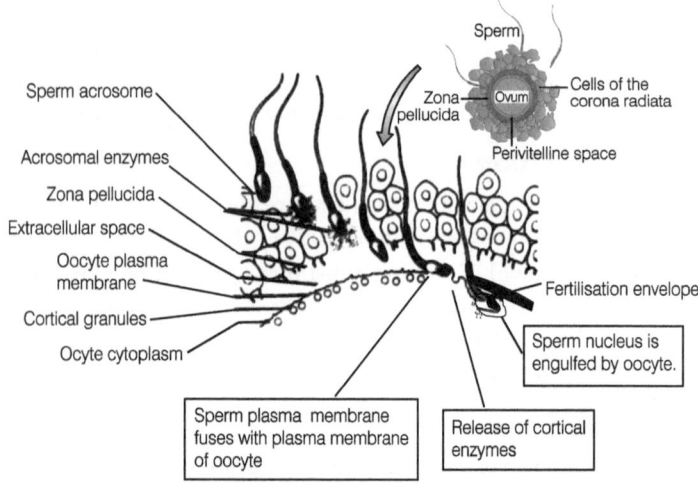

Series of events occurring in fertilisation envelope

Zygote Formation

Sperm contact with the plasma membrane of the oocyte triggers the second meiotic division and convert the secondary oocyte to **ovum**, which rapidly converts into **zygote** after the entry of the sperm nucleus.

Zygote contains 46 chromosomes, one set from each parent.

Pre-Embryonic Development

It involves all the changes that occur from fertilisation to the time just after an embryo implants in the uterine wall.

This process starts with **Cleavage**.

Cleavage

It is a series of rapid mitotic divisions of the zygote which convert the zygote into a multicellular structure blastocyst or blastula. The pattern of cleavage in human is **holoblastic**.

Significance of Cleavage

(i) Distribution of the cytoplasm amongst the blastomeres,

(ii) Restoration of the cell size and nucleocytoplasmic ratio.

Detailed events occurring in pre-embryonic development are shown below

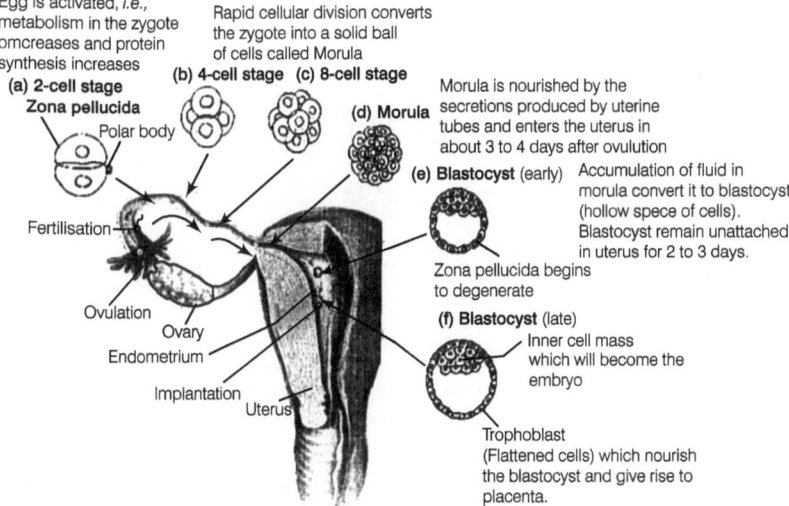

Development of morula and blastocyst

Implantation

It is the attachment of blastocyst to the uterine lining and digesting its way into the thickened layer of uterine cavity using enzymes released by the cells of blastocyst.

It occurs 6 to 7 days after fertilisation.

The process looks like

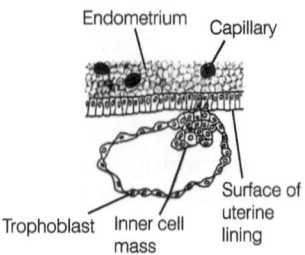

Cells of trophoblast contact the endometrium if it is properly primed by estrogen and progesterone, cells of uterine cavity at the contact point enlarge and thicken. Blastocyst usually implants high on the back wall of the uterus.

(a)

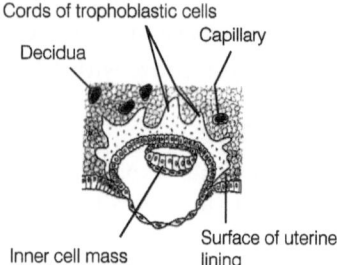

Trophoblast cells release enzymes, digest a hole in the thickened endometrial living and blastocyst bores its way into deeper tissue of uterine cavity. During this process, blastocyst feed on nutrients released from the cells it digests.

(b)

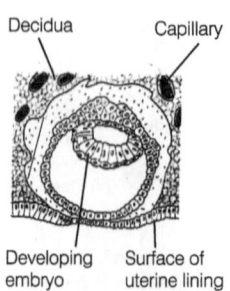

By day 14, the uterine endometrium grows over the blastocyst, enclosing it completely. Endometrial cells produce certain prostaglandins which stimulate the development of uterine blood vessels. Soon after that, placenta develops.

(c)

Trophoblast in various stages of implantation

Implantation fails to occur in the following conditions

(i) If endometrium is not properly primed by estrogen and progesterone.

(ii) If endometrium is not ready or is 'unhealthy' because of the presence of an IUD, use of a "morning after pill" or an endometrial infection.

(iii) If the cells of blastocyst contain certain genetic mutations.

Handbook of BIOLOGY

Unimplanted blastocysts are absorbed (phagocytised) by the cells of uterine lining or are expelled during menstruation.

Embryonic Development

It involves the transformation of the blastocyst into the gastrula by the process called **gastrulation**. The formation of the primary germ layers marks the beginning of embryonic development.

Gastrulation involves the cell movements called **morphogenetic movements** which helps the embryo to attain new shape and morphology. These movements results in the formation of three germ layer namely **ectoderm, mesoderm** and **endoderm**.

Key events occuring during embryonic development are shown below

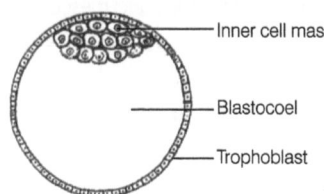

Cells of inner cell mass differentiate into 2 layers around 8 days after fertilisation. These 2 layers are **hypoblast** (primitive endoderm) and **epiblast** (primitive ectoderm).

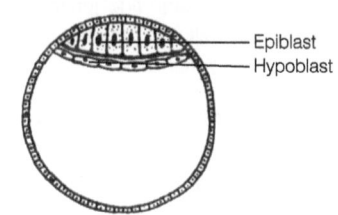

Hypoblast contain columnar cells and epiblast contains cuboidal cells. Together these two layers forms the **embryonic disc**.

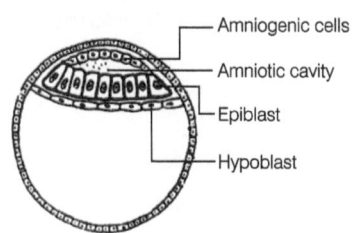

A space called **amniotic cavity** appears in between epiblast and trophoblast containing amniotic fluid. Cavity's roof is lined by **amniogenic cells** derived from trophoblast and its base is formed by epiblast.

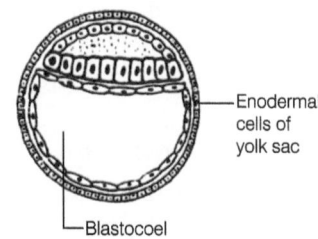

The cells of trophoblast give rise to the mass of **extraembryonic mesoderm** cells. It is differentiated into outer **somatopleuric** and inner **splanchnopleuric** mesoderm.

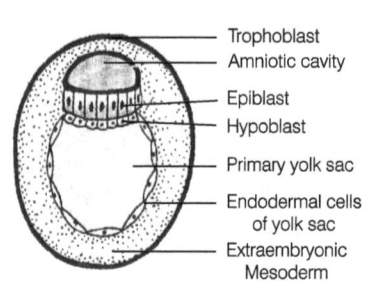
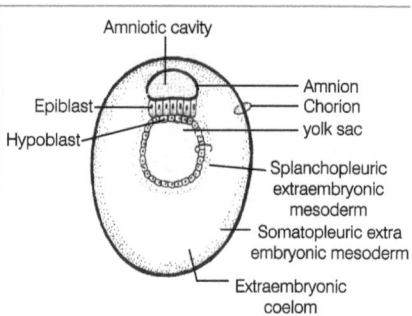

Yolk sac is derived from hypoblast cells (Primary Yolk sac). Later on, due to the appearance of extraembryonic coelom (formed by outer and inner mesoderm), the yolk sac becomes smaller (secondary yolk sac).

The **amnion** is formed from the inner cell mass, **chorion** from somatopleuric mesoderm and **atlantois** from trophoblast (inside) and splanchnopleuric mesoderm (outside).

The primary germ layers of the embryo gives rise to the organs in a process called **organogenesis**.

Various organs derived from different germ layers are as follows

End Products of Embryonic Germ Layers

Ectoderm	Mesoderm	Endoderm
Epidermis	Dermis	Lining of the digestive system
Hair, nails, sweat glands	All muscles of the body	Lining of the respiratory system
Brain and spinal cord	Cartilage	Urethra and urinary bladder
Cranial and spinal nerves	Bone	Gall bladder
Retina, lens, and cornea of eye	Blood	Liver and pancreas
Inner ear	All other connective tissue	Thyroid gland
Epithelium of nose, mouth, and anus	Blood vessels	Parathyroid gland
Enamel of teeth	Reproductive organs kidneys	Thymus

Role of Extraembryonic Membranes (Foetal Membranes)

The growing foetus develops 4 associated membranes called foetal membranes or extraembyonic membranes. Which are specialised to perform different functions.

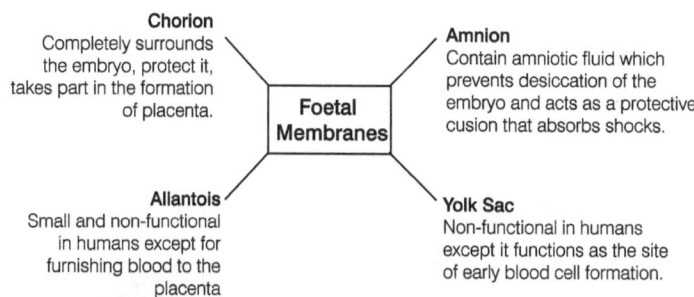

Foetal Development

It involves the continued organ development and growth and changes in body proportions. It begins in the eight week of pregnancy and ends during parturition.

Gestation Period and Parturition

Gestation period is the time period during which the foetus remains in the uterus. In humans, this period is about 280 days (38-40 weeks).

Parturition is the process of giving birth to a baby. It begins with mild uterine contractions. During labour pains, contractions increases in strength and frequency until the baby is born.

Following factors plays a major role in parturition

(i) Increased level of hormone oxytocin from the foetus and the mother.

(ii) Increase in oxytocin receptors by estrogen.

(iii) Blocking of calming influence of the progesterone by estrogen.

(iv) Expansion of cervix by hormone relaxin.

The stepwise approach with oxytocin feed back mechanism in birth is as follows

Step 1. Baby moves further into mother's vagina.

Step 2. Receptors in cervix gets excited.

Step 3. Impulses sent to hypothalamus.

Step 4. Hypothalamus sends impulses to posterior pituitary

Step 5. Posterior pituitary releases stored oxytocin to blood which stimulates mother's uterine muscles to contract.

Step 6. Uterine contractions become more vigrous (labour pians). The cyclic mechanism continues until the birth of the body.

Stages of Childbirth

Childbirth consists of three stages namely *i.e.,* dilation, expulsion and placental.

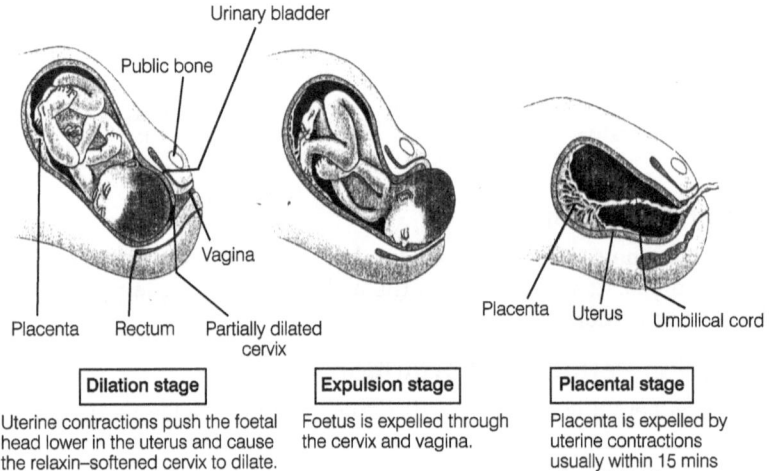

Placenta

It is the intimate connection between the foetus and the uterine wall of the mother.

It develops from chorion.

Chorionic villi are the number of finger-like projections which develop from the outer surface of chorion and penetrate the uterine walls to form placenta.

The **foetal part** of placenta is chorion and the **maternal part** is decidua basalis.

Types of Placenta

The placenta can be classified into different types on the following basis

(i) Nature of Contact

On the basis of nature of contact, placenta is of two types **indeciduate** and **deciduate**.

(a) **Indeciduate placenta** Chorionic villi are simple, lie in contact with uterus, they have loose contact, and there is no fusion. At the time of birth, uterus is not damaged, *e.g.*, Ungulate, Cetaceans, Sirenians, Lemurs, etc.

(b) **Deciduate placenta** The allantochorianic villi penetrate into the uterine villi. They are intimately fused. Hence, at the time of birth, the uterus is damaged and bleeding occurs, *e.g.*, Primates, Rodentia, Chiroptera, etc.

(ii) Distribution of Villi

On the basis of villi distribution, placenta is of five types as follows

Placental Types on the Basis of Villi Distribution

Diffused
Villi are distributed uniformly on the blastocyst surface except at extreme ends, e.g., Pig, horse (indeciduate type)

Cotyledonary
Villi are arranged in groups, each group is called cotydon which fits into the caruncles (maternal contact sites) of uterus, *e.g.*, sheep, cow, deer (indeciduate type)

Zonary
Villi are in the form of transverse bands or zones and penetrate in the uterus wall, *e.g.*, cat, dog, bear, elephant, carnivoses. (deciduate type)

Intermediatey
Rare type, shows free villi on cotyledons, indeciduate type; e.g., camel, giralffe.

Discoidal
Villi are present as disc on the entire surface of blastocyst, when embryo grows it moves away from the uterus hence, it look like a disc, deciduate type, *e.g.*, Rat, Bat, Rabbit

(iii) Histology

Placenta is classified into 5 types on the basis of number of layers present between the foetus and uterus.

The six layers in between foetal and materal parts are (i) endothelium of mother blood vessel, (ii) maternal syndesmose connective tissue, (iii) maternal epithelium, (iv) chorion of foetus, (v) foetus syndesmose connective tissue, (vi) endothelium of foetal blood vessel.

The five placental types are as follows

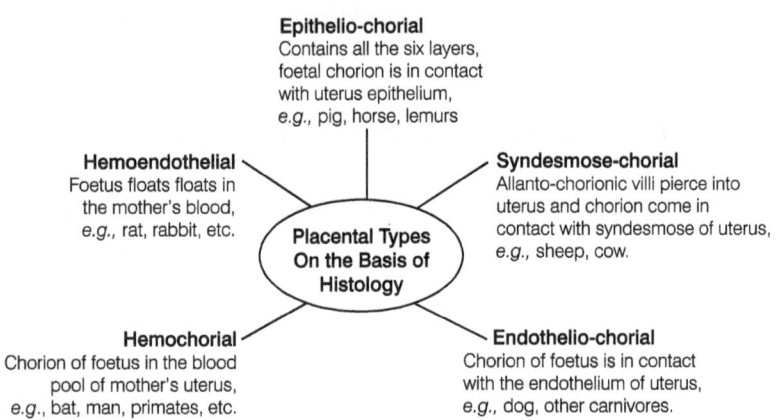

Human placenta is deciduate and hemochorial type and it produces various hormones whose functions are as follows

Hormones Produced by the Placenta

Hormone	Function
Human Chorionic Gonadotropin (HCG)	Maintains corpus luteum of pregnancy, Stimulates secretion of testosterone by developing testes in XY embryos
Estrogen (also secreted by corpus luteum during pregnancy)	Stimulates growth of myometrium, increasing uterine strength for parturition (childbirth) Helps prepare mammary glands for lactation
Progesterone (also secreted by corpus luteum during pregnancy)	Suppresses uterine contractions to provide quiet environment for foetus Promotes formation of cervical mucous plug to prevent uterine contamination Helps prepare mammary glands for lactation
Human chorionic somatomammotropin	Helps prepare mammary glands for lactation Believed to reduce maternal utilisation of glucose so that greater quantities of glucose can be shunted to the foetus
Relaxin (also secreted by corpus luteum of pregnancy)	Softens cervix in preparation of cervical dilation at parturition Loosens connective tissue between pelvic bones in preparation for parturition.

Other functions performed by placenta are listed below

(i) **Nutrition** It helps to supply all the nutritive elements from the maternal blood to pass into the foetus.

(ii) **Excretion** The foetal excretory products diffuses into maternal blood through placenta.

(iii) **Barrier** Placenta serves as an efficient barrier and allows only necessary material to pass into foetal blood.

(iv) **Storage** Placenta stores glycogen, fat, etc.

Summary of Human Pregnancy from Fertilisation to Birth of the Baby

Week 1	Week 2	Week 3
Fertilisation, cleavage to form a blastocyst 4-5 days after fertilisation. More than 100 cells. Implantation 6-9 days after fertilisation.	The three basic layers of the embryo develop, namely ectoderm, mesoderm and endoderm. No research allowed on human embryos byond this stage.	Woman will not have a period. This may be the first sign that she is pregnant. Beginnings of the backbone. Neural tube develops, the beginning of the brain and spinal cord (first organs). Embryo about 2 mm long.

Week 4	Week 5	Week 6
Heart, blood vessels, blood and gut start forming. Umbilical cord developing. Embryo about 5 mm long.	Brain developing. 'Limb buds', small swellings which are the beginnings of the arms and legs. Heart is a large tube and starts to beat, pumping blood. This can be seen on an ultrasound scan. Embryo about 8 mm long.	Eyes and ears start to form.

Week 7	By Week 12	By Week 20
All major internal organs developing. Face forming. Eyes have some colour. Mouth and tongue. Beginnings of hands and feet. Foetus is 17 mm long.	Foetus fully formed, with all organs, muscles, bones, toes and fingers. Sex organs well developed. Foetus is moving. For the rest of the gestation period, it is mainly growing in size. Foetus is 56 mm long from head to bottom. Pregnancy may begin to show.	Hair beginning to grow, including eyebrows and eyelashes. Fingerprints developed. Finger nails and toe nails growing. Firm hand grip. Between 16 and 20 weeks baby usually felt moving for first time. Baby is 160 mm long from head to bottom.

Week 24	By Week 26	By Week 28
Eyelids open. Legal limit for abortion in most circumstances.	Has a good chance of survival if born prematurely.	Baby moving vigorously. Responds to touch and loud noises. Swallowing amniotic fluid and urinating.

By Week 30	40 Weeks (9 months)
Usually lying head down ready for birth. Baby is 240 mm from head to bottom.	Birth

Lactation

The production and release of milk after birth by woman is called lactation. The first milk which comes out from the mother's mammary glands just after child birth is known as **colostrum**.

Colostrum is rich in proteins and energy along with antibodies that provides passive immunity for the new born infant. Milk synthesis is stimulated by pituitary hormone, prolactin.

The release of milk is stimulated by a rise in the level of oxytocin when the baby begins to nourish. Milk contains inhibitory peptides which accumulates and inhibits milk production, if the breasts are not fully emptied.

The Lactating Breast

The glandular units enlarge considerably under the influence of progesterone and prolactin. Milk is expelled by contraction of muscle-like cells surrounding the glandular units. Ducts drain the milk to the nipple.

17

Reproductive Health

Reproductive Health
According to World Health Organisation (WHO), reproductive health means a total well-being in all aspects of reproduction, *i.e.*, physical, emotional, behavioural and social.

Problems Related to Reproductive Health
There are various factors which may lead to reproduction health problems, *These are as follows*

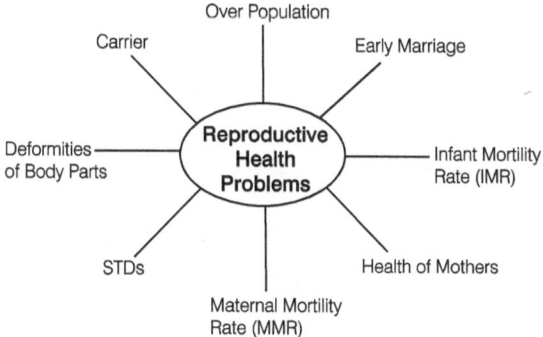

Population Explosion
It is the rapid increase of a population attributed especially to an accelerating birthrate, decrease in infant mortality and an increase in life expectancy.

Reasons for High Population Growth

(a) **Spread of education** Persons of the country are being educated about the diseases.
(b) **Control of diseases** Control of various communicable diseases is in practice.
(c) **Advancement in agriculture** Farmers are educated to develop high yielding crops.
(d) **Storage facilities** A good quantity of grains can be stored easily.
(e) **Better transport** This protects from famines.
(f) **Protection from natural calamity** It decreases death rate.
(g) **Government efforts** Government is making efforts to provide maximum informations to the farmers.

Effects of Population Explosion

Over population leads to the number of national and individual family problems. *These are as follows*

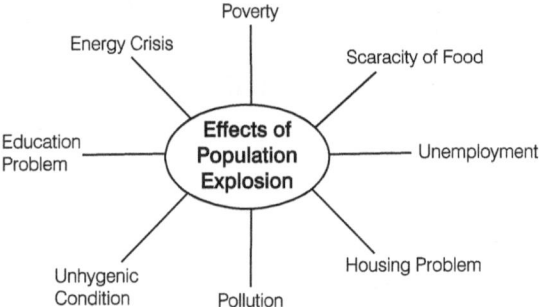

It may also lead to socio economic problems due to shortage of space, food, educational and medical facilities.

Strategies to Improve Reproductive Health

(i) Reproductive and Child Health Care (RCH) Programmes

They aim to create awareness among people about various reproduction related aspects and provide facilities and support for building up a reproductively healthy society.

This programme is a part of **family planning** programme which was initiated in 1951.

The various parameters of these programmes are as follows

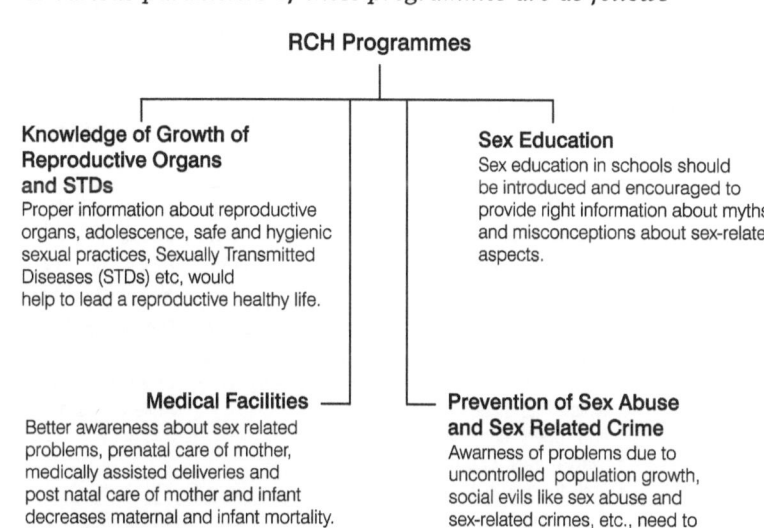

(ii) Research in Reproductive Health Area

It should be encouraged and supported to find out new methods. 'Saheli' a new oral contraceptive for the females was developed by our scientists at Central Drug Research Institute (CDRI) in Lucknow, India. It is a non-hormonal prepration.

(iii) Birth Control

It refers to the regulation of conception by preventive methods or devices to limit the number of offsprings.

Contraception It includes the contraceptive methods, *i.e.*, the methods which deliberately prevent fertilisation.

The various methods of birth control are listed in the following table

Methods of Contraception and Birth Control

Methods	Basis of Action	Note on Uses	Relative Disadvantages
Barrier Methods			
Condom	A thin, strong rubber sheath, prevents the sperm to entering the vagina.	Placed over erect penis just before sexual intercourse.	Not as reliable as the pill. Relies on male. May tear or slip off.
Femidom	Female condom-a thin rubber or polyurethane tube with a closed end, which fits inside vagina and open end has two fixable rings, one on each end, to keep it in place.	Inserted before intercourse and removed any time later.	Difficult to insert. Can break or leak. Expensive than male condom.
Diaphragm/Cap	A flexible rubber dome which fits over the cervix and prevents entry of sperm to uterus. Used with a spermicidal cream or jelly (a spermicide is a chemical which kills sperms).	Inserted before intercourse. Must be left in place at least 6 hours after the intercourse.	Suggestion of doctor is must for proper size selection. Its training is required to fit. Occasionally causes abdominal pain. It should not be left for more than 30 hours as it may cause toxic shock syndrome. Examination required after every 6 months that cap is of right of size.
Spermicide	Chemical which kills sperm.	Placed in vagina to cover the lining of vagina and cervix. Effective for about 1 hour.	High failure rate if used on its own.
Sponge	Polyurethane sponge impregnated with spermicide, fits over cervix, disposable.	Fits up to 24 hours before intercourse. Leave in place for at least 6 hours after intercourse.	High failure rate.

Methods	Basis of Action	Note on Uses	Relative Disadvantages
Hormonal Methods			
Pill	Contains the female sex hormones- oestrogen and progesterone. Prevents development of eggs and ovulation by inhibiting the secretion of FSH. Act on cervical mucus to prevent the penetration of sperm. Prevent the blastocyst implantation.	One taken orally each day during first 3 weeks of cycle. After week 4, menstruation starts and the pill is started again.	Short-term side effects, may include nausea, fluid retention and weight gain. Long-term side effects not fully understood, but increased risk of blood clotting may occur in some women. Not recommended for older women.
Minipill	Contains progesterone only. Ovulation may occur, but cervical mucus is thickened, preventing entry of sperms.	Must be taken within 3 hours after inter-course everyday.	May cause headache, nausea, weight gain.
IUD (Intra-Uterine Device) or Coil	Ist generation (non-medicated, e.g., lippes loops, rings). 2nd generation (copper devices, e.g., copper T-220). 3rd generation (hormonal devices, e.g., progestasert).	It is placed in cervix, acts as spermicide within the uterus.	May cause bleeding and discomfort. IUD may slip out.
Natural Methods (NFP stands for natural method of family planning)			
Abstinence	Avoid sexual Intercourse.	—	Restricts emotional development of a relationship.
Rhythm method	Avoid sexual intercourse around the time of ovulation (total abstinence for about 7-14 days).	—	High failure rate, even higher if periods are irregular. Requires good knowledge of body and good record-keeping. Requires a period of abstinence.

Methods	Basis of Action	Note on Uses	Relative Disadvantages
Temperature method	Note the rise in temperature at ovulation (due to rise in progesterone) and avoid sexual intercourse at these times.	—	As above.
Coitus interruptus (withdrawl)	Penis is withdrawn from vagina before ejaculation.	—	High failure rate. Requires much self-discipline. Penis may leak some sperm before ejaculation.
Lactational amenorrhea	Sucking stimulus prevents the generation of normal preovulatory LH surge hence, ovulation does not occur.	—	—

Sterilisation (Surgical methods)

Vasectomy	Vas deferens are severed and tied.	—	Very difficult to reverse. Need to use alternative method upto 2 to 3 months after vasectomy
Tubectomy	Both oviducts are severed and tied (now laproscopic method are used).	—	Even more difficult to reverse than vasectomy.

Termination (Its not a part of contraception)

Morning-after Pill	Contains RU486, an antiprogesterone.	Taken within 3 days of sexual intercourse.	For use only in emergencies. Long-term effects not known.
Abortion (discussed later in this chapter as MTP)	Up to 24 Weeks	Premature termination of pregnancy by surgical intervention.	Risk of infertility and other complications. Emotionally difficult and ethically wrong.

Medical Termination of Pregnancy (MTP)

MTP or induced abortion is the termination or removal of embryo from the uterus by using pharmacological or surgical methods. It is considered safe during the first trimester, *i.e.,* up to 12 weeks of pregnancy.

```
                          MTP
           ┌───────────────┴───────────────┐
       Significance                    Drawbacks
```

Significance
- Play significant role in decreasing human population.
- Helps in getting rid of unwanted and harmful pregnancies.

Drawbacks
- Misused to abort the normal female foetuses.
- Raises many emotional, ethical, religious and social issues.

Sexually Transmitted Diseases (STDs)

These are the diseases or infections which are transmitted through sexual intercourse. They are also called **Veneral Diseases (VD)** or **Reproductive Tract Infections (RTI)**.

Various STDs are as follows

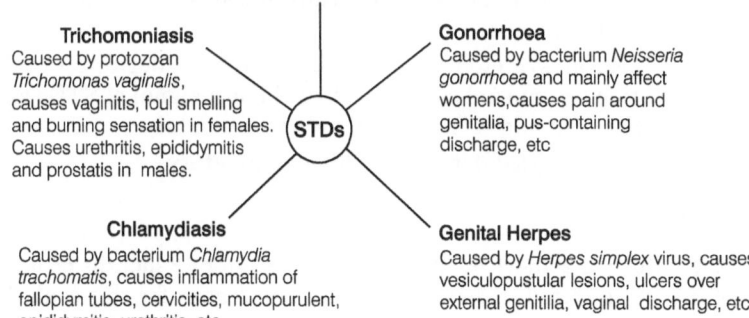

Syphilis
Caused by bacterium *Treponema pallidium* which grow and multiply in warm, moist area of reproductive tract, causes skin lesions, swollen joints, heart trouble, etc.

Trichomoniasis
Caused by protozoan *Trichomonas vaginalis*, causes vaginitis, foul smelling and burning sensation in females. Causes urethritis, epididymitis and prostatis in males.

Gonorrhoea
Caused by bacterium *Neisseria gonorrhoea* and mainly affect womens, causes pain around genitalia, pus-containing discharge, etc

Chlamydiasis
Caused by bacterium *Chlamydia trachomatis*, causes inflammation of fallopian tubes, cervicities, mucopurulent, epididymitis, urethritis, etc.

Genital Herpes
Caused by *Herpes simplex* virus, causes vesiculopustular lesions, ulcers over external genitilia, vaginal discharge, etc.

Other STDs are as follows

STDs	Pathogen	Symptoms
Chancroid	*Haemophilus ducreyi* bacterium	Ulcers over external genitalia.
Genital warts	Human Papilloma Virus (HPV)	Warts over external genitalia, vaginal infection.
Hepatitis–B	Hepatitis–B Virus (HBV)	Fatigue, jaundice, cirrhosis etc.
Candidiasis	*Candida albicans* (vaginal yeast)	Inflammation of vagina, thick, cheesy discharge etc.

Acquired Immuno Deficiency Syndrome (AIDS)

It is a fluid transmitted disease with possibility of transmission through body fluids like blood, semen, etc.

As sexual intercourse is the best suitable mode of fluid transmission that's why it is misleaded to be one of the STDs. Other transmission modes include blood transfusion, use of same syringes and needles, etc.

Preventive Measures (Prophylaxis) of STDs

Prevention of sexually transmitted diseases can be done by the simple practices given below

(i) Avoid sex with unknown partners/multiple partners.
(ii) Always use condoms during coitus.
(iii) Use sterilised needles and syringes.
(iv) Education about the sexually transmitted diseases should be given to the people.
(v) Any genital symptoms such as discharge or burning during urination or unusual sore or rash could be a signal of STDs and the person should seek medical help immediately.
(vi) Screening of blood donors should be mandatory.

Infertility

It is the failure to achieve a clinical pregnancy after 12 months or more of regular unprotected sexual intercourse. The reason for this could be physical, congenital, diseases, drugs, immunological or psychological.

Handbook of BIOLOGY

Primary Infertility
If the conception has never occurred, the condition is called primary infertility.

Secondary Infertility
If the patient fails to conceive after achieving a previous conception, the condition is called secondary fertility.

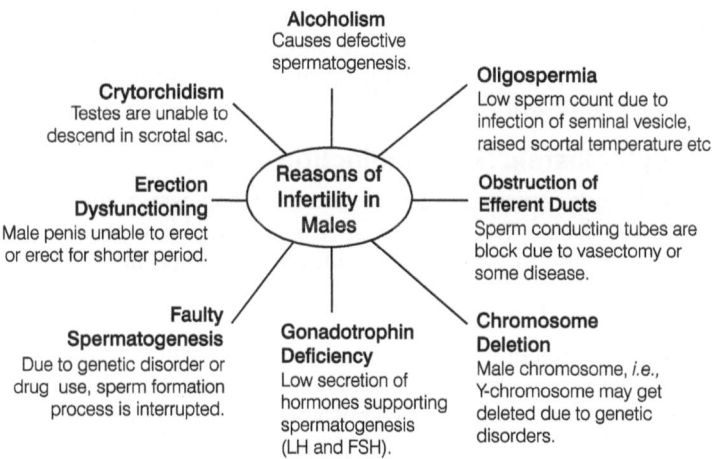

Reasons of infertility in males

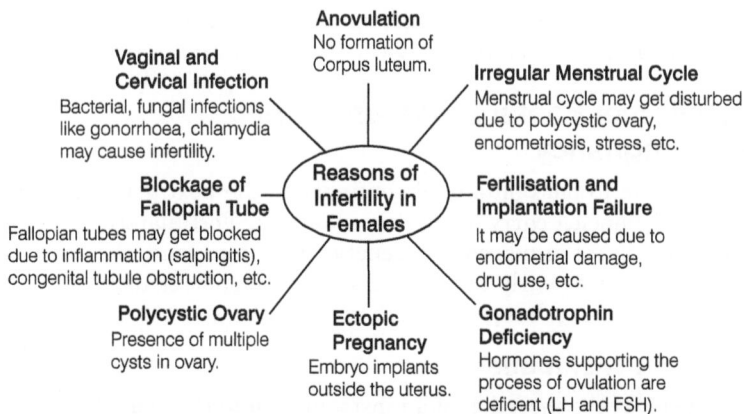

Reasons of infertility in females

Assisted Reproductive Technology (ART)

These are the applications of reproductive technologies to solve infertility problems.

They include the following techniques

1. *In Vitro* Fertilisation (IVF)

It is used as a remedy for infertility. A woman's egg cells are combined with sperm cells outside the body in laboratory conditions to become fertised. The fertilised egg (zygote) is then transferred to the patient's uterus. Hence, IVF refers to any biological procedure that is performed outside the organism's body.

2. Intracytoplasmic Sperm Injection (ICSI)

In this technique, sperm is injected into the cytoplasm of an egg using microinjection. It is effective when sperms are unable to penetrate the egg on its own due to low sperm count, abnormal sperms etc.

3. Intra Uterine Transfer (IUT)

It involves the transfer of an embryo to the uterus when it is with more than 8 blastomeres. Similarly, when the zygote is placed in the fallopian tube, the technique is known as **Zygote Intra Fallopian Transfer** (ZIFT).

4. Gamete Intra Fallopian Transfer (GIFT)

In this technique, eggs are removed from the ovaries and placed in one of the fallopian tube along with the sperm. This allows the fertilisation to occur within the woman's body (in *vivo* fertilisation).

Detection of Foetal Disorders During Early Pregnancy

No one wants to pass on any abnormality to the next generation, but all the pregnancies carry some degree of risk. Fortunately, it is now possible to detect hundreds of genetic mutations and chromosomal abnormalities very early in the course of development using invasive and non-invasive techniques, *which are as follows*

1. Invasive Techniques

These involves the insertion of an instrument into the body. It involves amniocentesis, Chronic Villi Sampling (CVS), etc. Amniocentesis (also referred to as Amniotic Fluid Test or AFT) is a medical procedure used in prenatal diagnosis of **chromosomal abnormalities** and

foetal infections. A small amount of amniotic fluid, which contains foetal tissues is extracted from the amnion or amniotic sac surrounding the developing foetus and the foetal DNA is examined for genetic abnormalities. Using this process, the sex of a child can be determined and hence, this procedure has some legal restrictions in some gender biased countries.

2. Non-Invasive Techniques

These techniques do not involves the introduction of any instruments into the body. It involves ultrasound imaging, maternal blood sampling, etc.

In ultrasound imaging, high frequency sound waves are utilised to produce visible images from the pattern of the echos made by different tissues and organs.

Maternal blood sampling technique is based on the fact that few foetal blood cells leak across the placenta into the mother's blood stream. A blood sample from the mother provides enough foetal cells that can be tested for genetic disorders.

18

Human Health *and* Disease

Human Health

Health is defined as a state of complete physical, mental and social well being. It is not merely the absence of disease or infirmity.

Balanced or good health is a state of **optimum physical fitness, mental maturity, alertness, freedom from anxiety** and **social well being** with freedom from social tensions.

Health can be affected by the following factors

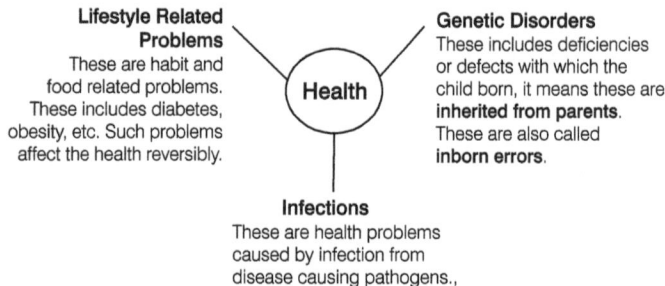

Factors which affect health

Healthy people are more efficient at work with increased longevity. This lead to reduced **Infant Mortality Rate (IMR)** and **Maternal Mortality Rate (MMR)**. There are some other factors also, which have major impact on our health, such as awareness about diseases and their effects on different functions of body, vaccination against infectious diseases, proper disposal of waste, maintenance of hygienic food and water resources.

Handbook of **BIOLOGY** 307

Common Diseases in Humans

Any deviation from normal state of health is called **disease**, in which the functioning of an organ or body got disturbed or deranged.

These disease are caused by microorganisms like bacteria, virus, fungi, protozoans, worms, etc. These disease causing organism are called as **pathogens**. *Diseases can be classified as*

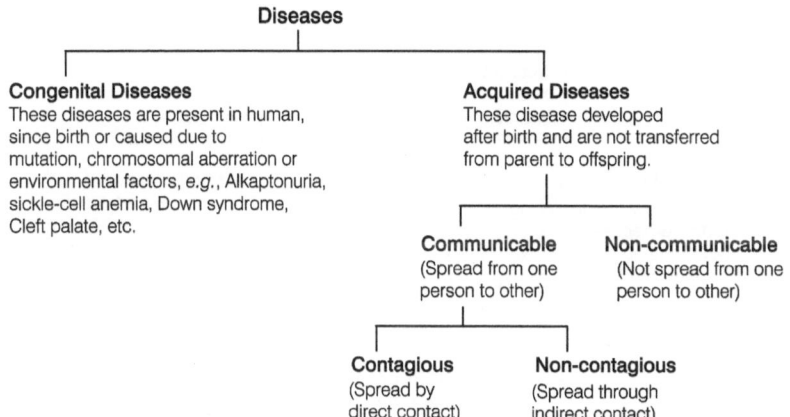

The detailed account of these diseases are as follows

Communicable or Infectious Diseases

These are transferred from one person to another. *On the basis of types of causative agent (pathogen), communicable diseases are of following types*

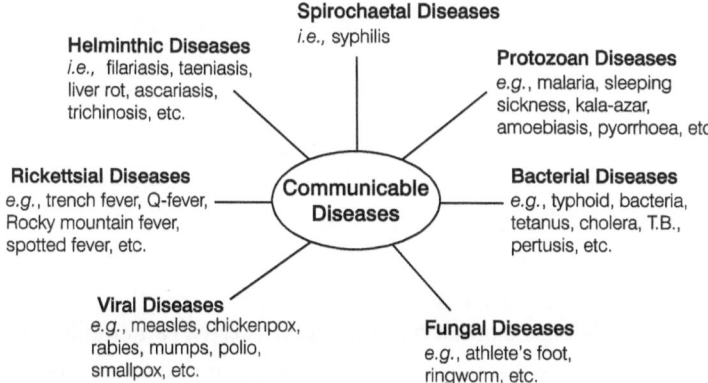

Communicable diseases

Non-Communicable or Non-Infectious Diseases

These diseases are not transferred from an affected person to healthy person. Among non-infectious diseases, cancer is the major cause of death.

Non-communicable diseases can be categorised as follows

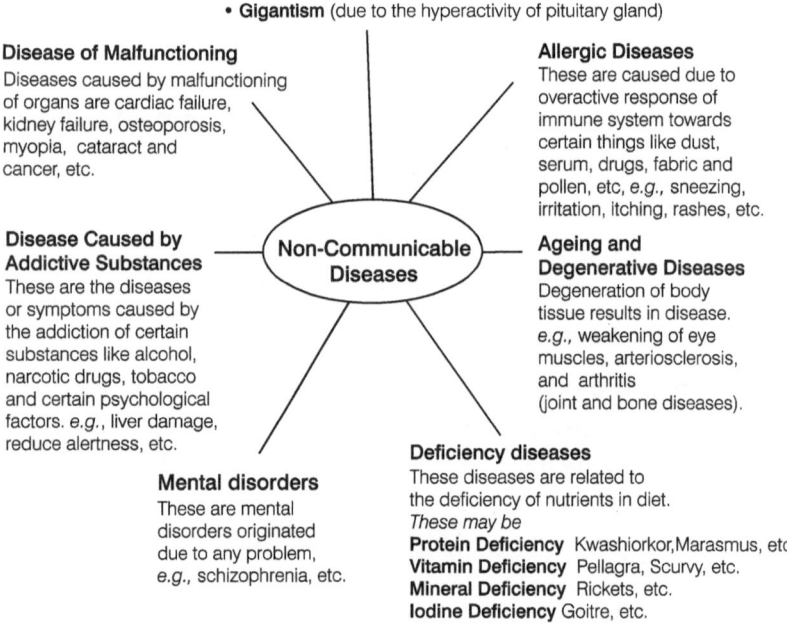

Non-communicable diseases

Immunity and Immune System

Immunity can be defined as

'The self-preparedness (of the body) against invasion by microbes. It also includes defense against non-microbial antigens and malignancy.'

Antigens are the substances, which evoke an immune response when introduced in the body.

Criterias for Antigenicity
  (i) Molecular size should be > 5000 d.
  (ii) Chemical nature (usually protein and polysaccharide).
  (iii) Susceptibility to tissue enzyme.
  (iv) Foreignness.
  (v) Iso and auto specificity (except lens protein and sperm).

Antibodies are protein produced within the body by the plasma cells against antigens.

Structure of Antibodies

The basic unit of all immunoglobulin (Ig) molecules consists of four polypeptide chains linked by disulphide bonds.

The structure is represented diagrammatically as

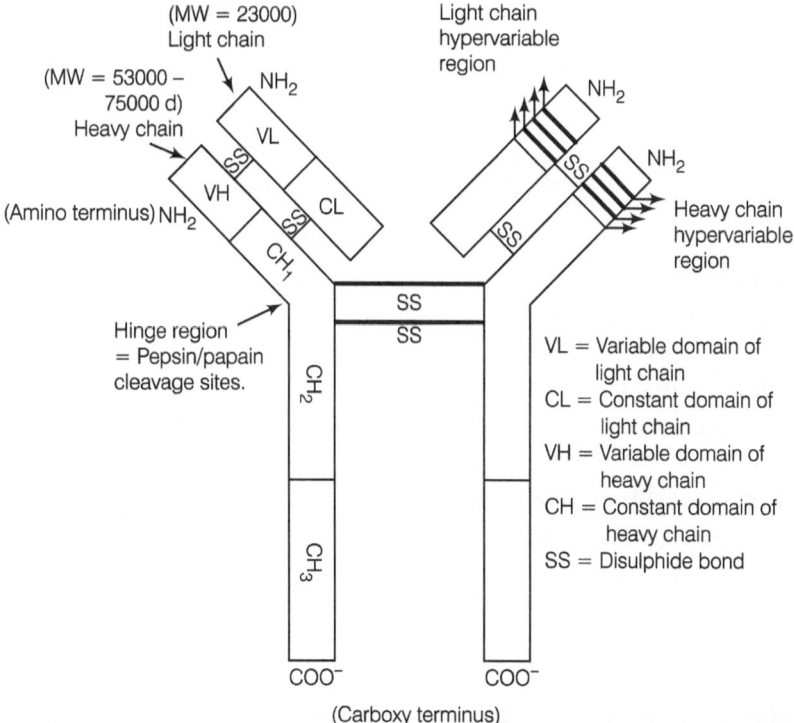

Antibody structure

Most of the antibodies are **euglobulin** and is usually **gamma** (γ) **globulin**. All antibodies are immunoglobulin, but all immunoglobulins may not be antibodies. Immunoglobulin constitutes 20-25% of total serum proteins.

Classes of Immunoglobulins

There are five classes of immunoglobulins. These are described as follows

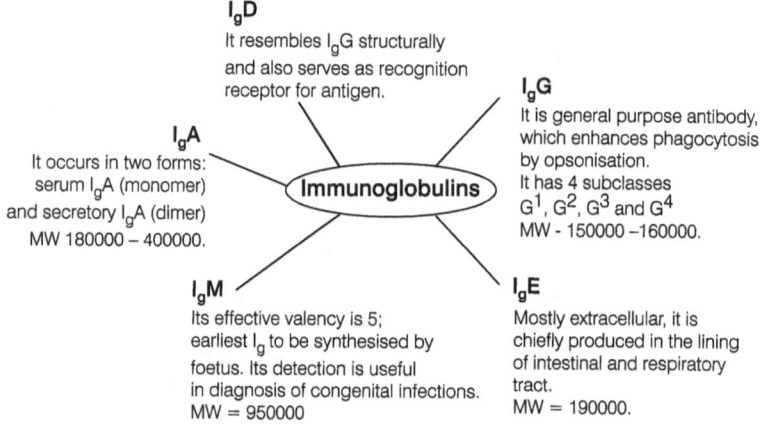

Types of immunoglobulins

Note

IgG-Protects body fluids

IgA-Protects body surface and

IgM-Protect the bloodstream

The action/response of antibodies against antigens is known as immune response or immunity. *Classically it is divided into two categories*

(a) Non-specific or Innate Immunity

It is not affected by the prior contact with the antigen and effective against all without recognising the specific identities of the enemies. *e.g.*, skin, sebum, sweat, mucous and acids in stomach are non-specifically protective.

(b) Specific or Acquired Immunity

This immunity is the primary function of the lymphocytes which is carried out by other cells also. It has separate mechanisms for each and every enemy. To develop immunity, the prior contact with the specific antigen is essential. It develops against only to those antigens, which are not recognised as self.

Handbook of **BIOLOGY**

*The specific immunity may be **active** or **passive**.*

(a) Active Immunity

It is developed within the body by the introduction of attenuated (heat suppressed) antigens, which are against lymphocytes. Active immunity can also be activated through vaccination. *e.g.,* polio vaccine, tetanus vaccine, etc.

On the basis of action of responding cell, active immunity is of two types

Active Immunity

Cell Mediated Immunity (CMI)
This immunity is due to T-lymphocytes, which got matured in thymus.

Humoral Immunity (HI)
It is due to B-lymphocytes, which got matured in bone marrow.

T-lymphocyte

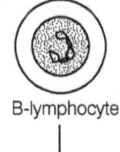
B-lymphocyte

It produce antibody on their surface when exposed to antigen.

It produce specific antibody on their surface when exposed to antigen.

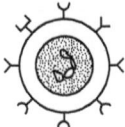

After producing various types of antibodies, T-cell itself goes to antigen and degrade it. No antibody is released.

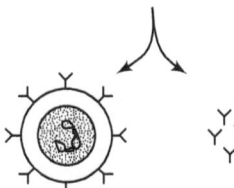 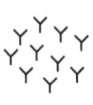

Saved as memory cell for further response against same antigen.

Released antibodies goes to antigen and digest it.

Demonstration of active immunity in organisms

(b) Passive Immunity

It occurs due to the transfer or introduction of antibodies (Immunoglobulins) from outside. *e.g.,* injection of serum against specific antibodies as Anti-Tetanus Serum (ATS), Anti-Venom Serum (AVS), etc.

During this, readymade antibodies are directly given to protect the body against foreign agents. The yellowish fluid colostrum secreted by mother during the initial days of lactation has abundant antibodies (*i.e.,* IgA) to protect the infant.

The foetus also receive some antibodies from their mother through the placenta during pregnancy. This is also an example of passive immunity. Immune system is biologically, reticuloendothelial system.

The detailed description of reticulendothelial system is as follows

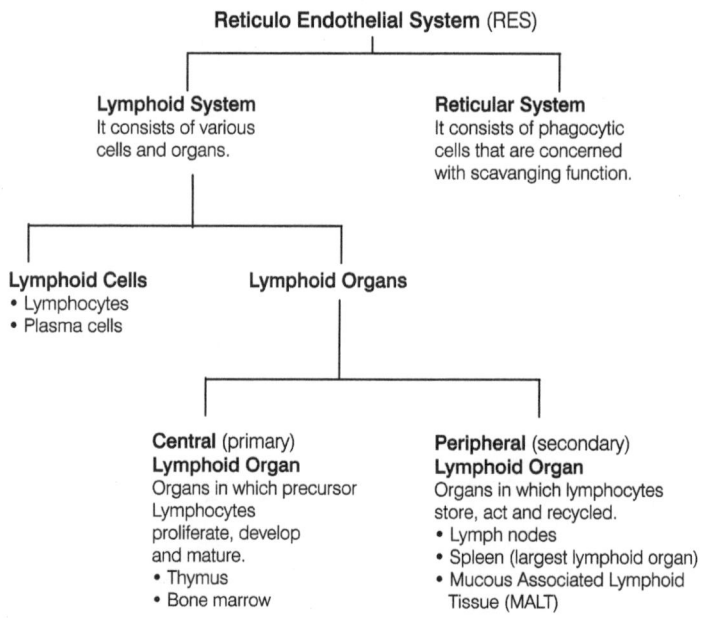

Components of reticuloendothelial system

Cells of Immune System

The various cells performing different functions constitutes the immune system.

A close look of structure and functions of these cells are described below

Cells of Immune System

Dendritic Cells
These are Antigen Presenting Cells (APCs) to T-cell during primary immune response. They are **bone marrow derived cell.** These have little or no phagocytic activity.
These are of three types
(i) Interdigitating dendritic cells.
(ii) Langerhans cell.
(iii) Follicular dendritic cell.

Null Cell or LGL
(Large Granular Lymphocyte)
They do not bear surface Ig, non-adherent and non-phagocytic with macrophage, they constitute innate immunity

Phagocytic Cells
It is two types
(i) **Mononuclear macrophage of blood and tissue**
These are the largest lymphoid cells with half life of 1 day. While lifespan of tissue macrophage is ~7 months. These are important for chronic inflammation and cell mediated immunity.
(ii) **Microphages**
These are polymorphonuclear leucocytes of blood neuterophil, eosinophil and basophil. They do not have any role in specific immune process.

Lymphocyte
Human body contains about 10^{12} lymphocytes, out of which 10^9 are renewed daily.
They are of two types
(i) **T-lymphocyte**
Thymus derived and constitutes about 60-70% of peripheral lymphocytes. It is present in paracorticalarea of lymph nodes and periarteriolar sheath of spleen.
(ii) **B-lymphocyte** 10-20% of peripheral lymphocytes, responsible for humoral immunity. In spleen and lymph node, they forms lymphoid follicles.

Major Histocompatibility Complex (MHC)

- Located on short arm of **chromosome six**, which code for histocompatibility (transplantation) antigen.
- Main function of MHC molecule is to bind peptide fragments of foreign proteins for presentation to antigen specific **T-cells.**

MHC *gene products are classified as*

Class-I Antigen	Class-II Antigen	Class-III Antigen
These are glycoproteins expressed in all nucleated cells. It is the principle antigen involved in **graft rejection** and **cell mediated cytolysis**.	They are glycoproteins restricted to antigen presenting cell only. These are responsible for graft versus host response and **Mixed Leucocyte Reaction** (MLR)	These are soluble proteins of complement system. e.g., heat shock protein and TNF (α and β).

Complement System

The complement system is an enzyme cascade that helps to defend against infections. Many complement proteins (C1-C9) occur in serum as inactive precursors (zymogens). At the sites of infection, these zymogens are activated locally and trigger a series of potent inflammatory events.

Activities of Complement System

The complement system shows various activities to digest the antigens. Phagocytes have important role in this system.

These activities are shown in following figure

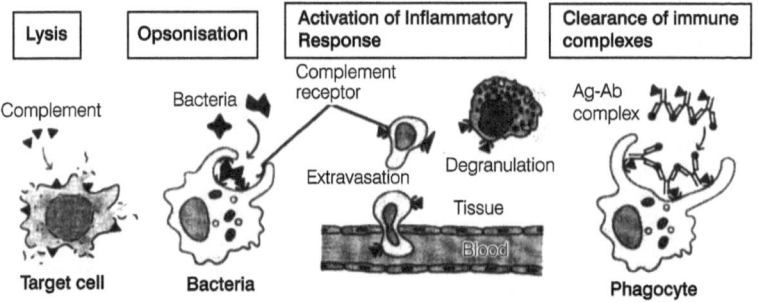

Activities of complement system

Vaccination and Immunisation

It is based on the property of the memory of the immune system.

During vaccination, a preparation of antigenic protein or pathogen or inactivated/weakened pathogen are introduced into the body.

Memory B-cell and T-cells are generated by vaccines that recognises the pathogen quickly on further contact and digest the invaders with a massive production of antibodies. If the preformed antibodies against any antigen are introduced into the body, it is called passive immunisation.

Allergies

The exaggerated or overactive response of immune system to certain antigen or pathogen is called **allergy**. The substances which causes such immune response are called **allergens**.

During allergies from-pollens, animal dander and mites in dust, etc., the I_gE type of antibodies are produced. The use of drugs like anti-histamine, adrenaline and steroids helps in reducing such allergic response.

Autoimmunity

Sometimes due to genetic or other reasons, the immune system of body is unable to differentiate between self and foreign substance and start killing the self tissues or cells. This is called autoimmune disease. *e.g,*. rheumatoid arthritis, etc.

Acquired Immuno Deficiency Syndrome (AIDS)

AIDS is a cell mediated immune disorder caused by Human Immunodeficiency Virus (HIV). HIV causes reduction in the number of **helper T-cells** which stimulates the antibody production by B-cell and ultimately reduces the natural defence against viral infectious.

First incidence of AIDS was reported from California, USA (1981). **Prof. Luc Montagnier** isolated HIV in 1983 at Pasteur Institute, Paris.

Various names are given to AIDS *causing agent by different scientist as*

LAV-II (Lymphadenopathy-Associated Virus-II) by **Luc Montagnier** (1983) France.

HTLV-III (Human T-lymphotropic Virus III) by **Dr RC Gallo** (1984) USA.

HIV (Human Immunodeficiency Virus) Common name for LAV and HTLV by international committee of viral nomenclature (1986) (WHO).

Structure of HIV

HIV belongs to retrovirus (RNA containing) family of viruses. The detailed description of the *structure of virus is as follows*

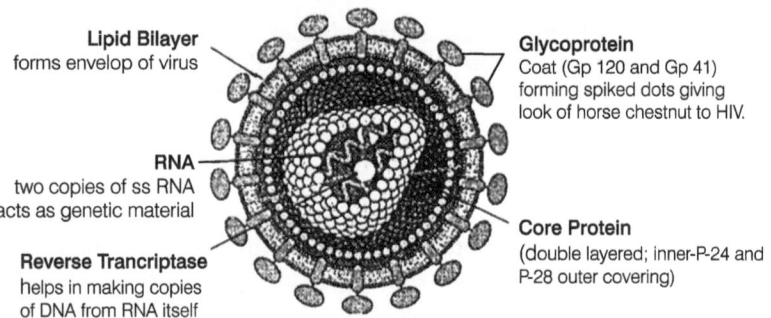

Lipid Bilayer forms envelop of virus

RNA two copies of ss RNA acts as genetic material

Reverse Trancriptase helps in making copies of DNA from RNA itself

Glycoprotein Coat (Gp 120 and Gp 41) forming spiked dots giving look of horse chestnut to HIV.

Core Protein (double layered; inner-P-24 and P-28 outer covering)

Structure of HIV

Transmission of HIV

AIDS is a fluid transmitted disease.

The modes of transmission of HIV can be pointed as
 (i) Unprotected sexual intercourse
 (ii) Use of contaminated needles or syringe
 (iii) Use of contaminated razors
 (iv) Transfusion of infected blood
 (v) Artificial insemination
 (vi) Prenatal transmission from mother to baby

HIV is found in blood and semen but it is not transmitted through
 (i) Mosquito bites
 (ii) Shaking hands with AIDS patients
 (iii) Sharing meals towels and toilets
 (iv) Hugging or dry kissing with patients

Mechanism of HIV Infection

Mechanism of HIV infection can be described diagrammatically as follows

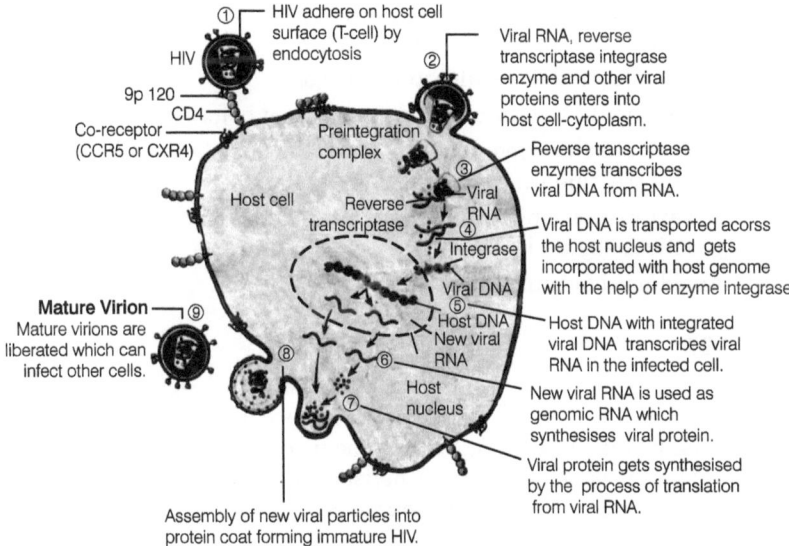

Steps in HIV infections

Incubation period It ranges from 6 months to 10 yrs. Average timing is 28 months.

Symptoms Chief symptoms includes fever, lethargy, pharyngitis, nausea headache, rashes, etc.

Treatment Although there is no cure for AIDS, it can be manifested in two major ways.

(i) **Antiviral therapy** Drugs against causative agent.

Azithmidine and **Ribovirin** are the drugs, which seems to be promising against AIDS. **Zidovudine** or AZT was the first drug used for the treatment of AIDS. **Didanosine** (dideoxyionosine-DDI) is another drug employed to treat AIDS.

(ii) **Immunostimulative therapy** Increases the number of resistance providing cells in the body.

Prevention

Following steps may help in the prevention of AIDS as there is no vaccine against AIDS. *These are as follows*

(i) Health education–people should be educated about AIDS transmission. December 1st is celebrated as World's AIDS Day to spread the information about AIDS.

(ii) Use of disposable needles and syringes.

(iii) Blood should be quarantined or screened before transfusion.

(iv) Use of sterilised equipments must be insisted while getting dental treatment.

(v) In sexual relationship one should be monogamous or safe sexual practices should be done.

(vi) Avoid use of common blades at barber's shop.

Cancer

Cancer is defined as an uncontrolled proliferation of cells without any differentiation. Cancer is a group of more than 200 different diseases, where malignant growth or enlargement of tissue occurs due to unlimited and uncontrolled mitotic division of certain cells and invades surrounding tissues, forming **tumours**. Simply cancer can be defined as **mitosis run amok**.

Characteristics of Cancerous Cell

Following are the characteristics of a cancerous cells

- Self sufficiency in growth signaling.
- Insensitivity to anti-growth signals.
- Evasion of apoptosis.
- Limitless replicative potential.
- Induction and sustainment of angiogenesis.
- Activation of metastasis and invasion of tissue.

Types of Tumors

There are two types of tumors

(i) **Benign Tumors or Non-Malignant Tumors**

These remains confined to the site of its origin, do not spread to other parts of body, grows slow and causes limited damage to the body. It is non-cancerous.

(ii) Malignant Tumors or Cancerous Tumors

It contains cancerous cells which break away from their site and can spread to the other part of the body through the blood stream and lymphatic system by the process called metastasis. It grows fast.

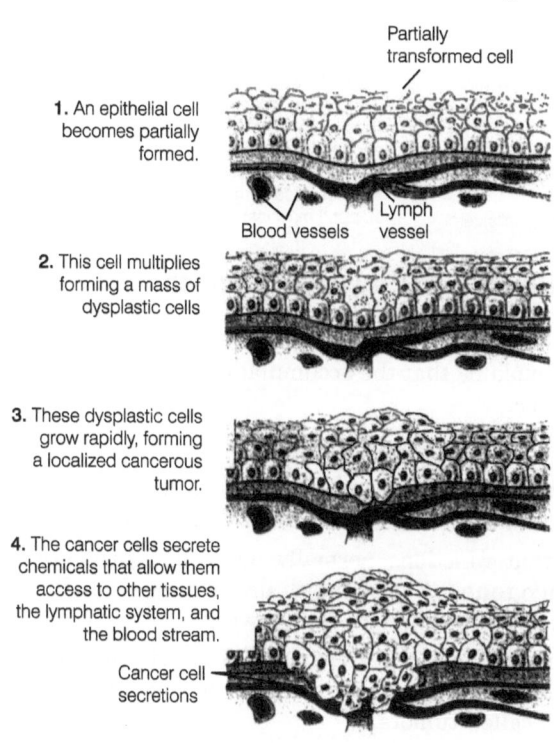

1. An epithelial cell becomes partially formed.
2. This cell multiplies forming a mass of dysplastic cells
3. These dysplastic cells grow rapidly, forming a localized cancerous tumor.
4. The cancer cells secrete chemicals that allow them access to other tissues, the lymphatic system, and the blood stream.

Cancer growth and metastasis

Cancers grow by cell division. Cells can break free from the tumor and lymphatic systems to other parts of the body, where they establish secondary tumors. Secondary tumors often develop in the liver, lungs and lymph nodes.

Types of Cancer

On the basis of its origin cancer is of following types

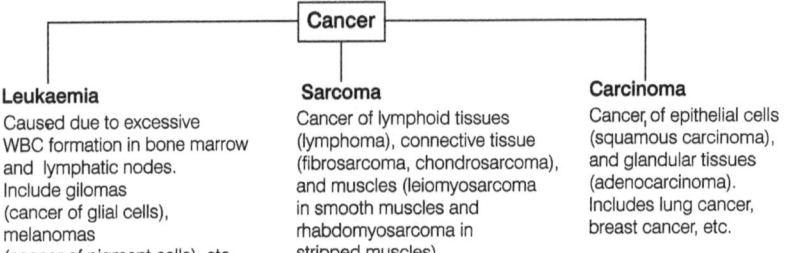

Leukaemia
Caused due to excessive WBC formation in bone marrow and lymphatic nodes. Include gilomas (cancer of glial cells), melanomas (cancer of pigment cells), etc.

Sarcoma
Cancer of lymphoid tissues (lymphoma), connective tissue (fibrosarcoma, chondrosarcoma), and muscles (leiomyosarcoma in smooth muscles and rhabdomyosarcoma in stripped muscles).

Carcinoma
Cancer of epithelial cells (squamous carcinoma), and glandular tissues (adenocarcinoma). Includes lung cancer, breast cancer, etc.

Theories Related to Causes of Cancer

(i) Mutation Theory

This theory explains that the accumulation of mutation over years may produce cancer.

(ii) Selective Gene Activation Theory

This theory explains that certain genes that are not normally expressed, suddenly become active and their product causes cancer.

Oncogenes that functions normally are called **proto-oncogenes** or **cellular oncogenes** (C-onc), which under normal conditions codes for protein that are necessary for cell growth.

Mutation in proto-oncogenes changes its activity and they looses the control on growth and division and continuously divides giving rise to a mass of cells called tumors.

Carcinogens are the agents that causes cancer. The can be physical, chemical or biological.

Different carcinogens are as follows

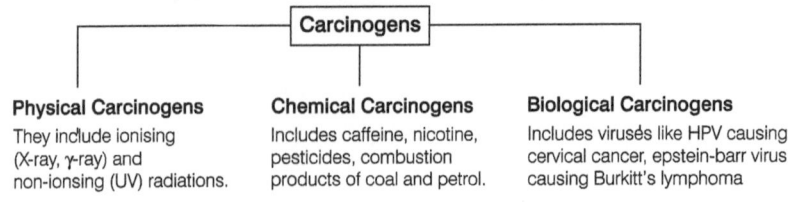

Physical Carcinogens
They include ionising (X-ray, γ-ray) and non-ionsing (UV) radiations.

Chemical Carcinogens
Includes caffeine, nicotine, pesticides, combustion products of coal and petrol.

Biological Carcinogens
Includes virusés like HPV causing cervical cancer, epstein-barr virus causing Burkitt's lymphoma

Cancer Detection and Diagnosis

Successful treatment of cancer requires early detection of the disease. Histopathological studies of the tissue and blood, bone marrow tests for increased cell counts and biopsy are the methods for detecting cancer. Besides these radiography, Computed Tomography (CT) (generates 3-D image of internal organs by using X-rays) and Magnetic Resonance Imaging (MRI) are used to detect cancer of internal organs.

Treatment of Cancer

Surgery, radiation therapy, chemotherapy are the common treatments of cancer.

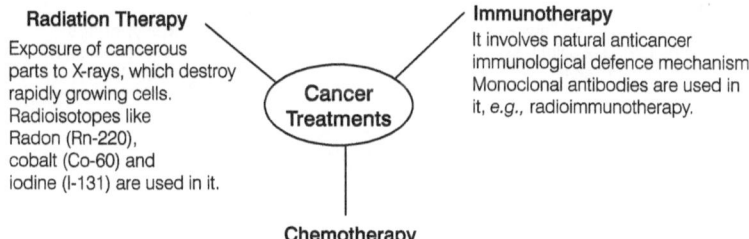

Radiation Therapy
Exposure of cancerous parts to X-rays, which destroy rapidly growing cells. Radioisotopes like Radon (Rn-220), cobalt (Co-60) and iodine (I-131) are used in it.

Immunotherapy
It involves natural anticancer immunological defence mechanism. Monoclonal antibodies are used in it, *e.g.*, radioimmunotherapy.

Cancer Treatments

Chemotherapy
Involves the administration of certain anticancer drugs, which check cell division. These drugs have side effects like hair loss, anaemia, etc. Patients are given substances called biological response modifiers (*e.g.*, interferon) which activate immune system and destroy tumor.

Drugs

Drugs are the chemicals used in the diagnosis, prevention, treatment and cure of diseases. They change the working style of the body. These are also called **additive substances** or **habituating substances**.

World Health Organisation (WHO) *define drugs as follows*

'Drug is any substance or product that is used or is intended to be used to modify or explore physiological systems or pathological states for the benefit of the recipient'.

Drugs can be classified into two major categories as follows

(a) **Psychotropic drugs** Mood altering drugs, affect behaviour and mental activity of a person.

(b) **Psychedelic drugs** Hallucinogens, produce dream like state with deorientation and loss of true sensory stimulus. They often make users of **See Sound** and **Hear colour**. These are also called **Vision Producing Drugs** as they produce false imagination.

Psychotropic Drugs

These are classified into four major categories *i.e.,* tranquillizers, sedative and hypnotics, opiate narcotics and stimulants.

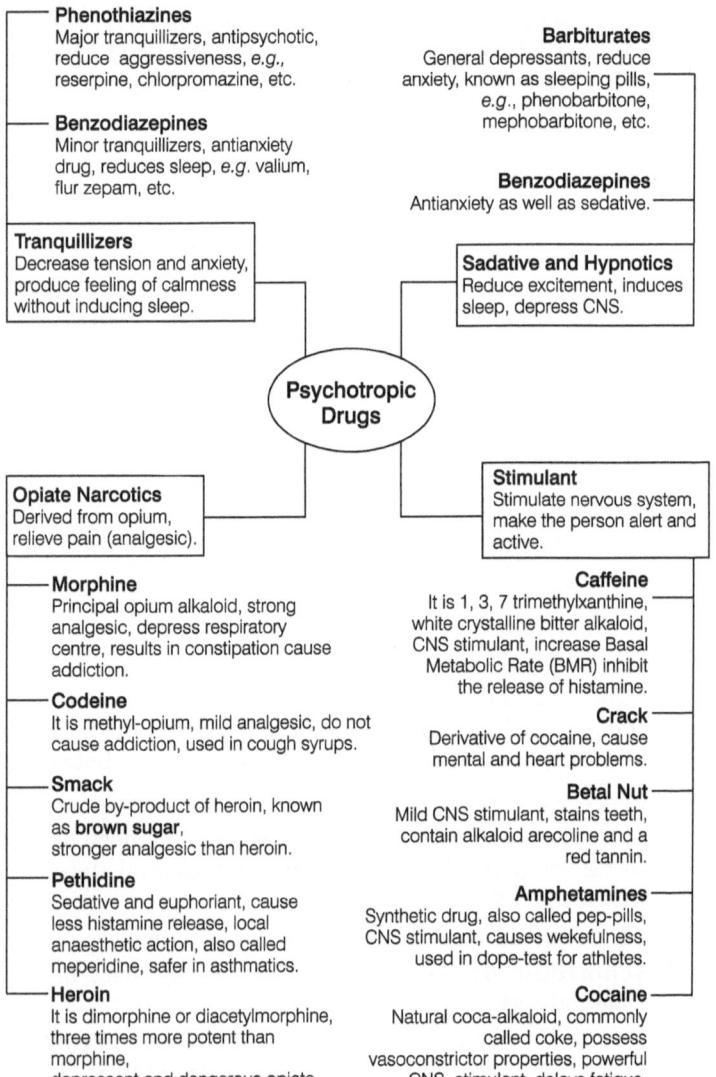

Psychedelic Drugs

They are broadly classified into two groups

(i) Natural Hallucinogens

They include Lysergic acid diethylamine (LSD), mescaline, psilocybin, cannabinoids and belladona (*Datura*).

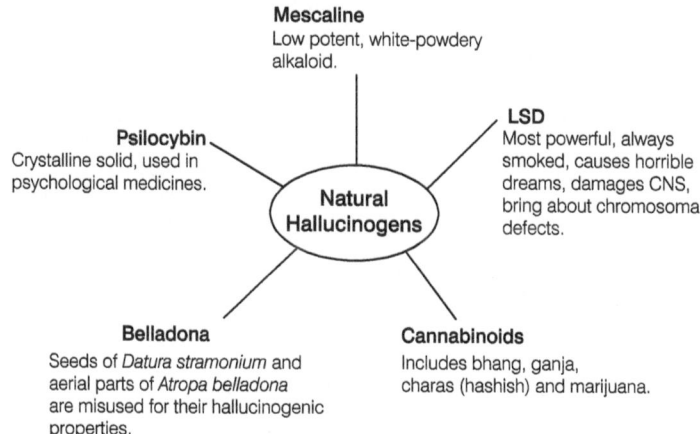

(ii) Synthetic Hallucinogens

They include Phencyclidine Piperidine (PCP) and Methylenedioxy Methamphetamine (MDMA).

(i) **PCP** (Phencyclidine Piperidine)

It is widely used in veterinary medicine to briefly immobilise large animals. PCP is available to addicts as **angel dust** (white granular powder).

It has stimulant, depressant, hallucinogenic and analgesic properties. Higher dose of PCP may produce hypersalivation, vomiting, fever and even coma.

(ii) **Methylenedioxy Methamphetamine** (MDMA)

MDMA has CNS-excitant and hallucinogenic properties. MDMA has become popular in students under the name 'ecstasy' drug.

Some Drug Yielding Plants

Common Name	Botanical Name	Parts of the Plant from which the Product is Obtained	Product Obtained
Hemp plant	Cannabis sativa or Cannabis indica (cannabinoid)	Leaves and flowers	**Hallucinogenic products** Bhang from fresh/dried leaves and flowering shoots of both male and female plants. **Ganja** from unfertilised female inflorescence. **Charas** from flowering tops of generally female plants. **Marijuana** from dried flowering plants.
Poppy plant (opium poppy)	Papaver somniferum	Unripe capsules (fruits)	Opium (Afeem) and its derivatives, (e.g., morphine, codeine, heroin, pethidine and methadone)
Ergot fungus	Claviceps purpurea	Fruiting bodies	LSD
Mexican mushroom	Psilocybe mexicana	Fruiting bodies	Psilocybin (Psilocybine)
Tea plant (a shrub)	Thea sinensis	Dried leaves	Tea
Coffee plant	Coffea arabica	Dried seeds	Coffee
Cocoa plant (sacred mushroom) (small tree)	Theobroma cacao	Dried seeds	Cocoa
Coca plant (cocaine plant)	Erythroxylon coca	Leaves and young twigs	Cocaine (Commonly called coke and crack)
Spineless cactus (peyote cactus)	Lophophora williamsii	Dried tops (called mescals)	Mescalin (mescaline)

Addiction

It is the continued repetition of a behaviour despite of its adverse consequences. Addiction to any substance is a disease and is difficult to beat.

Drug/Alcohol Addiction (or Abuse)

It is the state of periodic or chronic intoxication or dependency of a person on the regular consumption of drugs and alcohol either in low or high concentration.

Reasons of Drug/Alcohol Addiction

There are various reasons causing drug/alcohol addiction. *They include*

Peer Pressure
If friends describe about the good feeling of alcohol or drugs, such inspiration from peer groups acts as a pressure to start with the drugs.

Excitement or Adventure
Young blood look for some exciting work and these addictive substances attract them for such tasks.

Frustation or Depression
People start taking drugs or alcohol to get solace or relief from personal problems.

Reason of Drug/Alcohol Addiction

Apathy
Lack of interest in day to day activities of an individual may lead to such addictions.

Family History
Examples of parents or members of the family using these substances acts as the natural stimutant.

Desire to do more Physical or Mental Work
Some people think that the use of such substances provide them mental relief and increase their working power.

Causes of drugs/alcohol addiction

Effects of Drug/Alcohol Abuse

Drug/alcohol addiction is a sign of disgrace in society. The addicts are not liked by friends, colleagues and family.

Effects of drug/alcohol abuse

Withdrawal Symptoms Include anxiety, nervousness, irritability, depression, insomnia, dryness of throat, disturbed bowels, lack of concentration, increased appetite and craving for tobacco.

De-addiction

Addiction to drugs or alcohol vary widely according to the types of drugs involved, amount of drugs or alcohol used, duration of the drug alcohol addiction, medical complications and the social needs of the individual.

The following four ways can cure the drug/alcohol addicts

1. Addiction treatment is a methodical and slow process. *e.g.,* if an addict is used to smoke fifteen cigarettes a day, make sure that he/she reduces three cigarettes by the end of the month. This is because his body would not be able to bear the strain of more cigarettes. This may lead to serious complications.

2. Addiction rehabilitation centre can provide a temporary relief to the addicts problems.
3. De-addiction help can be provided through the means of friends and family members. Active interest in de-addiction process can help the addict tremendously by means of counselling.
4. There are many natural therapies available to cure the patient. These therapies are permanent. These therapies work well in the mindset of an addict. Once the patient's mindset is changed, he can take control of his life without any external assistance.

Adolescence

The World Health Organisation (WHO) defines adolescene as the period of life between 12 and 19 yrs of age. Adolescence is the formative period of both physical and psychological health and is the preparatory phase for the adult life. That's why a healthy adolescence is a critical juncture for a healthy adulthood.

Characteristics of Adolescence

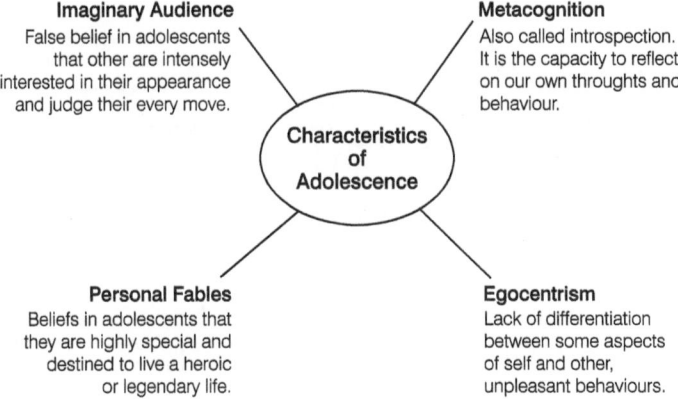

Adolescence: characteristics

Adolescence and Drug/Alcohol Abuse

Adolescence is accompanied by several biological and behavioural changes.

Curiosity, need for adventure and excitement and experimentation may constitute the common causes, which motivate adolescents to start taking drugs and alcohol.

Other causes include peer pressure, family history, media, etc.

19
Morphology of Flowering Plants

Plant Morphology : An Overview

Flowering plants or angiosperms shows large diversity of external structure or morphology, *a generalised morphology of these plants is as follows*

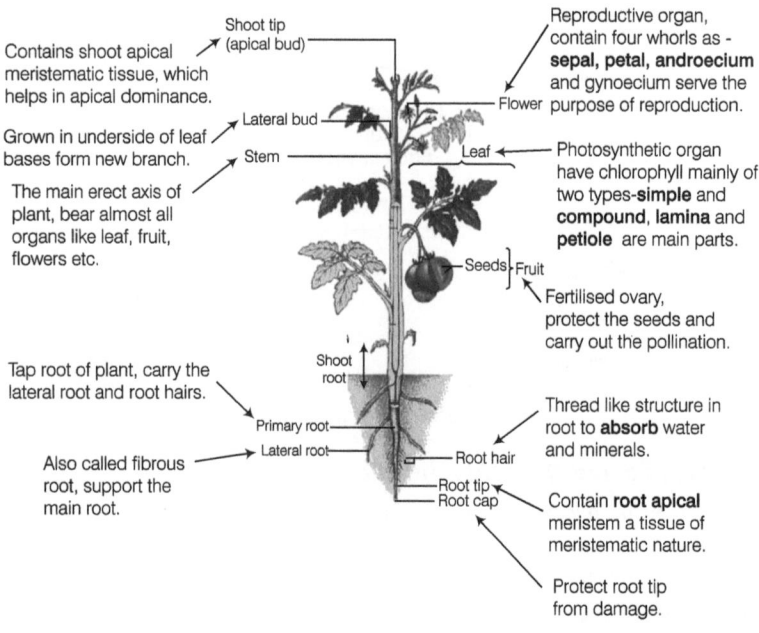

A typical flowering plant

Various components of plant's morphology and their structures are discussed here.

The Root Root is generally non-green, underground positively geotropic, positively hydrotropic and negatively phototropic, descending cylindrical axis of the plant body which develops from the redicle of the embryo. It is without node, internode, leaves, buds flowers and fruits.

Structure of the Root Generally, the root in plants is divided into three main regions. *These are*

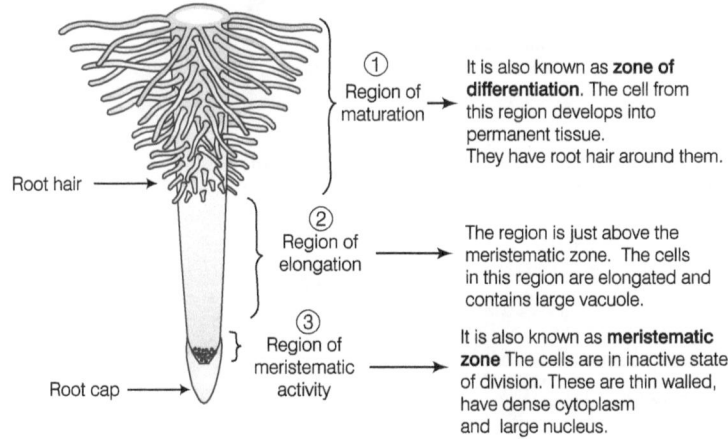

The regions of the root-tip

Root Cap A smooth cap shaped structure to provide protection to the young apical cells against soil particles in called root cap.

Types of the Root

There are two types of root

1. **Tap Root** Primary root further branches into secondary and tertiary root. *e.g.,* dicotyledonous root.
2. **Adventitious Root** In this, the radicle dies immediately after germination, hence these roots are arised from different portion of the plant, *e.g.,* monocotyledonous root.

Modifications of Roots

Both, tap roots and fibrous roots are modified, according to the need of peanuts.

1. Modifications of Tap Root System

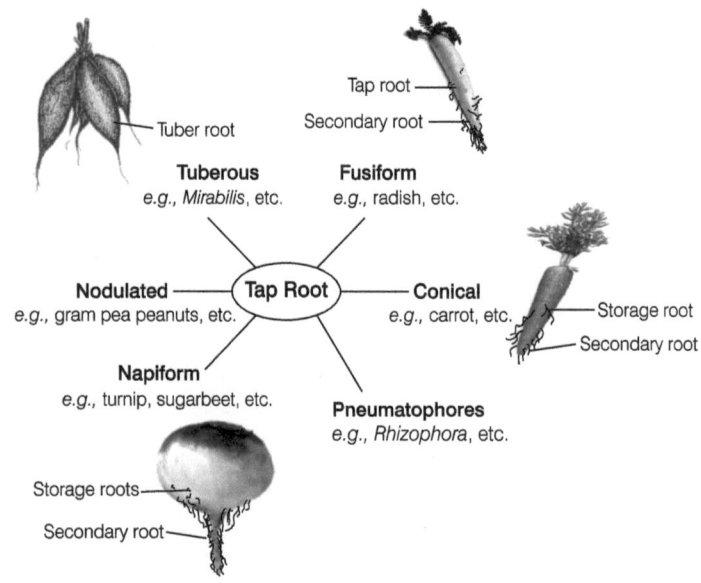

Various tap root modifications

- **Pneumatophores** are present in plants of coastal habitat. These roots absorb oxygen.
- **Nodulated root** in leguminous plants are forming nodule after combining with nitrogen fixing bacteria. They are meant for nitrogen fixation.

2. Modification of Adventitious Root

(i) **Tuberous** From the nodes of the stem, *e.g.*, sweet potato.
(ii) **Fasciculated** Arise in bunches, *e.g., Asparagus, Dahlia.*
(iii) **Beaded root** Swells at different places, *e.g., Vitis*, etc.
(iv) **Nodulose** Apical portion swells up, *e.g, Curcuma*, etc.
(v) **Annular** Ring structure formed, *e.g. Psychortia.*
(vi) **Prop root** Root hang from branches and penetrate into soil, *e.g. Ficus.*

Handbook of BIOLOGY

(vii) **Stilt Root** From stem they arise and enter into soil, *e.g.* maize, etc.
(viii) **Climbing root** Arise from nodes, *e.g. Pothos*, piper bettle.
(ix) **Buttress root** Arise from basal part of main stem, *e.g. Ficus*
(x) **Contractile root** Underground and fleshy, *e.g.*, onion, etc.
(xi) **Sucking root** In parasites, *e.g., Cuscuta.*
(xii) **Epiphytic root** Found in epiphytes, *e.g., Orchids.*
(xiii) **Floating root** Arise from nodes, help in floating, *e.g., Jussiaea.*
(xiv) **Photosynthetic root** Have chlorophyll, *e.g., Trapa, Tinospora.*
(xv) **Reproductive root** Develop vegetative buds, e.g., *Trichosanthes dioica.*
(xvi) **Mycorrhizal root** With fungal hyphae, *e.g., Pinus.*
(xvii) **Thorn root** Serves as protective organ, *e.g., Pothos.*
(xviii) **Clinging root** Arise from node and pierce into host plant, *e.g., Orchid, Ivy* etc.
(xix) **Leaf root** From margin of leaves, *e.g., Bryophyllum.*

The Stem

The stem is the ascending cylindrical axis of plant body which develops from the plumule of the embryo and grows by means of terminal bud. This is usually negatively geotropic and positively phototropic.

Stem Branching

There are two types of branching

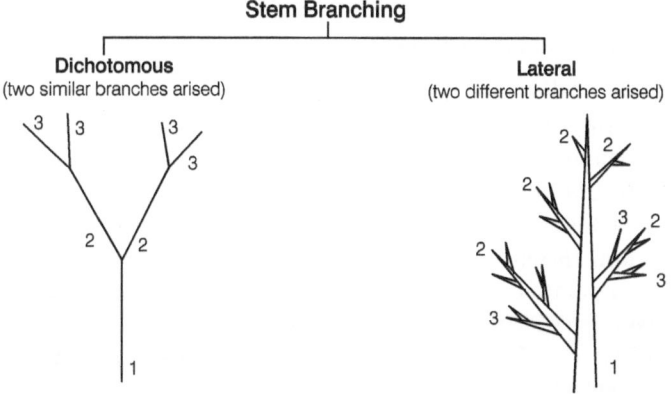

Branching patterns in stem

Types of Stem

Stems are of three types
1. Aerial 2. Sub-aerial 3. Underground

Different types of stem, actually are the modified stem. The modifications are to serve various purposes like **perennation, vegetative reproduction** and **storage of food**.

1. Underground/Subterannean Stem

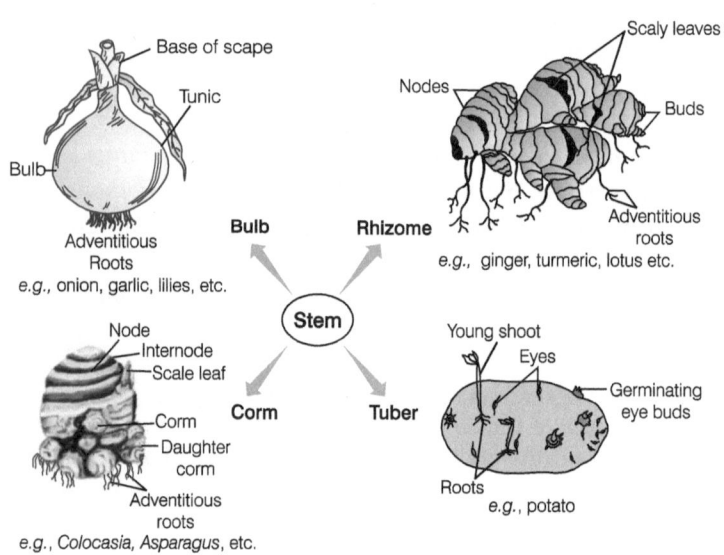

Underground modifications in stem

2. Aerial/Epiterranean Stem

These are as following types

(i) **Stem tendril** In weak plants with weak stem, the apical bud is modified into tendril for climbing. *e.g., Vitis, Passiflora*, etc.

(ii) **Phylloclade** In this the stem is modified into flat, fleshy and green leaf like structure. *e.g., Opuntia, Cocoloba, Ruscus*, etc.

(iii) **Stem thorn** Axil of the leaf or apex of the branch is modified into pointed structure called thorn. *e.g., Citrus, Bougainvillea*, etc.

(iv) **Cladode** Stem modified into leaf like structure, *e.g., Asparagus*.

(v) **Bulbil** A multicellcular structure, function as organ of vegetative reproduction, *e.g., Oxalis, Dioscorea*, etc.

Handbook of BIOLOGY

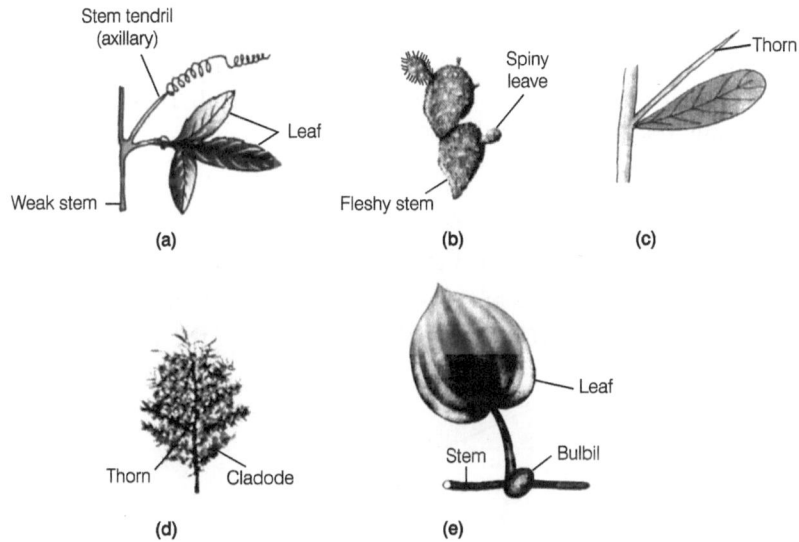

Aerial stems : (a) Stem tendril in *Vitis*, (b) Phylloclade of *Opuntia*, (c) Stem thorn of *Bougainvillia*, (d) Cladode in *Asparagus*, (e) Bulbil in *Dioscorea*

3. Sub-Aerial/ Prostrate Stem

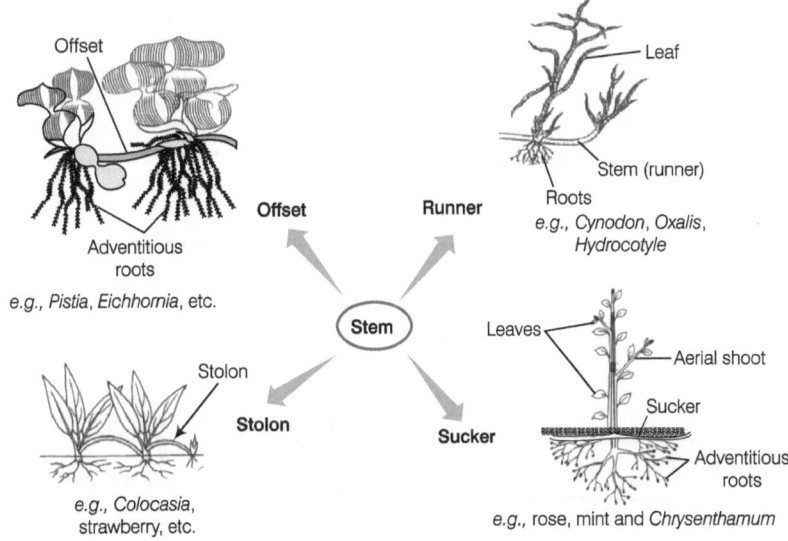

Sub-aerial modifications in stem

The Leaf

Leaf is exogenous, lateral, generally flattaned outgrowth that arise from the node of the stem and bear a bud in its axil. These are most important vegetative organ for photosynthesis.

Structure of Leaves

A typical leaf has three main parts

(i) **Leaf base** Part of leaf attached to the stem.

(ii) **Petiole** Part of leaf that connect lamina to stem.

(iii) **Lamina or leaf blade** Flattaned part of the leaves, which contain veins.

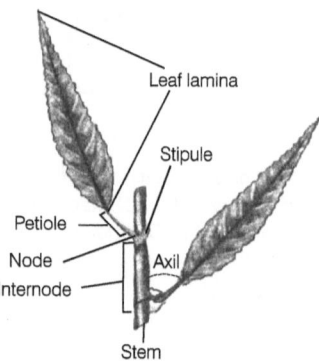

Typical leaf with its part

Leaf Venation

The arrangement of veins in lamina is known as venation

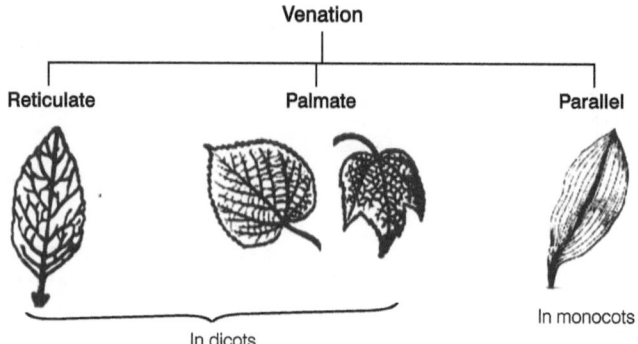

Different venation patterns in leaves

Types of Leaves

On the basis of incision of lamina, leaves may be of two types

Simple Leaves
In this, there is a single lamina, which is usually entire, *e.g.,* mango, guava, *Cucurbita.* etc. fig.(a)

Compound Leaves
In this type of leaf, the incision of lamina, reach up to midrib or petiole. *e.g.,* rose, neem, lemon, etc.

These are of two types

   (i) Pinnately compound leaves. fig. (b)
   (ii) Palmately compound leaves. fig. (c)

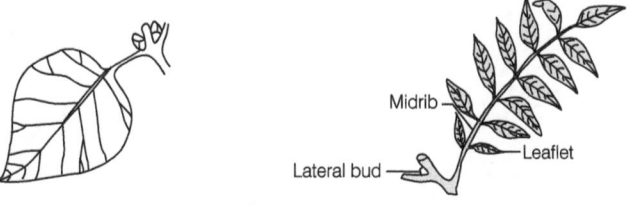

(a) Simple leaf of liliac

(b) Pinnately compound leaf of neem

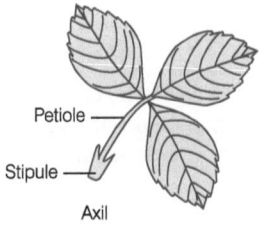

(c) Palmately compound leaf of strawberry

Type of leaves

On the basis of origin and function leaves are of the following types

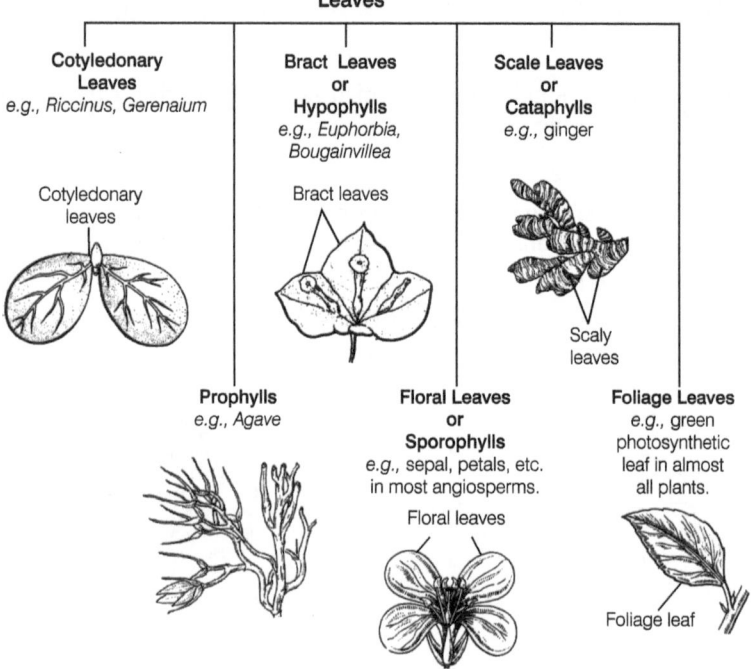

Types of different functional leaves

Phyllotaxy

Arrangement of leaves on main stem or branches is known as phyllotaxy, there are 5 main types of phyllotaxies, can be reported in plants. *The various phyllotaxies can be understood through following figure*

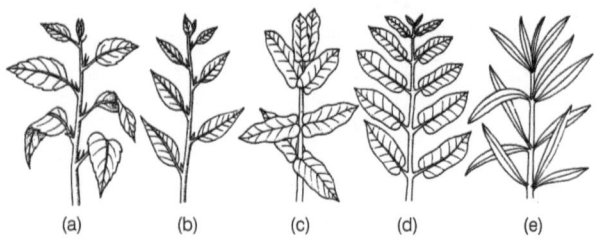

Types of phyllotaxy (a) Spiral (b) Alternate (c) Opposite decussate, (d) Opposite superposed (e) Whorled or verticillate

Modification of Leaves

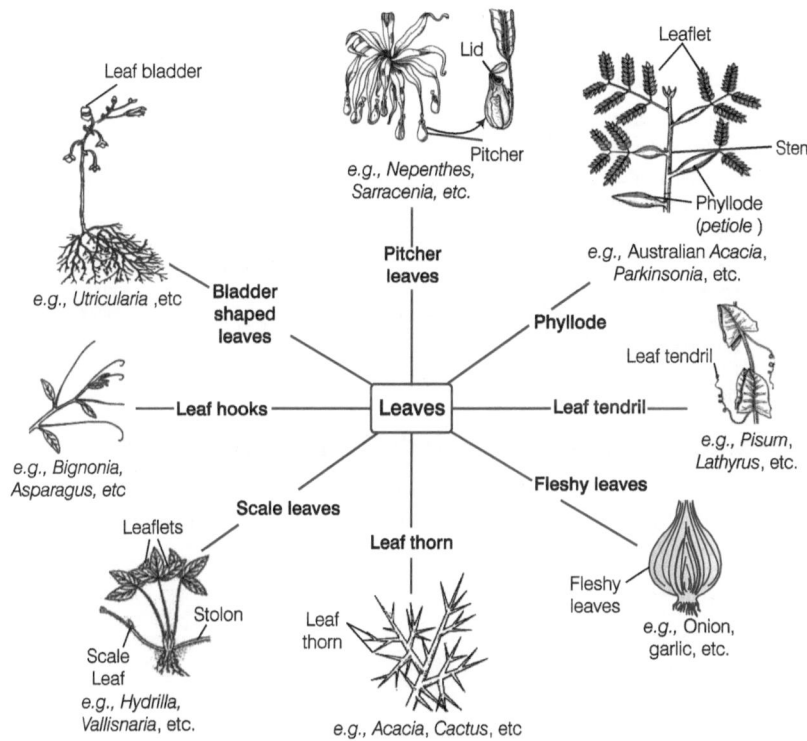

Various leaf modifications

The Inflorescence

The Shoot Apical Meristem (SAM) changes into floral meristem to form a flower and this flower bearing branch is called **peduncle**. The arrangement of flowers on floral axis is termed as **inflorescence**

It can also be defined as 'system of branches bearing flower.'

Types of Inflorescence

On the basis **modes of branching** and **modification of the peduncle.** *The inflorescence is of following types*

Handbook of BIOLOGY

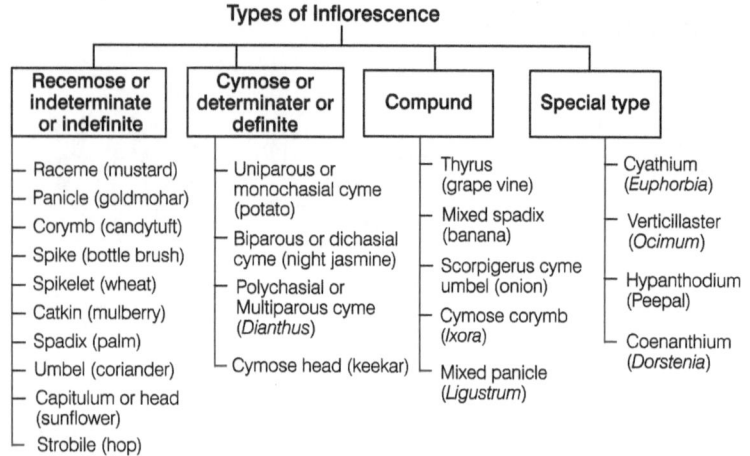

Racemose/Indeterminate/Indefinite Inflorescence

The peduncle continues to grow, forming new bracts and flowers in succession (acropetal manner). In this the oldest flower is near to base and youngest near the growing point.

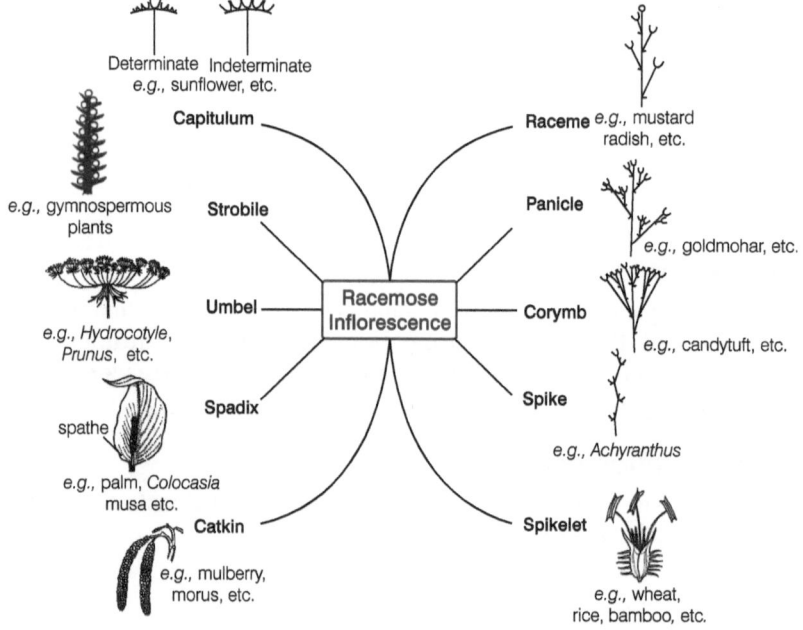

Various types of racemose inflorescence

Handbook of BIOLOGY

Cymose/Determinate/Definite Inflorescence

In this type of inflorescence the apical meristem of peduncle produce the first flower, the other flowers are originating from lateral branches from the axis below. Oldest flower remains in centre and youngest towards periphery, this arrangement is called centrifugal or basipetal sequence.

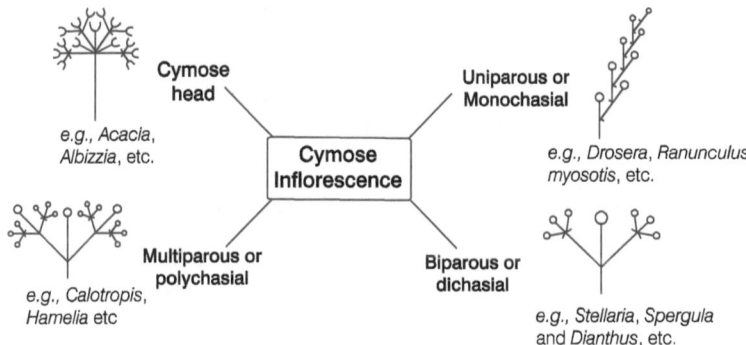

Various types of cymose inflorescences.

Compound/Mixed Inflorescence

In this the peduncle or main axis branched repeatedly once or twice in racemose or cymose manner.

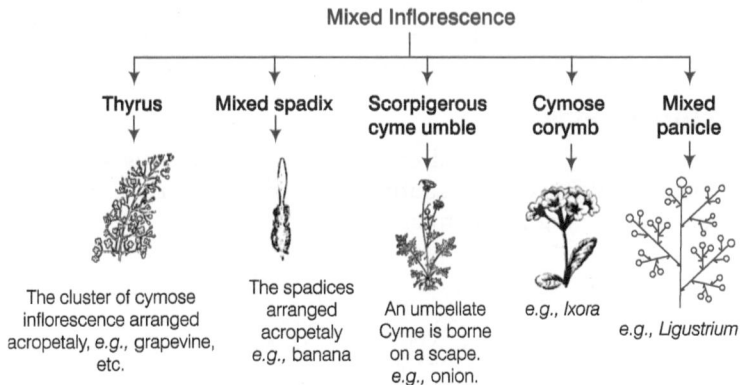

Various types of compound inflorescences

Special Inflorescence

These are of unique type of inflorescences.

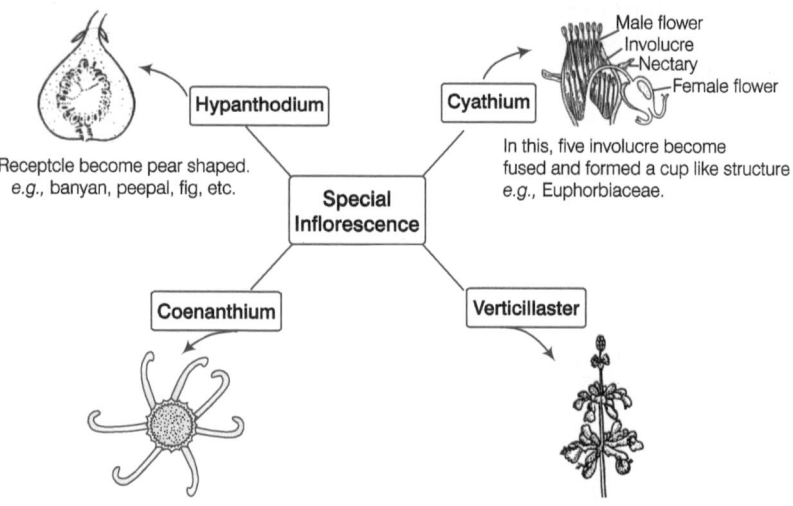

Various types of special inflorescences

The Flower

The flower is the reproductive part of an angiospermic plant. It develops in the axis of a small leaf like structure called **bract**.

Structure of Flower

A complete flower is modified condensed shoot, which is situated on receptacle (thalamus). A beautiful, reproductive organ serve the purpose of attracting pollinators.

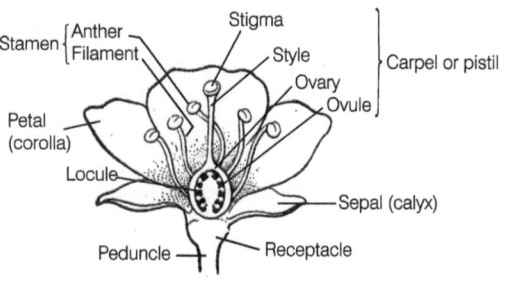

A flower showing detailed structure

Parts of a Typical Flower

Every flower normally has four floral whorls, *i.e,* **calyx, corolla, androecium** and **gynoecium**. All whorls arranged on the swollen ends of the stalk called **thalamus**.

The details of these parts are as follows

Calyx (Sepal)

The outermost whorl of floral leaves and the individual segment is called sepal. Mostly they are green in colour, but sometime coloured like petals (petaloid).

- Sepals free from each other – Polysepalous
- Sepals fused with each other – Gamosepalous

Modifications of Sepals

Sepals undergoes following modifications

(a) **Pappus** Hair-like modified sepals particularly for the dispersal of fruits, *e.g.,* sunflower, *Tagetes, Tridex.*

(b) **Spinous** Spine like, *e.g., Trapa.*

(c) **Tubular** Tube like, *e.g., Datura.*

(d) **Spurred** A tubular outgrowth called spur, arised at the base of one of the sepals, *e.g., Delphinium* (larkspur).

(e) **Campanulate** Ball-shaped, *e.g.,* China rose.

(f) **Leaf** One sepal becomes leaf-like, *e.g., Mussaenda.*

(g) **Hooded** One sepal becomes hood-like, *e.g., Aconitum.*

(h) **Cupulate** Cup like, *e.g., Gossypium.*

(i) **Bilabiate** Like two lips of mouth, *e.g., Salvia, Ocimum.*

(j) **Infundibuliform** Like funnel-shaped, *e.g., Atropa.*

(k) *Ureolate* Urn Like, *e.g., Silene.*

Corolla (Petals)

This is the second whorl, arise inner to the calyx. The petal and sepal together form the floral envelop.

Note Both petals and sepals combinely called **perianth**. When petal and sepals are not differentiated clearly, it is called **tepal.**

Shape of Corolla

Shape of polypetalous corolla

1. **Cruciform**
   e.g., mustard, etc.
2. **Caryophyllaceous**
   e.g., *Dianthus*, etc.
3. **Papilionaceous**
   e.g., pea, gram, etc.
4. **Rosaceous**
   e.g., rose, etc.
5. **Campanulate**
   e.g., *Physalis* etc.

Shape of gamopetalous corolla

1. **Tubular**
   e.g., sunflower etc.
2. **Funnel shaped**
   e.g., *Datura*
3. **Rotate**
   e.g., brinjal, etc.
4. **Salver shaped**
   e.g., ,mussaenda, *Ixora*, etc.
5. **Bilabiate**
   e.g., *Adhatoda Ocimum* etc.

6. **Ligulate**
   e.g., *Helianthus*
7. **Personate**
   e.g., *Antirrhinum*
8. **Urceolate**
   e.g., *Erica*
9. **Spurred**
   e.g., *Utricularia*

Different shapes of corolla

Aestivation of Petals

The arrangement of petals is called aestivation. *On the basis of its arrangement/pattern, aestivation can be of following types*

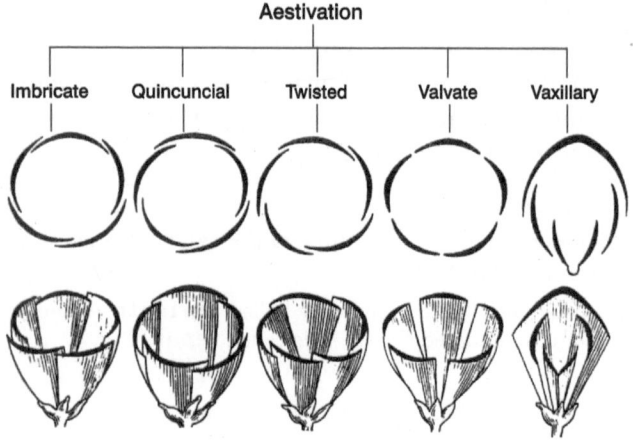

Various aestivations in flowering plants

Androecium (Male Reproductive Organ)

This is third whorl of floral appendages, that arise inner to corolla. Individual appendage is called **stamen** which represent the male reproductive organ.

There are various types of stamens, on the basis of various criteria

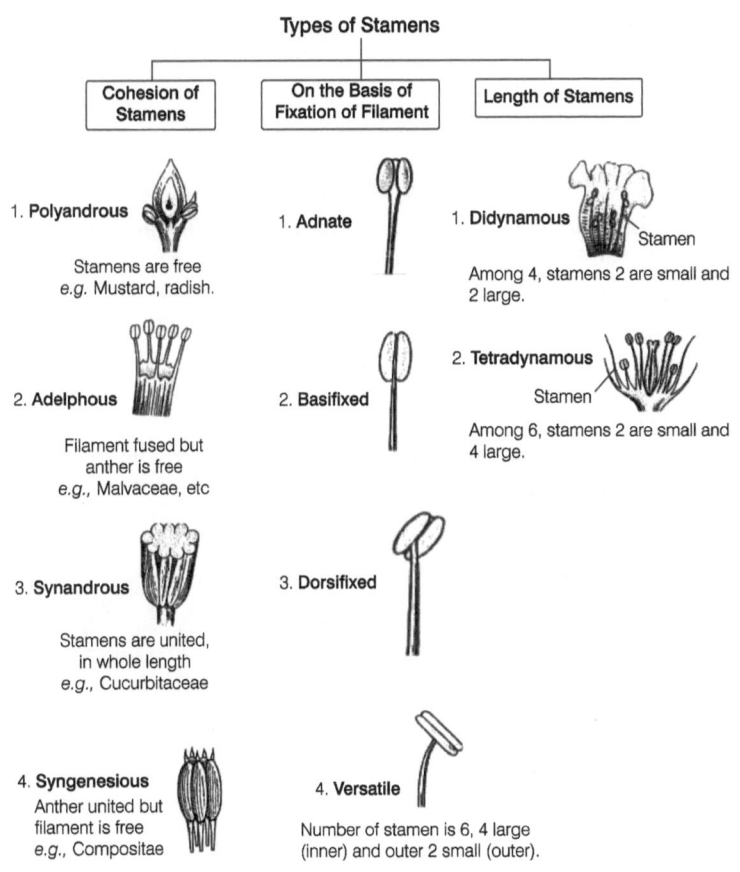

Various types of stamens

Gynoecium (Female Reproductive Organ)

It is the innermost floral whorl, acts as female reproductive organ of flower. On the basis of number of carpel and its arrangement, *the gynoecium is of following types*

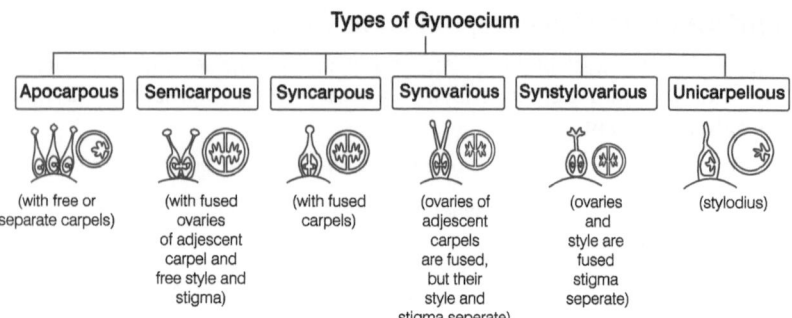

Terms Related to Flower Structure

1. **Actinomorphic flower** When the flower is regular and radially symmetrical. It is termed as actinomorphic, *e.g.,* mustard (Cruciferae), onion (Liliaceae), brinjal (Solanaceae).
2. **Zygomorphic flower** When the flower is bilaterally symmetrical, *i.e.,* divisible into only two equal halves by a single vertical plane, it is termed as zygomorphic, *e.g., Adhatoda*, pea, larkspur, *Ocimum*.
3. **Asymmetric flower** Flowers, which can not be divided into two equal halves by any vertical division, *e.g., Canna*.

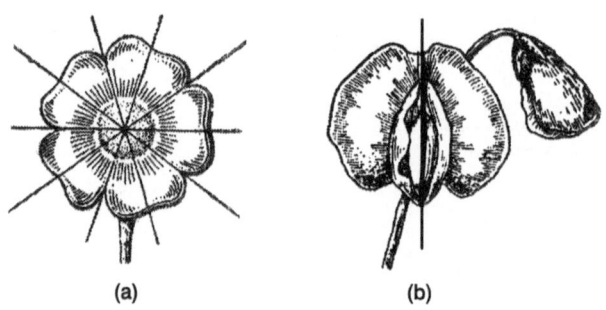

Symmetries in flower (a) Actinomorphic (b) Zygomorphic

4. **Hermaphrodite or intersexual or bisexual or monoclinous flower** A flower is called bisexual when it contains both male and female reproductive organs, *e.g.,* China rose, mustard, etc.
5. **Unisexual or dioecious flowers** A flower is called unisexual when it has only one essential floral whorl, either androecium (staminate or pistalloide) or gynoecium (pistillate or staminoide), *e.g., Morus alba,* papaya, *Cucurbita,* etc.
6. **Complete and incomplete flowers** A flower is called complete when it contains all the floral whorls, *i.e.,* calyx, corolla, androecium and gynoecium, *e.g., Solanum,* mustard. While the flower in the absence of any one of these four floral whorls, is called incomplete flower, *e.g., Cucurbita.*
7. **Regular and irregular flowers** When the flowers of a plant have same size, shape, colour and arrangement of various floral whorls/organs, then the flowers are called **regular**. If flower of a plant shows dissimilarity in any of its part or trait, then the flowers are called **irregular**.
8. **Cyclic and acyclic flowers** When the floral parts of a flower are arranged in a whorl, the flower is called **cyclic**, *e.g., Solanum.* If the floral part of a flower are arranged spirally and not in whorls, the flower is called **acyclic**, *e.g., Ranunculus, Opuntia, Nymphaea.*
9. **Achlamydeous, monochlamydeous and dichlamydeous flowers** In **achlamydeous** flowers, the accessory floral whorls (calyx and corolla) are absent, *e.g., Piper* sp. (Piperaceae).

    When a flower contains only one accessory whorl (either calyx or corolla) or **perianth** (a collective term given to a group of undifferentiate calyx and corolla), it is called **monochlamydeous**, *e.g., Polygonum* (Polygonaceae), onion (Liliaceae).

    The condition **dichlamydeous** is used when both the accessory whorls (calyx and corolla) are present, *e.g.,* in most of the flowers.
10. **Isomerous and heteromerous flowers** When the parts of a floral whorl are found in a particular basic number or its multiple, the situation is called **isomery** and the flower is **isomerous**.

An isomerous flower may be **dimerous** (2 or multiple of 2), *e.g.*, poppy or **trimerous** (3 or multiple of it), *e.g., Argemone* or **tetramerous** (4 or multiple of 4), *e.g., Solanum*. A flower is called **heteromerous**, when different parts of different floral whorls have different basic number of its multiple.

11. **Hypogynous, perigynous and epigynous ovary** A flower is called **hypogynous,** when the innermost floral whorl (gynoecium) occupies the highest position (superior) corolla and calyx are successively arise below it (inferior). *e.g., Brassica*, China rose, *Papaver, Citrus, Solanum*, cotton, etc.

    In **perigynous** flower, the all floral whorls are occurred at the same level of height on the thalamus so, they are called half superior or half inferior, *e.g.*, rose, peach, *Prunus*. In an **epigynous** flower, the innermost whorl, *i.e.*, gynoecium is covered by the elongated margins of thalamus.

    Thus, their position is inferior in relation to other floral whorls, which arise above the ovary and thus superior, *e.g.*, sunflower, *Cucurbita*, coriander, etc

12. **Bracteate and ebracteate flowers** Bract is a small leaf-like structure, whose axil bears a pedicel (flower stalk). A flower containing bract, is called bracteate, *e.g., Adhatoda* and without bract, it is called ebracteate, *e.g., Solanum*.

13. **Bracteolate, ebracteolate** A pedicel sometimes bears a pair of bracteoles, which are often green, sepal-like structures. A flower with bracteoles, is called **bracteolate** and without bracteolate, it is termed as **ebracteolate**.

14. **Epicalyx** It is an additional whorl of bracteole-like structures, which are found exterior to the sepals, *e.g.*, China rose, cotton (Malvaceae).

Placentation

The arrangement of ovule within the ovary is called placentation. It is a tubular structure to supply nutrient to growing embryo.

It is of following type

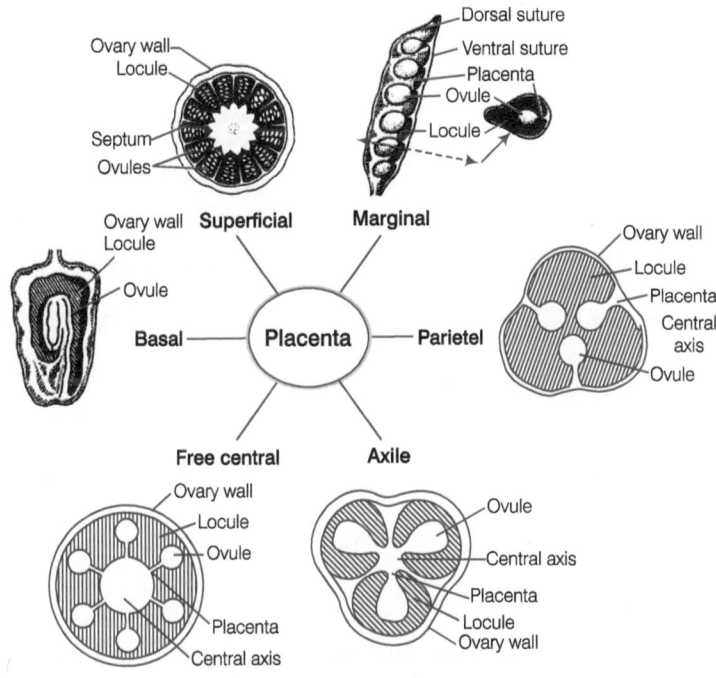

Types of placentation in flowering plants

The Fruit

After fertilisation of ovary, ovule is changed into seed and ovary into fruit. The fruit is a characteristic feature of the flowering plants. A true fruit is a ripened ovary. At this stage, the perianth and stamens fallen off, the gynoecium rearranged and ovary become extended.

Generally the fruit consists of a **wall or pericarp** and **seeds**. *Sometimes this pericarp is differentiated into three layers*

1. Outer – Epicarp 2. Middle – Mesocarp 3. Inner – Endocarp

On the basis of their development, the fruits are of two types

1. **True Fruits** These fruits are developed from the ovary of flower. *e.g.*, mango, orange, etc.
2. **False Fruits** The floral parts, other than ovary develops into fruit, *e.g.*, apple and pears, etc.

A general classification of true fruits, can be seen in following flow chart

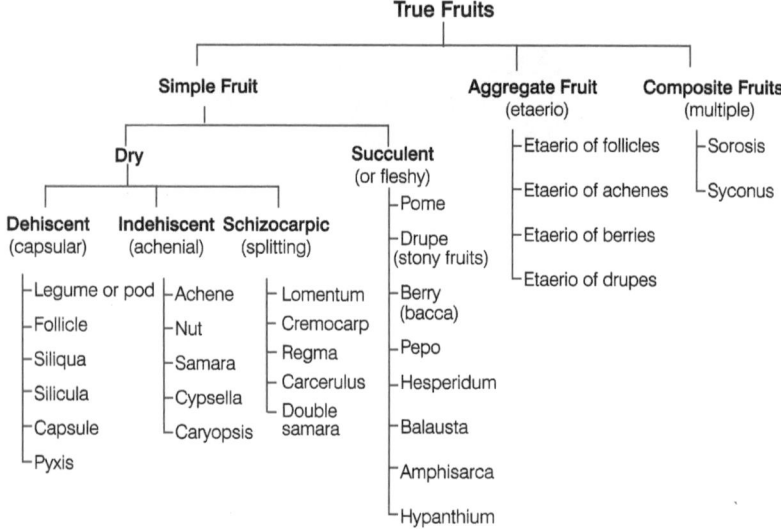

Simple Fruit

Simple fruits develop from the monocarpellary or polycarpellary syncarpous ovary of a flower. They are divided into dry and succulent categories.

Dry Fruits

In dry fruits, the pericarp is dry and not differentiated into epicarp, mesocarp and endocarp. These are classified into three categories – capsular (dehiscent), achenial (indehiscent) and schizocarpic (splitting).

(i) **Capsular** (Multiseeded, Dehiscent Fruits)

In these, the pericarp split open after ripening, and seeds are exposed. *They are divides as*

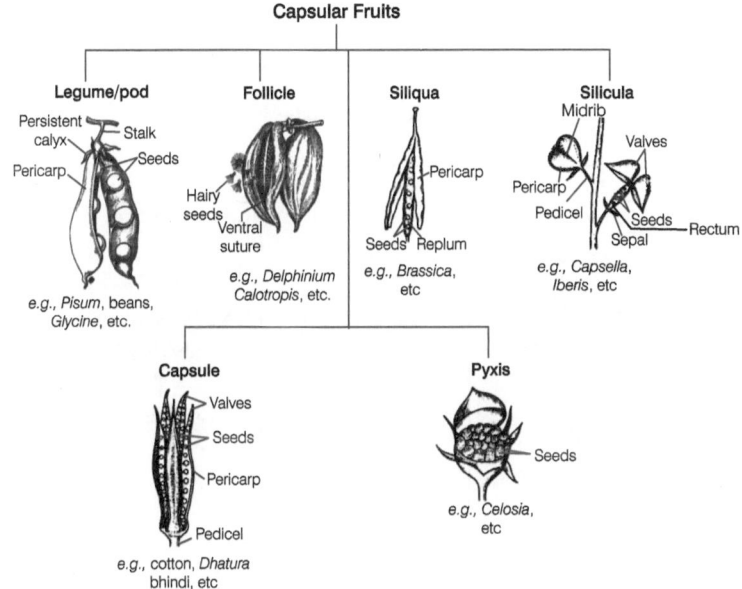

(ii) **Achenial Fruit** (Single Seeded, Indeshiscent Fruits)

They develops from single ovulated ovary having basal placentation. The seeds remain inside pericarp after ripenning.

These are of following types

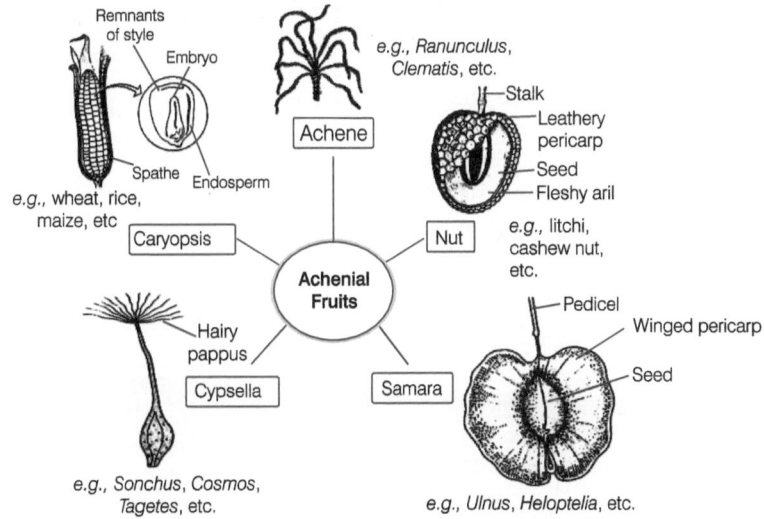

Achenial fruits and their types

(iii) **Schizocarpic Fruits** (Multiple Seeded, Splitting Fruits)
These are simple, dry, which break up into single seeded parts.

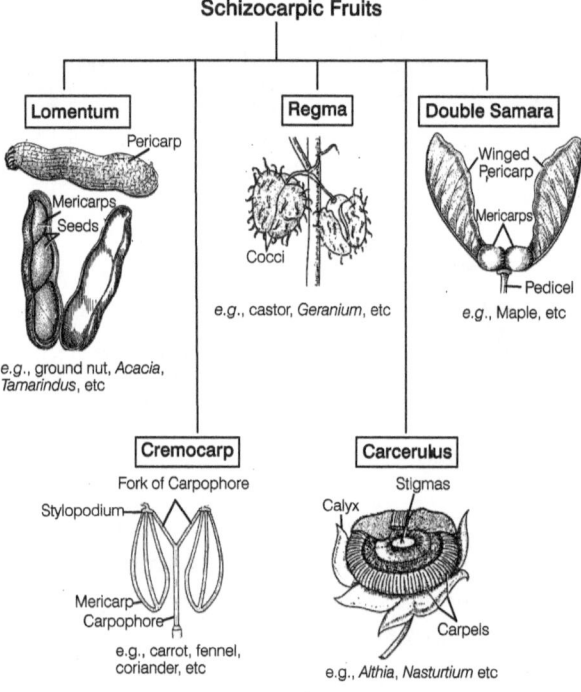

Succulent Fruit (Fleshy Fruits)

These have fleshy pericarp, which is divided into epicarp, mesocarp and endocarp.

They are of following types

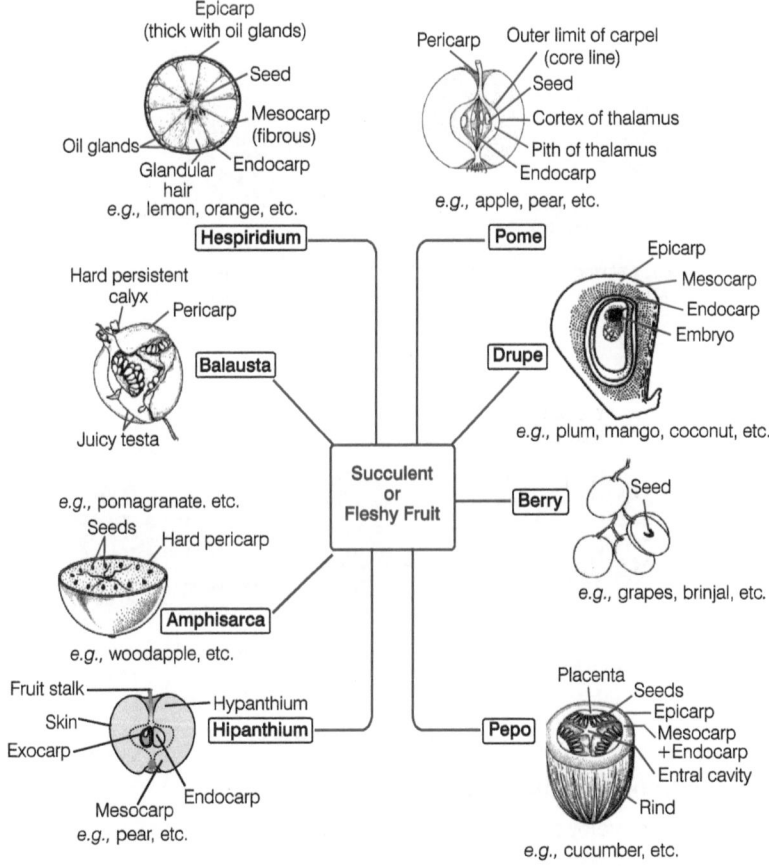

Different types of fleshy fruit

Aggregate Fruit (Etaerio)

Originally, these fruits are the group of fruitlets, which develops from the multicarpellary, apocarpous ovary. Individual carpel or pistil develops into fruitlet, but these matured in cluster on a single receptacle.

These can be categorised as

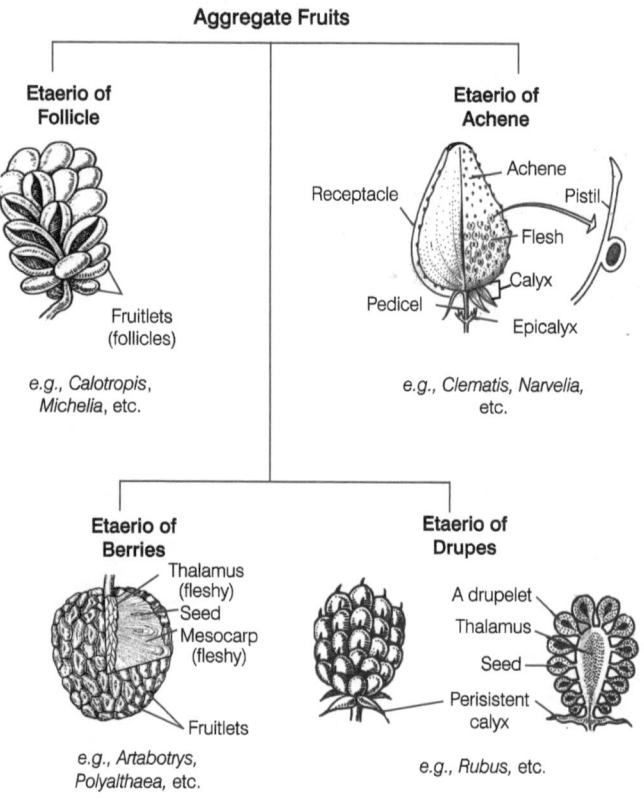

Various aggregate fruits

Composite or Multiple Fruit

These fruits develops from the whole inflorescence, hence they are also known as **infructescence**.

These are of following types

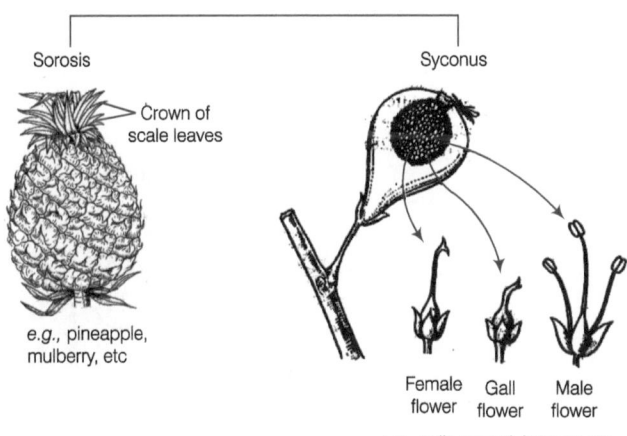

Multiple fruits

The Seed

A seed is a small embryo enclosed in a covering called seed coat, usually with some stored food. The formation of seed completes the process of reproduction in seed plants.

Parts of a Seed

A seed contains an embryo, an endosperm and a seed coat.

Embryo It represent an embryonic plants. It consists of an axis called **tigellum** to which embryonic leaves or **cotyledons** are attached.

Endosperm Endosperm, it present acts as the food storage tissues of a seed.

Seed coat It is a protective covering of the seed made up of one or two layers. The outer layer is called **testa** and inner is called **tegmen**. A minute opening called **micropyle** present in seed coat.

Types of Seed

Following flow chart provides the detailed, account of types of seed

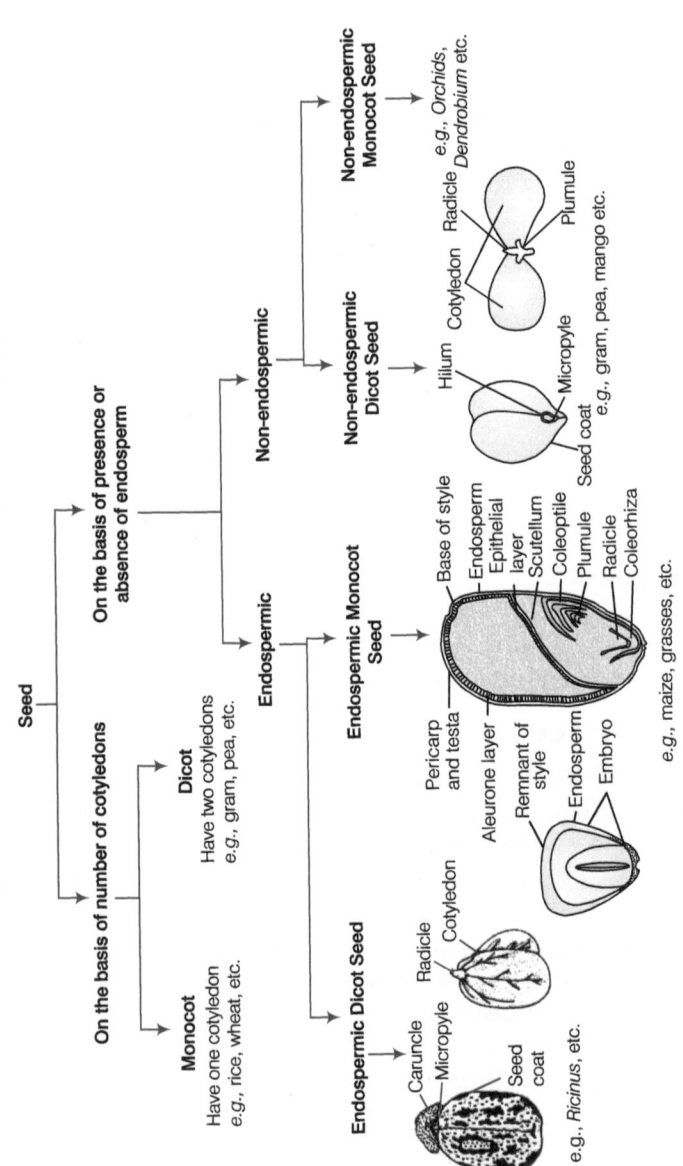

Various types of seeds in plants

Handbook of BIOLOGY

Viability of Seed
Germination power retaining ability of a seed is called the viability of seed, *i.e.*, a viable seed germinate during favourable condition.

Semitechnical Description of a Flowering Plant
Various morphological features of a plant, need to be described in a scientific language. *Following table clearly explains almost every sign used in floral description*

Br	Bracteate	$\overline{C}A$	Epipetalous stamens
Ebr	Ebracteate	$\overline{P}A$	Epiphyllous stamens
Brl	Bracteolate	Std	Staminodes
Epi	Epicalyx	G_4	Tetracarpellary, free carpels, apocarpous
0 (zero)	Absence of a particular whorl	$G_{(\underline{4})}$	Tetracarpellary, syncarpous (superior)
∞	Indefinite number	$K_{(n)}$	Calyx united (gamosepalous)
⊕	Actinomorphic	$G(\underline{4})-$	Tetracarpllary, syncarpous (semi inferior)
%	Zygomorphic	$C_{(n)}$	Corolla united (gamopetalous)
♂	Male flower	Ebrl	Ebracteolate
♀	Female flower	$G(\overline{4})$	Tetracarpelary, syncarpous ovary inferior (epigynous)
⚥	Bisexual flower, or hermaphrodite condition	$G(\overline{\underline{4}})$	Tet3racarpellary, syncarpous, ovary either superior or inferior
K_n	Calyx, where, *n*-is number of sepals	Pistd.	Pistillode
C_n	Corolla, where, *n*-is number of petals	$\overline{AG}$	Androecium and gynoecium are united
P	Perianth	$A_{(n)}$	Androecium with fused stamens
A_n	Androecium, where H = number of stamens	2+4	2 in one set and 4 in another
G_n	Gynoecium, where n = number of carpels	2–4	2 or 4
( )	Cohesion of floral parts in a whorl	X	Variable

Description of Some Important Families
Various workers have divided both monocots and dicots into several families. For proper understanding of these families, the comparative account of 5 families presented here.

Description of Some Important Families

Characteristics	Fabaceae	Solanaceae	Liliaceae	Cruciferae	Malvaceae
General Description.	The family also termed as **pea family**. It distributed all over the world.	Commonly known as **potato family**. It distributed in tropics and subtropics.	Commonly called as **lily family**. It is a representative of monocots.	It is known as **mustard family** or Brassicaceae. Mainly distributed in tropics.	Also known as **Mallow family**. Present in tropic and subtropics.
Plant structure	Tree, shrub, herb.	Herb, shrub and small trees.	Perennial herb.	Annual, biennial and perennial herbs.	All herb, shrub and trees.
Root structure	Root with root nodules.	Taproot system.	Root with underground bulb, corb and rhizomes.	Tap root, fusi form and napiform.	Profusely branched tap root.
Stem structure	Erect or climber.	Herbaceous, rarely woody, hairy, hollow, underground (potato).	Stem may be underground partially.	Herbaceous stem with pungent watery fluid. Have stellate hairs.	Erect, branched sturdy with trichomes, sometimes decumbent.
Leaves	Alternate, pinnately compound or simple venation reticulate.	Alternate, simple exstipulate, venation reticulate.	Mostly basal, alternate linear parallel venation.	Simple, alternate dissacted rarely opposite, reticulate venation.	Simple, palmately lobed, reticulate venation.
Inflorescence	Racemose.	Solitary, axillary or cymose.	Solitary/cymose often umbellate clusters.	Raceme or corymb.	Cymose or Raceme.
Flower	Bisexual, zygomorphic.	bisexual, actinomorphic.	bisexual, actinomorphic.	Bisexual, actinomorphic (may be zygomorphic).	Bisexual, Actinomorphic pentamerous.
Calyx	Five, gamosepalous imbricate.	Five united persistent, velvate.	6 tepals arranged in two whorls (3 + 3). Free or rarely united velvate.	Four polysepalous in two whorls.	Calyx like whorl called epicalyx.

Description of Some Important Families

Characteristics	Fabaceae	Solanaceae	Liliaceae	Cruciferae	Malvaceae
Corolla	Five, polypetalous, papilionacous.	Five united velvate.	—	Four, polypetalous cruciform.	5 petals, free but basally adnate.
Androecium	Ten, diadelphous, anther dithecous.	Stemans five epipetalous.	Steman 6 (3 + 3)	6 stamens arranged in two whorls.	Numerous stamens monoadelphous reniform
Gynoecium	Ovary superior monocarpellary, unilocular	Bicarpellary syncarpous, superior.	Tricarpellary, syncarpous, superior.	Bicarpellary syncarpous superior.	A compound pistill of 1 to many carpel.
Fruit	Legume seed one to many non-endospermic.	berry or capsule.	Capsule, rarely berry.	Fruit siliqua or silicula.	Capsule or schizocarp.
Seed	One to many non – endospermic	Many, endospermous.	Endospermous.	Small non – endospermic.	Seed with curved embryo and scanty endosperm.
Floral Formula	% ⚥ $K_{(5)} C_{1+2+(2)} A_{(9)+1} G_1$	⊕ ⚥ $K_{(5)} C_{(5)} A_{(5)} \underline{G}_{(2)}$	⊕ ⚥ $P_{3+3} A_{3+3} \underline{G}_{(3)}$	⊕ ⚥ $K_{2+2} C_4 A_{2+4} \underline{G}_{(2)}$	⊕ ⚥ Epik$_{3-9 \text{ or } (3-9)}$ $K_5 C_5$ $A_{(\infty)} \underline{G}_{(2-5)}$
Floral diagram					

20
Anatomy *of* Flowering Plants

Anatomy (Gk. *ana* – up; *tome* – cutting) is the study of internal structure of organism. There is a large variety of plants having diverse structure both morphologically and anatomically.

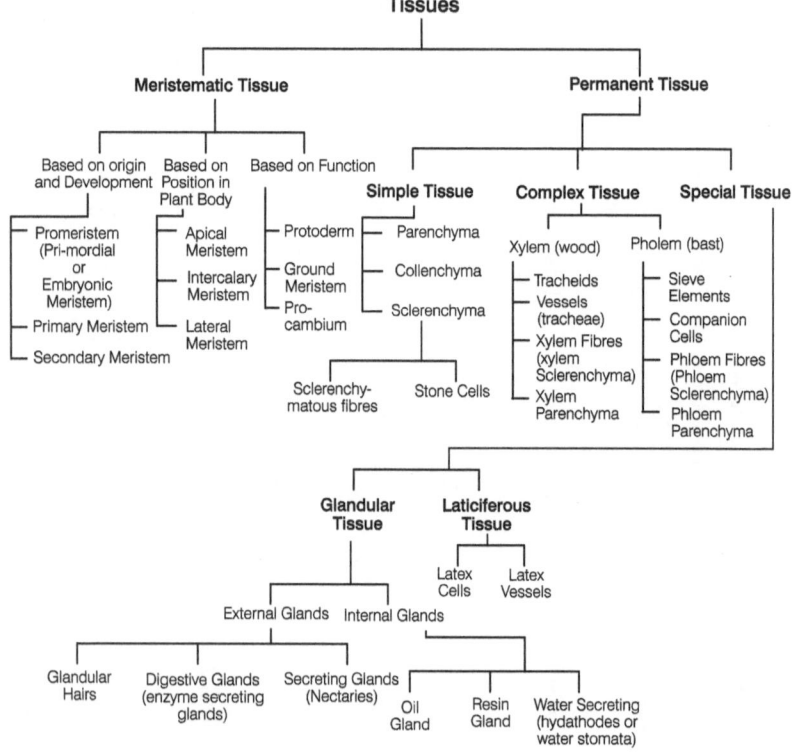

Handbook of BIOLOGY

Cell is the basic unit of organisation of all organisms and these are organised into tissues and above level of structure. The plant body is made up of various categories of tissues to comply the division of labour. Given flow chart shows the outlines of various tissues and their components in plants.

The Tissues

A group of cell having a common origin and cooperating with one another to perform a similar function is described as a tissue. The term 'Tissue' was coined by **N Grew.**

The cells constituting a tissue are connected together by plasmodesmata for proper coordination among them. The study of tissue is called histology. On the basis of constitution of cells, the tissues are of two types, *i.e.,* simple and complex. A **simple tissue** is made up of similar cells, which carry out the same function, whereas the **complex tissue** is made up of two or more than two types of cells which carry out the similar functions. *Tissues can be conveniently grouped into two categories*

    1. Meristematic tissues   2. Permanent tissues

Meristematic Tissues

A meristem or meristematic tissue (Gk. *meristos* – divided) is a simple tissue composed of 'a group of cells that are in continuous state of division resulting in new cells or retain their power of division'.

The term 'Meristem' was coined by **C Nageli** (1858) to designate dividing cells. *The chief characteristics of these tissues are*

    (i) Rounded, oval, polygonal or rectangular-shaped immature cells and small in size.
    (ii) Intercellular spaces are absent in meristematic cells.
    (iii) They do not store reserve food material and are in **active state of metabolism.**
    (iv) They have abundant and dense cytoplasm with small endoplasmic reticulum and simple mitochondria.
    (v) Plastids are present in proplastid stage.
    (vi) Nucleus is large and conspicuous.
    (vii) Vacuoles absent in protoplasm or if present, they are very small in size.
    (viii) The cells of cambium are highly vacuolated and they are large in size.
    (ix) Cell walls are thin, elastic and made up of cellulose.

The meristematic tissues can be classified on the basis of origin and development, functions and the position in plants body.

On the basis of origin and development

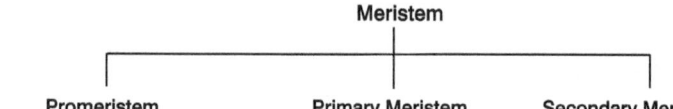

Promeristem Primordial meristem
It is also known as **urmeristem** or **embryonic meristem**. It is situated at the apices of root and shoot. It consists of thin walled, isodiametric cells with dense cytoplasm and large nuclei.

Primary Meristem
It is the first derivative of promeristem and forms the fundamental parts of the plant. The cells of these tissues divide in all possible planes.

Secondary Meristem
It develops later in the stages of development and **always lateral in position**. This meristem develop either at emergency or to affect secondary growth or formation of cork cells.

On the basis of function

Meristem

Protoderm
It is outermost meristematic layer of young growing region. It develops into **epidermis, stomata** and **root hairs**.

Procambium
It is composed of narrow elongated cells. It develops into primary vascular tissue.

Ground Meristem
It is the precursor of ground tissue system and has large and thin walled cell.
There meristems develops into hypodermis, cortex, pericycle pith and medullary rays.

On the basis of location in plant body

Meristem

Apical Meristem
These are present at the apices of primary and secondary shoots and roots of the plant. These meristems are responsible for increasing plant length and all the primary tissues of plant body, originated from them.

Intercalary Meristem
These meristems lies between the regions of permanent tissues. They may be present either at **nodes** or at the **base** of **leaf**. These are also known as **detached meristem**, as it originate from the apical meristem.

Lateral Meristem
These meristems are present along the side of the organs. They divide only in radial direction. These meristems are responsible for increasing girth of stem and roots.

Handbook of BIOLOGY

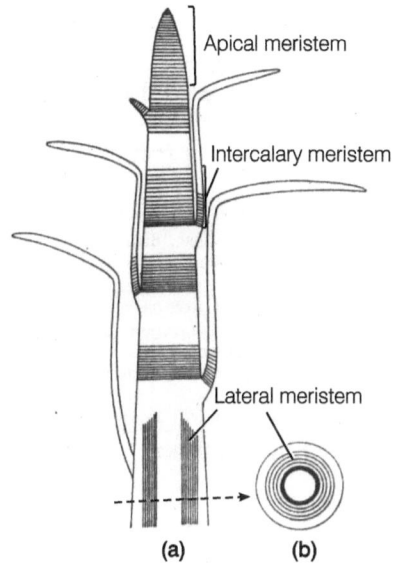

Position of meristems : (a) Longitudinal view (b) Cross-section

Various theories have been proposed to explain the organisation of both root and shoot apical meristem. The important theories among these are discussed here.

Chief Theories related to SAM and RAM

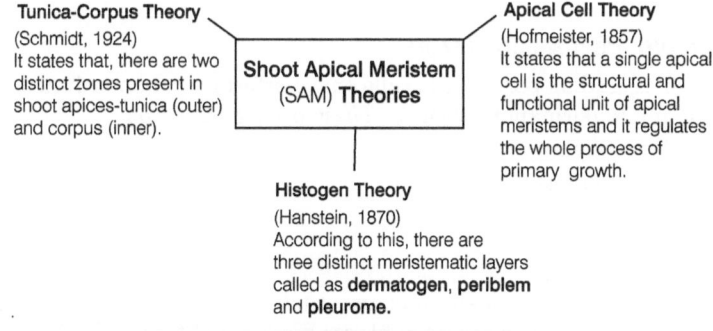

Tunica-Corpus Theory (Schmidt, 1924)
It states that, there are two distinct zones present in shoot apices-tunica (outer) and corpus (inner).

Apical Cell Theory (Hofmeister, 1857)
It states that a single apical cell is the structural and functional unit of apical meristems and it regulates the whole process of primary growth.

Histogen Theory (Hanstein, 1870)
According to this, there are three distinct meristematic layers called as **dermatogen**, **periblem** and **pleurome**.

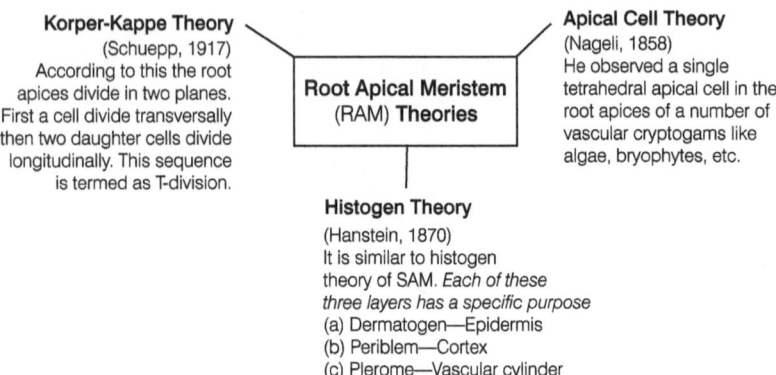

Note Haberlandt (1914) proposed the name **protoderm, ground meristem** and **procambium** respectivily to histogens.

Permanent Tissues

Permanent tissues are formed as a result of division and differentiation in meristematic tissues. These have assumed a definite, shape, size and function and have temporarily or permanently lost the power of division. The cells of these tissues are either living or dead, thin-walled or thick-walled.

Permanent tissues are of following three types
   (i) Simple tissues
   (ii) Complex tissues
   (iii) Special tissues

(i) **Simple** (Permanent) **Tissue**

A group of similar permanent cells that perform a common function is called simple permanent tissues. *These are classified as*
   (a) Parenchyma
   (b) Collenchyma
   (c) Sclerenchyma

(a) **Parenchyma**

Parenchyma (Gk. *para*–beside; *en, chein*–to pour in) is the most abundant and common tissue of plants made up of thin walled, usually living cells possessing distinct nucleus. Typically, the cells are isodiametric (all sides equal).

Handbook of BIOLOGY

These may be oval, rounded or polygonal in outline. The cell wall is made up of cellulose. These cells may or may not have intercellular spaces. Parenchyma is morphologically or physiologically **unspecialised tissue** that form the ground tissue in various parts of the plants.

Note *On the basis of their origin, the intercellular spaces are of two types*
- **Schizogenous** formed by the splitting of middle lamella.
- **Lysogenous** by the breakdown of cells.

Types of Parenchyma

Parenchyma cells are modified to perform various functions. *These functions are mentioned in following figure*

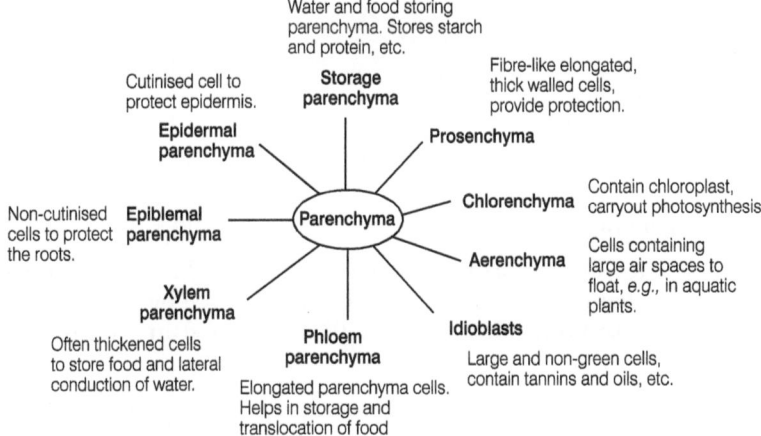

(b) Collenchyma

Collenchyma (Gk. *kolla* – glue; *en, chein*–to pour in) is a specialised, supporting simple permanent tissues. These cells have uneven thickening of cellulose, pectin and hemicellulose on their walls. **Schleiden** (1839), discovered and coined the term 'Collenchyma'.

These cells are often elongated, circular, oval or angular in transverse section. Collenchyma is found below the epidermis in the petiole of leaves and stems.

Collenchyma provides both mechanical strength and elasticity to the plants, hence it is also known as **living mechanical tissue**.

Types of Collenchyma

Collenchyma is of three types on the basis of structure of wall thickenings.

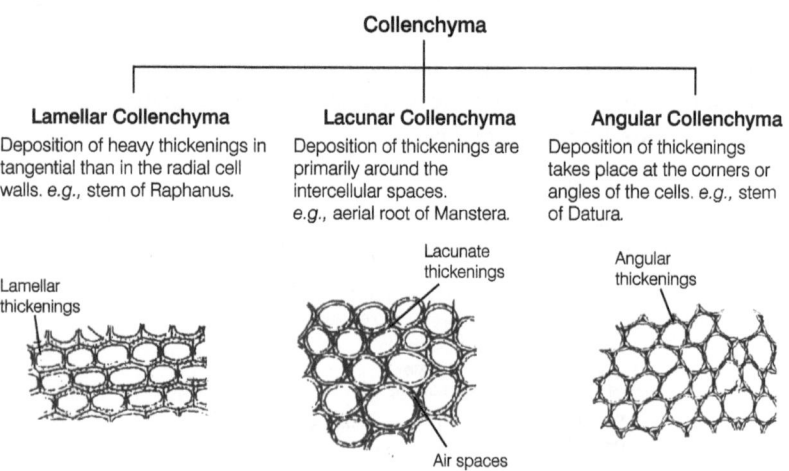

(c) Sclerenchyma

Sclerenchyma (Gk. *scleros*–hard; *en, chein*–to pour in) are considerable thick walled, lignified, supportive tissue characterised by the **absence of living protoplast**. **Mettenius** (1805) discovered and coined the term 'Sclerenchyma'.

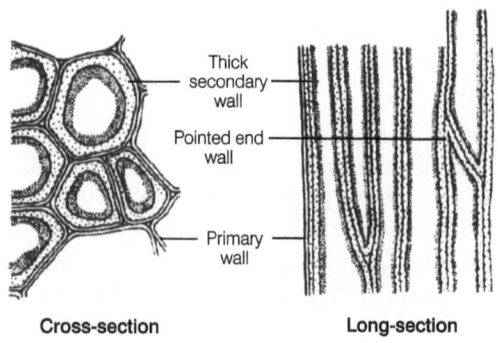

Structure of sclerenchyma

Types of Sclerenchyma

These are as follows

- **Sclerenchyma fibre** These are specialised cells being long, narrow, thick and lignified with pointed or blunt ends. They have great tensile strength, elasticity and flexibility.
- **Sclereids** The term 'Sclereid' was given by **Tscherch (1885).** These are also known as **stone cells** or **sclerotic cells.** They are dead cells with small lumens.

Differences between Parenchyma, Collenchyma and Sclerenchyma

Parenchyma	Collenchyma	Sclerenchyma
Cells are living and filled with protoplasm.	Cells are living and filled with protoplasm.	Cells are dead and empty.
No wall thickening.	Wall thickenings not uniform and consists of cellulose.	Wall thickening uniform and consists of cellulose, lignin or both.
Found in both the outer and inner parts of plant organs.	Found restricted to the outer parts of plant organs.	Found in both the outer and inner parts restricted to the areas, which have stopped elongation.
Provide mechanical strength only, when they are fully turgid.	Provide mechanical strength as well as elasticity.	Provide only mechanical strength.
No high refractive index	High refractive index.	Comparatively low refractive index.
Have ability to dedifferentiate and produce secondary meristem.	Ability to dedifferentiate is almost absent.	No dedifferentiation at all.

(ii) **Complex** (Permanent) **Tissues**

A complex permanent tissue is the collection of different types of cells that perform or help to perform a common function. These are the conducting tissues and classified as **xylem** and **phloem**.

(a) **Xylem** (Gk. *xylos* – wood; Nageli, 1858)

It is a complex permanent tissue mainly performing the function of conduction of water and solutes from the roots upto the top of plants. Simultaneously, it provides strength to the plants.

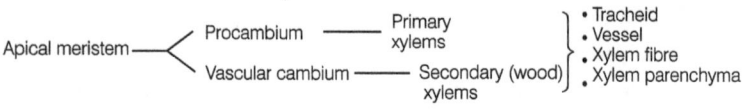

Xylem: origin and components

Components of Xylem

The components of the xylem are discussed as under

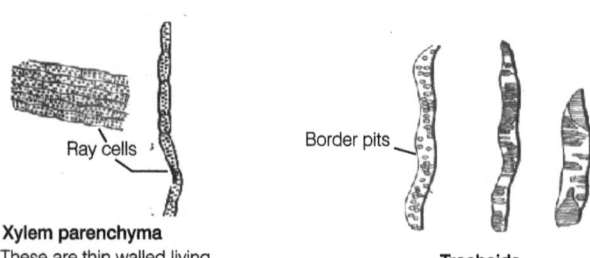

Xylem parenchyma
These are thin walled living cells, store food material and helps in lateral conduction of water. Ray parenchyma cells helps in conduction of water.

Tracheids
These are 5-6 mm long dead cells with wide lumen. The inner walls have various thickenings to provide mechanical strength. It constitutes 90-95% wood in gymnosperms and 5% wood in angiosperm.

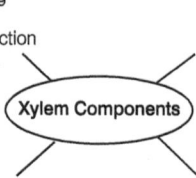

Xylem fibres
Also known as xylem sclerenchyma. They are long, narrow and tapering at both the ends. These provide mechanical support and have wall pits (simple).

Tracheae (xylem vessels)
These cells perform same functions as tracheid, but they are much elongated. These are formed by the fusion of short wide and thick walled vessel elements.

Xylem components

Types of Xylem

- *On the basis of the time of origin*

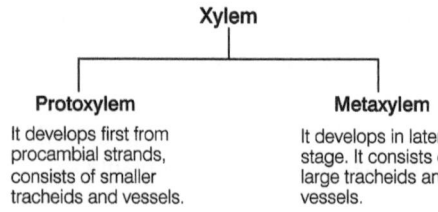

- On the basis of position of protoxylem with respect to metaxylem

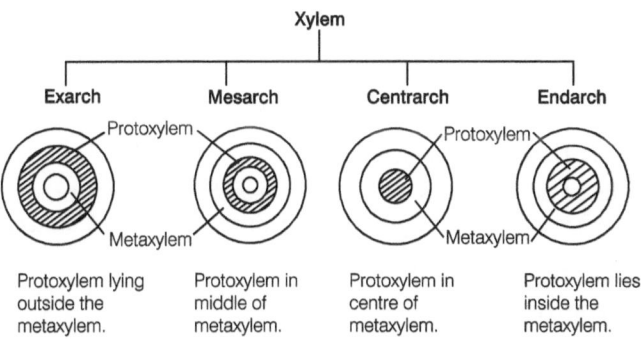

(b) **Phloem** (Gk. *phlois* – inner bark ;Nageli, 1858)

A complex permanent tissue which principally transports organic food in plants. It is also known as **bast**, because fibres of some plants are used for binding purpose.

It consists of four components. A new cell type called **transfer cells** has recently been reported from phloem. Transfer cells are much folded cell adjacent to sieve cells. They provide large area for the transfer of solutes.

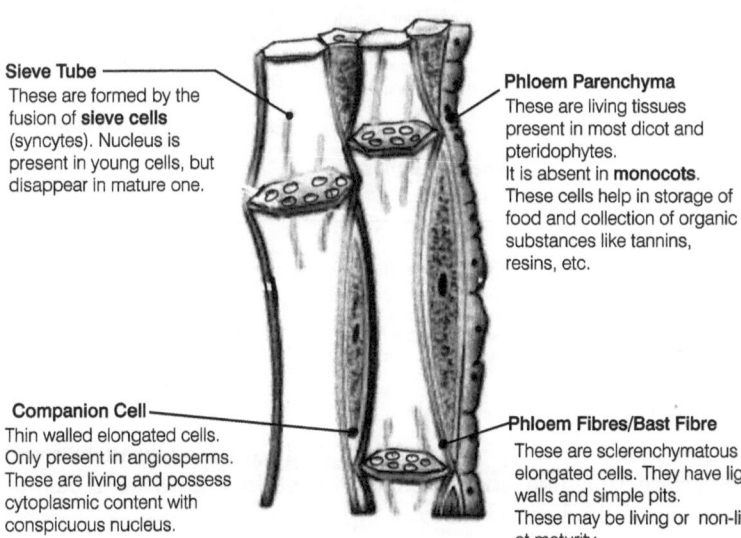

Components of phloem

Protophloem and Metaphloem

Protophloem is first formed part, which develops in parts that are undergoing enlargement. During elongation the protophloem elements get stretched and become non-functional.

Metaphloem are formed in the organs when they stopped enlargement.

(iii) Special Tissues (Secretory Tissues)

These cells or tissues are specialised to secrete or excrete products. The secreted substance may be useful for plants or may not be useful.

These tissue are of two types

(a) Glandular Tissues

These are present in form of glands (a gland is a group of specialised cells, which have capacity to secrete or excrete products).

The glandular tissues are of two types
- External glands
- Internal glands

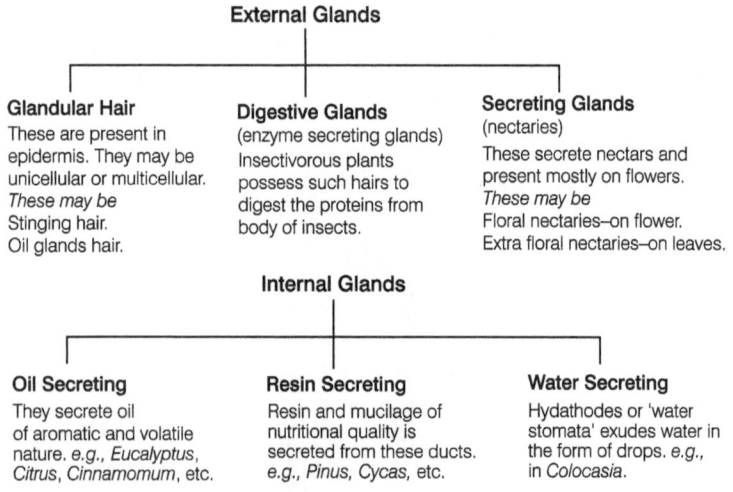

(b) Laticiferous Tissues

This tissue is mainly composed of thin-walled elongated, branched and multinucleate tube-like structures that contain colourless milky or yellow coloured fluid called **latex**.

They are scattered throughout the ground tissue of the plant and contain stored organic matter in the form of starch, rubber, tannins, alkaloids, mucilage, enzymes, protein, etc.

Handbook of BIOLOGY

This tissue is of two types

- **Latex cells** These are uninucleate cells, may be branched or unbranched. These cells are also known as non-articulated laticifers, e.g. *Euphorbia, Thevetia*, etc.
- **Latex vessels** These are formed by large number of cells placed end to end with their transverse wall dissolved so as to form long vessels. e.g., *Papaver, Hevea*, etc.

The Tissue System

The functions of the tissues depends on their location in plant body. The tissues or a group of tissue which perform a common function, constitutes the tissue system.

The principal tissues of a plant can be categorised into three important tissue system (Sachs; 1875). *These are as follows*

Epidermal Tissue System (Dermal Tissue System)

It is derived from **protoderm.** It perform several functions like mechanical support, absorption, excretion, etc., in plants. *Following flow chart provide the detail account of these tissues in plants*

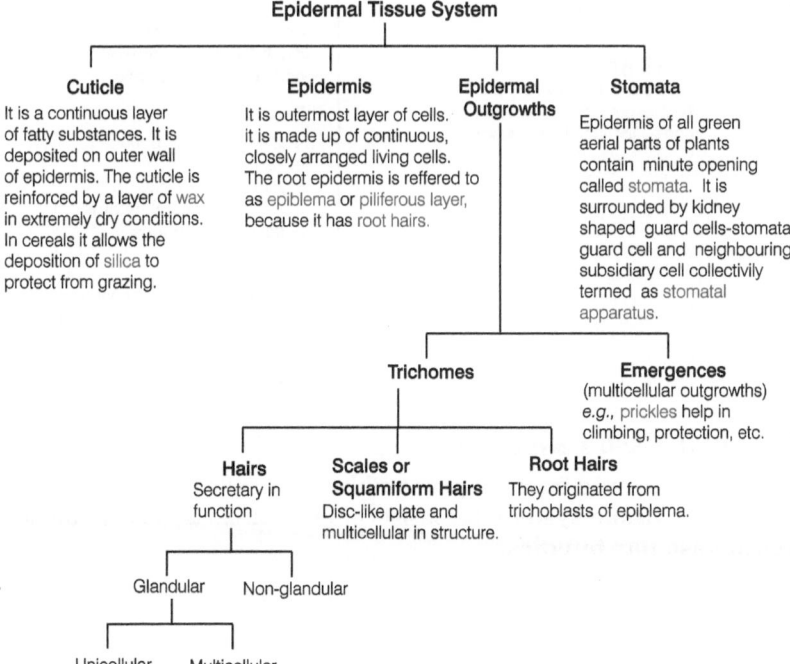

Ground Tissues System (Fundamental Tissue System)

It is partly derived from the **periblem** and partly from **plerome**. It constitutes the **main bulk of the body**. If consists of **simple permanent tissues** like parenchyma, collenchyma and sclerenchyma.

Following flow chart present the detailed view of ground tissue system in plants

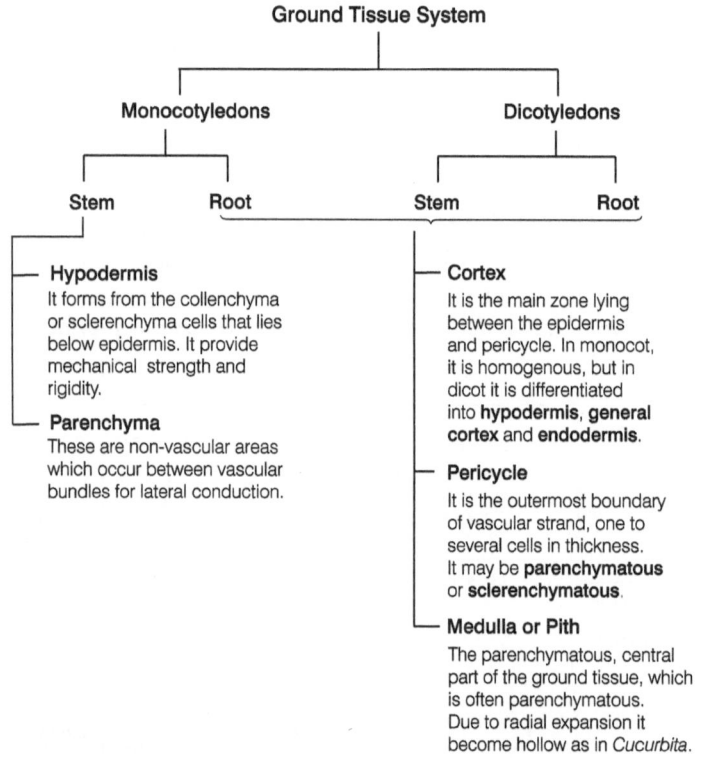

Vascular Tissue System (Fascicular Tissue System)

The tissues derived from the **procambium** are called the **vascular** or **fascicular tissue system**. It consists of number of strands or bundles called **vascular bundles**.

Handbook of BIOLOGY

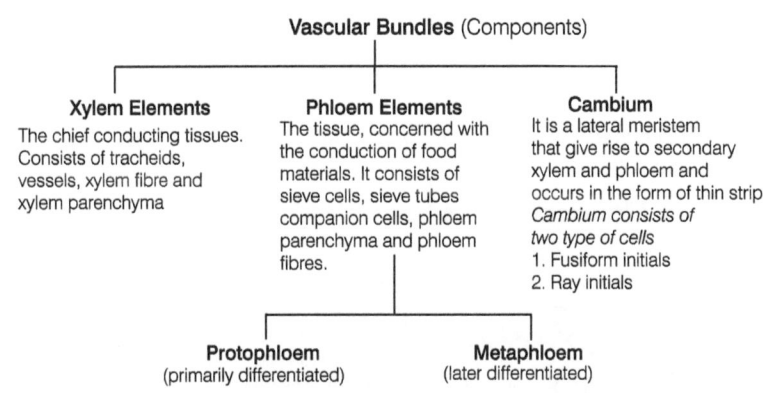

Vascular Bundles (Components)

Xylem Elements
The chief conducting tissues. Consists of tracheids, vessels, xylem fibre and xylem parenchyma

Phloem Elements
The tissue, concerned with the conduction of food materials. It consists of sieve cells, sieve tubes companion cells, phloem parenchyma and phloem fibres.

- **Protophloem** (primarily differentiated)
- **Metaphloem** (later differentiated)

Cambium
It is a lateral meristem that give rise to secondary xylem and phloem and occurs in the form of thin strip. *Cambium consists of two type of cells*
1. Fusiform initials
2. Ray initials

The vascular bundles are classified into three categories on the basis of relative position of xylem and phloem.

Vascular Bundles

Radial
These are mostly found in roots. The separate bands of phloem and xylem are present.

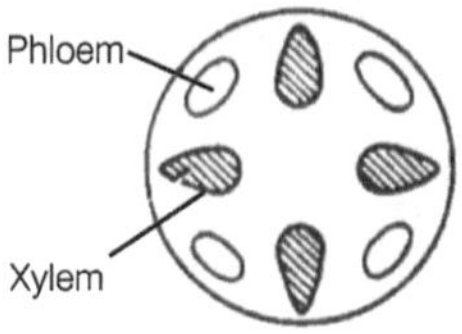

Conjoint
These are mostly found in stem and leaves. Both the xylem and phloem situated at same radius, as they are produced by layer division in vascular cambium.

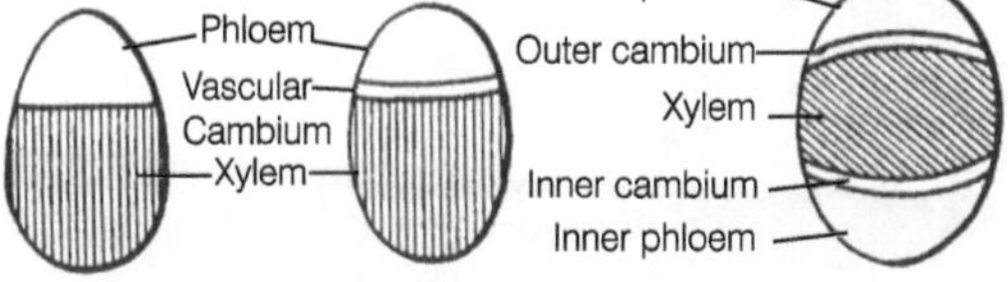

Concentric
In this, either xylem surrounds the phloem completely or phloem surrounds xylem completely.

- Amphivasal
- Amphicribral

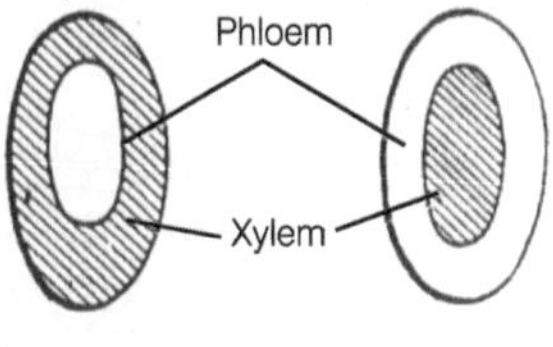

Collateral
- Closed
- Open
  - Phloem
  - Vascular Cambium
  - Xylem

Bicollateral
- Outer phloem
- Outer cambium
- Xylem
- Inner cambium
- Inner phloem

Anatomy of Dicot and Monocot Plants

Various plant organs (*i.e.*, root, stem, leaves, etc.) have characteristic structures.

The comprehensive account of these, structure with their internal details is as follows

Dicot and Monocot Roots

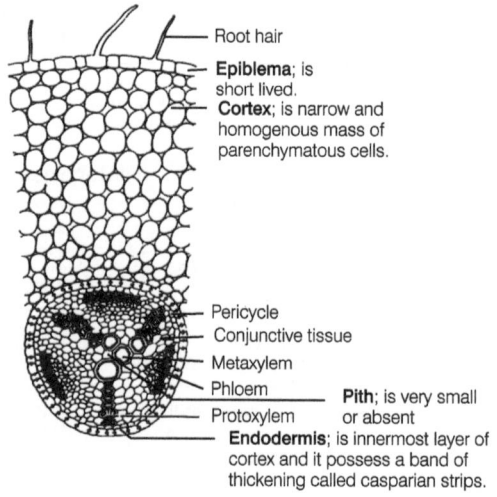

(a) TS of dicot root

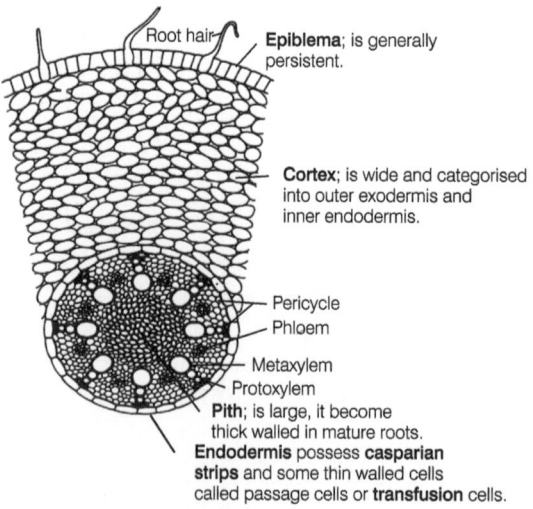

(b) TS of monocot root

Handbook of BIOLOGY

Dicot and Monocot Stems

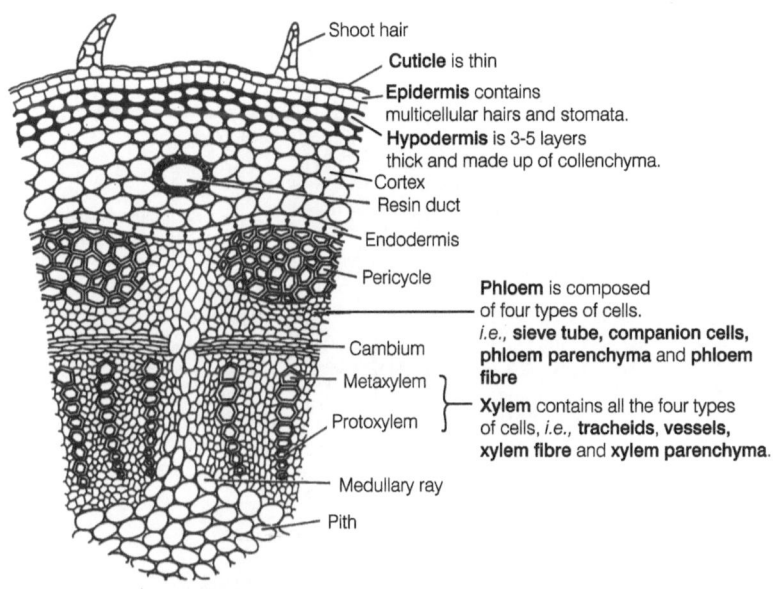

(a) TS of dicot stem

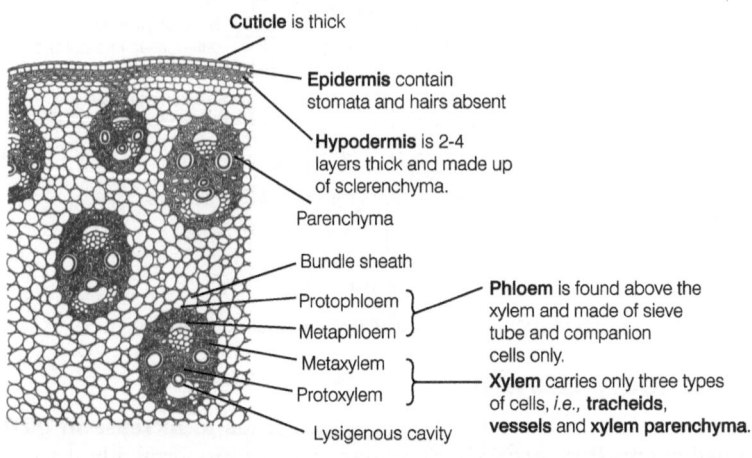

(b) TS of monocot stem

Dicot and Monocot Leaves

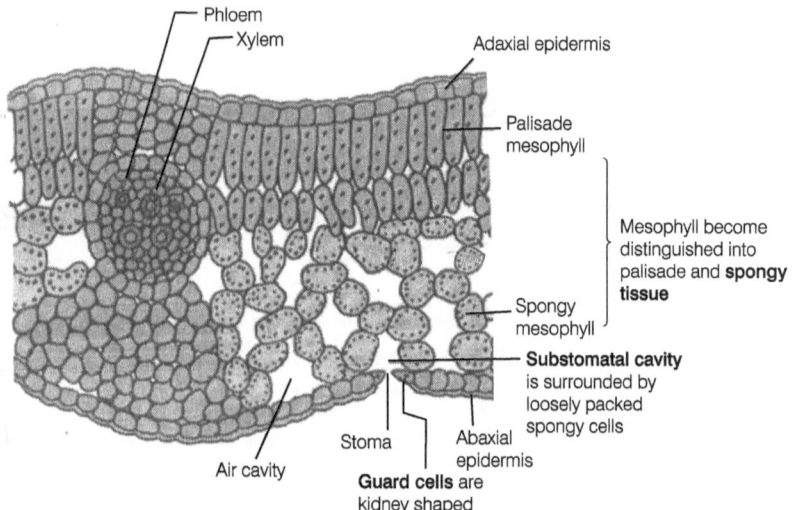

(a) TS of dicot : dorsiventral or bifacial leaf

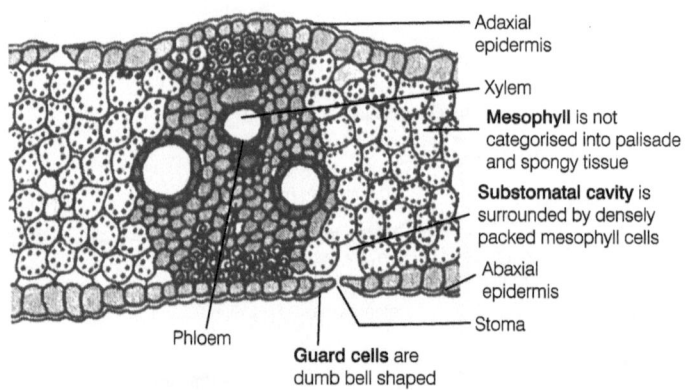

(b) TS of monocot : isobilateral or equifacial leaf

Secondary Growth

The formation of secondary tissue which leads to increase in girth is called **secondary growth**. Secondary tissues are formed by two types of lateral meristems– *vascular cambium and cork cambium.*

Cork cambium (phellogen) produces cork cells (phellem) on outerside and phelloderm on innerside. Phellem, phellogen and phelloderm together constitute the **periderm.**

Secondary Growth in Dicot Root

The secondary growth in dicot roots takes place in both stelar (by vascular cambium) and in extrastelar region (by cork cambium).

The whole process can be discussed as under

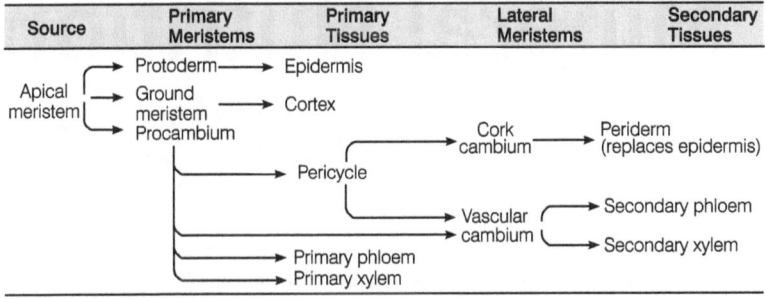

Summary of primary and secondary growth of root in a vascular plant

Secondary Growth in Dicot Stem

Secondary xylem produced by cambial ring is called **wood**. The wood formed in a single year is called **annual ring** or **growth ring**. *The whole process of growth can be discussed as under*

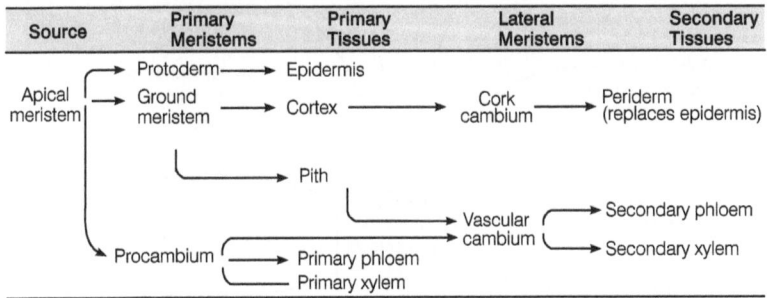

Summary of primary and secondary growth in stem of a vascular plant

Types of Wood

On the basis of time of formation

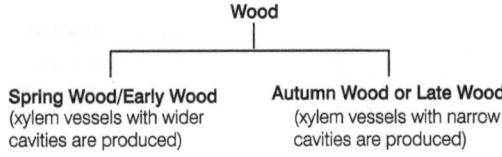

21
Mineral Nutrition *in* Plants

Almost all organisms require several elements to operate various functions in their body. The elements of biological importance and their absorption is the theme of mineral nutrition.

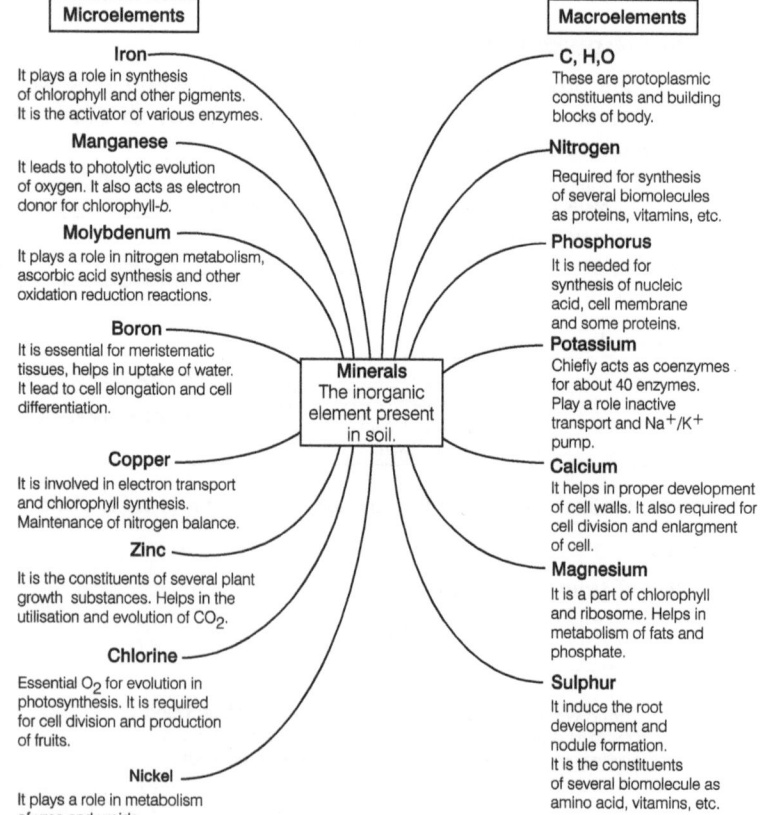

Microelements

Iron
It plays a role in synthesis of chlorophyll and other pigments. It is the activator of various enzymes.

Manganese
It leads to photolytic evolution of oxygen. It also acts as electron donor for chlorophyll-*b*.

Molybdenum
It plays a role in nitrogen metabolism, ascorbic acid synthesis and other oxidation reduction reactions.

Boron
It is essential for meristematic tissues, helps in uptake of water. It lead to cell elongation and cell differentiation.

Copper
It is involved in electron transport and chlorophyll synthesis. Maintenance of nitrogen balance.

Zinc
It is the constituents of several plant growth substances. Helps in the utilisation and evolution of CO_2.

Chlorine
Essential O_2 for evolution in photosynthesis. It is required for cell division and production of fruits.

Nickel
It plays a role in metabolism of urea and ureids.

Minerals
The inorganic element present in soil.

Macroelements

C, H, O
These are protoplasmic constituents and building blocks of body.

Nitrogen
Required for synthesis of several biomolecules as proteins, vitamins, etc.

Phosphorus
It is needed for synthesis of nucleic acid, cell membrane and some proteins.

Potassium
Chiefly acts as coenzymes for about 40 enzymes. Play a role inactive transport and Na^+/K^+ pump.

Calcium
It helps in proper development of cell walls. It also required for cell division and enlargment of cell.

Magnesium
It is a part of chlorophyll and ribosome. Helps in metabolism of fats and phosphate.

Sulphur
It induce the root development and nodule formation. It is the constituents of several biomolecule as amino acid, vitamins, etc.

Classification of Mineral Nutrients

- *On the basis of their essentiality in body, the minerals can be categorised into*

Mineral Elements

Essential mineral elements
(17 in number)
These elements have specific structural or physiological role. These are indispensable for plants to complete their life cycle, *e.g.*, nitrogen, phosphorus, etc.

Non-essential mineral elements
(other than 17 essential)
The elements are required in some plants, but not all. Their absence does not produce any major deficiency symptoms in plants. *e.g.*, cobalt, silicon, sodium, etc.

- *On the basis of their occurrence in dry matter of living organism, minerals are of following types*

Mineral Elements

Micronutrients/Microelement/Trace-element
(equal to or less than 100 mg/kg of dry matter)
These acts as cofactors or activators for the functioning of enzymes. These are **eight in number**.
e.g., Zn, Mn, B, Cu, Mo, Cl, Ni and Fe.

Macronutrients/Macroelements
(1000 mg/ kg of dry matter)
These are involved in the synthesis of organic molecule. These are **nine in number**.
e.g., C, H, O, N, S, P, K, Mg and Ca.

- *On the basis of their diverse functions, the essential elements can be classified into four different categories*

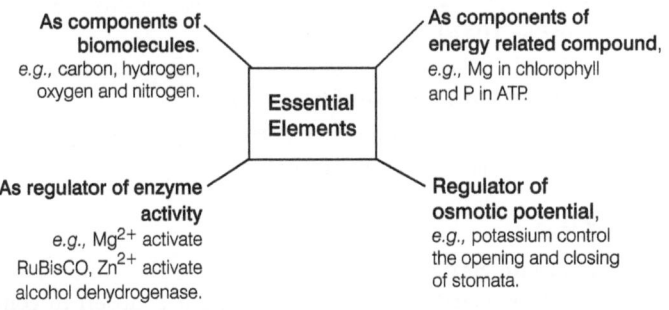

As components of biomolecules.
e.g., carbon, hydrogen, oxygen and nitrogen.

As components of energy related compound,
e.g., Mg in chlorophyll and P in ATP.

As regulator of enzyme activity
e.g., Mg^{2+} activate RuBisCO, Zn^{2+} activate alcohol dehydrogenase.

Regulator of osmotic potential,
e.g., potassium control the opening and closing of stomata.

Deficiency Symptoms of Essential Mineral Nutrients

These symptoms appear in plant when the mineral supply of an essential element becomes limited. The minimum concentration at which plant growth is retarded is termed as **critical concentration**.

A detailed account of certain symptoms are as follows

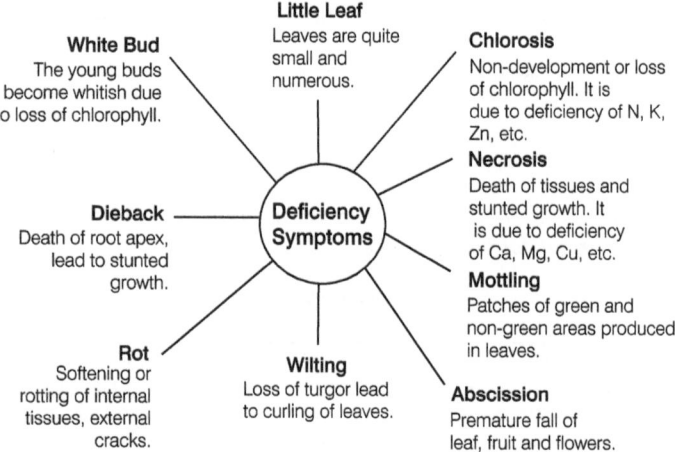

Toxicity of Micronutrients

1. The moderate increase in concentration of micronutrients cause its toxicity.
2. Any tissue concentration which reduce dry weight of tissue by 10% is called **toxic concentration'**.
3. The critical toxic concentration is different for different micronutrient as well as different plants.
4. The toxicity of one mineral, mostly lead to the inhibition of absorption of other micronutrients.

Hydroponics

In 1860, **Julius von Sachs** demonstrated for the first time that plant could be grown to maturity in a defined nutrient solution in complete absence of soil.

The soilless production of plants is called **hydroponics**. It is also known as **soilless culture** or **solution culture (Georick; 1940)**.

There are three methods for growing plants with nutrient solutions
1. **Hydroponic Culture** Using nutrient solution in this culture, an air tight container is supplied by air through a tube and nutrient through a funnel.

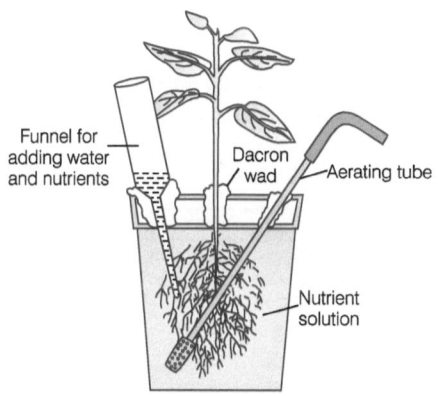

Hydroponic culture

2. **Slop Culture** Nutrient solution using sand. In this the plants are grown on sand column, the nutrient solution poured on regular interval from upside.
3. **Nutrient Film Technique** The nutrient solution drains through plant roots, through a channel. In this process, the plant roots do not have any substratum but they are bathed regularly with nutrient solution.

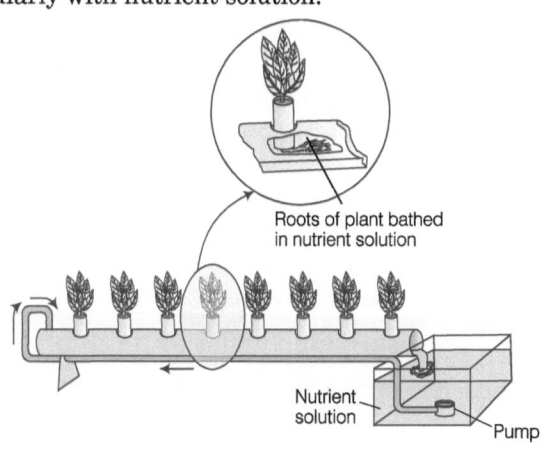

Nutrient film technique

Metabolism of Nitrogen

Nitrogen Cycle

Nitrogen cycle is an example of gaseous biogeochemical cycle, which lead to the cycling of nitrogen in various pools (*i.e.,* atmosphere, soil and living organisms).

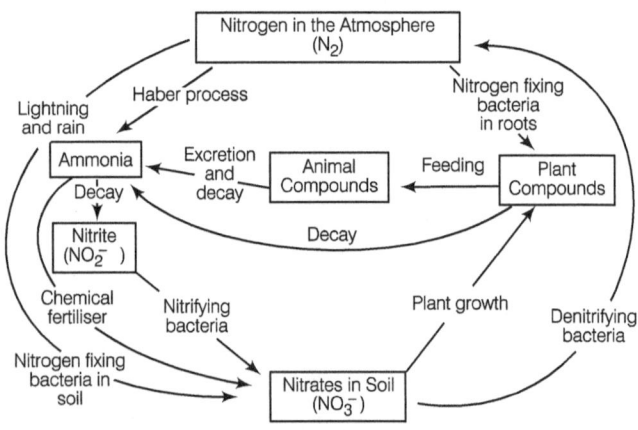

Nitrogen cycle

A regular supply of nitrogen to the plant is maintained through nitrogen cycle. Plant obtain nitrogen from soil as NO_3^- (nitrate), NH_4^+ (ammonium) and NO_2^- (nitrite) ions.

Nitrogen Fixation

Conversion of **free nitrogen** into **nitrogenous salts** to make it available for absorption by plants.

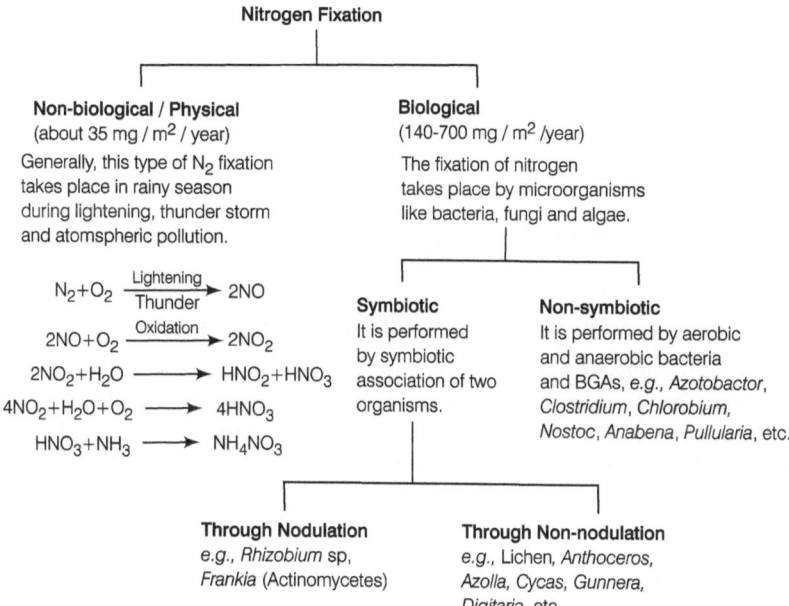

Biochemistry of Nitrogen Fixation

Schneider *et al.* (1960) and **Carnahan *et al.*** (1960) studied the nitrogen fixation by radiolabelling and confirmed the conversion of nitrogen into ammonia.

Basic requirements of N_2-fixation are
 (i) Nitrogenase and hydrogenase enzyme.
 (ii) A mechanism which protect **nitrogenase** from oxygen.
 (iii) Ferredoxin.
 (iv) Constant supply of ATP.
 (v) Coenzyme and cofactors like TPP, Co-A, iP and Mg^{+2}.
 (vi) Cobalt and molybdenum.
 (vii) A carbon compound to trap released ammonia.

The most important requirement of N_2-fixation is nitrogenase enzyme which has two sub-units. *These are*
 (i) **Fe containing unit**   Dinitrogen reductase.
 (ii) **Mo containing protein**   Dinitrogenase.

The enzyme nitrogenase is highly sensitive for molecular oxygen (O_2) and gets inactivated when exposed to it. The nodule formation is to provide anaerobic condition to this enzyme.

The basic N_2 fixing reaction is as follows

$$N_2 + 8e^- + 8H^+ + 16ATP \xrightarrow{\text{Dinitrogenase enzyme complex}} 2NH_3 + 2H^+ + 16ADP + 16Pi$$

The chemically fixed nitrogen is used by both plants and animals to synthesise various biomolecules of diverse uses.

Soil as Reservoir of Essential Elements

Soil acts as most stable reservoir for both nutrients and organisms to harbour in it. Various inorganic salts and ions, derived from rock minerals present in soil, are known as **mineral nutrition**. **Natural process** like weathering and humification enrich the nutritional content of soil, while some **artificial processes** like fertilisers (*i.e.*, chemical and organic) also lead to nutritional enrichment of soil.

22

Photosynthesis *in* Higher Plants

Photosynthesis is the only mechanism of energy input into living world. Only exception occurs in chemosynthetic bacteria that obtain energy by oxidising inorganic substances.

The synthesis of organic compounds like carbohydrates or glucose by the cells of green plants in presence of sunlight with the help of CO_2 and H_2O is called **photosynthesis**.

Photosynthesis sometimes called as **carbon assimilation** and is represented by following equation.

$$6CO_2 + 6H_2O \xrightarrow[\text{Green plants}]{\text{Light energy (686 kcal)}} 6O_2 + C_6H_{12}O_6$$

The whole process can be demonstrated as

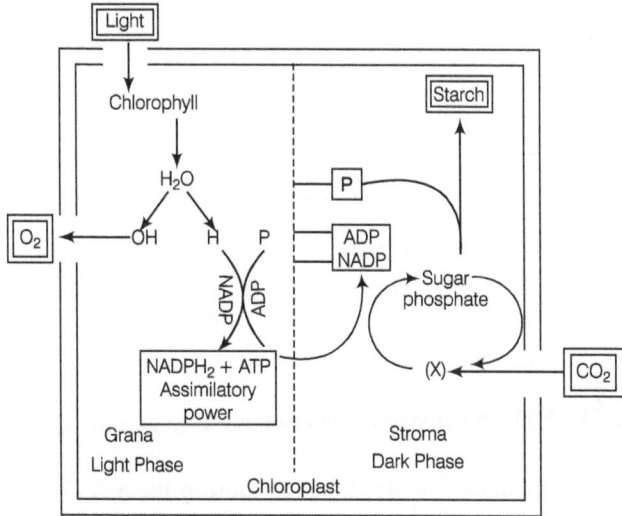

Demonstration of light dependent and light independent phases during photosynthesis

Chemistry and Thermodynamics of Photosynthesis

Photosynthesis is a chemical oxidation-reduction process in which water molecules are oxidised to form O_2, and CO_2 molecules are reduced to form carbohydrate. It is an enzyme regulated, anabolic process of producing organic compounds.

The annual CO_2 fixation is about 70 billion tonnes which require about 1.05×10^{18} kcal of energy. The total solar energy falling on earth is 5×10^{20} kcal/year. The plants are thus able to utilise only 0.2% of the solar energy received by the surface of earth.

Historical Timeline of Photosynthesis

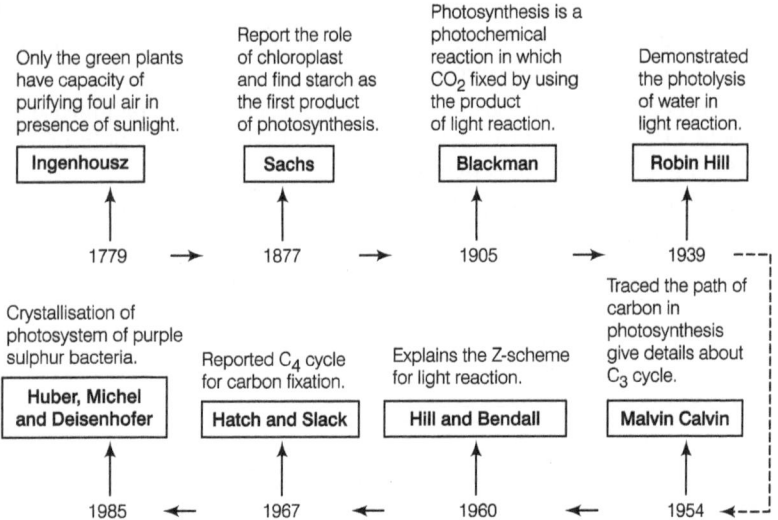

Landmark discoveries related to photosynthesis

Chloroplast : Photosynthetic Organ of Cell

Chloroplasts are the green plastids which occur in all green parts of the plants. These are the actual sites of photosynthesis.

These occurs mostly in chlorenchymatous cells (particularly in mesophyll) of leaves and young stem. It is a double membranous organalle in which the envelops encloses a liquid proteinaceous matrix called stroma.

It is a semi-autonomous organalle as it contain its own DNA and is a characteristic feature of plant cells only. As complete food synthesis takes place in chloroplast, it is also known as **kitchen of the cell.**

Handbook of BIOLOGY

Internal Structure of Chloroplast

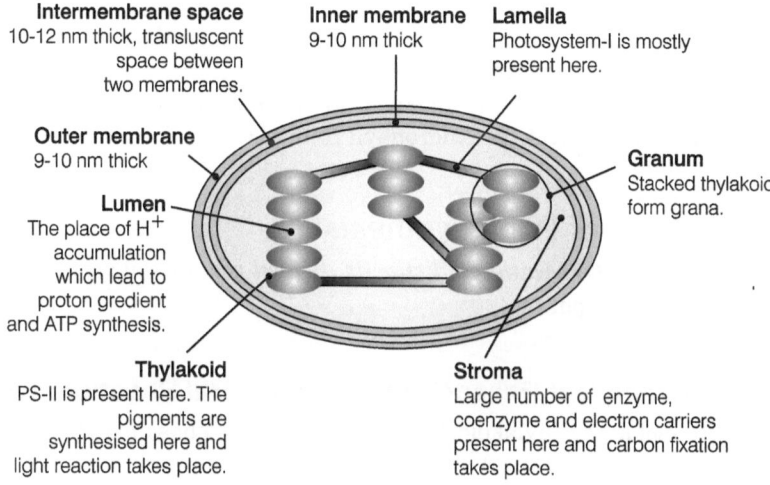

Detailed structure of chloroplast

Photosynthetic Pigments

The pigments present in plants are of two types

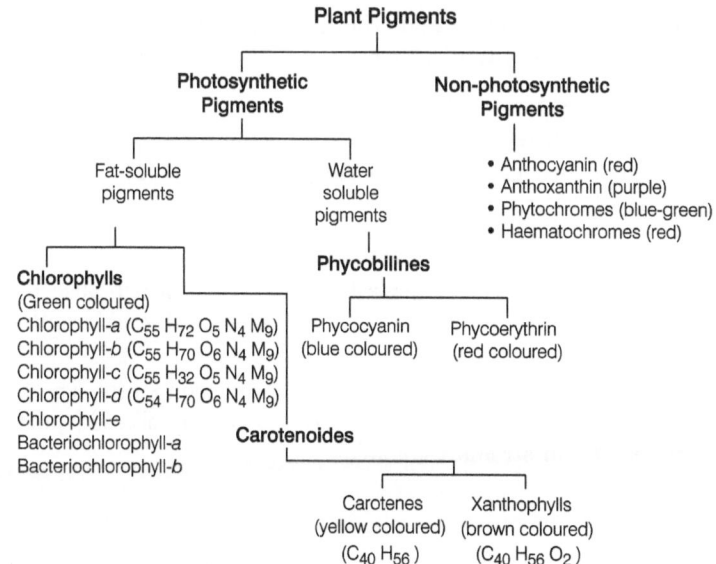

Pigments involved in photosynthesis

1. Both **chlorophyll-a** and **β-carotene** are universal photosynthetic pigment.
2. The heaviest pigment of chloroplast is **chlorophyll-b** and the lightiest one is **carotene**.
3. Chlorophylls directly involves in trapping of sunlight, while carotene protect the chlorophyll from photo-oxidation by bright sunlight.

Mechanism of Photosynthesis

The process of photosynthesis distinctly divided into two phases
- Photochemical phase
- Biosynthetic phase

1. Photochemical Phase/Light Reaction/Hill Reaction

It occurs inside the thylakoids, the function of this phase is to produce assimilatory powers (*i.e.,* ATP, NADPH, etc).

It includes
  (i) Light absorption
  (ii) Splitting of water
  (iii) Release of oxygen
  (iv) Formation of high energy chemical intermediates

Several complexes of protein and other pigments are involved in **light reaction** or **photochemical** phase.

(i) Light Absorption

The molecule which is responsible for absorption of light is a protein based complex called **Light Harvesting Complex** (LHC), which are organised into PS-I and PS-II.

(a) Photosystem-I or Pigment System-I

The **reaction centre** in this pigment system is P_{700}, which absorb the light of wavelength 700 nm. It has more of chlorophyll-*a* chlorophyll-*b* and carotenoids are comparativily less.

PS-I can carry on cyclic photophosphorylation independently. The PS-I with electron carriers is located on both the non-appressed part of grana thylakoid and stroma thylakoids.

(b) Photosystem-II or Pigment System-II

P_{680} functions as reaction centre in this photosystem. The photons of lower wavelength is absorbed by this photosystem. It is located in appressed part of thylakoid and carryout non-cyclic photophosphorylation with PS-I.

PS-II has chlorophyll-a, b and carotenoids (according to some physiologists, **xanthophyll** also functions as antenna in this system).

The other three sub-stages of photochemical phase can be studied in the head of electron transport.

(ii) Photolysis of Water/Splitting of Water

In photosynthesis, water is used as a source of hydrogen required for the reduction of CO_2 to form carbohydrate.

$$CO_2 + 2H_2O \xrightarrow[\text{Chlorophyll}]{\text{Light}} CH_2O + H_2O + O_2$$

$$4H_2O \xrightarrow[\text{Chlorophyll}]{\text{Light}} 2H_2O + 4H^+ + 4e^- + O_2$$

The first demonstration of photolysis of water was done by **R Hill** (1937) and it is described by **Van Niel** (1931).

As a result of photosynthesis the oxygen is released.

(iii) Formation of High Energy Chemical Intermediate

These intermediates are reduced molecule which provides energy during biosynthetic phase. There are various such intermediates, as $NADPH_2$, NADPH and ATP.

These are produced by two types of reaction

(a) Photophosphorylation

(b) Chemiosmosis

(a) Photophosphorylation

The formation of ATP molecule from ADP and H_3PO_4 in presence of light and chlorophyll-a is called **photophosphorylation.**

$$ADP + H_3PO_4 \xrightarrow[\text{Chl-}a]{\text{Light}} ATP$$

ATP formation takes place through the following two types of phosphorylation reactions

Non-Cyclic Photophosphorylation

Both ATP and NADPH$_2$ produced in this reaction, this takes place as follows

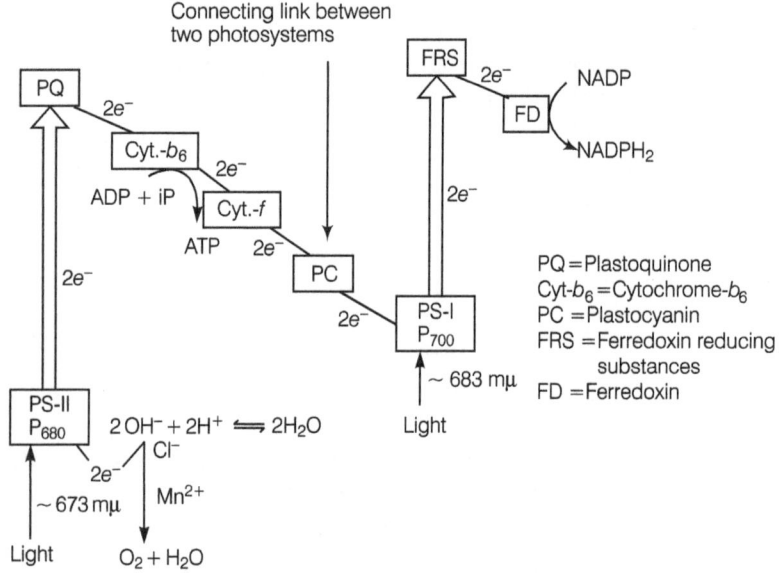

Diagrammatic representation of the non-cyclic photophosphorylation process (Z-scheme)

During non-cyclic photophosphorylation, the initial donor and final acceptor of electrons are different. After the illumination of PS-II the released electrons passed to PS-I *via* various electron carriers.

From PS-I, electron is finally provided to ferredoxin (FD), which help in synthesis of NADPH$_2$ from NADP. It is known as **Z-scheme**, due to its characteristic shape.

Cyclic Photophosphorylation

In this process, the initial donor and the final acceptor of electron is the same chlorophyll-*a* of PS-I. Only PS-I is involved in this phosphorylation.

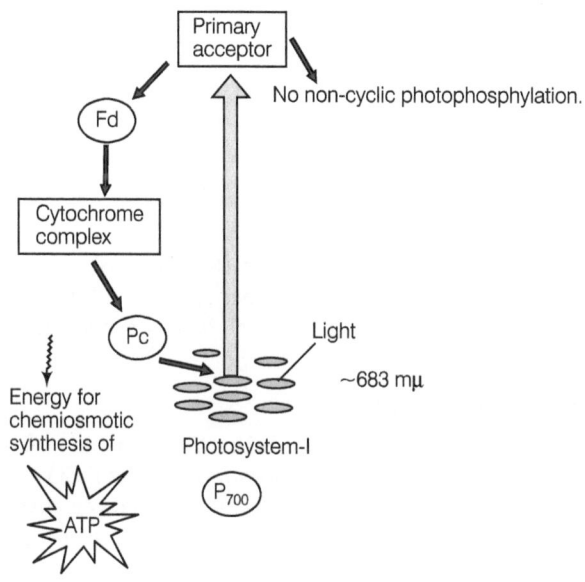

Diagrammatic reproduction of the cyclic photophosphorylation process

This occurs when activity of PS-II gets ceased or non-cyclic photophosphorylation stopped due to certain reasons. The electron emitted after illumination of PS-I return back to its original place *via* several electron carriers which ultimately lead to the synthesis of NADPH.

Three Diverse Methods of Synthesising ATP

Process	Energy Source	Site
Photophosphorylation	Sunlight	Chloroplast
Substrate level phosphorylation	Reaction not involving oxygen	Cytosol
Oxidative phosphorylation	Oxidation with oxygen	Mitochondria

(b) **Chemiosmosis**

Like respiration, in photosynthesis too, ATP synthesis is linked to development of a proton gradient across a membrane.

2. Biosynthetic Phase/Dark Reaction/Blackman's Reaction

It occurs in stroma or matrix and the chief function of this phase is to produce carbohydrate by using the assimilatory powers (*i.e.*, product of light reaction).

It includes

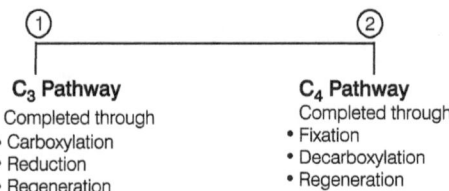

This process does not directly depend on the presence of light but it is dependent on the products of light reaction, *i.e.,* ATP and NADPH, besides CO_2 and H_2O. *There are three different pathways for CO_2 fixation in plants*

(i) C_3 - Pathway or Calvin Cycle

The cycle was discovered by **Calvin Benson** *et. al.,* through experimenting with *Chlorella* and *Scendesmus* with CO_2 containing radioactive ^{14}C. In this pathway the assimilatory power NADP(H) and ATP produced in light phase is used to reduce CO_2 into carbohydrate.

The scheme of C_3 pathway is as follows

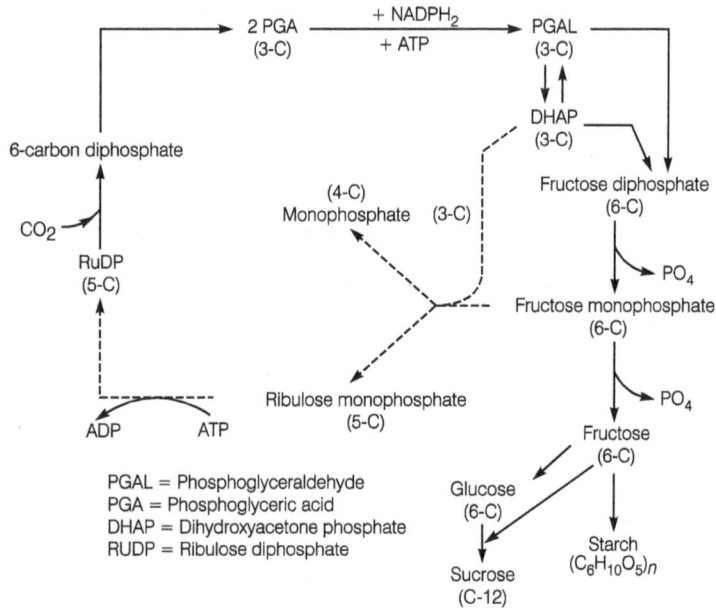

Diagrammatic representation of Calvin cycle, regeneration of RuDP is indicated by broken lines

In this cycle, 6 molecule of CO_2 is used and one molecule of fructose - 6 -P is produced as a byproduct at the expense of 12 molecules of NADPH and 18 molecules of ATP.

The overall reaction is expressed as

$6\ CO_2 + 12\ NADPH + 12\ H^+ + 18\ ATP + 11\ H_2O$

$\rightarrow F - 6 - P + 12\ NADP^+ + 18\ ADP + 17 Pi$

(ii) C_4 - Pathway or Hatch-Slack Cycle

This cycle is present in those plants, which are adapted for hotter climatic regions. Plants also possess a specific anatomy called **Kranz anatomy** to fulfill the structural demand for C_4-pathway.

These plants have Oxaloacetic Acid (OAA) as their first CO_2 fixation product. Through processes like fixation, decarboxylation and regeneration, the carbohydrate is synthesised in bundle sheath cells of leaf.

The schematic representation of C_4-cycle is as follows

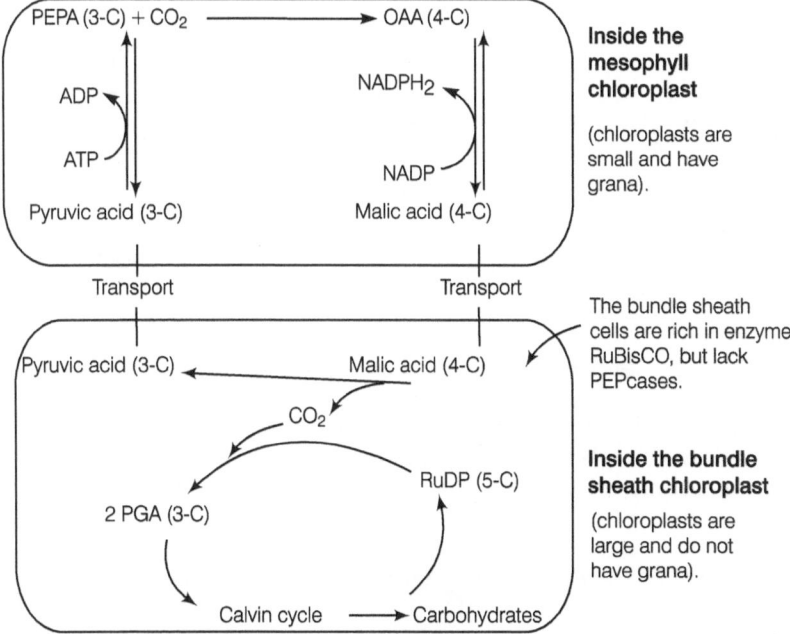

Schematic representation of Hatch and Slack pathway

(iii) CAM (Crassulacean Acid Metabolism) Pathway

The pathway mostly present is the succulent xerophytes, such as the members Crassulaceae, Euphorbiaceae, etc.

In this process, during night time, the stomata is open and **CO_2 enters through it, which is accepted by OAA** and converted into malic acid.

The schematic representation of CAM pathway is as follows

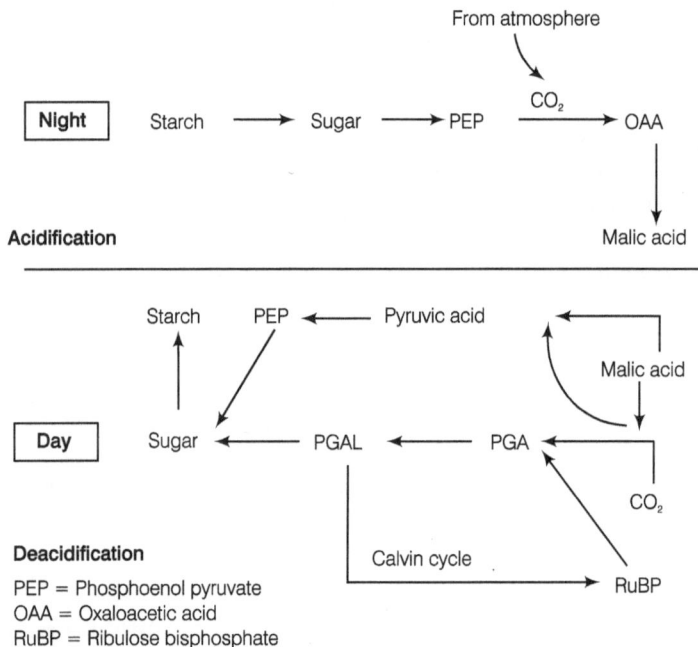

Schematic representation of the CAM pathway

During day time the malic acid produced both pyruvic acid and CO_2 after **decarboxylation**. The pyruvic acid enter into glycolysis, while CO_2 enter into calvin cycle.

Factors Affecting Photosynthesis

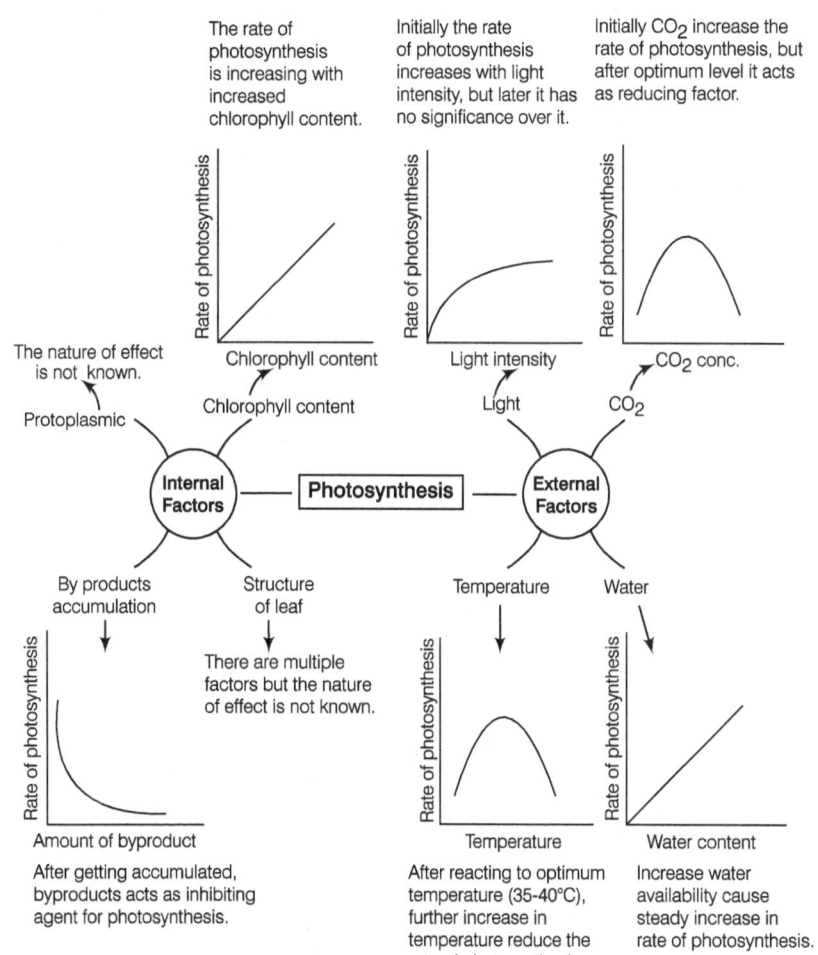

Law of Limiting Factors (Blackman; 1905)

It a chemical process is affected by more than one factor, then its rate will be determined by the factor which is nearest to its minimal value it is the factor which directly affect the process.

Photorespiration (C_2-Cycle)

It was discovered by **Dicker** and **Tio** (1959) in tobacco plants.

The **chloroplast, peroxisome** and **mitochondria** are required to complete this reaction.

The schematic representation of photorespiration is a follows

The CO_2 in form of output reach to the chloroplast and run the calvin cycle smoothly.

This reaction is also termed as **glycolate metabolism.**

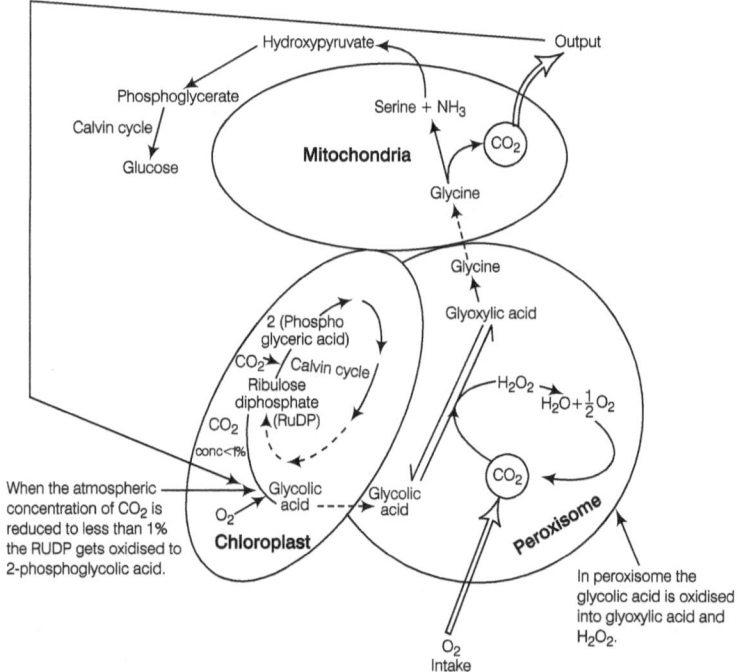

Diagrammatic representation of various steps of photorespiration

23
Transport in Plants

In plants, substances like growth regulators, nutrients, water, food, etc., have to be transported from one plant parts to another.

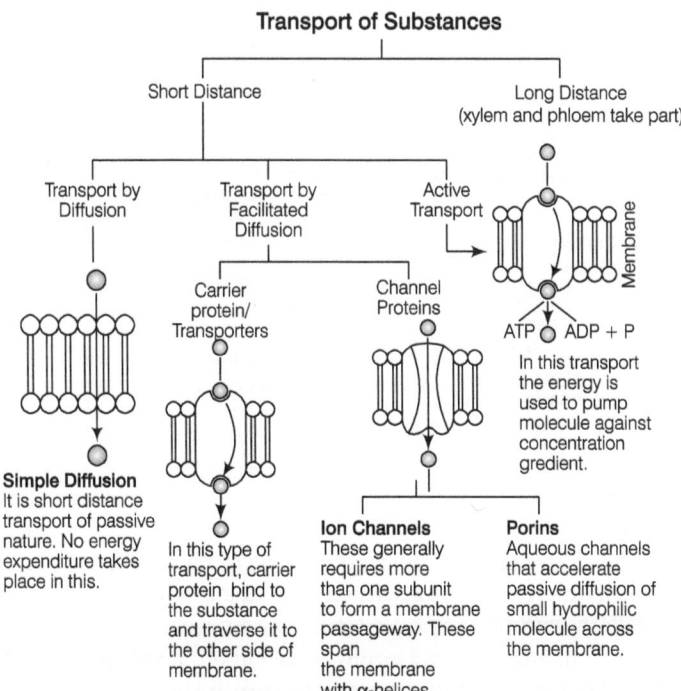

Several methods of transport of substances

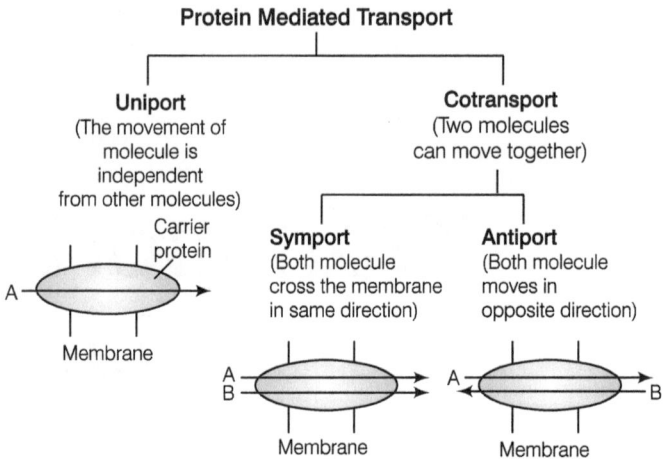

Types of protein mediated transports

Plant Water Relation

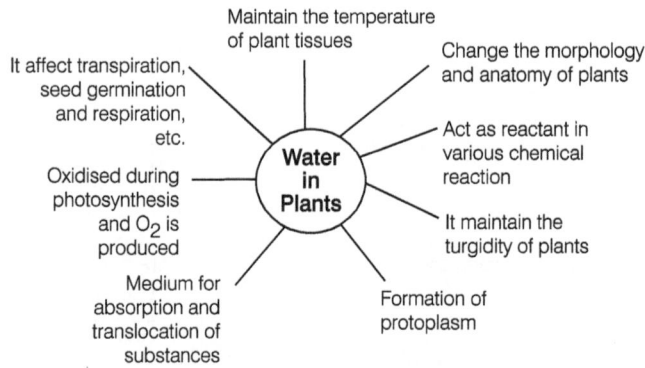

Roles of water in plants

Imbibition

It is absorption of water by the solid particle of an adsorbant causing it to enormously increase in size without forming a solution, *e.g.,* swelling of dry seeds in water.

   (i) Solid substance or adsorbants is called **imbibants** and the liquid which imbibed is known as **imbibate**.
  (ii) The swelling imbibant also develops a pressure called **imbibition** pressure (matric potential).

Diffusion

The tendency of even distribution of solid, liquid or gaseous molecule in available space is called **diffusion**. It is driven by **random kinetic motion**. Diffusion is defined as the movement of particle of substance from the region of their higher concentration.

Diffusion Pressure (DP); The pressure exerted by the even distribution of particle

DP ∝ concentration of diffusing particle.

Factors Affecting Diffusion

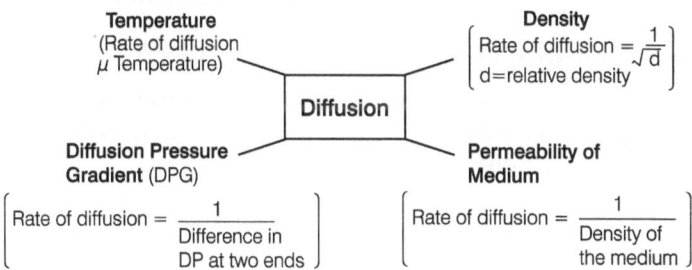

Osmosis

Osmosis is a special type of diffusion of solution/water that occurs through a semipermeable membrane.

The phenomenon of osmosis was discovered by **Nollet** in 1748.

Osmotic Pressure (OP; Pfeffer, 1750)

The actual pressure, that develops in a solution, when it is separated from pure water by means of semipermeable membrane.

OP depends upon–
- Concentration
- Ionisation
- Hydration
- Temperature

It is measured in terms of atmosphere (atm)

$$1 \text{ atm} = 14.7 \text{ pounds/inch}^2$$
$$= 760 \text{ mm Hg}$$
$$= 1.013 \text{ bar}$$
$$= 1.013 \times 10^5 \text{ Mpa.}$$

Osmotic pressure $\boxed{OP = m\,i\,R\,T}$

where, m = Molar concentration
i = Ionisation constant
R = Gas constant
T = Temperature

Chemical Potential

It is quantitative expression of the free energy associated with water.

'It is the difference between the potential of a substance in a given state and the potential of same substance in standard state.'

Water Potential (Stalyer and Taylor, 1960)

The total kinetic energy of water molecules present in a system is known as its water potential. Hence, the **pure water will have the highest water potential**.

'It is the difference in the free energy or chemical potential per unit molal volume of water in a system and that of pure water at the same temperature and pressure.

Chemical potential of pure water at normal temperature and pressure (NTP) is **zero**. It is represented by ψ (psi) or more accurately ψ_w.

Unit of ψ_w = bars or pascal (1 mpa = 10 bars)

$$\psi_w = \psi_s + \psi_p + \psi_g$$

Water potential — Solute potential — Pressure potential — Potential due to gravity

Water potential is a tool which inform us about the plant cells and tissues. The lower the water potential in a plant cell or tissues, the greater is its ability to absorb water.

Osmotic Potential (OP)/Solute Potential (ψ_s)

'It is the decrease in chemical potential of pure water due to the presence of solute particle in it.'

It can be calculated by

$$\psi_s = C \times R \times T$$

where, C = Concentration of solute particle
R = Gas contant
T = Temperature

It always have **negative value**.

Turgor Pressure (TP)/Hydrostatic Pressure/Pressure Potential (ψ_p)

This can be understood by following scheme diagram

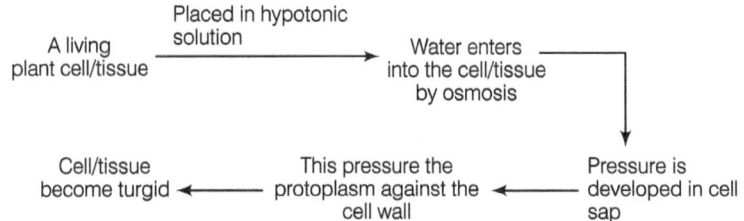

This pressure is called **turgor pressure.**

Diffusion Pressure Deficit (DPD) Meyer, 1938

The difference between the diffusion pressure of the solution and its solvents at a particular temperature and atmospheric conditions is called **DPD**. It determine the direction of net movement of water.

DPD has a **positive value.**

DPD $\propto$ Concentration of solution.

It is also known as **suction pressure** as it is a measure of the ability of a cells to absorb water.

$$DPD/SP = OP - WP$$
$$WP = TP$$
$$DPD = OP - TP$$

Now-a-days the term 'Water potential' is used which is equal to DPD.

Long Distance Transport of Water

Long distance transport of substances within a plant can not be by diffusion alone. Special systems are necessary to move substances across long distance and at a much faster rate.

Water, minerals and food are generally moved by a **mass** or **bulk flow system.**

Mass Flow System

According to this theory, 'An increase in transpiration increase the rate of absorption of ions'. The bulk flow of substances through vascular system is called **translocation.**

Absorption of Water by Plants

Water is absorbed along with mineral solutes by the root hairs, purely by diffusion. Once water is absorbed, it can move through different pathways.

There are three pathways for the movement of water in plants.
1. Apoplast pathway
2. Symplast pathway
3. Transmembrane pathway

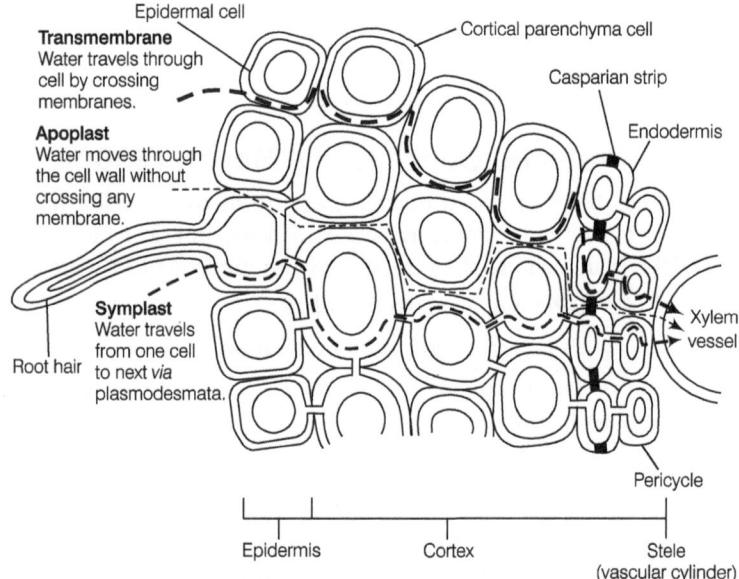

Three routes of lateral transport in plant tissues or organ

Mechanism of Water Absorption

Water absorption is of two types

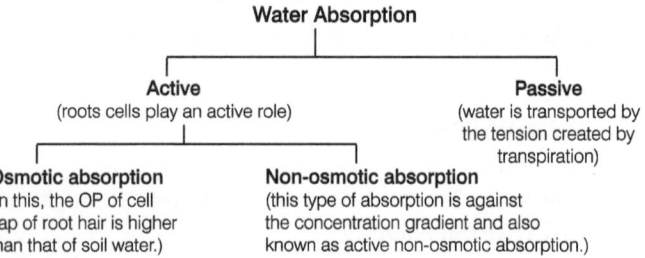

Factors Affecting the Rate of Water Absorption

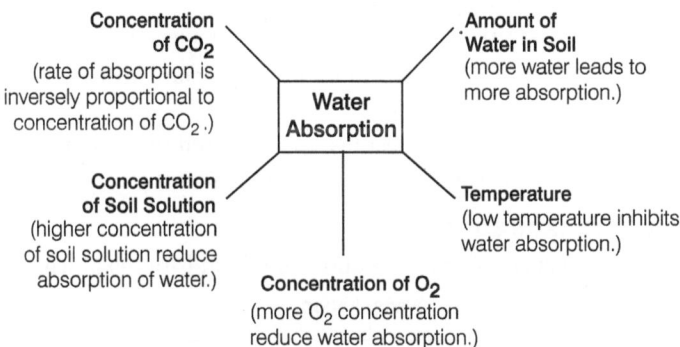

Upward Water Movement in a Plant

For distribution to various parts of the plant, water has to be move upward in a stem against gravity. There are two forces which provide the energy for this movement of water. *These are*

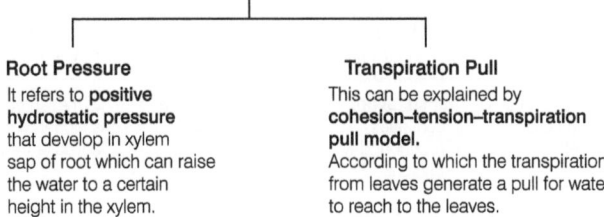

Guttation

It is the loss of water in the liquid state from uninjured parts of plants, usually from tips and margins of leaves. In this, water exudes from the group of leaf cells called **hydathodes.**

A hydathode is an opening or pore in the leaf epidermis, around, which are grouped as several thin-walled parenchyma cells. It occurs during night or early morning when there is high atmospheric humidity and transpiration is less.

Transpiration

It is an evaporative loss of water by plants, occurs mainly through stomata. Since transpiration reduce the water levels in soil, but is necessary for water and mineral absorption *i.e.*, ascent of sap. Therefore, it is also known as **necessary evil.**

The transpiration driven ascent of xylem sap depends mainly on the following physical properties of water

Cohesion Mutual attraction between water molecules.

Adhesion Attraction of water molecules to polar surfaces (such as the surface of tracheary elements).

Surface Tension Water molecules are attracted to each other in the liquid phase more than to water in the gas phase.

Types of Transpiration

(i) On the basis of part of the plant in which it takes place.

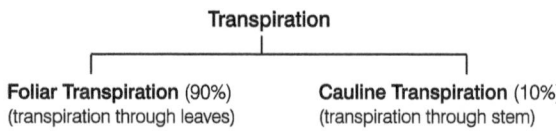

(ii) On the basis of surface of plant

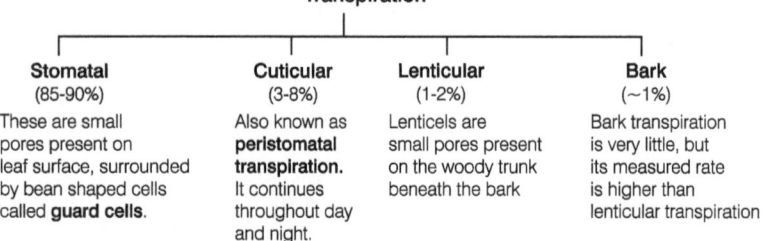

Significance of Transpiration

Advantages

(a) **Ascent of sap** Ascent of sap mostly occurs due to transpiration pull exerted by transpiration of water. This pull also helps in absorption of water.

(b) **Removal of excess water** It has been held that plants absorb far more amount of water than is actually required by them. Transpiration, therefore, removes the excess of water.

(c) **Cooling effect** Transpiration, by evaporating water, lowers down their temperature by 10°-15° C

(d) **Mechanical tissue** The development of mechanical tissue, which is essential for providing rigidity and strength to the plant, is favoured by the increase in transpiration.

(e) **Distribution of mineral salts** Mineral salts are mostly distributed by rising column of sap.

(f) **Increasing concentration of mineral salts** The loss of water through transpiration increases the concentration of mineral salts in the plant.

(g) **Root system** Transpiration helps in better development of root system which is required for support and absorption of mineral salts.

(h) **Quality of fruits** The ash and sugar content of the fruit increase with the increase in transpiration.

(i) **Resistance** Excessive transpiration induces hardening and resistance to moderate drought.

(j) **Turgidity** Transpiration maintains the shape and structure of plant parts by keeping cells turgid.

(k) **Photosynthesis** Transpiration supplies water for photosynthesis.

Disadvantages

(a) **Wilting** Wilting or loss of turgidity is quite common during noon due to transpiration being higher than the rate of water absorption. Wilting reduces photosynthesis and other metabolic activities.

(b) **Reduced growth** Transpiration reduces availability of water inside the plant.

(c) **Reduced yield** As reported by **Tumarov** (1925), a single wilting reduces growth by 50%.

(d) **Abscisic acid** Water stress produces abscisic acid. Abscisic acid prevents several plant processes and promotes abscission of leaves, flowers and fruits.

(e) **Wastage of energy** Since most of the absorbed water is lost in transpiration, it is energy wastage.

Factors Affecting Transpiration

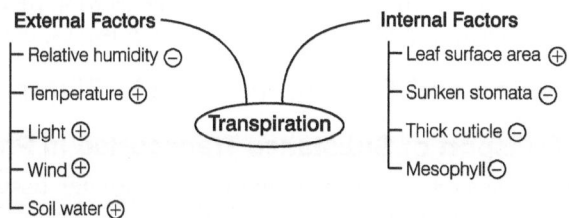

⊕ = increase the transpiration with increasing related factors.

⊖ = decrease in the transpiration with increase in related factor.

Uptake and Transport of Mineral Nutrients

Mineral Salt Absorption

Early scientists have opinion that inorganic salts are passively carried into plants with the absorption of water and the absorbed salts are translocated to the different parts of the plant through transpiration stream.

Now-a-days, it has been established that mineral salt absorption is an active process rather than passive as it was considerd earlier.

Active Mineral Absorption

The absorption of ions against the concentration gradient or with the help of metabolic energy is known as **active absorption**.

Following theory have been proposed to explain the phenomenon of active absorption.

The Carrier Concept (Vanden Honert, 1937) According to this theory 'The carrier molecules of ions combine with ions in outer free space to form carrier-ion complex. This complex move through intermediate space into inner space where it release ions. The carrier compound return back to outer space, but ions cannot'.

The observations like **isotopic exchange, saturation effect** and **specificity,** greatly support the carrier concept of active absorption of mineral salts.

Translocation of Mineral Ions

The translocation of mineral salts/ions takes place both by xylem and phloem. The upward movement usually occurs through xylem while bidirectional movement occurs through phloem.

pH $\begin{cases} \text{Decrease — Lead to absorption of anions} \\ \text{Increase — Lead to absorption of cations} \end{cases}$

The chief sinks for the mineral elements are the growing regions of the plant such as apical and lateral meristem, young leaves, etc.

Translocation and Storage of Food in Plants

Phloem Transport or Substance Transported in Phloem

Food, primarily sucrose, is transported by the vascular tissue phloem from source to a sink. The transport of food from the production centre (leaves) to the consumption centre (apices, roots, fruits, tubers) is called **translocation of organic solutes**.

Routes of Translocation

Solutes are translocated in various directions within the plants. *These may be*
- (i) Downward translocation of organic solute – From leaves to root and other parts of plant.
- (ii) Upward translocation of organic solute – Root to leaves or other apical region.
- (iii) Upward translocation of mineral salts – Occurs through xylem by active transport.
- (iv) Upward movement of solute – Movement of salts to the leaves.
- (v) Lateral translocation of solutes – Translocation in tangential direction, in woody stems.

Mechanism of Translocation

There are several theories have been put forward to explain the mechanism of organic solute movement.

The most accepted theory which explains the mechanism of translocation is **Mass Flow Theory.** *Some of the theories including mass flow are as follows*

Mass or Pressure Flow Theory (Ernst Munch; 1930)

It is also known as **pressure flow hypothesis** or **Munch hypothesis.** According to this hypothesis, *the organic solute translocate in following steps*

- (a) **Phloem loading** is an active transport mechanism. It is carried out by a specific carrier protein molecules in the cell surface membrane of companion cells that uses energy of ATP from the photosynthesising mesophyll cells to the sieve tubes in the veins of a leaf.
- (b) **Long distance transport** of sucrose in the stem and root phloem.
- (c) **Phloem unloading** is a passive transport mechanism from the sieve tubes to the cells at the root tip. It takes place passively down a concentration gradient of sucrose. The transfer cells are often present at unloading sites. Phloem unloading also requires metabolic energy, that is used by sink organs for respiration and biosynthetic reactions.

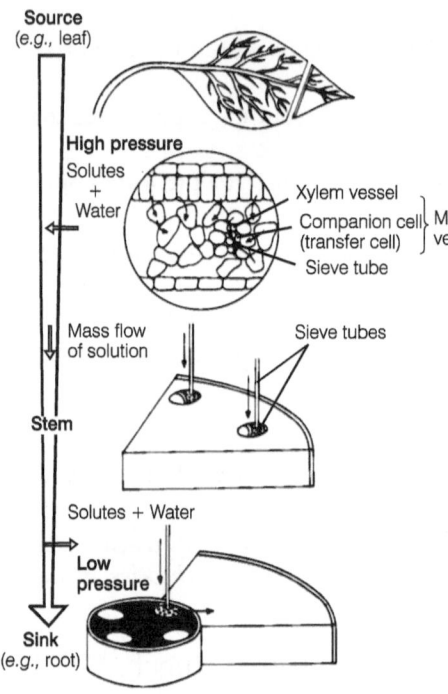

Loading of sieve tubes takes place here. Photosynthetic cells make sugars, particularly sucrose, and other organic solutes. Companion cells use energy to collect solutes by active transport. As solute concentration increases in the companion cells, water enters by osmosis. A pressure is created, which pushes the solutes through plasmodesmata into the sieve tubes.

Translocation Pressure inside sieve tubes is greatest at the source and lowest at the sink. It pushes sucrose, etc., from source to sink.

Unloading of the sieve tubes takes place at the sink. Solute is removed for use, thus maintaining the pressure gradient in the sieve tubes.

Sinks are any region where solutes are being used, *e.g.*, roots, fruits, storage organs and regions of growth.

Movement of solutes such as sucrose through the phloem of a plant. Three stages are involved, namely movement of solutes from photosynthetic cells to sieve tubes (loading), translocation in phloem and unloading at a sink.

Diffusion Theory (Mason and Maskell; 1928)
Translocation through transpiration stream.

Transcellular Streaming Theory (Thaine; 1962, 1969)
Translocation through peristaltic movement in continuous tubular strands in sieve tubes.

24

Respiration in Plants

Respiration is the most important, cellular, enzymatically controlled, catabolic process which involves the liberation of energy by oxidative breakdown of food substance inside living cells.

It has two phases. **First phase** is gaseous exchange between environment and organism through body surface or special respiratory organs and the **second phase** is cellular respiration.

Cellular Respiration

In this process, the oxidation of organic food takes place inside living cell for the liberation of energy. On the basis of requirement of oxygen. *This may be categorised as*

Cellular Respiration

Aerobic Respiration
Organic food is completely oxidised with the help of oxygen. It takes place in mitochondria and the products are CO_2 **and water**.
(~ 673 kcal/mol, energy released)

$C_6H_{12}O_6 + 6O_2 \xrightarrow{Enzymes} 6CO_2 + 6H_2O$
+686 kcal/2810 kJ

Anaerobic Respiration
Organic food is broken down incompletely to release energy in absence of oxygen. The products are CO_2 **ethyl alcohol and lactic acid**.
(~ 21 kcal/mol, energy released)

$C_6H_{12}O_6 \xrightarrow{Enzymes} 2CO_2 + 2C_2H_5OH$ (ethyl alcohol)
+59 kcal/247 kJ

$C_6H_{12}O_6 \xrightarrow{Enzymes} 2C_3H_6O_3$ (lactic acid)
+36 kcal/150 kJ

Respiratory Substrate

The substrate which are used as fuel in respiration are called **respiratory substrates**. The main respiratory substrates are carbohydrates and fat, but proteins can also be used in special circumstances. The most common respiratory substrate is **glucose**.

On the basis of respiratory substrate they used, *the respiration is of two types*

1. **Floating Respiration** Carbohydrate and fat are used as respiratory substrate.
2. **Protoplasmic Respiration** Protein is used as respiratory substrate.

Respiratory Quotient

It is the ratio of volume of CO_2 released to volume of oxygen absorbed. The value can be zero, one, less than one or more than one.

RQ can be calculated as

$$RQ = \frac{\text{Volume of } CO_2 \text{ evolved}}{\text{Volume of } O_2 \text{ absorbed}}$$

Aerobic Respiration

It is stepwise catabolic process of complete oxidation of organic food into CO_2 and water with oxygen acting as a terminal oxidant.

It is completed in two pathways—**Common pathway** and **Pentose Phosphate Pathway** (PPP).

Aerobic respiration consists of three steps

1. Glycolysis
2. Krebs' cycle
3. Electron transport chain and terminal oxidation.

Glycolysis (Gk. *glycos* – sugar; *lysis* – dissolution)

Glycolysis was discovered by three German scientists **Embden, Meyerhof** and **Paranas**, so also called **EMP Pathway**. Glycolysis occurs in **cytoplasm.**

Glycolysis is a major pathway for ATP synthesis in tissues lacking mitochondria, *e.g.*, erythrocytes, cornea, lens, etc.

Schematic Representation of EMP Pathway

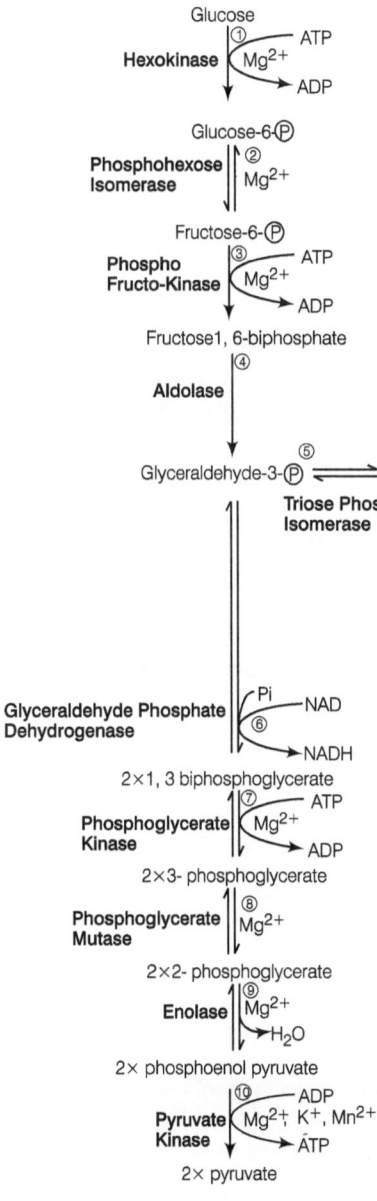

1. It is an irreversible reaction in which terminal phosphate of ATP is transferred to an acceptor nucleophile. Hexokinase is present in all cells of all organisms. In liver cells it is called as **glucokinase**. It is **first priming reaction**.

2. This is a reversible reaction which can proceed in either direction by small change in standard free energy.

3. It is **second priming reaction** of glycolysis and first 'committed' step. Some bacteria and protists have a phosphofructokinase that use ppii not ATP as the **phosphoryl group donor**.

4. This reaction is an example of **reversible aldol condensation**. Zn^{2+} is the cofactor which cleaves the fructose 1, 6 biphosphate into two 3-carbon units.

5. As only glyceraldehyde-3-(P) can proceed in further reaction of glycolysis, the dihydroxy acetone phosphate converted reversibly into glyceraldehyde-3-(P). It is last reaction of preparatory phase.

6. The **first step of payoff phase** that eventually lead to the formation of ATP. This reaction is irreversibly inhibited by Hg^{2+}

7. It is an **exergonic reaction** which is in combination with step-(6) constitute an energy coupling process. It is an example of **substrate level phosphorylation**.

8. In this reaction the enzyme, phosphoglycerate mutase catalyse a reversible shift of phosphoryl group between C_2 and C_3.

9. The enzyme enolase promotes reversible removal of H_2O mol from 2 phosphoglycerate to produce phosphoenol pyruvate.

10. In this **substrate level phosphorylation** the product first appear in its enol form the rapidly and non-enzymatically to its keto form at pH 7.

Net Result of Glycolysis
- Two molecules of pyruvic acid
- Two molecules of ATP
- Two molecules of $NADH_2$
- Two molecules of H_2O

$\qquad$ ATP released– 2 ATPs
$\qquad$ From 2 $NADH_2$– 6 ATPs
$\qquad$ Total released = $\overline{8\ ATPs}$
$\quad$ Total ATPs consume = 2 ATPs
$\qquad\qquad\qquad$ 6 ATP Net yield of glycolysis

Krebs' Cycle or Tricarboxylic Acid Cycle

It is also known as **citric acid cycle** because citric acid (tricarboxylic acid) is the first product of this cycle. In eukaryotic organisms, all the reactions of Krebs' cycle takes place in matrix of mitochondria because enzymes of this cycle are present in matrix except succinic dehydrogenase (situated in inner membrane of mitochondria).

In prokaryotes, the Krebs' cycle occurs in cytoplasm. It is basically a **catabolic reaction** as it oxidise acetyl Co-A and organic acid into CO_2 and H_2O.

It acts as an **amphibolic pathway** because it serves in both catabolic and anabolic processes. It is a series of 8 reactions which occurs in **aerobic environment.**

Handbook of BIOLOGY

The scheme of reaction with its detail is explained as follows

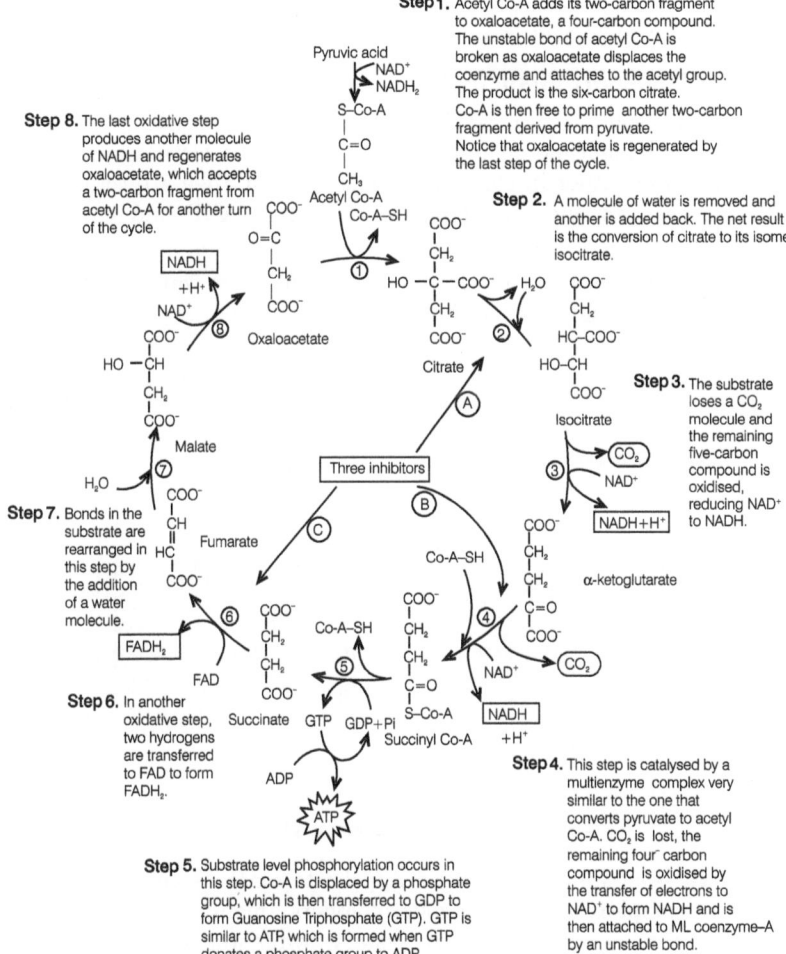

The Krebs' cycle

The enzymes involved in these reactions are
1. Citrate synthase
2. Aconitase
3. Isocitrate dehydrogenase
4. α-ketoglutarate dehydrogenase
5. Sunccinyl Co-A synthetase
6. Succinate dehydrogenase
7. Fumerase
8. Malate dehydrogenase

Three inhibitors are
A. Fluoroacetate
B. Arsenic dehydrogenase
C. Malonate

One molecule of pyruvic acid after entering into mitochondria undergoes **three decarboxylations** and **five oxidations**. One molecule of pyruvic acid through Krebs' cycle yields 15 ATP.

Electron Transport Chain (ETC)

Electron Transport Chain (ETC) or Respiratory Chain (RC) is present in the inner membrane of mitochondria. When the elctron pass from one carrier to another in electron transport chain, they are coupled to ATP synthase for the production of ATP from ADP and inorganic phosphate.

A diagrammatic representation of electron flow *via* various electron carrier complexes is shown in figure.

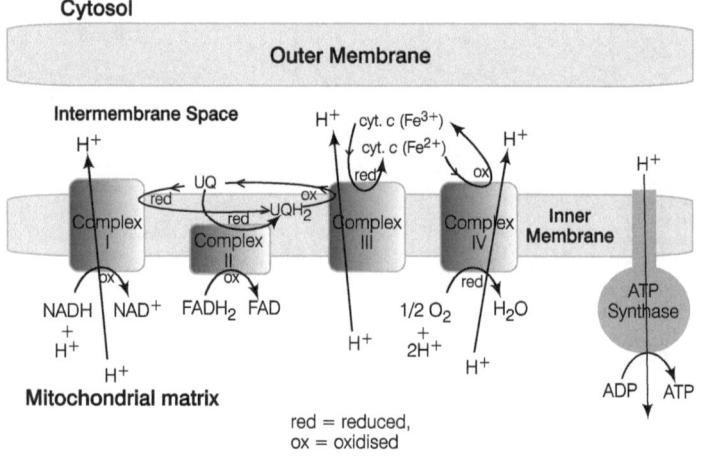

Electron transport chain in plants

The enzymes of inner membrane appear to exist as components of these five complexes. The first four members among these complexes constitute the electron transport system, while the 5th complex is connected with oxidative phosphorylation, *i.e.,* conservation and transfer of energy with ATP synthesis. *These complexes are*

(i) Complex I — NADH/NADPH : CoQ reductase
(ii) Complex II — Succinate : CoQ reductase
(iii) Complex III — Reduced CoQ (CoQH$_2$) Cytochrome-*c* reductase
(iv) Complex IV — Cytochrome-*c* oxidase
(v) Complex V — ATP synthase system

The complex V is ATP synthase complex which has a head piece, stalk and a base piece. Out of these, the head piece is identified as the coupling factor 1 (F_1) by **Racker** (1965). It contains 5 subunits namely — α (MW 53000), β (MW 50000), γ (MW 33000), δ (MW 17000) and ϵ (MW 7000). In addition to these, an ATPase inhibitor protein is also seen in this portion.

The stalk portion contains OSCP (*i.e.,* Oligomyosin Sensitivity Conferring Protein) and is necessary for binding F_1 to the inner mitochondrial membrane. The base piece is isolated as F_0 and present within the inner mitochondrial membrane. It provides the proton channel. *Thus, the complete complex looks like*

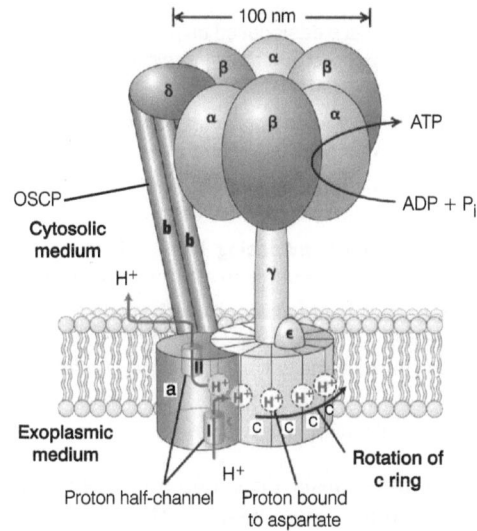

$F_0 - F_1$ complex (γ, ϵ and c constitutes the rotatory part

Oxidation phosphorylation was discovered in 1939. There are three hypothesis regarding the mechanism of oxidative phosphorylation. *These are*
 1. The chemical coupling hypothesis
 2. The chemiosmotic hypothesis
 3. The conformational hypothesis

The most accepted among these hypothesis is the **conformational hypothesis**.

According to conformational coupling hypothesis, the membrane of cristae found to assume different forms during functional states of mitochondrion as shown in following figure.

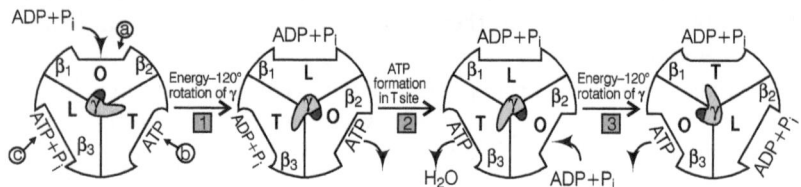

The binding change mechanism of ATP synthesis from ADP and P_i by the $F_0 - F_1$ complex.

The β subunit of head piece are designated as $β_1$, $β_2$ and $β_3$ as shown. *Look at the middle γ subunit structure which show different appearance in three different β subunits as*

(a) **Darker pointed portion indicating open conformation** (O) of β-subunit with suppressed margins so that, ADP and iP can attach easily.

(b) **Lighter pointed portion indicating tight conformation** (T) with elevated tight margins helpful in converting ADP + iP to ATP.

(c) **Lighter rounded portions indicating low conformation** (L) with sides elevated than open conformation but less elevated than tight conformation.

The movement of γ subunit is possible only with the help of energy. See the conformational changes step by step with ATP formation. The energy provided for γ subunit movement is through proton translocation as shown in first diagram.

A formation of 3 ATP molecules occur for every 360° rotation of γ.

The conformational hypothesis does not affect the central theme of Mitchell's chemiosmotic hypothesis. **Mitchell** (1976) himself considered the involvement of conformational changes in chemiosmotic coupling. Infact Mithell's hypothesis become more convinced when coupled with conformational processes.

Oxidative Phosphorylation

The aerobic respiration is ended with the oxidation of 10 molecules of $NADH + H^+$ and 2 molecules of $FADH_2$ generated from a molecule of glucose. In this, the oxygen from atmosphere is used for the oxidation of reduced coenzyme and it is called as **terminal oxidation**. The production of ATP with the help of energy liberated during oxidation of reduced coenzyme and terminal oxidation is called **oxidative phosphorylation**.

Summary of Aerobic Respiration
1. Glycolysis produces 2ATP molecule and 2 NADH +2 H$^+$.
2. Pyruvate oxidation yields 2 NADH + 2H$^+$.
3. Krebs' cycle produces 2GTP molecules 6 NADH + 6H$^+$ and 2FADH$_2$.
4. Electron transport system
   (i) 2 NADH + 2 H$^+$ from glycolysis yield 4 ATP *via* route-2 of ETC (glycerol-phosphate shuttle) or six ATP *via* route-1 (malate-aspartate shuttle).
   (ii) 2 NADH + 2H$^+$ from pyruvate oxidation yield 6ATP molecules in route-1 of ETC.
   (iii) 6 NADH + 6H$^+$ molecules from TCA (Krebs' cycle) yield 18 ATP molecules in route-1 of ETC.
   (iv) 2 FADH$_2$ molecules from TCA cycle yield 4 ATP molecules in route-2 of ETC (Electron Transport Chain).

Hence, ETS alone produces 32 or 34 ATP.

$$\underset{\text{(Glycolysis)}}{2\text{ATP}} + \underset{\text{(TCA cycle)}}{2\text{GTP}} + \underset{\text{(ETS/ETC)}}{32/34\,\text{ATP}} \rightarrow 38/36\,\text{ATP}$$

34 or 36 ATP + 2 GTP are produce from one glucose molecule.

A cytoplasmic enzyme **nucleoside diphosphate kinase** readily converts the GTP formed in TCA cycle to ATP.

In prokaryotic cells, oxidation of glucose molecule always yields 38 ATP molecules as NADH + H$^+$ is not to enter mitochondria, which are absent here.

Overall Result of Aerobic Respiration
Complete oxidation of one molecule of glucose results into the following products
1. Release of 6 carbon dioxide molecules
2. Utilisation of 6 oxygen molecules.
3. Formation of 12H$_2$O molecules.

So, overall process of aerobic respiration may be shown by the following equation

$$C_6H_{12}O_6 + 6O_2 + 10H_2O \rightarrow 6CO_2 + 16H_2O + 686 \text{ kcal energy.}$$

Fermentation

It is the general term for such processes which extract energy (as ATP), but do not consume oxygen or change the concentration of NAD^+ or NADH. It is similar to anaerobic respiration.

Generally the fermentation is of four types

Fermentation

Alcoholic Fermentation
It is common in yeast in which breakdown of the substrate takes place outside the cell. The end products are ethyl alcohol, CO_2 and energy.

Butyric Acid Fermentation
This pathway is common in *Clostridium butyricum*. This type of fermentation is normally occurs in rotten butter due to which it give fowl smell.

Lactic Acid Fermentation
It is common in lactic acid bacteria. Enzyme involved in fermentation is lactic acid dehydrogenase. Here only lactic acid, NAD and energy is produced.

Acetic Acid Fermentation
This pathway is common in acetic acid bacteria. The oxygen is used in this fermentation process. The end products are ethyl alcohol and acetic acid.

Pentose Phosphate Pathway (PPP)

This pathway is a major source for the NADPH required for anabolic processes. There are three distinct phases – **Oxidation, isomerisation** and **rearrangement**. Gluconeogenesis is directly connected to the PPP.

Pentose phosphate pathway (Warburg-Lipman-Dickens cycle) is an alternate method of aerobic respiration, which occurs in the cytoplasm of mature plant cells. This pathway accounts for 60% total respiration in liver cells. In this, for every six molecules of glucose, one molecule is completely oxidised in CO_2 and reduced coenzymes, while five are regenerated.

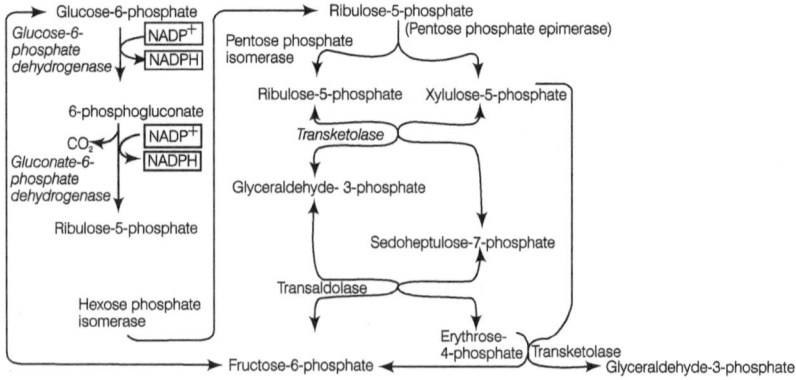

Reactions of the oxidative pentose phosphate pathway in higher plants

The Pentose Phosphate Pathway (PPP) is an alternate path to generate ATP than glycolysis and Krebs' cycle.

Amphibolic Pathway

The pathway in which both breakdown (catabolism) and build up (anabolism) is used. Krebs' cycle is amphibolic in nature, as its intermediates are used in other anabolic processes.

A general representation of amphibolic pathway is as follows

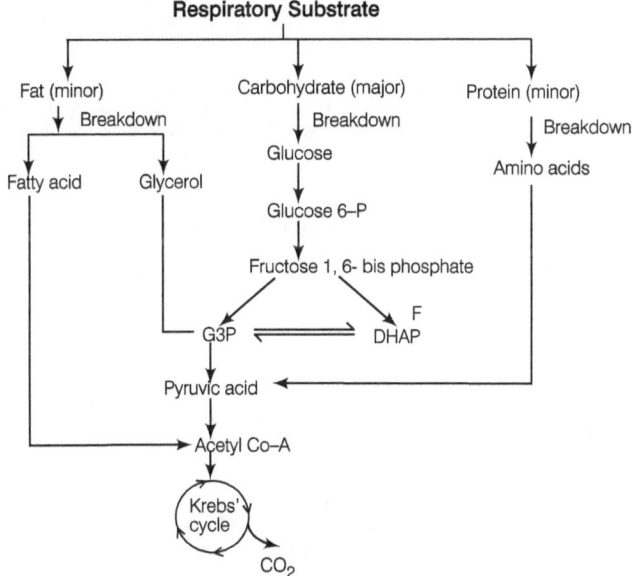

Amphibolic pathway of respiration

Factors Affecting Respiration

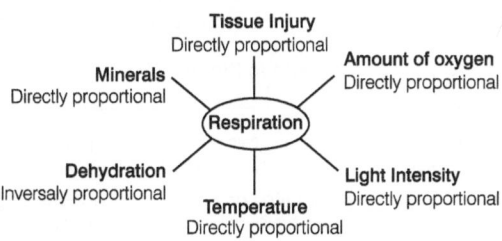

Conclusively, respiration is a vital phenomenon in almost all living organisms involved in breakdown of different substances, *i.e.,* respiratory substrates. In all of the organisms it is involved in both catabolism and anibolism. Respiration and its strategies are also the determining factor for several physical, physiological and geographical adaptation in animal and plant varieties.

25
Plant Growth *and* Development

Every living organism shows growth which can either be in size or in number. Hence, we can say that the growth is a characteristic of life.

Growth

It can be defined as 'an irreversible permanent increase in size of an organ or its part or even a cell'. It is accomplished by metabolic processes that utilised energy obtained by nutrition. The **development** is actually the sum of two processes, *i.e.,* growth and differentiation.

During growth anabolic processes exceed catabolic processes or growth is final end product of successful metabolism. Characteristically, the **growth is intrinsic in living beings**.

Types of Growth

The growth in an organism can be divided on the basis of various criteria. *These growths can be understood through following flow chart*

Growth in Plants

On the basis of sequence of growth
- **Primary growth**
  The division at the root and shoot apex.
- **Secondary growth**
  The growth in diameter because of cambium.

On the basis of continuity of growth
- **Unlimited growth**
  The growth of root and stem length in plant.
- **Limited growth**
  The growth of leaves, fruit and flower after getting certain size.

On the basis of growing organ
- **Vegetative growth**
  The growth of vegetative parts like leaves, stem and roots.
- **Reproductive growth**
  The growth of flower, fruits and other reproductive parts of plants.

Types of Growth Curves

By plotting the size or weight of an organism against time, the growth curve can be obtained. On the basis of their shapes, these curves can be of — **J-shaped curve** and **S-shaped curve**. Through these curves, the pattern of growth in an organism can be traced out.

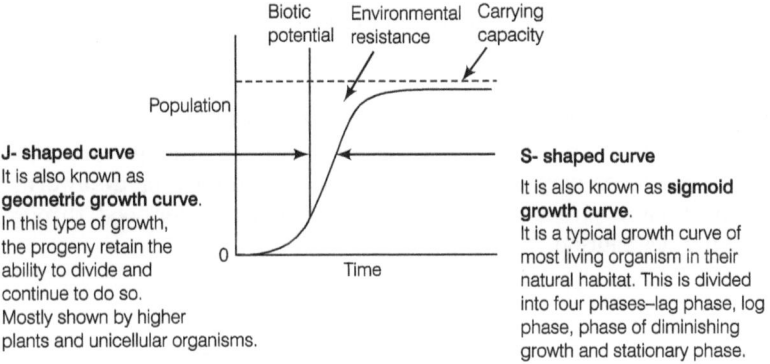

J- shaped curve
It is also known as **geometric growth curve**. In this type of growth, the progeny retain the ability to divide and continue to do so. Mostly shown by higher plants and unicellular organisms.

S- shaped curve
It is also known as **sigmoid growth curve**. It is a typical growth curve of most living organism in their natural habitat. This is divided into four phases–lag phase, log phase, phase of diminishing growth and stationary phase.

Phases of Growth

The sigmoidal growth curve can be categorised into four distinct phases. *These growth phases and their details are discussed in following figure*

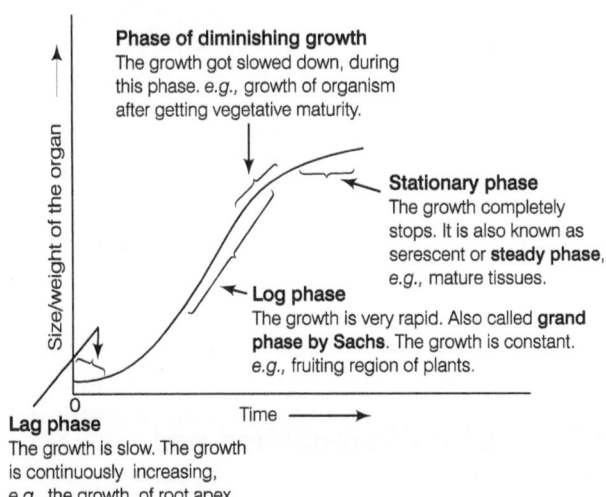

Phase of diminishing growth
The growth got slowed down, during this phase. e.g., growth of organism after getting vegetative maturity.

Stationary phase
The growth completely stops. It is also known as serescent or **steady phase**, e.g., mature tissues.

Log phase
The growth is very rapid. Also called **grand phase by Sachs**. The growth is constant. e.g., fruiting region of plants.

Lag phase
The growth is slow. The growth is continuously increasing, e.g., the growth of root apex and shoot apex region.

Handbook of BIOLOGY

Measurement of Growth

(i) The growth can be measured by horizontal microscope and an instrument called **auxanometer**.

(ii) **Bose** develop an instrument called **crescograph** for measuring growth. It magnifies growth up to 10000 times.

(iii) Growth can also be measured by calculating increase in cell number, weight, volume and diameter.

Growth Rate

'The increased growth per unit time is called as growth rate.'

With pasage of growth phases of an organism, the growth rates show increase or decrease, which may be **arithmetic** or **geometric**. The increasing pattern of growth rates can be understood through following description.

```
                     Growth
          ┌────────────┴────────────┐
     Arithmatic                 Geometric
```

Arithmatic

In such growth pattern, after mitotic cell division only one cell is continue to divide, while the other differentiate and mature, e.g., constantly elongating root.

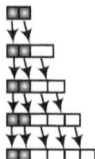

It can be represented mathematically as–

$L_t = L_0 + rt$

L_t = Length at time 't'

L_0 = Initial length

r = Growth rate

Geometric

Here both the progeny cells resulted after mitosis, continue to divide. However with limited nutrient supply the growth slows down and become stationary.

It can be represented mathematically as

$W_1 = W_0 e^{rt}$

W_1 = Final size (weight, height, number.)

W_0 = Initial size

r = Growth rate

t = Time of growth

e = Base of natural logarithms.

Here, r is the **relative growth rate** and also measure of the ability of the plant to produce new plant material, referred to as **efficiency index**.

Differentiation, Dedifferentiation and Redifferentiation

The three phases of cellular growth are **cell division, cell enlargement** and **cell differentiation**, which bring maturity to the cells.

Differentiation

It is the permanent qualitative change in structure, chemistry and physiology of cell wall and protoplasm of cells, tissue and their organ. It is the result of repression of genes. *e.g.,* to form a tracheary element, the cells would lose their protoplasm.

Dedifferentiation

It is the process of despecialisation of differentiated cell so, that they regain the capacity to divide and form new cells, *e.g.,* cork cambium.

Redifferentiation

It is the structural, chemical and physiological specialisation of cells derived from dedifferentiated meristematic cells, *e.g.,* secondary phloem, secondary cortex, etc.

Development

The sequence of events from seed germination to senescence of a plant is called **development**.

Every organism has capacity to adapt its environment through some changes among themselves in response to prevalent environmental conditions. The capacity to change under influence of environment is called **plasticity**.

Plant Hormones/Phytohormones/ Plant Growth Regulators

A plant hormone is an organic compound synthesised in one part of a plant and translocated to another part, where in very low concentration it causes a physiological response.

Plant hormones can be broadly divided into two groups based on their functions in a living plant body. One group is involved in **growth promoting activities**, *e.g.,* auxin, gibberellins and cytokinin. The other group involved in **growth inhibiting activities**, *e.g.,* abscisic acid, etc.

Note
 (i) K^+, Ca^+ cause important function and also transported from one place to another, but they are not hormones.
 (ii) Sucrose is also synthesised and translocated in plant, which causes growth at higher concentration, but not regarded as hormone.

Auxins

The term 'Auxin' (Gk. *auxein* —to increase) was first used by **Frits Went**. These hormones are found in meristematic regions of plant, *e.g.*, in coleoptile tips, in buds, etc.

Chemically the auxin is Indole 3–Acetic Acid (IAA). **Kogl** and **Haagen-Smit** (1931) isolated the active compound of molecular weight 328 from human urine, which was called as **auxin-A** (Auxanotriolic acid).

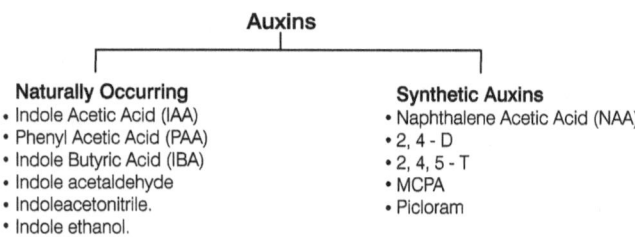

Naturally Occurring
- Indole Acetic Acid (IAA)
- Phenyl Acetic Acid (PAA)
- Indole Butyric Acid (IBA)
- Indole acetaldehyde
- Indoleacetonitrile.
- Indole ethanol.

Synthetic Auxins
- Naphthalene Acetic Acid (NAA)
- 2, 4 - D
- 2, 4, 5 - T
- MCPA
- Picloram

The natural auxin in plant is synthesised by the amino acid **tryptophan**.

Auxins are applied in very low concentration for good results. Higher concentration inhibit growth and exert toxic effects in plants.

Gibberellins

These growth regulators were not discovered in plants, but first became known as the metabolites of fungus.

The first pure Gibberellic Acid (GA) was isolated by **Cross** (1954) and **Borrow et al.** (1955) in Britain.

The GAs are diterpenoid acids derived from the tetracyclic diterpenoid hydrocarbon, **ent-Kaur 16-ene** having 20-carbon atoms.

Cytokinins

Miller et al. (1954) isolated the third growth substance from autocloved herring sperm DNA. Because of its cell division activity on tobacco pith callus it was called as **kinetin**.

Chemically, it is a derivative of adenire with a furfuryl group at C-6 and is called as 6-furfurylaminopurine.

The kinetin is formed from deoxyadenosine, a degradation product of DNA.

Abscisic Acid

It is most recent discovered plant hormone. **Okhuma et al.** (1965) first isolated it from young cotton fruit. Abscisic acid is sesquiterpene. It inhibit the action of **auxin, gibberellins** and **cytokinin**, hence it is also a growth inhibitor.

Ethylene

It is a ripening hormone and is produced in traces in form of gas by almost all tissues. The secretion of ethylene can be detected by gas chromatography.

These are synthesised by amino acid methionine as

$$\text{Methionine} \xrightarrow{\text{oxidative deamination}} \text{Methionol} \to \text{Ethylene}$$

The plant hormones, their functions and location in plant is given in following table

Plant Hormones, their Functions and Location

Hormone	Major Function	Location in Plant
Auxin (IAA)	Promotion of stem elongation and growth; formation of adventitious roots; inhibition of leaf abscission; promotion of cell division (with cytokinins); inducement of ethylene production; promotion of lateral bud dormancy (Apical dominance).	Apical meristems; other immature parts of plants.
Cytokinins	Stimulation of cell division, but only in the presence of auxin, promotion of chloroplast development; delay of leaf ageing; promotion of bud formation.	Root apical meristems; immature fruits.
Gibberellins	Promotion of stem elongation (bolting is cabbage), stimulates enzyme production in germinating seeds.	Roots and shoot tips; young leaves; seeds.
Ethylene	Promotion of fruit ripening, control of leaf, flower and fruit abscission.	Roots, shoot apical meristems; leaf nodes; ageing flower, ripening fruits.
Abscisic acid	Inhibition of bud growth; control of stomatal closure; some control of seed dormancy; inhibition of effects of other hormones.	Leaves, fruits, root, caps, seeds.
Brassinosteroids	Overlapping function with auxins and gibberellins.	Pollen, immature seeds, shoot, leaves.
Oligosaccharides	Pathogen defence, possibly reproductive development.	Cell walls

Other plant hormones are

Florigen	Flowering hormone
Vernalin	Vernalisation hormone
Anthesins	Flowering hormone
Calines	Formative hormone
Traumatic acid	Wound healing hormone

Applications of Phytohormones

Stem Elongation

It is induced by auxin, cytokinin and gibberellins. The process is extensively used in horticulture and other vegetative growth. The increased plant height, helps in the production of increased biomass where required.

The process of stem elongation is mainly accomplished by **apical dominance**, which helps in proper growth of plant. In absence of apical dominance the plant require physical support for growth and development.

Seed Dormancy

The inhibition of seed germination of a normal or viable seed due to internal factor, even when it is placed under favourable conditions required for germination is called **seed dormancy**.

The dormancy period for a seed may vary from days to years as the seeds of mangroves lacks any dormancy period and in most cereal grains it is of several months long.

Causes of Seed Dormancy

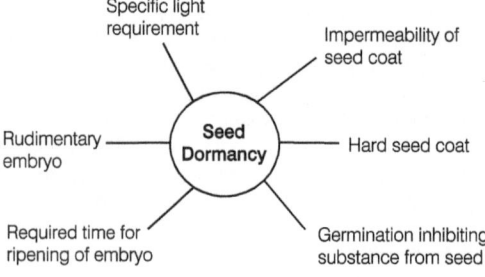

Processes to Break Seed Dormancy

Following process are employed to break seed dormancy

(a) **Scarification** Mechanical or chemical breakdown of seed coat.

(b) **Stratification** Exposure of seed to well aerated, moist condition.

(c) **Alternating temperature** Treatment of seed with low or high temperature.

(d) **Light** Exposure of suitable (red or far red) light to seed.

(e) **Pressure** Exposure of high hydraulic pressure (~2000 atm) at low temperature.

(f) **Growth regulator application** Kinetin and gibberellins are used to induce germination.

Biological Significance of Seed Dormancy

(i) It allows storage of seeds in viable state for longer duration.

(ii) It helps to retain seed viability in extreme conditions as well.

(iii) It helps in distant spreading of seeds.

(iv) It is useful in desert conditions for the postponement of seed germination.

Photoperiodism

The phenomenon of photoperiodism was first discovered by **Garner** and **Allard** in 1920. It has been discovered that duration of light also plays a major role in inducing flowering in plants. This flowering response in plants to the relative length of light and dark periods within a 24 hour cycle is called **photoperiodism**.

Every plant has a specific critical period of light duration needed for flowering. In order to flower they must be exposed to either more or less light hour than that of critical period. Based on flowering response to light duration, plants have been classified into **long-day plants, short-day plants** and **day neutral plants**.

Long-Day Plants (LDP)

They are plants which produce flowers only when they are exposed to light duration more than the critical period (12 hours). These plants produce flower in summer, *e.g.*, rye, oat, etc.

Short-Day Plant (SDP)

These plants produce flower only when they are exposed to light duration shorter than critical period. They produce flower in spring or winter, *e.g.,* coffee, tobacco, *Chrysanthamum*, etc.

Day Neutral Plants (DNP)

These plants produce flowers throughout the year irrespective of length of light hours to which they are exposed, *e.g.,* tomato.

Vernalisation

It is the promotion of flowering by low temperature treatment. Spraying gibberellins is a substitute to cold treatment and biennials can be made to flower in one year without the cold treatment.

Vernalisation stimulus is perceived by the apical meristem. This stimulus is believed to be a hormone called **vernalin**.

Abscission of Plant Parts

Abscission can be selectively used to control the growth of some parts of plant. It can also helps in timely harvesting of fruits and other products and to induce productivity.

Delay of Leaf Ageing and Promotion of Chloroplast Development

It is induced by cytokinin and helps to **improve productivity** as the chloroplasts in leaf are the sites of food production.

Formation of Adventitious Roots

This is performed by auxin. More adventitious roots helps in **vegetative propagation** of several plants.

Promotion of Lateral Buds Development

It is induced by hormone cytokinin. Lateral bud development have significance in production of bushy plants, which can be equally used in **horticultural** and **ornamental plants**.

26
Reproduction in Organisms

Reproduction is the process of producing offspring similar to itself. It is a characteristic of living organisms.

Biologically it means the **multiplication and perpetuation of the species.**

According to the conditions available in environment, organisms have adapted the processes of reproduction. Generally, two types of reproduction mechanisms are present in organisms.

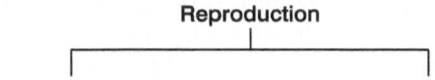

Asexual Reproduction
• Uniparental (single parent involved).
• Gamete formation does not occur.
• Syngamy (gametic fusion) absent.

Sexual Reproduction
• Biparental (both parents involved).
• Gamete formation always occur.
• Syngamy characteristically occurs.

Reproduction in Animals
Animal reproduce by both asexual and sexual methods.

Asexual Reproduction
It is the primary means of reproduction among the **protists, cnidarians** and **tunicates.** *The process of asexual reproduction can be occur through following methods*

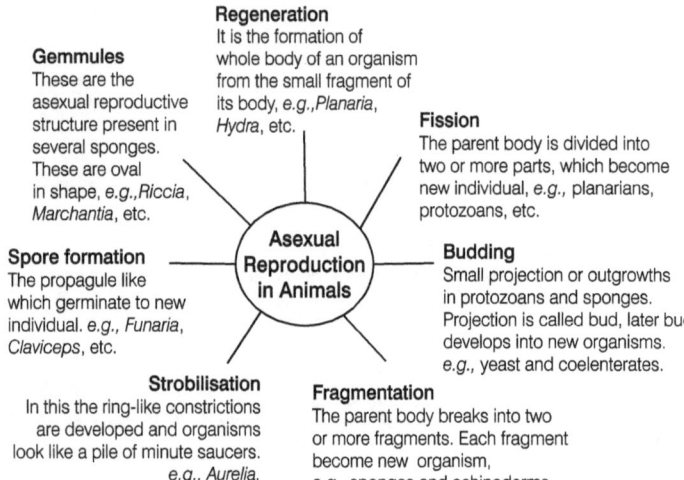

Sexual Reproduction

In animals, the sexual reproduction occurs by the fertilisation of **haploid sperm** and **haploid egg,** generating a diploid offspring. In most individuals (*i.e.,* **dioecious**), the female produce **eggs,** (*i.e,* large non-motile cells contain food reserve) and the male produce **sperms** (*i.e.,* small, motile cell and have almost no food reserve).

In other individual, (*i.e.,* **monoecious**) such as **earthworm** and **many snails,** single individual produce both sperm and egg. These individuals are called as **hermaphrodite.** The union of sperm and egg occurs in variety of ways, depending on the mobility and the breeding environment of individual.

Sexual reproduction is two types

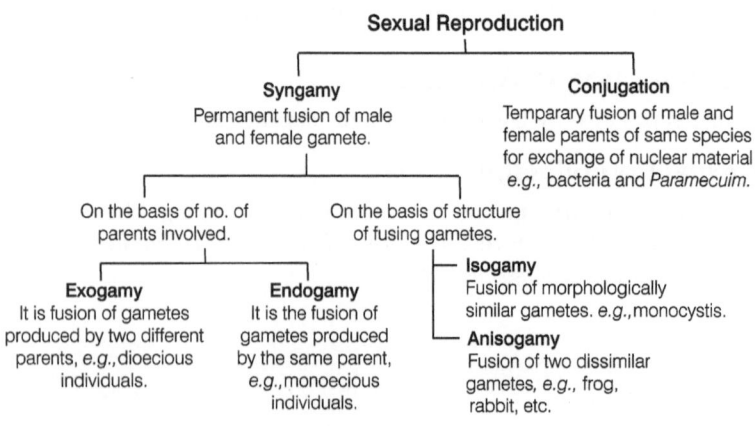

Other Modes of Sexual Reproduction

(i) **Autogamy** Fusion of male and female gametes produced by same individual, *e.g., Paramecium.*
(ii) **Hologamy** Fusion of entire mating individuals acting as gametes, *e.g., Chlamydomonas.*
(iii) **Paedogamy** Fusion of young individuals, *e.g., Actinosphaerium.*
(iv) **Merogamy** Fusion of small and morphologically dissimilar gametes.
(v) **Macrogamy** Fusion of two macrogametes takes place.
(vi) **Microgamy** Fusion of two microgametes takes place.
(vii) **Cytogamy** Fusion of cytoplasm of two individuals, but no nuclear fusion, *e.g., P. aurelia.*
(viii) **Plasmogamy** Fusion of related cytoplasm, *e.g.,* Fungi.
(ix) **Karyogamy** Fusion of nuclei of two gametes, *e.g., Mucor.*
(x) **Automixis** Fusion of gamete nuclei of the same cell, *e.g.,* Phasmids.

Reproduction in Plants

Plants also reproduce by both asexual and sexual methods.

Asexual Reproduction

The asexual reproduction in plants is also known as **vegetative propagation.** In both lower and higher plants, *it occurs by following methods*

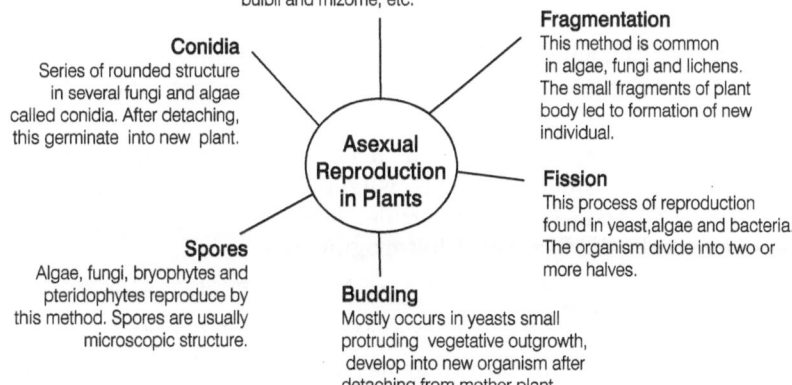

Vegetative Propagules
There are various vegetative propagules involved in asexual reproduction are discussed in chapter 19. These may be tuber, runner, sucker corm, stolons, offset, bulbil and rhizome, etc.

Conidia
Series of rounded structure in several fungi and algae called conidia. After detaching, this germinate into new plant.

Spores
Algae, fungi, bryophytes and pteridophytes reproduce by this method. Spores are usually microscopic structure.

Budding
Mostly occurs in yeasts small protruding vegetative outgrowth, develop into new organism after detaching from mother plant.

Fragmentation
This method is common in algae, fungi and lichens. The small fragments of plant body led to formation of new individual.

Fission
This process of reproduction found in yeast, algae and bacteria. The organism divide into two or more halves.

Sexual Reproduction

Like animals, the plants also reproduce sexually in which fertilisation of male and female gametes takes place and zygote is formed. Gametic cells, (*i.e.,* sperm and egg) are produced by the meiotic division.

In lower plants these gametes fuse directly through their cells then showing **isogamy** (fusion between similar gametes), **anisogamy** (fusion between dissimilar gametes) and **oogamy** (fusion between well defined gametes).

In higher plants on the other side these gametes are formed in well defined structure like antheridia (for male gametes) and archegonia (for male gametes) while in phanerogames these are situated inside more pronouned structures like androecium (for male gametes) and gynoecium for female gamete).

Events in Sexual Reproduction of Both Plants and Animals

The events of sexual reproduction though elaborate and complex, but follow a regular sequence. For easy understanding of the process, the process of sexual reproduction (*i.e.,* fertilisation) can be divided into three distinct stages. *These are as follows*

1. Pre-fertilisation
2. Fertilisation
3. Post-fertilisation event.

Pre-fertilisation Events

The events which occur before the fertilisation (*i.e.,* gametic fusion) are included in this. These include **gametogenesis** and **gamete transfer**.

Gametogenesis

The process of gamete formation is known as gametogenesis. The gametes are generally of two kinds **male gamete** and **female gametes.**

In some lower organisms, both male and female gametes are morphologically similar called **isogametes** or **homogametes**. In higher organisms both male and female gametes are morphologically distinct called **heterogametes.**

Heterogametes ⟨ Small—Microgamete/Male gamete—Spermatozoa
　　　　　　　　Large— Macrogamete/Female gamete—Ova

The gametes are usually formed by meiotic division, therefore they are haploid in nature.

Gamete Transfer

In most of the organisms, male gamete is motile and the female gamete is non-motile. The male gametes are produced in large number because large number of male gametes are failed to reach female gamete. In flowering plants through the process of **pollination**, male gamete reaches to female gamete.

Fertilisation Events

In this stage the most important event is the fusion of gametes (haploid) and formation of diploid **zygote.** This process is called **syngamy** or **fertilisation**.

The process of fertilisation may occur outside the body of organisms called **external fertilisation,** (*e.g.,* algae, amphibians, fishes, etc).

If the syngamy occurs inside the body of organisms, it is called **internal fertilisation,** (*e.g.,* fungi, reptiles, birds, higher animals and plants).

In organisms like rotifers, honeybees, lizard and some birds, the female gametes form **new organisms without fertilisation,** this phenomenon is called **parthenogenesis.**

Post-Fertilisation Events

The events which occurs after the formation of zygote are included in this phase.

Zygote

The zygote is formed in all sexually reproducing organisms. Further the development of zygote depends upon the types of life cycle and the environment of organisms.

27

Sexual Reproduction *in* Flowering Plants

All flowering plants show sexual reproduction and to comply this, they have adopted various features in form of coloured flowers, minute pollen grains and nector, etc. Before discussing sexual reproduction in flowering plants, we must take a close look of the most pivotal structure for sexual reproduction, *i.e.,* a flower.

Flowers are formed over mature plants in response to hormone induced structural and physiological changes in shoot apices.

Following flow chart will provide the detailed information about flower

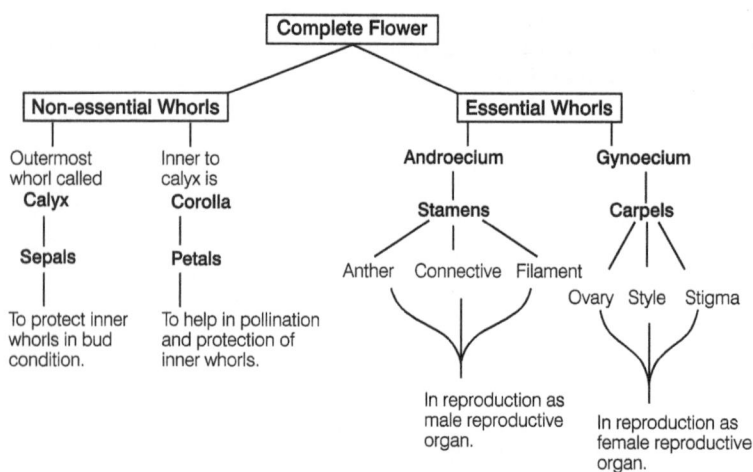

Floral whorls and their functions

Handbook of BIOLOGY

The whole process of sexual reproduction in flowering plants can be divided into following four steps
- Pollen grain formation
- Pollination
- Embryo sac formation
- Fertilisation

Pollen Grain Formation

Pollen grains are formed in pollen sacs of anther. The anther is bilobed and the lobe encloses four pollen sacs or **microsporangia**. The four pollen sacs in a dithecous anther appear to lie in four corners of an anther, thus a typical anther is tetrasporangiate.

Anther develops from a homogenous mass of hypodermal cell. These cells at each angle some how contain a prominent nucleus and abundant protoplasm.

These cells are called **archesporial cells**. Archesporial cells are divide by **periclinal division** and produce **parietal cells** on outer side and **sporogenous cells** on inner side.

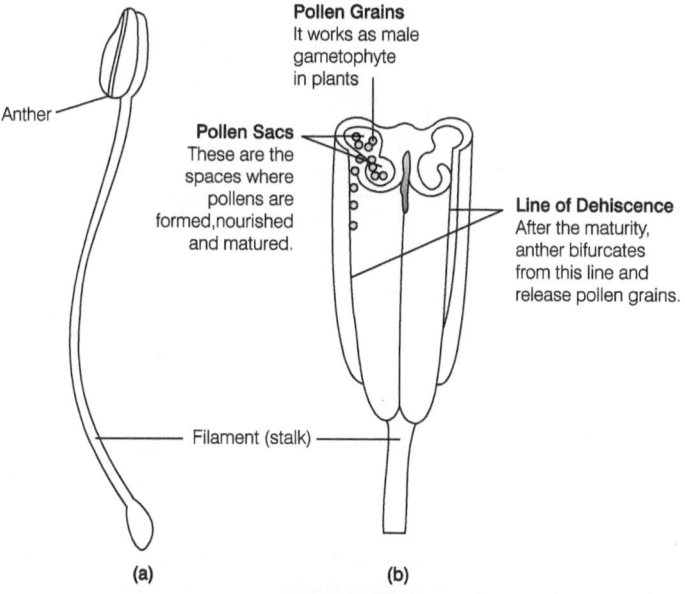

Pollen grain (a) A typical stamen; (b) three-dimensional cut section of an anther

Development of Pollen Grain

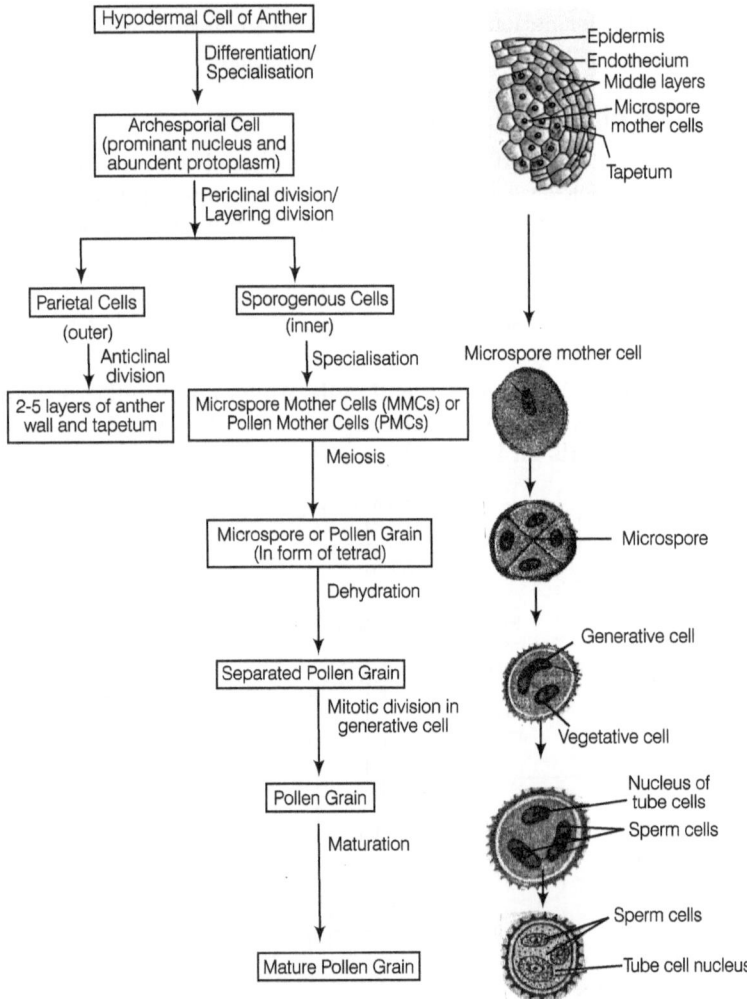

Note : About 60% angiosperms shed their pollen in 2-celled stage and remaining shed the pollen in 3-celled stage.

The newly formed microspores are arranged mostly in tetrahedral manner with following arrangements

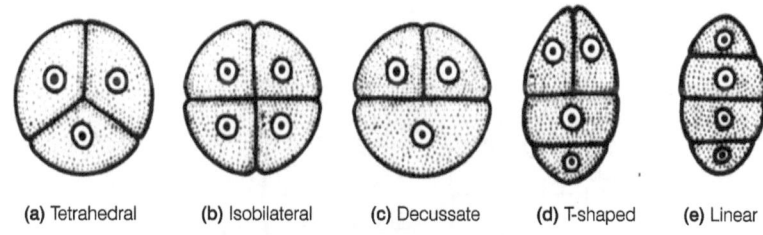

(a) Tetrahedral (b) Isobilateral (c) Decussate (d) T-shaped (e) Linear

Different types of microspore tetrads

Pollen Wall

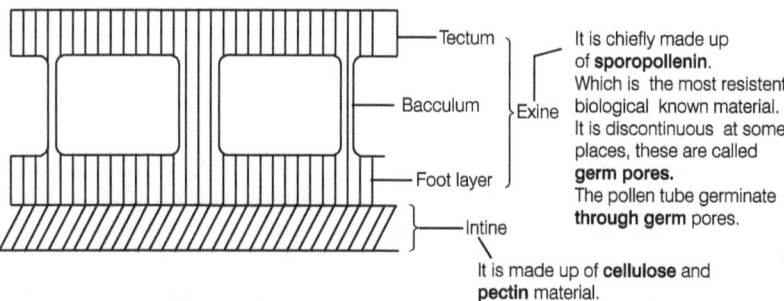

Exine: It is chiefly made up of **sporopollenin**. Which is the most resistent biological known material. It is discontinuous at some places, these are called **germ pores**. The pollen tube germinate **through germ pores**.

Intine: It is made up of **cellulose** and **pectin** material.

Pollen kitt is the matter produced by tapetal cells, which provide specific colour and odour to pollen grains and helps in attracting pollinating insects.

Embryo Sac Formation

A mature ovule or megasporangium contains a **nucellus**, **integuments** and **funiculus** through which it adhere to the placenta. The ovule develops into seed after fertilisation.

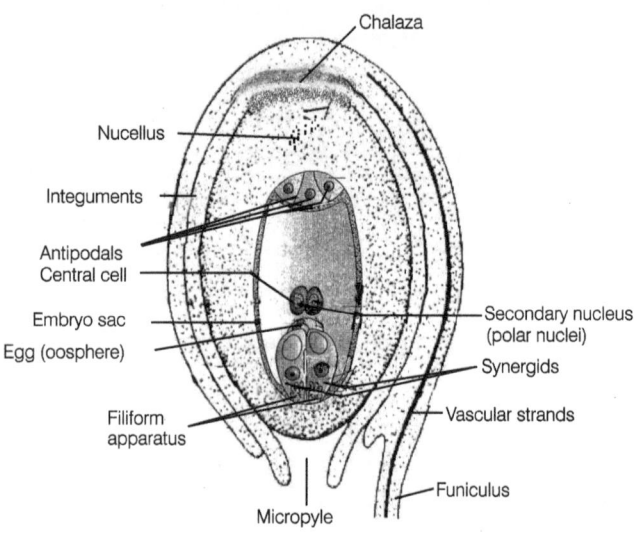

Structure of a typical ovule

A large oval cell lying embedded in the nucellus towards the micropylar end is the **embryo sac** or **female gametophyte**. This make the most important part of mature ovule. It is the embryo sac, which bears the embryo later on.

On the basis relative position of funiculus, chalaza and micropyle, *the ovules can be classified into following six types*

1. **Atropous** Simple and primitive type, *e.g.,* Gymnosperms, *Piper nigrum, Rumex* and *Polygonum.*
2. **Anatropous** Most common types of ovule. The ovule is rotated 180°. *e g.,* Solanaceae, *etc.*
3. **Campylotropous** The body of ovule is more or less at right angle to funicle. *e.g.,* Chenopodiaceae and Capparidiaceae.
4. **Amphitropous** The curvature is like anatropous ovule but, the embryo sac is horse shoe shaped. *e.g.,* Butamaceae and Alismaceae.

Handbook of BIOLOGY

5. **Hemianatropous** Here, body of ovule turned 90°, *e.g.,* Primulaceae and Plumbiginaceae.
6. **Circinotropous** In this type of ovule the length of funiculus is increased and cover whole ovule. *e.g.,* Cactaceae, etc.

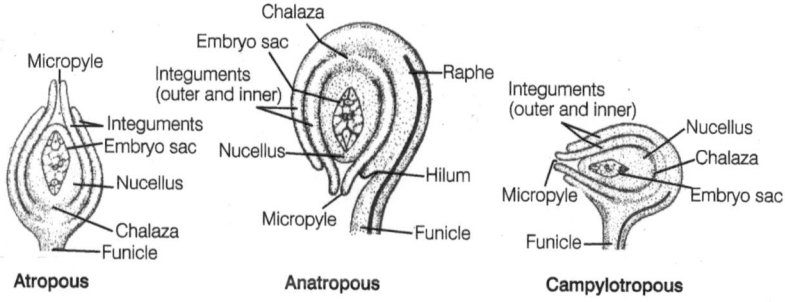

Development of Embryo Sac

It is a two step process

(i) Megasporogenesis

(ii) Megagametogenesis

Megasporogenesis in the devepment of megaspore *i.e.*, embryo sac while megagametogenesis is development of gamete within the megaspore. The development of megaspore takes place from specialised hypodermal cell called archesporial cell.

This cell after various mitotic division form a megaspore tetrad (a cluster of 4 cell) out of which 3 are degenerated while remaining one develops to functional megaspore or emrbyo sac.

Further development in embryo sac results into a functional embryo.

The events in this process looks like

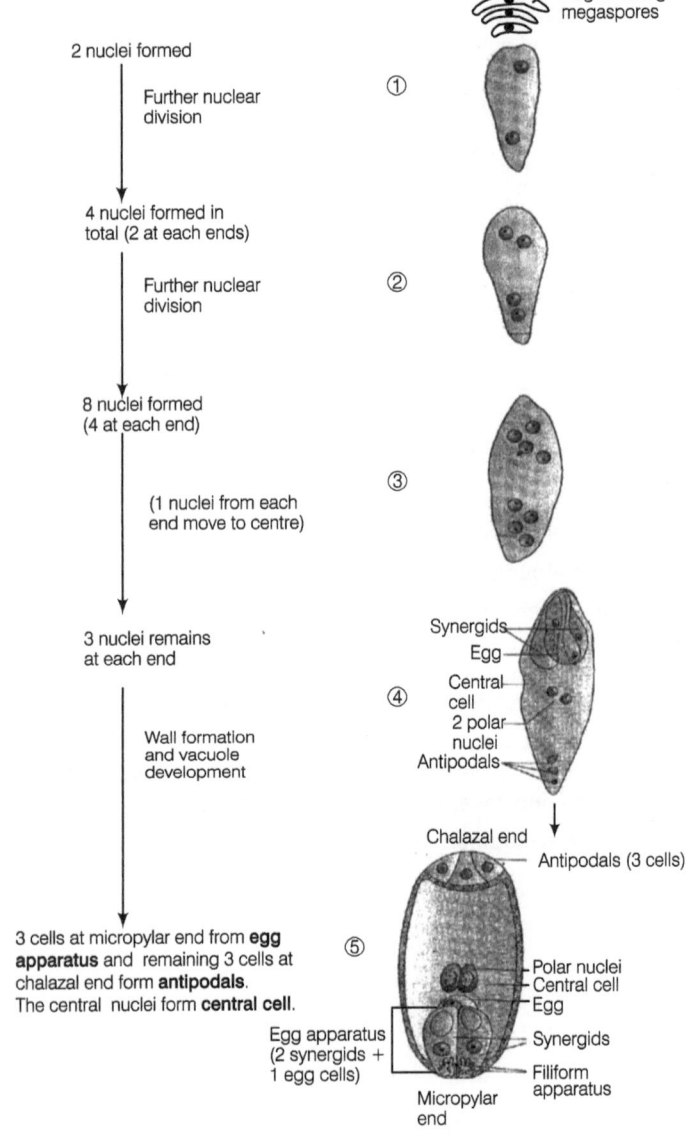

Embryo sac

Pollination

It is the transfer of pollen grains from the anther of a flower to the stigma of same or other flower.

It is of two types

1. Self-Pollination

It is the transfer of the pollen grain from the anther of a flower to the stigma of either the same or genetically similar flower.

Adaptations for Self-Pollination

Autogamy	Geitonogamy	Cleistogamy	Xenogamy
Transfer of pollen to the stigma occurs in the same flower, e.g., rice.	Pollen of one flower are deposited on the stigma of another flower of the same plant.	Flowers never open. The pollen from anther lobe fall on the stigma of the same flower, e.g., Commelina bengalensis.	Pollen grains from the anther of a flower are transferred to the stigma of another flower on a different plant. e. g., papaya, Cannabis
Direct contact of anther and stigma occurs by bending of filaments and style of the two organs respectively, e.g., Mirabilis jalapa.		Anthers do not dehisce; germinated pollen tube pierces anther wall and enter the stigma of same flower.	

2. Cross-Pollination

It is the deposition of pollen grain from anther of a flower to the stigma of a different flower of another plant of same or different species.

Adaptations for Cross-Pollination

Dichogamy	Dicliny	Herkogamy	Self Sterility or Self Incompatibility
The condition, where maturation time of stigma and anthers in such that either stigma becomes receptive before anthers mature (protogyny) or the anthers are ready for the dehiscence before stigma becomes receptive (protandry), e.g., in *Aristolochia* and *Scrophularia*, protogyny occurs and in rose, sunflower, *Impatiens*, etc., protandry is found.	Presence of only one kind of reproductive whorl in a flower is called dicliny or **unisexuality**. A plant may be **monoecious**, *i.e.*, carrying male and female flowers on the same plant. In such case, both cross and self-pollination can occur. In **dioecious** plants, *i.e.*, plants either with male or female flowers are borne on different plants, in such a case cross-pollination is the only way of pollination.	In some flowers, a mechanical barrier exists between the compatible pollen and stigma so that self-pollination becomes impossible, Sometimes, a hood-like, covering covers the stigma as in Iris and in *Calotropis*. The pollen are grouped in pollinia and stick to the surface till they are carried away by the insects.	The pollen of a flower has no fertilising effect on the stigma of the same flower. e.g., *Thea sinensis* (tea), *Passiflora*, etc.

Agents of Pollination

The pollination can be occur through following agents

Various Agencies of Pollination

Pollinating Agency	Process	Agent	Examples
Abiotic agents	Anemophily	Wind	Grasses, maize and gymnosperms
	Hydrophily	Water	*Vallisneria* and *Hydrilla*
	Entomophily	Insects	Rose, poppy and *Salvia*
Biotic agents	Ornithophily	Birds	*Erythrena* and *Maregravia*
	Cheiropterophily	Bats	Baobab tree (*Adansonia*)
	Malacophily	Snails	*Chrysanthemum* and *Lemma*
	Myrmecophily	Ants	*Myrmecophilus acervarum*
	Anthrophily	Human	Various ornamental plants

Handbook of BIOLOGY

Flowering plants have adapted various features to support their pollinators in the process of pollination as insect pollinating plants have strong necteriferious gland to attract the insects. on the other hand wind pollinating plants very light and non-sticky pollen grains to fly freely in air.

Fertilisation

Through the process of pollination the pollen lands on the stigma of a female flower. Pollen grain germinate and tube cell elongate and grows down into style towards the ovule in ovary.

The process of fertilisation, presented diagrammatically as

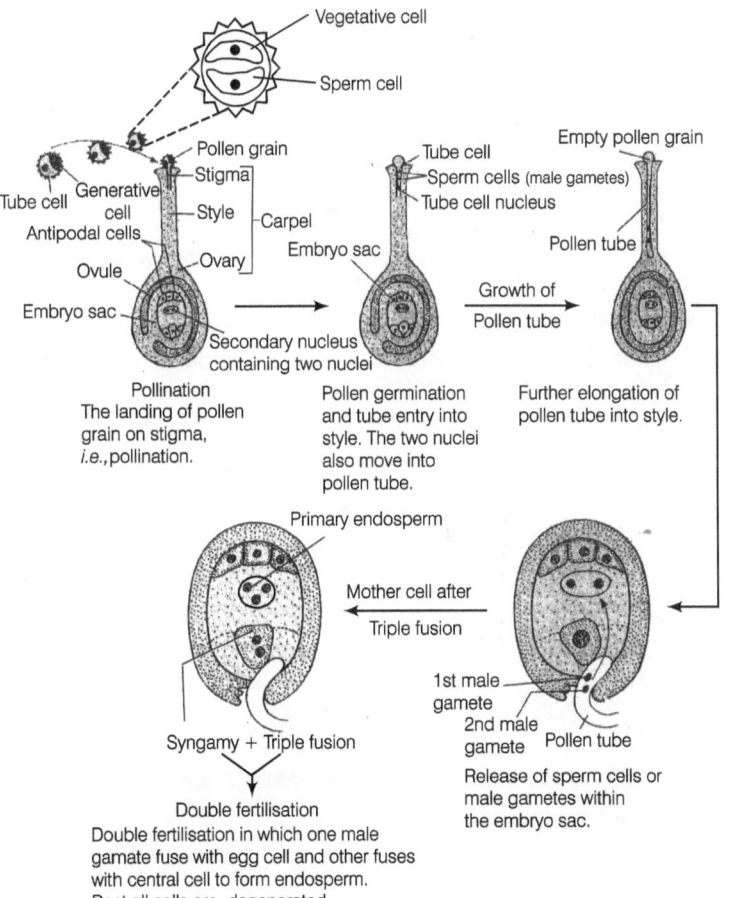

The process of fertilisation and double fertilisation

Entry of Pollen Tube into Ovule

The pollen tube can enter in ovule through three alternate ways. These are

(i) **Porogamy**; Entry through micropyle

(ii) **Mesogamy**; Entry through integuments

(iii) **Chalazogamy**; Entry through chalazal end.

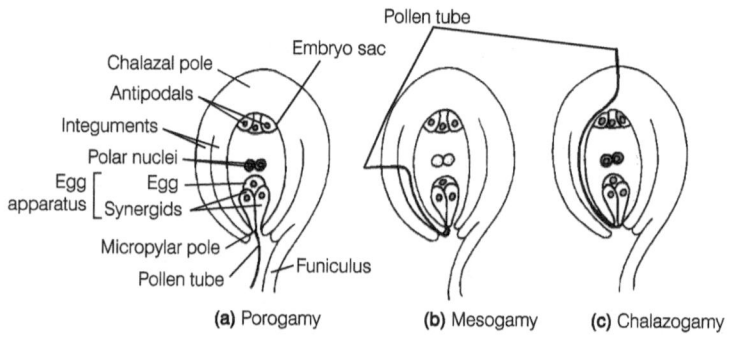

Various routes of pollen tube entry into the ovule

Endosperm

As a result of triple fusion, a triploid structure called Primary Endosperm Mother Cell (PEMC) is formed that finally produce a mass of nutritive cell called **endosperm** through **mitotic division**.

On the basis of development, endosperm is of three types

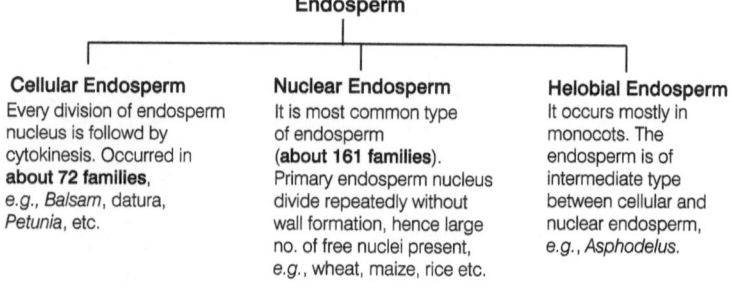

Functions of Endosperm

The important function of endosperm is to provide nutrition to the embryo and support its growth.

Development of Embryo/Embryogenesis

Before going into detail of embryogenesis, we first understand the embryo.

Embryo

The embryo of a plant is a miniature plant tucked into a foetal position in the seed. It is actually one of the earliest stage in the development of a plant, where nutrient provided to the seed enable it to germinate into a plant.

The embryogenesis is the sereis of specialisation and differentiation of cells. *The whole process of embryogenesis can be understood through following flow chart*

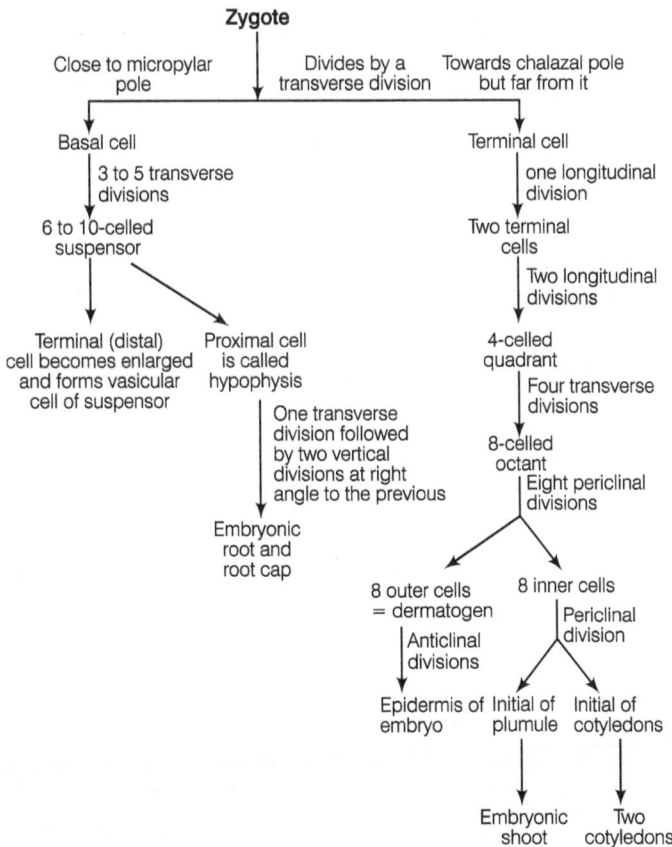

Embryo development in dicots

Seed

'A seed typically consists of seed coat, cotyledon(s) and an embryo axis.' In angiosperm, it is the final product of sexual reproduction and they are formed inside fruit. Although in most of the species, fruits are the result of fertilisation, some species develops fruit without fertilisation. Such fruits are called **parthenocarpic fruit**. *e.g.,* banana.

Additional Terms

(i) **Parthenocarpy** It is the process of producing fruit without fertilisation.

On the basis of its causes, it is three types

```
                        Parthenocarpy
        ┌───────────────────┼───────────────────┐
   Genetic            Environmental         Chemical Induced
 Parthenocarpy        Parthenocarpy          Parthenocarpy
Parthenocarpic fruits  The environmental condition  The artificial
are produced because   like fog, frost, high temperature  application of IAA,
of hybridisation or mutation.  and freezing led to   α-NAA, gibberellin
                       non-functioning of     leads to production
                       reproductive organ     of parthenocarpic fruit.
                       and results into parthenocarpy.
```

(ii) **Apomixis** The term 'Apomixis' was introduced by **Winkler** (1908).

'Apomixis is the substitution of sexual reproduction, which does not involve meiosis and syngamy.'

It is of two types

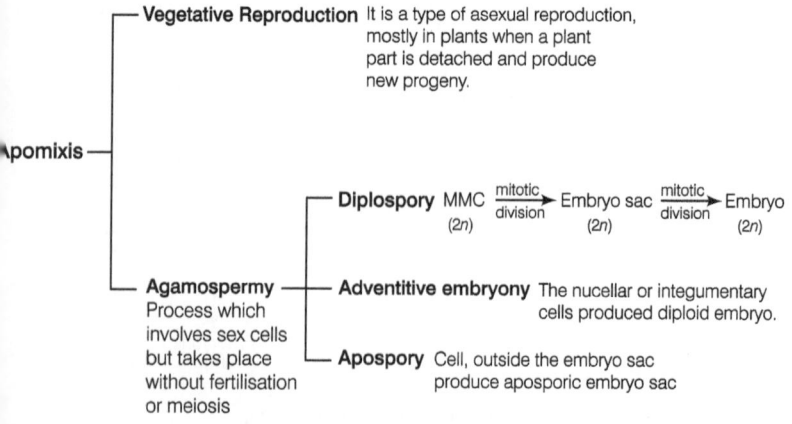

Apomixis
— **Vegetative Reproduction** It is a type of asexual reproduction, mostly in plants when a plant part is detached and produce new progeny.
— **Agamospermy** Process which involves sex cells but takes place without fertilisation or meiosis
  — **Diplospory** MMC (2n) $\xrightarrow{\text{mitotic division}}$ Embryo sac (2n) $\xrightarrow{\text{mitotic division}}$ Embryo (2n)
  — **Adventive embryony** The nucellar or integumentary cells produced diploid embryo.
  — **Apospory** Cell, outside the embryo sac produce aposporic embryo sac

(iii) **Polyembryony** The process of occurrence of more than one embryo in a seed is known as polyembrgony. It was first observed by **Anton von Leeuwenhoek** in 1917 in orange seed.

On the basis of originating cell, it is of two types

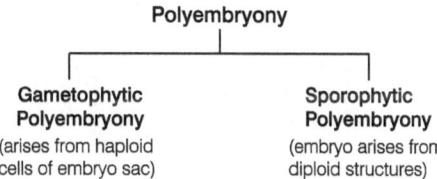

(iv) **Xenia** The term 'Xenia' was coined by **Wilhelm Olbers Focke** in 1881.

It is the effect of pollen on maternal tissues including seed coat and pericarp.

When one allele in the pollen is able to mask the effect of double dose of other, the former is called **xenia** over the latter.

(v) **Metaxenia** It is a condition during hybridisation where the alleles of one locus behaves as a double dose for the other and make it as a recessive.

This condition is found in aneuploids where segregation is prevented.

28
Principles of Inheritance and Variation

Through the process of reproduction, all organisms produce same type of organisms. The transfer of characters from one generation to next generation is the central idea of this chapter.

Heredity

It is the study of transmission of characters from parents to offspring or from one generation to the next. Thus, the transmission of structural, functional and behavioural characteristics from one generation to another is called heredity.

Basis of Heredity

Mendel (1866) proposed that, inheritance is controlled by paired germinal units or **factors**, now called **genes**. These represent small segments of **chromosome** *i.e.,* chromosomal basis of heredity.

The genetic material present in chromosome is DNA. Genes are segment of DNA called **cistrons**. Therefore, DNA is regarded as the chemical basis of heredity.

Inheritance

It is the process by which characters or traits pass from one generation to the next. Inheritance is the basis of heredity.

Variations

It is the differences in characteristics shown by the individuals of a species and also by the offspring or siblings of the same parents.

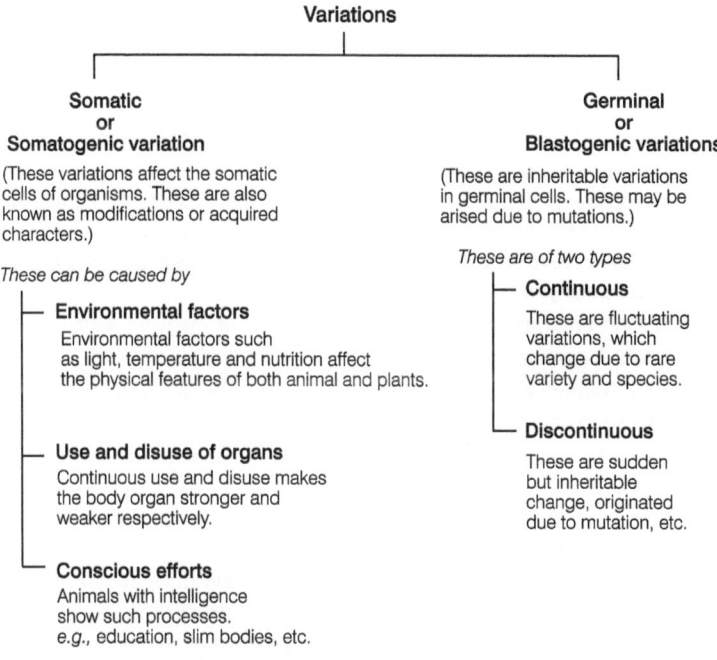

Terms Related to Genetics

1. **Characters** It is a well defined morphological or physiolo gical feature of an organism.
2. **Trait** Trait is the distinguishing feature of a character.
3. **Gene** Inherited factor that determines the biological character of an organism.
4. **Allele** A pair of contrasting character is called alleles or alternate form of genes is called alleles.
5. **Dominant allele** The factor or an allele pair which can express itself in both homozygous and heterozygous state.
6. **Recessive allele** The factor or allele pair which can express only in homozygous state.
7. **Wild allele** The allele which was originally present in the population and is dominant and widespread.

8. **Homozygous condition** The state in which organism has two similar genes or alleles of a particular character. (*e.g.,* TT or tt)
9. **Heterozygous condition** In this the organism contains two different alleles for a particular character. (*e.g.,* Tt)
10. **Monohybrid cross** When only one allelic pair is considered in cross breeding.
11. **Dihybrid cross** When two allelic pairs are used in crossing it is called dihybrid cross.
12. **Genotype** Genetic constitution of an individual is called in genotype.
13. **Phenotype** External features of organism.
14. **Punnet square** It is a checker board which was invented by RC Punnet and used to show the result of a cross between two organisms.
15. **Polyhybrid cross** Involvement of more than two allelic pair in a cross is called polyhybrid cross.
16. **F_1 or First Filial generation** The second stage of Mendel's experiment is called f_1-generation.
17. **Hybrid vigour or heterosis** The superiority of hybrid over either of its parents in one or more traits.
18. **Gene pool** All the genotype of all organisms in a population are combinely called gene pool.
19. **Genome** It is the complete set of chromosomes where every gene chromosome is present singly as in gamete.
20. **Pure line or pure breeding line** It is a strain of individuals homozygous for all genes considered. The term was coined by Johannsen.
21. **Haploid, diploid and polyploid cell** A single genome is present in haploid, two in diploid and many genomes present in polyploid cells.
22. **Test cross** The cross of F_1 offsprings with recessive parents is called test cross.
23. **Back cross** The cross of an organism with the organism of its previous generation is known as back cross.
24. **Reciprocal cross** A cross in which same two parents are used in such a way that if in one experiment 'A' is used as female parent and 'B' is used as the male parent, in other experiment 'A' will be used as male parent and 'B' is used as female parent.

Gregor Johann Mendel

He was born on July 22, 1822 in Austria. He graduated from gymnasium in 1840. In 1843, Mendel was admitted to the augistinian monastery at Brunn, where he took the name **Gregor**. From 1851-53 he studied mathematics and natural science.

In spring of 1856, he began experimenting with pea plant. In 1866, his paper **'Experiment on plant hybridisation'** published in volume IV of the proceedings of the natural society. He died on January 6, 1884 and was buried in Brunn central cemetery.

Mendel's experiment involved four steps

1. **Selection** The selection of characters for the hybridisation is the first and an important step.
2. **Hybridisation** The pollination and hybridisation between the individuals of two different /contrasting characteristics.
3. **Selfing** It is the specific hybridisation between the organisms of same origin (siblings).
4. **Calculation** The counting and categorising the products on the basis of character identified takes place in calculation.

Mendel performed his experiment on pea plant and he choose seven contrasting characters in it for observation.

These are

1. Colour of seed
2. Shape of seed
3. Flower colour
4. Colour of pod
5. Shape of pod
6. Position of flower
7. Height of plant

450　　　　　　　　　　　　　　　　　　Handbook of BIOLOGY

These characters and their inheritance pattern is given in the following table

Character or Trait Studied	Parent forms Crossed (F_1 Cross)	F_1 Phenotype	F_2 Products Dominant form, Recessive form	Total	Actual Ratio	Chromosome Location
Colour of seed	Yellow (cotyledon) × Green	All yellow	6022 yellow, 2001 green	8023	3.01 : 1	1
Shape of seed	Round (cotyledon) × Wrinkled	All round	5474 round, 1850 wrinkled	7324	2.96 : 1	7
Flower colour	Purple × White	All purple	705 purple, 224 white	929	3.15 : 1	1
Colour of pod	Green × Yellow	All green	428 green, 152 yellow	580	2.82 : 1	5
Shape of pod	Inflated × Constricted	All inflated	882 inflated, 299 constricted	1181	2.95 : 1	4
Position of flower	Axial × Terminal	All axial	651 axial, 207 terminal	858	3.14 : 1	4
Height of plant	Tall × Dwarf	All tall	787 tall, 277 dwarf	1064	2.84 : 1	4

Emasculation and Bagging

Mendel required both self and cross fertilisation within the plant for his experiments. Due to its self fertilising nature, the anthers of pea plants required removal before maturity (emasculation) and the stigma is protected against any foreign pollen (bagging). Through the process of emasculation and bagging, the pollen of only selected parent can be used for cross fertilisation.

Inheritance of One Gene/Monohybrid Cross

Mendel performed several experiments on pea, by considering one character at a time.

It is a cross made to study simultaneous inheritance of a single pair of Mendelian factors.

The schematic presentation of the monohybrid cross is as follows

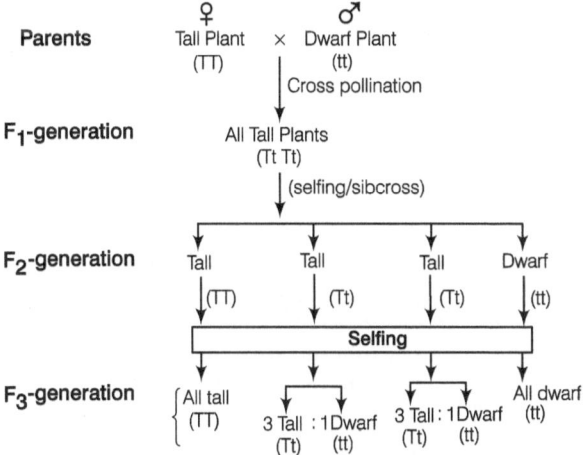

Monohybrid cross in pea plant

Mendel's Laws of Inheritance in which Monohybrid Cross is Applied

From the three laws of inheritance (*i.e.,* Law of dominance, Law of segregation and Law of independent assortment), the first two laws are based on the monohybrid cross.

These are explained in detail as follows

1. Law of Dominance

According to this law, 'when a cross is made between two homozygous (pure line) individuals considering contrasting trait of simple character then the trait that appears in F_1 hybrids is called dominant and the other one that remains masked is called recessive trait'.

In pea plant, out of the 7 characters, Mendel studied the dominant and recessive trait. These characters are discussed as earlier.

The dominant and recessive traits are also found in other animals, *e.g.*,

Cat	(a) Skin colour	Tabby colour is dominant over black or blue.
	(b) Length of hair	Short hair are dominant over long hair (Angora).
Cattle	(a) Colour of face	White face colour is dominant over coloured face.
	(b) Horn	Polled or hornless are dominant over horned cattle.
Dog	(a) Skin colour	Grey colour is dominant over black colour.
	(b) Tail	Stumpy tail is dominant over normal tail.
Drosophila	(a) Eye colour	Red colour is dominant over white.
	(b) Wings	Flat and yellow wings are dominant over curled and white.
	(c) Body colour	Grey body colour is dominant over white.
Salamander	Body colour	Dark body colour is dominant over light.

The law of dominance explains why individuals of F_1-generation express the trait of only one parent and the reasons for occurrence of 3:1 ratio in F_2 individuals.

Exceptions to Law of Dominance

These are as follows

(i) **Incomplete Dominance/Blending Inheritance** (Correns, 1903)

It is also known as **Intermediate** or **Partial** or **Mosaic** inheritance.

When F_1 hybrids exhibited a mixture or blending of character of two parents, it is termed as blending inheritance.

It simply means that the two genes of allelomorphic pair are not related as dominant or recessive, but each of them expresses partially, *e.g.*, **4 O'clock plant** (*Mirabilis jalapa*), **snapdragon** (*Antirrhinum*) and **homozygous fowl**. In 4 O'clock plant when a cross in made between dominant (red) and recessive (white) variety, the result of F_2 generation show deviation from Mendel's predictions.

Here, both phenotypic and genotypic ratios came as 1 : 2 : 1 for Red : Pink : White.

(ii) **Codominance**

The phenomenon of expression of both the alleles in a heterozygote is called **codominance**.

The alleles which do not show dominant-recessive relationship and are able to express themselves independently when present together are called **codominant allele'**. *e.g.*, coat colour in short horned cattles and MN blood group in humans.

In short horned cattle when a cross is made between white (dominant) and red (recessive) variety appearence of all Roan offsprings in F_1 generation and then white, Roan and Red in 1:2:1 ratio in F_2 generation show codominance of both the colours in Roan.

The roan coloured F_2 individual in above cross have both red and white hairs in form of pathes but no hair is having the intermediate colour.

(iii) **Pleiotropic Gene**

The ability of a gene to have multiple phenotypic effect, because it influences a number of characters simultaneously, is known as pleiotropy and such genes are called pleiotropic gene.

It is not essential that all traits are equally influenced, sometimes it is more evident in case of one trait (major effect) and less evident in other (minor effect).

e.g., In garden pea the gene controlling flower colour, also control the colour of seed coat and presence of red spot on leaf axil.

2. Law of Segregation/Law of Purity of Gametes

According to this law, 'In F_1 hybrid the dominant and recessive characters though remain together for a long time, but do not contaminate or mix with each other and separate or segregate at the time of gamete formation, thus the gamete formed receive either dominant or recessive character out of them.'

For proper understanding of Mendel's law of segregation the formation of hybrid is considered from pure line homozygous parents through monohybird cross given before first law.

As the purity of gametes again established in F_2 generation, it is called law of purity of gametes.

Inheritance of Two Genes/Dihybrid Cross

These crosses are made to study the inheritance of two pairs of Mendelian factors or genes.

The schematic representation of the dihybrid cross is as follow

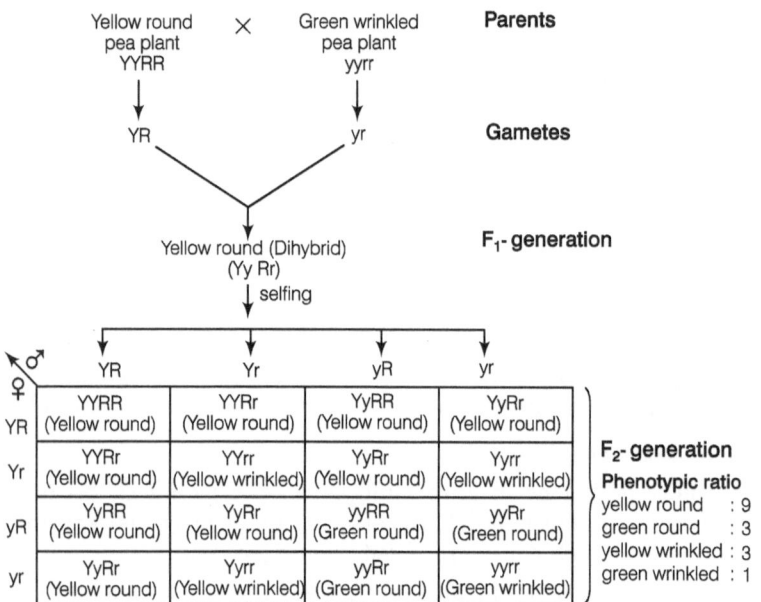

Dihybrid cross in pea plant

Exceptions to Law of Segregation

These are as follows

(i) Complementary Genes

The two pairs of non-allelic dominant genes, which **interact to produce only one phenotypic trait**, but neither of them (if present alone) produces the trait in the absence of other. It shows the phenotypic ratio 9 : 7.

Handbook of BIOLOGY

This cross is shown as

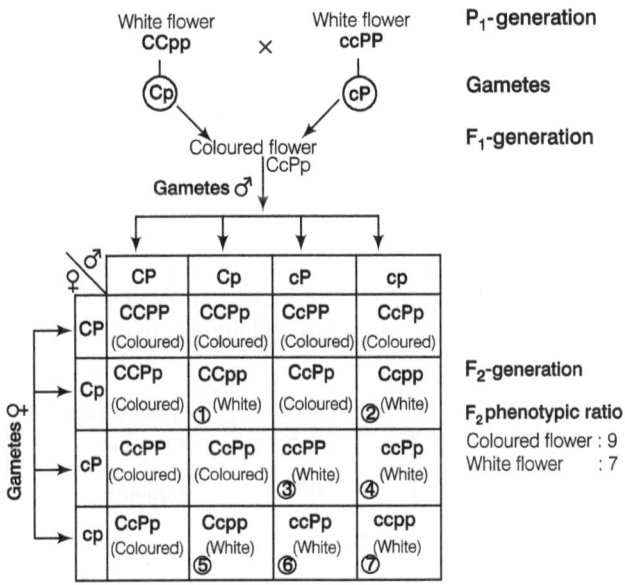

The results of an experiment to show the operation of complementry genes in the production of flower colour in sweet pea (*Lathyrus*)

(ii) Epistatic Gene or Inhibitory Gene

It is the interaction between two non-allelic genes, in which one gene masks or suppresses the expression of other. The gene which got suppressed is called hypostatic factor and the suppressor gene is called epistatic factor such an interaction is called epistasis.

The epistasis may be

(a) **Dominant epistasis** In this, out of two pairs of genes, the dominant one masks the expression of other gene pair.

The ratio obtained in this may be 12 : 3 : 1 or 13 : 3, *e.g.*, coat colour gene in dog.

(b) **Recessive epistasis** In this, out of the two pairs of genes, the recessive epistatic gene masks the activity of dominant gene of the other gene locus. The ratio obtained in this may be 9 : 3 : 4, *e.g.*, coat colour gene in mice.

3. Law of Independent Assortment

This law is defined as 'The inheritance of one character is always independent to the inheritance of other character within the same individual'. The dihybrid cross of Mendel can be a very good example of independent assortment.

Exceptions to Law of Independent Assortment

These are as follows

(i) Supplementary Genes

Two independent dominant gene pairs, which interact in such a way that one dominant gene produces its effect irrespective of the presence or absence of other, *e.g.*, the coat colour in mice. *The cross is represented as*

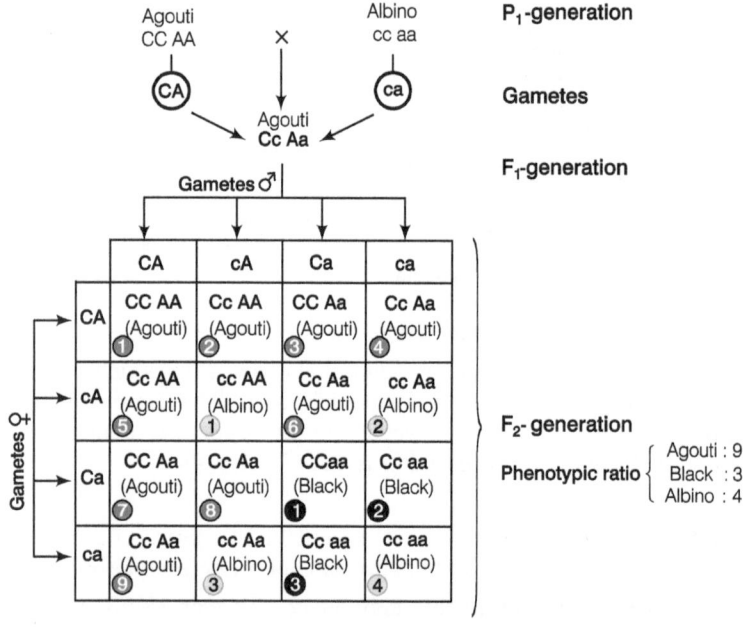

Interaction of supplementary genes in mice for coat colour

Here, presence of gene C produces black colour which along with gene A changes its expression in agouti colour. Thus in all combination with at least one C and one A produce agouti colour.

(ii) Duplicate Gene

The two pairs of genes which determine same or nearly same phenotype, hence either of them is able to produce the character. The duplicate genes are also called **pseudoalleles**. *e.g.,* fruit shape in shepherd's purse.

The inheritance can be seen as

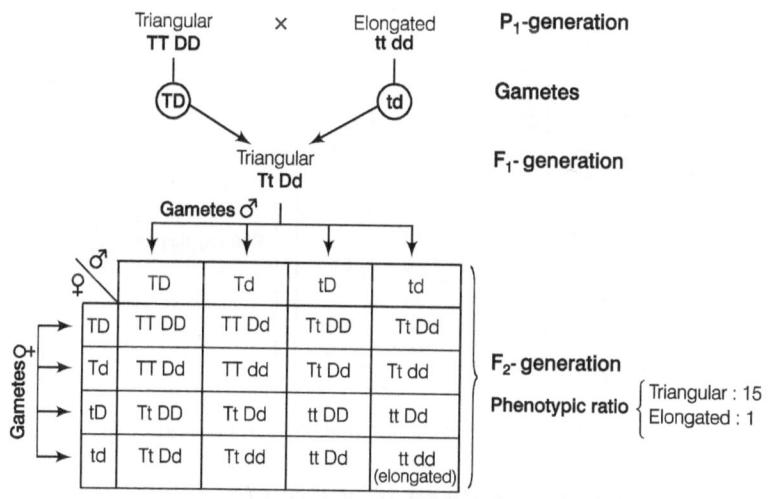

Interaction of duplicating genes in Shephered's purse for seed pod's shape

(iii) Collaborator Gene

In this the two gene pairs which are present on separate locus but interact to produce totally new trait or phenotype.

e.g., inheritance of comb in poultry.

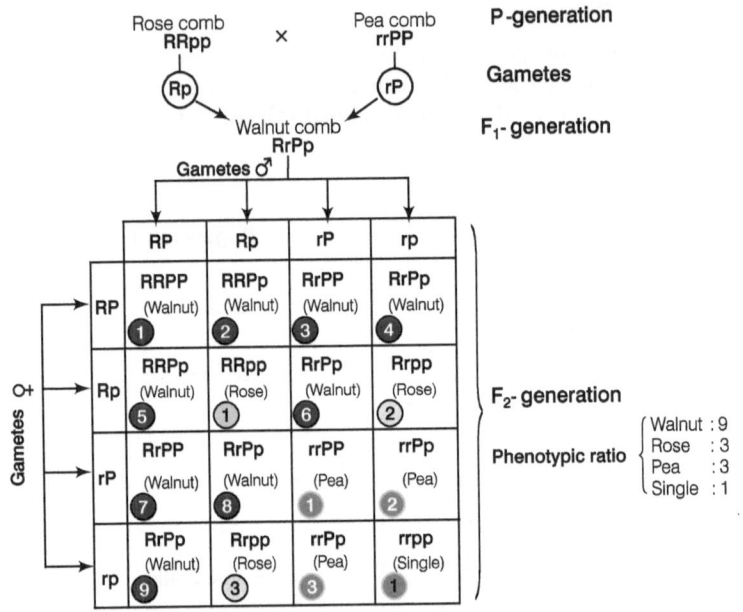

Inheritance of rose and pea comb in poultry

Chromosomal Theory of Inheritance

Walter Sutton and Theodore Boveri in 1902 united the knowledge of chromosomal segregation with Mendelian principles and called it chromosomal theory of inheritance.

According to this theory
  (i) All hereditary characters are carried with sperms and egg cells as they provide bridge from one generation to the other.
 (ii) The herditary factors are carried in the nucleus.
(iii) Chromosomes are also found in pairs like the Mendelian alleles.
(iv) The two alleles of a gene pair are located on homologous sites on the homologous chromosomes.
 (v) The sperm and egg have haploid sets of chromosomes, which fuse to reestablish the diploid state.
(vi) The genes are carried on the chromosomes.

(vii) Homologous chromosomes synapse during meiosis and get separated to pass into different cells. This is the basis for segregation and independent assortment.

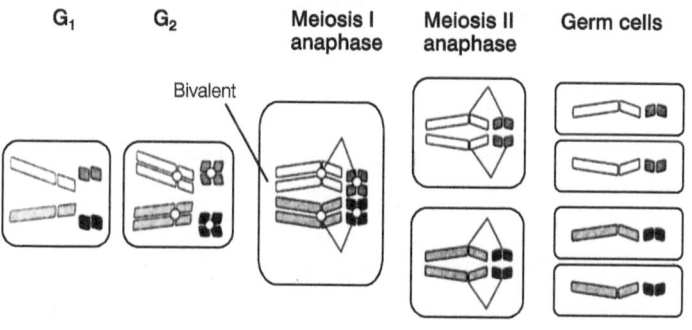

Meiosis and germ cell formation in a cell with four chromosomes

Sex Determination

It is the method by which the distinction between male and female is established in a species. It is usually under genetic control of specific chromosomes called **sex chromosomes** or **allosomes**.

There are five main genetic mechanisms of sex determination

(i) XX-XY Method

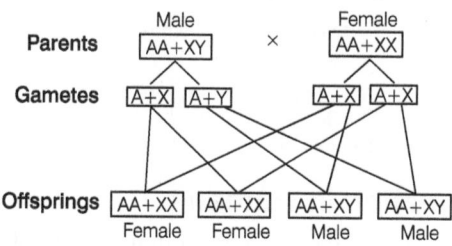

e.g., mammals (as in humans).

(ii) XX-XO Method

In this, female has XX and produces homogametic eggs, while male has only one chromosome and produces two types of sperms, *e.g.*, **Gynosperms** (with X) and **androsperms** (without X) *e.g.*, insects and roundworm.

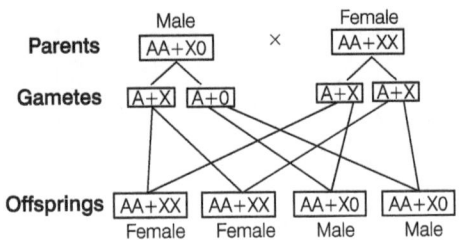

(iii) ZW-ZZ Method

In this, the male is homogametic and female is heterogametic, *e.g.*, certain insects, fishes, reptiles and birds.

(iv) ZO-ZZ Method

In this, female is heterogametic while the male is homogametic, *e.g.*, moths and certain butterflies.

(v) Haploid-diploid Method

In this method, the unfertilised egg develops into male (Arrhenotoky) while fertilised egg develops into female. This type of sex determination is the characteristic feature of insects like honey bees, ants etc.

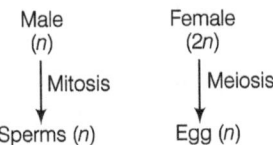

Sex Determination in Humans

The human shows XY type of sex determination. Out of total (23 pairs) chromosomes, 22 pairs are exactly similar in both males and females, known as **autosomes**.

The female contains a pair of X-chromosome and male contains both X and Y-chromosomes. The sex is determined by the genetic make up of sperm.

During spermatogenesis among males, two types of gametes are produced, 50% of the total sperm carry X-chromosomes and the rest 50% carry Y-chromosomes.

Linkage (Exception to Independent Assortment)

Linkage is the phenomenon of certain genes staying together during inheritance through generations without any change or separation. In other words, 'It is the tendency of genes staying together during inheritance.'

Morgan (1910) clearly proved and defined linkage on the basis of his breeding experiment in fruitfly *Drosophila melanogaster*.

Linked genes that are inherited together with the other genes as they are located on the same chromosome.

Linkage group is equals to the number of chromosome's pair present in cells. (*e.g.*, human have 23 linkage groups).

According to Morgan et. al. the linkage can be

1. **Complete or perfect** In this, genes remain together for at least two generations.
2. **Incomplete or imperfect** In this, genes remain together within same chromosome for less than two generation.

Crossing Over/Recombination

Those genes which show non-linkage, results into non-parental combinations in F_1. Presence of such combinations indicates that in linked gene, the process of interchange of alleles within non-sister chromatids of homologous chromosomes takes place, this is known as crossing over.

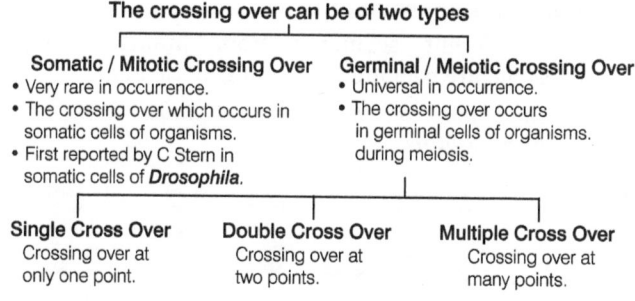

The mechanism of crossing over is explained by various theories, some of them with their propounders are listed below

(a) **Copy choice theory** — J Lederbreg (1955)
(b) **Precocity theory** — C D Darlington (1931)
(c) **Belling hypothesis** — Belling
(d) **Break and exchange theory** — Stern and Hotta (1969)
(e) **Hybrid DNA Model** — R Holliday (1964)

Linkage Maps/Genetic Maps/Chromosomal Maps

'It is the graphic representation of the relative distance between the genes in a linkage group'. The first likage map was given by **Strutevent** and **Morgan** in 1920s. In linkage maps, the integenic distances can be explained through arbitary unit of measurement called **map unit** to describe the distance between linked genes.

$$1 \text{ map unit} = 1\% \text{ of crossing over}$$

one map unit is now referred as cM (centiMorgan) in honour of Morgan's contribution.

Steps to Construct Genetic Map

Step 1 Determination of linkage group and total number of genes

By hybridising wild and mutant strains, we can determine the total no. of gene and link group in an organism.

Step 2 Determination of map distance

for determining of map distances, the test crosses are performed. The relative distance can be calculated according to the percentage of crossing over, as cross over frequency is directly proportional to the distance between the genes.

Step 3 Determination of gene order

After determining the relative distance the genes can be place in proper linear order.

Step 4 Combining map segments

Finally different segments from linkage group of a chromosome are combined to form genetic map.

Thus, *chromosomal map of chromosome number 2 of Drosophila melanogaster can be seen as*

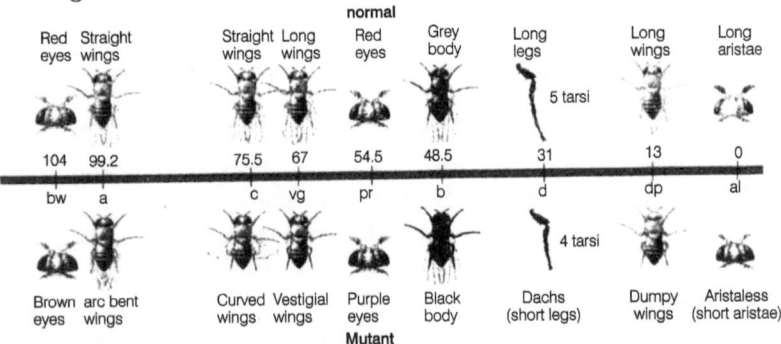

The genetic map of chromosome of *Drosophila melanogaster*

Cytoplasmic Inheritance/Extranuclear Inheritance

The total self replicating hereditary material of cytoplasm is called **plasmon** and cytoplasmic unit of inheritance are described as plasma genes.

Cytoplasmic inheritance have two distinct features
  (i) It is a maternal inheritance, *i.e.,* only maternal parent contribute for inheritance.
  (ii) The reciprocal crosses are not same due to participation of female parents only. *e.g.,* sigma particle inheritance in *Drosophila*, Kappa particle inheritance in *Paramecium* and breast tumor in mice, etc.

In *Drosophila* one strain show more sensitivity toward CO_2 (these are comparatively easily immobilised by exposing them to CO_2). This more sensitivity was discovered by L heritier and Teissier. The sensitive trait is regulated by a heat labile substance present in cytoplasm called sigma. *The inheritance of sensitive fly can be seen as*

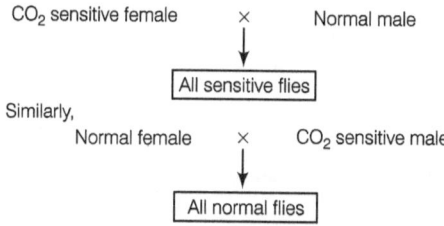

Results of reciprocal crosses clearly indicates the inheritance of more CO_2 sensitivity through females. The mammary cancer or breast tumour in mice has been found to be maternally transmitted. It was noted by **JJ Bitiner**. *He performed following crosses regarding cancer in mice*

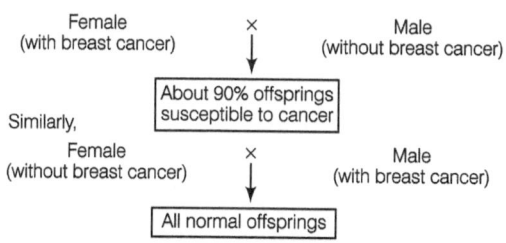

Such a difference in reciprocal crosses suggest the presence of maternal inheritance.

Mutation (Hugo de Vries; 1901)

A sudden inheritable discontinuous variation which appear in an organism due to permanent change in their genotypes.

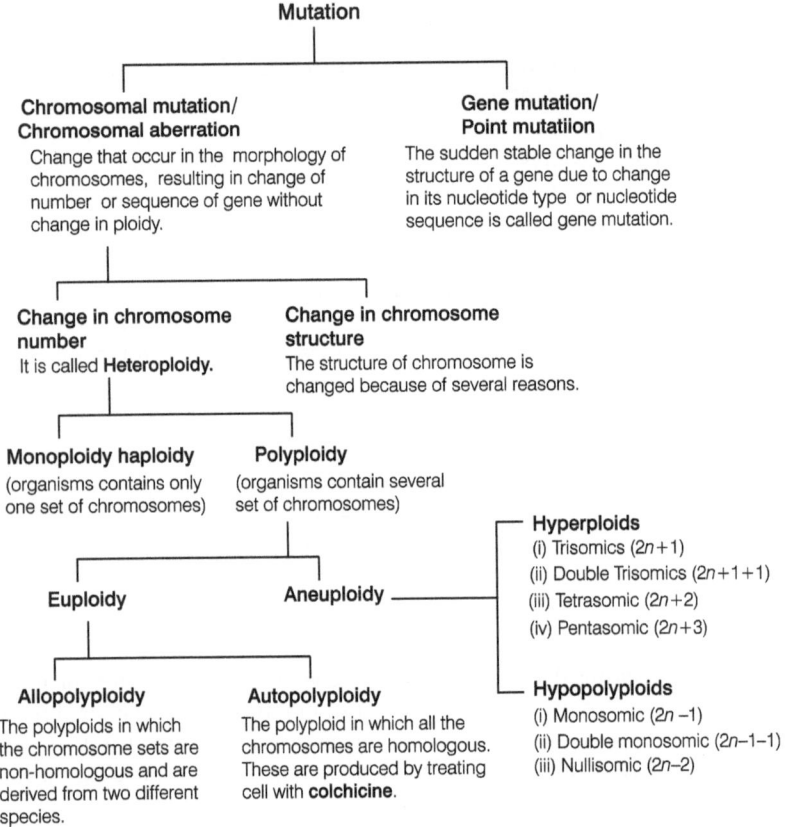

Change in Chromosomal Structure

The variations occurs due to following four proceses

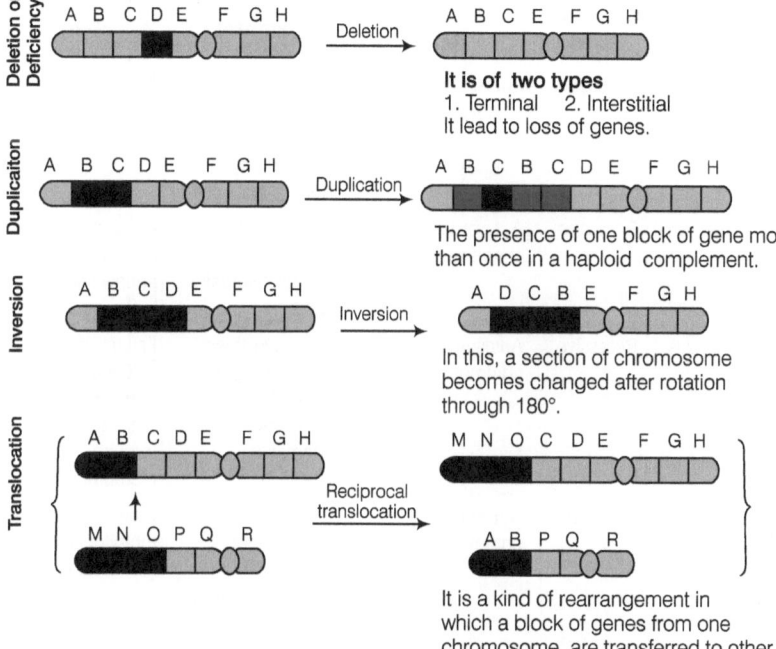

Diagram showing the forms of chromosomal mutations

Gene Mutation

The intragenic or point mutations involve alterations in the structure of gene by altering the structure of DNA. *It is of two types*

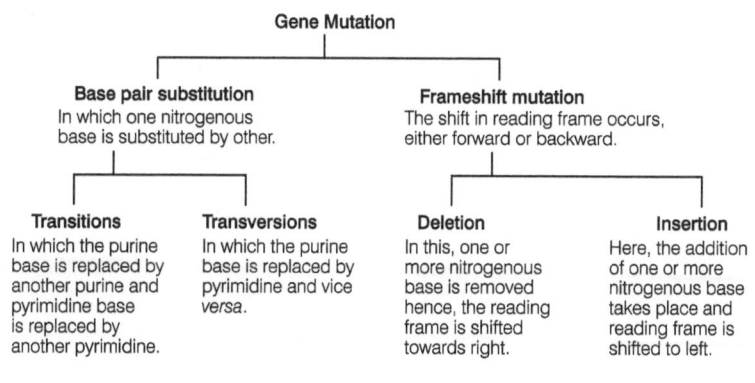

All these mutations cause various genetic disorders. *A list of some important genetic disorder is given as follows*

Disorder	Dominant/ Recessive	Autosomal/ Sex linked	Symptom	Effect
Sickle-cell anaemia	Recessive	Autosomal, gene on chromosome 11	Aggregation of erythrocytes, more rapid destruction of erythrocytes leading to anemia.	Abnormal haemoglobin in RBC's.
Phenylketonuria	Recessive	Autosomal, gene on chromosome 12	Failure of brain to develop in infancy, mental retardation, idiots	Defective form of enzyme phenylalanine hydroxylase.
Cystic Fibrosis (CF)	Recessive	Autosomal, gene on chromosome 7	Excessive thick mucus clogging in lungs, liver and pancreas anomalies.	Failure of chloride ion transport mechanism through cell membrane.
Huntington's Disease (HD)	Dominant	Autosomal, gene on chromosome 4	Gradual degeneration of brain tissue in middle age, loss of motor control.	Production of an inhibitor of brain cell metabolism.
Haemophilia A/B	Recessive	Sex-linked, gene on X-chromosome	Failure of blood to clot.	Defective form of blood clotting factor VIII/IX
Colour blindness	Recessive	Sex-linked, gene on X-chromosome	Failure to discriminate between red and green colour.	Defect in either red or/ and green cone cells of retina.
Down's syndrome		Autosomal, aneuploidy (trisomy+21)	Mongolian eyefold (epicanthus), open mouth, protruded tongue, projected lower lip, many loops on finger tips, palm crease	Retarded mental development IQ below 40.

Turner's syndrome		Sex chromosomal monosomy 44+X0	Short stature females (<5'), webbed neck, body hair absent menstrual cycle absent, sparse pubic hair, under developed breasts, narrow lips, puffy fingers.	Sterile, hearing problem
Klinefelter's syndrome		Sex chromosomal aneuploidy (Tri/tetrasomy of X chr) 44+ XXY, 44+XXXY	These males are tall with long legs, testes small, sparse body hair, barr body present, breast enlargement.	Gynaecomastia, azospermia, sterile

Pedigree Analysis

Scientists have devised another approach, called pedigree analysis, to study the inheritance of genes in humans. This is also useful when studying the population when progeny data from several generations is limited. It is also useful in studying the species with long generation time. A series of symbols are used to represent different aspects of a pedigree. *These are as follows*

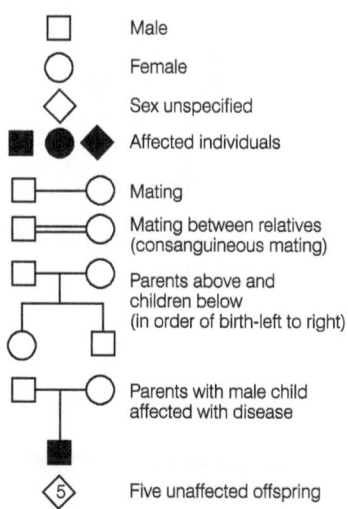

Symbols used in the human pedigree analysis

Once phenotypic data is collected from several generations and the pedigree is drawn, careful analysis will allow you to determine wheather the trait is dominant or recessive.

For those traits exhibiting dominant gene action
- Affected individuals have at least one affected parent.
- The phenotype generally appears every generation.
- Two unaffected parents only have unaffected offspring.

It is called dominant pedigree and shown as

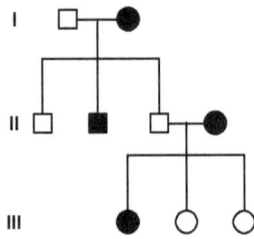

Those traits which exhibits recessive gene action
- Unaffected parents can have affected offspring.
- Affected progeny are both male and female and it is called **recessive pedigree** and shown as

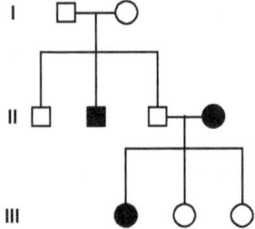

In due course of time the genetics and its principles will helps in the solution of several heredity problems.

29

Molecular Basis *of* Inheritance

Early in 20th century, scientists knew that the genes are situated on chromosomes, but they did not know the composition of genes. The identification of the molecules of inheritance was a major challange to biologists.

DNA and proteins were the candidate for the genetic material, but protein seemes stronger because of its complexity and variety.

The scientists knew that the genetic material should have following characteristics

1. It should be able to **store information** that pertains to the development, **structure and metabolic activities** of the cell or organisms.
2. It should be stable, so that it **can be replicated** with high fidelity during cell division and be **transmitted from generation to generation**.
3. It should be able to undergo rare genetic changes called **mutations** that provide the genetic variability **required for evolution** to occur.

DNA as Genetic Material

The chromosomes, which are described as hereditary vehicles are the condensed form of DNA and proteins.

The characteristics of DNA as genetic material can be proved through following experiments

1. Bacterial Transformation (Frederick Griffith; 1928)

This experiment was performed with two strains of *Streptococcus pneumoniae* (the pneumonia causing bacteria).

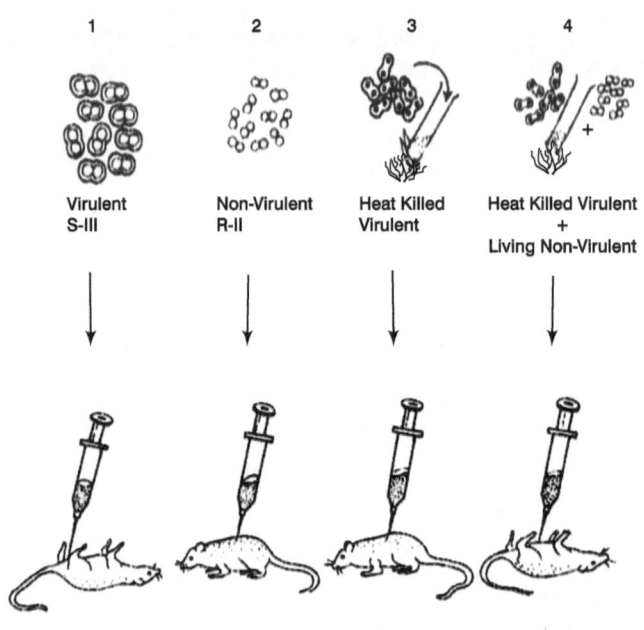

S = Smooth walled
R = Rough walled

Transformation experiment

2. Blender Experiment
(Alfred Hershey and Martha Chase; 1952)

The diagrammatic presentation of this experiment is given below

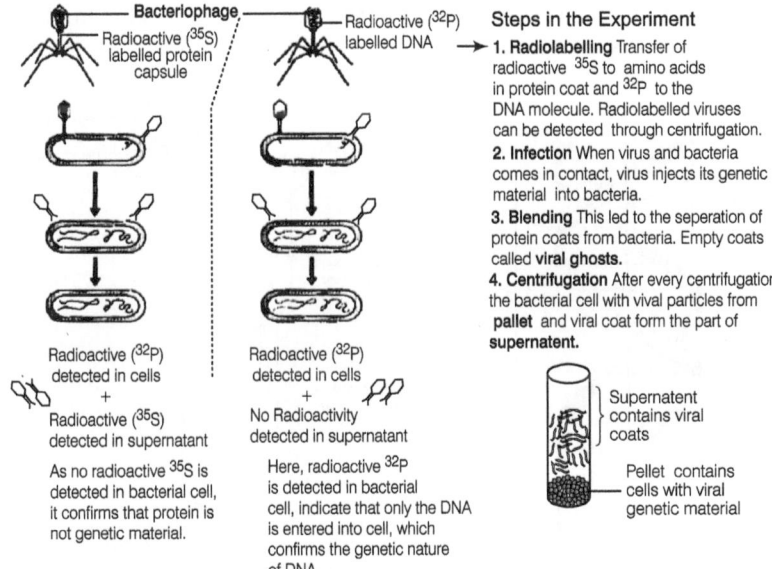

Blender experiment of Hershey and Chase

3. Transformation Experiment
(Avery, Mac Leod and Mc Carty; 1944)

Through this experiment, they showed that the genetic characteristics of bacteria could be altered from one type to another by the treatment with purified DNA.

The experiment can be understood by following cases

(Case-1) R-type + Protein S-type = R-Type

(Case-2) R-type + Carbohydrate S-type = R-Type

(Case-3) R-type + DNA of S-type + DNase = R-Type

(Case-4) R-Type + DNA of S-type = R-Type + S-Type

The experiment of **Avery, Mac Leod** and **Mc Carty** was based on the same principle as Griffith's experiment. R indicates the rough walled bacteria (*i.e.,* avirulent), while S indicate the smooth walled bacteria (virulent). In the experiment, in every case the resultant is modified according to the DNA (*i.e.,* R-type).

DNA

The chromosomes are chemically DNA molecule, which acts as the genetic material in most of the organisms. The DNA was discovered by a German chemist **F Meischer** in 1869. Before discussing the molecular basis of inheritance in detail, we need to understand the structure of DNA molecule.

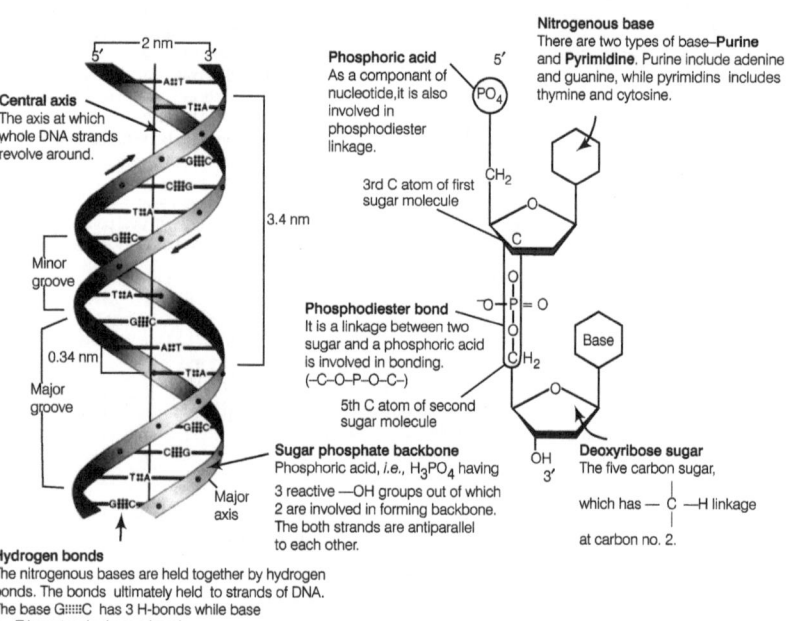

DNA double helix

The DNA molecule consists of two helically twisted strands connected together by base pairs, which align themselves in such a manner just like the steps of ladder.

The antiparallal polynucleotide chain running $5' - 3'$, in opposite direction. The $5'$ end carry phosphate group attached on 5th carbon of sugar and $3'$ end carry OH-group attached to 3rd carbon of sugar.

- The joining of bases creates two types of grooves called **major grooves** and **minor grooves**. Each turn of DNA helix accommodate 10 base pairs.

- On the basis of various criteria, there are different types of DNA exists, *these are given in following table*

Comparative Structure of DNA

Characters	A	B	C	D	Z
Handedness	Right	Right	Right	Right	Left
Base pairs / Turn	11.0	10.0	9.3	8.0	12.0
Helix diametar (Å)	23	19	19	16.7	18
Helix rise per bp	2.92	3.36	3.32	3.03	3.52-4.13
Occurrence in biological world	Rare	Common	Less common	No	In some cells

Packaging of DNA Helix

The haploid human genome contains approximately 3 billion base pairs of DNA packaged into 23 chromosomes. In a diploid cell, it makes about 6 billion base pairs per cell.

As each pair of base is around 0.34 nm long, each diploid cell therefore contains about 2 metres of DNA $[(0.34 \times 10^{-9}) \times (6 \times 10^9)]$. To accomodate such a large amount of DNA in our body the packaging is required, *which can be expressed through following figure*

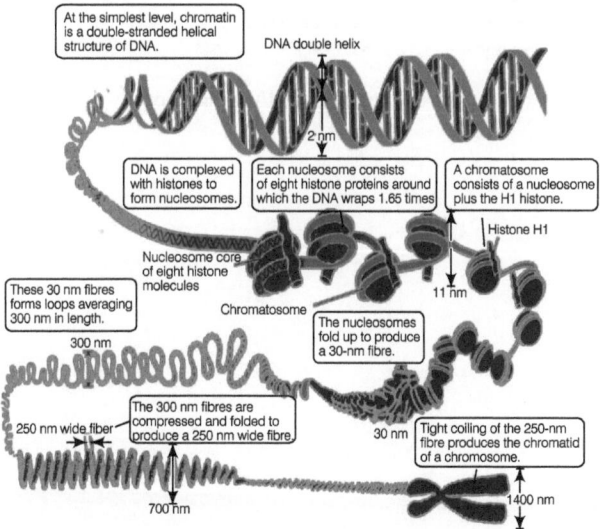

Packaging of DNA at different levels

DNA Replication

The DNA dependent DNA synthesis (*i.e.*, copying) is called DNA replication. It occurs in S-phase of cell cycle.

In DNA it was found that replication in of semiconservativ type, although it can be thought of to operate in conservative or dispertive mode too. *All the three possibilities are given below*

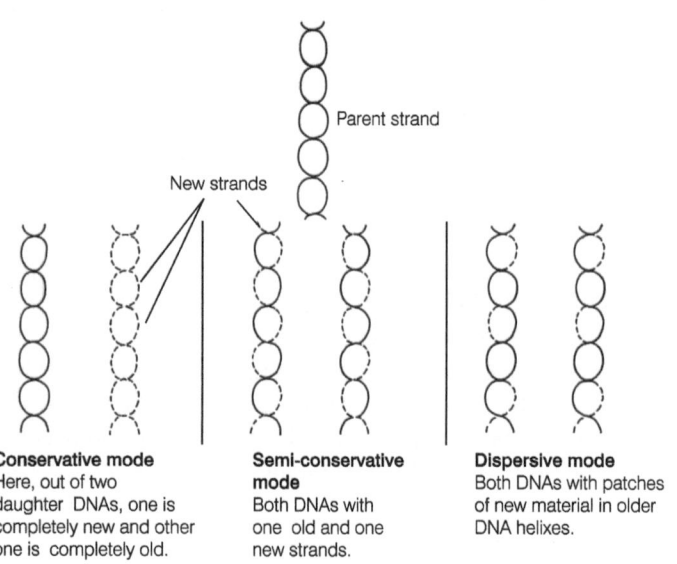

Conservative mode
Here, out of two daughter DNAs, one is completely new and other one is completely old.

Semi-conservative mode
Both DNAs with one old and one new strands.

Dispersive mode
Both DNAs with patches of new material in older DNA helixes.

Three modes of DNA replication

Handbook of BIOLOGY

The schematic presentation of DNA replication in prokaryotes is given below

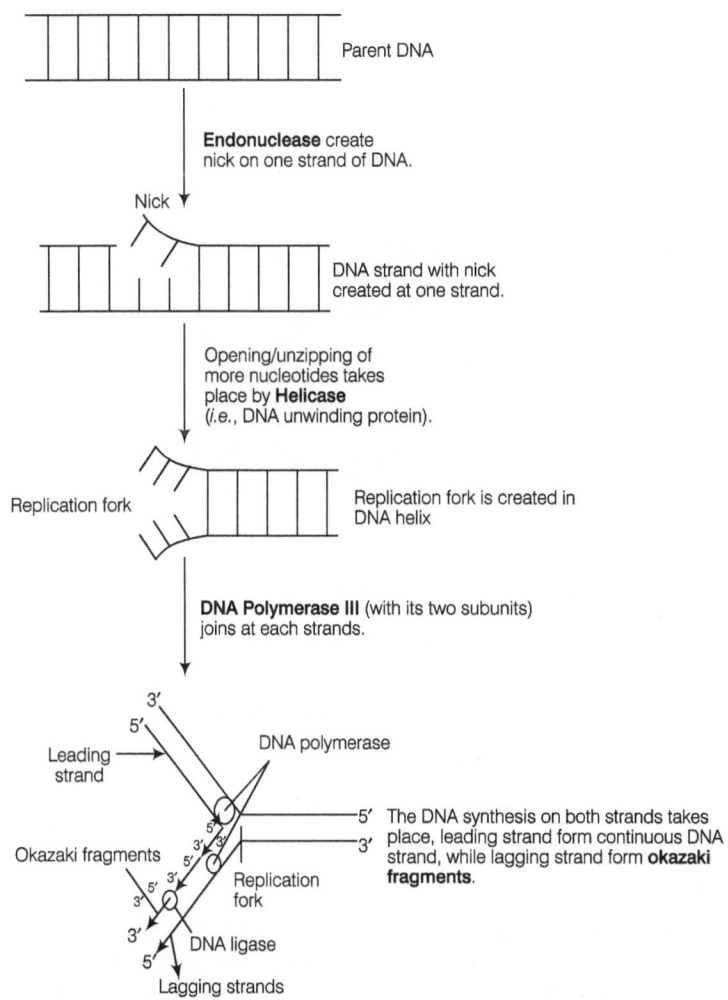

Process of DNA replication

As DNA replication can only occur in $5' \rightarrow 3'$ direction, hence it is continuous on one strand (leading) and in form of small fragments, by forming loop (trombone loop) at another strand (lagging strand).

The DNA synthesis on both the strands can be seen clearly through following figure

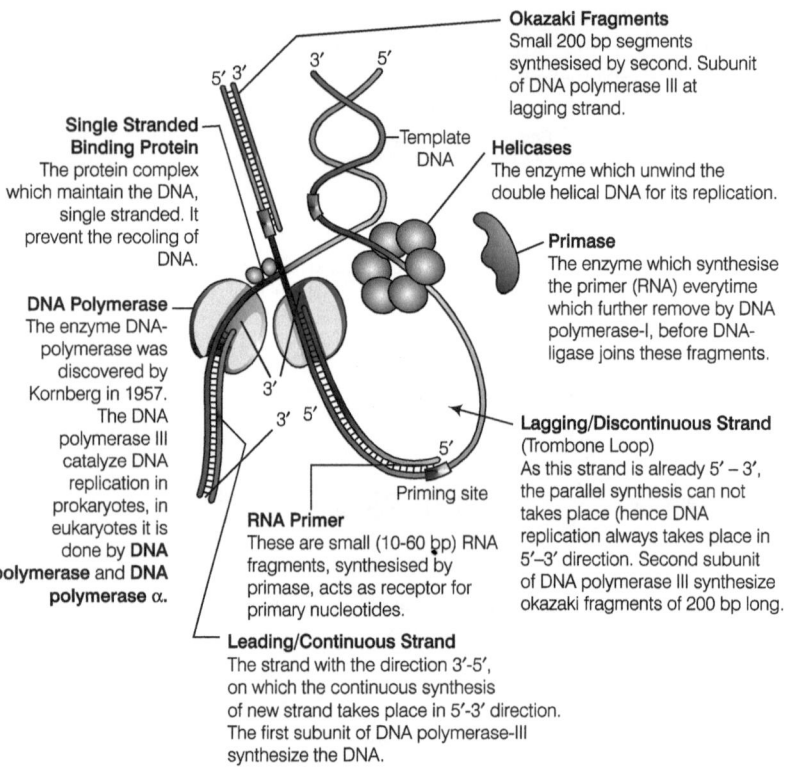

Mechinary of DNA replication (clearly showing trombone loop)

RNA

The other nucleic acid present in cell is RNA, *i.e.*, ribonucleic acid. It is present predominantly in cytoplasm and mostly in form of single strand. The pyrimidine, **thymine of DNA is replaced by uracil in RNA**. All normal RNA chains begin with adenine or guanine.

The RNA can be of following three types
1. *m*RNA or messenger RNA or template RNA.
2. Ribosomal RNA or *r*RNA.
3. Soluble RNA or transfer RNA or *t*RNA.

1. Messenger or *m*RNA or Template RNA

It makes 3 – 5% of total cellular RNA. The sedimentation coefficient of *m*RNA is 8S. The name messenger RNA was proposed by **Jacob** and **Monod** (1961).

The structural components of mRNA includes
  (i) CAP (at 5′ end)
  (ii) Non-coding region-1
  (iii) Initiation codon (AUG)
  (iv) Coding region
  (v) Termination codon
  (vi) Non-coding region - 2
  (vii) Poly A sequence (at 3′ end)

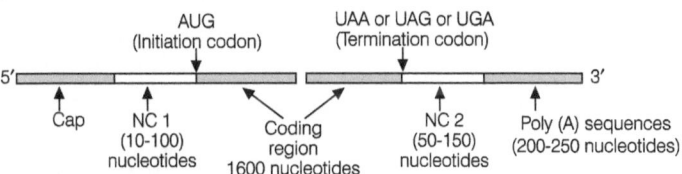

Structure of *m*RNA

The *m*RNA formed in nucleus, comes out with proteins into cytoplasm and normally swim as spherical balls, known as **informosomes**.

2. Ribosomal RNA or *r*RNA

It makes about 80% or more of total cellular RNA. It is the basic constituents of ribosomes and developed from the Nucleolar Organiser Region (NOR) of chromosomes in eukaryotes. It prokaryote, it is developed from *r*DNA.

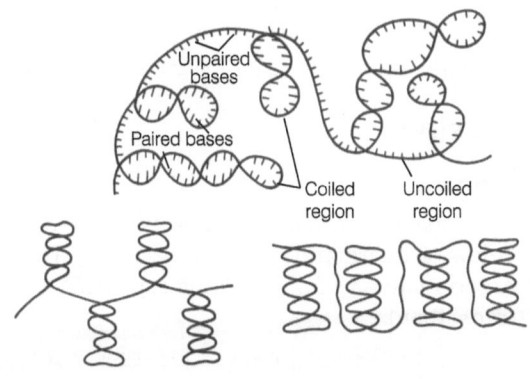

Structure of ribosomal RNA (schematic)

There are three types of rRNA present
  (i) High molecular weight rRNA (mol. wt > 1 million)
      e.g., 21S – 29S rRNA.
  (ii) High molecular weight rRNA (mol. wt < 1 million)
      e.g., 12S – 18S rRNA.
  (iii) Low molecular weight rRNA (mol. wt ~ 40000) e.g., 5S rRNA.

3. Transfer or *t*RNA or Soluble RNA

It makes about 10 – 20% of total cellular RNA with sedimentation coefficient of 3.8 S. It contain 73 – 93 nucleotides.

*t*RNA is synthesised in nucleus on DNA templetes. About 0.25% of DNA codes for *t*RNA. The chief function of *t*RNA is to carry amino acids to ribosomes for protein synthesis.

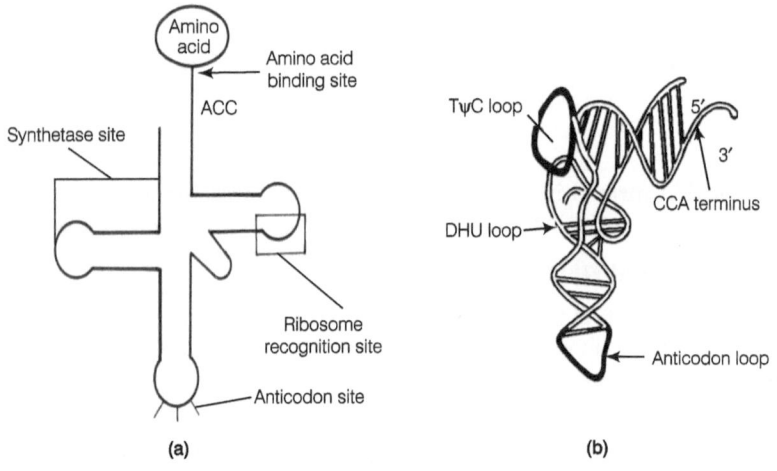

*t*RNA (a) The binding sites (b) The tertiary structure

Gene Expression

Central Dogma

Central dogma of molecular biology states that there is one way or unidirectional flow of information from master copy DNA to working copy RNA (transcription) and from working copy RNA to building plan polypeptide (translation).

$$\text{DNA} \xrightarrow{\text{Transcription}} m\text{RNA} \xrightarrow{\text{Translation}} \text{Polypeptide}$$

Central dogma of molecular biology was proposed by **Crick** (1958). *It is also written as follows*

DNA $\xrightarrow{\text{Replication}}$ DNA $\xrightarrow{\text{Transcription}}$ mRNA $\xrightarrow{\text{Translation}}$ Polypeptide

In this dogma genetic information is stored in the 4 letters language of DNA and same is transferred during transcription to 4 letter language of messenger.

Commoner (1968) suggested a circular flow of information.

DNA ⟶ RNA ⟶ Proteins ⟶ RNA ⟶ DNA

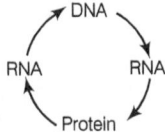

Temin (1970) found that **retroviruses** perform Central Dogma reverse that involves reverse transcription (forming DNA from RNA).

DNA $\underset{\text{Reverse Transcription}}{\overset{\text{Transcription}}{\rightleftarrows}}$ RNA $\xrightarrow{\text{Translation}}$ Polypeptide

Transcription or RNA synthesis occurs over DNA. Translation or protein synthesis occurs over ribosomes. These two are separated in time and space. This protects DNA from respiratory enzymes and RNAs from nucleases.

Transcription

The transfer of information from DNA strand to RNA is termed as transcription. It occurs in the nucleus during G_1 and G_2-phases of cell cycle.

Like DNA replication, it also proceeds in 5' → 3' direction and it require the enzyme **RNA polymerase**. In prokaryotes, only one RNA polymerase is involved in transcription (with its 5 polypeptide subunits – σ, β, β' and 2α), while in eukaryotes, *the transcription performed by three RNA polymerases*

  (i) **RNA polymerase-I**   Synthesise large rRNAs.
 (ii) **RNA polymerase-II** Synthesise small rRNA and mRNA.
(iii) **RNA polymerase-III** Synthesise small rRNA and tRNA.

Transcription Unit

The segment of DNA that take part in transcription is called transcription unit. *It has three components*

1. A promoter   2. The structural gene   3. A terminator

A schematic presentation of the process of transcription is as follows

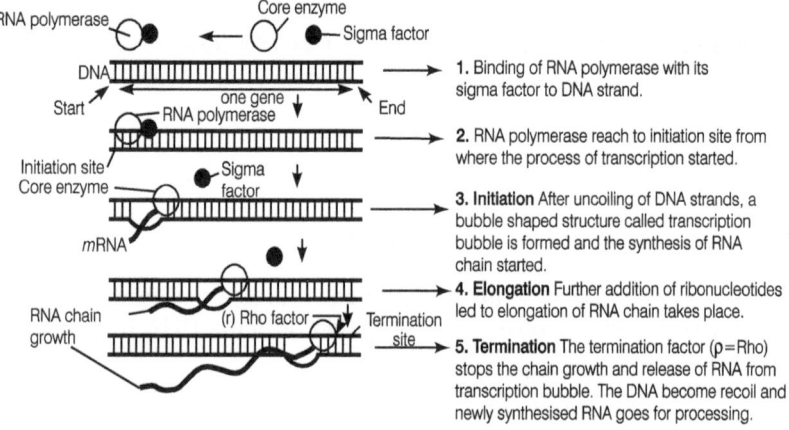

Outline of transcription process

RNA Processing

In Prokaryotes

In prokaryotes there are three enzymes, **RNAse III, RNAse E** and **RNAse P** are responsible for the most of primary endonucleolytic RNA processing events. The first two are proteins, while RNAse P is a **ribozyme**.

These enzymes have unique functions and in their absence the processing events are not performed. On the other hand a large **exonuclease** participate in the trimming of the 3' end of tRNA precursor molecule and they can substitute for each others.

In Eukaryotes

The initial processing steps involves the addition of a cap at 5' end and a tail at 3' end. The primarily synthesised RNA (*i.e.*, Pre mRNAs), these constitute the group of molecule found only in nucleus. *i.e.*, heterogenous nuclear RNA (*hn*RNA). These RNA molecule, in combination with proteins form heterogenous nuclear ribonucleoprotein particles (*hn*RNPs). In general any RNA having sedimentation coefficient more than 8 is called *hn*RNA.

Handbook of BIOLOGY

Capping involve the **formation of a cap at 5′ end** by the condensation of guanylate residues. **Addition of tail at 3′ end** occurs in the form of adding **polyadenylate sequences.**

Genetic Code

The genetic code was discovered by **Nirenberg** and **Matthaei** (1961). The 64 distinct triplets determines the sequence of 20 amino acids on polypeptide chains..

It is defined as

'The nucleotide sequences of nitrogenous bases, which specifies the amino acid sequence in a polypeptide molecule'.

Features of Genetic Code

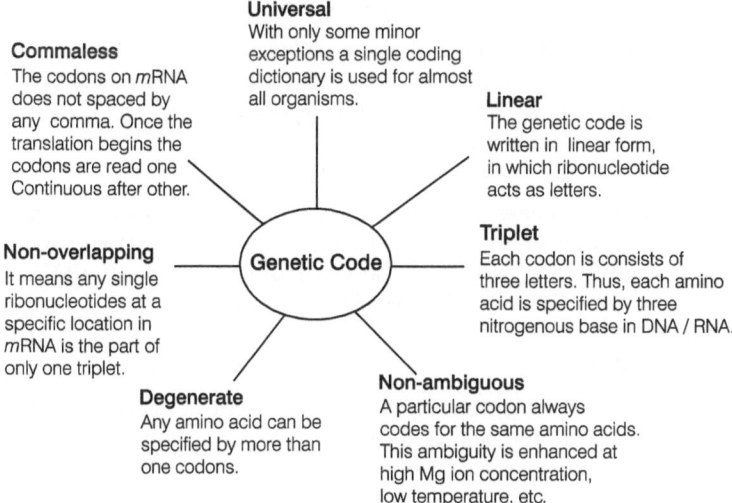

Characteristics of genetic codes

As a result of triplet combination of all ribonucleotides, 64 codons are generated.

Out of these 64 triplet codons, 3 codons are **stop or non-sense codon** (or termination codon). These are nucleotide triplets within the *m*RNA that signals the termination of translation. *These stop codons are as*

UAG (Amber), UAA (Ochre) and UGA (Opal).

Sometimes genetic codons shows deviation from their university. *e.g.*, in *Mycoplasma capricolum*, yeast and humans, the stop codon UGA codes for tryptophan while in several prokaryotes it codes for amino acid **Selenocysteine**. In humans the codon AGA (for arginine) acts as **stop codon**.

Mostly codons are non-ambiguous (*i.e.*, particular codon codes for same amino acid), But in certain rare cases the genetic code is found to be **Ambiguous** *i.e.*, some codons, codes for different amino acids under different conditions, for example, in streptomycin sensistive strain of *E. coli*, the codon UUU, normally codes for phenyl alanine but, it may also codes for isoleucine, leucine or serine when ribosomes are treated with **Streptomycin**. This ambiguity is enhanced, at high Mg ion concentration, low temperature and in the presence of ethyl alcohol.

Wobble Hypothesis (Crick; 1966)

According to this 'The major degeneracy occurs at the third position, while first two bases does not change. The third base is called **Wobble base**.' This wobble base of codon lacks specificity and the base in the first position of anticodon is usually abnormal, *e.g.*, inosine, pseudouridine and tyrosine.

These abnormal bases are able to pair up with more than one nitrogenous bases at the same position, *e.g.*, inosine (I) can pair up with **A**, **C** and **U**. The pairing between unusual base of *t*RNA and wobble base of *m*RNA is called **wobble pairing**.

Translation

The process in which genetic information present in *m*RNA directs the order of specific amino acid to form a polypeptide chain.

Handbook of BIOLOGY

The process of translation can be summarised as

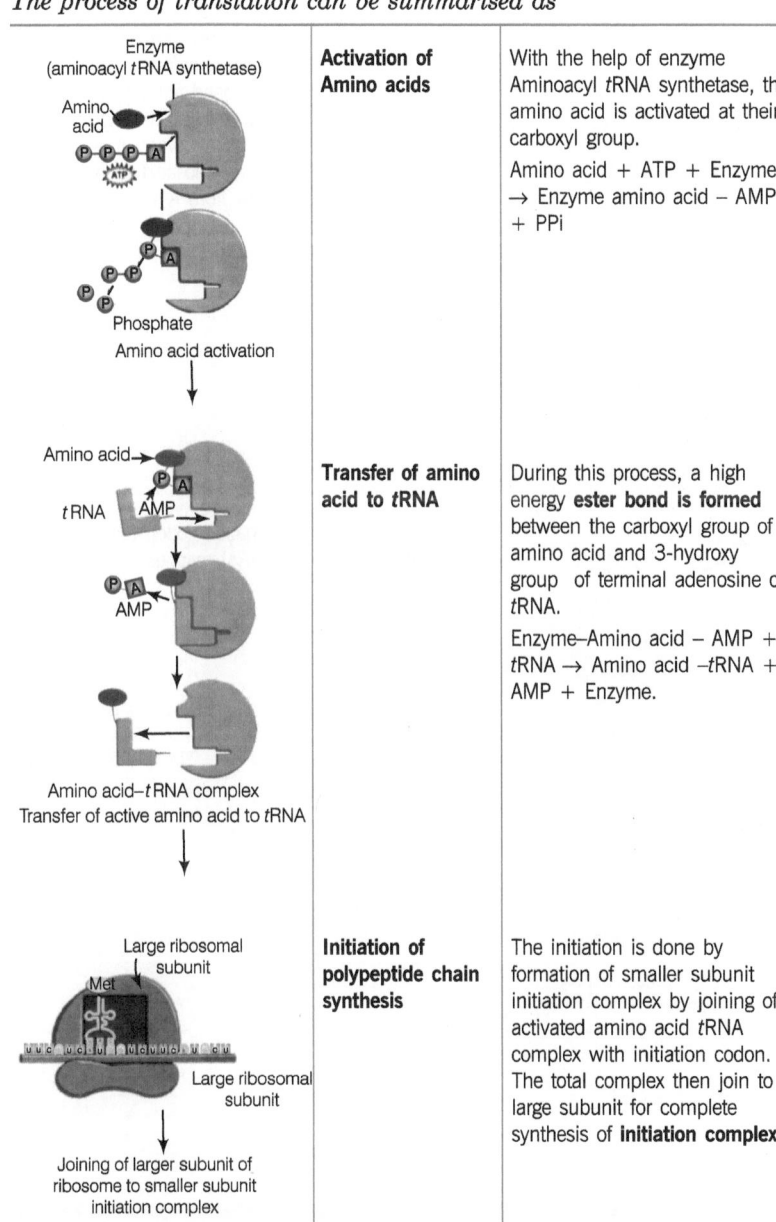

Amino acid activation figure	**Activation of Amino acids**	With the help of enzyme Aminoacyl tRNA synthetase, the amino acid is activated at their carboxyl group. Amino acid + ATP + Enzyme → Enzyme amino acid − AMP + PPi
Transfer of active amino acid to tRNA figure	**Transfer of amino acid to tRNA**	During this process, a high energy **ester bond is formed** between the carboxyl group of amino acid and 3-hydroxy group of terminal adenosine of tRNA. Enzyme–Amino acid − AMP + tRNA → Amino acid −tRNA + AMP + Enzyme.
Joining of larger subunit of ribosome to smaller subunit initiation complex figure	**Initiation of polypeptide chain synthesis**	The initiation is done by formation of smaller subunit initiation complex by joining of activated amino acid tRNA complex with initiation codon. The total complex then join to large subunit for complete synthesis of **initiation complex**.

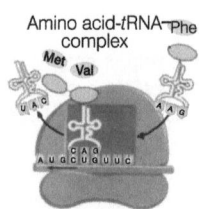 Chain elongation	**Elongation of polypeptide chain**	The enzyme which helps in **peptide bond formation** is peptidyle transferase. After peptide bond formation, translocation occurs, which involve the movement of second amino acid tRNA complex from A-site to P-site.
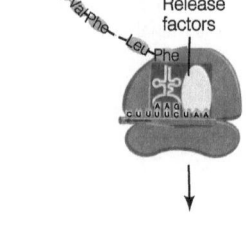 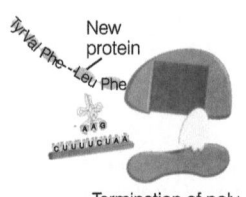 Termination of poly peptide chain formation	**Termination of polypeptide chain formation**	Termination codon (UAG, UGA and UAA) reaches the ribosome and terminate the polypeptide synthesis.

Regulation of Gene Expression

Gene regulation is the mechanism of **switching off** and **switching on** of the gene depending upon the requirement of cells and the state of the development.

(A) Control of Gene Expression in Prokaryotes

The hypothesis of this regulation was given by **F Jacob** and **J Monad** the hypothesis is known as **Operon model**. The theory was given on the basis of study of *lac* (lactose) **operon** in *E. coli*.

The operon consists of following components
  (i) Regulator gene
  (ii) Promoter gene
  (iii) Operator gene
  (iv) Structural gene

The first three genes among above genes are producing three compounds, *i.e.*, repressor, inducer and corepressor.

Repressor has capacity to bind on operator gene only after activation by **corepressor**. Another protein **inducer** have the capacity to blind on operator as well as **repressor**.

The complete operon looks like

Regulator	Promoter	Operator	Structural Gene		
			z	y	a
1200 bp	30 bp	35 bp	3063 bp	800 bp	800 bp
Regulator is responsible for the synthesis of protein called **repressor**. The **active repressor** is seen in inducible system, while **inactive repressor** is seen in repressible system.	It is the segment at which RNA polymerase binds. It initiate the transcription of structural gene and control the rate of *m*RNA synthesis.	This segment of DNA impose control over the transcription. This region works like 'on' and 'off' switch for protein synthesis.	This region of the DNA codes for the synthesis of proteins. These determine the primary structure of polypeptide.		

On the basis of their activity principles, the operons are of two types

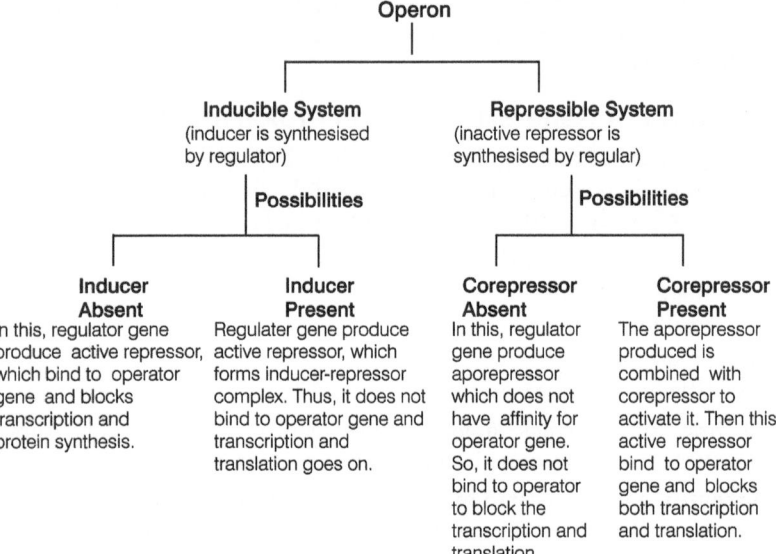

(B) Control of Gene Expression in Eukaryotes

In eukaryotes, the most accepted theory, *i.e.,* **Operon-Operator Model** of **Britton-Davidson** (1969).

According to this model, the eukaryotic operon contain four basic type of genes

(i) **Sensor** These gene segment are sensitive to cellular environment.

(ii) **Interogator** These acts as carrier of signal from sensor to receptor.

(iii) **Receptor** The signal is received by these genes. These are associated with produce.

(iv) **Producer** These are output control centre.

The gene regulation can be occur at various levels

1. At the level of transcription
2. At the level of RNA processing and splicing
3. At the level of translation

Human Genome Project (HGP)

HGP was the international, collaborative research programme, whose goal was the complete mapping and understanding of all the genes of human beings, *i.e.*, genome.

HGP has revealed that there are probably about 20500 human genes. The completed human gene sequence can now identify their locations. The ultimate result of HGP is 'The detailed information about structure, organisation and function of the complete set of human gene.'

The **International Human Genome Sequencing Consortium** published the first draft of the human genome in the journal **nature** in February 2001 with the sequence of the entire genome's 3 billion bp some 90% complete. The full sequence was completed and published in April 2003.

Following processes involved in completion of HGP
- DNA sequencing
- The Employment of Restriction Fragment Length Polymorphisms (RFLP)
- Yeast Artificial Chromosomes (YAC)
- Bacterial Artificial Chromosomes (BAC)
- The Polymerase Chain Reaction (PCR)
- Electrophoresis

30
Biotechnology : Principles *and* Processes

Biotechnology is the scientific technology which uses living organisms in the systems or processes for the manufacturing of useful products/services for human beings.

The term **biotechnology** was coined in 1917 by **Karl Ereky** to describe a process for large scale production of pigs.

Principle of Biotechnology

Among many, the two core techniques that enabled the birth of modern biotechnology are

1. Alternation of constituents of genetic material (DNA or RNA) to change the phenotype of resultant organisms.
2. Production of the large number of microbes/eukaryotic cells in controlled environment to manufacture various products.

Research Areas of Biotechnology

1. Production of improved organisms or pure enzymes.
2. Creating optimal conditions for a catalyst to act.
3. Technologies to purify proteins, organic compounds, etc.

Genetic Engineering/Recombinant DNA Technology/Gene Cloning

It is the technology involved in the synthesis of artificial genes, repair of genes and all other types of manipulation in genes and genomes of any organism.

The method of genetic engineering is completed in following stages/steps
 1. Isolation of a particular gene segment or DNA from an organism.
 2. Introduction of identified DNA into vector DNA to form rDNA.
 3. Introduction of rDNA into host.
 4. Selection of host progeny in which rDNA is present (*i.e.*, selection of hybrids).
 5. Formation of multiple copies of these hybrids (*i.e.*, cloning).

For the isolation of particular gene or DNA, specific enzymes, called **endonucleases** are used. The obtained fragments may be **blunt** or **sticky ended**.

For the transfer of the desired DNA from one organism to other, it should be **added with the microbial vector**. As a result of integration of vector DNA and desired DNA, rDNA is produced. These rDNAs are formed primarily in vectors.

Through vectors, these rDNAs are transferred to host where they integrate with the host DNA and copied several times. Among the total progeny organisms, only some of the organisms/cells have rDNA present in it, called hybrids.

After selecting these hybrids, the process of cloning takes place in which several copies of the same genetic constituents are produced, called **clones**. As a result of insertion of these clones, the **desired phenotypes/products** can be obtained.

A large number of products of various categories and applications are obtained from biotechnological processes. These products are used in various fields as agriculture therapeautics, textiles, environmental management, etc.

490 Handbook of BIOLOGY

Diagrammatic presentation of process of gene cloning is given below

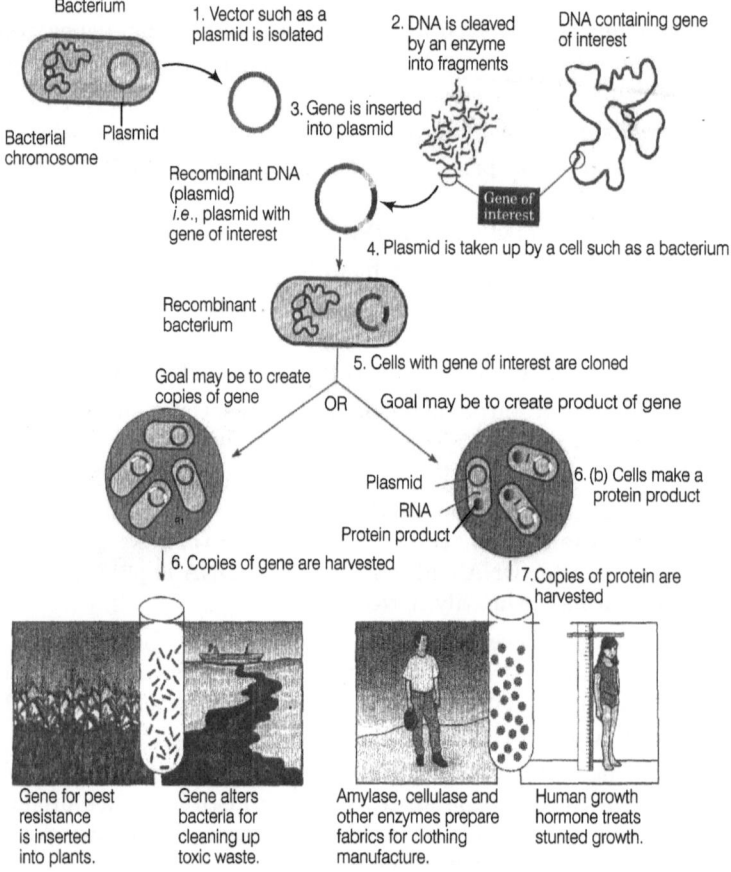

Basic steps in biotechnology

Tools of rDNA Technology

1. Restriction Endonucleases

The most important tool in biotechnology is restriction enzymes. These belongs to the large family of enzymes called **nucleases**. These were discovered by **Arber** in 1962.

These enzymes have the ability to recognise the certain nucleotide sequence and make 4-8 bp long cuts on these sequences. They were named restriction endonuclease because they have the ability to **restrict phage infection among bacteria**. Due to their function, they are also **known as molecular scissors** or **chemical scalpals**.

W Arber, H Smith and **D Nathans** in 1978, were awarded with Nobel Prize in medicine and physiology for their pioneering work in the study of restriction endonucleases.

The restriction enzymes can be of 3 types, on the basis of their chemical and physiological properties.

The comparative account of these enzymes is given in the following table

Features	Type I Enzyme	Type II Enzyme	Type III Enzyme
Protein structure	Bifunctional enzyme with 3 subunits	Separate endonuclease and methylase	Bifunctional enzyme with 2 subunits
Recognition site	Bipartite and asymmetrical (e.g., TGAC and TGCT)	Short sequence (4-6 bp), often Palindromic	Asymmetrical sequence of 5-7 bp
Cleavage site	Non-specific >1000 bp from recognition site	Same as or close to recognition site	24-26 bp down stream of recognition site
Restriction and methylation	Mutually exclusive	Separate reactions	Simultaneous
ATP needed for restriction	Yes	No	Yes
Mg^{2+} needed for restriction	Yes	Yes	Yes
Commonly used in	Random cutting and fragments making	Gene manipulation	Gene cloning

As a result of treatment with restriction endonucleases, *two types of DNA fragments are produced*.

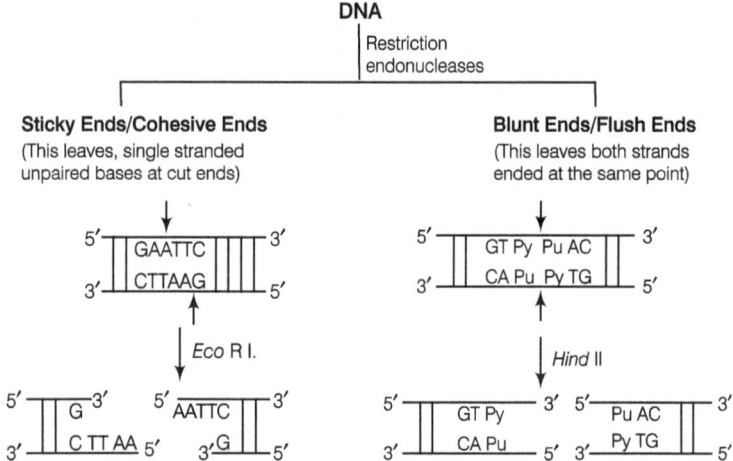

Nomenclature of Restriction Endonucleases

The name of the enzyme is derived from the name of organism from which it is isolated.

(a) The first letter of the genus become the first letter of the name (written in capital letter).

(b) First two letters of the species make second and third letter of the enzyme (written in small letters).

(c) All these three letters are written in italics.

(d) The fourth letter of the name of enzyme is the first letter of strain (written in capital latter).

(e) The roman number written at the end of the name indicates the order of discovery of enzyme from that strain.

2. Exonucleases

These enzymes remove nucleotides from the terminal ends (either 5' or 3') of DNA in one strand of duplex.

3. Lysing Enzymes

These enzymes are used for the isolation of DNA from cells. *e.g.,* lysozyme is used to digest the bacterial cell wall for the extraction of cellular DNA. Protease, lipase and other degrading enzymes comes in this category.

4. Synthesising Enzymes

With the help of these enzymes the synthesis of DNA takes place on the suitable templates. *They are of two types*

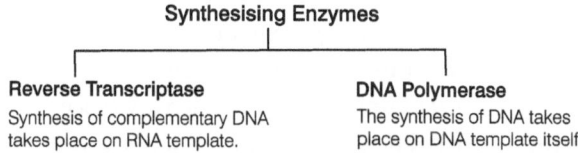

Reverse Transcriptase
Synthesis of complementary DNA takes place on RNA template.

DNA Polymerase
The synthesis of DNA takes place on DNA template itself.

5. DNA Ligase/Sealing Enzyme/Joining Enzyme

These enzymes help in sealing the gaps in DNA fragments, which are joined by complementary base pairing. They act as **molecular glue**, join DNA fragments by **forming phosphodiester bond**, *e.g.*, T_4-liagse of bacteriophage can join both cohesive and blunt ended fragments, hence used in DNA cloning. The ligase of *E.coli* is ineffective to join blunt end DNA, hence, it is not used in gene cloning.

6. Alkaline Phosphatase

These catalyses the removal of 5' phosphate group from the DNA and thus modify the terminus of DNA.

$$5' G_{OH} \ 3' \qquad \xrightarrow{\text{Alkaline Phosphatase}} \qquad 5' G_{OH} \ 3'$$
$$3' C_p T_p T_p A_p A_p \ 5' \qquad\qquad\qquad 3' C_p T_p T_p A_p \ \boxed{A_{OH}} \ 5'$$

After the treatment of alkaline phosphatase to the DNA, both **recircularisation** and **plasmid dimer formation** can be prevented as DNA ligase can not join the ends.

7. S_1- Nuclease

This enzyme converts cohesive ends of the duplex DNA to blunt or flush ends by trimming away the single strand.

8. Linkers and Adapters

Linkers are **single stranded**, synthetic oligonucleotide which self associate to form symmetrical double stranded molecule containing the recognition sequence for a restriction enzymes.

Adaptor molecules are chemically synthesised DNA molecule. They are used in 5' hydroxyl form to prevent self polymerisation.

9. Plasmid Vector

Plasmids are **double stranded**, closed **circular** DNA molecules which exist in the cell as **extra chromosomal units**. They are self replicating and found in variety of bacterial species.

There are three general classes of plasmids

(i) **Virulence plasmids** Encode toxic genes.

(ii) **Drug resistance plasmids** Provide resistance.

(iii) **Conjugation related plasmids** Encode genes for bacterial conjugation.

It was discovered by **William Hayes** and **Joshua Lederberg** in 1952. Plasmids ranges in size from 1-200kb and depends on the host protein for their maintenance and replication function.

10. Cosmid Vector

Cosmids are formed by the combination of plasmids and 'cos' sites of phage lambda (λ). It has the capacity to transfer the DNA of up to 45 kbp. This vector can be packaged into λ-phage. This is more efficient than plasmid transformation.

A typical plasmid vector contains

(i) A plasmid origin of replication

(ii) Selectable markers

(iii) Suitable restriction enzyme sites.

(iv) Lambda (λ) 'cos' site.

11. Phagemid Vectors

It is a composite structure made up of bacteriophage and plasmids. These have the capacity to carry larger DNA molecules.

12. Shuttle Vectors

Plasmid vectors can replicate only in *E. coli*. The cloning vectors which can transfer the genes into eukaryotic organisms are shuttle vectors.

13. Artificial Cloning Vectors

These vectors are artificially constructed.

Following are some artificial cloning vectors

(i) $_p$BR 322 Vector

This was the first artificial cloning vector constructed in 1977 by **Boliver** and **Rodriguez**.

It possesses the following characteristics
  (a) **Size** 4.36 kb (double stranded cloning vector)
  (b) *Contains two antibiotic resistasnce gene*
     - Ampicillin resistance (amp^R)
     - Tetracycline resistance (tet^R)

It contain 20 unique recognition sites for restriction endonucleases.

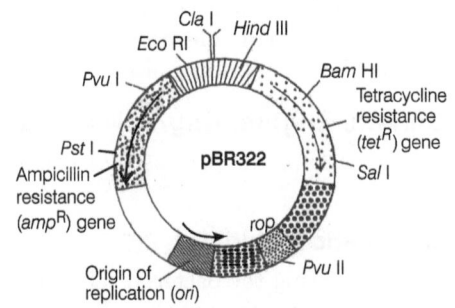

Diagram showing essential features of plasmid $_p$BR 322

(ii) Bacterial Artificial Chromosome (BAC)

This vector is based on the natural, extra chromosomal plasmid of *E.coli*. It can accomodate up to 300-350 kbp of foreign DNA and it can also be used in genome sequencing project.

It contain genes for **replication and maintenance of F-factor.**

(iii) Yeast Artificial Chromosomes (YAC)

These vectors **contain telomeric sequences**, the centromere and the autonomously replicating sequence from yeast chromosomes. It is used to clone the DNA fragments of **more than 1 mb** in size.

14. Transposons

These are the DNA sequences which can change their location in the genome and hence, known as **mobile DNA** or transposons. The activator (Ac) and dissociated (Ds) are the popular transposons of maize which are also called **Ac-Ds elements**. The transposons of *Drosophila* are known as **P-elements**.

Characteristics of a Cloning Vectors

The following features are essential to facilitate cloning into a vector

(i) A vector should contain a **replicon** that enable it to replicate in the host cells.

(ii) It should have several **marker gene**s.

(iii) It should have a unique **cleavage site** within one of the marker gene.

(iv) For the expression of cloned DNA, the vector DNA should contain **suitable control elements** such as promoter, terminators and ribosome binding sites.

Processes of Genetic Engineering/rDNA Technology

Genetic engineering is a complex process which can be studied in following steps

(i) Isolation of the Genetic Material

This can be achieved by treating the bacterial cells/plant/animal tissues with enzymes such as lysozyme (bacterial), cellulase (plant cells) and chitinase (fungus), etc.

The complete schematic representation of the process is as follows

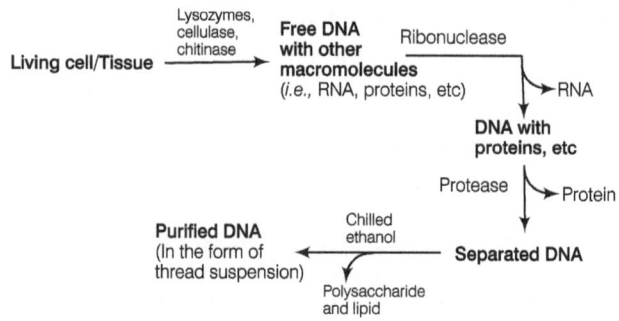

Method to isolate DNA

In order to cut the DNA with restriction enzyme, it needs to be in pure form.

(ii) Cutting of DNA at Specific Location

The purified DNA fragments are treated with restriction enzyme at optimal conditions of that enzyme. After certain period, **agarose gel electrophoresis** is employed to check the progression of restriction enzyme digestion and separation of DNA fragments.

Gel Electrophoresis

Electrophoresis is a technique of separation of charged molecules under the influence of an electrical field so that, they migrate in the direction of electrode through a medium/matrix.

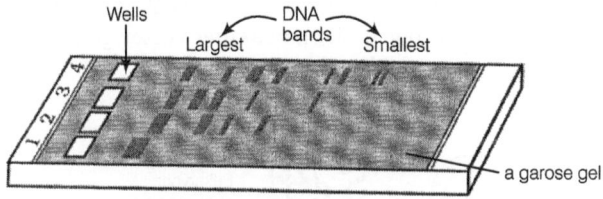

A typical gel electrophoresis showing undigested and digested DNA fragments.

The smallest fragments of DNA settle down fastly to the lowest regions while the largest DNA fragments become undigested and remain at topmost region of the agarose gel column.

(iii) Amplification/Copying of Gene of Interest Using PCR

Polymerase Chain Reaction (PCR) is a technique of synthesising multiple copies of the desired gene (or DNA) *in vitro*. This was developed by **Kary Mullis** in 1985. *The procedure of this reaction is as follows*

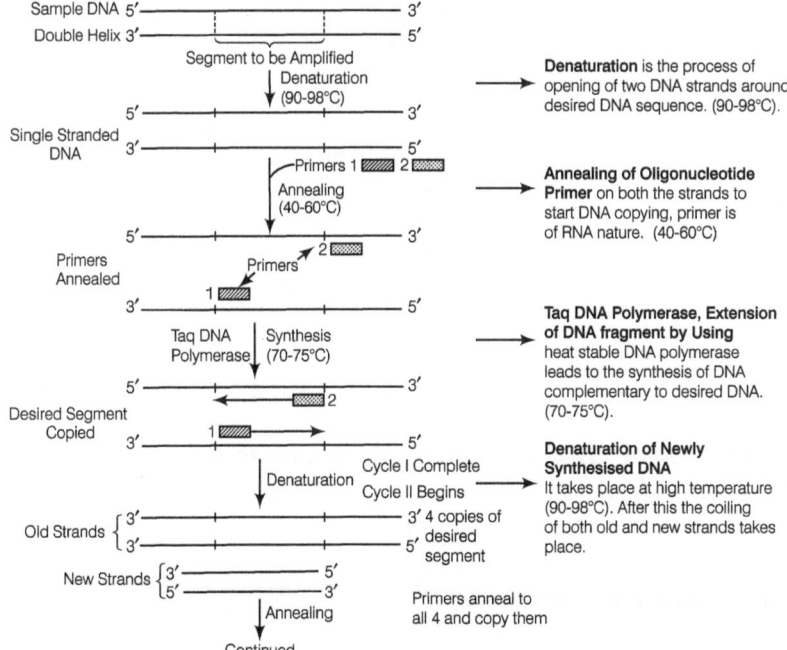

Operation of PCR

(iv) Insertion of DNA Fragments into Vector DNA to form rDNA

After the isolation of target DNA fragment, DNA ligase can be used to join it to a vector digested by the same restriction endonuclease, *e.g.*, a fragment generated by *Eco* RI only join with the cloning vector digested by *Eco* RI, and not with the cloning vector generated by *Bam* HI. *The complete process looks like*

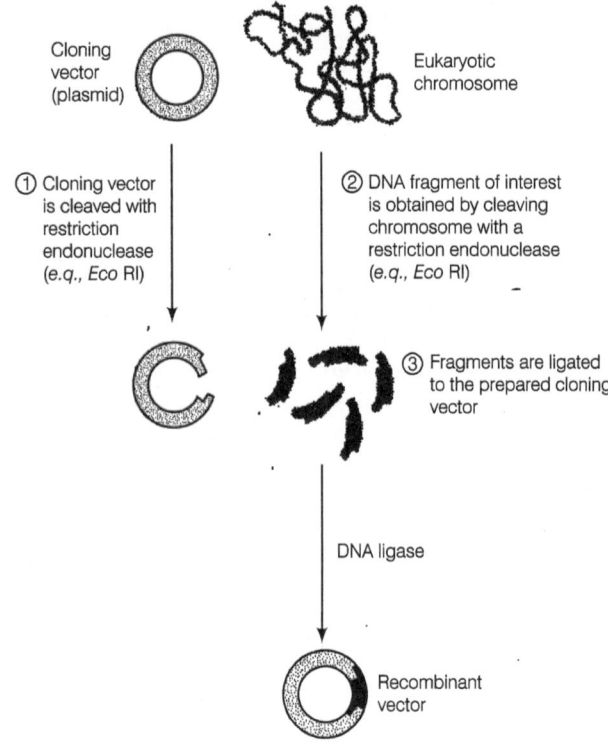

The process of formation of r DNA

(v) Insertion of rDNA into Host Cells/Organisms

The rDNA can be inserted into the host cell through various methods. *Broadly these can be categorised into*

(i) Vector mediated gene transfer
(ii) Vectorless gene transfer.

Handbook of BIOLOGY

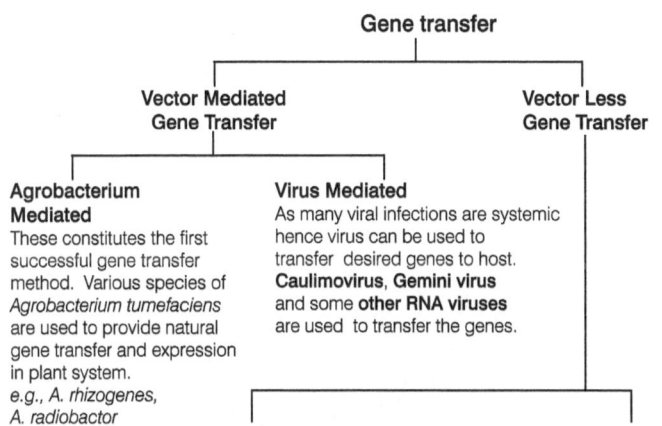

- **Physical Gene Transfer Methods Electroporation**
  Here high electrical impulses (1-1.5 kV) are used to insert the DNA into host.
- **Particle Bombardment/Biolistics**
  In this, the DNA coated on gold or tungsten is fired on host through gene gun.
  Macro injection
  It is the injection of DNA solution (5-10 μl) by micro pipette into the host tissues.
- **Microinjection**
  It is the direct mechanical introduction of DNA into the target cell.
- **Liposome Mediated Transformation**
  Artificial lipid vasicles are used to transfer DNA to host.
- **Silicon Carbide Fibre Mediated Transformation**
  The fibres of 10-80 μm length are used to deliver DNA into target cells.
- **Ultrasound Mediated Transformation**
  An acoustic intensity of 0.5 W/cm^2 for 30 mins. is sufficient to take foreign DNA by protoplast.
- **Pollen Mediated Transformation**
  The introduction of DNA into gametes can occur through this method.

- **Chemical Gene Transfer Methods**
  PEG (Poly ethylene glycol mediated transfer) The first integration of isolated Ti-plasmid DNA into plant protoplast was reported in the **Petunia** and **tobacco** in the presence of **PEG**. The 40% solution of PEG creates small pores in the plasma membranes which helps in the integration of linear DNA into random sites on host DNA.
- **Calcium Phosphate Coprecipitation**
  In this, the DNA CaPO$_4$ complex is added to dividing cells to transfer DNA.
- **Polycation, DMSO Technique**
  Use of polycation to increase adsorption of DNA on host cell.
- **DEAE Dextran Procedure**
  DNA complexed with diethyl amino ethyl. This method does not produce stable transformants.

(vi) **Selection/Screening of Hybrids**

The selection of hybrid with rDNA can be made by the treatment of resulted solution with the antibiotics (the resistance gene of which antibiotic is already inserted in rDNA). All the hybrids will die which do not contain rDNA and only recombinant hybrids will be reported in the resultant solution.

Bioreactors (Fermenters)

Bioreactors are the vessels in which the raw materials are biologically converted into specific products by microbes, plants and animal cell in a controlled way.

Following figure will give the idea about the structure and operation of a typical bioreactor

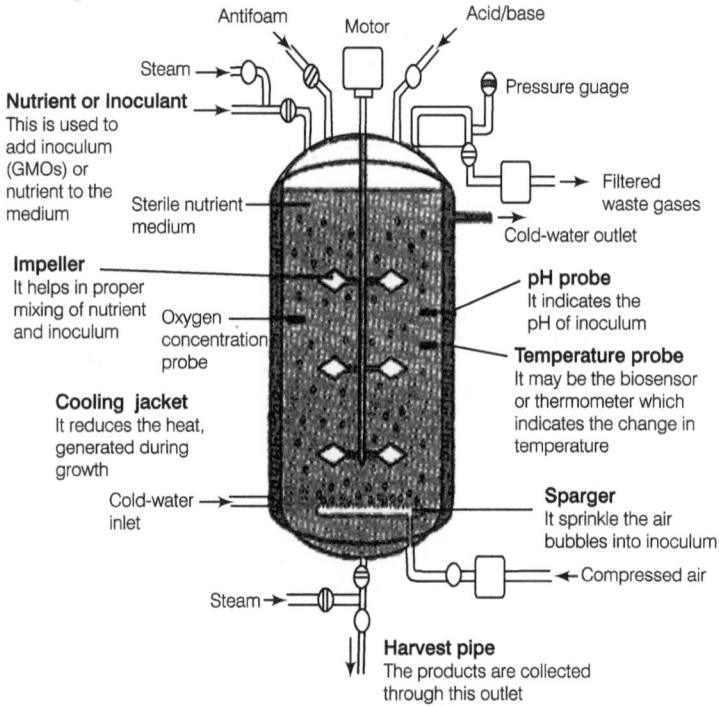

A typical bioreactor

Down Stream Processing

It is the process of separation and **purification** to make a biotechnological product ready for marketing.

After the purification, the product is mixed with certain preservative and taken for comprehensive trials on target individuals.

Before **releasing into the market**, every product has to take the approval by Genetic Engineering Approval Committee (GEAC).

31

Biotechnology and Its Application

Biotechnology is the application of biological system in technology that can only be achieved through the integration of biological, physical and engineering sciences. Biotechnology has tremendous applications in certain areas like healthcare, agriculture, industries, etc.

Red Biotechnology
It is medical biotechnology, applied in designing organisms used to which produce antibiotics or genetic cure products through genomic manipulation.

White Biotechnology
It is the industrial use of biotechnology.

Green Biotechnology
It is the agricultural use of biotechnology.

The applications of biotechnology in various fields are discussed as follows

Application of Biotechnology in Crop Improvement
There are mainly three benefits of biotechnology to agriculture
1. Reduction of duration of breeding period.
2. New methods of hybridisation
3. Application of rDNA technology in agriculture.

(a) Transgenic Crops or GM Crops

It is a crop which contain and expresses a transgene. A more popular term for transgenic crop is **genetically modified crops** or **GM crops**.

The genetic modification may leads to following changes in crops

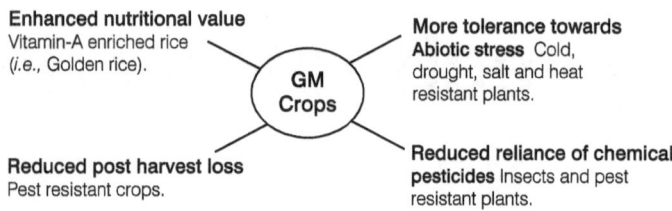

After its integration into host DNA, transgene can perform one of the following functions

(i) **Produces a protein of interest** The gene which produces the protein of our interest is inserted into other organism. *e.g.*, hirudin, a protein that prevent blood clotting. The gene producing hirudin is inserted into the plant *Brassica napus* where the hirudin is synthesised and stored in seeds.

(ii) **Produces a desired phenotype** It produces a protein that, on its own produces the desired phenotype. *e.g.*, crystal (*cry*) protein produced by *Bacillus thuringiensis* (*Bt*) in plants is toxic to the larvae of certain insects.

(iii) **Modify an existing biosynthetic pathway** By this modification, a new end product is obtained. *e.g.*, transgenic rice and transgenic potato produces higher content of vitamin-A and protein, respectively.

(iv) **It masks the expression of native gene** A protein expression masks the existing native gene. *e.g.*, in the tomato variety '*Flavr savr*', the function of the gene producing **polygalacturonase** (pectin degrading enzyme) is blocked which results in the delayed ripening and better nutrient quality.

Other examples of GM crops are

1. ***Bt cotton*** Pest resistant, herbicide tolerant and high yielding plant. It is also resistant to bollworm infestations.
2. **Golden rice** Vitamin-A rich rice.
3. **Potato** With higher protein content.
4. **Corn, brinjal** Insect resistance provided.
5. **Soyabean, maize** Herbicide resistance provided.

(b) Genetically Modified Organisms (GMOs)

The GMOs have various modifications in their metabolism and may have altered phenotypes.

Following table describe the detailed information about several GMOs

Some Genetically Modified Organisms

Organism	Modification
Long life tomatoes	There are two well-known projects, both affecting the gene for the enzyme polygalacturonase (PG), a pectinase that softens fruits as they ripen. Tomatoes that make less PG, ripen more slowly and retain more flavour.
	The American *'Flavr savr'* tomato used **antisense technology** to silence the gene, while the British **Zeneca tomato disrupted the gene**. Both were successful and were on sale for a few years, but neither is produced any more.
Insect-resistant crops	Genes for various powerful protein toxins have been transferred from the bacterium *Bacillus thuringiensis* to crop plants including maize, rice and potatoes.
	These *Bt* toxins are thousands times more powerful than chemical insecticides, and since they are built-in to the crops, insecticide spraying (which is non-specific and damages the environment) is not unnecessary.
Virus-resistant crops	Gene for virus coat protein has been cloned and inserted into tobacco, potato and tomato plants.
	The coat protein seems to 'immunise' the plants which are much more resistant to viral attack.
Herbicide resistant crops	The gene for resistance to the herbicide BASTA has been transferred from *Streptomyces* bacteria to tomato, potato, corn and wheat plants making them resistant to BASTA.
	Fields can safely be sprayed with this herbicide, which will kill all weeds, but not the crops.
Pest-resistant legumes	The gene for an enzyme that synthesises a chemical toxic to weevils has been transferred from *Bacillus* bacteria to the *Rhizobium* bacteria that live in the root nodules of legume plants.
	These root nodules are now resistant to attack by weevils.
Nitrogen-fixing crops	This is a huge project, which aims to transfer about 15 or more genes required for nitrogen fixation from the nitrogen-fixing bacteria *Rhizobium* into cereals and other crop plants.
	These crops would then be able to fix their own atmospheric nitrogen and not need any fertiliser. However, the process is extremely complex.

Organism	Modification
Crop improvement	Proteins in some crop plants, including wheat, are often deficient in essential amino acids (that's why vegetarians have to watch their diet so carefully). So the protein genes are being altered to improve their composition for human consumption.
Mastitis-resistant cattle	The gene for the enzyme lactoferrin, which helps to resists the infection that causes the udder disease mastitis, has been introduced to **Herman-the first transgenic bull**. Herman's offspring inherit this gene and do not get mastitis hence, produce more milk.
Tick-resistant sheep	The gene for the enzyme chitinase, which kills ticks by digesting their exo skeletons has been transferred from plants to sheep. These sheep should be immune to tick parasites and may not need sheep dip.
Fast-growing sheep	The human growth hormone gene has been transferred to sheep, so that they produce human growth hormone and grow more quickly. However, they are more prone to infection and the females are infertile.
Fast-growing fish	A number of fish species, including salmon, trout and carp, have been given a gene from another fish (the ocean pout) which activates the fish's own growth hormone gene so that, they grow larger and more quickly. Salmon grows to 30 times their normal mass at 10 times more than the normal rate.
Environment cleaning microbes	Genes for enzymes that digest many different hydrocarbons found in crude oil have been transferred to *Pseudomonas* bacteria so that they can clean up oil spills.

Bt Cotton (Insect Resistant Cotton)

The bacterium *Bacillus thuringiensis* (*Bt*) is a family of over 200 different proteins which naturally produce chemical harmful to certain insects (as larvae of moths, cotton bollworm and flies) and harmless to other forms of life.

The *Bt* cotton variety, contains a foreign gene obtained from *Bacillus thuringiensis*. This gene protects the plants from bollworm. The worm feeding on the leaves of a *Bt* cotton plant become lethargic and sleepy thereby causing less damage to the plant.

Farmers who grew *Bt* variety, obtained 25-75% more cotton than those who grew the normal variety. The inserted foreign genes are **CryI Ac** and **Cry IIAb** (control the bollworm) and **Cry IAb** (controls the corn borer).

Handbook of BIOLOGY

There are two methods to introduce cry genes into target cells

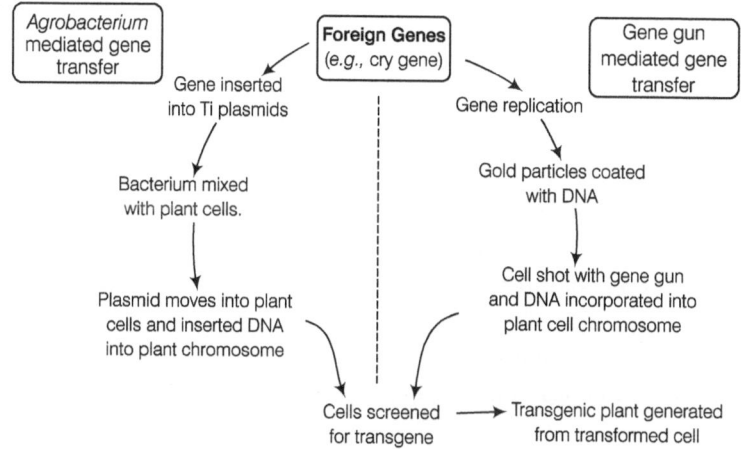

Generation of *Bt* cotton

Application of Biotechnology in Plant Tissue Culture

Plant tissue culture is a novel and innovative technique to grow high quality, disease free plants quickly and in a large quantity by culturing various plant parts. This method is used mostly when the planting material is in scarce amount.

Followings are the methods used in plant tissue culture

(i) **Meristem culture** It is the method of cultivation of axillary or apical shoot meristem. It involves the development of an already existing shoot meristem and subsequently the regeneration of adventitious roots from the developed shoot.

The process of meristem culture is shown in the following flow chart

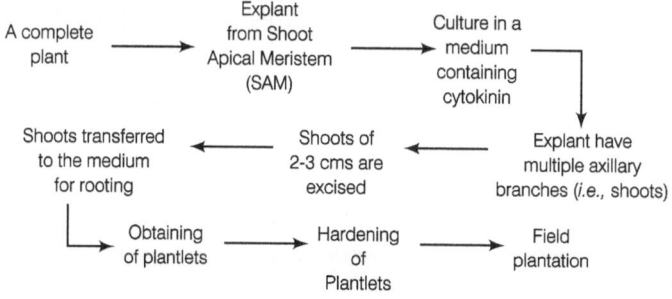

Steps in meristem culture

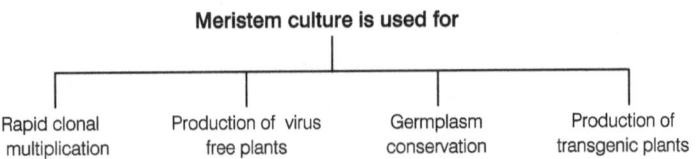

(ii) **Embryo culture** In this method, the embryos removed from the developing seeds are placed on a suitable medium to obtain seedlings.

Embryo culture can be applied to
1. Recovery of interspecific hybrids.
2. Propagation of orchids.
3. Overcoming dormancy.
4. Anther culture and haploid production.

Embryo-nurse Endosperm Technique
The embryo from mature seeds are cultured *in vitro* on developing endosperm. The fresh endosperm is the primary requirement of the developing embryo.

(iii) **Protoplast culture and somatic hybridisation** The production of hybrid plants through the fusion of protoplasts of two different plant species is called somatic hybridisation and the produced hybrids are known as **somatic hybrids** or cybrids.

Protoplast, also known as **naked plant cell** refers to all the components of a plant cell excluding the cell wall.

The technique of somatic hybridisation have following four steps
1. Isolation of protoplasts
2. Fusion of the protoplasts
3. Selection of hybrid cells
4. Culture of hybrid cells (regeneration of hybrid plants).

Handbook of BIOLOGY

The diagrammatic representation of the process of somatic hybridisation is as follows

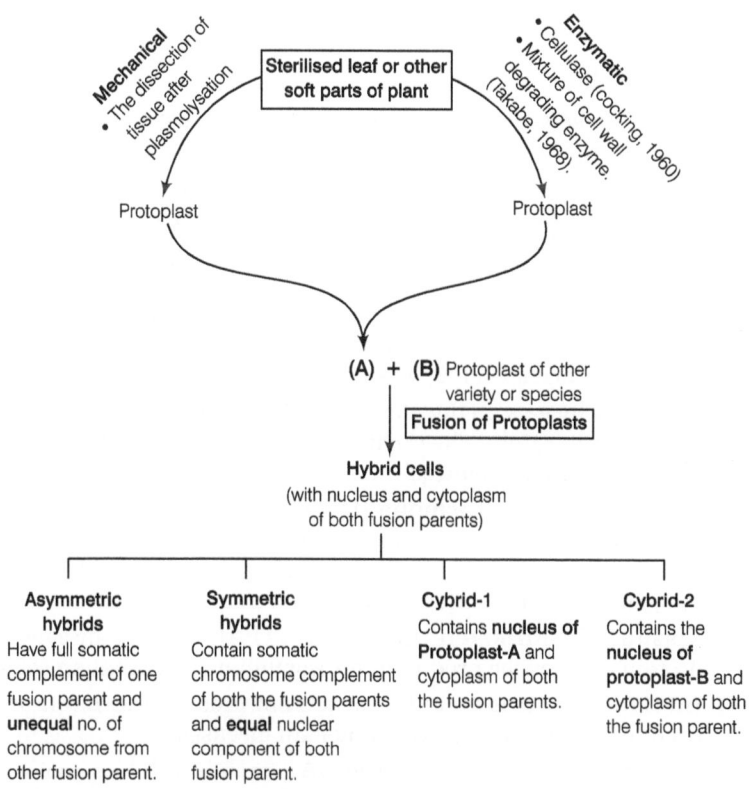

Somatic hybrids have following uses
1. Used for gene transfer and transfer of cytoplasm.
2. Used in the production of useful polyploids.
3. In the development of new crop plants, *e.g.,* pomato (hybrid of potato and tomato), rabbage (hybrid of raddish and cabbage) etc.

Application of Biotechnology in Medicine

With the help of following services, biotechnology imposes immenssse impact on healthcare sector. *It helps in*

(i) Enabling mass production of safe and more effective therapeutic drugs.

(ii) The early diagnosis of diseases for its effective treatment.

The biotechnological applications can be categorised into two groups.
 1. Gene products
 2. Gene therapy

Gene Products

Description of some genetically engineered products are as follows

(a) **Human Insulin** (Humulin) The pancreas produce insulin in humans to regulate the blood sugar concentration. In the absence of enough insulin, the patient develops **wasting symptoms** and **eventually dies.**

Humulin is synthesised for the management of **adult-onset diabetes.** In 1983, an American company **Eli-lily produced first genetically engineered insulin** by synthesising two DNA sequences corresponding to A and B chain of insulin.

This DNA fuses with the plasmid of *E.coli* where both the chains produce separately. These chains are joined by Disulfide Bonds and **humulin** is produced.

(b) **Human Growth Hormone** (HGH) The HGH gene is cloned into *E.coli*, which helps in the treatment of dwarfism in human. This is synthesised by adding a single sequence which causes the gene to be translated and secreted from the cell.

(c) **Tissue Plasminogen Activator** (TPA) A clot dissolving protein can now be produced in recombinant mammalian cells.

(d) **Interferon** It is an antiviral protein produced in *E.coli* and used to fight certain cancers and skin diseases.

(e) α-1 **Anti Trypsin** (AAT) The AAT protein inhibits protease enzymes like trypsin and elastase. Because of mutation (base substitution), the **AAT fails to inhibit elastase** hence, elastase digest the elastic tissue of alveoli and cause **emphysema.**

AAT is now produced in GM sheep where the gene for AAT is coupled with milk producing gene. The AAT is purified from the milk of **GM sheep** (*i.e.*, Tracy).

(f) **Vaccines** It represent another application of *r*DNA technology. The hepatitis-B vaccine (now in use) is composed of viral particles manufactured by yeast cells and recombined with viral genes.

- (g) **Antibiotics** These are produced by fungi such as *Penicillium* and *Cephalosporium* etc., to treat infections caused by bacteria and certain other parasites.
- (h) **Biochips** These are single stranded DNA chains or repeated DNA segments which firmally struck to silica (glass chips) for matching and studying DNA components of unknown composition.
- (i) **ELISA** (Enzyme Linked Immuno Sorbant Assay) It uses an enzyme conjugated to an antibody for the detection of specific antigen/antibody based on antigen-antibody interaction.

Gene Therapy

It is the technique of genetic engineering in which we **replace a faulty gene by a normal healthy functional gene.** This therapy has been tried for sickle-cell anaemia and **Severe Combined Immuno Deficiency (SCID).**

The first clinical gene therapy was performed on a 4-year old girl with Adenosine Deaminase (ADA) deficiency in 1990.

Gene therapy can be visualised in following flow chart

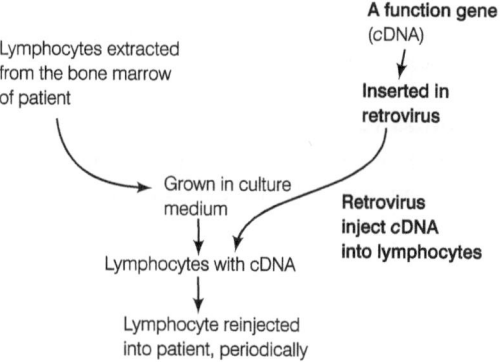

Schematic representation of gene therapy

Cystic Fibrosis

It is the most common genetic disease caused by the mutation in the gene for protein called CFTR (Cystic Fibrosis Transmembrane Regulator).

The gene for CFTR was identified in 1989 and soon after that a cDNA clone was made. This cDNA cloned gene is delivered to epithelial cells of the lungs, where they gets incorporated into nuclear DNA and make functional CFTR chloride channels.

Stem Cells

These cells are present in multicellular organisms that can divide through mitotic division and differentiate into specialised cells.

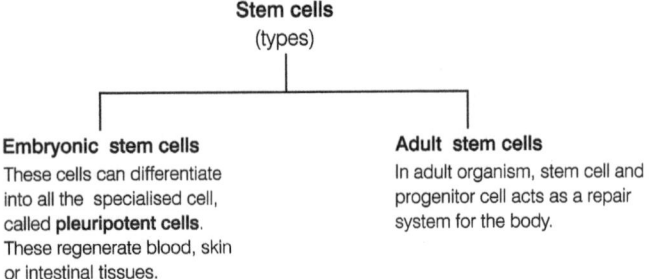

Molecular Diagnostics

It includes all the test and methods to identify a disease analysing DNA or RNA of an organism, e.g., rDNA technology, PCR, ELISA etc.

Application of Biotechnology in Industry

The industrial application of biotechnology is explained in the following presentation

Enzymes
Various enzymes are produced at industrial level such as amylase, used in **brewing**, **baking** and **textile industry**. Other enzyme is *protease*, which is used in **meat**, **leather** and **detergent** industries.

Other Food Items
A food product, sauerkraut (sour cabbage) is produced by the microbial action of *Leuconostoc* and *Lactobacillus* bacteria. Some microbes also used in *pickles* and

Miscellaneous
Amino acids, nucleotides, vitamins and organic acids are also produced by the **microbial action** *Lysine* (used to treat Herpes simplex infection) is a product of the bacterium *Corynebacterium glutamicum*. Viatmin-B_{12} and B_2 are produced by **bacterium** and **mould** respectively. **Xanthan** (use to stabilise and thicken food is produced by *Xanthomonas compestris*.

Mining
Microorganism are highly important to leach low grade ores, to extract their valuable metals. *For example* **copper** and **uranium** can be extracted by *Trichobacillus*.

Biotechnology in Industry

Beverages
Wine, is the aged product of alcoholic fermentation of fruits. The crushed fruit is combined with the *Saccharomyces*. Fermentation takes several days and produce alcoholic product called wine. The **beer** is produced by soaking grains with *Saccharomyces*. The other beverages are **vodka**, **whisky**, **rum**, **sake** etc.

Bakery Industry
It this, the flour, water, salt and yeast are used to make the dough. *Saccharomyces cerivisiae* is used to ferment carbohydrate in the dough and produce CO_2, which creates the soft texture of bread.

Dairy industry

Cheese
The protein portion of the milk, the **casein** is used to produce cheese and cheese products. The **protein curd** which is precipitated from milk is an unripened cheese.

Buttermilk
The dairy product that result from the souring of low fat milk by lactic acid. The flavour is due to substance such as **diacetyl** and **acetaldehyde**. It is produced by *Streptococcus, Leuconostoc* and *Lactobacillus*, etc.

Yogurt
It is a fermented milk product with pudding like consistency. It is produced by *Streptococcus thermophilus* and *Lactobacillus bulgaricus*.

Cheese Product
- **Soft cheese** Such as camembert is a product of growth of the fungus *Penicillium camemberti*.
- **Hard cheese** Have less water and ripened by bacteria or fungi.
- **Swiss cheese** It is ripened by various bacteria such as *Propionibacterium* which produce gas holes in the cheese.
- **Blue cheese** It is produced by *Penicillium roqueforti* which produces vein in the cheese as it.

Application of Biotechnology in Environment

Biotechnology has tremendous potential for unique, efficient, ecofriendly and economically viable options for waste treatment and degradation of hazardous waste into relatively less harmful products. Following biotechnological products helps in the protection of environment.

Biosurfactants

These are **surface active substances** synthesised by several microorganisms like bacteria and yeast. These have the property to **reduce surface tension**, stabilising emulsions and **promoting foaming**.

Biosurfactants have the potential to solubilise hydrocarbon contaminants and increase their availability for microbial degradation. In some bacterial species such as *Pseudomonas neruginosa*, biosurfactants are also involved in a group motility behaviour called swarming motility.

Superbug

It is a modified strain of **oil eating bacteria** which was developed by **Prof. Anand Mohan Chakraborty**. The process of working through which GMOs cleanup several environmental contaminants is known as **bioremediation**. A more general approach to cleanup oil spills is by the addition of fertilisers to facilitate the decomposition of crude oil by bacteria.

Mycofilteration

It is the process using fungal mycelia to filter the toxic waste.

Phytoremediation

It refers to the natural ability of certain plants called **hyperaccumulators** to bioaccumulate, degrade or render harmless contaminants in soil water or air. *e.g,* mustard plants, pigweeds, etc.

Biosensors

These referred as engineered organism (usually a bacterium) that is **capable of reporting some environmental phenomenons** like presence of heavy metals or toxins.

Biofuels

These are a wide range of fuels, which are in some way derived from biomass. Biofuels are gaining increased public and scientific attention driven by factors such as high fuel prices, need for increased energy security and concern over green house gas emission from fossil fuels.

These fuels can be categorised as

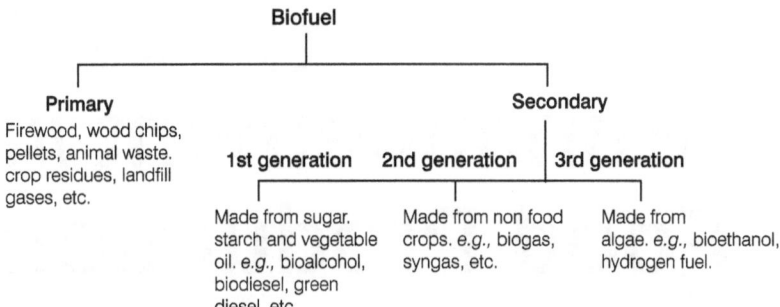

The manipulation of living organisms by the human race needs some regulation on both **ethical** and **moral grounds**. As genetic modification of organisms can have unpredictable results when such organisms are introduced into the ecosystem.

The modification/usage of living organisms for public services has also created problems with **patent** granted for the same.

Biopiracy is the term used to refer to the use of bioresources by companies and other organisation without proper authorisation from the countries and people concerned without compensatory payment.

Biotechnology provides several products of high utility values. Major part of applied biotechnology still remains unex plored which surely will provide the solution of various problems related to humans and their environment.

32

Strategies *for* Enhancement *in* Food Production

According to the theory given by **TR Malthus**, the world's population is increasing geometrically, *i.e.,* 2, 4, 8, so on. As the cropping area isnot increasing significantly, the search for alternate food resources and strategies for enhancement in food production plays an important role.

The advanced techniques in **animal husbandry** and **plant breeding** plays an important role in enhanced food production. Several methods of enhanced food production and their detailed descriptions are given here.

Animal Husbandry

It is the science of rearing, caring, feeding, breeding improvement and utilisation of domesticated animals. It deals with the raising of livestock, poultry farming, fisheries, sericulture, apiculture and lac culture. The animals used for transport, milk, meat and agriculture are collectively called **livestock.**

Despite having large portion of livestock population, India contribute only 25% of world's farm produce, it means that the productivity per unit area is very low.

Management of Farms and Farm Animals

In farm management, we deals with the processes and systems that increases the yield and improve the quality of products.

Better yield primarily depend upon the quality of breed in the farm. For the yield, potential have to be realised and the farm animals have to be well looked after. *Following things should be kept in mind for proper farm management.*
- Farm animals should be housed well.
- They should have proper, scientific diet.
- Farm animals must avail adequate water.
- They should be maintain, disease free.
- Proper maintenance of hygiene and sanitation.

Even after ensuring above measures, a farm should be inspected in regular intervals and the record keeping of these inspection should be maintained.

Livestock

The term 'livestock' is used for domesticated animals and it is a part of modern agriculture. *On the basis of utilities, livestock can be categorised into*

(a) **Milk yielding animals** Cows, buffaloes and goats provides us milk, which is used to obtain animal protein and serves as a perfect natural diet.

(b) **Meat and egg yielding animals** Sheeps, goat, pigs, ducks and fowls provide us meat and eggs.

(c) **Animals utilised as motive power** Buffaloes, horses, donkeys, bullocks, camels and elephants are used in transport and ploughing the fields.

(d) **Wool giving animals** Sheeps are reared for obtaining wool from their hide.

(e) **Miscellaneous uses** The hides of cattle are used for making a variety of leather goods.

Here, several animals of livestock category are described with their detailed descriptions here.

Cow or Zebu

Zebu is sometimes known as **humped cattle**. Cow (*Bos indicus*) is one of the most important milk yielding cattle in the country.

The castrated cow males, *i.e.,* bullocks are used in **farm practices** and **drawing carts**.

Handbook of BIOLOGY

The important Indian breeds and their related aspects are as follows

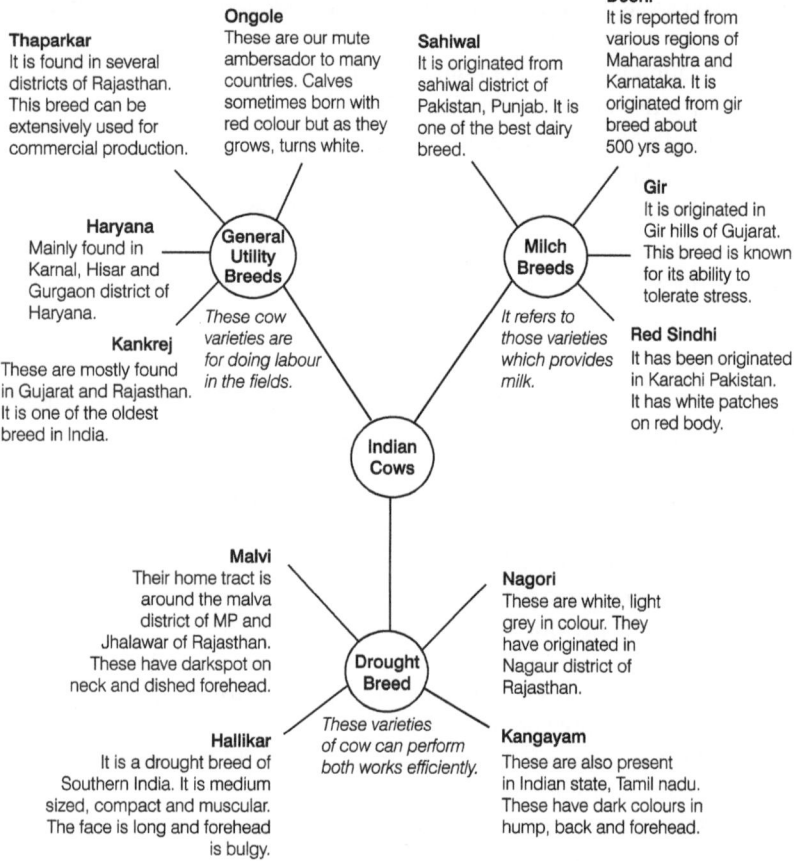

Various cow varieties in India

Buffalo

Indian buffalo is a major cattle raised for milk production. 26 breeds of buffalo are found in India.

Handbook of BIOLOGY

The important Indian breeds are

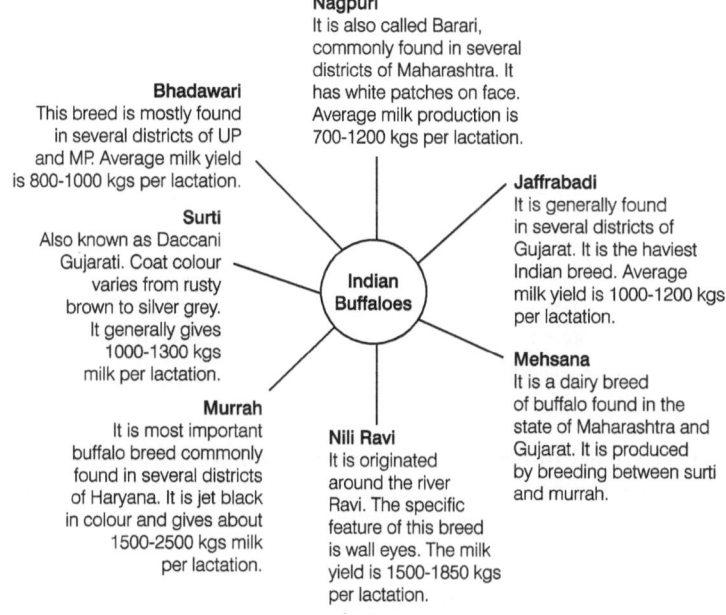

Various buffalo varieties in India

Horse

Horse (*Equus caballus*) is the first beast of burden. Physically it is firm footed, strong, fast runner, intelligent and barns easily. Breeds of Indian horses and the regions in which, *they are found is shown in the following table*

Breeds of Indian Horses

Name	Regions
Manipuri	North-Eastern mountains
Marwari	Rajasthan
Zanskari	Ladakh
Kathiawari	Rajasthan and Gujarat
Bhutia	Punjab and Bhutan
Spiti	Himachal Pradesh

Sheep

Sheep (*Ovis aries*) is reared for wool and mutton. It is herbivorous in nature and feed on farmwaste, oil cake and other cattle feeds.

Important Indian sheep breeds are as follows

Breeds of Indian Sheep

Breed	Distribution	Uses
Bhakarwal	Jammu and Kashmir	Under-coat used for high quality woollen shawls
Lohi	Punjab, Rajasthan	Good quality wool, milk
Deccani	Karnataka	Mutton, no wool
Rampur-Bushair	Uttar Pradesh, Himachal Pradesh	Brown coloured wool
Marwari	Gujarat	Coarse wool
Nali	Haryana, Punjab, Rajasthan	Superior carpet wool
Patanwad	Gujarat	Wool for army hosiery
Nellore	Maharashtra	Mutton, no wool

Camels

It is mostly used in deserts and commonly known as 'ship of deserts'. Its main uses are transport, ploughing and drawing water, etc. Some of the species of camels are *Camelus dromdarius* (Arabian camel), *Camelus ferus* (Bactrian camels) etc.

Improvement of Animals through Breeding

Scientific methods are used for the improvement of animals, *some of these scientific methods are as fallows*

Breeding

Breeding is the cross between animals of two breeds (*i.e.,* a group of animals related by descent and similar in most characters).

It can be sub-categorised as

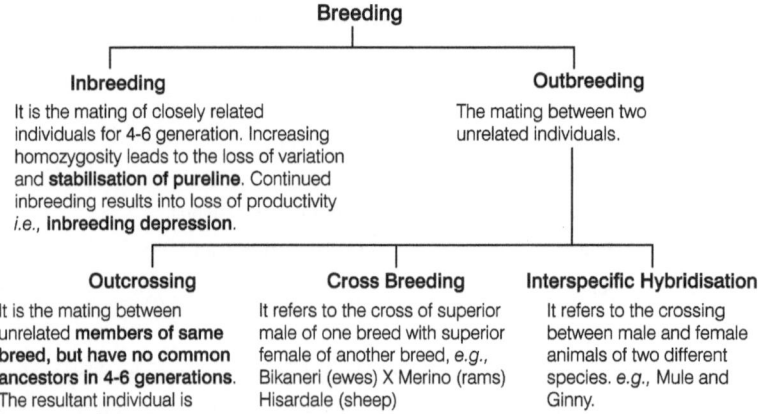

Advanced Methods of Breeding

There are three following advanced methods of breeding

(i) **Artificial Insemination** (AI)

It is a method of controlled breeding in which semen from the selected male parent is injected into the reproductive tract of selected female parent.

Advantages of artificial insemination are
  (a) Semen collected can be frozen for later use.
  (b) Semen collected can be transported in frozen form.
  (c) Helps us to overcome several problems of normal mating.

(ii) **Multiple Ovulation Embryo Transfer Technology** (MOET)

It is a programme for herd improvement in animals like cattle, sheep, etc. In this method, the hormones like FSH-activity are injected into female to promote super ovulation which can be fertilised by either superior male or artificial insemination. The fertilised egg of 8-32 cells can be transferred to receptive **surrogate mothers**.

(iii) **Transgenesis**

It involves the transfer of gene into special cell or embryos. In this case, the unfertilised egg is enucleated by treating it with **cytochalasin-B** and the blastula stage nuclei are obtained from embryo donor.

Poultry

The term **Poultry** refers to rearing of fowl, geese, ducks, turkeys and some variety of pigeons, but more often it is used for fowl rearing. Fowls are reared for food or for their eggs.

- Poultry birds reared for meat are called **broilers**.
- Female fowls raised for egg production are called **layers**.
- **Cockerel** is a young male fowl and **rooster** is mature male fowl.

The hens normally start laying eggs from February and continue till August. The average production by an Indian breed is about 60 eggs per annum.

Poultry Feed

Poultry feed includes bajra, jowar, barley, maize, wheat, rice bran, oil cake, fish meal, bread, green residue of vegetables, salt, vitamins and minerals. Now-a-days, readymade poultry feed is also available in the market.

Poultry Products

The fowls are reared to obtain following useful products for human

Eggs

These are the rich source of easily digestable animal protein. Eggs are the good sources of calcium, protein, iron, vitamins and a moderate amount of fat. Each egg consists of shell and shell membranes (12%), albumin and chalaza (56%) and yolk (32%).

Poultry meat

It is a good source of nutrition for non-vegetarians.

Feathers

They are used for commercial purposes such as for making pillows and quilts.

Manure

It is obtained from dropping of poultry birds and is highly valuable for field crops.

Some indigenous breeds of fowls includes

- **Assel** (best table bird) It has high endurance and fighting qualities.
- **Chittagong or Malay** It grows faster and have good taste.
- **Ghagus** Big and hardy breed found in South India.
- **Bustra** It is minor breed found in Gujarat and Maharashtra.

Large increase in egg production in India has been named as **silver revolution.**

Pisciculture/Fish Farming/Culture Fishery

It can be defined as

'The scientific rearing and management of fishes in water bodies under controlled conditions'. It is establish to capture, preserve, exploit and utilise various types of fishes, prawns, lobsters, crabs, oysters, other molluscs, etc.

Handbook of BIOLOGY

Fishery can be categorised into

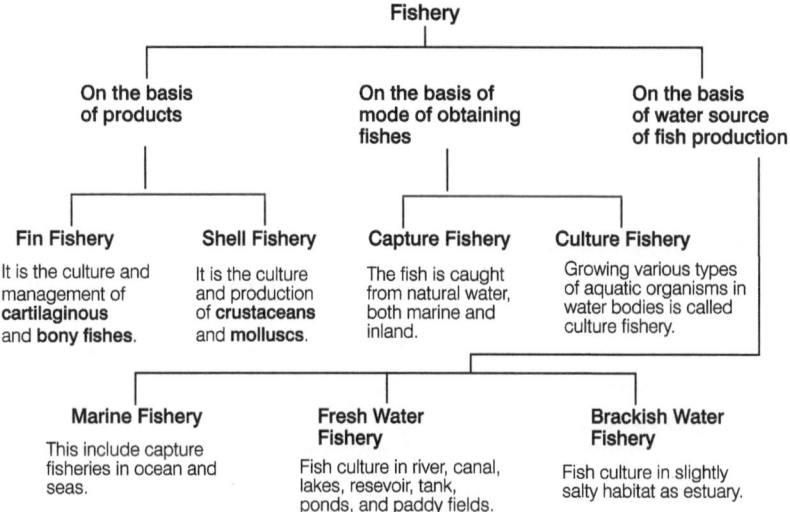

Steps used in Pisciculture

The following steps are used in fish farming or pisciculture

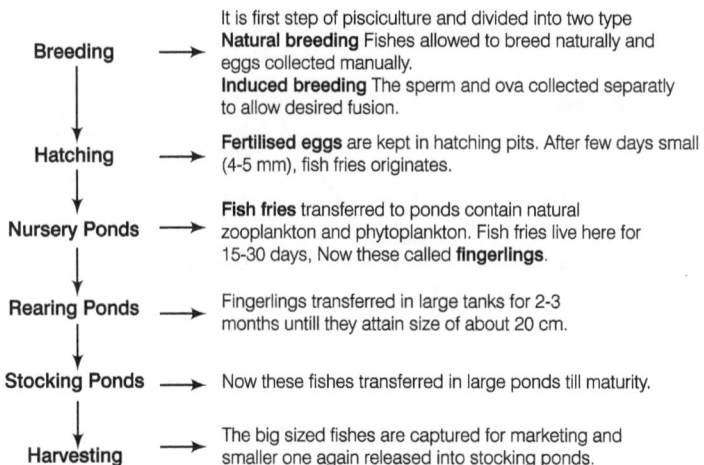

Fishes are used as food, in controlling diseases and in production of fish oils (cod-liver oil, rich in vit A and D), fish manure (bones of fishes), fish glue, shagreen (Sharp placoid scales of shark used for polishing), lather (skin of sharks) and artificial pearl.

Apiculture/Bee-Farming

'Apiculture is the rearing, management and care of honeybees for obtaining honey, wax and other substances'

For apiculture large places called **apiaries** or **bee farms** are established scientifically.

The Khadi and Village Industries Commission (KVIC) and the Indian Council of Agricultural Research (ICAR) are making efforts to raise the commercial production of honeybees products.

Species of Honeybees

Four species of honeybees are reported in different parts of India, *which are as follows*

  (i) *Apis florea F.* (Little bee) Docile bee rarely stings and can be easily used for honey extraction.
  (ii) *Apis indica F.* (Indian bee) It can be easily domesticated and most commonly used for honey production. Therefore, it is reared in artificial hives.
  (iii) *Apis dorsata F.* (Rock bee) It is a giant bee and yields maximum honey.
  (iv) *Apis mellifera F.* (European bee) Best species from commercial point of view.

Products Obtained from Apiculture

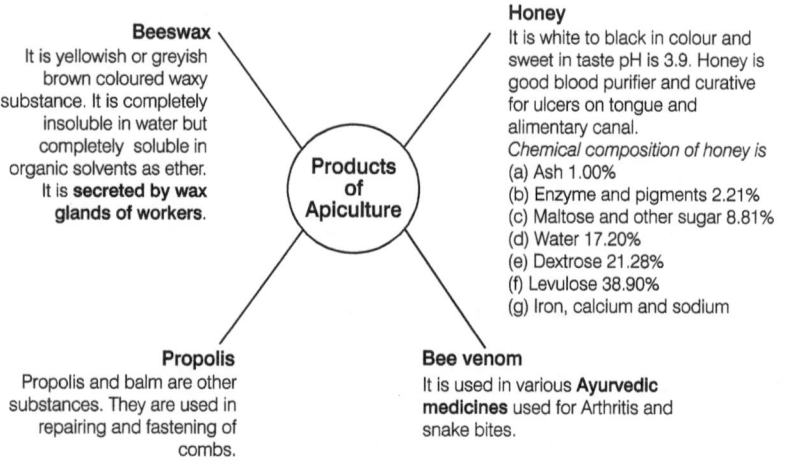

Colony and Castes/Social Organisation of Honeybees

Honeybees are **social** and **polymorphic** insects, they live in highly organised colonies. An ordinary colony has about 40-50 thousand individuals, *consisting of three* main types.

Queen

The queen is large sized bee, responsible for laying eggs. She lays up to 2000 eggs everyday of each season. Queen lay both fertilised ($2n$) and unfertilised (n) egg. The workers and queen originates from fertilised egg while drones are originated from unfertilised egg.

Drone

It is haploid fertile male. Drones are larger than workers and are quite noisy. They fail to collect food but eat voraciously. These are stingless and their main role is to mate with queen.

Worker

These are diploid, sterile female. There size is the smallest among all castes.

Total indoor and outdoor activities are performed by workers only. *For this purpose, they have been provided with some specific features such as*

(a) They have a **powerful sting** for defence.
(b) They have **long proboscis** for sucking the nectar.
(c) They have **strong wings** for fanning.
(d) For collection of pollens, they have **pollen baskets**.
(e) They have four pairs of pocket like **wax** secreting glands on ventral surface of second of fifth abdominal segment.

Workers live for 3-12 months. The function of workers changes with age. During first half of their life they remain engaged in indoor duties as **scavangers, nurse bees, fanner bees** and **guard bees**.

During the second half of their life, they perform outside duties as **scout bees** and **forager bees**.

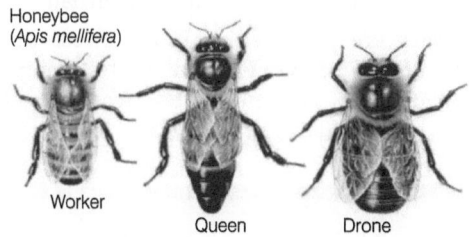

Colony members of honeybees

Life Cycle of Honeybees

The life cycle of honeybees have 4 prominant stages. The eggs layed by queen hatched into larva within 24 hrs of formation. The larva metamorphosed into pupa which later matured into adult bee. *The diagrammatic representation of life cycle of honeybnee is as follows*

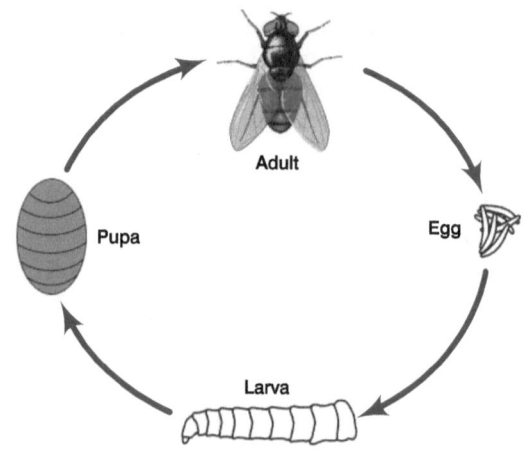

Life cycle of honeybees

Sericulture

It is the production of raw silk on commercial scale by rearing practice of the silkworm.

Silk

It is a pasty secretion of caterpillar of silkworm during cocoon formation. It is secreted from the salivary glands of silkworms.

Silk is composed of following two types of proteins

(i) **Fibroin** Constitutes 80% of the silk thread.
(ii) **Sericin** Constitutes 20% of the silk thread.

Four types of silk are produced in India. These are **mulberry silk** (contributes about 91.7%) **eri silk** (contributes about 6.4%), **tasar silk** (contributes about 1.4%) and **muga silk** (contributes about 0.5%).

Species of Silkworm

Some species of silkworm are as follows

(i) **Mulberry silkworm** *(Bombyx mori)* Bombyx mori belongs to family–Bombycidae, native to China but now it has been introduced in different countries.

(ii) **Tasar silkworm** *(Antheraea paphia)* It is found in China, India and Sri Lanka. Caterpillars of this silkworm feed on oak, sal, ber and fig plants. It belongs to the family–Saturniidae.

(iii) **Muga silkworm** *(Antheraea assama)* Native to Asom (India), it belongs to family–Saturniidae. Caterpillars feed on *Machilus, Cinnamon* plants. Silk produced by this moth is known as muga silk.

(iv) **Eri silkworm** *(Attacus ricinii)* It feeds on castor leaf and belongs to family–Saturniidae. Life history of this worm resembles with that of mulberry worm.

(v) **Oak silkworm** *(Antheraea pernyi)* Oak silkworm is found in Japan and China and feeds on oak plant. It also belongs to the family–Saturniidae.

(vi) **Giant silkworm** *(Attacus altas)* This worm is found in India and Malaysia and is the largest of living insects.

Process of Sericulture

The sericulture includes following steps

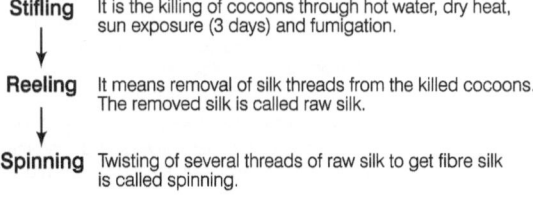

Lac Culture

The lac is obtained from the **Indian lac insect** *Laccifer lacca* (*Tachardia lacca*).

The lac insect feed on the sap of the host tree (palash).

Chemical Composition of Lac

It contains large amount of resins, sugar, water and other alkaline substances, *which are given below*

Resin	68 to 90%
Dye	2 to 10%
Wax	6%
Albuminous matter	5 to 10%
Mineral matter	3 to 7%
Water	3%

Shell lac is used in the preparation of varnishes, paints and polishes and is also used in making gramophone records, printing ink, buttons and pots, and in filling ornaments such as bangles and bracelets. It is also used as insulating material.

Plant Breeding

Plant breeding is purposeful manipulation of plant species in order to create desired plant types that are better suited for cultivation, give better yield and are disease resistent. Plant breeding programmes are carried out in systematic way worldwide.

The main steps in breeding a new genetic variety of a crop are

Collection of variability
↓
For effective exploitation of natural genes available in the population, the collection and preservation of all the different wild varieties, species and relatives of the cultivated species takes place. The collection is called germplasm collection.

Evaluation and selection of parents
↓
The germplasm is evaluted to identify the parent with desirable characters, which is further used in the process of fertilisation.

Cross hybridisation among the selected parents
↓
The set of different desired characters can be combined through hybridising these parents. It is very time consuming and tedious process. One among several progeny individual is true hybrid.

Screening and testing of superior recombinants
↓
It is the process of selection of hybrid with desired character combination. It is crucial process and requires careful scientific evaluation of the progeny.

Testing, release and commercialisation of new cultivers.
The newly selected variety is evaluated on the basis of various performance parameters in varied conditions. Later these are released as the product in market for commercial purpose.

Steps in plant breeding

Plant Breeding for Disease Resistance

Resistance of the host plant is the ability to prevent the pathogens from causing diseases and is determined by the genetic constitution of the host plant.

The disease resistance can be developed in plants through **conventional breeding technique** or **mutation breeding**.

During conventional breeding technique, *the following steps takes place*

1. Screening germplasm for resistance resource.
2. Hybridisation of selected parent.
3. Selection and evaluation of the hybrids.
4. Testing and release of new varieties.

The plant variety of various crops and their disease resistance is shown in the following table

Disease Resistant Varieties

Crop	Variety	Resistance to Diseases
Wheat	Himgiri	Leaf and stripe rust, hill bunt
Brassica	Pusa Swarnim (Karan rai)	White rust
Cauliflower	Pusa Shubhra, Pusa Snowball K-1	Black rot and Curl blight black rot
Cowpea	Pusa Komal	Bacterial blight
Chilli	Pusa Sadabahar	Chilly mosaic virus, tobacco mosaic vrius and leaf curl

Plant Breeding for Resistance Against Insect Pests

For the development of insect pest resistance, the similar steps as the collection of resistant gene from the cultivated or wild varieties and transfer of these genes to targeted host.

Some released crop varieties bred by hybridisation and selection for insect pest resistance are given below

Insect Resistant Crops

Crop	Variety	Insect Pests
Brassica (rapeseed mustard)	Pusa Gaurav	Aphids
Flat bean	Pusa Sem 2, Pusa Sem 3	Jassids, aphids and fruit borer
Okra (Bhindi)	Pusa Sawani Pusa A-4	Shoot and fruit borer

Plant Breeding for Improved Food Quality

According to a survey, about 840 million people in the world do not have adequate food to meet their daily requirements. A far greater number, *i.e.,* about 3 billion people suffer from deficiency of micronutrients, vitamin and proteins. This deficiency is called **hidden hunger**. Diet lacking micronutrients increases the risk for diseases, reduce life span and mental abilities.

Biofortification

The breeding methods have been used to produce crops with high levels of vitamins, proteins and minerals, to improve the public health. *Breeding for improved nutritional quality is undertaken with the objectives of improving*

(i) Protein content and quality

(ii) Oil content and quality

(iii) Vitamin content

(iv) Micronutrient and mineral content

In 2000, maize hybrids that had twice the amount of the amino acids, lysine and tryptophan, compared to existing maize hybrids were developed. Wheat variety **Atlas-66** having a high protein content has been used as a donor for improving cultivated wheat.

Single Cell Protein (SCP)

Conventional agricultural production of cereals, pulses, vegetables, fruits etc., may not be able to meet the demand of food as the rate at which human and animal population in increasing.

The shift from grain to meet diets also creates more demand for cereals as it takes 3-10 kg of grain to produce 1 kg of meat by animal farming. One of the alternate sources of proteins for animal and human nutrition is Single Cell Protein (SCP). Microbes are being grown on industrial scale as a source of good protein.

Microbes like *Spirulina* can be grown easily on materials like waste water from potato processing plants (containing starch), straw, molasses, animal manure and even sewage to produce large quantities and can serve as food rich in protein, minerals, fats, carbohydrate and vitamines.

Such utilisation also reduces environmental pollution. It has been estimated that in a day, 250 g of microorganisms like *Methylophilus methylotrophus,* because of its high rate of biomass production and growth, can be expected to produce 25 tonnes of protein.

33

Microbes in Human Welfare

A large variety of microorganisms constitutes the major component of biological system, as they are present everywhere like soil, water, air, inside our bodies and of animals and plants.

The branch of science which deals with the study of different aspects of microorganisms is known as **microbiology** and **Louis Pasteur** is considered as **Father of Microbiology**.

Various microorganisms can tolerate extreme conditions like **high salinity** (halophiles), **deep inside temperature** (thermophiles) and in **highly acidic atmosphere** (thermoacidophiles).

By infecting the living organisms, microorganisms causes serious diseases in plants, animals and humans. Thus, microorganisms affect human beings both directly and indirectly.

Many microorganisms are also very useful to human beings. We use several microbial products almost everyday.

The uses of microorganisms in various fields are discussed here

Microbes in Household Products
(Domestic Microbiology)

The microbes have been used to make several products such as curd, cheese, butter, vinegar, etc.

Some important products produced by microorganisms are mentioned below

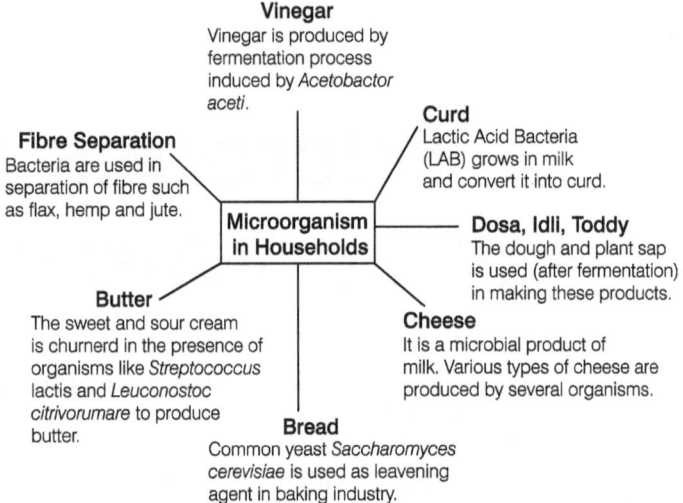

Household applications of microbes

Microbes in Industrial Products
(Industrial Microbiology)

Microorganisms such as bacteria, fungi, yeasts, etc., are now used in a wide range of industrial processes. The study of microorganisms in industrial production processes is known as **industrial microbiology**.

The microorganisms are usually cultured in large fermentation chambers called as **fermentors**, under controlled conditions.

Following are the products synthesised industrially through microbes.

(a) **Antibiotics** 'Antibiotics are chemical substances which are produced by microorganisms and can kill or inhibit the growth of other disease causing microorganisms.'

A microorganism which produce antibiotic is called **antibiont**. The term **'Antibiotic'** was first defined by **Waksmann** in 1942.

The first antibiotic was **penicillin** (wonder drug), isolated from *Penicillium notatum* (a mould), by **Alexander Flemming** in 1928.

Chief antibiotics and their source organisms are given in following table

Antibiotics and Their Source

Antibiotic	Source
Penicillin	P. notatum and P. chrysogenum
Streptomycin	S. griesus
Erythromycin	S. erythreus
Viomycin	S. floridae
Chlorotetracycliin	S. aurofaciens
Terramycin	S. rimosus

(b) **Alcohols** The most important alcohol, *i.e.*, ethanol or ethyl alcohol, (CH_3CH_2OH) is used as solvent, a germicide, a beverage, an antifreeze, a fuel, a depressent and is a versatile chemical intermediate for other chemicals.

The most widely used sugar for ethanol fermentation is **blackstrap molasses**, contains about 35-40% sucrose 15-20% invert sugars such as glucose and fructose and 28-35% of non-sugar solids. The whole process of ethanol production can be summarised as follows

$$C_6H_{12}O_6 + \text{yeast} \rightarrow 2\underset{\text{Ethanol}}{C_2H_5OH} + CO_2 + \text{Energy}$$

Several organisms like **yeast** (*i.e., Saccharomyces cerevisiae, S. uvarum*) and **bacteria** (*i.e., Clostridium sporogenes, C. indolis, C. sphenoides, Zygomonas mobilis* and *Leuconostoc mesentroides*, etc.) are involved in ethanol production, industrially.

(c) **Nutritional supplements** Microorganisms are also used as a source of several nutritional supplements.

These are given in following table

Microbes as Food Supplements

Product	Microbe	Use (s)
Amino acids		
Glutamic acid	*Corynebacterium glutamicum*	Flavour enhancer monosodium glutamate
Lysine and methionine	*Brevibacterium flavum*	Ceral food supplement
Phenylalanine and aspartic acid	*Corynebacterium* sp. and *E.coli*	Ingredients of an artificial sweetener aspartame (nutrasweet)
Vitamins		
Vitamins-B_{12}	*Pseudomonas* sp.	Health supplement
Riboflavin (B_2)	*Ashbya gossypii*	Health supplement
Vitamin-C	*Acetobacter* sp.	Health supplement
Proteins	*Chlorella*, *Spirulina*	Food additive

(d) **Organic acids** Several organic acids are produced by microorganisms.

Lactic Acid
The first organic acid produced by fermentation process. It is produced by *Streptococcus lactis*, *Lactobacillus* sp. and *Rhizopus*.

Citric Acid
It is first isolated in 1784 by **Carl Wilhelm Sheele** from lemon juice. Industrially, the fungus *Aspergillus niger* produces citric acid.

Kojic Acid
It is produced industrially by *Aspergillus oryze*. It is used as **skin whitener** and **flavour enhancers**.

Acetic Acid (vinegar)
It is produced in two steps
(i) Conversion of suger into alcohol by yeast.
(ii) Conversion of alcohol to aceticacid by bacteria, *Acetobactor* sp.

Gluconic Acid
Gluconic acid is produced industrially by *Aspergillus niger*. It is used in **metal cleaning** and therepy for calcium and iron deficiencies.

[Central node: Organic Acids by Microorganisms]

Some Other Organic Acids Synthesised by Various Microbes

Organic Acids	Microorganism
Propionic acid	*Bacterium propioni*
Butyric acid	*Clostridium acetobutyricum*
Oxalic acid	*Aspergillus* sp.
Gallic acid	*Aspergillus niger*
Itaconic acid	*A. terreus*

(e) **Enzymes** Microbes synthesises large number of enzymes, which have significant economic importance. *Some of these enzymes are given in the following table with their source organism and uses*

Enzyme Producing Microorganisms

Enzymes	Organisms	Uses
α-amylase	*Aspergillus* sp.	Laundry detergent
β-amylase	*Bacillus subtilis*	Brewing
Cellulase	*Trichoderma viride*	Fruit juices, coffee, paper
Invertase	*Saccharomyces cerevisiae*	Sweet manufacture
Lactase	*Saccharomyces fragilis*	Digestive aid, sweet manufacture
Oxidases	*Aspergillus niger*	Paper and fabric bleaching
Lipase	*Aspergillus niger*	Washing powders, leather tanning, cheese production
Pectinase	*Aspergillus niger*	Fruit juice
Proteases	*Aspergillus oryzae*	Meat tenderiser, leather tanning
Rennin (chymosin)	*Mucor* and *E. coli*	Cheese production

Microbes in Healthcare and Medicine
(Medical Microbiology)

Microbes are used to produce **insulin, growth hormones** and **antibodies**. They are also helpful in the treatment of diseases such as cancer. Research shows that, *Clostridia* can selectively target cancer cells.

Various strains of non-pathogenic *Clostridia* have shown to infiltrate and replicate within solid tumours. *Clostridia*, therefore have the potential to deliver therapeutic proteins to tumours.

Lactobacillus species has therapeutic properties including **anti-inflammatory** and **anticancer** activities.

Serum and **vaccines** produced by various microorganisms are used to induce immunity among human beings.

The alkaloid, released from *Cleviceps purpurea* called **ergotinine**, stimulates the **muscles of uterus** and is used to assist child birth and controls uterine haemorrhage.

Some Other Important Products of Microorganisms

Products	Microorganisms
Cyclosporin A 11-membered cyclic oligopeptide an immunosuppressive that inhibits activation of T-cell response to transplanted organs	*Trichoderma polysporum* and *Tolypocladium inflatum*
Statins Inhibitor of enzyme HMG Co-A reductase of liver, lowers LDL cholesterol level.	Yeast-*Monascus perpureus*

Microbes as Biofertilisers and Biocontrol Agents
(Agricultural Microbiology)

To protect the environment and control soil pollution, the biofertilisers and manures are used in modern agriculture, termed as **organic farming**.

Biofertilisers

These are the nutrient materials obtained from the living organisms or their remains, used for enhancing the fertility of soil.

Biofertilisers contain some organisms which can bring about nutrient availability to the crop plants.

The main sources of biofertilisers are

(a) Nitrogen fixing bacteria (free living and symbiotic)
(b) Nitrogen fixing cyanobacteria (free living and symbiotic)
(c) Mycorrhizal fungi

Note
- Natural processes fix about 190×10^{12} g per year of nitrogen through lightning (8%) photochemical reactions (2%) and biological nitrogen-fixation (90%). Biological nitrogen fixation provides about 1750 million tonnes of nitrogen, free of cost naturally in the form of biofertilisers.
- N_2 fertilisers are often not required for rice cultivation as the fern *Azolla* has *Anabaena azollae* as symbiont, which fixes N_2 and grows thickly into rice fields.

Nitrogen fixation in plants with their symbiotic host is given in following table

Some Symbiotic Nitrogen-fixing Organisms

Host Plants	Nitrogen-fixing Symbionts
Leguminous Legumes and Parasponia	Azorhizobium, Bradyrhizobium, Photorhizobium, Rhizobium and Sinorhizobium
Actinorhizal Alder (tree), Ceanothus (shrub), Casuarina (tree) and Datisca (shrub)	Frankia
Gunnera	Nostoc
Azolla (water fern)	Anabaena
Sugarcane	Acetobacter diazotrophs

Biopesticides

Microorganisms such as bacteria, fungi, viruses, protozoan, etc., and their products are which used to control the pests are known as biopesticides.

These biopesticides can be of following types

Bacterial	— e.g., *Bacillus thuringiensis*
Fungal	— e.g., *Metarhizium, Beauveria* and *Verticillium*
Protozoam	— e.g., *Schizogregrine*
Viral	— e.g., Nuclear Polyhedrosis Virus (NPV) and Granulosis Viruses (GV).

Bioherbicides

These are the organisms which destroy weeds without harming the useful plants. The first bioherbicide was a **mycoherbicide**, which was based on a fungus *Phytopthora palmivora*.

Bioherbicides can be categorised as

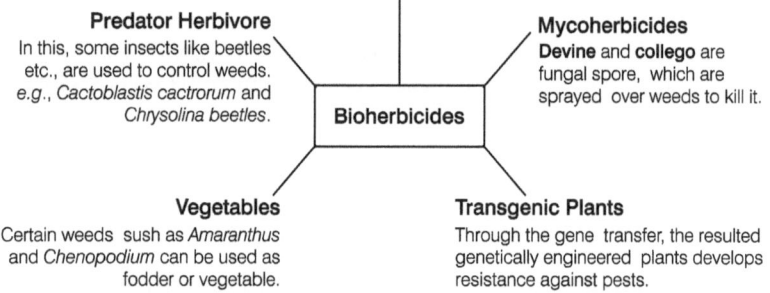

Bioinsecticides

Living organisms and their products used for insect control are called bioinsecticides. These includes **pathogen /parasites** and **predators.**

Some important bioinsecticides are as follows.

1. **Sporeine** First commercial bioinsecticides obtained from *Bacillus thruingiensis*.
2. **Doom** It is the mixture of *Bacillus papillae* and *Bacillus lentiborbus*, which has been used to control japanese beetles papillae.
3. **Ladybug** (lady bird beetle) and praying mantis can control scale insect or aphid pests of vegetables, cotton and apple.
4. **Vedalian Beetle** (*Radiola cardinalis*) has been found effective against cottony cushion scale (*Icerya purchasi*).
5. **Mycar** is a product obtained from the fungus *Hirrutella thompsoni* and used to control citrus rust mite.
6. **Predator bug** (*Cystorhinus mundulus*) has been successfully used to control sugarcane leaf hopper in Hawaii.
7. **Bacillus sphaericus** is toxic to larva of *Anopheles* mosquito.
8. **Boverin** is obtained from a fungus *Beauveria bassiana* and used for controlling colorado potato beetle (*Leptinotarsa decemlineata*) and codling moth.

    The fungus *Entomophthora ignobilis* may be used for controlling green peach aphid.

    The fungus *Coelomomyces* is useful to control mosquito larvae.

Some of the natural insecticides are listed below

Natural Insecticides and Their Sources

Natural insecticides	Sources
Rotenones	Roots of *Derris elliptica* and *Lonchocarpus*
Nicotine	From tobacco (*Nicotiana tabacum*)
Salanin, azadirachtin, meliantiol	From neem (*Azadirachta indica*)
Pyrethrin and cineria	From capitulum of pyrethrum (*Chrysanthemum cinerarifolium*, *C. coccineum* and *C. marashalli*)
Ryania	Roots and stem of *Ryania speciosa*

Microbes in Sewage Treatment
(Environmental Microbiology)

Municipal waste water is called sewage. It contains large amount of organic matter and microbes. Treatment of waste water is done by the **heterotrophic microbes** which are naturally present in the sewage.

The treatment of sewage is carried out in following two stages

1. Primary Treatment
In involves the **physical removal of large and small particles** from the sewage through **filteration** and **sedimentation**.

2. Secondary or Biological Treatment
The primary effluents is aerated in large tanks, through this aeration, the Biological Oxygen Demand (BOD) of water increases, (which got decreased by growing microbes).

Microbes in Biofuels

Biofuels are fuel of biological origin which are used for the production of heat and other forms of energy. The energy derived from biofuels is called **bioenergy**.

The biofuels offers following advantages

1. These are renewable energy resources.
2. They release relatively low greenhouse gases including carbon dioxide emission than fossil fuels.
3. The raw materials used in biofuel production are often wastes, including municipal waste. Therefore, it helps in pollution control.

Various biofuels, their substrate and microorganisms from which they are produced are given in following table

Biofuels and Related Microorganisms

Biofuels	Substrate	Microorganisms (s)
Bioethanol	Starch, sugar crops	*Bacillus licheniformis* (amylase activity)
	Cellulosic wastes	*Saccharomyces cerevisiae, Zymomonas* (sugar fermentation)
	(a) Enzyme hydrolysis	*Trichoderma reesei* (cellulase)
		S. cerevisiae (hexose fermentation)
		Recombinant *E. coli* (pentose fermenation)
		Clostridium sp., *Fusarium oxysporum* (consolidated processing)
	(b) Acid hydrolysis	*S. cerevisiae, Zymomonas* (for fermentation) *Clostridium jungdahlii*
Methane	Farm and human wastes, municipal solid wastes, effluents from food and dairy industries, etc.	A group of anaerobic microorganisms
Butanol	Soluble carbohydrates	*Clostridium acetobutylicum, C. beijernickii*
Hydrogen	Sunlight and water sugars and fatty acids (from starch, cellulose)	*Chlamydomonas reinhardit, C. moewusii* anaerobic bacteria like *Clostridium*
Biodiesel	Sunlight and carbon dioxide	*Monoraphidium minutum, Cyclotella cryticum, Euphorbia* plants, *Copaifera* tree, etc.

Microorganisms with their large population provide the products of several categories to serve human kind. Despite having the list of large number of products, the field remains unexplored in several ways.

The ultimate list of products and services will be different through which the humanity can be served in better ways. The combination of microbiology with biotechnology would be the lead outcome in this field.

34

Evolution

The term **evolution** is derived from two latin words, *e* = from *volvere* = to roll/unfold, and was first used by english philosopher **Herbert Spencer**.

*The **principle of evolution** implies* " The development of an entity in the course of time through a gradual sequence of changes, from a simple to more complex state".

Biopoiesis refers to origin of life from non-living substances, while **biogenesis** is the term used to refer to the origin of life from already existing life forms.

There are **two theories** which have been given to explain the mechanism of origin of life. First is spontaneous generation from the non-living material (abiogenesis) and second is the origin of life from the parental organism by reproduction (biogenesis). Presently the view of biochemical origin of life is widely accepted.

The history of life comprises two events
 1. Origin of life
 2. Evolution of life

Before discussing above events in detail we must take a close look on the 'origin of universe'.

Origin of Universe

Several theories have been given to explain the origin of universe and the most accepted one is Big-Bang theory.

Big-Bang Theory (Abbe Lemaitre; 1931)

According to this theory

About 15 billion years ago, a fiery explosion took place in the condensed cosmic matter and its fragments got scattered into space at an enormous velocity.

Arno Allan Penzias supported the Big-Bang theory and discovered evidences for this theory. Our **galaxy** (*i.e.,* cluster of stars), contains about **100 billion stars** and called as **Milky way**.

Origin of Life

Ancient Theories of Origin of Life

Theories of Abiogenesis (origin of living organisms from non-living matter)	**Theories of Biogenesis** (origin of living organisms from pre existing living organisms Non-living matter)
Theory of Special Creation These are mythological theories, who belives that the life was created by supernatural powers.	Theories of biogenesis were supported by various scientist, through experiments performed by them. *Some of them are discussed here*
Theories of Spontaneous Generation This is also known as **autobiogenesis** The theory was supported by **Plato, Aristotle**, etc, They believed that the snails, fishes, frogs arose spontaneously from mud.	**Francesco Redi's Experiment** (1668) He placed well cooked meat in three jars. First jar is **uncovered, Second** by **parchment and third** is covered by **muslin cloth**. After some days, he observed that the maggots developed only in uncovered jar.
Theory of Cosmozoic Origin According to this theory, the life is coeternal with matter without any beginning. The living protoplasm reached to Earth from other part of universe.	**Lazzaro Spallanzani's Experiment** (1767) Spallanzani, taking organic liquid (boiled nutritive both) in the vessels, then sealed them. But he always found that, if proper care is taken, no living things appear.
Theory of Panspermia Arrhenius (1908) proposed this theory. It also support the process of coming living material from other planet.	**Louis Pasteur's Experiment** (1860-1862) He disproved the theory of spontaneous generation by performing a well designed experiment called **swan-necked flask experiment.**

Modern Theory of Origin of Life (Al Oparin)

It is also known as **modern theory** or **abiogenic origin** or **naturalistic theory** or **physicochemical evolution**. It was hypothesised by **Al Oparin** and supported by **JBS Haldane, Miller** and **Urey** and **Sydney F Fox**.

According to this theory, the life was originated in deep sea hydrothermal vents. Through these vents, the sea water seeps through the cracks in bottom, untill the water comes close to hot magma.

The **super heated water** expelled forcibly, with variety of compounds such as H_2S, CH_4, iron and **sulphide ions**.

Oparin wrote the book **Origin of Life** in 1936. In his book, he admitted abiogenesis first, but biogenesis ever since. Therefore, oparin's theory is also known as **primary abiogenesis.**

The schematic presentation of physicochemical evolution is as follows

Chemical Evolution

Primitive Earth
(Hot revolving ball of the gas) Free atoms like hydrogen, oxygen, carbon, nitrogen, sulphur, phosphorus, etc., are present.
↓
Inorganic Molecule
These molecules are produced by the combination of elements. *e.g.*, H_2, O_2, N_2 etc.
↓
Simple Organic Molecule
Formation of water, methane, ammonia and hydrogen cyanide took place. The environment became reducing.
↓
Complex Organic Molecule
By the **polymerisation** of simple organic molecule, larger organic molecule were formed. These are polypeptide, nucletides and polysaccharides, etc.
↓
Coacervates
The large organic molecule synthesised abiotically on primitive earth. These form colloidal aggregrates due to intermolecular attraction. These colloids were called coacervate by Oparin and microsphere by Sydney F. Fox.
↓
Protobionts
These are also known as protocell or eobiont. These are nucleoprotenoid having free living gene and were similar to present mycoplasma.
↓
Progenotes
The protobiont give rise ot Monera, which in turn give rise to prokaryotes with naked DNA, protoribosomes, etc.

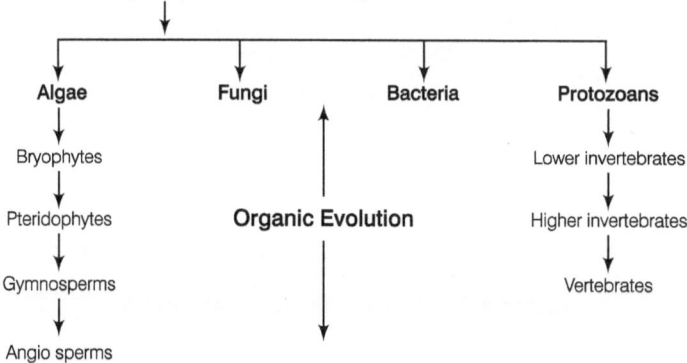

Modern theory of origin of life was supported by **Miller** and **Urey** with their experiment in 1953.

Miller and Urey's Experiment

In 1953, **Miller** built an apparatus of glass tubes and flasks in the laboratory. He created an atmosphere containing hydrogen (H_2), ammonia s(NH_3), methane (CH_4) and water vapour (H_2O) in one big flask and allowed the condensed liquid to accumulate in another small flask. The ratio of methane, ammonia and hydrogen in the large flask was $2:1:2$.

Energy was supplied to the apparatus by heating the liquid as well as by electric sparks from tungsten's electrodes in the gaseous flask (larger flask). The conditions of apparatus resembled the atmosphere present on the early earth. The experiment was conducted continuously for about one week and then the chemical composition of the liquid inside the apparatus was analysed.

The diagrammatic representation of Miller's experiment is as follows

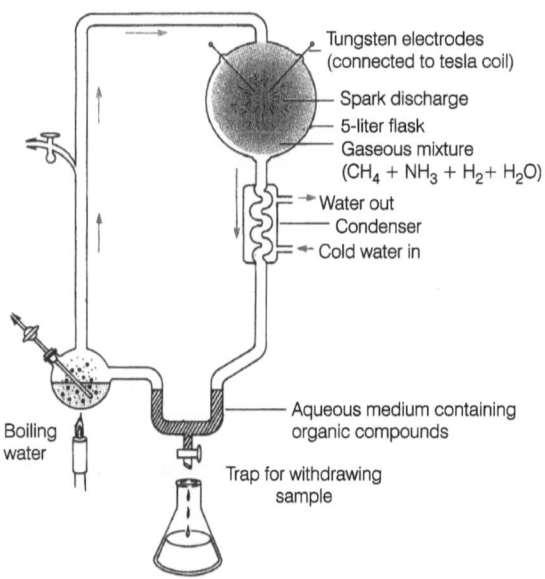

Diagrammatic represtation of the apparatus, stanley used to demonstrate the synthesis of organic compounds by electrical discharge in a reducing atmosphere.

Following categories of products were formed under the prebiotic conditions in Miller's experiment apparatus.

Some Products Formed Under Prebiotic Conditions

Carboxylic Acids	Nucleic Acid Bases	Amino Acids	Sugars
Formic acid	Adenine	Glycine	Straight and branched
Acetic acid	Guanine	Alanine	Pentoses and hexoses
Propionic acid	Xanthine	α-amino butyric acid	
Straight and branched fatty acids ($C_4 - C_{10}$)	Hypoxanthine	Valine	
Glycolic acid	Cytosine	Leucine	
Lactic acid	Uracil	Isoleucine, proline	
Succinic acid		Aspartic acid, serine, threonine	

Which Came First RNA or Protein?

It is a matter of great controversy among biologists to decide that which came first RNA or protein. There are three views regarding this problem as follows

1. **RNA world** (the group of scientists, who focus on RNA as the first molecule). RNA world group feels that without a hereditary molecule, other molecules could not have formed consistently. This view is supported by the discovery of **ribozyme**, a catalytic RNA molecule, which have the ability to act like enzymes.

2. **Protein world** (the group of scientists, who focus on protein as the first molecule). The protein group argues that without enzymes (which are proteins), nothing could be replicated at all, or heritable. They are in view that the nucleotide is very complex therefore, it can not be formed spontaneously.

3. **Peptide-Nucleic Acid** (PNA) **world** (the group of scientists, who focus on the combination of RNA and protein.) The PNA world believed that there must have been a pre-RNA world, where the peptide, (nucleic acid) was the basis for life. PNA is simple and able to self-replicate.

Evidences for Evolution

Scientists proposed many evidences through which the evolution of life forms can be proved. Several different lines of evidences convinced **Darwin** and his contemporary scientists that the modern organisms arose by evolution from more ancient forms.

Darwin documented evolutionary evidences mainly on the basis of **geographical distribution of species** and fossil records.

Some significant convincing evidences for the occurrence of descent with modification come from
1. Palaeontology
2. Morphology and comparative anatomy
3. Geographical distribution
4. Embryology
5. Taxonomy
6. Connecting links
7. Cytology
8. Biochemistry and Physiology
9. Genetics

1. Evidences from Palaeontology

Palaentology is the study of fossils of prehistoric life. According to **Charls Lyell** 'Fossil is any body of trace of body of animals or plants buried and preserved by the natural causes.' Fossils are generally preserved in **sedimentary rocks**, which are formed by the deposition of **silt, sand** or **calcium carbonate** over millions of years.

Determination of Age of Fossils

The age of fossils can be determined by following methods

- **Radioactive Carbon** (C^{14}) **Dating Method** This was discovered by **WF Libby**. As the half life of carbon is relatively short, this isotope is only reliable for dating fossils less than 70000 years.
- **Electron Spin Resonance** (ESR) **Method** It is a relatively new, precise and accurate method. It is based on the fact that the background radiation causes electron to dislodge from their normal positions in atoms and trapped in crystalline lattice of material, it is mostly used to date $CaCO_3$ and lime stone.
- **Radioactive Clock Method** This was discovered by Boltwood (1907) and based on the disintegrating property of radioactive elements.
- **Potassium-Argon Method** The transformation of potassium into argon; rubidium into strontium has been used for dating fossils bearing rocks of any age and any type.

Geological Time Scale

The evidence of the evolution can also be taken through geological time scale. The complete life span of earth (*i.e.*, 4600 million years) is known as geological time, which have been divided into **eras**. Eras are divided into **periods** and periods into **epoches**. An Italian scientist **Giovanni Ardulna**, developed first geological time scale in 1760.

Geological Time Scale with Notes on Events in the Evolution of life and Environment

Rocky Mountain Revolution (Little Destruction of Fossils)

Era	Period	Epoch	Geological and Climatic Conditions	Flora (Plant Life)	Fauna (Animal Life)
Cenozoic (Age of Mammals)	Quaternary	Recent (Holocene)	End of last ice age; climate warmer; climatic zones distinct.	Dominance of herbs.	Age of man; development of human cultures.
		Pleistocene	Periodic continental glaciers in North.	Increase of herbs spread of herbs and grassland.	age of man, extinction of many large mammals.
	Tertiary	Pliocene	Cool and temperate climate away from equator, continuous rise of mountains of Western-North America.	Decline of forest, great decrease of woody plants.	Abundant mammals man evoluing elephant, horses and camels almost like modern models.
		Miocene	Cooling of climate.	Development of grasses reduction of forests.	Mammals at height of evolution, first man-like apes.
		Oligocene	Lands lower, climate warmer.	Worldwide tropical forests, rise of monocots and flowering plants.	Archaic mammals extenct appearange of modern mammals.
		Eocene	Zoned climatic belts well established.	Extension of angiosperms.	Placental mammals. diversified and specialised; hoofed mammals and carnivores established.
		Palaeocene	Development of climatic belts.	Modernisat of angiosperms.	Evolutionary explosion of mammals.

Era	Period	Epoch	Geological and Climatic Conditions	Flora (Plant Life)	Fauna (Animal Life)
Rocky Mountain revolution (Little Destruction of Fossils)					
Mesozoic (Age of Reptiles)	Cretaceous	—	Birth of modern reptiles, development of climatic diversity.	Rise of flowiering plants especially monocotyledons, decrease of gymnosperms.	Dinosours reached keat, become extinct toothed birds became extinct; beginning of loteost fishes and modern birds; archaci mammals common.
	Jurassic	—	Culmination of worldwide warm climates.	Cycades and conifers common; appearance of first known flowering plants.	Dominance of dinosous appearance of first toothed birds; rise of insectivorous morsupials.
	Triassic	—	Continents exposed, world subtropical climates.	Gymnosperms dominant, declining towards the end extinction of seed fern.	Transction of reptiles to mammals, rise of progressive reptiles andegg laying mammaly extinction of primitive amphitoians.
Appalachian Revolution (Some Loss of Fossils)					
	Permian	—	Rise of continents; climate became arid and varied, glaciation in Southern hemisphere.	Dwindling of ancient plants, decline of lycopods and horse tails.	Extinction of ammonites and trilobites, abundance of primitives reptiles; appearance of mammals; like reptiles, decline of amphibians.
	Pennsylvanian	—	Uniform climate throughout world.	Great forests of seed-ferns and gymnosperms (great tropical coal forests).	Amphibians dominant on land, insects common, appearance of first reptiles.

Era	Period	Epoch	Geological and Climatic Conditions	Flora (Plant life)	Fauna (Animal life)
	Mississippian (Carboniferous)	—	Climate uniform, humid at first, cooler, later as land rose; spread of tropical seas.	Mosses and seed ferns dominant, gymnosperms increasingly widespread (early coal forest).	Rise of insects, sea lilies at peak. spread of ancient sharks.
	Devonian	—	Broad distribution of uniform climates; increased temperature.	First forests, first gymnosperms and first known liverworts, horsetails and ferns.	Diversification in fishes; sharks and lung fishes abundant, evolution of amphibians.
	Silurian	—	Slight climate cooling extensive continental seas.	First known land plants club mosses, algae dominant.	Wide expansion of invertebrates first insects, rise of fishes.
	Cambrian	—	Warm climate, great submergence of land.	Land plants probably first appeared, marine algae abundant.	First indication of fishes, corals and trilobites abundant, diversified molluscs.
	Ordovician	—	Climate became progressively warmer.	Algae, fungi and bacteria; first fossils of plant life.	Invertebrates numerous and varied, most modern phyla established.
Protero-zoic		—	Cool climate, volcanic eruptions, repeated glaciating.	Primitive aquatic plants algae, fungi and bacteria.	Shelled Protozoans, Coelenterates, flatworms, primitive annelids.
Archae-ozoic		—	Great volcanic activities, no recognisable fossils, indirect evidence of living things form some sedimentary deposits of organic material in rocks. e.g., *Eubacterium isolatum*, *Archaeospheroides barbertonis*.		

2. Evidences from Biogeography

Biogeography is the study of distribution of animals and plants.

According to **continental drift** or **plate tectonics theory** given by **Alfred L Wegener** (1912), the total landmass of modern world is originated from a large mass called **Pangea**.

This separation was started in **caboniferous period** and ended till **mesozoie era**.The shape of coastal areas and the species of plants and animals present in different continents supports the theory. The continental drift theory is also known as **Jigsaw fit theory**.

3. Evidences from Morphology and Comparative Anatomy

These includes followings

(a) Homology and Homologous Organs

Those organs which have the **same embryonic origin** and **basic structure**, though they may or may not perform the same function.

This is the result of **divergence** due to **Adaptive radiation**. *On the basis of its occurrence, homology is of following types*

Various examples of homologous organs are given with their function in following diagram.

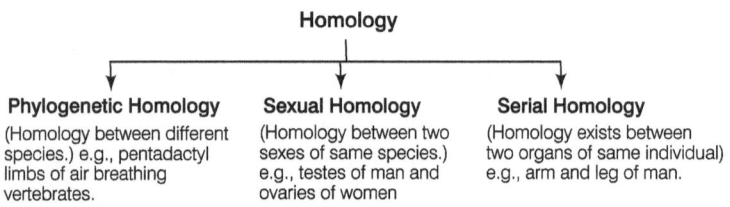

Handbook of BIOLOGY

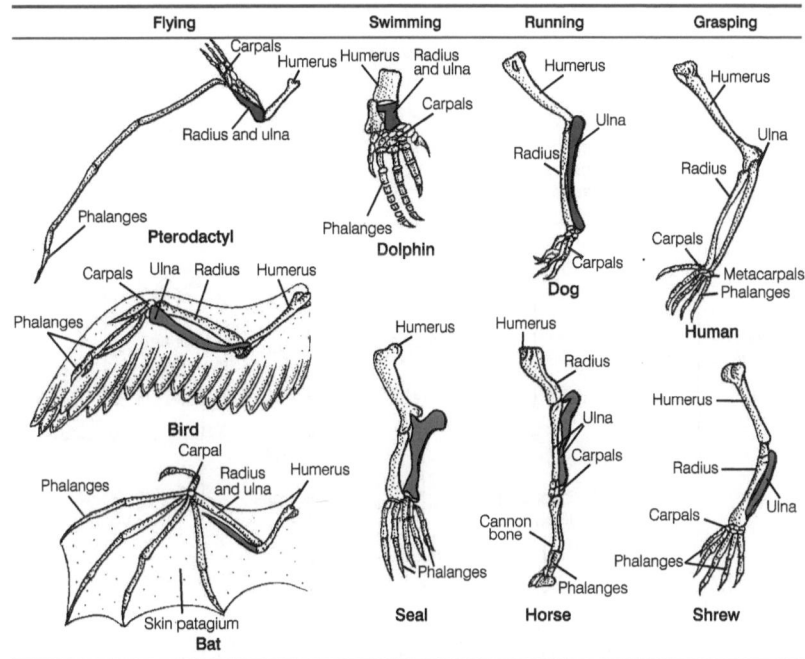

Forelimbs in vertebrates

Adaptive Radiation

HF Osborn (1898) developed the concept of **adaptive radiation** or **divergent evolution,** *i.e.,* the development of different functional structures from a common ancestral form.

The significance of adaptive radiation is that, it leads to the modification of homologous structures which ultimately results into divergent evolution.

Following figure of adaptive radiation in Darwin finches clearly indicates the process of divergent evolution

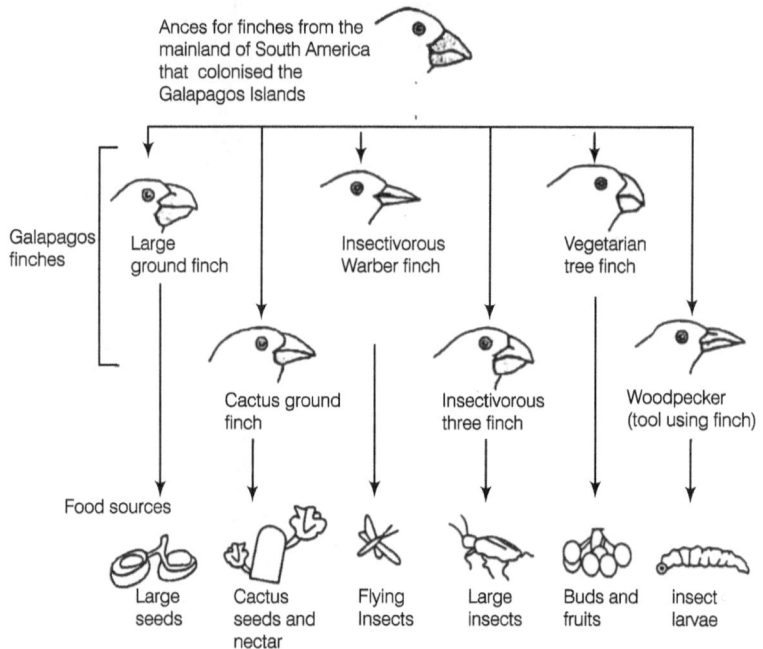

Adaptive radiation in Darwin finches

(b) Analogy or Analogous Organ

These are the structure which are different in their basic structure and developmental origin but appear similar and perform similar functions. This relationship between structure and function is known as **analogy** or **convergent evolution**.

Adaptive Convergence (Convergent Evolution)

In adaptive convergence, separate lineage show similar morphology under the influence of similar environmental factors.

'When a species of distinct lineages closely resemble on overall morphology it is called as **homeomorphs**'.

e.g., wings of birds, insects and bats are homeomorphs.

Handbook of BIOLOGY 551

Analogy in the wings is shown in the following diagram

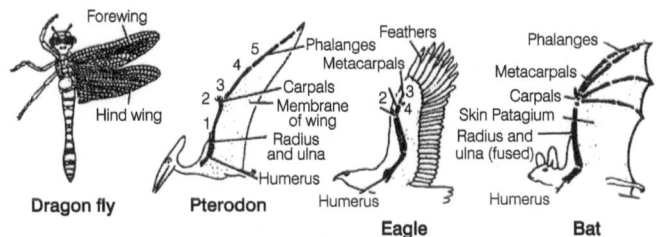

Analogy in the wings

(c) Vestigial Organs

These are non-functional organs, which were functional in their ancestors.

There are more than 90 vestigial-organs in the human body. Some examples are **coccyx** (tailbone), **nictitating membrane** (3rd eyelid), caecum, vermiform appendix, canines, wisdom teeth, body hair, auricular muscles, mammary glands in males, etc.

Vestigial organs are also present in some other animals, e.g., splint bones in horse, hind limbs and pelvic girdle in pythan, wings and feathers in flight in python, wings and feathers in flight less birds, etc.

Atavism or Reversion

It is the sudden reappearance or refunctioning of some ancestral organs, which have either completely disappeared or are present as vestigial organ. *e.g.,*

(i) Long and dense hair

(ii) Birth of human baby with small tail.

(iii) Development of power of moving pinna in some individuals.

4. Evidences from Embryology

Through the comparative study of life histories of individuals, the evidences of evolution can be collected.

A comparative study of the ontogeny of various forms of animals reveals the phylogenetic relationship and thus confirms evolution. To varify this, following points can be considerd.

(a) The zygote of all metazoans are single celled and similar to the body of protozoans.

(b) The stages of embryonic development *i.e.*, **morula, blastula** and **gastrula** are basically similar in all **metazoans**.

552   Handbook of BIOLOGY

   (c) In fishes, the young individuals develop from gastriles is almost like the adult but the tadpole of amphibials is similar to young fishes.
   (d) The early postgastrula stages are quite similar in the members of all the different classes *viz*-fishes, amphibians, reptile, birds and mammals.
   (e) Possession of **pharyngeal gill slits** and gill pouches are one of the three diagnostic characters of all chordates.

Due to the similarity among early embryos of all vertebrates, it is very difficult to differentiate a human embryo from other vertebrates.

The comparative account of several vertebrate embryo is given as follows

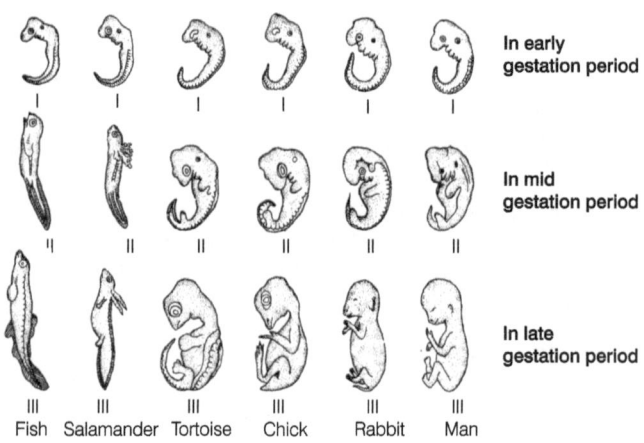

Depicting the remarkable similarity in the early embryos of some vertebrates

Recapitulation Theory of Biogenetic Law

It states that

Ontogeny (development of the embryo) is the recapitulation of phylogeny (the ancestral sequences).

For example
   (i) Presence of fish-like characters (*i.e.*, gills, gill slits, tail, tail fin, lateral line and sense organs) in tadpole larva of frog.
   (ii) Presence of filamentous green algae-like structure, **protonema** during the development of *Funaria* (moss).

5. Evidences from Connecting Links

A connecting link demonstrates the characteristics of more than one group. These organisms indicates the transition of characters from one to another group of organisms.

Following table give the number of organisms (*i.e.*, links) and their disputed positions between groups.

S.No.	Link	Between the groups
1.	Virus	Living and non-living
2.	*Peripatus* (walking worm)	Annelida and Arthropoda
3.	*Balanoglossus*	Chordates and Non-chordates
4.	*Archaeopteryx*	Reptiles and Birds
5.	*Cycas*	Pteridophytes and Gymnosperms
6.	*Echidna* (spiny ant eater)	Reptiles and Mammals
7.	*Euglena*	Animals and Plants
8.	*Gnetum*	Gymnosperms and Angiosperms
9.	Hornworts	Protista and Fungi
10.	*Neopilina*	Annelida and Mollusca
11.	*Ornithorhynchus* (duck billed platypus)	Reptiles and Mammals
12.	*Proterospongia*	Annelida and Arthropoda
13.	*Protopterus* (lung fishes)	Bony fishes and Amphibia
14.	*Xenoturbella*	Protozoa and Metazoa
15.	Trochophore larva	Annelida and Mollusca
16.	Tornaria larva	Echinodermata and Chordata
17.	*Sphenodon* (living fossil lizard)	Amphibia and Reptilia
18.	*Seymouria*	Amphibia and Reptiles
19.	*Latimeria*	Pisces and Amphibia
20.	Myxomycetes	Protista and Fungi
21.	Actinomycetes Rickettisa	Bacteria and Fungi
22.	*Chimera* (rabbit fish/rat fish)	Cartilaginous and Bony fishes
23.	*Club moss*	Bryophytes and Pteridophytes
24.	Ctenophora	Coelentarates and Platyhelminthes

6. Evidences from Taxonomy

During classification, organisms are grouped according to their resemblance and placed from simple organisms towards the complexity.

There was no difference among animal and plants during the origin of unicellular stage of organisms. Thus, *Euglena* is a common ancestor of both plants and animals.

7. Other Evidences

Several other evidences also supports the process of evolution. These may by **Biochemical or physiological** (*i.e.,* study of different products and physiology among organisms), **cytological** (*i.e.,* deep observation of cellular composition among related organisms) and **genetical** (*i.e.,* have the **mutation** and variation as their theme for evolution) nature.

Theories of Evolution

Organic evolution implies that 'present day organism are modified but lineal descendents of species that lived in former geological time, and the more complex and highly differentiated forms have evolved from the simpler organism by gradual modifications'.

Lamarckism

It is the first theory of evolution which was proposed by **Jean Baptiste de Lamarck** (1744-1829), a french biologist.

It was published in 1809 in his book "Philosophie zoologique".

Central Idea The characteristics that are acquired by organisms during their life times in response to environmental conditions are passed on to their offspring.

4 basic propositions of Lamarck

Lamarckism includes 4 basic propositions

1. Internal vital force
2. Effect of environment and new needs.
3. Use and disuse of organs.
4. Inheritance of acquired characters.

Handbook of BIOLOGY 555

The diagrammatic representation of Lamarck's theory is as follows

	The ancestors of giraffe were bearing **small neck and forelimbs** and were like horses. These have **internal vital force** to increase their size and become relatively large in due course of time.
	Probably, due to some reasons, the surface vegetation was removed which lead to the stretching of neck to reach to the branches of trees. This stretching is induced by the **scarcity of food in environment and need for the food**. The changing environmental conditions always generate new needs. To fulfill new needs, an organism needs to make some changes in their structure.
	As the neck is comprehensively used to reach to the branches of trees, the elongation takes place. This is based on the proposition of **use and disuse of organs** the other organs of body say tail is not used so much hence reduced or become unchanged. The continuous stretching of neck lead to permanent elongation and character is acquired.
	The acquired character (*i.e.,* long neck) is transmitted in next generation as the **inheritance of acquired character** is given by **Lamarck**. After several generations, the variations/modifications are accumulated upto such extent that they give rise to new species. This process of new species formation is called **speciation**.

Criticism of Lamarckism

(Evidences against the inheritance of acquired characters)

Mendel's laws of inheritance and **Weismann's theory of continuity of germplasm** (1892) discarded the Lamarck's concept of inheritance of acquired characters.

Theory of continuity of germplasm (August Weismann, 1834-1914) According to Weismann "the characters influencing the germ cells are only inherited".

There is a **continuity of germplasm** (protoplasm of germ cells), but the **somatoplasm (protoplasm of somatic cells) is not transmitted** to the next generation. He cut the tails of rats for as many as 22 generations and allowed them to breed but tailless mice were never born.

Neo-Lamarckism

In full agreement with Weismann's theory, neo-Lamarckism proposes that

(i) Environment influences an organism and changes its heredity.

(ii) Some of the acquired variation can be passed on to the offsprings.

(iii) **Internal vital force** and **appetency** (*i.e.,* a desire) do not play any role in evolution.

(iv) Only those variations are passed on to next generation, which also affects **germ cells.**

Darwinism (Charles Robert Darwin; 1809-1882)

The second most famous theory of evolution was given by **Charles Robert Darwin**. It was published in 1859 in his book "**Origin of species by means of natural selection. The preservation of races is the struggle for life**".

Five Basic Propositions of Darwinism

Darwinism includes five basic propositions

1. Rapid multiplication/overproduction
2. Limited resources
3. Variations
4. Natural selection
5. New species formation

Handbook of BIOLOGY

The diagrammatic presentation of above five propositions are given in following figure

The multiplication of individual of a species occurs in a geometric proportion. Due to this tendency of multiplication, in a very short time the earth would be overcrowded. Despite having the rapid rate of reproduction by a species its number remains about constant under fairly stable environment.

Due to this geometric population growth and their demands, the resources got depleted rapidly and lead to deficiency. As most of the natural resources are limited, it led to the adjustment among organisms for their needs. *The struggle for resources occurs at three levels*

1. **Intraspecific struggle** Struggle among individuals of same species. It is most intense.

2. **Interspecific struggle** Struggle between the individuals of two different species.

3. **Struggle with environment** It is the struggle of living forms against the environment.

Variations are the differences among the individuals. These variations can help to adjust with the environment.
There are two types of variations

1. **Continuous variation** It shows the whole range of variation among particular character.

2. **Discontinuous variation** These appears suddenly and shows no gradation.

Variations can be conclusively termed as environment induced adaptation by an individual.

The organisms which adapt useful variation are successfully survive in changing environment and those which fails to put those changes are not selected and stunted or removed from the population after death. This process is termed as **natural selection** by Darwin. The giraffes with small neck are failed to survive and died. The phrase **survival of the fittest** was given by **Herbert Spencer**.

The survived population radiated in different environment and establised as different species with changed/modified characters. This process of **establishment of new species** is called as speciation by Darwin. The new species is originated by combination of **struggle for existance, continuous variation** and **inheritance**.

Criticism of Darwin's Natural Selection Theory
Followings are the criticism against Darwin's theory
1. Darwin emphasised on **inheritance of small variation** which are non-inheritable and useless for evolution.
2. Darwin fails to explain the survival of the fittest.
3. Darwin fails to differentiate between **somatic** and **germinal variations**.
4. Natural selection does not explain the **co-ordinated development** and **co-adaptation**.
5. Darwin fails to explain the occurrence of vestigial organs.

Neo-Darwinism
It may be defined as the theory of organic evolution by the natural selection of inherited characteristics.

The theory of evolution given by **Darwin** and **Wallace** has been modified in the light of modern studies like genetics, molecular biology, palaentology and ecology, etc.

Postulates of Neo-Darwinism
These are as follows
(i) Neo-Darwinism distinguished between the germplasm and somatoplasm.
(ii) Neo-Darwinism explained that the adaptations result from the multiple forces and natural selection is one of them.
(iii) As per Darwinism, characters are not inherited as such, instead there are character determiners which control the development.
(iv) The characters are the result of determiner's (genes) of organisms and the environment during its development.

Mutation Theory (Hugo de Vries, 1848-1935)
To explain the process of evolution, **Hugo de Vries** proposed mutation theory, which was published in 1901 in his book 'Die Mutation Theorie'.

He gave much importance to the **discontinuous variations** or **saltatory variations**. He coined the term **mutation** for suddenly appearing saltatory variations.

Main Features of Mutation Theory

As the mutation theory is more emphasised on mutation's the features, **can be diagrammaticaly represented as**

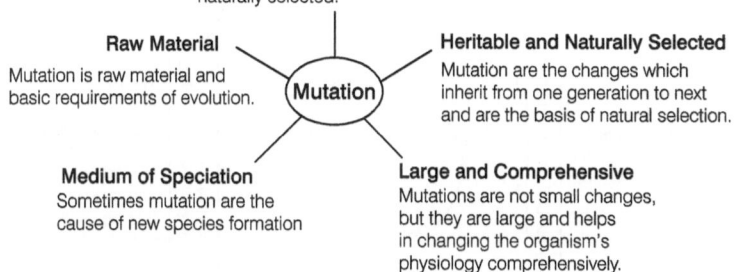

Criticism against Mutation Theory

(i) The **Oenothera lamarckiana** of **Hugo De Vries** was not a normal plant, but a complex heterozygous form with chromosome aberrations.

(ii) Natural mutations are not the common phenomenon.

(iii) Most mutations are **recessive** and **retrogressive**.

(iv) Mutation theory fails to explain the role of nature in the process of evolution.

Modern Synthetic Theory of Evolution

The modern theory of origin of species or evolution is known as **modern synthetic theory** of evolution.

The modern synthetic theory of evolution evolved in 1937, with the publication of Dobzhansky's **Genetics and the Origin of Species** which was supported by **Huxley** (1942), **Mayr** (1942) and **Stebbins** (1950), etc.

Main Postulates of Modern Synthetic Theory of Evolution

This theory has four basic types of processes, this can be represented diagrammatically as following

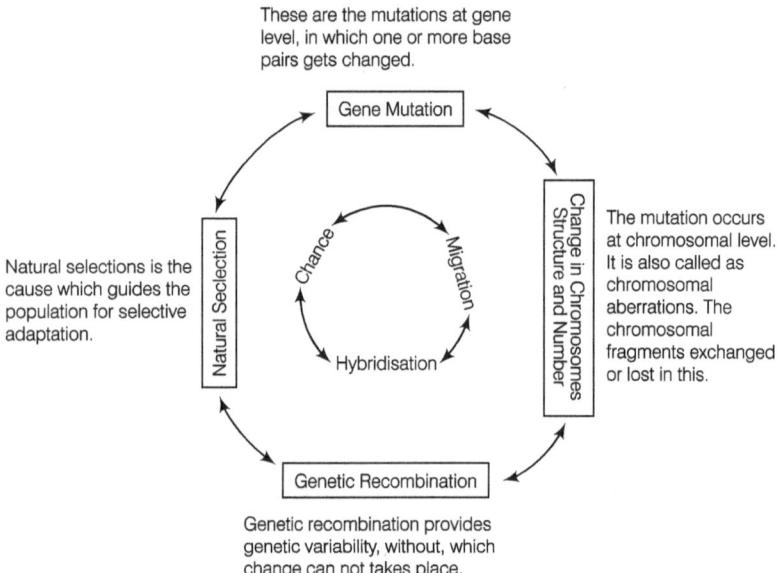

Causes and processes of evolution (causes with bold and processes in boxes)

Mechanism of Evolution

Evolution is a change in a populations alleles and genotype from generation to generation. There are four basic mechanisms by which evolution takes place. These includes **mutation, migration, genetic drift** and **natural selection**.

Agents of evolutionary change *Various agents of evolutionary changes are as follows*

Mutation It is **sudden** and **heritable change** in an organism, which is generally due to change in the base sequence of nucleic acid in the genome of the organisms. It is the ultimate source of variations.

Mutation may be harmful or beneficial for the organism. It helps in the accumulation of variations which later results in large variations and new species formation.

Gene Migration (Gene Flow)

The movement of individuals from one place to another is called migration. It can be a powerful agent of change because the members of two different populations may exchange genetic material.

Sometimes **gene flow** is obvious when an animal moves from one place to another. When a newcomer individual have unique gene combination and is well adapted, it alter the genetic composition of receiving population.

Genetic Drift or Random Drift In small population, frequencies of particular allele may change drastically by chance alone. Such change in allele frequencies occurs randomly as if the frequencies were drifting and are thus known as **genetic drift**. It continues until genic combination is fixed and another is completely eliminated.

There are two special cases of genetic drift

1. **Founder Effect/Founder Principle** It is noted that when a small group of persons called founders, leaves their place of origin and find new settlements the population in the new settlement may have unique genotypic frequency from that of the parent population.

   Formation of a different genotype in new settlement is called **founder effect.**

2. **Bottle Neck Effect** Due to several natural causes, the population decline even if the organisms do not move from one place to another.

   A few surviving individuals may constitute a random genetic sample of the original population. The resultant alterations and loss of genetic variability has been termed as bottleneck effect.

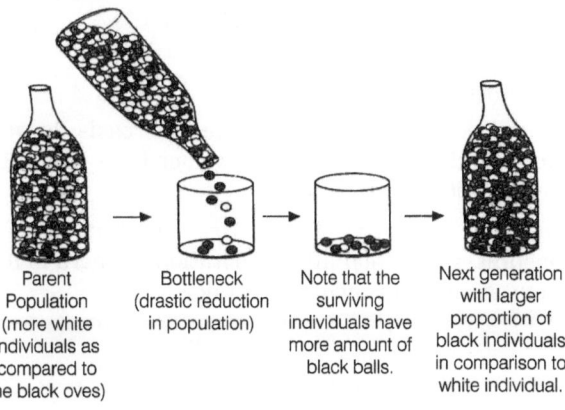

Parent Population (more white individuals as compared to the black oves) → Bottleneck (drastic reduction in population) → Note that the surviving individuals have more amount of black balls. → Next generation with larger proportion of black individuals in comparison to white individual.

Selection Darwin and Wallace explained the differential reproduction as the result of selection. *It is of two types*

1. **Artificial selection** In this the breeder select for the desired characterisitics.
2. **Natural selection** Environmental conditions determine that which individual in population produces the maximum number of offsprings.

On the basis of environmental conditions, natural selection can be categorised as follows

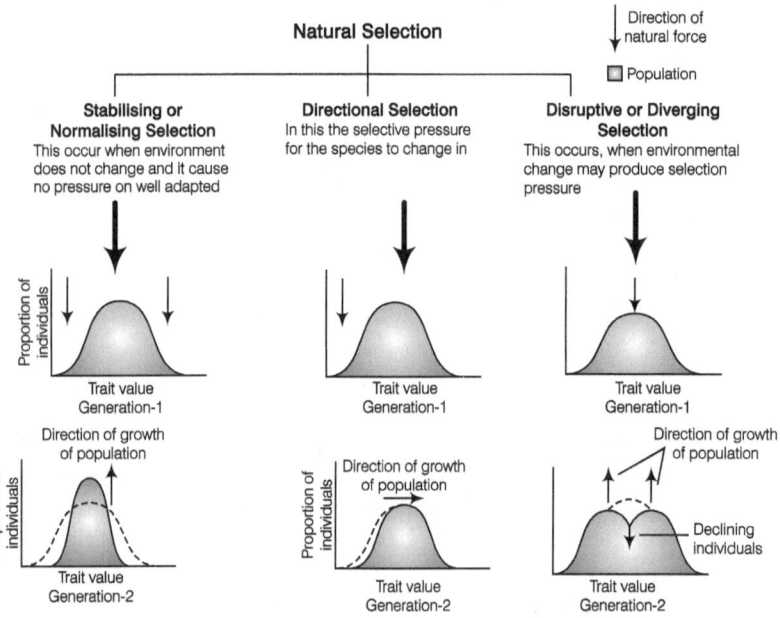

Hardy-Weinberg Law

It is the fundamental law which provides the basis for studying the **Mendelian populations**. It was developed by **GH Hardy** and **G Weinberg** in 1908. It states that

'W'The gene and genotypic frequencies in Mendelian population remains constant, generation after generation, if there is no selection, migration, mutation and random drift takes place."

Handbook of BIOLOGY

Followings are the conditions for **Hardy-Weinberg equilibrium**.

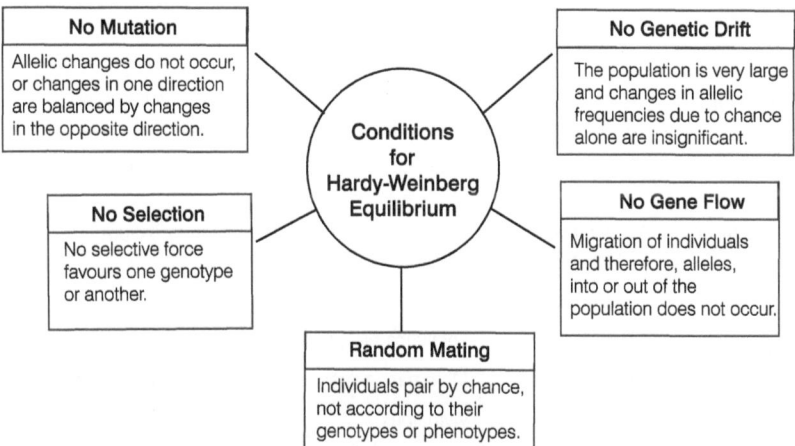

Hardy-Weinberg principle is a tool to determine when evolution is *occurring*. To estimate the frequency of alleles in a population, we can use the Hardy-Weinberg equation.

According to this equation

P = the frequency of the dominant allele (represented here by A)

q = the frequency of the recessive allele (represented here by a)

For a population in genetic equilibrium

$p + q = 1.0$ (The sum of the frequencies of both alleles is 100%)

$(p+q)^2 = 1$

So, $p^2 + 2pq + q^2 = 1$

The three terms of this binomial expansion indicates the frequencies of the three genotypes

p^2 = frequency of *AA* (homozygous dominant)

$2pq$ = frequency of *Aa* (heterozygous)

q^2 = frequency of *aa* (homozygous recessive)

Evolution of Human

The human beings belong to a single family-**Hominidae**, which include a single genus *Homo* which have a single living species *sapiens* and a single living subspecies sapiens. All the racial groups **mongoloid, Negroid, Caucasoid** and **Australoid** are the types of *Homo sapiens sapiens*.

The detailed classification of human with their general characteristics are mentioned in following table

Classification of Human

Kingdom	Animalia	Absence of chlorophyll, cell wall, presence of locomotion and intake of complex food.
Phylum	Chordata	Presence of notochord and dorsal hollow central nervous system.
Sub-phylum	Vertebrata (Craniata)	Presence of vertebral column and cranium (brain box).
Section	Gnathostomata	Jaws are present.
Super-class	Tetrapoda	Forelimbs are present.
Class	Mammalia	Mammary glands, ear pinna and hair are present.
Sub-class	Theria	Viviparous.
Infraclass	Eutheria	Presence of true placenta.
Order	Primata	Presence of nails over the digits.
Sub-order	Anthropoidea	Facial muscles are present for the emotional expression.
Family	Hominidae	Posture is erect and bipedal locomotion.
Genus	*Homo*	Man
Species	*Sapiens*	Wise
Sub-species	*Sapiens*	Most wise

Human and Other Primates

The primates originated in the beginning of the tertiary period (palaeocene epoch) about 65 million years ago from a small terrestrial shrew like **insectivore**.

The begining of primate evolution is presumed in eocene of tertiary period. (75-60 million years ago) in evergreen forests. The place of origin of human is great controversy.

The fossils of humans were obtained from Africa, Asia and Europe, but most probably the origin of human occurred in central Asia, China, Java and India (Shivalik hills).

Handbook of BIOLOGY

Following primate tree, throw a light on human evolution

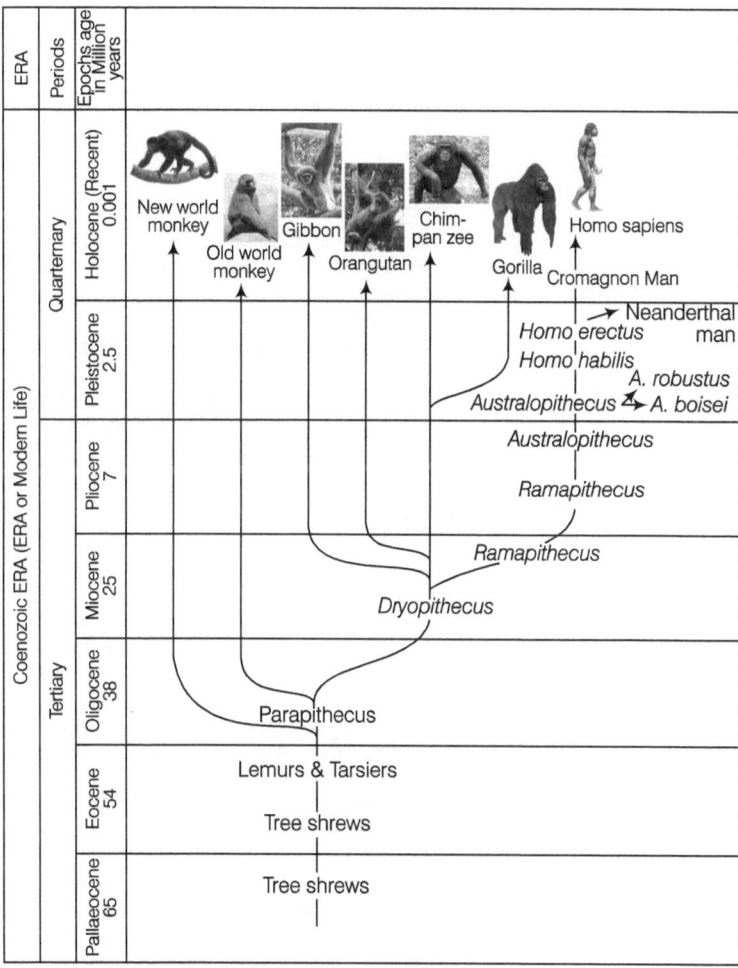

Human evolution can be explained through the series of following intermediates of early humans. From the earliest ape like ancestors to the modern man, the evolution is slow and dynamic process.

The common ancestry of both **ape** and **human** got differentiated after *Dryopithecus* and the first man like primate was Ramapithecus, it was the oldest man's ancestor and the first hominoid.

Australopithecus, constitute the first **ape man**, which had both man and ape characters. *Australopithecus* gave rise to *Homo habilis* approximately 2 million years ago.

Homo habilis (handy man or able man or skillful man or the tool maker)  *Homo habilis*	**Discovery** • Mary Leakey (1961) obtained the fossils of *Homo habilis* from Pleistocene rocks of Olduvi Gorge in East Africa. • Richard Leakey (1972) also obtained fossils of *Homo habilis* from East side of Lake Turkana in Kenya **Characteristics** • *Homo habilis* man was about 1.2 to 1.5m tall. • Its cranial capacity was 700-800 cc, which lived in Africa about two million years ago. • *Homo habilis* was carnivorous and had begun hunting for meat. • *Homo habilis* lived in small community or groups in caves. • Perhaps they showed sexual division of labour and communicated with visual signals and simple audible sounds.
Homo erectus (erect man)  *Homo erectus*	**Discovery** • Fossils of *Homo erectus* obtained from diverse sites from Olduvai Gorge in Africa to java, Algeria, Germany, Hungary and China. • Fossils were 800000 to 30000 years ago. • *Homo erectus* is considered as the direct ancestor of modern man. It evolved from *H. habilis* about 1.7 million years ago in the Pleistocene. • Homo erectus species include the fossils of Java man, peking man, Heidelberg man, Algerian of Atlantic man. **Characteristics** • They were the oldest known early human to have modern human like body proportion. • They were the first human species to have fleshy nose. They had flat skull was with prominent ridges over the brow. • They had short arm and long legs. The short arms depicts that the tree climbing ability was lost completely in them. The long legs depicts that they are better suited for long distance migrations. • They were the first one to walk upright and stood erect thus, named so, Also known as *Homo ergaster*. • They were the first hominid to live in hunter-gatherer society.

(a) Java man or *Pithecanthropus erectus* or *Homo erectus* (ape man that walks erect) 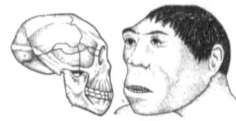 Java man	**Discovery**<ul><li>In 1891, Eugene Dubois obtained fossils (some teeth, skull cap and femur bone) from Pleistocene deposits (500000-1500000 years back) in central java (an island of Indonesia).</li><li>It was named *Pithecanthropus* erectus (ape man that can walk erect) by Eugene Dubois and *Homo erectus* by **Mayer** (1950).</li></ul>**Characteristics**<ul><li>Java man was more than 25 feet tall and weight about 70 kg.</li><li>Its legs were ling and erect, but body slightly bent during movement.</li><li>Java man was the first pre-historic man, who began the use of fire for cooking, defence and hunting.</li><li>Its cranial cavity was 940cc, which is about intermediate between Australopithecus (600-700cc) and modern man (1400-1600cc).</li></ul>
(b) Peking man (*Homo erectus Pdkinensis* or *Pithecanthropus pekinensis* or *Sinanthropus Pekinensis*) 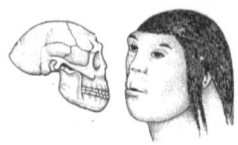 Peking man	**Discovery**<ul><li>The fossils (skulls, jaws and post cranial bony fragments) of peking man were discovered by WC Pai (1924) from the lime stone caves of Choukoutien near peking (peking is the former name of China's capital Beijing).</li><li>These fossils of peking man were about six lakh years old.</li></ul>**Characteristics**<ul><li>Peking man was 1.55 to 1.60m tall, *i.e.,* slightly shorter, lighter and weaker than java man.</li><li>The cranial cavity of Peking man was 850-1200cc that is more than java man.</li></ul>
(c) Heidelberg man (*Homo erectus heidelbergensis*)  Heidelberg man	**Discovery**<ul><li>The fossil of Heidelberg man is represented by lower jaw, which was found from the middle Pleistocene rocks of Heidelberg (Germany).</li><li>Credit for the discovery of Heidelberg man goes to Otto Schoetensack.</li></ul>**Characteristics**<ul><li>It had ape like lower jaw with all the teeth. The teeth were human like.</li><li>The jaw was large, heavy and lack a chin.</li><li>Its cranial cavity was probably about 1300cc, intermediate between erect man (H. erectus) and Neanderthal man (*H. sapiens neanderthalensis*).</li><li>Heidelberg man is regarded as an ancestor to Neanderthal man and contemporary to Homo erectus.</li></ul>

Neanderthal man
(*Homo sapiens neanderthalensis*)

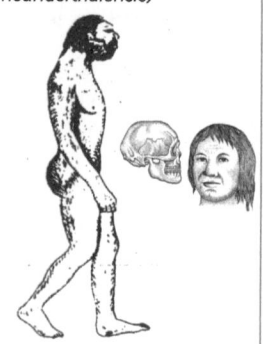

Neanderthal man

Discovery
- Fossils of Neanderthal man was discovered by C Fuhlrott (1856) from Neander valley in Germany.
- Neanderthal man arose about 150000 years ago and flourished in Asia, Europe and North Africa. Neanderthal man extinct about 25000 years ago.

Characteristics
- Neanderthal man existed in the late Pleistocene period.
- Neanderthal walked upright with bipedal movement.
- **Cro-magnon man** (*Homo sapiens fossilis*) or fossil man closest to modern man or direct ancestor of living modern man.

Cro-magnon man

Discovery
- Mac Gregor discovered the fossil of cro-magnon man from Cro-magnon rocks of France in1868.

Characteristics
- Cro-magnon man was almost similar to modern man with about 1.8m height. Orthognathous face, broad and arched forehead, strong jaws, elevated nose and well developed chin as well as dentition.
- Cranial capacity was about 1650cc, *i.e.*, much more than modern man (1450cc).
- Probably they succeeded from Neanderthal man and distributed in Africa, Europe and Middle East.
- Cro-magnon lived during old stone age which is also known as palaeolithic. (began more than 2 million years ago).

Living Modern man
(*Homo sapiens sapiens*)

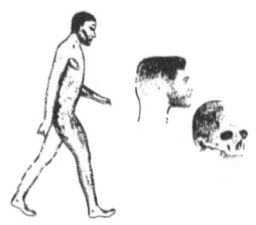

Modern man

Discovery
- It is believed that living modern man first appeared about 10000 years ago in the regions of Caspian sea and Mediterranean sea.

Characteristics
- Its cranial capacity is average 1450cc, which is lesser than cro-magnon.
- It is distinguished from cro-magnon merely by slight raising of skull cap, reduction in volume of cranial cavity (1300-1600cc) thinning of skull bones and formation of four curves in the vertebral column.
- Human species (*sapiens*) have white or caucaroid, mongoloid and black or negroid races.

Future Man (*Homo sapiens futuris*)

The organic evolution is a continuous process of nature, which is still continued at present and probably will remains in future too. It is believed that in future, human could change as a result of the factors like **gene mutation, gene recombination** and **natural selection**.

An American anthropologis **HL Sapiro** named the future man, (*Homo sapiens futuris* which may possess following characteristics

   (i) Height will be higher.
  (ii) Hair will reduce and skull may become dome-shaped.
 (iii) Body and cranium will be more developed.
 (iv) The fifth finger may reduce.
  (v) The age will increase.

35
Ecosystem

An **ecosystem** consists of biological community that occurs in some locale and the physical and chemical factors that make up its non-living or abiotic environment.

'Ecosystem is normally an **open system** because, there is a continuous entry and loss of energy and materials'.

The term **ecosystem** was first used by **AG Tensley** in 1935 to describe the whole complex of living organisms living together as a sociological units and their habitats.

The ecosystem is also called as **biocoenosis** (Mobius; 1877), **microcosm** (Forbes; 1887) and **biogeocoenosis** (Sukachey).

It is also known as **ecocosm** or **biosystem**.

Classification of Ecosystem
On the basis of origin, the ecosystem can be classified in following ways

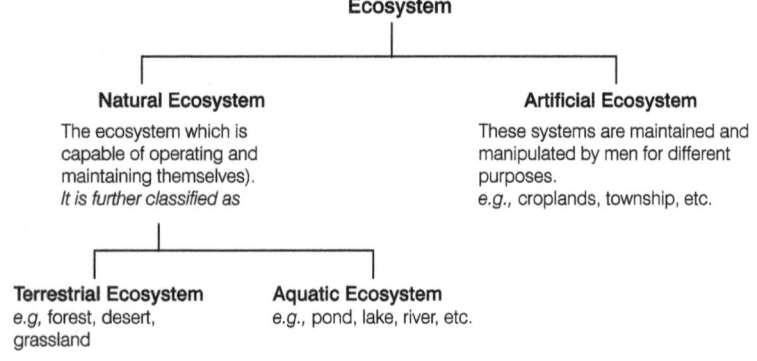

Components of Ecosystem

Eugene P. Odum explained the components of ecosystem on the basis of trophic level as follows

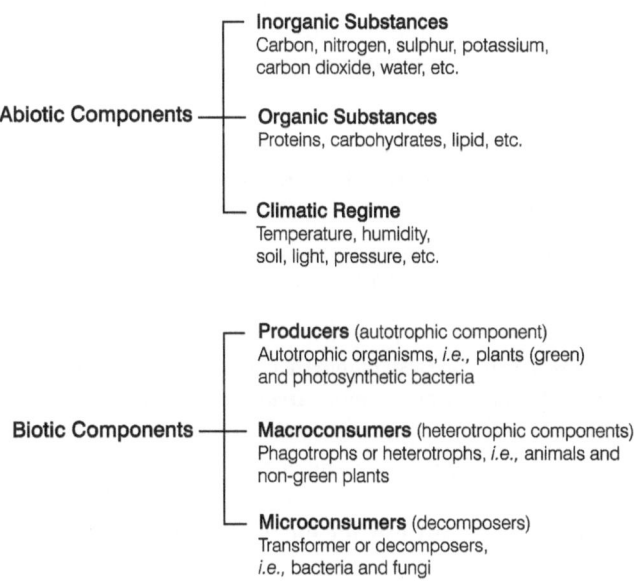

Components of ecosystem

Abiotic Components

Abiotic components of an ecosystem consists of two things, the **material** and **energy**.

The important abiotic components include, temperature, wind, light, water, soil and mineral, etc.

Temperature

It is the most ecologically relevant environment factor. **Latitude, altitude, topography, vegetation** and **slope aspects** are some factors which influence the temperature.

Temperature regulated periodic activities are reported from animals. *e.g.,* **diurnal** (active during day), **nocturnal** (active during night), **auroral** (active at dawn), **vesperal** (active during evening) and **crepuscular** (active in twilight).

Water

It is the most important for all living processes. Infact the life on earth is originated in water and without water, it is unsustainable.

Water constitutes most part of our body and blood. On the basis of water availability in plants, they are grouped into three communities namely **hydrophytes**, **mesophytes** and **xerophytes**.

Light

Light with wavelength between 400–760 nm is the **visible light**. The part of light which is effective in photosynthesis (*i.e.*, 400-700 nm) is termed as Photosynthetically Active Radiation (PAR).

This band of energy provides radiant energy for photosynthesis and thus **support all autotrophic organisms**.

Soil

It is weathered top surface of earth's crust constituted by **mineral matter** (sand, silt and clay), **organic matter** (humus) and **microorganisms** (bacteria, fungi, etc).

Soil is the medium of anchorage and supply of **nutrients** and **water** to plants and plants are ultimate source of energy for animals and human. Hence, soil constitutes the important life support component of the biosphere.

Biotic Components

The biotic components are divided into following categories

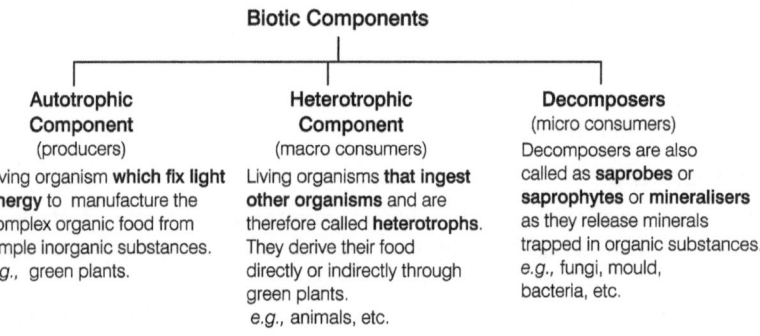

Handbook of BIOLOGY

On the basis of role in trophic structure, macroconsumers or consumers are categorised as

Consumers

Primary Consumers (herbivore)	Secondary Consumers (carnivore)	Tertiary Consumers (top carnivore)	Detritivores
These organisms feed directly on producers. These are also known as **key industry animals**. e.g., **protozoans** (pond ecosystem), **deer** (forest ecosystem), etc.	The group of organisms which feed on primary consumers. e.g., insects, game fishes, etc.	These animals eat other carnivores. Some ecosystems have **top carnivores** like lion and vulture.	These organisms depend on the organic detritus. e.g., earthworm.

Ecosystem : Structure and Characteristics

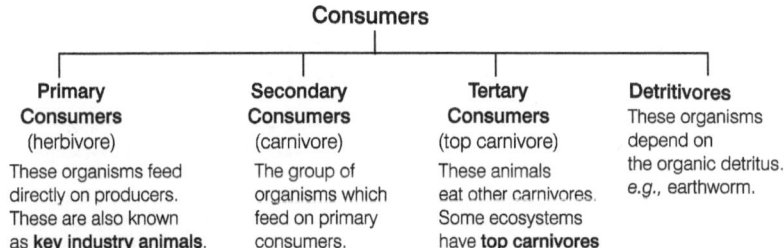

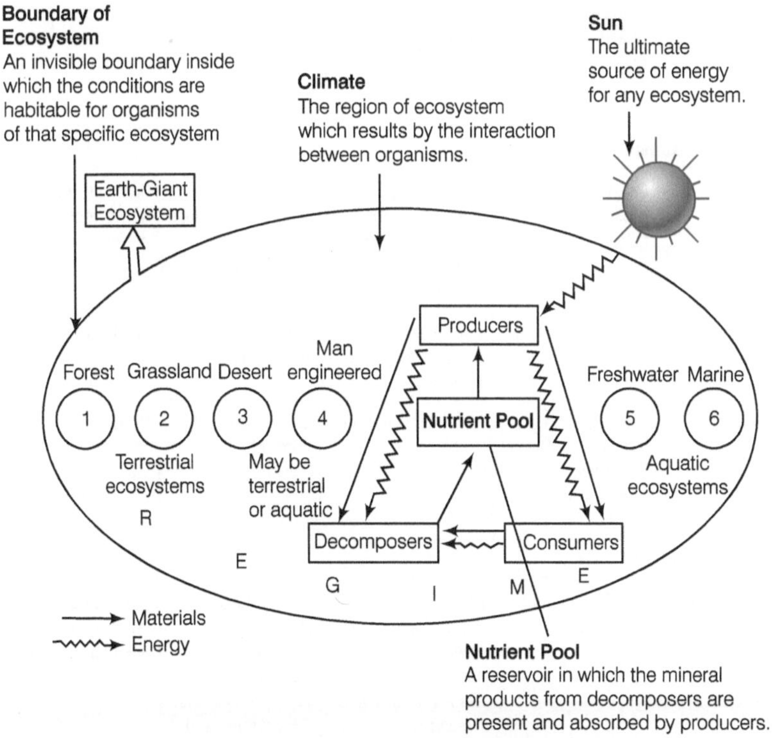

Structure of an ecosystem (generalised)

Features of Ecosystem

A comparative account of several ecosystems are given in the following table

Comparative Summary of Marine, Grassland, Forest and Desert Ecosystems

Component	Marine Ecosystem	Grassland Ecosystem	Forest Ecosystem	Desert Ecosystem
Abiotic components	Temperature zones, air, O_2, minerals rich salts, etc	CO_2, H_2O, nitrate, phosphate and sulphates, roughly 19% of the earth's crust	Soil and atmosphere.	Rainfall less than 25 cm, extreme of temperature and cold
Biotic components	Phytoplanktons, diatoms and dinoflagellates	*Dichanthium* and *Cynodon*	Mainly trees teak, sal	Shrubs, bushes, some grasses and very few trees.
Producers	Microscopic algae, members of phaeophyta and rhodophyta	*Digitaria*, *Dactyloctenium*, *Setaria* and also few shrubs.	*Quercus* in temperate forest *Pinus*, *Abies*, *Cedrus*, *Juniperus* and *Rhododendron*	Cycads, cacti, palm, coconut, etc.

Macro Consumers

Component	Marine Ecosystem	Grassland Ecosystem	Forest Ecosystem	Desert Ecosystem
Primary	Crustaceans, molluscs and fishes	Deer, sheep, cow, buffaloes, rabbit, mouse. Also some insects, termites and millipedes.	Leafhoppers, flies, beetle, bugs spider deer, mouse and moles	Animals, insects, some reptiles and camel
Secondary	Carnivorous fishes	Fox, jackal, snake, frogs, lizards and birds.	Lizard, fox snake and birds	Reptiles
Tertiary	Harring, shad and mackeral carnivore fishes like cod, haddock, halibut, etc.	Hawk and vulture	Lion, tiger, wild cats, etc.	Vultures

Micro Consumers

Component	Marine Ecosystem	Grassland Ecosystem	Forest Ecosystem	Desert Ecosystem
Decomposers	Chiefly bacteria and fungi	*Mucor*, *Aspergillus*, *Penicillium*, *Fusarium*, *Cladosporium* and *Rhizopus*	Mostly fungi, *Aspergillus*, *Polyporus*, *Fusarium*, Bacteria *Bacillus*, *Clostridium* and *Streptomyces*	Fungi and bacteria, which are thermophilic

Functions of Ecosystem

Following four are the important functional aspects of the ecosystem

(i) Decomposition
(ii) Productivity
(iii) Energy flow
(iv) Development and stabilisation
(v) Nutrient cycle

Before going in detail about the functional aspects of ecosystem, we need the better understanding of **food chain** and **food web**.

Food Chain

As the biotic factors of the ecosystem are linked together by food, a particular linking makes a chain called **food chain**, *it is* 'A group of organisms in which there is a transfer of food energy takes place through a series of repeated process of eating and by eaten'.

It is always **straight** and usually contain 4-5 trophic level.

Types of Food Chain

On the basis of habits of organisms involved, the food chain can be categorised as

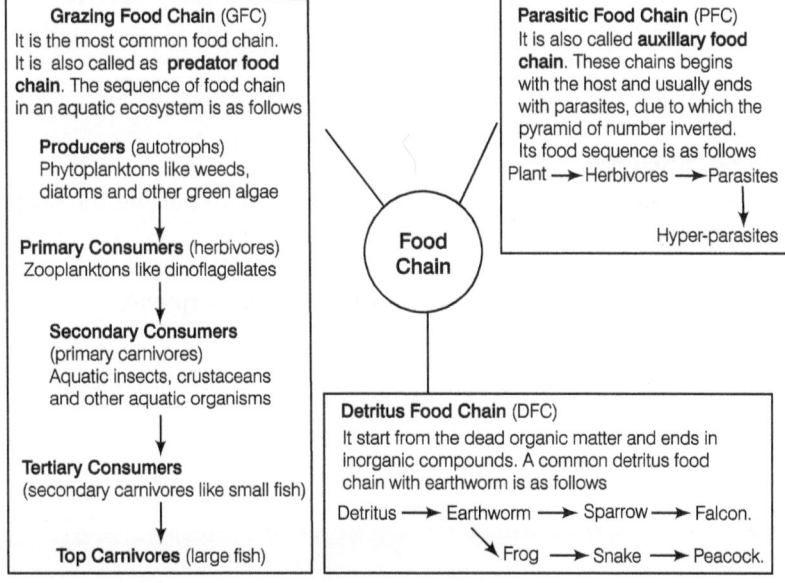

Types of food chain

Food Web

Food web is the network of food chains which become interconnected at various trophic levels. In any complex food web, one can recognise several different trophic levels.

In a food web, a given species may occupy more than one trophic levels. The complexity of food web vary greatly and this can be expressed by a measure called connectance of the food web.

$$\text{Connectance} = \frac{\text{Actual number of interspecific interaction}}{\text{Potential number of interspecific interaction}}$$

A typical food web can be represented as follows

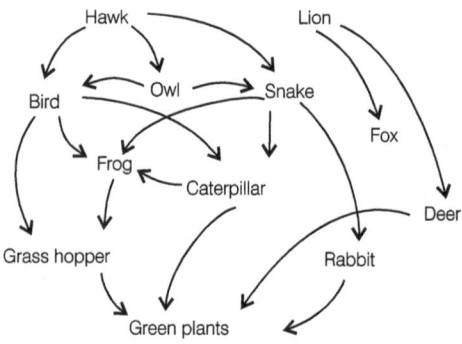

Food web

1. Decomposition

The process of decomposition completely takes place outside the body of decomposers.

They digest the organic substances outside their body and then absorb it. Hence, they are also known as **osmotrophs** (absorptive).

Process of Decomposition

There are three processes which occur simultaneously during decomposition.

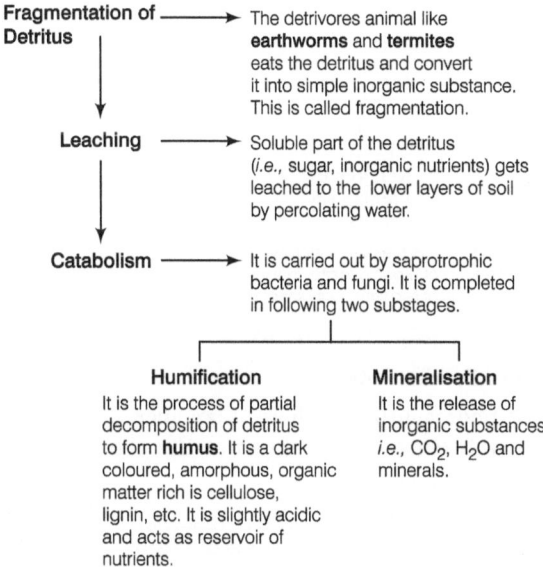

Factors Affecting Decomposition

(i) **Chemical nature of detritus** Slow decomposition, (cellulose, lignin, tannin, resin) fast decomposition (protein, nucleic acid).

(ii) **Soil pH** Acidic (slow decomposition), alkaline soil (fast decomposition).

(iii) **Temperature** Temperature $\propto$ rate of decomposition.

(iv) **Moisture** Amount of moisture $\propto$ rate of decomposition.

(v) **Aeration** Amount of air $\propto$ rate of decomposition.

2. Productivity

It refers to the rate of biomass production, i.e., the rate at which the sunlight is captured by the producers for the synthesis of energy rich organic compounds.

'It is the amount of organic matter accumulated per unit area per unit time.'

Production Ecology is the branch of ecology that deals with the rate of production of organic matter in ecosystem.

It is of following types

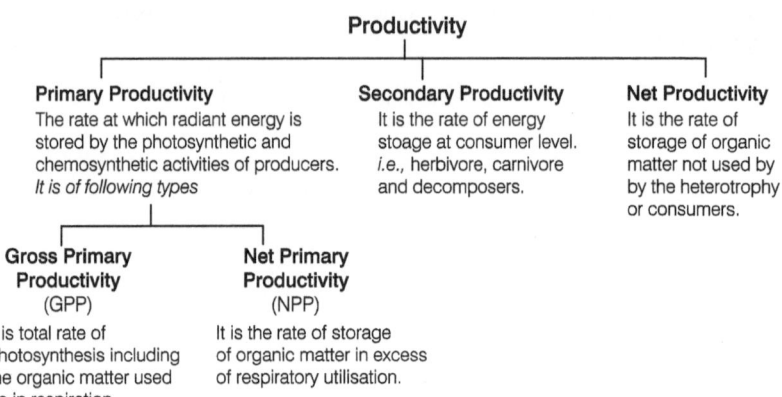

Measurement of Productivity

As a result of photosynthesis, there is an increase in dry mass. The **Relative Growth Rate** (R) is defined as the gain in mass per unit of plant mass in unit time.

$$R = \frac{\text{Increase in dry mass in unit time}}{\text{Dry mass of plant}}$$

The increase in dry mass in unit time is equal to $\frac{w_t - w_0}{t}$

w_t = dry mass after time t,
w_0 = dry mass at the start of time period.

The **Net Assimilation Rate** (NAR) relates increase in dry mass to leaf area.

$$\text{NAR} = \frac{\text{Increase in dry mass in unit time}}{\text{Leaf area}}$$

Biomass is the total dry mass of all organisms in an ecosystem.

Total biomass = Biomass of primary producers + Biomass of consumers
+ Biomass of decomposers + Biomass of dead organisms.

3. Energy Flow

'The movement of energy in ecosystem is termed as **energy flow**'

(It is unidirectional energy transformation). The flow of energy in ecosystem is controlled by two laws of thermodynamics.

First Law Energy can neither be created, nor be detroyed, but can be transferred or transformed to another form.

Second Law In every activity involving energy transformation, dissipation of some energy takes place.

The **incident radiation** of plant is about 1×10^6 kJ/m^2/yr and of this, about 95–99% is immediately lost by plant through **reflection, radiation** or **heat of evaporation**.

The remaining 1–5% is used in the production of organic molecules. Organism at each trophic level depends on those belongs to the lower trophic level for their energy requirements.

Each trophic level contains certain mass of living matter at a particular time called **standing crop**. The standing crop is measured as the mass of living organism (biomass).

The number of trophic level in the food chain is restricted as the transfer of energy which follows 10% **law** given by **Raynold Lindeman**.

Following diagram clearly describe the flow of energy in a food chain applying 10% law

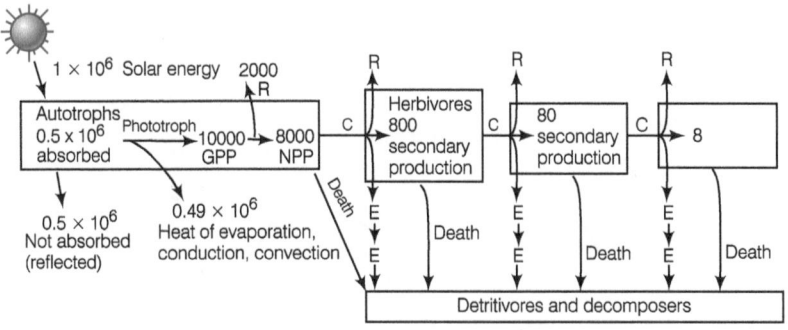

Energy flow through a grazing food chain

R = Energy loss through respiration, **E** = Energy loss from grazing food chain to detritivores and decomposers through excretion,

C = Consumption by organisms.

Here, biomass 800, 80 and 8 kJ/m^2/yr NPP shows that only 10% energy is transfered to the next trophic level.

Ecological Pyramids

It is the diagrammatic representation of the relationships among numbers, biomass and energy content of the producer and consumers of an ecosystem. The concept was proposed by **Charls Elton** (1927) hence, these are also known as **Eltonian pyramids**.

Types of Pyramids

Pyramids can be of different types including upright or inverted or spindle shaped.

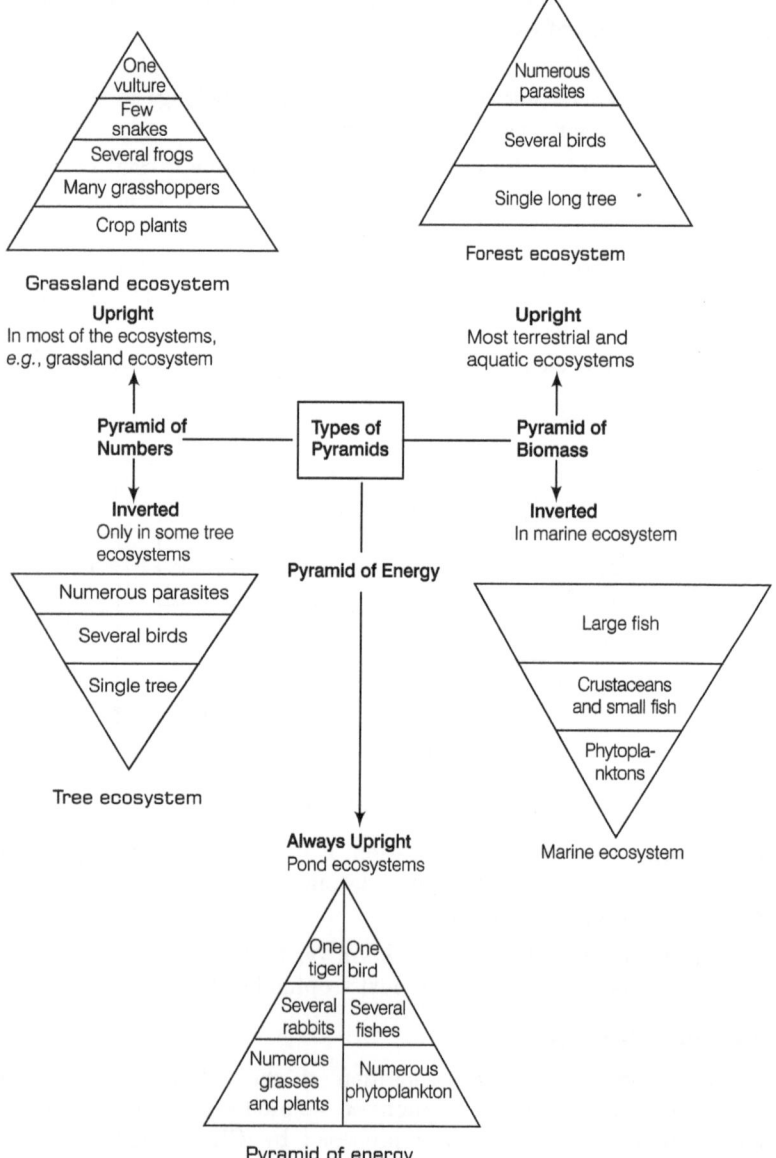

Handbook of BIOLOGY

Spindle shaped pyramid is seen in the forest ecosystem where the number of produces are lesser in number and support a greater number of herbivores and which in turn support a fewer number of cornivores.

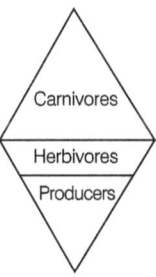

Partly upright pyramid of number

4. Development and Stabilisation

An ecosystem develops and stabilise through the process of **ecological succession**.

Ecological Succession

It is a sequence of **seres** (developmental stage of a community) from baren land to the climax.

The initial community of the area which is replaced in time by a sequence of succeding communities until the climax is reached is called **pioneer stage** or **pioneer community**. The intermediate stages between pioneer and climax stages (*i.e.*, final stage) are called as **seral stages**.

Causes of Succession

The causes of ecological succession can be of three types as follows

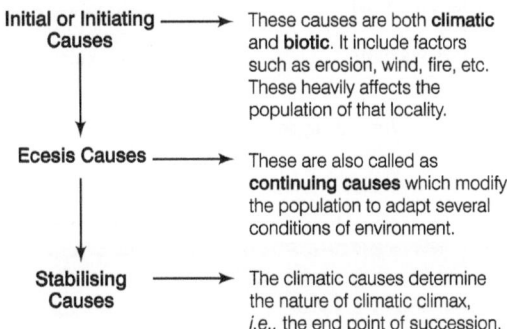

Changes During Biotic Succession

The following changes may occur due to ecological succession
(a) Small short lived plants to large long lived plants.
(b) Unstable biotic community to stable biotic community.
(c) Little diversity to high diversity.
(d) Greater niche specialisation.
(e) Increase in biomass.
(f) Increase in soil differentiation.
(g) Increase in humus content of the soil.
(h) Aquatic or dry conditions to mesic conditions.
(i) Simple food chains to complex food webs.

Types of Succession

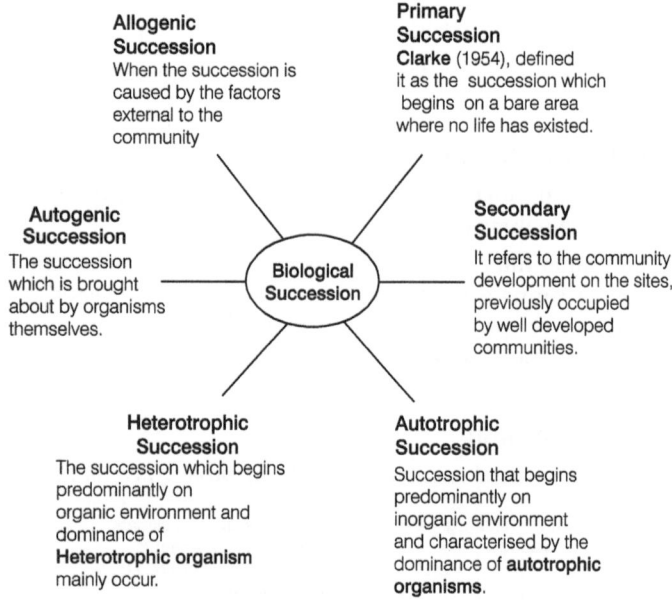

Various types of succession

Process of Succession

The succession is a slow and complex phenomenon, *which is categorised into following stages and substages*

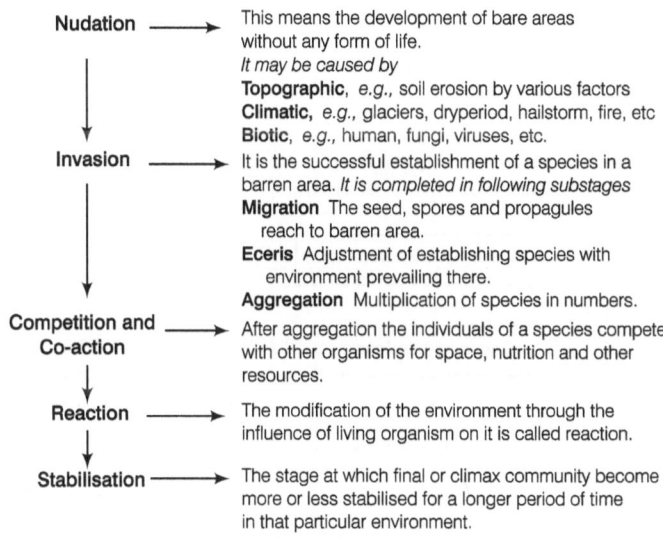

The processes involved in succession

Examples of Biological Succession

Hydrosere and **xerosere** are the two main biological succession. *They are discussed below*

Hydrosere/Hydrarch Succession

In this succession, a pond and its community are converted into a land community.

Developments in Hydrosere/Hydrarch can be represented as follows

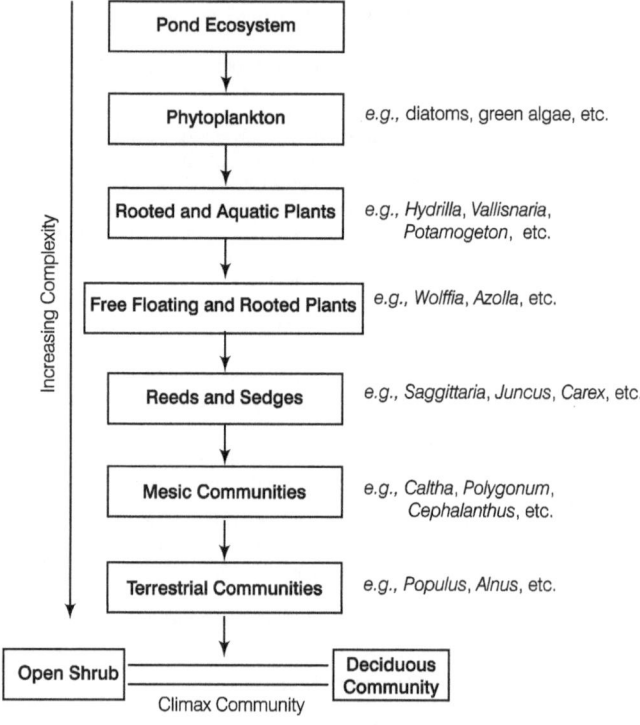

Succession in aquatic ecosystem

Xerosere/Xerarch Succession

Xerosere occurs on bare rock surface where the original substratum is deficient of water and lacks organic matter.

Handbook of BIOLOGY

Developments in Xerosere/Xerarch occurs in following stages

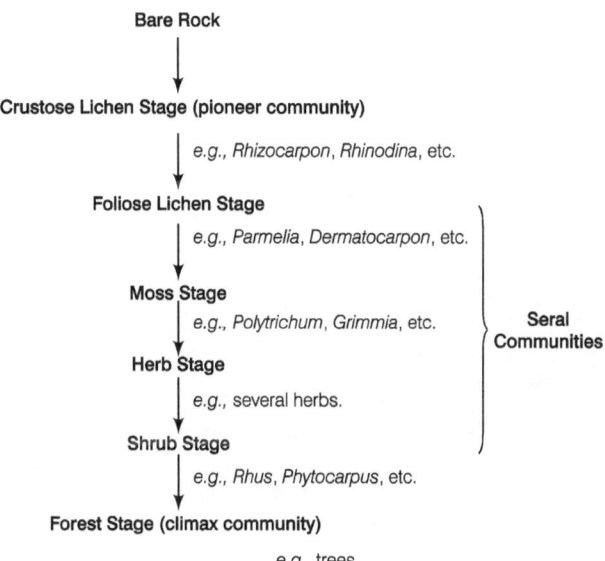

Succession on bare rock

5. Nutrient Cycling

For the maintenance of ecosystem, the nutrient gets recycled in ecosystem. The cycling of nutrients are also known as **biogeochemical cycling**.

This can be categorised as

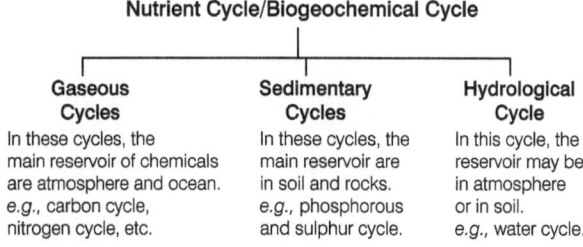

Carbon Cycle

The atmospheric carbon dioxide is virtually the only source of carbon. This gas is used by all the plants in photosynthesis and the end products (organic substance) of this complex process are used in the construction of living matter. *The complete carbon cycle looks like*

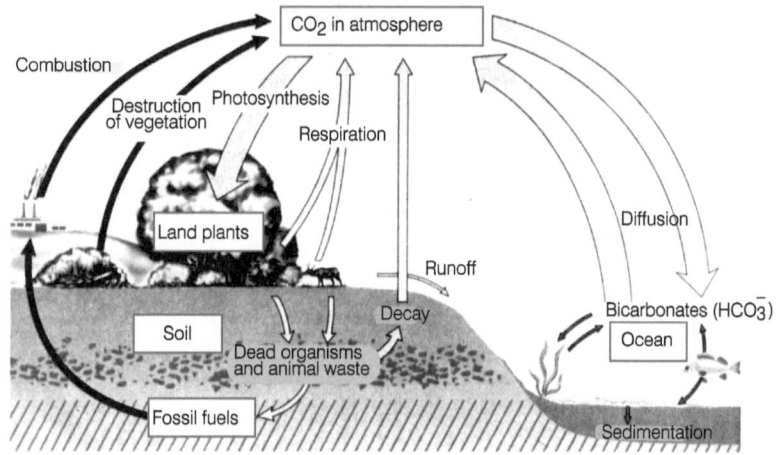

The carbon cycle

Phosphorus Cycle

Phosphorus cycle lacks an atmospheric component. The basic source and the great reservoir of phosphorus are the **rocks** and other deposits, which have been found in the **past geological ages**.

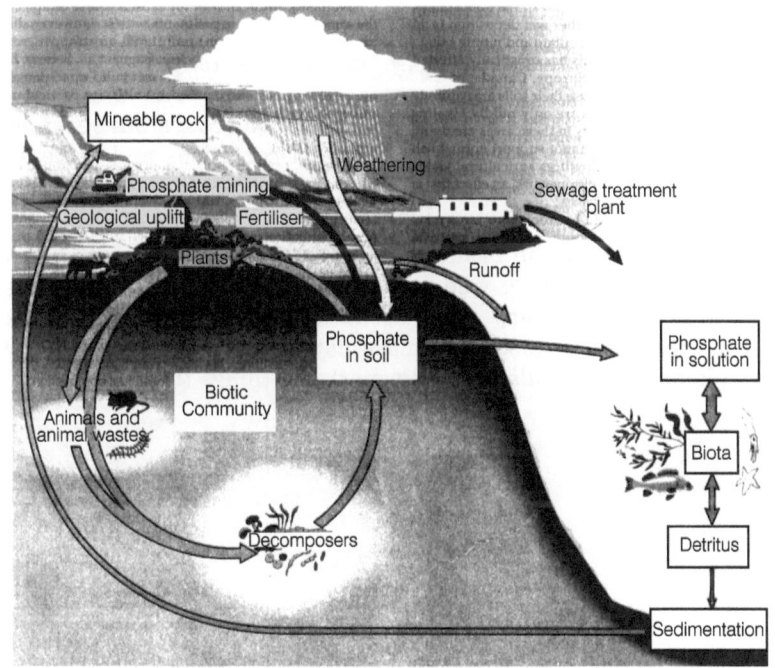

Phosphorus cycle in nature

Hydrological (Water) Cycle

Water moves in ecosystem through various reservoir. *i.e.,* ocean, atmosphere and living organisms. Following diagrammatic representation gives the idea of water cycle.

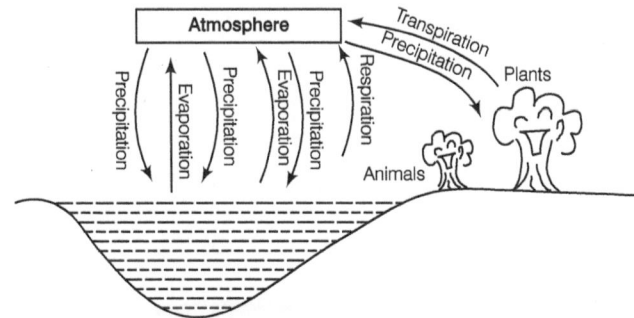

Water cycle in nature

Ecosystem Services

Healthy ecosystems are the base for a wide range of economic, environmental and aesthetic goods and services. The products of ecosystem processes are named as **ecological** or **ecosystem services**. Ecosystem service refer to a wide range of conditions and processes through which natural ecosystems, and the species that part of then, help sustain and fulfill human life.

These services maintain biodiversity and the production of ecosystem goods, such as seafood , wild game, forage, timeber, biomass fuels, natural fibres, and many pharmaceuticals, industrial products, and their precursors. It is also the transformation of a set of natural assets (soil, plants and animals, air and water) into things that we value.

36

Organisms and Population

Organism

An isolated, biological entity (*e.g.*, unicellular or multicellular) which is able to perform biological process independently called as **organism**. Individual organism is the basic unit of ecological hierarchy.

Organism and its Environment

Organism's life exists not just in a few, favourable habitats, but even in extreme and harsh conditions, *e.g.*, desert, rainforests, deep ocean and other unique habitats.

The suitability of environment directly affect the growth of residing population and manifested in from of various biological communities.

Following diagrammatic representation clearly indicates the relationship between environmental conditions and its impact on population which ultimately results into different types of communities.

Grasslands
Temperature. 20-30° with increasing rain precipitation up to 75-80 cm, the species richness and productivity increased with high biomass.

Deserts
Lack of water, temperature is very high/very low, less precipitation, arid climate lead to sparse population with desert adapted feature like spine, etc.

Tropical Forest
Most suitable combination of Temperature. (20-30°C) and precipitation (150-430 cm) lead to well adapted community with evergreen plants and animals.

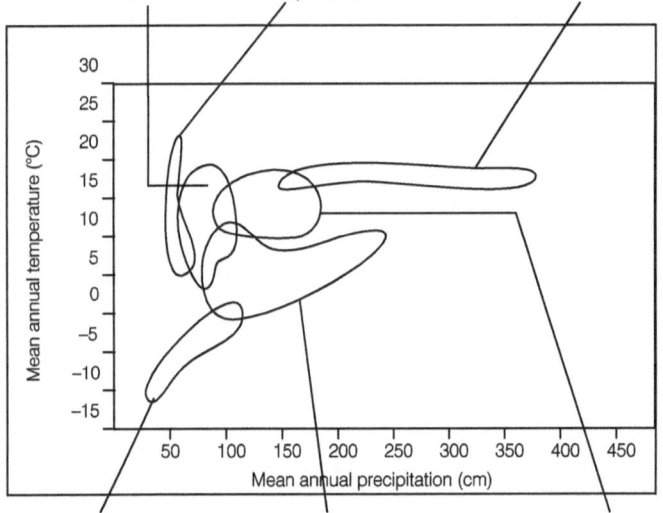

Arctic and Alpine Tundra
Very low temperature and precipitation, therefore very low biodiversity as present at high latitundes in Northern hemisphere.

Coniferous Forest
Low temperature and high precipitation results in to marshy floors in forest because of high humus deposition, which support high biodiversity

Temperate Forest
Moderate temperature and pracipitation therefore soft woody and hard woody plant and all type of animals are present.

Climatic adaptation among floral and faunal communities

Responses to Abiotic Factors

Organism cope up with the stressful conditions or possibilities to manage with the adverse situation.

With following set of modifications, an organism can stabilised its relationship with environment.

Regulate

Some organisms are able to maintain a constant body temperature and constant osmotic concentration despite changes in the external environment. *e.g.,* **Thermoregulation**, as human is an isothermic organism, it regulate the temperature, in summer by sweating and in winter by shivering. The process of regulation mostly occurs in birds and higher animals.

Conform

It is the strategy to adjustment of organisms towards environmental conditions. In this an organism control their physiology in the tune of environmental conditions. *e.g.*, poikilotherms (*i.e.*, an organism which fails to maintain their body temperature constant) changes their body temperature with environment. *e.g.*, fishes.

Migrate

It is the movement of an organism from less favourable conditions to more favourable conditions.

On the basis of driving factors of migration, it is of following four types

1. **Diurnal migration** When migration is controlled by cycle of day and night. *e.g.*, the movement of planktons towards the surface of aquatic bodies during night and descent to deapth during day.
2. **Metamorphic migration** Migration is controlled by stage of life, *e.g.*, Salmon fishes living in Pacific ocean ascends fresh water stream once in life for spawning and after laying eggs, breedes die and offspring returns back to the ocean to develop for period of years before they again repeat the event.
3. **Periodic migration** These migration controlled by size and population. *e.g.*, several insects migrate from there place of origin when population increases beyond carrying capacity of that place.
4. **Annual migration** Migration regulated by time of year. *e.g.*, Siberian Cranes migrate to India at specific period (July to September month).

Suspend

To suspend unfavourable condition, organism slowed down their metabolic process *e.g.*,

1. Lower plant produce spore with thick covering to sustain unfavourable condition and germinates in favourable condition.
2. Polar bears undergoes **hibernation** during winters.

Camouflage

It is the ability of an organism to blend with the surrounding or background. Organism use camouflage to mask their **location**, **identity** and **movement**.

e.g., many insects, reptiles and mammals (like military colouration dress), insects (like butterfly).

Adaptation

Organisms adapted morphologically, physiologically, behaviourally to survive and reproduce in its habitat by making adjustment with environment.

Adaptation are of two types

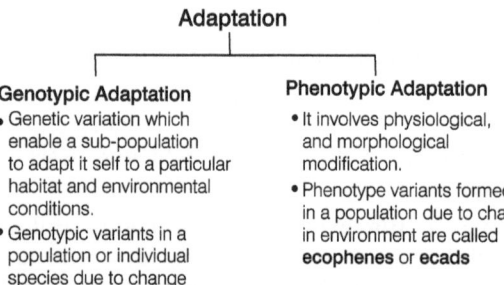

Strategic Adaptation in Plants

Plant Adaptation to Light Region

(a) **Heliophytes/Sun Loving Plants**

(i) Stem short internode, leaves thicker, bladed phototropism.

(ii) High respiration rate.

'Plant growing in bright light', but some heliophyte plant will grow in partial shade. *e.g.,* sugarcane, sunflower, maize and *Bougainvillea* etc.

(b) **Sciophytes/Shade Loving Plants**

Stem thin, long internode sparsely branched, poorly developed conducting and machenical tissue.

- 'Plant growing in partial shade or low light', but some sciophytes which are not damaged by bright light. *e.g., Drosera, Nepenthese*, birch, spruce, etc.
- These are aerobic, shows low rate of respiration.

(c) **Stratification**

In a forest, plant get arranged in various strata (layers/ arrangement their size, *i.e.,* grasses, herbs, shurbs and trees) according to their **shade tolerance** called as **stratification**.

Plant Adaptations to Aquatic Environments

The plant growing in aquatic habitat are called as **hydrophytes** or **aquatic plants**. *Hydrophytes are of five types*

Emergent Hydrophytes
(Amphibious Plants)
- Plants grows in shallow water of marshy area/swamps.
- Long shoot, aerial leaves with stomata, root well-developed rhizome present.
- Cuticle present to avoid dessication, developed vascular bandles e.g., *Ranunculus*.

Anchored Hydrophytes with Floating Leaves
- These plants are floating on surface but rooted at bottom of shallow water body.
- Large leaves, long petiole, vascular system are well-developed
- Large air cavities, leaves with wax to avoid wetting.
- Stomata present on upper surface of leaves e.g., *Nymphoides*,
- *Potamogeton* species.

Types of Hydrophytes

Submerged Hydrophytes
- Poorly developed roots.
- Thin leaves, stomata are absent
- Leaves are finaly dissected.
- Stem soft, flexible, spongy with no cuticle layar in epidermal cells.
- Aerenchyma occurs in the roots and stem. Vascular tissues are reduced.
- e.g., *Hydrilla, Vallisneria.*

Free-floating Hydrophytes
- Plant free floting in water, No connection with bottom.
- Plants have air storing organs (e.g., inflated petiole in Eichhornia)
- Roots help in balancing and root tips are covered by root pockets.
- Stomata are present on the upper surface of leaves. e.g., *Azolla, Trappa, Eichhornia* etc.

Suspended Hydrophytes
- Roots are absent
- Never contact with the bottom.
- In all characters, they resemble with the submerged hydrophytes. e.g., *Utricularia, Lemna* species.

Plant Adaptations to Water Scarcity and Heat

Xerophytic Plants

Plants which live in dry conditions and shows high rate of transpiration than absorption of water. Deep root system, woody stem, green photosynthetic leaves reduced to spine to prevent water loss.

They are mainly of four types of xerophytic plants which are discussed below

1. **Ephemarals or Drought Escapers**
   - The plant live for a brief period during the rain.
   - Small size and larger shoots and roots.
   - They are generally found in arid zone.
   - e.g., *Euphorbia* species, *Solanum, Argemone mexicana*.

2. Annuals or Drought Evaders
- These plants live for a few month even after stop-page of rain.
- They need small quantity of water for their growth and development.
- Similar to ephemeral xerophytes, but grows for longer periods.
- e.g., *Echinops echinatus* and *Solanum surattense*.

3. Succulent or Drought Resistant
- These plants store water and mucilage in fleshy organs.
- They have water storage region made up of thin walled parenchymatous cells.
- Stem is green, photosynthatic and have thick cuticle.
- They are called **phylloclades** (stems of indefinite growth) and **cladodes** (1-2 internode long stems).

e.g., *Opuntia* and *Euphorbia*.

4. Non-succulent Perennial Xerophytes or Drought Endurers
- These are true xerophytes or euxerophytes.
- They have smallar short system and root very extensive.
- Leaves of leaflets are often small, vertical, thick and leathery.
- e.g., *Nerium* and *Calotropis procera*.

Plant Adaptation to Saline Environment (Halophytes)

Halophytes show following characteristics as their adaptations

1. Accumulation of Several Compounds	Growing with NaCl, MgCl$_2$, and high concentration of salt
2. Maintain high Osmotic Pressure	They have a high osmotic pressure (minimum of 40 bars)
3. Structural Adaptation	Succulent leaves, stem or both, thick cuticle sunkun stomata. These have substances like tannins and other wax substances to reduced insolation and prevent desiccation.
4. Secretion of Some Products	They secrete salt like atriplex, spartina through **chalk** or **salt glands**

Halophytic adaptation through structural and physiological modification are explained through the example of **mangroves**.

Handbook of BIOLOGY

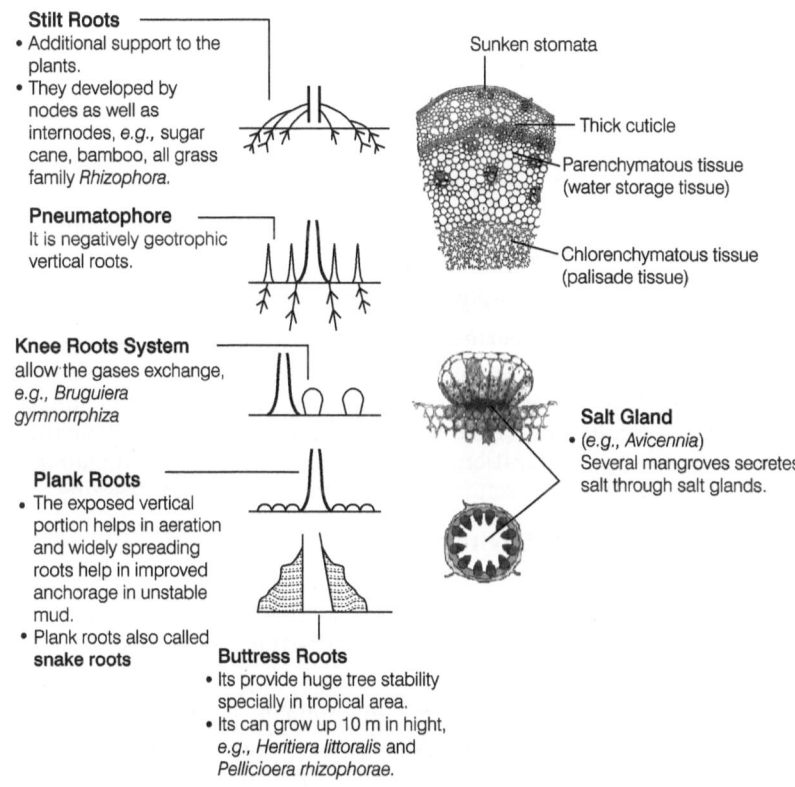

Stilt Roots
- Additional support to the plants.
- They developed by nodes as well as internodes, *e.g.*, sugar cane, bamboo, all grass family *Rhizophora*.

Pneumatophore
It is negatively geotrophic vertical roots.

Knee Roots System
allow the gases exchange, *e.g.*, *Bruguiera gymnorrhiza*

Plank Roots
- The exposed vertical portion helps in aeration and widely spreading roots help in improved anchorage in unstable mud.
- Plank roots also called **snake roots**

Buttress Roots
- Its provide huge tree stability specially in tropical area.
- Its can grow up 10 m in hight, *e.g.*, *Heritiera littoralis* and *Pellicioera rhizophorae*.

Sunken stomata
Thick cuticle
Parenchymatous tissue (water storage tissue)
Chlorenchymatous tissue (palisade tissue)

Salt Gland
- (*e.g.*, *Avicennia*) Several mangroves secretes salt through salt glands.

Structural modifications in plants to saline environment

Plant Adaptation to Oligotropic Soils

- Oligotropic soil are **poor in nutrients**.
- One such type of soil, which supports dense vegetation is the one found in tropical rain forests.
- Top soil of oligotropic region has shallow while sub soil has dence cley mixed with Fe - Al (iron-aluminium) compounds.
- Major adaptations of tropical plants is the presence of **mycorrhizae** (plant roots with fungi).

Mycorrhizae are of two types
  (i) **Ectomycorrhiza** When the fungal hyphae present outside the host cell that is called ectomycorrhiza.
  (ii) **Endomycorrhiza** When the fungal hyphae present inside the host cell that is called endomycorrhiza.

Strategic Adaptations in Animals
- Animal also develops strategies to live better in their environment.
- *Animal adaptations may be of two type*
  (i) **Short term** It is temporary like increase of heart beat.
  (ii) **Long term** It is permanent in nature like typical type of beak claw etc.
- In animal, most adaptations occurs against environmental changes and stress conditions. These may be physiological and behavioural adaptations, *e.g.,* migration, hibernation, aestivention, camouflage, mimicry, echolocation, water scarcity and prevention of freezing.

Adaptation to Cold Environment
Some animals protect themselves from excessive cold by developing hard covering as they can not undergo hibernation and can not migrate, *e.g.,* barnacles and molluscs of intertidal zone of cold areas, several insects and spiders.

Some animal are adapted to colder environment by developing extra solutes in the body fluids and spacial ice nucleating proteins in the extracellular spaces.

These extra solutes which prevent freezing, are glycerol and antifreeze protein. Ice fish (*Chaenocephalus*) or Antarctic fish (*Trematomus*) remains active even in extremely cold sea water due to this hardness.

Adaptation to Water Scarcity in Animal
- Animal face with water scarcity in desert area, shows two type of adaptation reducing waterloss and ability to tolerate arid conditions. Camel has a number of adjustment to desert conditions like water consumption, tolerance with temperature, etc.
- The animal produces dry feaces and urine.
- Camel can rehydrate itself quickly. Its storage of water about 80 litres.

Mimicry

- It is resemblance of species with another in order to obtain advantage, especially, against predation.
- The species which is copied is called **model**, while the animals which copy as a **mimic** or **mimictic**.

These are of two type

1. Batesian Mimicry

In this mimicry the **mimic is defenseless**, *e.g.*, viceroy butterfly mimics unpalatable toxic monarch butterfly.

2. Mullerian Mimicry

In this mimicry there is the resemblance between two animal species, especially insects to their mutual benefit, *e.g.*, monarch butterfly and queen butterfly.

Population and Community

As combination of several population in a area makes community, the relationship between these two is established.

The comparative account of both population and community is given below.

Differences between Community and Population

Community	Population
It is a grouping of individuals of different species found in an area.	It is a grouping of individuals of a single species in an area.
Interbreeding is absent amongst different members of a community.	Individuals interbreed freely.
Different members of a community are morphologically and behaviourly dissimilar.	Morphological and behaviourly similar species are found in a population.
It is a large unit of organisation.	It is a small unit of organisation.
In a biotic community, there is often a relationship of eating and being eaten.	There is no relationship of eating and being eaten.

Characteristics of Population

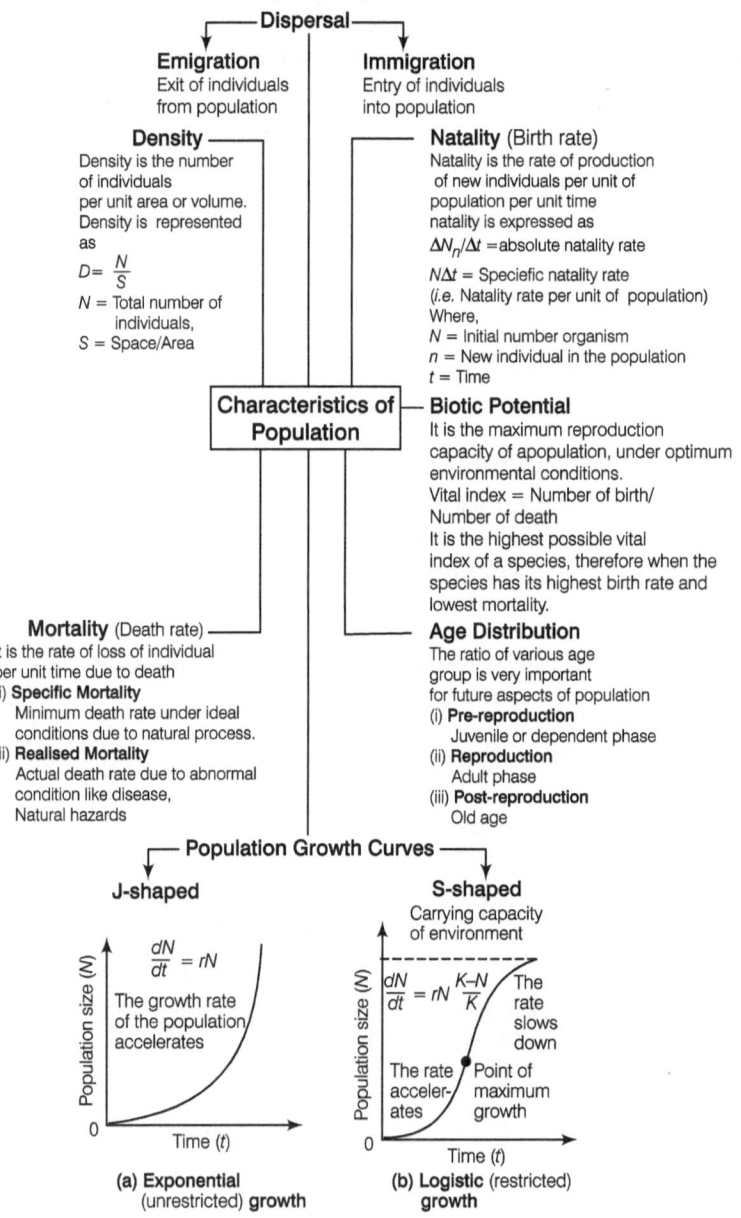

Population Interaction

Organism belonging to different population interact for their necessities

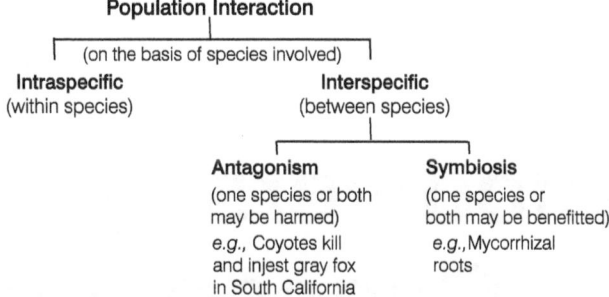

Population interactions can also be categorised on the basis of its nature.

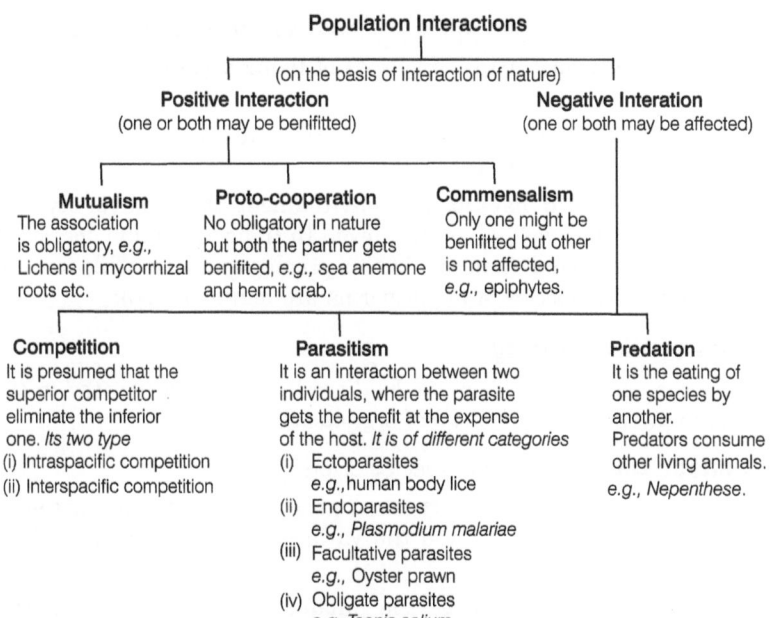

Interaction and adaptation of organisms into their environment can be accomplished by various strategies. These strategies ultimately helps in the establishment of new communities. Detailed study of these process of establishments throws light on several new fields of environmental studies.

37
Biodiversity and Conservation

Biodiversity (Gk. *bios*–life; *divsersity*–forms) or Biological diversity can be defined as the vast array of species of living organisms present on the earth.

The term, 'Biodiversity, was coined by **WG Rosen** (1985), but later popularised by **EO Wilson**.

Due to difference in habitat and environment the biodiversity can studied at global as well as country level. In India maximum species of Arthropods are found (approx 68389) among animals while among plants maximum species of angiosperms are found (17500).

Levels of Biodiversity

For the convenience of study, *the biodiversity can be categorised in the following three levels of biological organisations*

(i) **Genetic Diversity** (within species diversity)

The diversity in number and types of genes as well as chromosomes present in different species and the variation in the genes and their alleles in same species.

It is useful as it involves the adaptation to change in the environmental conditions and is also essential for healthy breeding. It also helps in speciation.

(ii) Species Diversity (between species diversity)

It means the species richness in any habitat. Greater the species richness, grater will be their diversity. India is among the world's 15 nations that are exceptionally rich in species diversity. Number of individuals of different species represents the species evenness and species equitability.

(iii) Community and Ecosystem Diversity (ecological diversity)

It is the diversity at ecosystem or community level. An ecosystem is referred to as natural when it is undisturbed by human activities.

- Diversity at the level of community or ecosystem has three perspective, *i.e.*, α, β and γ (Whittaker; 1965).

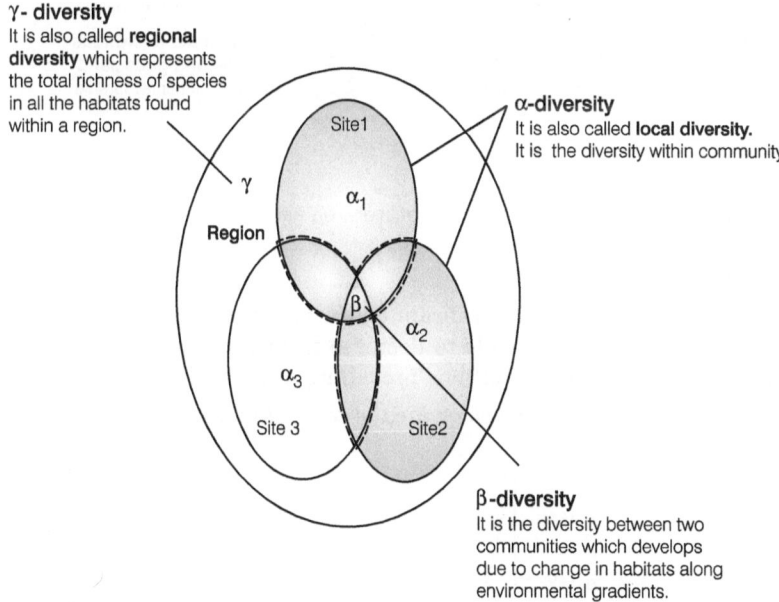

Schematic representation of various levels of diversity

Patterns of Biodiversity

1. Latitudinal Gradient

Generally, species diversity decreases as we move away from the equator towards poles.

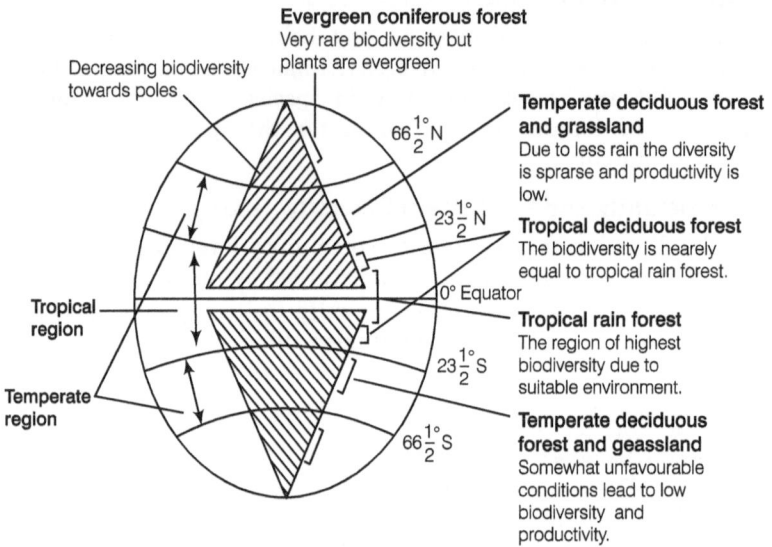

Biodiversity pattern on earth

2. Altitudinal Gradient

The impact of altitude is significant on the types of biodiversity. Mostly the increasing altitude leads to decrease in biodiversity as only some species can adapt the conditions prevailing at high altitude.

Following graph gives the clear idea of this relationship

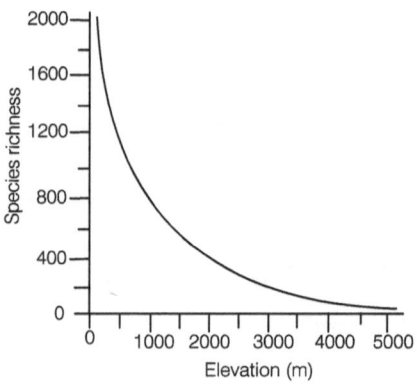

Effect of altitude on biodiversity

3. Species-Area Relationship

According to German naturalist and geographer **Alexander Von Humboldt** "Species richness increases with increasing explored area, but only up to a certain limit".

The relationship between species richness and area gives a rectangular hyperbola curve for a wide variety of taxa like birds, bats, freshwater fishes and flowering plants.

On a logarithmic scale, the relationship is a straight line and is described by the following equation

$$\log S = \log C + Z \log A$$

Here, S is species richness, Z is slope of line or regression co-efficient, C is Y intercept while A is area.

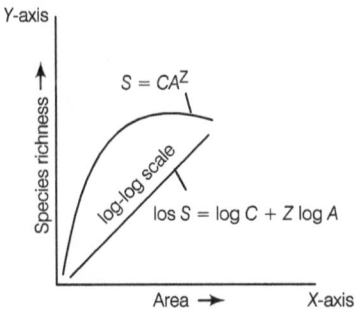

Species-area relationship

Ecologists have discovered that the value of Z-line is similar for a small region or area particular, regardless of taxonomic group or region (*i.e.*, 0.1–0.2). But if we consider a large area (*i.e.*, whole continent), the value of Z deviates between 0.6–1.2.

Importance of Biodiversity

Biodiversity is essential not only for ecosystem, but also for the survival of human race. It maintains high productivity and human health.

The detailed description of importance of biodiversity is given below

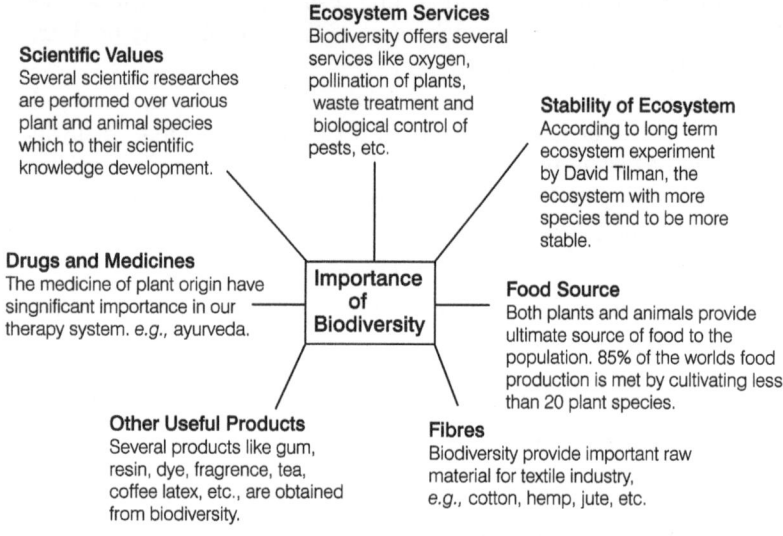

Importance of biodiversity

The importance of biodiversity is described through an analogy (the 'rivet popper hypothesis') used by Paul Ehrlich, in which he compare ecosystem with airplane and the species with rivets.

Loss of Biodiversity

The loss of biological diversity is a global crisis. Out of the 1.6 million species known to inhabit the earth, about 1/4 to 1/3 is likely to get extinct within the next few decades. Tropical forests are estimated to contain 50 to 90% of the world's total biodiversity.

The IUCN (International Union for Conservation of Nature and Natural Resources) Red List (2004) documents the extinction of 784 species (including 338 vertebrates, 359 invertebrates and 87 plants) in the last 500 years.

Some examples of recent extinctions include the **dodo** (Mauritius), **quagga** (Africa), **thylacine** (Australia). **Steller's sea cow** (Russia) and three sub species of tiger (Bali, Java, Caspian).

The last twenty years alone have witnessed the disappearance of 27 species. Careful analysis of records shows that the extinctions across taxa are not random; some groups like amphibians appear to be more vulnerable to extinction.

Adding to the grim scenario of extinctions, the fact is that more than 15500 species worldwide are facing the threat of extinction.

Presently, 12% of all bird species, 23% of all mammal species, 32% of all amphibian species and 31% of all gymnosperm species in the world face the threat of extinction.

In general, loss of biodiversity in a region may lead to
1. Decline in the plant production.
2. Lowered resistance to environmental perturbations such as drought.
3. Increased variability in certain ecosystem processes, such as plant productivity, water use and pest and disease cycles.

IUCN and Red List Categories

International Union of Conservation of Nature and Natural Resources (IUCN) is now called World Conservation Union (WCU), headquartered at Morges, Switzerland.

The Red Data Book, catalogue the taxa who face the risk of extinction. It was initiated in 1963. The red list contain 9 categories of individuals according to their threats. *There are*

1. Extinct (Ex)
2. Extinct in the Wild (EW)
3. Regionally Extinct (RE)
4. Critically endangered (CR)
5. Endangered (EN)
6. Vulnerable (VU)
7. Near Threatened (NT)
8. Least Concern (LC)
9. Data Defecient (DD)

Out of these category 4, 5 and 6 are the threatened category.

Causes of Biodiversity Loss

Unbalanced human activities lead to accelerated extinction of species from the world. The major causes of biodiversity reduction are termed as **'Evil Quartat'**.

Some important causes of biodiversity loss are given below

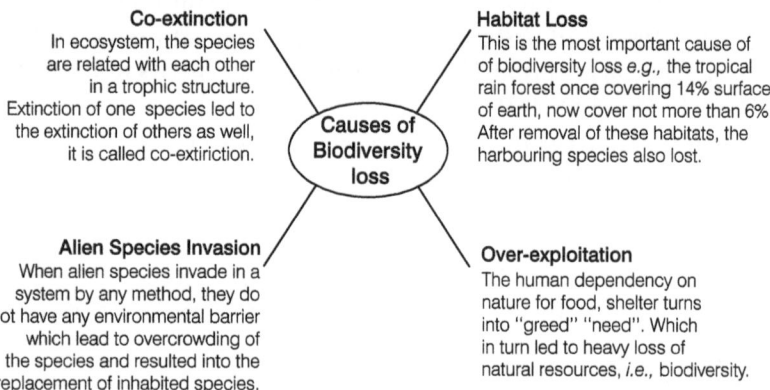

Factors causing biodiversity loss

Biodiversity Conservation

Conservation means **protection, upliftment** and **scientific management** of biodiversity so as to maintain it at its optimum level and derive sustainable benefits for the present as well as future strategies.

The following are the three major reasons to conserve biodiversity

Narrow utilitarian The useful human products like food, fibres, drugs and medicines are obtained from biodiversity.

Broadly utilitarian Biodiversity provides ecosystem services like providing oxygen, pollinating crops and controlling floods and erosions, etc.

Ethical utilitarian Every living species has an intrinsic value, through it may not have direct economic value and also every species has right to live.

Methods of Biodiversity Conservation

Some main strategies of conservation are as follows

(i) All the threatened species should be protected. Priority should be given to ones belonging to the monotypic genera, endangered over vulnerable, vulnerable over rare and rare over other species.

Handbook of BIOLOGY

(ii) All the possible varieties (old or new) of food, forage and timber plants, medicinal plants, livestock, aquaculture animals, microbes should be conserved.

(iii) Wild relatives of economically important organisms should be identified and conserved in protected areas.

(iv) Critical habitats for feeding/breeding/resting/nursing of each species should be identified and safeguarded.

(v) Resting/feeding places of migratory/wide ranging animals should be protected, pollution controlled and exploitation regulated.

(vi) National Wildlife Protection Law should be enacted (in India, 1972), wildlife protection strategies should be formulated (1983) and protection programmes should be integrated with the international programmes.

(vii) Ecosystems should be priortised.

(viii) The reproductive capacity of the exploited species and productivity of the ecosystem should be determined.

(ix) International trade in wildlife should be highly regulated.

(x) Development of reserves or protected areas should be initiated.

(xi) Introduction of new species should be in strict control of regulatory laws.

(xii) Pollution reduction and public awareness should be promoted.

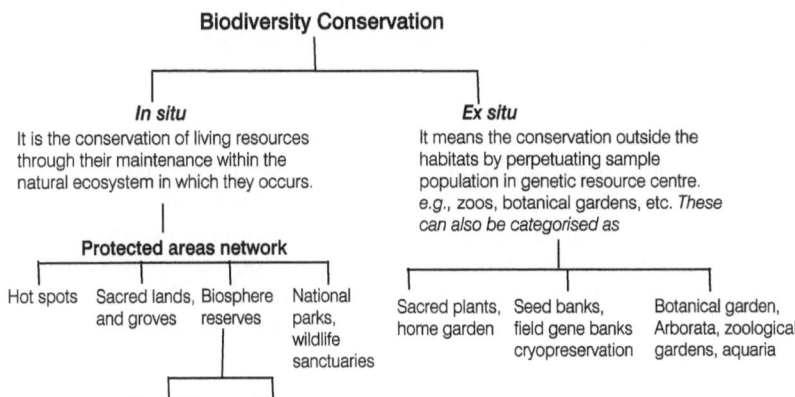

The detailed description of these protected areas is given below

(i) **Hot Spot**

The concept of hot spot was given by **Norman Myers** in 1988. Hot spots are the areas that are extremely rich in species diversity, have high endemism and are under constant threat.

Among the 34 hot spots (cover less that 2% of earth land area) of the world, two are found in India extending into neighbouring countries – **The Western Ghats/Sri Lanka** and the **Indo–Burma Region** (covering the Eastern Himalayas also known as cradle of speciation).

The key criteria for determining a hot spot are

(a) Number of endemic species, *i.e.,* the species which are found nowhere else.

(b) Degree of threat which is measured in terms of habitat loss.

Hot Spots in India

The following two hot spots in India are

(a) **Eastern Himalaya** The Eastern Himalayan hot spots extends to the North-Eastern India and Bhutan. The temperate forests are found at altitudes of 1780 to 3500 metres. Many deep and semi-isolated valleys found in this region are exceptionally rich in endemic plant species.

Besides being an active centre of evolution and rich diversity of flowering plants, the numerous primitive angiosperm families (*e.g.,* Magnoliaceae and Winteraceae) and primitive genera of plants, like *Magnolia* and *Betula*, are found in Easterns Himalaya.

(b) **Western Ghat** The Western Ghat region lies parallel to the Western coast of Indian Peninsula for almost 1600 km, in Maharashtra, Karnataka, Tamil Nadu and Kerala.

The forests at low elevation (500 m above mean sea level) are mostly evergreen, while those found at 500-1500 metres height are generally semi-evergreen forests. The Agasthyamalai hills, the Silent valley and the new Amambalam reserve, are the main centres of biological diversity.

(ii) Wetlands

Wetlands are an integral part of the watersheds and generally lie at the interface between the land and water. On the basis of their function of filtering water before entering into the large water bodies, they are also known as 'kidneys of ecosystem'.

A convention for the protection of wetlands held in Ramsar on 2nd february 1972, since then 2nd February was celebrated as **World Wetland Day**.

In India there are 26 Ramsar sites present.

(iii) National Parks of India

India's first national park (IUCN Category-II Protected area) was **Hailey National Park**, now known as **Jim Corbett National Park**, established in 1935. By 1970, India had only five national parks.

In 1972, India enacted the **Wildlife Protection Act** and **Project Tiger** to safeguard habitat. Further, federal legislation strengthening the protections for wildlife was introduced in the 1980s. As on April 2012, there are 102 national parks.

Some important national parks of India are mentioned in the following table with their belonging state

Some National Parks in India

Name	State
Bandipur National Park	Karnataka
Bannerghatta National Park	Karnataka
Bhitarkanika National Park	Odisha
Buxa Tiger Reserve	Paschim Bangal
Corbett National Park	Uttarakhand
Dachigam National Park	Jammu and Kashmir
Dibru-Saikhowa National Park	Asom
Gir National Park	Gujarat
Great Himalayan National Park	Himachal Pradesh
Gugamal National Park	Maharashtra
Hemis National Park	Jammu and Kashmir
Indravati National Park	Chhattisgarh
Intanki National Park	Nagaland

Name	State
Kanha National Park	Madhya Pradesh
Kaziranga National Park	Asom
Kanchenjunga National Park	Sikkim
Kishtwar National Park	Jammu and Kashmir
Madhav National Park	Madhya Pradesh
Manas National Park	Asom
Mouling National Park	Arunachal Pradesh
Namdapha National Park	Arunachal Pradesh
Nameri National Park	Asom
Nanda Devi National Park	Uttarakhand
Palani Hills National Park	Tamil Nadu
Periyar National Park	Kerala
Pine Valley National Park	Himachal Pradesh
Rajaji National Park	Uttarakhand
Rani Jhansi Marine National Park	Andaman and Nicobar Islands
Sariska National Park	Rajasthan
Silent Valley National Park	Kerala
Simlipal National Park	Odisha
Sri Venkateshwara National Park	Andhra Pradesh
Sundarbans National Park	Paschim Bangal
Tadoba National Park	Maharashtra
Valmiki National Park	Bihar

(iv) **Wildlife Sanctuary**

India has over 448 wildlife sanctuaries. Characteristically in wildlife sanctuaries the protection is given to animal life only.

Some important Sanctuaries of India are given in following table

Some Important Sanctuaries on India

Name and Location	Area (in sq km)	Key Vertebrate Species being Protected
Chilka Lake (Odisha)	990	Flamingoes, sandpipers, ducks, water fowls, cranes, golden plovers and ospreys.
Keoladeo Ghana Bird Sanctuary (Rajasthan)	29	**Migratory birds** Siberian crane, spoon bill, herons, egrets and variety of other local birds. **Mammals** Blue bull, wild boar, black buck and spotted deer. **Reptiles** Python.
Mudumalai Wildlife Sanctuary, Nilgiri (Tamil Nadu)	520	**Mammals** Flying squirrel, porcupine, elephant, sambhar, cheetal, barking deer, mouse, deer, four-horned antelope, giant squirrel wild dog, cat and civet. **Reptiles** Rat snake, python, flying lizard and monitor lizard.
Manas Wildlife Sanctuary, Kamrup (Asom)	—	Tiger, wild boar, sambhar, golden langoor, one-horned rhino, panther, swamp deer, wild dog and wild buffalo.
Periyar Sanctuary (Kerala)	777	**Mammals** Elephants, leopard, black langoor, sambhar, gaur, bison. **Birds** Egret and horn bills.
Sultanpur Lake Bird Sanctuary (Uttar Pradesh)	12	**Birds** Cranes, duck, green pigeon, drake and spot bill. **Reptiles** Python and crocodile.

(v) Biosphere Reserves

Biosphere reserves are a special category of protected areas of land and/or coastal environments, wherein people are an integral component of the system. These are the representative examples of natural biomes and contain unique biological communities within. Biosphere reserves represent a specified area zonated for particular activities.

These consists of

(A) **Core zone** No human activity is allowed in this zone.

(B) **Buffer zone** Limited activity is permitted.

(C) **Manipulation zone** Several human activities are allowed.

There are 14 biosphere reserves established in India, which are mentioned here.

The main biosphere reserve of India includes
- (a) Nilgiri Biosphere Reserve
- (b) Pachmarhi Biosphere Reserve
- (c) Manas Biosphere Reserve
- (d) Great Nicobar Biosphere Reserve
- (e) Nanda Devi Biosphere Reserve
- (f) Nokrek Biosphere Reserve
- (g) Agasthyamalai Biosphere Reserve
- (h) Kanchenjunga Biosphere Reserve
- (i) Dehang-Debang Biosphere Reserve
- (j) Dibru-Saikhowa Biosphere Reserve
- (k) Simlipal Biosphere Reserve
- (l) Sundarbans Biosphere Reserve
- (m) Gulf of Mannar Biosphere Reserve
- (n) Achanak Maar-Amarkantak Biosphere Reserve

(vi) **Zoos**

Zoo is the place where wild animals are kept for public viewing. Many of them have various rare species of animals and have recorded success in captive breeding of animals.

The following table will give the information about important zoos in India.

Zoos in India

Name	City	State
Arignar Anna Zoological Park	Chennai	Tamil Nadu
Asom State Zoo	Guwahati	Asom
Aurangabad Zoo	Aurangabad	Maharashtra
Bannerghatta Biological Park	Bangaluru	Karnataka
Children's Corner Zoo	Chennai	Tamil Nadu
Guindy Snake Park	Chennai	Tamil Nadu
Indira Gandhi Zoological Park	Vishakhapatnam	Andhra Pradesh
Indore Zoo	Indore	Madhya Pradesh
Jawahar Lal Nehru Biological Park	Bokaro	Jharkhand
Kamla Nehru Zoological Park	Ahmedabad	Gujarat
Kanpur Zoological Park	Kanpur	Uttar Pradesh
Nehru Zoological Park	Hyderabad	Andhra Pradesh
Sanjay Gandhi Biological Park	Patna	Bihar
Sri Chamarajendra Zoological Park	Mysore	Karnataka
Veermata Jijabai Udyan Zoo	Mumbai	Maharashtra

(vii) Botanical Gardens

This plays an important role in the conservation of plant species as that there are several instances when plants believed to be extinct, were found living only in a botanical garden. *Sophora toromiro* is the famous example.

Record of threatened plants that are in cultivation have been kept in Green Books. The **Indian Green Book** prepared by BSI which lists 100 such species which are rare, endangered or endemic, but all are growing in a living state in various botanical gardens.

With the help of above measure, we can easily protect the biodiversity present all around us. The protection of biodiversity can not be only accomplished by government organisation, but it is the cumulative responsibility of every individual.

38
Environmental Issues

Humans have always inhabited **two worlds**. One is the **natural world** of plants, animals, soil, air and waters that preceded us by billion of years and of which, we are a part. The other is the **world of social institutions** and artifacts that we create for ourselves using science, technology and political organisation.

Where earlier people has limited ability to alter their surroundings, we now have power to extract and consume resources, produce wastes and modify our world in a way that threatened both our continued existence and that of many organism with which we share the planet.

Environmental issues includes the aspects which adversely affects our biophysical environment. Pollution, global warming, deforestation, etc., are the topic of major concern in current perspective.

Pollution

Pollution is the addition of the harmful agents to the ecosystem, which has detrimental effect on it. Environmental pollution is any discharge of material or energy into air, water or land that causes or may cause **acute** (short term) and **chronic** (long-term) effect on the earth's ecological balance or that lowers the quality of life.

Pollution can be defined by different organisations, differently, *some of these are as follows*

WHO has defined 'Pollution is the introduction of harmful material into the environment'.

Handbook of BIOLOGY

According to Central Pollution Control Board (CPCB) Pollution means contamination of water, air and land in such a way that alter the physical, chemical and biological property of that resource.

Ministry of Environment and Forest (MOEF) defined pollution as 'Introduction of different harmful pollutant into certain environment that make it unhealthy to live in'.

Types of Pollution

On the basis of location of reservoir, or the area where these pollutants are present. *The pollution can be of following types*

(i) Air pollution
(ii) Water pollution
(iii) Soil pollution
(iv) Thermal pollution
(v) Radioactive pollution
(vi) Noise pollution
(vii) Genetic pollution

Pollution can also be categorised as

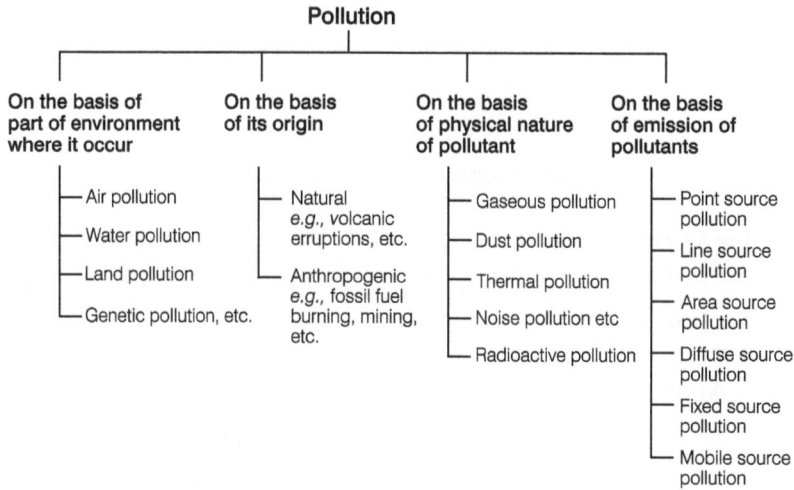

Air Pollution

It is undesirable change is the natural characteristics of the atmosphere due to contamination of indoor and outdoor environment by any chemical, biological or physical agent.

Sources of Air Pollution

The six air pollutants that account for most of the air pollution are called **criteria air pollutants**.

Various air pollutants and their originating causes are given in following figure

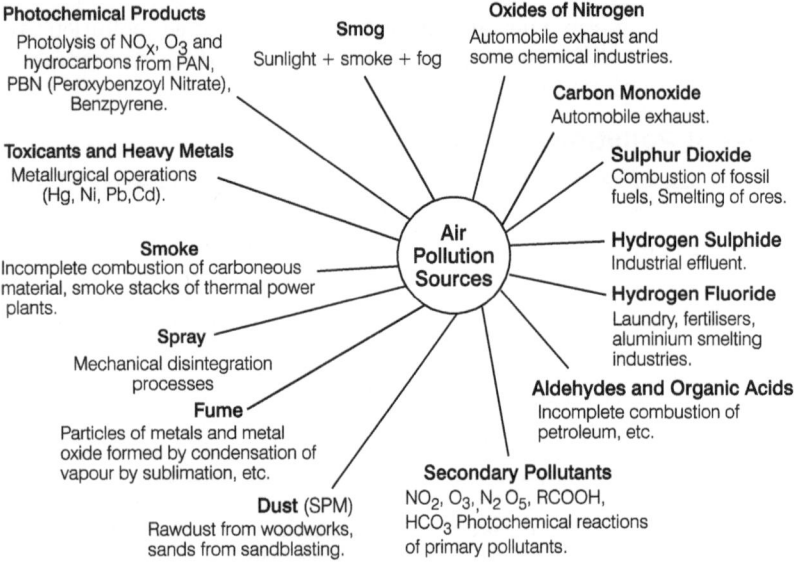

Chief air pollutants and their sources

Effects of Air Pollution

The air pollution has following effects on various organisms

(a) Effects on Humans

The following table, provides the list of various air pollutants and their effects on human body

Common Air Pollutants and their Effects on Human Body

Pollutants	Effect on Human Body
Aldehydes	Irritate nasal and respiratory tract.
Ammonia	Inflame upper respiratory passages.
Arsenic	Breakdown of red cells in blood, damage kidneys, causes jaundice, lung and skin cancer.
Carbon monoxide	Reduce O_2 carrying capacity of blood.
Chlorine	Attack entire respiratory tract and mucous membrane of eyes, cause pulmonary oedema.

Pollutants	Effect on Human Body
Cyanides	Interfere with nerve cells, resulting dry throat, indistinct vision, headache.
Fluorides	Irritate and corrode all body passages, causes osteoporosis.
Sulphides	Causes nausea, irritates eyes and throat.
Nitrogen oxides	Inhibit ciliary action of nose, causes bronchitis.
Phosgenes (carbonyl chloride $COCl_2$)	Induce coughing, irritation and sometimes fatal pulmonary oedema.
Sulphur	Causes chest constriction, headache, vomiting and death from respiratory ailments.
Suspended particles (ash, soot, smoke)	Causes emphysema, eye irritations and possibly cancer.

(b) **Effects on Plants**

Air pollution also causes several damages to plants.
These are listed below

Injury Thresholds and Effects of Air Pollutants on Plants

Pollutant	Effect on Plants	Concent Ration (ppm)	Sustained Exposure Time
Ozone (O_3)	Fleck, bleaching, bleached spotting, growth suppression. Tips of conifer needles become brown and necrotic.	0.03	4h
Sulphur dioxide (SO_2)	Breached spots, bleached areas between veins, chlorosis, growth suppression, reduction in yield, leaf curling.	0.03	8h
Peroxyacetyl Nitrate (PAN)	Glazing silvering or bronzing on the lower surface of leaves.	0.01	6h
Hydrogen Fluoride (HF)	Chlorosis, dwarfing leaf abscission, lower yield.	0.0001	5 weeks
Chloride (Cl_2)	Bleaching between venis, tips and leaf abscission.	0.01	2h
Ethylene (C_2H_2)	Withering, leaf abnormalities, flower dropping and failure of flower to open.	0.05	6h

(c) Effects of Climate

Air pollution causes **acid rain**. The acid rain has various negative effects. *The effects of acid preparation can be categorised as*

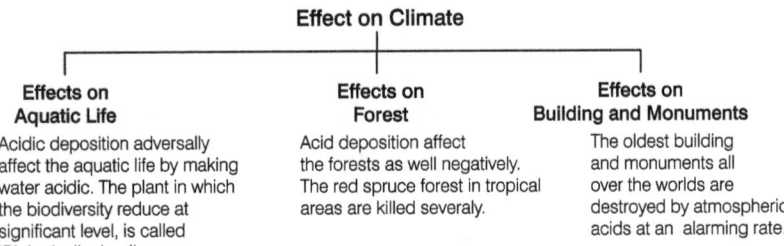

Effects on Aquatic Life	Effects on Forest	Effects on Building and Monuments
Acidic deposition adversely affect the aquatic life by making water acidic. The plant in which the biodiversity reduce at significant level, is called 'Biologically dead'.	Acid deposition affect the forests as well negatively. The red spruce forest in tropical areas are killed severaly.	The oldest building and monuments all over the worlds are destroyed by atmospheric acids at an alarming rate.

Effects of air pollution on climate

Control of Air Pollution

Several methods are used to control air pollution. *Some of them are as follows*

(1) Use of High Chimneys

For proper escaping of smoke, fumes and heated air the industrial plants should have high chimneys.

(2) Government's Norms for Emission

In the line of world standard, Government of India also has formulated new fuel policy everytime. *These fuel policies with their applicable regions are given as*

Standard	Reference	Date	Region
India 2000	Euro 1	2000	Nationwide
		2001	NCR*, Mumbai, Kolkata, Chennai
Bharat stage II	Euro 2	2003. 04	NCR*, 10 cities †
		2005. 04	Nationwide
Bharat stage III	Euro 3	2005.04	NCR*, 10 cities †
		2010.04	Nationwide
Bharat stage IV	Euro 4	2010.04	NCR*, 10 cities †

* National Capital Region (Delhi)

† Mumbai, Kolkata, Chennai, Bangaluru, Hyderabad, Ahmedabad, Pune, Surat, Kanpur and Agra

(3) Other Control Measures to Control air Pollution

These methods are characterised on the basis of physical nature of pollutant.

(a) Method to Control Particulate Pollution

Different technological equipments are used to control particulate pollution, *these are*

(i) **Cyclonic separator** In this, centrifugal force cause the settling of particulate matters.

(ii) **Trajectory separators** In this, heavier particle settle down, when dirty air is passed from a chamber as an oblique jet.

(iii) **Electrostatic precipitator** Particulate matter present in dirty air are charged electrically and passed through a chamber where these particles loose their charges and settle down.

(iv) **Filters** Particulate matter gets filter out by passing dry emissions under pressure through, polyester, teflon and polyamide bags which are large sized and porous.

(b) Methods to Control Gaseous Pollution

The gaseous pollution can be inhibited by following set of methods

Adsorption Technique	Combustion Technique	Absorption Technique	Scrubber	Catalytic Converter
The toxic gases from dirty air are removed by very fine solid particles (e.g., charcol).	The emission are burnt at high temperature to remove gaseous pollutants.	The packing materials, fixed in scrubber are used to absorb the gaseous pollutants.	The exhaust is passed through a spray of water or lime to remove gases like SOx.	It contains expensive metals like Platinum, Palladium and Rhodium as the catalyst. After passing through it, unburnt hydrocarbons are converted into CO_2 and water.

Water Pollution

Water is said to be polluted when its quality gets degraded due to addition of various inorganic, organic, biological and radiological substances, which makes it unfit and health hazard.

Impurities in form of variables are as follows

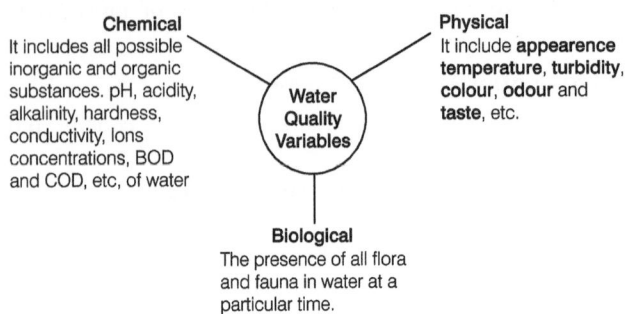

Categories of water pollutants

The comparative account of Biochemical Oxygen Demand (BOD) and Chemical Oxygen Demand (COD) is given as

Comparison of BOD and COD

Biochemical Oxygen Demand (BOD)	Chemical Oxygen Demand (COD)
It is the amount of oxygen used for biochemical oxidation by microorganisms in a unit volume of water.	It is the amount of oxygen required by organic matter in a sample of water for its oxidation by a strong chemical oxidant and is expressed as ppm of oxygen taken from the solution of potassium dichromate in 2 hours.
BOD value approximates the amount of oxdisable organic matter and therefore, used as a measure of degree of water pollution and waste.	This value is a poor measure of strength of organic matter, as oxygen is also consumed in the oxidation of inorganic matter such as nitrates, sulphates, reduced metal ions and also that some organic molecules such as benzene, pyridine and few other cyclic organic compounds are not oxidised by this test.
BOD test is influenced by many factors such as types of microorganisms, pH, presence of toxins, some reduced mineral matter and nitrification of microorganisms.	Presence of toxins and other such unfavourable conditions for the growth of microorganisms do no affect COD values.

Sources of Water Pollution

The various sources of water pollution can be explained through following diagram.

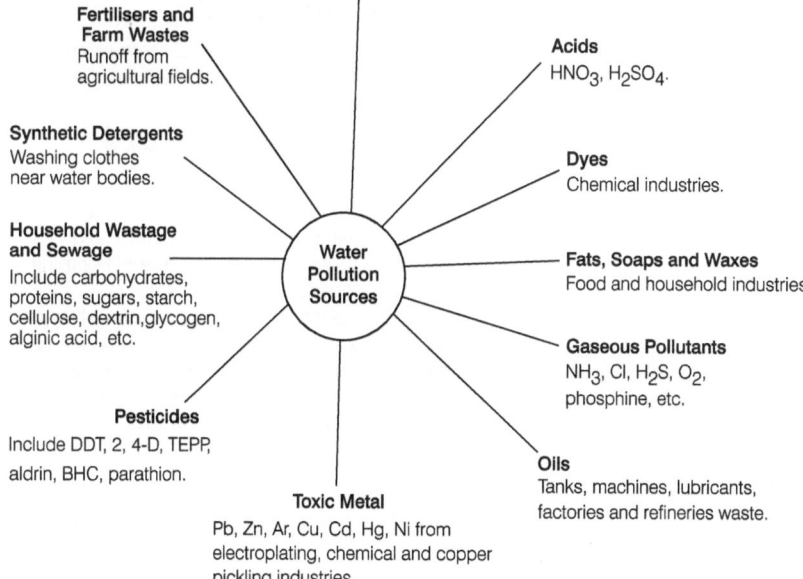

Industrial
Paper and Pulp Free chlorine.
Textile Minor acids, fats, oils and grease.
Food processing Starch.
Chemical Mineral acids OH, NH_3, tartaricacid and nitro compounds P, S, F.
Metal Fluorides, cyanogen and limestone are called nuisance.
Petroleum Hydrocarbons, phenols and fats.
Tanneries Sulphide, chromium, phenol and tannic acid.
Acid and Grease Bad taste and odour to H_2O.
Battery Lead mineral acids.
Wool Scouring Alkalis, fats, oils and, grease.

Fertilisers and Farm Wastes
Runoff from agricultural fields.

Acids
HNO_3, H_2SO_4.

Synthetic Detergents
Washing clothes near water bodies.

Dyes
Chemical industries.

Household Wastage and Sewage
Include carbohydrates, proteins, sugars, starch, cellulose, dextrin, glycogen, alginic acid, etc.

Water Pollution Sources

Fats, Soaps and Waxes
Food and household industries.

Gaseous Pollutants
NH_3, Cl, H_2S, O_2, phosphine, etc.

Pesticides
Include DDT, 2, 4-D, TEPP, aldrin, BHC, parathion.

Oils
Tanks, machines, lubricants, factories and refineries waste.

Toxic Metal
Pb, Zn, Ar, Cu, Cd, Hg, Ni from electroplating, chemical and copper pickling industries.

Water pollutants and their sources

Effects of Water Pollution

Water pollution affect individuals severally and cause various disease, which depends upon the nature of pollutant.

Chief pollutants and their toxic effects are given in following table

Some Elements and their Toxic Effects in Humans

Elements	Toxic effects
Aluminium	Interferes with phosphate metabolism, inhibit absorption of fluorides, Ca and iron compounds.
Arsenic	Loss of appetite, copious secretion of mucus in respiratory tract, **black foot disease**.
Cadmium	**Itai-itai disease** (Japan), kidney damage.
Fluorine	**Fluorosis**, about 5-12 ppm is toxic, enamel becomes brittle bones lose their elasticity and are prone to fractures, impairs glycolysis, knock-knee disease.
Lead	**Anaemia** and mental retardation due to degenerative changes in motor nerves.
Mercury	**Minamata disease**, main site of injury is CNS leading to tremors inability to coordinate, impairment of vision and loss of hearing. Two major episodes of mercury poisoning having occurred in Japan, in Minamata bay and Nigata. Mercury was absorbed, bioaccumulated and biomagnified to high levels. Fish collected from this bay had 10-12 mg of Hg per kg of their flesh and bones. The largest mercury epidemic occurred in 1971-72 in Iraq, when 6000 people were affected and 500 died; infertility in human.

Control of Water Pollution

Water pollution can be controlled through various measure, some of them are discussed here.

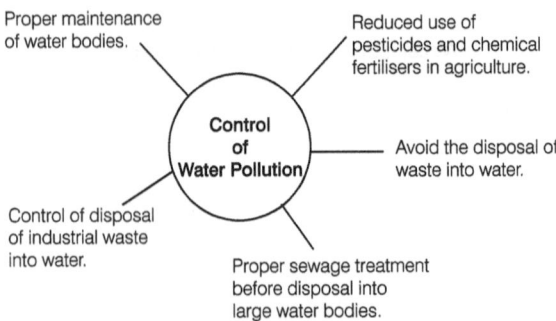

Special Cases of Water Pollution

Eutrophication and biomagnification are two special cases of water pollution.

Eutrophication

Eutrophic (*eu* + *trophic* = truely nourished) waters are rich in organisms and organic materials. Eutrophication is an **increase in nutrient level and productivity.**

As with BOD, eutrophication often results from nutrients enrichment. Sewage, fertiliser, run off, and other human activities caused increase in biological productivity is called **cultural eutrophication.**

The schematic representation of eutrophication is given as

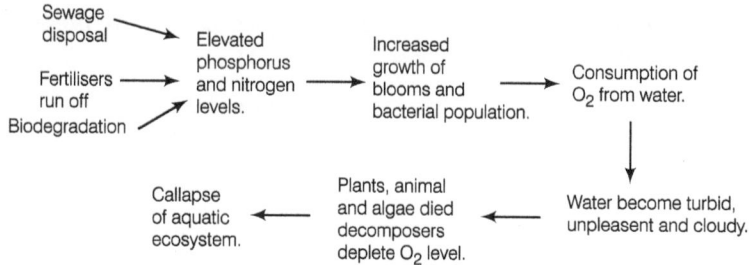

Events of eutrophication

Biomagnification/Bioaccumulation

Many pesticides such as DDT, aldrin and dieldrin have a long lifetime in the environment. These are fat soluble and generally non-biodegradable.

After incorporating into food chain, they gets magnified and accumulated in higher trophic level. The process of **biological magnification** is also reported for certain other pollutants such as lead (Pb), mercury (Hg), copper (Cu) and strontium-90.

The diagrammatic representation of bioaccumulation is shown as follows

	Water	Microscopic Aquatic Organisms	Small Fishes	Large Fishes	Fish Eating Birds
DDT levels	0.000003 ppm	0.04 ppm	0.5 ppm	2.0 ppm	25.0 ppm

Soil Pollution

Soil pollution is defined as the build up in soils of **persistent toxic compounds, chemical, salts, radioactive material** and **disease causing agents** which have adverse effects on health of inhabiting organisms.

It can be of following two types

1. **Negative soil pollution** It is the reduction is soil productivity due to erosion and overuse.
2. **Positive soil pollution** It is the reduction in soil productivity, because of addition of undesirable substances like fertilisers into soil.

Sources and Effects of Soil Pollution

The chief agents of soil pollution and their effects on soil are presented diagrammatically as follows

Biological Agents

Excreta of humans, animals and birds is the major one.
Pathogenic organisms are
(i) Excreted by man, bacteria and parasitic worms.
(ii) Excreted by animals, cow, pig, sheep, etc., bacteria and other worms.
(iii) Naturally found in soil due to some edaphic cause they develop.
Diseases caused by these agents are **dysentery, cholera, typhoid,** etc.

Industrial and Urban Waste

Examples of industrial and urban wastes are
(i) Coal and mineral mines, metal processing industries and engineering industries.
(ii) Domestic and community wastes, *i.e.,* sludge.
(iii) Garbage, rubbish materials such as paper, residues from home, fuels, street sweepings, glasses, rubber and abandoned vehicles, etc.

Dumping of solid wastes not only create, aesthetic problems but also public health problems *e.g.,* dysentery, diarrhoea, etc., are common diseases.

Sources of Soil Pollution

Radiological Agents

From nuclear explosion and radioactive wastes (nuclear testing and laboratories) like, ruthenium 106, rhodium 106, Lodine 131, barium 140, lanthanum 140, cerium 144, promethium 144, carbon 14, cesium 137, create several serious health hazards, *e.g.,* cancer.

Agricultural Practices

Fertilisers, pesticides, soil condition fumigant and other chemical agents. Farming phosphates, nitrates, DDT, BHC, endrin, aldrin, dieldrin, organosulphurous compounds, organic compounds with Pb, Hg, Ar are toxic to plants. Lindane has been reported so, taint carrots. Flies, insects and rodents multiply which in turn harm the crop.

Various factors causing soil pollution

Control of Soil Pollution

The control of soil pollution can be done through following steps
  (i) It involves safer land use, planned urbanisation, controlled developmental activities, safe disposal and the management of solid wastes.
  (ii) In recovering and recycling some waste items-like plastics, tin cans, other metals, glass, polyethylenes, rags, papers, etc., are picked up by rag pickers for recycling. All these items are recycled in recycling units to make new items. This reduces soil pollution.
  (iii) To reduce soil pollution solid waste is sometimes disposed off by burning. *The methods of burning are*
    (a) **Incineration** Carried out in very high temperature, *i.e,* 900-1300°C.
    (b) **Pyrolysis** It is a combustion at temperature 1650°C in the absence of oxygen.

Thermal Pollution

It is the degradation of water quality by any process that change the whole water temperature.

It can also be defined as 'warming up of an aquatic ecosystem to the point where desirable organisms are adversely affected (Owen, 1985).'

Causes of Thermal Pollution

Major sources of thermal pollution are many industries, thermal power plants, oil refineries, etc. The use of coolants and boilers in thermal power plants is the important cause of thermal pollution.

Effects of Thermal Pollution

Harmful effects of thermal pollution on aquatic ecosystem are as follows
  (i) Reduction in dissolved oxygen.
  (ii) Interference with reproduction of aquatic animals.
  (iii) Increased vulnerability to diseases.
  (iv) Direct mortality.
  (v) Invasion of destructive organisms.
  (vi) Undesirable changes in algal population.
  (vii) Elimination of flora and fauna of cold water.

Radioactive Pollution

The release of radioactive material into environment is called radioactive pollution. This can be very dangerous as radiation mutated the DNA, causing abnormal growth and sometimes cancer and this radiation remains in atmosphere for years slowly diminishing over times.

Causes of Radioactive Pollution

There are many causes of radioactive pollution. The most important one is inappropriately disposed radioactive wastes.

Some of these causes are as follows
1. Production of nuclear weapons
2. Decommissioning of nuclear weapons
3. Medical waste
4. Mining of radioactive ores
5. Coal ash
6. Nuclear power plants
7. Nuclear tests.

Effects of Radioactive Pollution

The nuclear radiation cause genetic variation (*i.e.,* mutation) and cancer in exposed organs or body parts. These radiations affect the future generations as it alter the DNA composition permanently.

Solid Wastes

These wastes are left over that goes out in trash. The various sources of solid wastes are municipal waste, mining waste, hospital waste, defunct ships, electronic wastes (e-wastes), etc.

Different modern industries are releasing large amount of solid waste which need to be managed in proper way to avoid environmental loss.

Control of Solid Wastes

There are various controlling measures of solid wastes, *some of them are discussed as follows*

(i) Dumping or landfilling is pilling of waste on selected low lying land. Open landfilling is dumping of waste material on uncovered low lying area. The waste is burnt periodically or compressed at intervals. In sanitary landfilling, wastes are dumped in a depression or trench after compactions and covered with dirt everyday.

Handbook of BIOLOGY

Most importantly the solid wastes can be treated after separation into three types
   (a) Biodegradable   (b) Recyclable   (c) Non-biodegradable
 (ii) A scientific method of treating e-wastes in an environment friendly manner is called **evencs**. E-wastes are buried in **landfills** or **incinerated**.
 (iii) Other methods of disposing wastes are source reduction, composting, recovery and recycling.
 (iv) **Ahmed Khan** in 1998, developed polyblend, a fine powder of recycled modified plastic, which can be used for road carpeting when mixed with bitumen in Bengaluru.

Greenhouse Effect (GHE)

It was first described by **Fourier** in 1827.

It is defined as

'The trapping of solar radiation by a layer of Greenhouse Gases (GHGs), which is important for maintenance of habitable temperature on earth'.

Greenhouse Effect (GHE) is a **positive cancept** as it is needed for existance of life on earth and in absence of it the temperature of earth would be $-18°C$.

Causes of GHE

The greenhouse effect is caused by several gases. *The share of greenhouse effect by different sources are given in following figure*

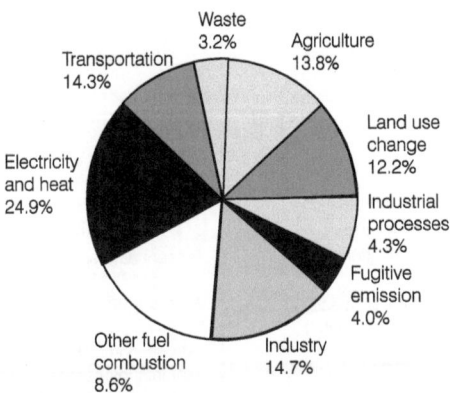

Annual global greenhouse gas emission in 2010, different by sector

Despite their differential concentrations, different gases causes varied level of greenhouse effect. This is called **differential greenhouse effect**. *Differential greenhouse effect caused by various substances are shown in following figure*

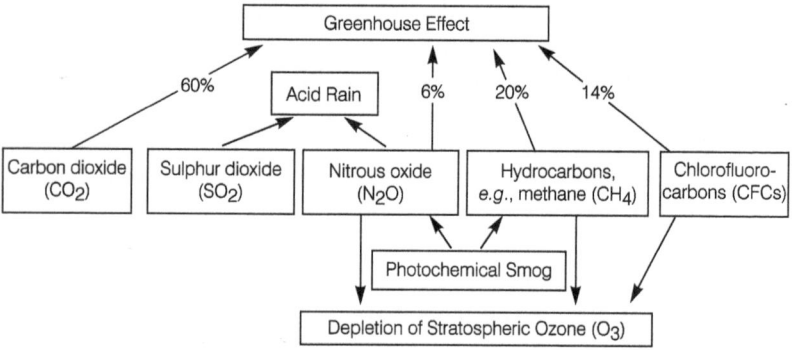

Differential greenhouse effect

The greenhouse effect is increasing day by day with increasing concentration of these substances into environment. *Chief greenhouse substances and their brief discription are given as follows*

Carbon Dioxide (CO_2)

Present level in atmosphere is 380 ppm (parts per million).

Atmospheric lifetime is 5-200 yr.

It is increasing due to fossil fuel's burning. Deforestation and change in land use.

High concentration may cause fertilisation effect, *i.e.*, increase in rate of photosynthesis and growth of plants decrease in stomatal conductance and transpiration rate.

Methane (CH_4)

Present level in atmosphere is 1750 ppb (parts per billion).

Methanogen bacteria increase greenhouse effect by producing methane.

The major sources are freshwater wetlands, enteric fermentation in cattle. Flooded rice fields along with biomass burning.

Greenhouse Gases (GHGs)

Nitrous Oxide (N_2O)

Present atmospheric concentration is 316 ppb (parts per billion).

Major sources are agriculture, biomass burning, nylon industries, nitrogen rich fertilisers and fuels.

Chlorofluorocarbons (CFCs)

Present atmospheric concentration is 282 ppt (Part Per Trllion).

Atmospheric lifetime is 45-260 yr.

Major sources leaking from air conditioners, refrigeration units, evaporation of industrial solvents, production of plastic foams and propellants in aerosol, spraycans.

Chief greenhouse gases, their sources and effects

In most scenerios, emissions continue to rise over the century, while in a few, emissions are reduced. Over the last three decades of 20th century, GDP per capita and population growth were the main driving factors in greenhouse gas emissions.

Global Warming

The gradual continuous increase in average temperature of the surface of earth as a result of increase in concentration of greenhouse gases is termed as **global warming**.

The global average surface temperature rose 0.6 to 0.9° C (1.1 to 1.6°F) between 1906 and 2005 and the rate of temperature increased has doubled in the last 50 years.

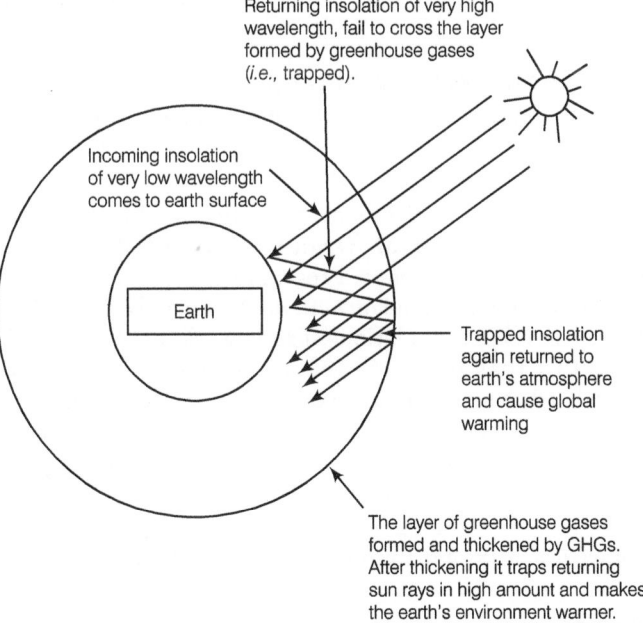

Schematic representation of global warming

Effects of Global Warming
Various effects of global warming are as follows
 (i) The temperature of the earth has increased by 0.6°C in last three decades, which will lead to changes in precipitation patterns.
 (ii) Rise in temperature leads to deleterious changes in environment resulting in odd climatic changes called **EI Nino effect.**
 (iii) The rise in temperature will lead to the increased melting of polar ice caps, which will cause the rise in sea level and many coastal areas will be submerged.
 (iv) Increased temperature will lead to increased weed growth, eruption of disease and pests. Thus, crop productivity will decrease.

Steps to Control Global Warming
 (i) Kyoto (Japan) hosted an international conference from December 1-10, 1997 of G-77 (a group of 140 developing countries) to discuss **global warming**.
 (ii) To assess the role of human activities in climate change, the **World Meterological Organisation** (WMO) and United Nations Environment Programme (UNEP) Set-up an Intergovernment Panel on Climate Change (IPCC) in 1988. The IPCC and United Nations Framework on Climate Change (UNFCC) that had reviewed the situation in October 1997, submitted their report in Kyoto in **Kyoto Protocol**.
 (iii) **Earth Day, 22 April** It was founded by **Gaylord Nelson** and organised by **Danis Hayes**. It markes the beginning of environment consciousness with clear focus on reducing pollution. The earth day network promotes environment awareness and year round progressive action.

Acid Rain
It is a broad term referring to a mixture of wet and dry deposition from the atmosphere containing higher than normal amount of **nitric** and **sulphuric acids**.

Acid rain occurs when these gases reacts in the atmosphere with water, oxygen and other chemicals to form various acidic compounds.

Handbook of BIOLOGY

Acidic deposition occurs in two ways i.e., wet and dry.

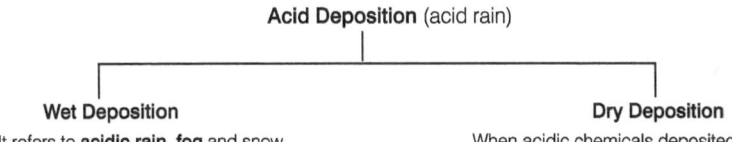

Wet Deposition
It refers to **acidic rain, fog** and snow. They resulted when acid chemical in air are blown into wet areas. The strength of the effect depends upon the acidity of water, chemistry and buffering capacity of soil, etc.

Dry Deposition
When acidic chemicals deposited in from of dust or smoke and fall to the ground through dry deposition.

Causes of Acid Rain

It may cause due to natural sources like volcanoes or by the combustion of fossil fuel in which SOx and NOx gets released.

Effects of Acid Rain

Acid rain have various adverse effects on several groups of organisms. The overall pH of water bodies and soil gets reduced by acidic rain. Acid deposition adversely affect the both floral and faunal biodiversity in various ecosystems.

Finally acid rain also cause the damage to several architecture and buildings. It cause the process of mineralisation, especially in limestone constructed buildings.

Ozone Layer Depletion

In the region of upper stratosphere (ozonosphere), 17-26 km above the earth's surface, exists a thin veil of renewable ozone O_3. This ozone layer absorb 99% of the harmful incoming UV radiations.

The energy of radiation got dissipated in following reaction

$$O_3 \rightleftharpoons O_2 + [O]$$

Ozone is being depleted by several man-made chemicals called **Ozone Depleting Compounds** (ODCs) or **Ozone Depleting Substance** (ODSs)

It was first detected by Farman *et al.* in 1984.

The process of formation and breakdown of ozone in stratosphere, diagrammatically represented as

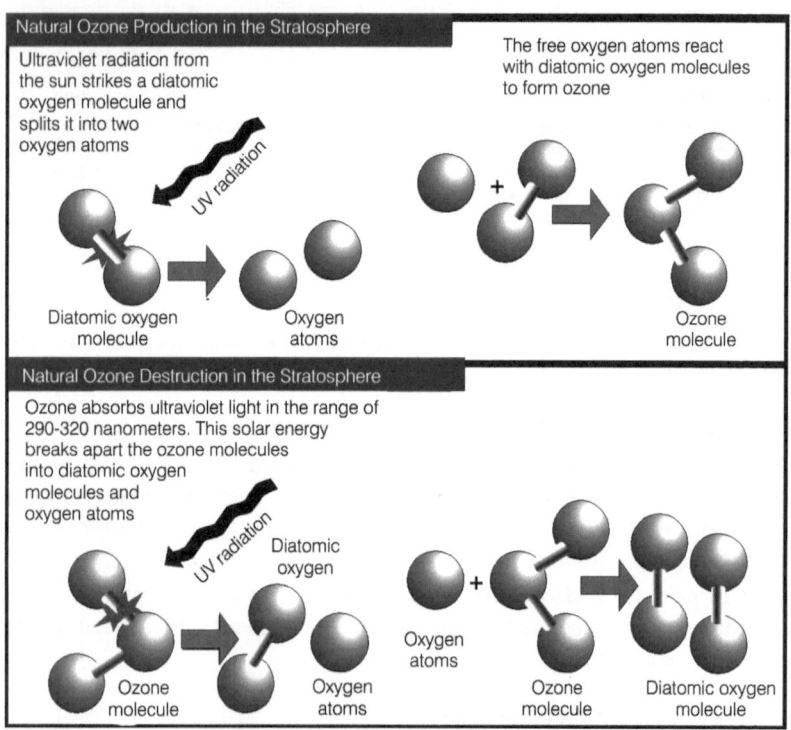

Ozone production and destruction in nature

Rather than a 'hole', ozone depletion is more a thinning, where ozone level decrease by 50% to 100%. Ozone loss is projected to diminish gradually until around 2050, when polar ozone holes will return to 1975 levels.

Mechanism of ozone depletion is as follows

$$CFCl_3 \xrightarrow{UV\text{-}C} CFCl_2 + Cl$$
$$CFCl_2 \xrightarrow{UV\text{-}C} CFCl + Cl$$
$$Cl + O_3 \rightarrow ClO + O_2$$
$$ClO + O_3 \rightarrow Cl + 2O_2$$

Harmful Effects of Ozone Layer Depletion

Depletion of ozone leads to various direct and indirect effects, *some of them are discussed as*

(i) **Rain failure** Due to depletion of ozone layer in stratosphere, the temperature of earth increases and it will be responsible for the failure of rainfall.

(ii) **Increase in radiation** Reduction of O_3 in stratosphere would allow UV rays to reach the earth.

(iii) **Cancer** Due to thinning of ozone layer, threat of skin cancer (melanoma) may increase. A 5% decrease in stratospheric ozone appears likely to lead 10% to 20% increase in skin cancer globally.

(iv) **High dose of UV-B** Causes inflammation of cornea (snow blindness) cataract, etc.

(v) **Other effects** Destruction of aquatic flora and fauna, loss of immunity and epidemic proportions of cataracts are some other effects of O_3 depletion.

(vi) Increased UV radiation's entry to earth's atmosphere lead to increased **global warming**.

Note

(i) To protect ozone depletion, **Montreal Protocol** was signed a Montreal (Canada) in 1967 (effective since 1989).

(ii) **Dobson Unit (DU)** It is a measurement of column ozone level. In tropics, it is 250-300 DU year around.

Deforestation

It is the conversion of forest area to non-forested area.

The prime region for deforestation is increase demands of humankind and its dependence on forest products. **Jhum cultivation** is such a technique in which mostly tribal population slash and burn forests to make it agricultural land. After sometime these population moves to different place and do the same practice again, hence this agriculture is also called **shifting agriculture**.

Effects of Deforestation

It caused loss of biodiversity as it lead to habitat destruction, soil erosion and sometimes desertification as well. Deforestation is also responsible for increased concentration of CO_2 in the atmosphere, because frees acts as since for CO_2.

Reforestation

It is the process of restoring forest that once existed, but was removed at some point of time in past.

Case Studies of Forest Conservation

(i) Amrita Devi Bisnoi in 1731 shown exemplary courage by hugging a tree and daring kings peop   le to cut her first, Government of India recently instituted **Amrita Devi Bisnoi Wildlife Protection Award** for individulals or communities, which protect and save forests.

(ii) **Chipko movement** was launched by **Chandi Prasad Bhatt** and **Sundar Lal Bahuguna** against large scale falling of trees by timber contractor in Uttarakhand hills.

These all protection movement led to introduction of **Joint Forest Management** (JFM) concept in 1980s for protecting and managing forests.

Appendix

1. Planes of the Body

Different sections of the body are termed as anatomical planes (flat surfaces) by the medical professionals. These planes are imaginary lines vertical or horizontal, which are drawn through an upright body. The terms are used to describe a specific body part.

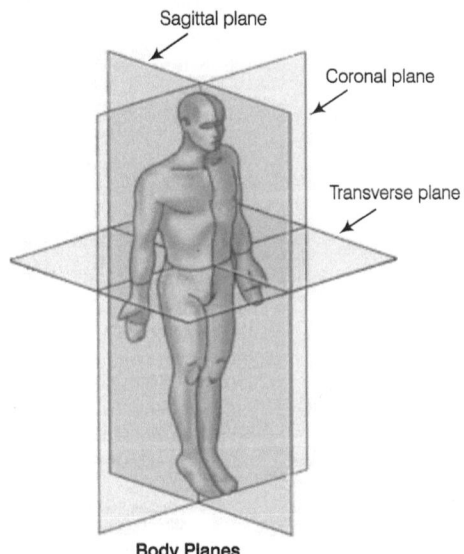

Body Planes

Coronal Plane

Coronary or frontal plane is a vertical plane running from side to side. It divides the whole body or any of its parts into anterior and posterior portions.

Sagittal Plane

Sagittal or lateral plane is a vertical plane running from front to back. It divides the body or any of its parts into right and left sides. Median plane is a sagittal plane that runs through the midline of body.

Transverse Plane

Transverse plane is a horizontal plane. It divides the body or any of its parts into upper and lower parts.

2. Comparison of Compound Microscope, Transmission Electron and Scanning Electron Microscope

Characteristic	Compound Microscope	Transmission E. Microscope	Scanning E. Microscope
Resolution (Average)	500 nm	10 nm	2 nm
Resolution (Special)	200 nm	0.5 nm	0.2 nm
Magnifying Power	Up to 1,500X	Up to 5,000,000X	~ 100,000X
Depth of Field	Poor	Moderate	High
Type of Object	Living or non-living	Non-living	Non-living
Preparation Technique	Usually simple	Skilled	Easy
Preparation Thickness	Rather thick	Very thin	Variable
Specimen Mounting	Glass slides	Thin films on copper grids	Aluminium stubs
Field of View	Large enough	Limited	Large
Source of Radiation	Visible light	Electrons	Electrons
Medium	Air	High vacuum	High vacuum
Nature of Lenses	Glass	1 electrostatic + a few em. lenses	1 electrostatic + a few em. lenses
Focusing	Mechanical	Current in the objective lens coil	Current in the objective lens coil
Magnification Adjustments	Changing objectives	Current in the projector lens coil	Current in the projector lens coil
Specimen Contrast	By light absorption	By electron scattering	By electron absorption

Light Microscope
Eyepiece
Objective lens
Specimen
Optical condenser
Focusing knob
Stage
Illuminator

Transmission Electron Microscope
Electron gun
Condenser
Electron beam
Specimen
Objective 'lens'
Projector 'lens'
Viewing binoculars
Fluorescent screen

Scanning Electron Microscope
Electron gun
Electron beam
Condenser
Scanning electro-magnets
Fluorescent screen
Detector
Amplifier
Secondary electrons
Specimen

3. Comparative Analysis of Various Phylums of Animal Kingdom

Phylum	Porifera	Coelenterata	Ctenophora	Platyhelminthes	Aschelminthes	Annelida	Arthropoda	Mollusca	Echinodermata	Hemichordata	Chordata
Organisation level	Cellular level	Tissue level	Tissue level	Organ and organ system level	Organ system level	Organ system level	Organ system level	Organ system level	Organ system level	Organ system level	Organ system level
Symmetry	No clear symmetry	Radial symmetry	Radial symmetry	Bilateral symmetry	Bilateral symmetry	Bilateral symmetry	Bilateral symmetry	Bilateral symmetry	Radial symmetry	Bilateral symmetry	Bilateral symmetry
Coelom	Absent	Absent	Absent	Absent	Pseudocoelomate	Coelomate	Coelomate	Coelomate	Coelomate	Coelomate	Coelomate
Segmentation	Absent	Absent	Absent	Absent	Absent	Present	Present	Present	Absent	Absent	Present
Digestive system	Absent	Incomplete	Incomplete	Incomplete	Complete	Complete	Complete	Complete	Complete	Complete	Complete
Circulatory system	Absent	Absent	Absent	Absent	Absent	Present	Present	Present	Present	Present	Present
Respiration	Absent	Absent	Absent	Absent	Absent	Absent	Present	Present	Present	Present	Present
Distinctive feature	Pores and canal system	Cnidoblast cells	Comb plate for movement	Suckers, floyd body and hooks	Elongated worm like	Segmented body	Joint appendage and exoskeleton	Shell present on body	Radical body with water vascular system	Worm like body with proboscis, collar and trunk	Notochord, nerve chord and gills lungs
Example	Sycon, Spongilla and Euspongia	Physalia, Adomsia and Pennatula	Ctenoplana and Pleurobrachia	Taenia and Fasciola	Ascaris, Wuchereria and Ancylostoma	Nereis, Pheretima and Hirudinaria	Apis, Bombyx, Anopheles and Locusta	Pila, Sepia and Octopus	Asterias, Echinus, Cucumaria and Ophiura	Balanoglossus and Saccoglossus	Fish, birds, amphibians, reptiles and mammals

4. Important Plant Products

Common Name	Botanical Name	Important Plant Part	Uses
A. Food yielding plants			
(a) Cereals			
1. Wheat	Triticum aestivum	Caryopsis a one seeded fruit	Flour for bread and chapatis, suji, maida.
2. Rice	Oryza sativa	" "	Rice is staple food for 70% of population of world, straw- paper, mats.
3. Maize	Zea mays	" "	Food for man and also fodder zeatin a cytokinin is obtained from grains in milk stage.
(b) Millets			
1. Bajra (Pearl millet)	Pennisetum typhoideum	Small sized grain	Food for poor.
2. Jawar (Great millet)	Sorghum vulgare	" "	Food for poor and also for cattle.
3. Ragi (Finger millet)	Eleusine coracana	" "	Flour used for preparing cakes and pudding.
(c) Legumes			
1. Matar (Garden pea)	Pisum sativum	Ovule or seed	Eaten green of canned or as vegetable.
2. Chana (Bengal gram= Chick pea)	Cicer arietinum	Seed	Used as besan, bread and also cattle feed.
3. Arhar (Red gram= Pigeon pea)	Cajanus cajan	Seed	Dal and as cattle feed.
4. Mung (Green gram)	Phaseolus aureus	Seed	"
5. Urd (Black gram)	Phaseolus mungo	Seed	"
6. Soya bean	Glycine max	Seed	Eaten roasted or as milk.
7. Mungphali (Ground nut = Peanut)	Arachis hypogea	Seed in (lomentum, underground)	Rich in proteins, eaten roasted or as vegetable ghee.
8. Lobia (Cowpea)	Vigna sinensis	Young pods and seeds	Used as vegetable.
9. Masur (Lentil)	Lens culinaris	Seeds	Used as dal.
(d) Nuts			
1. Almonds (Badam)	Prunus amygdalus	Seeds	Used in the preparation of various dishes.
2. Green Almond (Pista)	Pistacia vera	Seeds	As flavouring material in ice creams, candy and sweets.
3. Cashew nut (Kaju)	Anacardium Occidentale	Kernels	Sugared or salted kernels are consumed as table nuts, also used in confectionary.
4. English walnut (Akhrot)	Juglans regia	Kernels	Eaten raw, preparation of candy and ice creams.

Common Name	Botanical Name	Important Plant Part	Uses
B. Spices and condiments			
1. Red pepper (Chillies)	Capsicum sp.		Dried pepper is used as powder with most of the Indian foods, fresh also eaten.
2. Black pepper (Kali mirch = Black pearl)	Piper nigrum		Dried mature seeds used in cooking.
3. Turmeric (Haldi)	Curcuma domestica		Dried rhizome is very aromatic and used to colour pickles, food stuffs and also to prepare kumkum.
4. Cumin (Zira)	Cuminum cyminum		Aromatic fruits are used in soup, curries, cakes, pickles, oil is used for flavouring beverages and other food stuffs.
5. Coriander (Dhania)	Coriandrum sativum		Fruits and leaves are aromatic, used in making soup, pickles, etc.
6. Clove (Laung)	Syzygium aromaticum		Dried unopened flower buds are very aromatic, fine flavoured and imparts warming qualities.
7. Saffron (Kesar)	Crocus sativus		The dried stigma and tops of the styles make the saffron of commerce. It possesses pleasant aroma, used as spice and dye stuff.
8. Cardamom (Chhoti Ilaichi)	Elettaria cardamomum		Fruits and seeds are used for flavouring sweet dishes, beverages, etc.
9. Bengal cardamom (Badi Ilaichi)	Amomum aromaticum		Fruits and seeds are chief ingredient of 'garam masala'.
10. Asafetida (Hing)	Ferula assafoetida		Resin obtained from the roots is used for flavouring food products.
C. Edible oil			
1. Mungphali (Ground nut=Peanut)	Arachis hypogea		Seed yields edible oil, roasted seeds eaten, oil cake used as cattle feed and manure.
2.(a) Rape (b) Mustard	Brassica napus B.campestris		Seed oil used for cooking, oil cake a good manure and cattle feed.
3. Til (Sesame)	Sesamum indicum		Seed yield cooking oil, oil used for hairs as medicine.
4. Coconut	Cocos nucifera		Seed yield cooking oil. also used as hair oil. for soaps; fruit husk yields coir.
5. Cotton seed	Gossypium sp.		Oil is used as ghee and cake as fodder of animals.

Common Name	Botanical Name	Important Plant Part	Uses

D. Timber yielding plants

1. Sisham	*Dalbergia sisso*	Wood	For carved door pans, wooden statue.
2. Rosewood	*D. latifolia*	"	For furniture, houses.
3. Teak (Sagaun)	*Tectona grandis*	"	Furniture.
4. Sal	*Shorea robusta*	"	Door frame, beams, railway sleepers.
5. Mulberry	*Morus alba*	"	Sports goods, mainly hockey sticks, tennis rackets cricket stumps.
6. Walnut (Akhrot)	*Juglans regia*	"	Musical instruments, rifle butts.
7. White willow	*Solix alba*	"	Cricket bats.

E. Medicinal plants

1. Sarpgandha	*Roauwolfia serpentina*	Root	For blood pressure, snake bite, mental disorders.
2. Opium (Afeen)	*Papaver somniferum*	Latex from unripe fruit (capsule)	Narcotic, sedative, in relieving pain.
3. Quinine	*Cinchona officinalis*	Bark	For malaria.
4. Belladonna	*Atropa belladonna*	Dried leaves and roots	Narcotic, diuretic, antispasmodic, leaves stimulant of CNS relieving pain.
5. Datura	*Datura stramonium*	Fruit juice	For removing dandruff, for bronchial ailments.
6. Amla	*Emblica officinalis*	Fruit	Diuretic, laxative for haemorrhage, diarrhea dysentry.
7. Kuchla	*Strychnos nux-vomica*	Seed	In paralysis and mental disorders.
8. Isapgol	*Plantago ovata*	Seed husk	For constipation and peptic ulcers.
9. Liquorice (Mulhati)	*Glycorrhiza glabra*	Roots	For cough and bronchitis.
10. Santonin	*Artemesia cina*	Flowers	Antihelminthic and antimalarial, contains a variety of steroidal.
11. Yam	*Dioscorea* species	Tubers	Drugs, some of which are used to make birth control pills.
12. Digitalis	*Digitalis purpurea*	Leaves	Used as cardiac stimulant and toxic.
13. Sada bahar	*Catharanthus roseus*	Leaves	Treatment of leukemia and other cancers.

F. Sugar yielding plants

1. Sugarcane	*Saccharum officinarum*	Stem	Sugar, molasses, card board, paper.
2. Chukander (Beet sugar)	*Beta vulgaris*	Root	Paper, sugar, salad.